BACK TO THE ROUGH GROUND

REVISIONS

A Series of Books on Ethics

General Editors:

Stanley Hauerwas and Alasdair MacIntyre

Back to the Rough Ground

Practical Judgment
and the Lure of Technique

by

JOSEPH DUNNE

University of Notre Dame Press
Notre Dame, Indiana

Foreword to the Paperback Edition ©1997 by Alasdair MacIntyre
Paperback edition published in 1997 by University of Notre Dame Press

Reprinted in 2001, 2009

Library of Congress Cataloging-in-Publication Data

Dunne, Joseph.
    Back to the rough ground : practical judgment and the lure of
technique / by Joseph Dunne.
        p.   cm.
    Includes bibliographical references and index.
    ISBN 13: 978-0-268-00705-8 (paper : alk. paper)
    ISBN 10: 0-268-00705-5 (paper : alk. paper)
    1. Rationalism.   2. Reason.   3. Prudence.   4. Practice
(Philosophy).   5. Philosophy, Modern—18th century.   6. Philosophy,
Modern—20th century.   7. Aristotle. Nicomachean ethics.
8. Technical reason.   9. Practical reason.   I. Title.
B833.D86   1997
128'.3—dc21   97-35478
                                                                    CIP

To my mother and the memory of my father

Contents

Foreword to the Paperback Edition, by *Alasdair MacIntyre*   xiii

Preface   xv

Introduction   1

     1. Generative Context of the Study and Its Central Issue   1
     2. The Company of Philosophers   8
     3. Conversation as a Mode of Philosophical Inquiry   20

PART 1: THE RETRIEVAL OF PHRONESIS AND TECHNE IN MODERN PHILOSOPHY

A. Specific Domains: Religion, Art, and Politics

1. J. H. Newman's Appeal to Phronesis in *A Grammar of Assent*   31

     1. Newman's Critique of Rationalism: Preliminary Remarks   31
     2. Newman and Aristotle   33
     3. Newman and Contemporary Philosophy   38
     4. 'Incommensurability' in Philosophy of Science, Aristotelian Scholarship, and the *Grammar*   45
     5. Conclusion: Newman on Language   50

2. R. G. Collingwood's Critique of Techne in *The Principles of Art*   55

     1. 'The Technical Theory of Art'   55
     2. 'Imaginative Expression'   60
     3. Expression and Language   64
     4. Aesthetics and Ethics: Collingwood and Aristotle   69
     5. Collingwood's Subjectivism and Anti-Individualism   75
     6. Intersubjectivity and Language: What Collingwood Is 'Trying to Say'   81

3. Hannah Arendt's Distinction between Action and Making in *The Human Condition*   88

     1. Action and Behavior   89

2. Uncertain Stories and the Limits of Practical Knowledge   91
3. Tyranny and the Flight from Action into Making   93
4. Promising, Forgiving, and the Condition of Plurality   97
5. Arendt and Aristotle   100

B. The Universal Scope of Philosophical Hermeneutics

4. The Play of Phronesis and Techne in Hans-Georg
   Gadamer's *Truth and Method*   104

   1. Nineteenth-Century Hermeneutics   106
   2. The Heideggerian Background   109
   3. Finitude, Tradition, and the Hermeneutical Circle   110
   4. Conversation as the Medium of 'Effective-Historical
      Consciousness'   117
   5. The 'Fusion of Horizons' in the Act of 'Application'   121
   6. Aristotle as Mentor: The Centrality of the Appeal to Phronesis   123
   7. Gadamer's Account of Experience, in Relation to Aristotle   128
   8. Experience as Being-in-Play   132

5. Language, Hermeneutics, and Practical Philosophy   138

   1. The Unity of Thought and Language   138
   2. Finitude and the 'Infinity' of Language   144
   3. Limitations of the 'Statement' and the Synthesis of
      Hermeneutical Ideas in Reflection on Language   147
   4. Beyond 'Substance Metaphysics': Reflection on Language
      as a Way of Profiling Techne and Phronesis   152
   5. Theory and Practice: The Extent of Gadamer's Appeal
      to Aristotelian Practical Philosophy and Phronesis   156
   6. The Scope of Gadamer's Thought: Concluding Questions   164

C. The Challenge of Critical Theory

6. The Distinction between Praxis and Technique in
   the Early Philosophy of Jürgen Habermas   168

   1. Situating Habermas   168
   2. The Aristotelian Background   173
   3. Praxis Mediated through Modern Thought   177
   4. Habermas and Hermeneutics   182
   5. The Modern Loss of the Distinction between Praxis
      and Technique   186

7. Habermas's Later Philosophy: Ambiguities of Rationalization   193

   1. Critique and Praxis: The Shift to the Notion of
      Communicative Action   193

2. The 'Uncoupling of System and Life-World': Progress
   and Deformation   198
3. Habermas's Defense of the 'Rationalization of the Life-
   World': Technicism in a New Guise?   201
4. The Life-World and the Limits of Rationalization:
   The Shadow Side of Habermas's Thought   209
5. Conclusion: *Aporiai* in Habermas's Thought and the Point
   of a Return to Aristotle   216

Interlude   227

PART 2: PHRONESIS AND TECHNE IN ARISTOTLE

8. Theory, Techne, and Phronesis: Distinctions and Relations   237

   1. Aristotle's Conception of 'Theory'   237
   2. The Primacy of Theory and the Questionable Status of
      Practice   239
   3. The Place of Techne and Phronesis, and of the Distinction
      between Them, in Aristotle's Writings   244
   4. Aristotle's 'Official' Concept of Techne: Its Essential Reference
      to Fabrication and Its Closeness to Theory   249
   5. Technai of the *Kairos* and Their Affinity with Phronesis 253
   6. The Distinction between Techne *Poiētikē* and Phronesis   261
   7. Meeting Two Difficulties That Stem from Aristotle's Usage 269

9. The Circle between Knowledge and Virtuous Character:
   Phronesis as a Form of Experience   275

   1. Aristotle's Reserve about the Role of Knowledge in Virtue:
      The Emergence of a Circle between Phronesis and
      Character   275
   2. The Key to Understanding the Circle Is 'Experience'   279
   3. Interlude: The Nonassimilation of 'Experience' Raises
      Questions about Techne in *Metaphysics* 1.1   281
   4. The Appeal to Experience in *Nicomachean Ethics* 10.9
      and 1.3   285
   5. Phronesis and Character as Modalities of Experience   290
   6. *Nous*, or Perceptiveness with Regard to 'Ultimate
      Particulars,' as a Crucial Element in Phronesis   295
   7. Suggested Examples of 'Ultimate Particulars' Elucidated
      by Reference to *De Anima* and Wittgenstein   300
   8. The Openness of the Phronetic Approach, and How It Differs
      from Deductivism   304
   9. The Relationship between Universals and Particulars in
      the Sphere of Phronesis and *Eupraxia*   310

10. Beyond the 'Official' Notion of Techne: Recovering the
      Experiential Background   315

    1. Aristotle's Failure to Distinguish between Techne as an
          Ability to Analyze and Techne as an Ability to Make   315
    2. Evidence of Two Different Tendencies in Aristotle's
          Treatment of Techne   319
    3. Aristotle's Neglect of the Role of Experience in Techne
          Related to His Characteristic Approach to *Genesis*   326
    4. The Role of Matter in Aristotle's Thought Supports an
          Emphasis on Experience   329
    5. Implications of the Analogy between Techne and Nature   334
    6. Implications for 'Techne' of Aristotle's Account of Change 338
    7. Aristotle's Account of 'Soul' Supports a Conception
          of Techne as Embodied   343
    8. 'Deliberation' Reconsidered, and Conclusion   350

Epilogue   357

    1. The Main Themes   357
    2. Import for Practices   364
    3. Bearings in Philosophy   371

Notes   383

Bibliography to Introduction and Part 1   469
Bibliography to Part 2 and Epilogue   477

Index   485

Theuth said, "Here, O king, is a branch of learning that will make the people of Egypt wiser and improve their memories; my discovery provides a recipe for memory and wisdom." But the king answered and said, "O man full of arts, to one it is given to create the things of art, and to another to judge what measure of harm and of profit they have for those that shall employ them."

Plato, *Phaedrus*

We have got on to slippery ice where there is no friction and so in a certain sense the conditions are ideal, but also, just because of that, we are unable to walk. We want to walk: so we need *friction*. Back to the rough ground!

Ludwig Wittgenstein, *Philosophical Investigations*

Foreword to the Paperback Edition

Too many readers of, say, the table of contents of *Back to the Rough Ground* may conclude too easily and quite mistakenly that it is not a book that deserves their attention. Those with an interest in Aristotle may think that an approach to Aristotle's texts by way of an excursion through five very different nineteenth- and twentieth-century thinkers is likely to lead to a misreading of Aristotle. This is after all not how books about Aristotle normally proceed. And those who already have an interest in one or more of what at first sight is an assorted bunch of modern thinkers may suppose that they are being invited to revisit all too familiar territory and that these thinkers are being treated as no more than a prologue to Aristotle, and therefore mistreated.

Both responses will miss the point of this remarkable book, a book that certainly brings its author's own critical questions to the reading of the texts, but only in a way that is respectful of their integrity. A third kind of mistake will be made by those who have been provoked by their own experiences into asking persistent questions about the relationship of theory to practice and who think that they have learned from those attempts to find answers that all theoretical discussion of the relationship of theory to practice is barren and unhelpful. Disillusionment with theorizing, let alone philosophical theorizing, as any kind of guide to practice is widespread in our culture. But this book speaks to the concerns of the disillusioned by enquiring just what kind of philosophical theory it is that might after all inform and improve practice and even, on occasion, help to rescue it from its own perplexities. So while readers for whom this aspect of his book is unusually relevant may be among those most likely to be impatient with and even incredulous at the thought that their questions are best approached by an extended interrogation of philosophical texts, such readers are in fact among those who may have most to lose by ignoring this book.

What then does Dunne try to achieve? In the first part of his book he engages in a series of conversations, in each of which an author whose texts are addressed supplies clues and insights as to how to answer key questions about practical knowledge, yet always in a way that leads to a constructive reformulation of the problems rather than to a solution. And the careful choice of authors results in a progressive sharpening of the questions, so that when

Dunne approaches Aristotle's texts he has provided himself and his readers not only with a set of penetrating questions about theory's relationship to practice, but also with a statement of some central difficulties that will have to be resolved if those questions are to be adequately answered.

One obvious danger in Dunne's approach is that of an anachronistic misreading of Aristotle arising from a facile assumption that *our* questions are more or less the same as *his* questions. In fact he turns out to be much less guilty of this than some other recent writers on Aristotle who profess purely scholarly intentions, and he avoids this danger in part because he shows himself to be so well aware of it and consequently able to put the reader on her or his guard, and in part because his whole project derives from a large dissatisfaction with *our* questions, as they are usually framed.

With respect to Aristotle, Dunne is not only a sympathetic expositor but also a critic. He argues powerfully that, in order to make Aristotle's central positions on *phronēsis* (practical understanding) and *technē* (craft skills) fully intelligible and defensible, we badly need to expand upon Aristotle's own brief remarks about experience and about the specific kinds of experience that are required both for acquiring and for exercising practical knowledge and craft skills. He interprets *phronēsis* and *technē* so that the relationship between them is even closer than Aristotle himself allows. And he does all this in order to explain how we moderns may, through attention to the quality of our experience, embody *phronēsis* and *technē* both in *our* practice of theorizing and in *our* practice more generally, so that any sharp opposition between distinctively modern modes of practice and Aristotelian modes of practice, such as I and some others have suggested, is denied.

So Dunne's exploration leads him back finally to the practical questions that originally prompted his enquiry, questions not only about contemporary practice in general but about his own particular occupation, that of a teacher who is also a teacher of teachers. But his argument and its conclusions are relevant to many spheres of practice and his work will not disappoint either readers whose primary interest is in the philosophical issues for their own sake or readers whose primary interest arises from their practical concerns. Dunne's standpoint is, as I have already remarked, not my own. We are in significant respects at odds both about some aspects of Aristotle's thought and about the nature of modernity. So my admiration for his splendid book is not founded on agreement but instead on a recognition that there are not many books from which so very much can be learned. Sometimes that learning may take place by our appropriating his insights or as a result of our being convinced by his arguments, but sometimes too by our quarreling with his conclusions. His is a book that will provide unusually profitable reading for a very long time.

Alasdair MacIntyre
June 1997

Preface

In *The Reflective Practitioner* (New York: Basic Books, 1983) Donald
Schön draws attention to a considerable mismatch between an entrenched
picture of the kind of knowledge which successful practitioners are *supposed* to possess and the knowing-in-action which their practices actually
embody. "How comes it," Schön asks, "that in the second half of the twen-
tieth century we find in our universities, embedded not only in men's minds
but in the institutions themselves, a dominant view of professional knowledge as the application of scientific theory and technique to the instrumental problems of practice?" (p. 30). An important part of any adequate
answer to this question lies in philosophy, and in this book I attempt to
bring it into view. I shall be concerned with 'practice' in a wide sense em-
bracing both professional competence in specific domains and the actions
that in less defined settings give substance to a person's life. I hope not
only to account for the established, articulated — and largely misconceived
— notion of practical knowledge but also to make more explicit the knowledge that is implicit in good practice and that tends to *remain* implicit
or to receive only the most peremptory articulation. Schön suggests that
when people "use terms such as 'art' and 'intuition' they usually intend
to terminate discussion rather than to open up inquiry. It is as though
the practitioner says to his academic colleague, 'While I do not accept
your view of knowledge, I cannot describe my own'" (pp. vii–viii). My
purpose in this book is precisely "to open up inquiry" about practitioner's
knowledge and to look for adequate conceptual resources to "describe" it.

    I pursue the inquiry into practical knowledge through exploring a
particular tradition of philosophical reflection in which this inquiry has
already been under way for a long time and in which a great deal of work
has been done to develop and refine appropriate concepts. Hence, the
book has a double focus: as well as helping to elucidate problems of practical knowledge, it should also illuminate those thinkers whose writings
contribute to the philosophical tradition which I explore. An interesting
light may be shed on ideas of each of my main protagonists through the
way in which they are made to address the book's central topic — as well
as through the way in which they are brought *together* for this task. I have

not assumed familiarity on the reader's part with any of these authors. Readers with a discrete interest in one or other of them will find that chapters (or sets of chapters) devoted to each of them are relatively self-contained. At the same time, common themes run through different chapters and all are intended to contribute to a coherent, overall argument.

I owe an immense debt to Fergal O' Connor, O.P., of University College, Dublin, who shows by his example that philosophy can seriously address practical issues *and* be a form of play. His unique power as a teacher derives from an involvement in social practices outside the academy, combined with a passionate engagement with great texts of the philosophical tradition (especially Plato). He has kept the topic of this book green through countless hours of discussions and helped me in more ways than I can be aware of, let alone adequately acknowledge.

In St. Patrick's College, Dublin, I have enjoyed a convivial ethos and a recognition that in work of this kind "time is a good discoverer and partner" (Aristotle). I am indebted to the authorities of the college and in particular to its former president, John Doyle, C.M., for granting me in 1980 the sabbatical leave in which the idea of the book first germinated, and to my colleague Andrew Burke for his generous cooperation. I am deeply grateful to my head of department, John Canavan, for his steadfast support at all stages. I owe a great debt to many former students of the college, most particularly in recent years to experienced teachers attending in-service degree courses who have inspired me by their commitment to reflective practice and, by sharing with me their questions and insights about teaching, made me feel that the argument presented here was worth making.

St. Edmund's College, Cambridge, afforded congenial conditions for study when I was a visiting scholar there in the academic year 1980–81. I remember with particular gratitude the hospitality and friendship of Richard and Elspeth Giddens and the robust help of Professor Elizabeth Anscombe as I took my first steps—backward, as it seemed—into Aristotle's writings. I am grateful also to Professor Martha Nussbaum for her kind interest in my work during a visit to Dublin in the spring of 1988 and for her comments on draft chapters on Aristotle. Throughout, my task was made easier by the courteous and efficient help of staff at the University Library in Cambridge and at the libraries of University College, St. Patrick's College, and the Goethe-Institut in Dublin; I am especially grateful to Evan Salholm and Carola Hogreve.

Parts of the book were read and helpfully commented on, at different stages, by Pádraig Hogan, Lars Løvlie, Eoghan Mac Aogáin, Maurice Reidy, Denys Turner, and Gerard Watson. Hugh Gash, James Kelly, Liam Mac Mathúna, Mark Morgan, and Mary Thompson assisted me with final proof-reading. John Cleary has read all of Part 2 and been generous with various kinds of help. Jim Heney first advised me to use a computer and then, with a nice combination of techne and phronesis, dealt with unforeseen consequences of my doing so. At a crucial stage Siobhán Campbell was a bright spirit to the work, lightening the task of bringing order to a seemingly unmanageable typescript. Gerry Gaden and Frank Litton have read all of the typescript at various stages of its composition and in their different ways have given me warm and critical support. I owe special thanks to two friends from student days. John Doyle undertook the bulk of my teaching duties while I was on sabbatical and has enriched me over many years by the vigor and inventiveness of his conversation about philosophy and teaching. Jack Hanna's encouragement never allowed my enthusiasm to flag and, besides, his judgment on issues has been a kind of touchstone. Both helped me greatly by their constructive responses as I wrote consecutive chapters through the summers of the 1980s. Of other friends whose interest has sustained me over the years and the particular quality of whose support in each case I am conscious of, I must mention Joe Coyne, Paddy Daly, Laura O' Connor, Dilecta Planansky, O.S.B., Stephen Pryle, Isabelle Roe-Vallet, and Pat Walshe. My sister, Rosemary, did sterling work on the Index and her love and belief have supported me throughout.

My thanks are due, finally, to those who have made this book a *book*: to Stanley Hauerwas and Alasdair MacIntyre for accepting it in the *Revisions* series; to James Langford, Director of the University of Notre Dame Press, for his courteous help at all stages; and to Ann Rice for the insightfulness and care of her copyediting.

Gratitude, and the opportunity to express it, is one of the pleasures of completing a work such as this. But none of those who have so richly helped me is responsible for views expressed here, and the book's flaws are stubbornly my own.

· · ·

Parts of chapters 8 and 9 have been previously published in the *Irish Journal of Philosophy* 2.2 (Autumn 1985) in "Aristotle after Gadamer: An Analysis of the Distinction between Phronesis and Techne," a paper read to the Irish Philosophy Society at a conference on hermeneutics — attended, happily, by Professor Gadamer — in Belfast in March 1985.

Apart from the majority of notes which simply give references for the many citations in the text, notes to Part 1 and Part 2 serve broadly different functions. Notes to Part 1 contain material whose insertion in the main text would interrupt the broad flow of the discussion but which provide explanatory, illustrative, or comparative background to ideas introduced there; if the overall movement of thought is conceived as a 'conversation' (as it is in the Introduction) then these notes are devices enabling the conversation to 'breathe'—pauses allowing an idea to be rounded out, an aside to be made, or a connection adverted to. Many of the notes to Part 2 are of a different character because no great philosopher has received closer attention than Aristotle and especially over the past few decades an exceptional body of scholarship has accumulated around his work. Since one can hardly write responsibly on Aristotle now without acknowledging this literature, and since it only very rarely obtrudes in the main text here, the notes to Part 2 bear the burden of frequent, though inevitably selective, references to it.

Except where otherwise noted, translations of Aristotle are from the Revised Oxford Translation, edited by Jonathan Barnes (Princeton: Princeton University Press, 1984). I have taken the liberty of slightly altering translations to harmonize with my treatment of the four central Greek terms, 'phronēsis,' technē 'praxis,' and 'poiēsis,' as naturalized English words. Following established convention, references to Aristotle's texts indicate the pages, columns, and lines of the Bekker edition (Berlin 1831).

Introduction

1. Generative Context of the Study and Its Central Issue

What is carried on in this work is a philosophical conversation and I shall give some advance notice here of the kind of conversation it is, the voices that are party to it, and how it contributes—precisely as a conversation—to a deeper understanding of its central theme.

The first task is to identify this theme, by indicating what it was that first provoked the conversation and remains all the time at issue in it. I can do this now quite independently of the philosophical concepts and idioms that will claim the reader's attention later on. For what drew me toward the philosophers whose works will be considered in subsequent chapters was a problem that was not in the first instance philosophical: it was, rather, a problem that I encountered in a quite practical setting, *before* I came to see that it called for and could not be adequately resolved without the kind of historical and philosophical perspective that is developed in this book.

In the late 1970s, with my colleagues in the college of education where I worked, I was formally introduced to a model of teaching that promised, we were told, spectacular improvements in the quality of our students' teaching if only they (and we as their mentors) would use it as a blueprint in planning and conducting lessons. This model was called the behavioral objectives model. Teachers who used it would formulate very specific goals (in terms of demonstrable changes in their pupils) for each lesson or series of lessons and then plan their teaching as a series of instrumental steps toward the achievement of these goals. The pre-specification of intended learning-outcomes would be the primary requirement for effective teaching. It would be the basis on which teachers could determine how their instruction should be organized with respect to methods, classroom activities, and learning materials, and at the same time it would provide a clear-cut criterion for evaluating the success of their endeavors: to succeed now would simply mean to achieve one's objectives. The objectives model thus seemed to be the royal road to *efficiency* in teaching, to provide a proper basis on which teachers could be

1

made *accountable* for their performance, and, more fundamentally, to open the possibility of rescuing teaching from woolly-mindedness and muddle and of constituting it as a truly *rational* practice.

The foremost exponents of the behavioral objectives model were North American, though their ideas had been widely exported, and educationalists in other countries had not, indeed, been notably protectionist in relation to them. The antecedents of these ideas go back to the beginning of the century and to the attempts made then to forge a new science of education that would replace the mixture of rhetoric, traditional lore, and practical know-how that had constituted the old pedagogy. More proximately, the seminal work of the movement was Ralph Tyler's *Basic Principles of Curriculum and Instruction* (1949). Another volume that was eventually to become very influential—though, like Tyler's book, not immediately—was *The Taxonomy of Educational Objectives: The Cognitive Domain*, edited by Benjamin Bloom (1956). A companion volume to this, *The Taxonomy of Educational Objectives: The Affective Domain*, edited by D. Krathwohl, was published in 1964, and from about that time onward what had been a relatively insignificant emphasis within the educational establishment began to harden into a coherent movement with a reforming—not to say crusading—purpose. Writing in 1969, W. James Popham, one of the most prolific authors of the movement, had this to say:

> until the last few decades, educators have been approaching the task of describing educational objectives with a hand-axe mentality. It should not be surprising that the overall quality of instruction has been almost as primitive as that practiced by those Aboriginal tool-makers. . . . American educators have generally engaged in the same level of discourse regarding the specification of educational goals that one might derive from the grunts of a Neanderthal. . . . We are at the brink of a new era regarding the explication of instructional goals, an era which promises to yield fantastic improvements in the quality of instruction. One can only sympathize with the thousands of learners who had to obtain an education from an instructional system built on a muddle-minded conception of educational goals.[1]

Popham's confidence, if not his arrogance, was shared by fellow proponents of this model; any reservations they had about their project related only to what they saw as the recalcitrance of teachers and the inertia of school systems, and not to any issue of principle about the nature of teaching as a practice or the type of rationality, or relationship between knowledge and action, that may be appropriate to it. Despite this confident advocacy, however, I found that their claims ran up against intuitions that I had formed in the course of my experience in classrooms: not only was it the case that the good teachers whom I knew—or the students who had impressed me on teaching practice—did not seem to work in this way, but I fancied that if they had their teaching might have been a great deal less successful than I had deemed it to be. But what was the authority of these intuitions when set against the imposing rationality of the objectives model? Did they commit one to irrationality, with nothing less vague to appeal to than inspiration or 'flair' or the supposition (self-defeating for a teacher-educator) that good teachers are born and not made?

The issue which had thus been precipitated for me was the nature of rationality in teaching—and indeed, beyond this, the nature of any rational practice. It was through a close examination of representative texts of the behavioral objectives movement that the full dimensions of this issue became apparent. I shall sketch briefly the main points which emerged in this examination and show how they opened the larger philosophical context which is explored in this book.[2] By doing so, I hope not only to lay bare the original motivation of the book but also, by exemplary reference to the specific field of education, to illustrate its pertinence to practical engagements across a wide front.

My difficulties with the behavioral objectives model concerned not just its emphasis on *behavior* but more fundamentally the concept of *objective* from which this emphasis in fact derived. Written into the concept of an objective was the requirement that the latter's achievement should be verifiable—that unequivocal evidence should be available to establish it; and confining objectives to observable behavior ensured that this requirement could be met. The verification being insisted on was of a kind that could be carried out by a detached observer who could not be assumed to have any familiarity with the teacher's situation or background. The language in which objectives were to be formulated was to be precise and explicit and thus to preclude the possibility of misinterpretation by removing the need for interpretation itself. Through the medium of this language a teacher ought to envisage herself as being in virtual communication with an indeterminate community of observers or of other teachers who, solely by reference to her stated objectives—and without need to establish through discussion any shared contextual understanding—ought to be able, in the one case, to assess her teaching performance and, in the other, to replicate everything essential in it (since what is essential was taken to reside simply in a specified outcome or product). This language was being presented, then, as a tool not just for analyzing a teacher's activity *pre-factum* or *post-factum* but also for constructing and carrying out this activity *in actu*. The 'model' locates teaching activity squarely between two other processes: the framing of objectives which precedes it and evaluation which occurs after it (this was the core of Tyler's celebrated 'rationale'). The basic problems of teaching, then, are to be clarified by these two adjoining analytic activities; the latter offer, as it were, a secure *terra firma* on either side of the flux of teaching itself, on which one can anticipate, plan, and control the moves one will make, or — in the case of evaluation — discover how one has fared in one's previous moves and thereby have data to inform one's new plans.

Much of my skepticism concerned the quality of information that could be provided by these analytic activities for the actual conduct of teaching. A precise statement of objectives, it was claimed, can keep the teacher "on target." But how can a teacher know that the target set is a desirable or appropriate one? For all the exactness of its formulation, how can one avoid its being arbitrary? It seemed clear to me that one can do so only through a kind of judgment and good sense that neither depends on nor derives from a commitment to objectives formulation *per se*. Moreover, when advocates of the model suggest that objectives-based evaluation provides "empirical evidence" that either confirms that objectives have been well chosen or suggests a reorientation of the teacher's work, this claim seemed no less problematical. For whatever evidence is thrown up by an evaluation about the "learner's post-instructional behavior" will have to be interpreted for its significance with respect to the act of instruction; and guidance for such an interpretation is not forthcoming from this evidence itself. If the initial standards set for instruction were arbitrary, there is no way that subsequent empirical evidence, on its own, could exorcise this arbitrariness from them at a later stage. If, for instance, a teacher fails to achieve her objective, how is this to be interpreted or its significance for her activity to be judged? It could mean that the objective was too difficult for the class and that it should now be scaled down. Or it could mean that it was, in fact, an appropriate goal for the class — in which case her instruction may have been incompetent; and if so, we still have to find out in what respects. Or perhaps — for a complex set of reasons, maybe unknown to the teacher — members of the class were distracted on this particular day from their normal level of attention and achievement. Any number of factors may have intervened to produce the results that the evaluation gave back as empirical evidence. Accordingly, the teacher has to make a complex set of judgments, based on much more than the evidence of the learner's post-instructional behaviors, before she can rationally revise her decisions. Both the pre-specification of objectives, then, and subsequent evidence supplied by the approved form of evaluation would leave answers to the teacher's questions of the form "what shall I do?" massively underdetermined.

These difficulties with the behavioral objectives model seemed to arise from the exclusiveness of its concern with instructional outcomes and its corresponding neglect of teaching as an engagement or a process, as well as its inattention to the experiential dimension of learning. Framed within this model, the teacher and pupils appear to relate externally to educational 'content' as to an objectified *tertium quid*; one gets no sense of the pedagogic relationship as setting up a field of psychic tension, with its own forces of attraction and repulsion that must intrinsically affect whatever 'content' may loom up within it. It is not exactly that an affective dimension to education is denied; rather than entering into the pedagogic relationship and determining what can transpire within it, however, emotions are allowed to exist only as the content of certain 'affective objectives' which the teacher, with full explicitness and foresight, can plan and control. Nor is there any sense that (to change images) something might be at work in the pedagogic situation which cannot simply be made the object of analysis but must rather be lived through—a kind of subsoil which nourishes the fruits of explicit purposes but which is not itself a fruit. It is as if action can be resolved into analysis—that the problems of the first-person agent can be solved from the perspective of the third-person analyst. As a form of action, then, teaching is no longer seen as embedded in particular contexts or within cultural, linguistic, religious, or political traditions which may be at work in all kinds of tacit and nuanced ways in teachers and pupils as persons. Or, rather, it is suggested that everything essential in teaching can be disembedded from such contexts and traditions, as well as from the urgencies and contingencies of the classroom, and made transparent in a neutral model which, by isolating in precise terms the goals of the activity, provides the teachers with guidelines for controlling efficiency and straightforward criteria for evaluating success. It was in reflecting on all this that the appositeness of the words of Wittgenstein which provide the title for this book first struck me: one might teach by this model on ice but hardly in the rough ground of the classroom.

The logic whereby so much that seemed to me ineliminable from teaching could be so lightly disregarded was an *instrumentalist* one. In profiling a teacher's objectives, this model sought to separate ends and means, to repose everything of value that a teacher might accomplish in the ends (i.e., objectives) and then to construe all problems of teaching as ones simply of finding the most suitable means to the achievement of these ends. Every classroom activity could now be conceived as purely instrumental, i.e., as a means which was in itself neutral and therefore substitutable in principle by any other means, the only criterion for such substitutions being efficiency and economy in achieving the ends. All questions of value then were to be located at the level of ends—in deciding in the first instance what objectives were worth teaching. But once these decisions were made, further critical issues were precluded; for, since means were in themselves value-neutral, the only questions that could arise in relation to them concerned their *effectiveness* in achieving the chosen ends.

To thus demystify a teacher's activity so that it amounts to no more than neutralized means was possible, I believed, only because the 'ends' too — in being cast into objectives statements — had been severely attenuated. Ends alone were allowed to be intrinsically valuable, but it seemed clear that what made them valuable (if their value was to be more than merely stipulative, i.e., to accrue to them simply in virtue of their being set up as objectives) was something that could not be articulated within the discourse of this model. The model enjoins teachers to specify their goals as discrete, observable behaviors. Atomistic objectives may seem worthwhile, however, only if they aggregate over time into qualities of mind and character, such as an ability for independent thought and reflection, a habit of truthfulness, a sense of justice, a care for clarity and expressiveness in writing and speech. So far from giving one any reason to suppose that this aggregation will occur, however, the behavioral objectives model cannot offer grounds for supposing that qualities such as these — which I took to be the really significant achievements of education — even exist. For the language of the model is designed precisely to exclude them as being too vague or too open to divergent interpretations as to their meanings. This exclusion is ensured by the insistence that in formulating objectives "[t]he overt behaviour or the procedure for observing it must be described so that all who read the description can agree whether or not a given student's performance or product testifies to the presence of the objective in question";[3] or, as this same attempt to eliminate a hermeneutical dimension from teaching is urged by one of the more robust proponents of the model: "remember the iron-clad rule of objectives writing: if there is disagreement about the meaning, don't argue about it, fix it."[4] The highly specific behavioral objectives that a teacher formulates, then, either are not connected with any background sense on her part of dispositions and virtues to be fostered in the pupils — in which case there is no basis for considering them worth teaching — or else they are so connected — in which case much more is at play for the teacher than these objectives *per se*. And this 'more' will make it impossible for her to treat her instructional methods merely as instrumental means. For some methods that might be 'effective' in achieving the circumscribed objectives may be found to be incompatible with the larger aim which remains in the background (and gives the objective whatever educational import it may have); while other methods may be required as intrinsic to, or constitutive of, this aim—so that they are not at all 'neutral' or substitutable. (For example, could independent thought really be an aim in a classroom where pupils were given little scope to develop and discuss their ideas?)

The claim to neutrality here concerned not just particular teaching methods as means but also the whole model itself. In that the model was seen as carrying no substantive commitments with respect to educational values but as being equally hospitable to educators of any and every persuasion, it itself, as a framework for organizing teaching, could be presented as neutral; for it made no prescriptions about what should be taught but, rather, offered an instrument to all who had such prescriptions—however disparate or conflicting among themselves the latter might be—to implement them more successfully. In the words of one writer, "[t]hese are neutral instructional models in the sense that they are not tied to the attainment of particular objectives . . . the purpose . . . is to achieve more efficiently whatever goals have been selected." Or as the authors of a seminal text put it in relation to their own efforts "to avoid value judgments about objectives and behaviours": "Neutrality with respect to educational principles and philosophy ought to be achieved by constructing a system which, insofar as it was possible, would permit the inclusion of objectives from all educational orientations."[5]

Despite the protestations of its adherents, I did not believe that this model was in fact neutral "with respect to . . . philosophy." If this was to be shown, however, it became clear that what needed to be tackled was the conception of practical rationality held by these authors. For they could take their model to be neutral—i.e., to be at the service of different 'options' while not being itself an option at all—only because it appeared to them to be simply and incontestably rational. It appeared thus because they came to the problems of teaching already equipped with a conception of rational action whose credentials had already been established (they supposed) in the empirical sciences and in their applications in industry and in other fields. This conception being in no need of justification, their purpose was simply to extend its range so that it should come to prevail in the hitherto—by its standards—backward domain of education. Their fundamental commitment, then, was not to any vision of teaching but rather to certain presuppositions about rational action. These presuppositions were applied systematically in the development of their own model of teaching and appealed to as a norm in criticizing other approaches; they were taken to provide a universal standard such that any mode of thinking or acting that departs from it necessarily *falls short* of it and can thus be regarded as ripe for submission to it. Given all this, the problem confronting me was to show that this standard constituted *a* logic or *a* form of rationality—one which had its own biases, limitations, and (when these limitations were not acknowledged) distortions—and that it did not, therefore, define exclusively what is meant by 'logical' or coincide with rationality *as such*.

This problem was not confined to teaching; it was easy to discover that variants of it arose in other fields such as political activity, organizational and management practices, psychotherapy, and community development. The objectives model had to be recognized as a vehicle for importing into education a project which has quite general cultural significance and deep historical roots; the issue which it ultimately raises is about the nature of rationality and also at the same time the nature of practice, *any* practice. With this recognition I was no longer interested in the discourse of this model as such. I wanted, rather, to assemble a more ample discourse which would enable me to interpret and criticize, beyond the level of its own self-understanding—i.e., beyond the conceptual resources available in its own texts—the basic project that was being carried forward through this model, a project which, as I have indicated, far transcended in scope and significance what its exponents, wittingly or unwittingly, were trying to accomplish in the particular field of education. I wanted to articulate not only the nature of this project but also what I believed to be its severe limitations, as well as the basis of an alternative to it. My sense of these limitations and of the possibility of an alternative derived of course from what I have called an intuitive sense of the nature and texture of a practical engagement. And so what I also needed to be able to articulate, and justify, was precisely the intuitions which had initially prompted my unfavorable response to it, as well as my sympathy with some other approaches which it heavily criticized.

2. The Company of Philosophers

To find a discourse which would facilitate this articulation, I looked to philosophy. For the problem confronting me, I soon discovered, was one which had already been identified and reflected on, in different contexts and in varying styles, by several philosophers. These were philosophers who saw themselves as combatting a particular conception of the jurisdiction of reason in human affairs—or, rather, the attempt to establish a particular mode of reason as the necessary and sufficient guide in all areas of practice and indeed in the general conduct of life. 'Rationalism' is the term which may be given to this conception, and, following my chosen philosophers, the type of reason that it seeks to install may be called 'technical' reason. Now in contesting the hegemony of this mode of reason, these philosophers had both exposed its nature and limits and at the same time tried to evoke an alternative to it. Moreover, by trying to demonstrate the reasonableness of this alternative mode of informing and guiding practical activity, they had offered and attempted to justify a different—a larger and more differentiated—picture of human reason itself. Their arguments about reason were at the same time, of course, arguments about practice. It was because practice is in their view irreducible to technique that it calls for a distinctively practical and therefore nontechnical type of knowledge. Or, since technical rationality can be seen as an attempt to extend the standpoint and the benefits—in terms of detachment, explanatory power, universality, and control—of a certain kind of *theory* to the agent who is involved in practical situations, the issue here can also be construed in terms of the relationship between theory and practice. The philosophers I was interested in were ones for whom practice was not "merely an expression of embarrassment at the deplorable but soon overcome condition of incomplete theory," and who did not suppose that "to be consigned to practice means to have to make do as much as needs be without a perfect theory."[6]

There are five modern[7] philosophers who will guide us into an exploration of the distinctions and relations between technical and practical reason and who, in doing so, will direct us back to Aristotle. The classic articulation of the distinction between these two modes of reason is to be found in the analysis of the concepts of *technē* and *phronēsis* in book 6 of the *Nicomachean Ethics*. Aristotle there aligns techne with a kind of activity which he calls 'making' or 'production' (*poiēsis*). This activity issues in a durable outcome, a product or state of affairs (a house, a goblet, a person restored to good health) which can be precisely specified by the maker before he engages in his activity and which, as surviving the latter, provides it with its end or purpose (*telos*). Techne then is the kind of knowledge possessed by an expert maker; it gives him a clear conception of the why and wherefore, the how and with-what of the making process and enables him, through the capacity to offer a rational account of it, to preside over his activity with secure mastery. Aristotle elaborated this concept of techne with the help of a cluster of concepts—especially means (*ta pros to telos*) and end (*telos*) and matter (*hulē*) and form (*eidos*) —through which he may be said to have laid down the authoritative framework for the whole Western tradition of purposive rationality—at the level of 'common sense' as much as at that of philosophical conceptualization.

It was Aristotle's singular achievement, however, that having consolidated the notion of techne (which he very largely took over from Plato), and having given due recognition to it as the preeminent vehicle through which (in a whole range of specific areas) human beings contribute to the order of the material world, he nonetheless stopped short of according to it an unlimited jurisdiction in human affairs. Besides *poiēsis,* the activity of producing outcomes, he recognized another type of activity, *praxis,* which is conduct in a public space with others in which a person, without ulterior purpose and with a view to no object detachable from himself, acts in such a way as to realize excellences that he has come to appreciate in his community as constitutive of a worthwhile way of life. Now a person's relationship to his characteristic praxis was, Aristotle believed, different from the relationship that obtained between him and poiesis. As an activity that both involved one with other people and at the same time was a realization of one's self, praxis engaged one more intimately, or afforded one less detachment, than the poiesis over which one exercised an uncompromised sovereignty. And for this reason—that it, e.g., brought one's emotions so much more into play and both formed and revealed one's character—as well as because of its bringing one into situations that were very much more heterogeneous and contingent than the reliably circumscribed situations of poiesis, praxis required for its regulation a kind of knowledge that was more personal and experiential, more supple and less formulable, than the knowledge conferred by techne. This practical knowledge (i.e., knowledge fitted to praxis) Aristotle called phronesis, and in his analysis of it, in which he distinguished it explicitly from techne, he bequeathed to the tradition a way of viewing the regulation of practice as something nontechnical but not, however, nonrational.

Aristotle was the first to identify this theme of the distinction between what, following him, we call technical and practical reason, and he analyzed it with a power and subtlety which have since hardly been surpassed. I did not approach him directly, however, when this theme first came into focus for me. Indeed my relation to him then might be taken to confirm his view (which needs, I believe, to be qualified) that young people do not have what it takes to profit from moral and political philosophy: still filtered through my undergraduate perception, he was an ancient and not very interesting figure. He became interesting only as I discovered him, in solution as it were, in a number of modern philosophers who were tackling the problem of rationalism in ways that responded to my need. These are the five philosophers who will be met in the first part of this book, and I will introduce them briefly by indicating what it is in their works that makes them especially relevant to my theme and how each of them, with varying degrees of emphasis and explicitness, points back to Aristotle as the exemplary analyst of it and thus motivates my examination of his thought in Part 2.

In the first three chapers, attending not to the complete *oeuvre* but to a single work in which the theme is addressed with particular pointedness, I shall consider the ideas of three philosophers who grappled with the technicist phenomenon as they encountered it in three different areas with which they were respectively concerned. I shall begin with John Henry Newman's *A Grammar of Assent*. At a time when technical reason seemed to be bolstered by the full energy of the Industrial Revolution — reinforced by the utilitarianism of Bentham and Mill as well as by the confidence in science of what was still an Age of Progress — this book tried to expose its (i.e., technical reason's) flat-footedness in the myriad of cases where concrete matters are at issue and one must make judgments as best one can according to one's lights. It was *religious* practice that Newman was particularly concerned to vindicate — a practice which would disappear altogether indeed if technical reason had a legitimate monopoly on rational motives for action and belief. Religion figured in Newman's work, however, in a way not unlike the way in which education figures in my own: it was the area of his immediate and primary concern, but he could see that an adequate defense of it required an argument which, contesting the jurisdiction of technical reason on a quite general front, would demonstrate the need for, and the competence of, a more personal, committed, and at the same time more flexible type of intelligence, in matters not just of religion but of, for example, history, art, the law, and even the sciences. Newman's elaboration of this type of intelligence, which he called the "Illative Sense," will be the object of attention in chapter 1. I shall try to show there both how closely modeled on Aristotelian phronesis it is *and* — making a case for the prescience or contemporaneity of Newman — how much it anticipates a radical revisionism that has characterized the philosophy of science over the past few decades.

In chapter 2 I turn to a book, published nearly seventy years after the *Grammar*, which prosecutes the case against technical reason in the *aesthetic* field. In *The Principles of Art*, R. G. Collingwood argues that the most systematic source of misunderstandings of artistic processes is the technicist bias ingrained in our habits of thought by the overriding obviousness of fabrication and (what has in large part contributed to this obviousness) by the enduring influence of the conceptual schema worked out by the Socratic philosophers (especially Aristotle) around the concept of techne. This schema, which involves commonplace distinctions between end and means, form and matter, end product and raw material, planning and execution, is all too easily applied to an artist's work — or rather misapplied, since it distorts our understanding of the latter from the ground up. Collingwood brings techne into very clear relief, all the better to dissociate from it altogether the conception of artistic purposiveness that he himself goes on to formulate. He works out this formulation in terms of the crucial concepts of 'imagination' and 'expression', and in doing so he does not at all advert to Aristotle's analysis of phronesis. I shall try to show, however, that what motivates his conception of artistic purposiveness is similar to what motivates Aristotle's conception of purposiveness in the ethical sphere and that some of the points that we meet in his aesthetics are close to, and prepare our minds for, points which we shall find Aristotle making in his analysis of phronesis. Moreover, the philosophical context which Collingwood develops for his aesthetics reveals the theme of human finitude, and a particular way of understanding language, as inextricably bound up with the attempt to think beyond technique; and reflection on these themes deepens, as we shall see, in the attempts at such thinking that will be explored in subsequent chapters.

Chapter 3 brings us to a confrontation with the limits of technique in the field of *politics*. Hannah Arendt's book *The Human Condition* tries to show that the tradition of political thought in the West, beginning with ruthless clarity in Plato's writings and deriving an irresistible impetus from the rise of the modern bureaucratic state, has canonized 'making', at the expense of 'action', as the prototype of political activity. The maker — be it builder, cobbler or carpenter — operates within a framework which, when he gets it right, assures him stability, reliability, and predictability in the execution of his task. And it is this framework, Arendt suggests, that has served as the paradigm for dealing with political matters. At the heart of such a politics, we should then understand, is a desperate attempt to escape from the inherent vulnerability of human affairs. For what this politics entails — and now does so with such success that we scarcely have the resources any longer to recognize the fact — is the suppression of 'action' with the hazardousness, open-endedness, and irreversibility that are its unavoidable corollaries. Action, for Arendt, involves an enactment and a disclosure of an agent's uniqueness within a vibrating nexus of relationship with other agents. Its secret is that there is an element in it of 'happening' — so that one can never preside over it, or experience sovereignty through it, as one can in the case of making. From the perspective of this concept of action, Arendt's indictment of the Western political tradition is comprehensive. Since this concept itself, however, has clear affinities with Aristotle's concept of praxis — as her foil-concept of making clearly derives from his concept of poiesis — he is the one classical thinker on whom her verdict cannot be severe. And so in exploring the thesis of her book in chapter 3, I shall be broadening the scope of our consideration of limits and alternatives to the technical (or 'making') paradigm and at the same time picking up further resonances of the Aristotelian analysis.

Of these three philosophers whom I have just introduced, two were English (though comfortably outside the mainstream of English philosophy) and the other was a German Jewess whose productive life as a phi-

losopher was spent as an émigré in the United States. The two other thinkers whom we shall meet in Part 1, Hans-Georg Gadamer and Jürgen Habermas, are German—indeed they are almost certainly the most influential
German philosophers of the past few decades. I mention this fact because
when one steps into their work in this book, it may seem as if, after a
relatively comfortable jog in the foothills, one is being asked to run at
high altitude. And this is related not just to the fact that our other three
philosophers very deliberately wrote for the general reader, whereas these
two are irredeemably academic. Something endemic in German philosophy is also involved here: a propensity to speculative flights in which it
can seem to take off from itself, so to speak, rather than from any 'unmediated' reality, and hence to bring one into thin air, if not into cloud
and vapor.

   To speak of German philosophy like this is already, of course, to speak
of it from a characteristically English point of view or from what one writer,
in a tradition that goes back at least to Locke, calls "moderately plain speech."
This is a tradition (our author tells us) which puts a premium above all
on 'clarity' and which, in doing so, "distinguishes sharply between obscurity and technicality. It always rejects the first, but the second it sometimes
finds a necessity." When this same author goes on to speak of those who,
wanting "philosophy to be . . . profound . . . resent technicality but are
comforted by obscurity,"[8] it is a fair guess that German philosophers are
his main targets. Aware of the cultural divide here, I want to claim that
at least in the case of the two philosophers whom I shall be discussing
there is a kind of technicality which need not be mistaken for obscurity
simply because it differs from the kind of technicality that prevails in Anglo-
American analytical philosophy; and if I believe that the difficulty presented by this technicality is worth negotiating for the sake of something
profound that is expressed through it, I have at least sought to be clear
in attempting to vindicate this belief.

   The opening three chapters are intended to introduce our theme
and to illustrate its range by showing how it arises in a number of different fields. None of the three chosen philosophers is unaware of the general implications of the issue whose impact on a specific field (religion,
art, politics) is his/her particular concern, and all of them bring considerable philosophical resources to the task of analyzing it. It is only in chapters 4 and 5, however, that what may be called the universality of our theme
is brought into full relief and that its heaviness of consequence for, and
utter centrality to, philosophy is made the object of thematic reflection.
Like the other three books we shall have studied, Hans-Georg Gadamer's
Truth and Method has its own primary base from which it reflects on the
limits of technical reason. However, this base, namely, the work of inter-

pretation that is involved in the reading of texts, is soon absorbed into a more primordial background: the sustaining relationship in which we are bound to tradition and to language. And this relationship itself, it is quickly apparent, far transcends the work of the professional exegete or philologist which is Gadamer's proximate concern and embraces not only religion, art (to which an entire part of his book is actually devoted), and politics, but education, history, the sciences (natural and human), philosophy itself, and indeed all cultural pursuits.

Gadamer tries to show that when we set out to understand the past — paradigmatically in a canonical text — there is no method on which we can rely to guarantee the adequacy or truth of our interpretation. It is not that rigor is dispensable here but rather that the kind of rigor needed does not reside in rules or formulae that can be systematized — is not, in other words, within the custody of techne. And the reason for this has to do with the nature of our relationship with the past. For despite our so easily supposing that we inhabit a securely circumscribed 'present' from the vantage point of which we can objectify the 'past' as other, this past — in the form of 'prejudices' that we cannot avoid and can scarcely recognize — is already active within the (ostensibly impartial) thinking that we bring to it as 'object.' Our attempts to profile the past, then, always involve us in also re-identifying ourselves, and to acknowledge this fact is not so much to erase gratuitously the line between past and present as to appreciate that it is only by allowing it to float, as it were, and by floating with it ourselves — in a way that I shall try to clarify in chapter 4 — that we can discover where it is.

Gadamer's theme here (prompted by Heidegger) is 'historicity,' and it embraces our relationship to the future as well as to the past. Our mode of being in time puts severe limits on our ability to plan our lives. The continuing power of the past makes it impossible for us to frame, or at least to realize, radically new possibilities, and we benefit more by what comes into play in our experience without our having the power to summon it than by what results from our deliberate calculation and choice. What Gadamer is adverting to here is human finitude (a theme already met in Collingwood and Arendt), his account of which is the positive counterpart of his critique of technical reason: for to be finite is to find oneself participating in a condition over which one cannot exercise the kind of mastery that craftspersons exercise over their materials. His critique of technique deepens into a radical questioning of the whole standpoint of modern subjectivity. The primacy of consciousness and will, which has been so definitive for modern philosophy since Descartes, is undercut, and our mode of being is shown to be much more substantially one of participation or belonging rather than of self-definition or self-constitution.

Exploring this theme with Gadamer will involve us in pondering the nature of 'experience' and also of language, which, we might say, has become the central preoccupation of post-Cartesian philosophy (and which we shall already have met in Newman and in Collingwood). And it will also bring us back to the Greeks and especially to Aristotle. For Gadamer's expedient, when he is trying to articulate the kind of understanding that occurs when we come to grips with a text—and, by extension, that comes into play in all our dealings with the world—is to turn back to Aristotle's analysis of phronesis. At the heart of *Truth and Method* there is a long section on 'phronesis' in which Gadamer tries to clarify this concept precisely by leaning on the distinction between it and 'techne', and then claims that phronesis offers the best available model for illuminating the kind of understanding that is his own special concern. Moreover, in a long series of essays after the publication of his *magnum opus,* in which he reflects on the nature of hermeneutics (or the study of interpretation), he suggests that a far more helpful model for it than any modern science is Aristotle's 'practical philosophy'. (This philosophy—set out primarily in the *Ethics,* but also in the *Politics* and the *Rhetoric*—analyzes the ingredients of good practice (*eupraxia*) and concedes to phronesis a type of insightfulness that is able to make up for practical philosophy's own unavoidable imprecision and indeterminateness as a *theory* of the practical by fitting itself, with sensitivity and a 'good eye', to practice itself.) In encountering Gadamer, then, in chapters 4 and 5, we shall be exploring one of the undeniably great works of twentieth-century philosophy, whose deepest intention is to challenge the pretensions of technical reason and, as entirely integral to this challenge (at the level not just of scholarship but of real *philosophical* need), to retrieve Aristotle's notion of phronesis.

The four 'modern' philosophers whom I have so far introduced share (at least as I present them, putting a sharp focus on a single book of each) a unified undertaking, and when their contributions to this are considered successively one can discern a real continuity and also what might be called a cumulative development, for insights that are met in an earlier figure recur in a later one and without too much strain all these insights can be seen to converge and to find their ultimately most satisfying matrix in Gadamer's thought. In the two final chapters of Part 1, however, we shall meet a philosopher who can sympathize with the basic impulse behind this undertaking but who can himself share in it only by breaking up its unity—and thereby calling into question the integrity, and the contemporary plausibility, of its return to Aristotle. What I mean by the unity of the undertaking we have so far been considering stems from its assumption that to expose the limitations of the paradigm of fabrication or technique is *ipso facto* to rehabilitate practice and phronesis in a recognizably Aristotelian sense. It is just this assumption, however, that is questioned by Jürgen Habermas. In chapter 6 we shall see that Habermas, too, is a relentless critic of technical ascendancy—and, indeed, with much greater intrepidity and a more informed eye, tracks down its many different 'colonies' in complex and increasingly opaque industrialized societies. But while he too has used the term 'praxis' to designate the type of engagement in which the human capacities, needs, and aspirations that are abrogated by technique are still preserved, 'praxis' in his sense has traveled a long way from what it was in Aristotle; he has injected into it, we might say, the most liberating elements that he has been able to appropriate from modern thought, and increasingly this has implied for him not just a departure from, but a repudiation (as "neo-conservative") of, any Aristotelian revivalism.

No more than our other four thinkers, then, does Habermas accept technical reason as an adequate realization of 'reason'. His difficulty with any rehabilitation of phronesis, however, is that it sells short what the best of specifically modern thought has taught us to regard as the real and unrenegable demands of reason. It is not that he has been unable to learn from Aristotle and indeed from Gadamer. Quite early in his career he acknowledged the merits of Aristotelian practical philosophy insofar as it was a kind of theory that was still vitally related to life-practice, having illuminative and directive power with respect to it—whereas most modern social theory, frozen in methodological detachment and with its hands tied by a vow of value-neutrality, has abdicated any such role. And he has been happy to accept Gadamer's extension of this Aristotelian insight into hermeneutics, for it has helped him to deepen his critique of positivistic science, i.e., a science that is committed to being heedless of the historical presuppositions of its own genesis and application. And yet for all this, Habermas convicts Aristotle's ethics of incorrigible complacency; for it presupposes and accepts the ethos of an existing political order, and the *phronimos* (person who possesses phronesis), as formed by and as having deeply internalized this ethos, is not one who can ever criticize or think beyond it. And, as is only to be expected, the same kind of conservatism or stifling of critique reappears and is explicitly legitimated in Gadamer's endorsement of 'prejudice' and in the folding back of reason into tradition that it entails.

Habermas has wanted to envisage a practice, then, that is informed not by phronesis but by *critique:* a critique that will have *theoretical* rigor and, though never without presuppositions, a commitment to reflect relentlessly on just what these presuppositions are, and to dissociate itself from any that do not fall in with reason's ultimately ungainsayable in-

terest in mature autonomy (*mündigkeit*). In Habermas's earlier work, which
I shall consider in chapter 6, Marx and Freud (purged, it must be said,
of a residual technicism which he detects in both of them) appear as the
exemplary exponents of such an 'emancipatory' theory, and so praxis in
the Marxist sense of *theoretically* enlightened political intervention and
the enlightened therapeutic intervention of psychoanalytic procedure are
offered as paradigms for all practice. In a change of emphasis in his later
work (to be considered in chapter 7), however, Habermas frees himself
from over-reliance on either of these two particular traditions which have
made frontal assaults on what he calls "systematically distorted communication" and argues that implicit in every practice (or what he now calls
"communicative action") is an urge toward self-transparency, an urge that
was curbed in traditional societies but which 'cultural modernity' gives
us the hope of releasing and gratifying. Such self-transparency comes about
as agents 'decenter' themselves from given assumptions and identities and,
exposing all givens to discussion and testing, as well as opening up (primarily through artistic projections) new and more unconstrained possibilities of living, require discursive justification for any norms or policies to
which they will commit themselves. It is as a defender of modernity (or
of what loosely may be called the Enlightenment legacy), then, that Habermas takes his stand. He stands not only against what might be considered
the pre-modern impulse shared by our other thinkers, but against what
he sees as the wilder desertion of reason by 'post-modernist' thinkers (his
debate with Jacques Derrida has been fiercer than his earlier debate with
Gadamer) and also (like the defender of any great and complex movement) against the distortions to which modernity itself has succumbed,
thereby betraying its own best intentions.

Now it is clearly in an adversarial role that Habermas enters our overall conversation. There is indeed enough shared understanding between
him and our other interlocutors—his opposition, no less thorough than
theirs, to technicism, his appreciation of the strengths as well as the
weaknesses of Gadamer (and Aristotle) and his well-documented admiration for Arendt—to make him a genuine partner in the conversation. But
this cannot hide, and in fact only deepens, the challenge that he presents
to the whole line of thought which I have been charting. My response
to this challenge, in the second half of chapter 7, will be to scrutinize
closely Habermas's own very ambitious project, not only from a viewpoint
formed through the preceding stages of the conversation but, more particularly, with a view to his relationship with Aristotle.

Habermas has been as acute as anyone in recognizing the circularity
that obtains when the reasonableness that guides our practice is parasitic
on the integrity of this practice itself; but, unreconciled to this circularity,

he has sought tirelessly to break it. He has tried mightily to demonstrate the possibility of a practice which—unblinkered by technical reason and also avoiding the kind of complicity with an established way of life that goes with phronesis—will have a rigorously rational and in the end quasi-*theoretical* basis. I shall try to show, however, that the coherence of this whole enterprise is enormously threatened: that, in particular, it is not clear how—his own best intentions notwithstanding—the theoretical or 'discursive' undertakings that he projects can remain vitally connected with or embedded in a practical way of life at all or, if they can, how they do not turn out to be just another, albeit highly refined and sophisticated, form of technique. And I shall also ask whether his difficulties here are not caused—as within the context set by our other thinkers they must seem to be—by his attempting to do something which Aristotle was right to declare, at the very outset of his ethico-political reflections, to be simply impossible. Aristotle believed that if one's subject matter is the practical and communal life of persons then one must renounce the methodological purism and the possibilities of generalization and precision that are legitimate aspirations in properly theoretical endeavors. Habermas, Aristotle might say, cannot have his theoretical cake and eat it. He cannot have a form of knowledge which, constructed in the almost laboratory-like conditions of his 'ideal speech situation', enjoys the advantages of theory and at the same time, as practical, must be able to gear in with the motivational resources of a person's character and bend itself to the contingency and haphazardness of concrete situations. The circle cannot be broken and so must be accepted as part of the nature—the never fully disclosed and sometimes irredeemably tragic nature—of human life itself.

We shall already have met this circle under the rubric of the 'hermeneutical circle' in Gadamer. The difficulties in Habermas's position, the exposure of which will bring Part 1 of our study to a close, will provide the immediate stimulus, however, for a discussion of Aristotle's philosophy of practice and, in particular, for considering closely his way of handling this circle. And so the voice which will all the time have been echoing through other voices in Part 1 will join the conversation, in its own right, in Part 2.

I shall approach Aristotle, then, for the classic articulation of the position which Habermas has been trying to overcome and an understanding of the strength of which may shed light on the *aporiai* in Habermas's philosophy. It is not simply nor indeed primarily as a counter-response to Habermas, however, that we shall be going back to Aristotle in Part 2. For our direct concern there will be to illuminate Aristotle himself and to do so in the light of the whole conversation carried on in Part 1. The fact that I shall have demonstrated the range and depth of the retrieval

of key concepts of his practical philosophy will not make it otiose to return then to his own texts. On the contrary, what we get in our 'modern'
philosophers is not a full trawl of the riches (and problems) of Aristotle's
analysis, but rather an encouragement to do this trawling ourselves. These
philosophers (though this is certainly least true of Gadamer) do not so
much work on Aristotle as show through their works that, if I may so put
it, Aristotle is working in them. But the way that he works in them provides the basic orientation for the work that I shall do on him. For I shall
be approaching Aristotle with an eye firmly focused on the concepts of
phronesis and techne and on the distinction between them. It is a curious
fact, however, that this distinction is not one on which Aristotle himself
lavished much attention and so, rather than hearing it directly from him,
it is only by taking a quite active part ourselves in a conversation with
him about it—only by making explicit, that is, a good deal that remains
tantalizingly implicit in his own texts—that we shall come to a proper
understanding of it. Moreover, it is also the case that this distinction has
not been much profiled in the very considerable body of scholarship that
has accumulated around the *Ethics* over the past few decades. 'Phronesis'
has indeed been the subject of much detailed exegesis but its distinction
from or contrast with 'techne' has not been a very significant theme in
this work. This is no doubt related to the fact that 'techne' itself, despite
or rather perhaps because of its being one of the most solidly domesticated
of all the concepts in his philosophy, has received so little—so surprisingly
little—attention in Aristotelian scholarship. There is, then, a certain gap
between the interests of philosophers and of commentators with regard
to Aristotle's ethico-political thought, and it is this gap that I shall be
trying to bridge when, with the heightened sense of its philosophical significance gained from the conversation in Part 1, I turn to commentary
in Part 2.

The distinction I have introduced here between 'philosophy' and
'scholarship' or 'commentary' is by no means straightforward, of course,
and important questions arise about the relationship between the different things that are attempted in the two parts of this book. How legitimate is it to approach Aristotle in such an avowedly prejudiced manner
as I shall be doing—with anticipations formed by encounters with modern thinkers and motivated by a problem that arose in a contemporary
setting? Does each part stand independently or must they be read together? I shall address these and related questions not here but in a short
Interlude between Parts 1 and 2 (where the fuller reading of Gadamer
that we shall have undertaken in the meantime will have put us in a better position to answer them). Suffice it to say here—and to explain and
justify it there—that each part can indeed be read independently, since no

first-hand acquaintance with Aristotle's texts will be presupposed in Part 1, and the interpretation of these texts in Part 2 will be developed with scarcely any overt intrusions from the philosophers who will have been given their voices in Part 1. At the same time, it must also be said that the two parts are conceived as deeply complementary to each other. Rather than starting an entirely new conversation, Part 2 is a new phase of the same conversation that is going on in Part 1. My exchange with Aristotle there is indeed altogether concentrated on *his* texts, and the questions that I press upon him are ones whose sense, and pertinence to the texts, should at all stages be quite perspicuous (so that, if they are not, this is a fault and not an unfortunate necessity). It still remains true, however, that the overall thrust of these questions will have been suggested by the philosophers of Part 1. And so a reading of these last three chapters is likely to be enhanced if one can not only hear the conversation that is going on there but *overhear* the voices that from behind the scenes prompt this conversation—even if they are never allowed to derail or, I hope, to muffle it.

3. Conversation as a Mode of Philosophical Inquiry

I shall conclude this Introduction by saying something about the conception of philosophy—and the working assumptions it carries with it—that is implicit in this study. This will mainly involve reflection on my dominant metaphor of 'conversation.' For, as is by now quite apparent, my whole strategy, having come upon and identified an initial problem, is to engage a number of philosophers as partners in a conversation about it: so that to resolve the problem and to deepen the conversation with one's partners become one and the same thing. But is this only a metaphor or rather (given that 'only' here implies an epistemologically superior attitude to metaphor which some good recent philosophy might have disabused us of)[9] is it a weak, distracting, or misleading metaphor? How seriously is the notion of conversation to be taken, in what way does it condition our inquiry, and has it merits that outweigh what might seem like considerable constraints? The beginning of an answer to these questions is that I do intend 'conversation' to be taken in a serious and substantial sense; so that if this sense can now be clarified—and the questions therefore more fully answered—the reader should have a good idea of the nature and limits of this book.

Since the work is conceived as a conversation, each philosopher must be allowed to speak in his or her own voice (hence the very frequent, though seldom lengthy, quotations which are threaded through each chapter) and at the same time made to speak to a common issue or theme. My own obviously privileged partnership in the conversation carries the responsibility of ensuring that these two conditions are met with respect to the other partners: that the voice of none of them is distorted or falsified, while at the same time each one is disciplined by the conversation itself (so that no overconcern to present the full doctrine of any one thinker should overthrow the common theme). I need to clarify what 'discipline' means here, however. For while conversation certainly entails selection and direction, there is still an expansiveness about it which means that no one is really on a tight leash. When it is properly conducted it actually conducts itself; it comes to have a life of its own and to carry the partners along in its movement. And this fact has an important implication with respect both to my original purpose in entering the conversation and to the viewpoints of the philosophers whom I engage in it. With respect to the philosophers it can well happen that the point or significance of things said by each of them will be brought to light in new or revealing ways through the *context* that gradually accumulates and that is contributed to, of course, by the other voices; when viewpoints are brought together in conversation then, like the rubbing together of fire sticks (to use Plato's image),[10] they can sometimes produce the illuminative spark that no one of them can quite produce on its own.

With respect to our original purpose, the conversational effect is perhaps more disconcerting. For it was with a firm footing in the world of practical affairs (that of teaching and schools) that we first identified our problem and then went to the philosophers seeking a quite specific type of enlightenment. What we discover, however, is that philosophy will serve us only if we surrender to it. The original problem does not remain in a position to dictate what the terms of the conversation will be but is itself assumed into and transformed by it. It is as if one were to take up a game with the object of becoming fit and then to find that one has succumbed to the charm of the game itself so that one continues in a new and developing relationship to it—with one's original purpose not unfulfilled but transmuted in a way not anticipated. So here, too, our original problem of getting a purchase on a particular model of teaching—and, beyond that, of formulating the shortcomings of technical reason—once it is drawn into the discourse of our philosophers, is not suspended or abjured but is shown rather to open up, quite beyond our expectations, such large themes as finitude, the nature of experience as well as of language, and indeed the presuppositions of the whole modern philosophy of consciousness. And unless one is seduced into following out these themes with one's philosophers one will have little to gain from them with regard to the original problem.

There is a severe consequence here for the practice of applied philosophy such as, for example, the philosophy of education may be taken to be. The occupational hazard of a philosopher of education — and the case is similar, I suggest, in other applied fields — is, with the laudable intention of making one's work accessible to colleagues in education, to adopt a pusillanimous attitude to philosophy. Invariably this attitude serves education no better than it serves philosophy. Moreover, to eschew it does not imply a despotic role for philosophy nor consign it to some lofty perch where, practised by and intelligible only to initiates, it remains uncontaminated by the 'world.' It is just that one cannot start out with serious misgivings about the ascendancy of technical reason and with a correlative desire to vindicate the integrity of practice and then, when one turns to philosophy for confirmation of these misgivings and of this desire, to entertain an implicitly technical notion of philosophy. Philosophy is itself a practice, and, as in the case of any other practice, it is only when one gets caught up in doing it that one can learn to get out of it what it has to give. What it has to give is indeed a kind of insight into the structure of our other practical engagements and, moreover, far from its being the case that experience in any of these (e.g., teaching) must be left behind when one takes it up, such experience (as no one emphasized with greater clarity than Aristotle) is itself a prerequisite for fruitful participation in it. All our interlocutors were passionately concerned about the state of affairs in areas which they shared with their non-philosophical confreres (Newman in religion — and more specifically that of the Christian and Roman Catholic communities — Collingwood in the arts, Arendt in politics, Gadamer in the practice of reading and, beyond that, and in company with Habermas, in the general mode of organization and texture of life in advanced industrial societies) and they philosophized precisely out of this concern. And we in our turn shall be able to join them as active partners only if we too have our concerns in the pre-philosophical world; if we do not, we may handle their jargon, but it will not be a living discourse for us; we shall not have made it our own. Even though it is scarcely ever mentioned, and so remains inaudible, my own experience of teaching has shaped my response to these philosophers, directing — in ways I can scarcely be conscious of myself — the questions, consolations, cautions, and stresses (in both senses), that make up the course of the conversation.

I can clarify further the type of philosophical conversation which I am defending by reference to a recent book whose skillful and provocative advocacy has given some notoriety to conversation as an exemplary mode of philosophising. In *Philosophy and the Mirror of Nature* Richard Rorty canvasses a style of philosophizing that he calls "hermeneutics," and in distinguishing this from the more traditional type of philosophy that he calls "epistemology," he writes: "For epistemology conversation is implicit inquiry. For hermeneutics, inquiry is routine conversation."[11] Rorty is impressed by something I have already acknowledged: the self-sustaining energy, the élan, of good conversation. But he seems to think that a conversation is somehow hijacked as a conversation if, even implicitly, it is at the same time an inquiry. It may be interesting, engaging, inventive, witty, resourceful, and for all these qualities we may prize it; but the partners in it are not to be seen as "holding views on subjects of common concern,"[12] nor is it to be seen as in any sense driven by a desire for *truth* about these subjects. Here I differ from Rorty in that I see the protagonists in this conversation as having a "common concern," and moreover see the role of the conversation as being precisely to bring this out—despite, or rather through the interplay and fusing of, the differing idioms (responding to different contexts) that they each use to express it—and in bringing it out to reach a more truthful understanding of it. It is not important in the end, perhaps, to what we call our ways of doing philosophy, nor does any one figure have an imprimatur with respect to a particular title, but I may say that what is attempted here is, *pace* Rorty (for whom as implicit inquiry it would be convicted as 'epistemology'), an exercise in hermeneutics—in a sense of this word which is sanctioned by Gadamer. For Gadamer, who is much gestured to by Rorty, is the hermeneutical philosopher *par excellence,* who has done more than anyone to legitimate the place of conversation in philosophy (and in other disciplines too) and who has done so indeed while at the same time emphasizing its essential character as *play* (a notion to which Rorty is much drawn and which was present in my earlier image of the game). But for Gadamer, as we shall see, conversation remains the medium in which we search for truth; in Rorty's more radical deconstruction, on the other hand, the truth of a position (if we are so bewitched by epistemology as to still want to speak of 'truth' at all) simply *is* its ability to find a place in, and to further, an interesting conversation.

It is Aristotle himself who gives us the most famous expression of the ultimate undisplaceability of truth from philosophical conversation which I have just been affirming. Although our friends are dear to us, he tells us as he is about to confute Plato's idea of the Good, still as philosophers we must regard truth as even dearer still.[13] To bring out the distinctive way in which conversation mediates the truth, however, we need to give this remark a somewhat different turn. Aristotle is telling us that truth must take precedence even over friendship. But what we may add in the present context is that in the pursuit of truth friendship is a help and not a hindrance; it is through what Plato calls "*benevolent* disputation" that we can best reach it.[14] I make a clean breast of the fact, then, that all the philosophers who feature in this work are ones whom I deeply admire and have found over many years to be most profitable companions. If they were thinkers whose follies I supposed I could easily expose by clever arguments they would have found no place here. Also excluded of course is the kind of antagonist who is both formidable and extremely unsympathetic. There is no Thrasymachus or Callicles in this conversation,[15] and so cross-examination (*elenchos*), although by no means missing, is not its dominant mode, nor is it ever employed with the same oppositional intensity that this pair called forth from Socrates (they were not likely candidates for the Academy, of course, and it was the practice among his own students, sharing a common ethos and committed to a common search, that Plato characterized as "benevolent disputation").

In the kind of dialectical conversation that Plato left us as an example, the friendliness or hostility of one's interlocutor was less important, in fact, than that one's own attitude in the conversation should be friendly: in the sense first of all that one tried to hear without distortion what the other had to say (even when it was uncongenial; *dialegein* originally meant 'to welcome the difference')[16] and then tried to *strengthen* it. The eristic spirit in which, all the better to show one's own superiority, one tried to trip up the partner had no place in dialectic. To the contrary, truth was best served by making as good a case for the other's position as one could— if possible a better case, even, than he had made himself. In the end, then, one saw that it commanded one's assent; or, one's dissent, having been earned with greater exertion, was all the more illuminating. It is in the spirit of dialectic in this sense that I attempt to conduct the present conversation. I try to be hospitable to the particular idiom of each (or, in Rorty's phrase, to "take on the jargon of the interlocutor") and to let the conversation be enriched by the distinctiveness of what each has to say. At the same time I try to bring out affinites between them. And when it sometimes happens that weaknesses seem to remain in a position even when the effort has been made to demonstrate its strengths, it is *within* the conversation, i.e., from one of the other partners, that the remedy is sought—a remedy that may be more palatable and effective for the affinities with the latter already established.

Perhaps it is still a worry, however, not so much that I am so well disposed to the philosophers included here (as they are to each other) but rather that they were in the first instance so congenial to the task set for them, namely, that of confirming intuitions and convictions which experience had already taught me. Is such a task any more than an exercise in special pleading? If philosophy is to be asked to articulate certain intuitions, should it not also be expected—if the exercise is to be intellectually respectable—to *test* them?

This question bites deeper than one might suspect. The philosophers to whom I turn are ones whose theories do not just happen to vindicate the kind of intuitions with which I began. More seriously (and this is most conspicuously true of Newman, Gadamer, and Aristotle, but can also be detected, in a more subdued light, even in Habermas) they offer theories which very self-consciously clip their own wings as theories in the light of what they see as ineluctable constraints on them from the side of practice. These constraints are such as to impose on them, *qua* theories, a task, in relation to practice, which is reconstructive in the sense not of setting any radically new agenda for the latter but rather of simply bringing to light what is going on in it anyhow—often enough, it may be, behind the backs of the practitioners themselves and in spite of large ambitions which they may suppose themselves able to realize. The limitation on its own role which philosophy willingly accepts here affects its powers not only of (practical) redirection but also, and in the present case more significantly, of (theoretical) justification. Philosophy is without independent means of confirming, or disconfirming, the intuitions of practical life if, acknowledging its own dependence on these intuitions, it sees its task primarily as one of revealing or bringing them to light. And so how am I to answer the charge brought against my own project if the philosophers to whom I turn for help in it already seem to have foresworn the ground from which it might be answered?

I have just been trying to show that the problem here is more intractable than it might have appeared to be at first sight. But in honoring this intractability one is in fact on the way to resolving the problem. For the important consequence of the acknowledgment we have just seen by our philosophers is not that one cannot provide an answer to satisfy one's questioner but rather that the kind of answer she or he is looking for is simply unavailable. What sort of test, after all, should a philosopher be able to apply to prephilosophical intuitions and how, in particular, might this test be *independent?* The very notion of such a testing, where one is not already involved in what is being tested and can therefore survey it with complete impartiality, *itself belongs within the technical framework.* And so if one insists on this criterion in evaluating the respective merits of technical and practical approaches, then, in the name of disinterested inquiry, one has already shown oneself to be prejudiced in favor of the technical. And of course what I want to claim is not that my own inquiry is unprejudiced but rather that prejudice one way or another is inescapable. Philosophy cannot be brought in to arbitrate in a neutral way between these two approaches; for the dispute between them is already active and being fought out *within philosophy itself.*

Moreover, the matter need not be allowed to rest with a retort that the person who alleges *petitio principii* here is in fact hoist on his own petard. One can move beyond this logical stalemate when, having acknowledged the circularity of one's undertaking, one then assumes it as a theme into one's ongoing reflection and in doing so offers the only kind of justification that this kind of undertaking is susceptible of—a dialectical one. This is not indeed a justification with reference to an external criterion, but shows only that one's inquiry is taking responsibility for itself: it has made its own implicit procedure a theme for explicit reflection. And it is here that the express commitment of my philosophers to a certain understanding of the relationship between philosophy and practice, which at first sight seemed to deepen our problem, now—with the problem itself transfigured—turns to our advantage. I can the more easily confess to the circularity and prejudice of my own inquiry given that, as it proceeds, the inquiry itself (most notably in Newman and Gadamer) will explicitly develop a perspective within which one will more easily be able to see that circularity need not be vicious nor prejudice intellectually discreditable.

I have been trying to forestall an objection which the nature of my project, and in particular my selection of interlocutors, might seem to invite. Having just offered a justification for the kind of thinkers whom I invoke, I do not, however, want to make any special claim for the particular set of thinkers which is assembled here. I had indeed a certain kind of argument which I wanted to make, but I had no *a priori* checklist which threw up just *these* thinkers as uniquely suitable allies for the making of it. And I may say, more particularly, that I was not looking for, nor on the whole is it helpful to regard my interlocutors as, representatives of 'neo-Aristotelianism'—at least not if the latter is understood as an attempt to respond to a perceived groundlessness of contemporary moral discourse with a full-scale and unabashed restoration of Aristotle's doctrine. In the Epilogue I shall try to show how the kind of relationship to Aristotle established by my interlocutors distinguishes this work from 'neo-Aristotelianism.'

It is a consequence of the lack of very determinate advance criteria that there may well be—and indeed there certainly are—other thinkers who would fit comfortably into the present conversation; who would have no difficulty in, as we say, getting on its wavelength and, through their contribution to it, of course, making it a different, though for my purposes not a decisively different, conversation.[17] *This* conversation, facilitated by the particular complementarities that exist between my chosen thinkers, has indeed a certain structure or 'logic' which is, I hope, perspicuous. Nonetheless, I should confess that in the end there is something irredeemably contingent about the particular group that I have brought together, for they (I mean *just* they, i.e., all of them and no one else) are a function of books that came to hand at particular times while others remained at large, of some trails followed up while others were allowed to run dead, of influences, already established and scarcely recognizable, that disposed this way and not that; and all of this a matter of chance as well as of contrivance (or as Aristotle would say of *tuchē* as well as of techne). Still this very adventitiousness is after all inseparable from conversation which, however great the concentration it may demand, is something that one *falls* into—and that is most likely to fail just when it is too deliberately set up (or as we say 'staged') in order to succeed. And— one last advertence to the self-referential character of the book—this fact, as a general feature of life itself, will, under the name of 'finitude', be one of the themes developed *in* the particular conversation that will be conducted here.

I have been clarifying the nature of conversational philosophy not in order to claim that it is the best, much less the only, kind of philosophy, but simply in order to explain it as the kind that is essayed in the present work. Having done so, I turn now to our theme of practical reason and to the philosopher who will open our conversation about it.

PART 1

The Retrieval of Phronesis and Techne in Modern Philosophy

We accept the fact that the subject presents itself histori-cally under different aspects at different times or from a dif-ferent standpoint. We accept that these aspects do not sim-ply cancel one another out as research proceeds, but are like mutually exclusive conditions that exist each by themselves and combine only in us. Our historical consciousness is al-ways filled with a variety of voices in which the echo of the past is to be heard. It is present in the multifariousness of such voices: this constitutes the nature of the tradition in which we want to share and have a part.

H.-G. Gadamer, *Truth and Method*

Philosophy proclaims its devotion to the universal. But as the profession of cosmopolitan philanthropy which is not rooted in neighborly friendliness is suspect, so I distrust the universals that are not reached by way of profound respect for the significant features and outcomes of human experi-ence as found in human institutions, traditions, impelling interests, and occupations. A universal which has its home exclusively or predominantly in philosophy is a sure sign of isolation and artificiality.

John Dewey, "Context and Thought"

1. J. H. Newman's Appeal to Phronesis in *A Grammar of Assent*

1. Newman's Critique of Rationalism: Preliminary Remarks

In setting out to trace a line of resistance to modern rationalism that is at the same time an attempt to retrieve Aristotelian phronesis, I begin with the work of John Henry Newman. This may seem an unlikely starting point for a study that purports to address a crucial issue in contemporary culture that will bring us eventually very near the center of current philosophical reflection. Newman, after all, was a nineteenth-century Christian apologist whose work has been of, at most, only marginal interest to philosophers. Moreover, even in his own time (and notwithstanding his many public controversies—with prime ministers[1] no less than with leading academics and churchmen) the distinctive cast of his mind and his singular career made him an isolated figure. His being unconvinced by the rationalism that seemed irresistible to most contemporary intellectuals was only the broadest aspect of this isolation. Brought up an Anglican, and having become at Oxford the leader of the most vigorous theological movement in that church for a century, he was estranged from most of what by sentiment and affection was dearest to him when he converted to Roman Catholicism because of what he had come to regard—primarily through reflection on fifth-century theological disputes —as irremediable defects in the authoritativeness of the Anglican Confession. And as a Roman Catholic, the exigent intelligence which had led to his conversion (and by no means been forfeited through it) made him chronically suspect to the leaders of a church then deeply entrenched in anti-modernist reaction. From all this it may seem to be fairly judged that "Newman belongs to no school. In the history of philosophy and theology he appears as a great outsider."[2] Even if he did not write as a philosopher, however, and was out of season in his own time, I shall try to show that Newman is a particular beneficiary of the "temporal distance" which separates his age from ours and that the very factors which made him uncomfortable in the intellectual landscape of Victorian England fit him for intimate partnership in *our* philosophical debates.[3]

The fact that he was above all a religious thinker and that religion was the field which suffered the first and most obviously damaging encroachments of rationalism forced Newman into an early confrontation with a problem whose full brunt would be felt in other fields only when (as we shall see in later chapters)[4] the fuller expansion of rationalism had come to threaten the integrity of practice itself in any field whatever. Newman's significance lies precisely in his diagnosis of the problem as a generic one that required less a defense of religion than a challenge to the paradigm of rationality which would so summarily discredit it[5] — and in his consequent articulation of a rationality which would not only leave room for religious belief but, while doing so, would also do justice to the many ways of being reasonable that are embedded in our social practices. The rationalism that he set out to contest was not of course the exclusive preserve of the skeptical critics of religion; for it was hardly less evident in the kind of apologetics (for which Newman himself had no taste) that felt confident of trading arguments with atheistic all-comers and of making religion prevail just through the force of superior argument on what was supposed to be the level ground of "reason." Newman's own concern was not to provide explicit 'proofs' for theism or Christianity but, rather, through a kind of phenomenological analysis, to reconstruct the processes of inference and assent that ground the conviction of ordinary, intellectually unsophisticated believers[6] and to demonstrate their reasonableness as not being essentially different from the processes which operate in concrete reasoning in any field whatever, be it in a law court, in conducting a historical inquiry, in deciding the authenticity of an artwork, or in solving an engineering problem. If Newman was uninterested then in the 'God of the philosophers', this did not lead him to regard faith as an irrational 'leap'. It is a movement of the mind which indeed involves a venture — while at the same time being conditioned by previous commitments and anticipations — but Newman's purpose is to demonstrate that in this it is similar to the reasonings exemplified in all areas where people deal with matters concretely.[7]

My own interest here, then — since "when faith is said to be a religious principle, it is . . . the things believed, not the act of believing them, which is peculiar to religion"[8] — will not be in the specifics of Newman's defense of religious belief but in his general account of what it is to be reasonable. The core of this account is its denial of the possibility of our constructing — or even reconstructing from successful practice — a method or system (i.e., a techne) whose proper application would yield true knowledge or at least provide an unequivocal criterion of it. Rationalism, in its various versions, was the supposition that such a system existed, whether supplied by or modeled on logic, mathematics, or the hypothetico-deductive method of the empirical sciences. The most significant upshot of rationalism was its exclusiveness: its drastic contraction of the range within which assent can legitimately be given or, in other words, its withdrawal of the status of rationality from large areas in which people not only reason but suppose that they can (even if they do not actually) reason *correctly*. Newman's basic conviction was that in many areas "thought is too keen and manifold, its sources are too remote and hidden, its path too personal, delicate and circuitous, its subject-matter too various and intricate to admit of the trammels"[9] of any formal method, and that consequently "methodical processes of inference, useful as they are, as far as they go, are only instruments of the mind, and need, in order to their due exercise, that real ratiocination and present imagination which gives them a sense beyond their letter, and which, while acting through them, reaches to conclusions beyond and above them. Such a living *organon* is a personal gift, and not a mere method or calculus."[10] His purpose, then, being to counter the rationalist position with an account of reason as "an intrinsic and personal power, not a conscious adoption of an artificial instrument or expedient,"[11] his procedure is similar to Aristotle's in the *Ethics:* not to construct a theory which practice must accommodate to if it is to pass muster, but rather to articulate the structure and defend the integrity of what is already recognizable in the way of life of a community as good practice (in Aristotle's case: acting virtuously, in Newman's case: reasoning well—though, as we shall see, the two cases are closely akin).

In developing my outline of Newman's position, I shall confine attention to his main work, A *Grammar of Assent* (and, to a lesser extent, to the much earlier *University Sermons,* which contain his first published reflections on the problem of rationality and provide the essential background to the *Grammar*); and even with respect to the *Grammar,* my focus will be almost exclusively on the second part of the book, on "Assent and Inference."[12] What I shall try to bring out, in considering Newman's argument, is the way in which it is under Aristotle's influence, as well as the extent to which it anticipates—while at the same time, in certain respects, undeniably differing from—the major strand of contemporary European philosophy which we shall be exploring in later chapters.

2. Newman and Aristotle

Newman had no compunction about identifying "Aristotelic argumentation in its typical modes and figures" (or "the Aristotelic syllogism")[13] as a leading exemplar of the type of rationality whose limits he was seeking to expose, nor about writing: "In spite of Aristotle, I will not allow that genuine reasoning is an instrumental art [i.e., a techne, the techne of logic itself]."[14] Still, when he came, in a later part of the book, to sketch the unsupersedable personal capacity—which he called the "Illative Sense"—which informs reasoning and leads to correct judgment in all concrete matters, it was precisely Aristotle's concept of phronesis that he invoked. In 'phronesis' he found that Aristotle had long ago uncovered, in the field of moral practice, just that resourcefulness of mind and character which, through his own 'Illative Sense', he wished to recognize in all the fields and contexts in which we reason concretely. "Aristotle," he tells us, "calls the faculty which guides the mind in matters of conduct, by the name of phronesis"; and he then goes on to outline, as eloquently as anyone ever has, the peculiar nature of phronesis:

> What it is to be virtuous, how we are to gain the just idea and standard of virtue, how we are to approximate in practice to our own standard, what is right and wrong in a particular case, for the answers in fulness and accuracy to these and similar questions, the philosopher refers us to no code of laws, to no moral treatise, because no science of life, applicable to the case of the individual, has been or can be written. . . . An ethical system may supply laws, general rules, guiding principles, a number of examples, suggestions, landmarks, limitations, cautions, distinctions, solutions of critical or anxious difficulties; but who is to apply them to a particular case? Whither can we go, except to the living intellect, our own, or another's? What is written is too vague, too negative for our need. It bids us avoid extremes; but it cannot ascertain for us, according to our personal need, the golden mean. The authoritative oracle, which is to decide our path, is something more searching and manifold than such jejune generalizations as treatises can give, which are most distinct and clear when we least need them. It is seated in the mind of the individual, who is thus his own law, his own teacher, and his own judge in those special cases of duty which are personal to him. It comes of an acquired habit, though it has its first origin in nature itself, and it is formed and matured by practice and experience . . . it is a capacity sufficient for the occasion, deciding what ought to be done here and now, by this given person, under these given circumstances.[15]

Newman enthusiastically embraces that whole tendency in Aristotle's thought whose fullest expression is in the concept of phronesis because he finds confirmation in it of what long years of reflection had taught him to recognize in his own experience and in that of his friends: that "many of our most obstinate and reasonable certitudes depend on proofs which are informal and personal, which baffle our powers of analysis and cannot be brought under logical rule."[16] He quotes with approval the well-known remark in the methodological preface to the *Nicomachean Ethics* about its being the mark of an educated person to expect only that degree of accuracy which is appropriate in each field (and so not to make mathematical rigor the standard in all fields). And, in support of his conception of the necessary "elasticity" of concrete reasoning (which is "oppressed and hampered, as David in Saul's armour,"[17] if it is made to follow strict logical rules) he alludes to a nice metaphor which Aristotle uses in the discussion of justice which precedes his treatment of phronesis in the *Ethics*: "In old times the mason's rule which was in use in Lesbos was, according to Aristotle, not of wood or iron, but of lead, so as to allow of its adjustment to the uneven surface of the stones brought together for the work. By such the philosopher illustrates the nature of equity in contrast with law, and such is that phronesis, from which the science of morals forms its rules and receives its complement."[18] Or again, in the same vein, he quotes a remark from book six about the possibility of young men becoming accomplished mathematicians, but not *phronimoi* (people of practical wisdom), since phronesis — in Aristotle's words — "is concerned with . . . particulars, which become familiar from experience."[19]

Newman's emphasis on experience is all of a piece with his insistence on judgment as the crucial, unsubstitutable quality of a person who knows his way around an area: "Instead of trusting logical science, we must trust persons, namely those who by long acquaintance with their subject, have a right to judge. And if we wish ourselves to share in their convictions and the grounds of them, we must follow their history, and learn as they have learned. We must . . . depend on practice and experience more than on reasoning. . . . By following this we may . . . rightly lean upon ourselves, directing ourselves by our own moral or intellectual judgment, not by our skill in argumentation."[20] By way of precedent for this view — which flies in the face of modern rationalism and which, in particular, rules out the possibility of our ever devising anything that would even approximate to a person-proof method (or, in the case which launched my own inquiry here, a teacher-proof system of teaching) — he quotes the "grand words" of Aristotle: "We are bound to give heed to the undemonstrated sayings and opinions of the experienced and aged, not less than to demonstrations; because from their having the eye of experience, they behold the principles of things."[21]

A reader of the *Grammar* who comes to it already familiar with the *Ethics*, even when she does not find Aristotle quoted or directly alluded to, will still find him resonating throughout the work. She will read, for instance, that we are forced "instead of devising, what cannot be, some sufficient science of reasoning which may compel certitude in concrete conclusions, to confess that there is no ultimate test of truth besides the testimony borne to truth by the mind itself, and that this phenomenon, perplexing as we may find it, is a normal and inevitable characteristic of the mental constitution of a being like man on a stage such as the world"[22] — or in similar vein elsewhere that "in no class of concrete reasonings . . . is there any ultimate test of truth and error in our inferences besides the trustworthiness of the Illative Sense that gives them their sanction,"[23] so that in each subject-matter "our duty is to strengthen and perfect the special faculty which is its living rule." When she reads this she can hardly fail to connect it with the notoriously Aristotelian tenet that the *spoudaios* (or person of sound disposition and outlook) is not such because he keeps the moral rules, but rather that the rules are such because they are implied in the pattern of living of the *spoudaios;* or, more precisely, with the view that virtue is "to be determined by a rational rule and by that rule by which the *phronimos* would determine it"[24] — a rule (*logos*) which, when Aristotle comes to analyze it in book 6, turns out to be no rule at all but rather a capacity for insight and judgment which is inseparable from the character of the *phronimos* himself.

Or again, when she reads in Newman: "As to logic, its chain of conclusions hangs loose at both ends; both the point from which the proof should start, and the point at which it should arrive, are beyond its reach; it comes short both of first principles and of concrete issues . . . even its most careful combinations made to bear on a conclusion want that steadiness of aim which is necessary for hitting it,"[25] she must think of the equivalent point which Aristotle makes in book 6 of the *Ethics* when he points out a twofold need for intuitive mind (*nous*) in order to make up for a double deficiency in syllogistic or deductive reasoning: "*Nous* is concerned with the ultimates in both directions; for both the primary propositions and the ultimates are objects of *nous* and not of argument, and in demonstrations *nous* grasps the unchangeable and primary definitions, while in practical reasonings it grasps the last and contingent fact. . . . [Hence *nous* is both beginning and end; for demonstrations are from these and about these.]"[26] And she will notice too that Newman's metaphor of the archer (far too unreliable a model for a modern rationalist) is the same one that Aristotle uses quite unselfconsciously at the beginning of his discussion of phronesis in book 6: "in all the states of character we have mentioned, as in all other matters, there exists some mark, as it were, to be hit, upon which the man who has the rule keeps his eyes, and bends his bow more or less strongly accordingly. . ."[27]

As a further example of the deep affinity between the *Grammar* and the *Ethics* we may take the way in which in both of them a view fundamentally at odds with modern rationalism is proposed, namely, that in human affairs a merely calculative intelligence is no more capable of truth than it is of goodness — or, rather, that without goodness even the most subtle intelligence will find truth itself beyond its reach. This point is implicit in Newman's strictures on "mere skill in argumentation" as it is in Aristotle's strictures on that cleverness (*deinotēs*) which in Ross's translation is called "mere smartness." But it is also made ringingly explicit by both of them. Beside Newman's assertion "that truth there is, and attainable it is, but that its rays stream in upon us through the medium of our moral as well as our intellectual being; and that in consequence that perception of its first principles which is natural to us is enfeebled, obstructed and perverted by allurements of sense and the supremacy of the self,"[28] we may place Aristotle's point in the penultimate chapter of book 6: "And this eye of the soul acquires its formed state not without the aid of excellence . . . for inferences which deal with acts to be done are things which involve a starting-point . . . and this is not evident except to the good man; for wickedness perverts us and causes us to be deceived about the starting-points of action. Therefore it is evident that it is impossible to have phronesis without being good";[29] or his earlier advertence, in parenthesis, to the close etymological link between phronesis and *sōphrosunē* (temperance) so that in Greek 'temperance' literally means 'preserver of phronesis' (*sōizousa tēn phronēsin*) — a preserver which is necessary because the judgments with which phronesis is concerned are of such a kind as "pleasant and painful objects destroy and pervert."[30]

Given all this Aristotelian oil in his lamp, it is unsurprising to find Newman claiming, near the end of his work: "as to the intellectual position from which I have contemplated the subject, Aristotle has been my master";[31] the points which I have just made should make it plain how much substance there is in this claim. It should be noticed, however, that Newman does differ from Aristotle in *generalizing* the field of phronesis beyond *ta prakta* (i.e., ethical engagements) so that it "holds good in all concrete matters, not only in those cases of practice and of duty in which we are familiar with it [and which, for Aristotle, are its *only* cases] but in questions of truth and falsehood generally,"[32] and is at work, therefore, "in all concrete reasonings whether in experimental science, historical research or theology." He also differs from Aristotle in *dividing* phronesis so that it becomes proper to specific fields and a person "may possess it in one department of thought, for instance, history and not in another, for instance, philosophy."[33] In fact, Newman goes very much against Aristotle when he carries on this division even within the one field to which Aristotle confined it, for while Aristotelian phronesis exists seamlessly with all the virtues, for Newman it might be shown in the exercise of one virtue by a person who did not possess other virtues and so we might have someone who is "just and cruel, brave and sensual, imprudent and patient."[34]

My purpose here, however, is not to dwell on the measure of difference and even disagreement that exists between Newman and Aristotle, but rather to mark the very great resemblance, amply acknowledged by Newman himself, between their respective concepts of the Illative Sense and of phronesis, and to notice that even in his departures from Aristotle, far from downgrading phronesis, Newman was in fact installing it at the heart of all concrete reasoning (i.e., *all* reasoning apart from the strictly determined inferences of a formal system) and so endowing it with a quite unrivaled significance. Moreover, by doing this—by taking up so fully the 'phronetic' strand in Aristotle's thought, while at the same time registering his misgivings about another strand (that of techne, and in particular of logic, the techne of reasoning, of which Aristotle was the self-proclaimed founder)—and by making this particular way of appropriating Aristotle so central to his whole project of repudiating the rationalist paradigm, Newman was in fact anticipating, though I have not seen him given credit for it, a very vital strand in contemporary European philosophy. We shall be meeting this strand in later chapters, and here I should like to continue my account of Newman by indicating how it is anticipated in his work.

3. Newman and Contemporary Philosophy

In that it analyzes the nature of assent and of the inferences that accompany it, *A Grammar of Assent* might be taken as a work of epistemology. It does not, however, enter into the classic epistemological problematic that had been handed on and developed in a whole tradition of thought from Descartes through Berkeley, Hume, and Kant. In this tradition the epistemological standpoint was one which suspended belief in the power of the human subject to attain 'objective' knowledge, so that, in response to a radical doubt, 'reason' had to engage in the constructive task of adducing grounds on which the objectivity of knowledge could be based. This project might (adopting more recent jargon) be called a 'foundationalist' one. Now, so far from offering any solution within the terms of this project, *A Grammar of Assent* does not even entertain the problem which gives it its starting point. Newman does not attempt to set up for himself a vantage point from which he could ask whether knowledge is possible. He assumes that we *do* know, that knowledge is a practice that people are already involved in, and what he undertakes in his essay is what might be called a phenomenological analysis of this practice.[35] Had he attempted to provide some ultimate foundation for it, he tells us quite simply, "I should have been falling into metaphysics; but my aim is of a practical character."[36]

If unambitiousness, even to the point of a lack of philosophical seriousness, should be alleged against Newman here, this charge is unlikely
to come from the kind of thinkers whose work will be explored in our
later chapters. The clearest affinity is with Hans-Georg Gadamer, whose
avowedly 'post-metaphysical' philosophy, as we shall see, is a full-blooded
revival of 'practical philosophy' as an attempt — after the example of Aristotle's *Ethics* — neither to legislate nor to provide some more ultimate justification for good practice, but rather to articulate what is already operative
in it. This nonfoundationalist project involves for Gadamer a rehabilitation of the notion of 'prejudice': one cannot avoid being indebted to
assumptions and anticipations which form a kind of horizon within which
one understands and judges and which cannot, therefore, themselves appear within this horizon. Reason has no absolute standpoint from which
it could make all its assumptions transparent, and to accept one's bounded-
ness within tradition, therefore, far from being an abdication of reason,
is simply to resign oneself to the only kind of reasonableness that is available to a finite creature. In developing this viewpoint, Gadamer both gives
central importance to a retrieval of Aristotle's notion of phronesis and at
the same time opposes what he sees as a basic tenet of Enlightenment
thought; "the fundamental prejudice of the Enlightenment," he comments,
"is its prejudice against prejudice itself."[37] I shall be exploring Gadamer's
position in some depth in chapters 4 and 5 below; but perhaps I have
said enough about it to make it worthwhile here to show how much it is
anticipated by Newman:

> it is not unfair to urge . . . that tradition, though unauthenticated, being
> (what is called) in possession, has a prescription in its favour, and may
> *prima facie,* or provisionally, be received. Here are the matters for a fair
> dispute; but there are writers who seem to have gone far beyond this rea-
> sonable scepticism, laying down as a general proposition that we have no
> right in philosophy to make any assumption whatever, and that we ought
> to begin with a universal doubt. This, however, is of all assumptions the
> greatest, and to forbid assumptions universally is to forbid this one in par-
> ticular. . . . Of the two, I would rather have to maintain that we ought to
> begin with believing everything that is offered to our acceptance, than that
> it is our duty to doubt of everything.[38]

Here Newman is defending what, in one of the University Sermons, he
calls "previous notices, prepossessions, and (in a good sense of the word)
prejudices";[39] it is just this "good sense of the word" that Gadamer too
has been attempting to vindicate. Both of them are especially concerned
with the process through which one comes to understand or judge the
viewpoint of another (Gadamer's paradigm case of this is the reading of
texts, whereas Newman's is more the participation in intellectual contro-

versy),[40] and what both of them stress is the prior context which one always brings to the engagement, which is effective in one's interpretation and response and which has its roots in a subsoil of the mind which can never be fully turned over for inspection. Newman speaks of "subtle assumptions . . . accompanying the course of reasoning step by step, and traceable to the sentiments of the age, country, religion, social habits and ideas, of the particular inquirers or disputants, and passing current without detection, because admitted equally on all hands,"[41] or of "how little depends upon the inferential proofs and how much upon those pre-existing beliefs and views, in which men either already agree with each other or hopelessly differ, before they begin to dispute."[42]

Gadamer's thought is only one manifestation of a 'contextualism' which has been evident not only in a keener philosophical response to issues raised by anthropological studies (e.g., in Peter Winch's *The Idea of a Social Science and Its Relation to Philosophy* [London: Routledge and Kegan Paul, 1958]), but also in a major reorientation in the philosophy of science (most notoriously through the work of Thomas Kuhn and Paul Feyerabend).[43] It is indeed an irony of recent intellectual history that while modern rationalism has sought to establish science (or rather a particular image of science) as the ultimate standard of reason, what has done most in contemporary philosophy to undermine this standard has been not so much a rear-guard action against it on behalf of areas of thought and action which are discredited by it (as irrational or pre-rational — e.g., theology, jurisprudence, art criticism, or historical research) but rather work done precisely in the *philosophy of science* — where, in order to make sense of the kind of reasoning that actually goes on in the sciences, thinkers have increasingly canvassed the *affinities* or *analogies* between it and the kind of thinking that goes on in, for example, a law court or in the appraisal of an artwork. I shall now look briefly at some of this work and show how congenially Newman's work sits with it.

Consider first Hilary Putnam's reflections, in *Meaning and the Moral Sciences,* on the fact that an element of what he calls "practical knowledge" is inexpungible from the methodology of the human or 'moral sciences':

> it is a feature of 'scientific' knowledge (at least if we take *physics* as the paradigm) that we *use measuring instruments that we understand.* Our theory applies to our measuring instruments, and to their interactions with what they are used to measure, not just to the objects we measure. It is a feature of *practical* knowledge that we often have to use *ourselves* (or other people) as the measuring instruments — and we do *not* have an explicit theory of *these* interactions.[44]

As an example of the intrusion of 'practical knowledge', in this sense, into research in the 'moral sciences', Putnam takes the case of a historian who, on the basis of all the evidence he has amassed, concludes that "Smith was hungry for power." How does he reach this conclusion? *"Not* by applying 'general laws of history, sociology and psychology' to the data as positivist methodologists urge he should! Rather he has to absorb all his material, and then *rely on his human wisdom* that this shows power-hunger 'beyond a reasonable doubt' (as the courts say). In effect, he uses *himself* as a 'measuring instrument'. . . ."[45] If this historian should seem to be in a poor state with respect to the methodological rigor and hence the warrantability of his scholarly knowledge, he is not in fact any worse (though neither is he any better) off here than he is in the case of his commonsense judgments, and what Putnam wants to point out is the unassimilability of these latter judgments, too, to any 'scientific' standards — even though it would be entirely futile to doubt systematically their entitlement to count as *knowledge.* "The idea that what we know is co-extensive with what we can check 'publicly' following well-understood paradigms of scientific testing does not even fit some of the *simplest* facts we know."[46] As an example of one of these facts, Putnam takes the case in which it is "perfectly clear to everyone in a given situation that Jones is jealous of Smith's reputation," even though "one couldn't give *anything like* a 'scientific proof'" of this proposition.

> It isn't, for example, that 'Jones said blah-blah and people who say blah-blah are generally jealous'. Even if it is true that people who say blah-blah are generally jealous, one can easily envisage *an indefinite number* of situations in which someone might say blah-blah and *not* be jealous. So it is more like 'people who say blah-blah are likely to be jealous *unless special circumstances obtain* and no special circumstances obtained in this instance . . . one can't verify *Jones is jealous* in isolation: one would have to verify a *huge* 'psychological theory' which covered all the 'special circumstances'. And this of course is *implicit* in our knowledge of people, and our *ability* to use psychological descriptions — not something we can state explicitly.[47]

Now compare Putnam's viewpoint here with what we find in Newman. Taking the phrase, "the rational exclusion of any supposition that he is innocent," as used (or rather implied) by a distinguished legal author of the day, Newman glosses it thus: "'rational' is used in contradistinction to argumentative, and means 'resting on implicit reasons' . . . which for some cause or other, because they are too subtle or circuitous, we cannot put into words so as to satisfy logic."[48] In a law court, as in very many other situations, we are involved in "concrete reasonings," and are "in great

measure thrown back into that condition, from which logic proposed to
rescue us. We judge for ourselves, by our own lights, and on our own principles."⁴⁹ Or, as the same point is made elsewhere: "Everyone who reasons, is his own centre; and no expedient of attaining a common measure
of minds can reverse this truth;—but then the question follows, is there
any *criterion* of the accuracy of an inference such as may be our warrant
that certitude is rightly elicited in favour of the proposition inferred, since
our warrant cannot, as I have said, be scientific? I have already said that
the sole and final judgment on the validity of an inference in concrete
matter is committed to the personal action of the ratiocinative faculty,
the perfection or virtue of which I have called the Illative Sense."⁵⁰ There
is, in other words, no more ultimate or absolute standard than "the 'ju-
dicium prudentis viri.'"⁵¹ The affinity with Putnam which appears here
scarcely needs elaboration, but as a further evidence of it, here is how
Newman deals with one of his examples:

> They [i.e., inferences] come to no definite conclusions about matters of fact,
> except as they are made effectual for their purpose by the living intelligence
> which uses them. "All men have their price; Fabricius is a man; he has his
> price;" but he had not his price; how is this? Because he is more than a
> universal; because he falls under other universals; because universals are
> ever at war with each other; because what is called a universal is only a general;
> because what is only general does not lead to a necessary conclusion. Let
> us judge him by another universal. "Men have a conscience; Fabricius is
> a man; he has a conscience." Until we have actual experience of Fabricius,
> we can only say, that, since he is a man, perhaps he will take a bribe, and
> perhaps he will not. Latet dolus in generalibus; they are arbitrary and falla-
> cious, if we take them for more than broad views and aspects of things,
> serving as our notes and indications for judging of the particular, but not
> absolutely touching and determining facts.⁵²

The 'practical knowledge' whose role in moral science Putnam wants
to recognize is similar, he believes, to Dilthey's *'Verstehen'* (as well as to
Polanyi's 'implicit knowledge'); and it is worth noting how he goes on to
defend *Verstehen* against the standard objection that, as a mode of em-
pathic insight, it improperly displaces the verification or checking that
is the hallmark of science. He is on the offensive in making his point:
inductive testing of theories in 'proper' science, he asserts, *itself* "presupposes some a priori (in the sense of antecedent) weighting of the theories—
a weighting *prior* to the checking." He calls this "prior probability," affirms
his belief that it is "qualitative not numerical," and asserts that "no one
has been able to *formalize* the intuitive judgments which in *practice* constitute the 'prior probability metric.'" This prior probability, he then as-

serts, is precisely what is given by *Verstehen:* through the latter, one's judgments of people are given a certain 'plausibility'. And even though, as imbued with this prior plausibility, judgments should certainly not be regarded as immune to checking, still *"even this checking is ultimately intuitive."*[53]

Putnam's points here are strongly resonant of Newman: "If I have brought out one truth in anything I have written, I consider it to be the *importance of antecedent probability* in conviction."[54] So Newman claimed in 1853—a claim well justified by the key role played by this idea in the *University Sermons* and the *Essay on Development.* In the *Sermons* he continually draws attention to the way in which one "advances and decides upon antecedent probabilities," and so reaches "a judgment about facts . . . formed not so much from the impressions legitimately made upon the mind by those facts, as from the reaching forward of the mind itself towards them."[55] Evidence, though in itself far from overwhelming, when it is "supported by antecedent probabilities" may still be "enough."[56] Newman's chief concern here is with Faith, which he describes as "an exercise of presumptive reasoning, or of Reason proceeding on antecedent grounds."[57] But he does not fail to point out that the case is no different with unbelief which "really goes on presumptions and prejudices as much as Faith does, only presumptions of an opposite nature"—so that if unbelievers "call themselves rational," this is "not because they decide by evidence, but because, after they have made their decision, they merely occupy themselves in sifting it."[58] There may seem to be a sharp edge in this comment, but in fact what Newman attributes to unbelievers here is no different from what he attributes to believers throughout the *Sermons.* It is true of *both* groups that they "decide by the principles of thought and conduct which are habitual to them; that is, the antecedent judgment, with which a man approaches the subject of religion, not only acts as a bearing this way or that,—causing him to go out to meet the evidence in a greater or lesser degree, and nothing more,—but, further, it practically colours the evidence, even in a case in which he has recourse to evidence, and interprets it for him."[59] The phrase "antecedent probability" occurs only once in the *Grammar,*[60] but the idea is substantially retained there—as will be clear from the passages which I related earlier with Gadamer's notion of 'prejudice'. (Gadamer, it may be pointed out, is in the tradition of Dilthey—though, as we shall see later, he is far from uncritical of the idea of *Verstehen.*)[61]

In referring to Putnam, I have wanted to show how Newman's analysis of knowledge anticipates a significant contemporary viewpoint on the methodology of the human sciences. But that this analysis is congruent with recent philosophical reflection on the natural sciences, also, can be brought out by reference to the work of Thomas Kuhn. In the research of scientific communities, according to Kuhn, there is "no neutral algorithm for theory-choice, no systematic decision-procedure which, properly applied, must lead each individual in the group to the same decision."[62] For even though there are criteria which may be said to come into play in deciding between rival theories (Kuhn mentions accuracy, consistency, scope, simplicity, and fruitfulness) they "function not as rules, which determine choice, but as values which influence it."[63] In other words, the weight which each of them is to carry always remains to be decided in each particular case, a decision made all the harder by the fact that they can often be *in conflict with each other,* and that there is no higher meta-criterion which can effectively resolve such conflict. Commenting on Kuhn's position here, Richard Bernstein writes: "it is misleading to speak of proof (if our model of proof is a deductive argument). Rather, the cumulative weight of the complex arguments advanced in favor of a given paradigm theory, together with its successes, persuade the community of scientists."[64] Later in the same discussion Bernstein praises the American pragmatist C. S. Peirce for emphasizing (long before the current wave of antirationalist—or, in Bernstein's phrase, "post-empiricist"—philosophy of science, but some time *after* Newman) "the multiple strands and diverse types of evidence, data, hunches, and arguments used to support a scientific hypothesis or theory. Any one of these strands may be weak in itself and insufficient to support the proposed theory, but collectively they provide a stronger warrant for rational belief than any single line of argument—like a strong cable that is made up of multiple weak strands."[65]

All of this is remarkably foreshadowed in *A Grammar of Assent.* Corresponding to Kuhn's "neutral algorithm" is what Newman, in more vivid language, calls "a far-reaching and infallible rule," which attempts to "supercede the need for personal gifts" and to provide a "key [which] revolving through the intricate wards of the lock opens to us a treasure-house."[66] Newman was aware that "the processes of reasoning which legitimately lead to assent . . . are in fact too multiform, subtle, omnigenous, too implicit, to allow of being measured by rule";[67] and that "probable reasons viewed in their convergence and combination . . . constitute a real, though only a reasonable, not an argumentative, proof."[68] Newman allows himself to "hazard" thus:

> the conclusion in a real or concrete question is foreseen and predicted rather than actually attained; foreseen in the number and direction of accumulated premisses, which all converge to it, and as the result of their combination, approach it more nearly than any assignable difference, yet do not touch it logically (though only not touching it,) on account of the nature of its subject-matter, and the delicate and implicit character of at least

part of the reasonings on which it depends. It is by the strength, variety, or multiplicity of premises, which are only probable, not by invincible syllogisms,— by objections overcome, by adverse theories neutralized, by difficulties gradually clearing up, by exceptions proving the rule, by unlooked-for correlations found with received truths, by suspense and delay in the process issuing in triumphant reactions,— by all these ways, and many others, it is that the practised and experienced mind is able to make a sure divination that a conclusion is inevitable, of which his lines of reasoning do not actually put him in possession. This is what is meant by a proposition being 'as good as proved', a conclusion as undeniable 'as if it were proved', and by the reasons for it 'amounting to a proof', for a proof is the limit of converging probabilities.[69]

Newman's analysis here is clearly very close to what we have just seen in the work of our contemporary philosophers, and though he prefaced this passage with the fear that "to some minds it may appear far-fetched or fanciful" anyone who is acquainted with this work will be unlikely to regard it as such. Moreover, it is worth noticing that the self-same image which Bernstein takes from Peirce is also to be found in Newman: "The best illustration of what I hold is that of a *cable* which is made up of a number of separate threads, each feeble, yet together as sufficient as an iron rod. An iron rod represents mathematical or strict demonstration; a cable represents moral demonstration, which is an assemblage of probabilities, separately insufficient for certainty, but, when put together, irrefragable. . . . A man who said 'I cannot trust a cable, I must have an iron bar,' would *in a certain given case,* be irrational and unreasonable."[70]

4. 'Incommensurability' in Philosophy of Science, Aristotelian Scholarship, and the *Grammar*

What we have been meeting here is the idea of 'incommensurability'. Interestingly, this idea has come to loom large both in the recent work in philosophy of science to which I have been alluding and in recent philosophical work on Aristotle's *Ethics*. I want to point out Newman's relevance to both contexts of discussion.

To maintain the 'incommensurability thesis' is to insist on the plurality, heterogeneity, and irreducibility to any common measure, of the factors that must be taken into account in reasoning one's way to a judgment or conclusion. We have seen this thesis in Kuhn's denial that there can be a single 'algorithm of theory-choice', and in his willingness to characterize as 'values' (and thereby to expose himself to the charge of 'relativism' or 'subjectivism') the multiple criteria that are operative in scientific rea-

soning. Now a closely related thesis may be said to be propounded in
Aristotle's name by philosophers working on the *Ethics,* who show that
a distinctive, and entirely creditable, feature of his whole approach to practical deliberation was precisely its rejection of what might be called the
'commensurability thesis' famously propounded by Socrates in the *Protagoras.* As described by Nussbaum, this latter thesis was to the effect that
there could be "a techne in which all values were commensurable on a
single scale";[71] or, in Burnyeat's formulation, it was the assumption "that
there is only . . . one category of value, within which all goods are commensurable, as it were in terms of a single common coinage . . . [so that]
if, ultimately, only one factor counts—call it F—and we have measured
two actions X and Y in terms of F, and X comes out more than Y does,
there is nothing left to give value to Y to outweigh or compensate for
its lesser quantity of F."[72] Or, again, as formulated by Wiggins, it was the
supposition "that there is just one evaluative dimension φ, and one quantitative measure m, such that φ-ness is all that matters, and all courses
of action can be compared with one another by the measure m in respect
of φ-ness."[73] Aristotle's most explicit denial of commensuration was in a
passage in the *Politics* where he showed the absurdity of trying to establish a calculus which would enable one to reckon on a common scale, for
the purpose of assigning due quotas of political privilege, differences between people in respect of such natural or acquired goods as height, wealth,
freedom, and virtue.[74] But it is also implicit in his criticism of the Platonic idea of *the* Good and in his careful identification and analysis of
several different excellences of character (e.g., courage, justice, temperance,
magnanimity) each of which makes its own distinctive and irreducible contribution to the good life—a life, therefore, which only with the greatest
good fortune, if at all, can be preserved from painful conflict: conflict
that is painful precisely because of the unavailability of any "common measure" that would unambiguously resolve it.[75]

Now "common measure" is a phrase which recurs constantly throughout the *Grammar,* and Newman may indeed be the first writer in modern
times who carries the term 'incommensurability' outside its matrix in mathematics and gives it *epistemological* significance.[76] What he is arguing against
in the *Grammar* is the attempt to "invent a method which may act as
a common measure between mind and mind";[77] and when he has worked
out his own notion of reason in terms of the Illative Sense, he is careful
to point out that it "supplies no common measure of mind and mind."[78]
Newman (as is clear from the quotations at the end of section 3 above)
agrees with the point which we have just met in our other authors and
in Aristotle, namely, that there are many disparate factors that *a person*
must take into account when making certain judgments and that these

factors cannot be reduced to a single scale. It is clear, however, from two brief quotations immediately above, that the emphasis in his notion of incommensurability falls elsewhere: on the disparateness of the factors that will weigh with *different people* faced with the same situation and on the impossibility of establishing a truly common medium between these people in terms of which this disparateness can be expressed. This different emphasis which we find in Newman connects in fact with a more specialized sense that the term 'incommensurability' has come to have in recent discussion in the philosophy of science, and I want to look now at some of this discussion and at Newman's relevance to it.

This more specialized sense has come to prominence in association with Kuhn's notion of a 'paradigm' and the quite radical revision of the traditional conception of the scientific enterprise which he has elaborated around this notion. Scientists can make spectacular progress, Kuhn suggests, when they operate within a single paradigm, i.e., a shared set of commitments and assumptions that restricts for them the range of what constitutes a legitimate or worthwhile problem, defines what will count as an acceptable solution to it, and selects the kind of procedures, experiments, and instruments that may be useful in reaching this solution. The existence of such a framework of commitments virtually defines a scientific field and makes possible the steady, cumulative refinement of its concepts and laws that characterizes its 'normal' development. Adherence to the paradigm expedites progress in a scientific field by exempting its practitioners from the kind of preoccupation with first principles that seems such a stultifying feature of areas of inquiry where nothing as coherent as a paradigm has yet emerged or where no one of several competing paradigms has managed to establish its ascendancy. If Kuhn demonstrates that the research conducted *within* paradigms — once the latter have become established and thus made possible what he calls 'normal' science — is orderly, cohesive, and even, one might say, 'grooved', the real sting in his book, however, comes from what, primarily as a historian, he is able to say *about* paradigms, and *their nonparadigm-based* emergence. As a way of "seeing the world and of practicing science in it" a paradigm is not something as amenable to inspection as a fact, a theory, or even a rule. Even when it is firmly established (thus ensuring a fundamental consensus among the relevant scientific community) a scientist's allegiance to it is brought about through a process of *initiation* (i.e., professional education) and is a matter of having internalized certain exemplary achievements as models, rather than of being able to enunciate explicit rules that strictly determine practice. Moreover, in the *emergence* of paradigms — before they are available to give a stamp to the training of a generation of professionals and despite the fact that observation and experience still set limits to what can plausibly be proposed for scientific acceptance—"an apparently arbitrary element, compounded of personal and historical accident, is always a formative ingredient."[79]

It is here that 'incommensurability' becomes a key concept in Kuhn's understanding of science. A paradigm that has shown immense fruitfulness in the generation and solution of problems (or 'puzzles' as they become within the stable framework that it provides) eventually runs into problems (or 'anomalies') that prove intractable within its own (i.e., the paradigm's) terms and thereby induce a crisis. The attempt to resolve this crisis eventually leads not to a move within the old paradigm but rather to a revolutionary shift to a new one. The process through which the first bold spirits open up this new paradigm "cannot be justified by proof,"[80] "cannot be made a step at a time, forced by logic and neutral experience."[81] In language whose religious ancestry is undisguised, Kuhn writes of "the transfer of allegiance from paradigm to paradigm" as a "conversion experience."[82] And later on, in the same register, he writes: "The man who embraces a new paradigm at an early stage must often do so in defiance of the evidence provided by problem-solving. He must, in other words, have faith that the new paradigm will succeed with the many large problems that confront it, knowing only that the older paradigm has failed with a few. A decision of that kind can only be made on faith."[83] If the new paradigm is to prevail, it will eventually consolidate into procedures and canons whose success in generating and solving new puzzles (as well as preserving in a transformed framework what is still valuable in the solutions to old ones) will have its own persuasive force—will indeed have become the secure basis for the initiation of a new generation into what is now deemed to be 'normal' science. However, before its consolidation, "something must make at least a few scientists feel that the new proposal is on the right track, and sometimes it is only personal and inarticulable aesthetic considerations that can do that. Men have been converted by them when most of the articulable technical arguments pointed the other way."[84]

It is at points of such revolutionary change, when the old paradigm is still entrenched and the new one has not yet gained wide acceptance, that 'incommensurability' comes most sharply into focus. There are pioneers of the new paradigm to canvas its merits with unconverted adherents of the old one, but it will be found that there is no "common measure" in terms of which adjudication can be made between the two. And so both sides will find themselves "at least slightly at cross-purposes. Neither side will grant all the non-empirical assumptions that the other needs in order to make its case."[85] Both protagonists "inevitably talk through each other when debating the relative merits of their respective paradigms,"[86] for they will have run up against "the incompleteness of logical contact that consistently characterizes paradigm debates."[87] Because of this 'incompleteness', though "each may hope to convert the other to his way of seeing his science and its problems, neither may hope to prove his case. The competition between paradigms is not the sort of battle that can be resolved by proofs."[88] Instead of 'proof', Kuhn speaks of 'persuasion'—which is not an irrational process, but rather one of "argument and counterargument in a situation in which there can be no proof."[89] What makes these arguments and counterarguments fall short of proof is their circularity: each side unavoidably uses the very paradigm that it is supposed to be defending. This fact does not prevent some of these arguments from exhibiting a picture of scientific practice that is "immensely persuasive." But what Kuhn wants to point out is that "the status of the circular argument is *only* that of persuasion. It cannot be made logically or even probabilistically compelling for those who refuse to step into the circle. The premises and values shared by the two parties to a debate over paradigms are not sufficiently extensive for that."[90] And indeed it may not be sensible to speak of *refusing* to step into the circle of the new paradigm — any more than it is to speak of *choosing* to do so. For stepping into a paradigm (as Kuhn makes clear in the Postscript to his book) is like becoming at home in a second language so that one no longer needs to translate it back into one's mother tongue. And this transition is not "one that an individual may make or refrain from making by deliberation and choice, however good his reasons for wishing to do so. Instead, at some point in the process of learning to translate, he finds that the transition has occurred, that he has slipped into the new language without a decision having been made."[91]

Kuhn's focus, in his reflection on the history of science, is quite different from Newman's focus, in his more wide-ranging reflection on knowledge, in the *Grammar*. The picture of knowledge, however, which Kuhn's book has been so influential in undermining (science as the cumulative achievement, from one definitive standpoint, of universally binding knowledge based on publicly accessible evidence and rigorously logical argumentation) is a picture which Newman had already very acutely criticized, and Newman's own conception of knowledge has some strong affinities, which are I believe worth bringing out, with Kuhn's.[92] One cannot say that Newman articulated the notion of a 'paradigm', but he is no less aware than Kuhn that ideas emerge only within a particular matrix and that this is determined by "first principles, the recondite sources of all knowledge, as to which logic provides no common measure of minds — which are accepted by some, rejected by others, — in which, and not in the syllogistic exhibitions, lies the whole problem of attaining to truth."[93]

Because of the absence of a common measure, there is no 'proof' which will show one set of first principles to be superior to another, and so Newman writes of "how a controversy . . . is carried on from starting points, and with collateral aids, not formally proved, but more or less assumed, the process of assumption lying in the action of the Illative Sense, as applied to primary elements of thought respectively congenial to the disputants."[94] He is aware of how incorrigibly at odds with each other are those whose first principles differ, a difference which will determine what is seen as a problem, what counts as evidence, and what kind of argument persuades. He does not suppose that significant disagreements are to be resolved by one or other party's improving the tightness of its reasoning or the accuracy of its attention to the "facts"—as if the facts themselves were not already to some extent differently colored by the different perspectives from which they are approached: "taking the facts by themselves, probably, these authors would come to no conclusion at all; it is the 'tacit understandings' . . . the vague and impalpable notions of 'reasonableness' on his own side as well as on that of the others, which both make conclusions possible, and are the pledge of their being contradictory. The conclusions vary with the particular writer, for each writes from his own point of view and with his own principles, and these admit of no common measure."[95] And so, of the gulf between two thinkers separated by a difference of 'tacit understandings'[96] (his example is that between Pascal and Montaigne), he writes: "two characters of mind are brought out into shape, and two standards and systems of thought,—each logical, when analysed, yet contradictory of each other, and only not antagonistic because they have no common ground on which they can conflict."[97] Or again, the same thought, repeated near the end of the book: "the fact remains, that, in any inquiry about things in the concrete, men differ from each other, not so much in the soundness of their reasoning as in the principles which govern its exercise, that those principles are of a personal character, that where there is no common measure of minds, there is no common measure of arguments, and that the validity of proof is determined, not by any scientific test, but by the Illative Sense."[98]

5. Conclusion: Newman on Language

I have been elaborating Newman's antirationalist account of knowledge by bringing into relief the close convergence between it and some of the most influential developments in the philosophy of science over the past few decades. This has allowed me not only to demonstrate the contemporaneity of Newman's work, but also to corroborate one of his basic tenets: that the form of reasoning which he adumbrates in the context of a clarification of the grounds of religious belief is not essentially dissimilar from that which can be shown to operate in other areas of knowledge. Within the context of my overall study, the most significant point which has emerged from the discussion of our recent authors, with their profiling of the notion of 'incommensurability', is that although scientific knowledge, as an *outcome,* gives us great technical control over specific domains of nature, still in its own *development,* it is not fully assured by any established set of rules or technical procedures—and so, to this extent, partakes in the nature of *practical knowledge.* (This is the case not because science must have a practical import beyond itself, nor because it is not properly theoretical knowledge, but rather because the endeavor through which it itself is built up is a *practice.*) Newman himself is more central to our theme, however, and the references to contemporary writers have been intended to contribute to an understanding of the significance of his views because, more fully than they, he adverts to the practical nature of reasoning and, in doing so (as we have seen), very explicitly invokes, and extends the range of, Aristotle's analysis of phronesis.[99] In subsequent chapters I shall be going on to explore how other thinkers—in what I believe to be real, though not self-conscious or avowed, continuity with Newman—further extend and deepen his retrieval of this Aristotelian analysis. The extensions of it which we shall meet in the next two chapters are into art and politics—two areas that are scarcely touched in the *Grammar.* And the deepening of it will lead to a growing preoccupation with *language,* a theme which Newman often adverts to—though with less sustained attention, and more ambivalence, I think it can be said, than Collingwood and, especially, Gadamer, whose reflections on language will be met in the next chapter and in chapter 5, respectively. It is with a brief discussion of what seems to be Newman's view of language in the *Grammar,* and with a cursory anticipation of the conception of language that we shall meet later, that I conclude this chapter.

Newman's great concern in the book, as we have seen, is to expose the limitations of logical inference; but he sometimes seems to attribute these limitations to the fact that this type of inference is linguistic—and so to suggest that the more delicate and 'implicit' process of ratiocination which he seeks to vindicate is essentially extralinguistic. Language then appears as at best an *instrument* of the mind, and often enough, indeed, an unserviceable one—so that the mind runs freer and becomes more resourceful and accurate if, released from language, it realizes itself simply in thought. Thus, for instance, Newman writes: "great as are the services of language in enabling us to extend the compass of our inferences, to test their validity, and to communicate them to others, still the mind it-

self is more versatile and vigorous than any of its works, of which language
is one, and it is only under its penetrating and subtle action that the mar-
gin disappears . . . between verbal argumentation and conclusions in the
concrete";[100] or, again: "we proceed, as far indeed as we can, by the logic
of language, but we are obliged to supplement it by the more subtle and
elastic logic of thought."[101] Or, again, speaking of a complicated argument (about a literary text) he seems to suggest that it really registers only
with someone who can take it in by a kind of extralinguistic empathy:
"it requires rather to be photographed on the individual mind as by one
impression, than admits of delineation for the satisfaction of the many
in any known or possible language, however rich in vocabulary and flexible in structure."[102]

What kind of separation, we want to ask, on the evidence of passages
such as these, does Newman allow between language and thought? In the
next chapter we shall meet Collingwood's belief that to envisage any kind
of separation here is, *ipso facto*, to misunderstand both language and
thought; however, since Newman has, as I believe, stronger affinities with
Gadamer than with Collingwood, it will be more helpful here to ask about
Newman's view of language from the point of view of Gadamer's rejection of this separation. For Gadamer, language is not an instrument that
we can avail of or dispense with. It is neither external to thought nor a
'work' of the mind. Its limits, such as they are, are the limits of thought
itself. Even if we have to struggle hard to articulate our thought, what
we are trying to do is not to find an adequate verbal formulation for
something that we already possess extralinguistically, but rather—paradigmatically in speech—to bring thought itself into being. This view of
Gadamer's does allow for the implicit or tacit dimension of thinking and
reasoning which Newman rightly insists on; no less than Newman, he
is conscious that thought cannot be fully encapsulated in clear, self-sufficient
propositions and that a good writer or speaker is one who can suggest or
evoke the whole unspoken context which supports it. Gadamer makes this
point, however, through a critique of what he calls "the statement"—and
not through a critique of language itself. The tacit dimension, then, exists not outside language, but rather as a tension within it—language being not a set of labels or markers that are at our disposal but rather an
activity or game (indeed a whole set of games) that we are involved in.
And it is here that his treatment of language meets his interest in our
central Aristotelian distinction. For what he is arguing against is a *technical* (or instrumental) conception of language; and by seeking to replace
this with a conception of language as a form of activity, he is opening it
(language) as a crucial field for the exercise of *phronesis*.

Before turning to Gadamer, I had quoted a few passages where Newman seemed to regard language as a vehicle for thought, a vehicle that, although necessary to its communication, places unfortunate limits on its native resourcefulness and elasticity. If we look further in the *Grammar,* however, I think we shall see that it is unclear whether the limits which he wants to expose are those of language itself or, rather, only of a *technical approach to it.*

> Now without external symbols to mark out and to steady its course, the intellect runs wild; but with the aid of symbols, as in algebra, it advances with precision and effect. Let then our symbols be words: let all thought be arrested and embodied in words; and thought go for only so much as it can show itself to be worth in language. Let every prompting of the intellect be ignored, every *momentum* of argument be disowned, which is unprovided with an equivalent wording, as its ticket for sharing in the common search after truth. . . . Ratiocination thus restricted and put into grooves is what I call Inference. . . . Verbal reasoning, of whatever kind, as opposed to mental, is what I mean by inference. . . . It proposes to provide both a test and a common measure of reasoning; and I think it will be found partly to succeed and partly to fail; succeeding so far as words can in fact be found for representing the countless varieties and subtleties of human thought, failing on account of the fallacy of the original assumption, that whatever can be thought can be adequately expressed in words.[103]

In the process of inference, Newman seems to be saying here, it is ratiocination that is restricted — and linguistic formulation *per se* that provides the grooves. But is the logical process he is talking about not one in which *language, too, is "restricted and put into grooves"*? And in fact does he himself not acknowledge this when (a page or two after the above passage) he tells us that, with respect to words, the aim of inference is:

> to circumscribe and stint their import as much as possible . . . and to make them . . . the *calculi* of notions, which are in our absolute power, as meaning just what we choose them to mean, and as little as possible the tokens of real things, which are outside of us, and which mean we do not know how much but so much certainly as, (in proportion as we enter into them,) may run away with us beyond the range of scientific management. . . . Words . . . have innumerable implications; but in inferential exercises it is the very triumph of that clearness and hardness of head, which is the characteristic talent for the art, to have stripped them of all these connatural senses, to have drained them of that depth and breadth of associations which constitute their poetry, their rhetoric, and their historical life, to have starved each term down till it has become the ghost of itself, and everywhere one and the same ghost . . . so that it may stand for . . . a notion neatly turned

out of the laboratory of the mind, and sufficiently tame and subdued, because existing only in a definition.[104]

Here, at least, it seems clear that it is "definition" (which may be compared with Gadamer's "statement")[105] that is narrow, while language itself is endlessly expansive. And can there, indeed, be much stronger evidence of this latter fact than Newman's own writing? He is one of the great rhetoricians of the English language, and the *Grammar* (whose epigraph is St. Ambrose's "Non in dialectica complacuit Deo salvum facere populum suum") should be a beneficiary of the recent attempt — ably supported, as we shall see, by Gadamer — to heal the ancient quarrel between rhetoric and dialectic. And we may also of course bear in mind here that the essential thrust of what we have been meeting in the *Grammar* had been first enunciated by Newman in University Sermons: a fact which may be given some significance by a remark on preaching, in the *Idea of a University,* which also provides strong affirmation of the unity, rather than the separation, of thought and language: "Nothing that is anonymous will preach; nothing that is dead and gone; nothing even which is of yesterday, however religious in itself and useful. Thought and word are one in the Eternal Logos, and must not be separate in those who are His shadows on earth. They must issue fresh and fresh, as from the preacher's mouth, so from his breast, if they are to be 'spirit and life' to the hearts of his hearers."[106]

Here I conclude my consideration of Newman. His voice will in fact resonate at various points throughout the subsequent conversation; but my immediate task is to introduce another voice which changes the ground of the discussion from religion to art, and which, in doing so, extends the range of the argument about technical reason that has got under way here.

2. R. G. Collingwood's Critique of Techne in *The Principles of Art*

1. 'The Technical Theory of Art'

Whereas *A Grammar of Assent* moves toward the eventual enthronement of phronesis, the book I shall consider here begins from, and follows out the implications of, the dethronement of techne. It is R. G. Collingwood's contention, in *The Principles of Art,*[1] that a necessary prolegomenon to an adequate aesthetic is to expose what he calls "the technical theory of art" (i.e., "the theory that art is some kind of craft")[2]—or, in other words, to identify and dispel a whole cluster of technicist assumptions which tend to permeate and bedevil essays in the theory of art. These assumptions are deeply lodged in general habits of thought and it is on this account that they so easily provide the conceptual stock-in-trade in terms of which artistic matters are discussed. They are, however, as Collingwood tries to show, deeply uncongenial to these matters—so that no issue of aesthetics can be discussed in terms of them without at the same time being distorted. The most important task, therefore, before we can construct an adequate aesthetic, is to liberate our thinking from the systematic biases that stem from them. But such liberation itself requires a prior task: the identification of just what it is that we need to be liberated from.

When Collingwood sets about this task he finds that it has already been accomplished for him. For the classic articulation of the whole technicist framework already exists in "the philosophy of craft which was one of the greatest and most solid achievements of the Greek mind, or at any rate of that school, from Socrates to Aristotle, whose work happens to have been most completely preserved."[3] And so when Collingwood identifies as the key technicist elements: (1) a distinction between end and means, (2) a distinction between planning and execution, (3) a converse relationship between end and means in the respective processes of planning and of execution (so that in planning end is first and means are subsequent, whereas in execution the reverse is the case), (4) a distinction between form and matter, (5) a distinction between raw material and finished product or artefact and (6) a hierarchical relationship between various crafts (so that, e.g., the product of one provides the raw material or the tools for another),[4] he is but restating things that had already received their definitive statement in Aristotle's elaboration of the concept of techne. "It was the Greek philosophers who worked out the idea of craft [i.e., *technē*] and it is in their writings that the above distinctions have been expounded once for all."[5]

Collingwood believes that this idea of craft, whose tenacious hold over aesthetic thought he tries to loosen, was no less captivating in its effects on the Greek philosophers who invented it: "Once the Socratic school had laid down the main lines of a theory of craft, they were bound to look for instances of craft in all sorts of likely and unlikely places."[6] One of these places was art. In fact, for them, art simply *was* craft. "When they came to deal with aesthetic problems . . . both Plato and Aristotle . . . took it for granted that poetry, the only art they discussed in detail, was a kind of craft, and spoke of this craft as *[poiētikē technē]*, poet-craft."[7] In this conception, "the poet is a kind of skilled producer; he produces for consumers; and the effect of his skill is to bring about in them certain states of mind which are conceived in advance as desirable states."[8] It is just this ability of the maker to *conceive in advance* what the outcome of his activity will be that constitutes his making as 'craft' ("this is what . . . [techne] means in Greek: the power to produce a preconceived result by means of consciously controlled and directed action. . . . The craftsman knows what he wants to make before he makes it. This foreknowledge is absolutely indispensable to craft").[9]

Collingwood is well aware that the dominant notion of art in this century, "which carries with it all the subtle and elaborate implications of the modern European aesthetic consciousness,"[10] is very different from the Greek notion (for the Greeks conceived poetry, sculpture, drama, music, etc., not as 'fine arts' in our sense but "as in principle just like carpentry and the rest, and differing from one of these only in the sort of way in which any one of them differs from any other.")[11] He nonetheless contends that, in the way in which art is still thought about, the basic categories—whatever refinements may be put upon them—are still technical. For the fundamental idea of craft—the idea that the artist "deliberately sets himself to arouse certain states of mind in his audience"[12]—remains at the core of most contemporary approaches to art. This is "much encouraged by modern tendencies in psychology and influentially taught at the present day by persons in a position of academic authority; but after all it is only a new version, tricked out in the borrowed plumage of modern science, of the ancient fallacy that the arts are kinds of craft."[13]

Whether, *as an aesthetic theory,* the target of Collingwood's attack can still be regarded, more than fifty years after the publication of his book, as significant or influential is not of concern here. Notwithstanding the great advances in aesthetics itself since he wrote, there is still much truth in his assertion that the technical theory of art "is by no means of merely antiquarian interest. It is actually the way in which most people nowadays think about art; and especially economists and psychologists, the people to whom we look (sometimes vainly) for special guidance in the problems of modern life."[14] Even if few serious aestheticians would now defend 'the technical theory', art still exists in a world in which, like everything else, it is all too likely to be thought of in technicist terms. This wider technicism is the target of the present study, and the interest of Collingwood's book lies not so much in what it has to say specifically about art (any more than our interest in Newman's book was confined to its thoughts on religion) as in its very clear profile of the whole framework of thought and activity that hangs around the concept of techne, as well as in its attempt (which involves a protracted effort to avoid the traps of technicist thinking) to articulate a mode of intentionality that is radically different from the technical one.

In the course of this latter articulation, Collingwood nowhere alludes, by way of precedent, to Aristotle's analysis of phronesis. And, what is more curious, when he mentions early on "two brilliant cases of resistance"[15] in Greek philosophy to the "temptation," which we have already seen, "to look for instances of craft in all sorts of likely and unlikely places," this same analysis of phronesis is not one of them.[16] It will be instructive, nonetheless, within the general context of our concern with phronesis, to follow Collingwood's analysis of his notion of artistic intentionality. For this latter analysis and Aristotle's analysis of phronesis are motivated by a common need and are responding to a common problem, i.e, to transcend the framework of techne. And, this being the case, we may expect that points made by Collingwood in dealing with this problem in the *aesthetic* field and points made by Aristotle in dealing with it in the *practical-moral* field will throw light on each other. Besides, we shall find that, in tackling his problem in aesthetics, Collingwood cannot avoid raising issues of quite general philosophical significance (e.g., about experience, language, and the nature and limits of subjectivity) that will recur in later chapters as we follow the fortunes of phronesis and techne in our other thinkers.

Collingwood's quarrel with the 'technical theory' is that it not only leads to mistaken thinking about art objects (correctly identified as such) but, more basically, that it causes some things to be mistakenly considered artistic which in fact are not so. There are two types of things in particular which his critique of the technical theory seeks to expose — by showing not that they are bad art but that they may not be art at all. He calls these two types of things "amusement" and "magic."[17] Both of them are alike in that their aim is to arouse emotion; they differ in that in the case of amusement the emotion, once excited, is discharged or 'earthed' within the self-contained (and 'make-believe') frame of the amusement itself, whereas in the case of magic such catharsis is forestalled and the emotion is canalized into 'real' life, where its discharge lends energy to the performance of some practical task.[18] It might seem that only magic fits into the instrumental framework of 'craft' ("the central and primary characteristic of craft is the distinction it involves between means and end") for in it, clearly, emotions are aroused for their usefulness in achieving ends beyond themselves, whereas the sole end of amusement is the enjoyment of emotions for their own sake.[19] Collingwood makes it clear, however, that even if amusement can claim to be its own end, the so-called work of art which provides the amusement is strictly a means to the arousal, and harmless working off, of determinate emotions. And in fact he is much more hostile to amusement than to magic.[20] It is not the same thing as 'enjoyment'; or rather it is "enjoyment which is had without paying for it."[21] Nor is it the same as 'recreation'; for it dissipates, while the latter replenishes, the store of emotional energy available for practical life. It is something whose prevalence can be seen as both an index and a cause of emotional bankruptcy—and hence moral decay—in personal and social life. By contrast, 'magic' flourishes only in relation to a robust way of life —where the latter already exists, or where (as, e.g., among prominent left-wing writers of the 1930s)[22] there is a commitment to make it exist. Moreover, magic is altogether more likely than amusement to issue in good art—a fact which will be due, of course, not to its being magic per se, but rather to the existence of true artists (such as existed "among the Aurignacian and Magdalenian cave-men, the ancient Egyptians, the Greeks, and the mediaeval Europeans") in whom "the artistic and the magical motives are felt as one motive."[23]

Before asking what, according to Collingwood, actually constitutes the artistic motive, we may notice that the concession just made (i.e., that an object which is magical may also, though for different reasons, be artistic) is in fact part of a more general qualification which enters his critique of the technical theory of art. While magic is indeed practical or useful, still it is only obliquely so; its usefulness appears not in the magical object or activity itself (e.g., the patriotic statue, the religious hymn, the initiation rite, the war dance) but rather in the nonritualistic practical activities (discharging civic duties, practicing religious virtues, behaving as an adult, fighting bravely in battle) whose performance is animated by it. However, Collingwood also acknowledges that a craft product which is *directly* useful, e.g., a house or a jug, may also be a work of art. Just as a portrait-painter may do more than make a good likeness, and through this 'more'—which we still have to define—create a genuinely artistic work, so a builder or potter may do likewise; we must only remember that what makes something art is not the same as what makes it useful. And he also concedes, more significantly, that great works of art (e.g., the *Divina Comedia* or the cathedral at Chartres) often carry a "massive intellectual burden,"[24] which would be quite unsustainable by their creator(s) without a large element of planning and hence of technique. It is not this element, however, which makes them works of art, and his rejection of the technical theory implies not that "no planned work is a work of art" but rather that "unplanned works of art are possible."[25]

These qualifications aside, Collingwood's attack on the technical theory of art is quite radical. For whereas "most people who write about art today seem to think that it is some kind of craft,"[26] and are thus concerned to clarify the specific twists or nuances that it introduces into craft activity in order to make it 'artistic', his question, on the other hand, is "irrespectively of such details . . . whether art is any kind of craft at all";[27] or, as he elsewhere puts it, whether "we are only frustrating our study of it in advance if we approach it in the determination to treat it as if it were the conscious working-out of means to the achievement of a conscious purpose, or in other words technique."[28] His answer to this question is clear-cut—and underlies the whole theory of art which he himself sets about establishing: "The description of the unwritten poem as an end to which his technique is means is false; it implies that before he has written his poem, he knows, and could state, the specification of it in the kind of way in which a joiner knows the specification of a table he is about to make."[29] But if this is not the case with the artist, if, in other words, the work of art is made by him, but is "not made by transforming a given raw material, nor by carrying out a preconceived plan, nor by way of realizing the means to a preconceived end,"[30] then how *is* it made?

One possible way of answering this question is immediately excluded, namely, any recourse to romantic notions of 'genius' or 'inspiration' or to "the sentimental notion that works of art can be produced by anyone, however little trouble he has taken to learn his job, provided his heart is in the right place"[31]—a notion which ignores what is later described as "the vast amount of intelligent and purposeful labour, the painful and conscientious self-discipline that has gone to the making of a man who can write a single line as Pope writes it, or knock a single chip off a single stone like Michelangelo."[32] The confidence, not to say complacency, of many advocates of technical reason stems from their conviction that the only possible alternative to it is some form of irrationalism;[33] and if Collingwood's rejection of this alternative is no less explicit than his rejection of technicism itself, it will be worthwhile to consider now just what kind of positive account he offers, beyond this double negation, of the intelligence or purposefulness that is at work in the process of artistic creation.

2. 'Imaginative Expression'

"What is the nature of this making which is not technical making or, if we want a one-word name for it, fabrication?"[34] What is its nature, given that it is engaged in "deliberately and responsibly, by people who know what they are doing, even though they do not know in advance what is going to come of it"?[35] This, as we have just seen, is the question which Collingwood faces in taking up the constructive part of his task. His answer is that a work of art is made, or rather "created," through a process of what he calls "imaginative expression"—a phrase whose full meaning he can make clear only in the context of what turns out to be a comprehensive theory of 'experience', 'consciousness', 'imagination' and 'language'. It is to the construction of such a theory that the second, central book of *The Principles of Art* is devoted (the first book having been devoted to an exposition and demolition of the 'technical theory of art', and the third and final book being devoted to a detailed working out of the implications of this constructive theory for questions of art). In this section and the next, I shall try to sketch the main lines of this overall theory and to show how it fills out the meaning of 'imaginative expression' as the central artistic act.

'Imaginative' activity, in Collingwood's usage, is not the unusual activity which is concerned with 'imaginary'—as opposed to 'real'—objects; it is, rather, the quite usual activity through which I constitute myself as a *conscious* person. As such it exists at a level intermediate between two other levels: one, that of a psychic organism subject to ever-changing sensory impressions and the emotions with which these are invariably charged; the other, that of a thinker who interprets what originates at the psychic level, analyzes, relates, distinguishes, infers, explains—and thereby introduces general concepts as well as a binding distinction between truth and falsity. Consciousness, as such, is not yet thinking in the full sense of intellection, but neither is it a merely passive registering of what is simply 'given' at the psychic level; it is an active attention which, supervening on the latter, stabilizes and transforms it. What impresses itself at the psychic level is evanescent and importunate; if one could speak of a 'self' at this level it would be a self at the mercy of fleeting, and at the same time dominating, impressions and emotions. The *conscious* self, however, through the continuous focusing and refocusing of attention, gains a measure of control over impressions and emotions: impressions are rescued from an endless flux, made available for recall and anticipation, enhanced by being fused with other impressions and memories, and thus converted into a state in which they are material for the supervening activity of intellect or thought; at the same time emotions are made less violent, for the act of attention is also an act of self-assertion through which they are 'owned', or absorbed into a pattern of life which is consciously *mine* — even though its full elaboration can scarcely be accomplished without the further activity of intellect. Now it is through this activity of consciousness that we come to have what Collingwood calls 'imaginative' experience; "the work of consciousness converts impressions of brute sense and brute emotion into ideas, something which we no longer simply feel but feel in that new way which we call imagining."[36] And so, "[r]egarded as names for a certain kind or level of experience, the words consciousness and imagination are synonymous: they stand for the same thing, namely, the level of experience at which . . . feeling [i.e., sensation and emotion] . . . [is] transformed by the activity of consciousness."[37]

In its relation to the psychic base, "consciousness is absolutely autonomous: its decision alone determines whether a given sensum or emotion shall be attended to or not."[38] What Collingwood says here needs to be qualified. The freedom possessed at the level of consciousness resides in a person's not having to attend to the most stimulating of present sensations or to identify with the emotion of the moment, however powerful it may be. This freedom is not freedom of choice or decision, however. For I do not conduct a preliminary survey of different alternatives that can lay claim to my attention and then select one; rather in being conscious I have already selected. And so, as Collingwood acknowledges, "imagination is 'blind'"—in the sense that it "cannot anticipate its own results by conceiving them as purposes in advance of executing them. The freedom which it enjoys is not the freedom to carry out a plan, or to choose between alternative possible plans. These are developments that belong to a later stage [i.e., that of intellectual thought]."[39]

While it possesses a freedom which can be said to be blind, imagination is not entirely arbitrary, however. This can best be shown by dwelling on its relationships with the two other levels that bound on it, the lower psychic level and the higher level of intellect. Since it does not try to establish relationships between concepts, consciousness cannot be said to make truth-claims, and accordingly it might seem not to be open to the possibility of falsehood. Although it is not yet intellectual and so is not thought in the full sense (or "thought par excellence"),[40] Collingwood still wants to recognize it as thought—indeed "thought in its absolutely fundamental and original shape."[41] In its own way, therefore, it shares in the bipolarity of all thought: it has an intrinsic responsibility to be truthful while at the same time it can succumb to falsehood. To see what *kind* of truth and falsehood is in question here we need to look more closely at consciousness's relationship with the 'brute' sensations and more particularly emotions, which press upon it from the psyche. Once admitted into consciousness, the latter are transformed. So long as we do not grant them conscious recognition, they cannot be said, on that account, to be no part of our experience; but by being made conscious they become clearer and less oppressive. Not everything, of course, that stirs in our psychic life must have its conscious correlative: if (as we have seen) consciousness is a selecting, then it necessarily follows that some things should be selected *out;* and such simple exclusion is not due to any failure of consciousness but is, rather, a structural feature of consciousness itself. There is a type of exclusion, however, which is not so much an ignoring as a disowning. I attempt to admit something into awareness, but a conflict between it and some established feature of my consciousness causes me to balk, and the attempt miscarries. Now *this* exclusion, or denial, does not leave my consciousness unaffected. The price I have had to pay for it is in the form of a distortion in what I do admit into awareness: for example, denying feelings of anger towards my boss, I tell myself that my wife is giving me a hard time—so that I can feel angry at her. Of such psychic feelings it can be said that my "conscious self disclaims responsibility for them, and thus tries to escape being dominated by them without taking the trouble of dominating them."[42] If I can evade in this way, what I cannot do, however, is erase from consciousness the marks of this evasion; and so the "picture which consciousness has painted of its own experience . . . is a bowdlerized picture, or one whose omissions are falsifications."[43]

The falsity which we meet here is not that of error (which attaches to propositions asserted by intellect) or of deception (an act which presupposes self-possession as well as possession of a truth which is then consciously concealed)—though it might be said to be that of what we paradoxically call 'self-deception'. It exists at a more basic level in the self than either of the other two, and is in fact the "protoplasm of untruth"[44] out of which they develop. Clearly, it is very close to what other philosophers (e.g., Sartre) refer to as "false consciousness." Collingwood's own term for it, however, is "corrupt consciousness," by which he means to bring out the fact that it is a form not only of untruth but also of evil—though here again it must be distinguished from (even though it is closely related to) two more easily categorizable forms of evil with which we are familiar: that which we commit (wrong-doing) and that which we suffer (disease).

It has been most systematically analyzed, as Collingwood himself acknowledges,[45] by psychoanalysis (with its concepts of repression, dissociation, projection, etc.), and indeed the ambiguous position which the latter has occupied as between medicine and morality, or between therapy and education,[46] reflects its inherently ambiguous nature.

The phrase we set out to clarify—since it was Collingwood's formula for understanding the nature of art—was "imaginative expression." In dealing with consciousness we have been concerned, quite explicitly, with imagination; and, as I shall now try to show, we have also, though so far only implicitly, been concerned with expression. For, in Collingwood's view, to be conscious of an emotion is at the same time to have expressed it:

> until a man has expressed his emotion he does not yet know what emotion it is. The act of expressing it is therefore an exploration of his emotions. He is trying to find out what these emotions are. There is certainly here a directed process; an effort, that is, directed upon a certain end; but the end is not something foreseen and preconceived, to which appropriate means can be thought out in the light of our knowledge of its special character. *Expression is an activity of which there can be no technique.*[47]

This passage (which brings out clearly the nontechnical nature of expression) might be taken to mean that though we have certain emotions, we do not come to know or to be conscious of them until we express them. But later in the book it becomes clear that Collingwood's position is stronger than this. We simply do not *have* an emotion unless it is expressed—since "expression . . . is not . . . made to fit an emotion already existing, but is an activity without which the experience of that emotion cannot exist."[48] In Collingwood's view, then, "[t]here are no unexpressed emotions."[49] This is true at two levels. At that of the psyche, emotions in their crude state are expressed through automatic bodily changes and are never experienced without this concomitant expression, e.g., sudden fear through a sweat or shiver. At the level of consciousness—and this is the less obvious but more important point which he is concerned to argue—they are expressed through *language,* and so are experienced at all only as already linguistic.[50] There is a sense, of course, in which there must be unexpressed emotions—for, if there were not, the artist, whose task is to express emotion, would have nothing to do. This sense, however, does not cancel out Collingwood's main point, for "what are called unexpressed emotions are emotions at one level of experience, already expressed in the way appropriate to that level, of which the person who feels them is trying to become conscious: that is, trying to convert into the material of an experience at a higher level, which when he achieves it will be at once an emotion at this higher level and an expression appropriate to it."[51]

3. Expression and Language

The implications of Collingwood's notion of expression can be brought out more fully if we go on to examine that through which, as we have just seen, emotions are imaginatively expressed, that is, language. Coming at language from the side of expression, Collingwood is in immediate collision with the view that language consists of a set of signs which have, or ought to have, clear and precise meanings and whose combinations are, or ought to be, subject to invariant rules—a double 'ought' which at the limit would sanction the abandonment of natural languages altogether as "ill designed for their purposes", and their replacement by a "scientifically planned 'philosophical language'."[52] Collingwood saw this view as that of Hobbes, Locke, and Berkeley[53] (though the most consequential version of it perhaps was Leibniz's) and as being still, at the time he was writing, "almost an orthodoxy." It has since been drastically undermined, of course, most notably in English philosophy by Wittgenstein and Austin and successors such as Grice and Searle; and, though the systematic aims that Collingwood inherited from British Idealism would never allow him to be counted among 'analytic' philosophers,[54] he can be seen to be moving in their direction. The orthodox view, he believed, was an intellectualist prejudice which saw language through the abstractions of lexicography, grammar, and logic. Not that he had any quarrel with these disciplines—provided that their limitations were correctly seen in relation to language in actual use, or as an activity (what de Saussure called *la parole*);[55] like Wittgenstein in *Philosophical Investigations,* he gets at the limitations of logic not by "bargaining any of its rigour out of it" but rather by seeing that "*[t]he preconceived* idea of crystalline purity can only be removed by turning our whole examination round. (One might say: the axis of reference of our examination must be rotated, but around the fixed point of our real need)."[56]

Collingwood turns the examination of language round by seeing that verbal language—which can indeed be intellectualized by a process in which lexicography, grammar, and logic play significant parts—far from being coterminous with language as such is in fact only a specialized "offshoot" of it; in its original state language consists of bodily activities which, because they are not simply "autonomisms of our psycho-physical organisms" (which express merely psychical experiences), have a freedom corresponding to the imaginative conversion which, as we have seen, is performed by consciousness. In the simplest instances, a bodily action that expresses a purely psychic experience may, *materially,* differ very little, if at all, from an action that can properly be called linguistic: e.g., the *cry* of a baby who is simply lost in his distress may sound much like the *utterance* of a baby into whose crying an element of purposiveness has crept, who has transformed his distress by taking up an attitude to it—be it one of demandingness or of self-pity. But (as Rousseau tells us in *Emile* and as any experienced parent will know) *formally,* or in relation to the total structure of experience, the two actions are quite different. In fact, very simple instances aside, material identity is quickly transcended as imaginative experience becomes incomparably more elaborated than psychic experience and "creates for itself, by an infinite work of refraction and reflection and condensation and dispersal, an infinity of emotions demanding for their expression an infinite subtlety in the articulations of the language that it creates in expressing them."[57]

When he says that the "language of total bodily gesture" is "original" language (or, what comes to the same thing, that "the dance is the mother of all languages")[58] the claim he is making is not about how language has evolved in our history or pre-history but rather (irrespectively of what this natural history may have been) about the order of priority that obtains for us now as languaged beings. What has become the privileged case of verbal language will be misunderstood if we do not see its roots in a wider language of bodily movement. When Collingwood begins his reflection on language by taking Hobbes and Locke to task for understanding words as labels that are available to be tied on to items of experience, the point he is making is close to Wittgenstein's point at the beginning of the *Investigations* when he attacks (what he takes to be) St. Augustine's similar viewpoint: what both of them bring out is that words could not work for us at all outside the context of activities or gestures (such as pointing) that are intuitively understood or (in Collingwood's phrase) that we simply "tumble to."[59] From a standpoint already within verbal language, Collingwood believes, one is likely to regard expressiveness as dispensable—something which, if it is not always undesirable, then is at least displaceable into a special category of language use that can be clearly recognized as 'emotive', 'rhetorical' or 'poetic'. From Collingwood's standpoint, on the contrary, what is exceptional is the attempt to intellectualize language into a system of univocal signs where expressiveness would be annulled, and this attempt, in any case, no matter to what lengths it may be pushed, can never finally succeed: "Scientific discourse insofar as it is scientific tries to rid itself of its function as discourse or language, emotional expressiveness: but if it succeeded in this attempt it would no longer be discourse."[60]

What Collingwood is objecting to here is not only the theory that scientific language is normative for all languages (is, so to speak, the ideal state to which others ought to aspire) but also the apparently more neutral view (which he attributes to I. A. Richards) that 'scientific' picks out one 'use' to which language may be put—just as 'emotive' or 'expressive' picks out another, different use. This is, he believes, just another version of what he has most wanted to expunge from our understanding of art; it is, in other words, the "technical theory of language [which] is as complete an error as the technical theory of art, if indeed they are two errors and not one."[61] It suggests that "language is not an activity, but something which is 'used', and can be 'used' in quite different ways while remaining the same thing, like a chisel that is used either for cutting wood or for lifting tacks."[62] Since language is not a thing that we can use—and *might* use in an expressive way—but rather an activity in which we are caught up that is already expressive, no distinction can be made in the end between scientific discourse and expressive discourse; for the former will always itself be expressive. This fact can be obscured by the relative dominance in a scientific culture of the written over the spoken word—which is a further stage in the process whereby speech itself is abstracted from its matrix in the whole body. However, even though silent reading is now the stock response to writing, the written word is dead unless the reader can convert it into (at least virtual) speech[63]—a speech, moreover, which is itself dead unless it carries a whole range of emphasis and inflection which is not registered on the page. As Collingwood says of words on the page (and this includes technical terms which are indeed purged of emotional expressiveness precisely as part of their becoming technical, but which acquire expressiveness the moment they are taken into *use*— i.e., become part of actual or virtual speech): "If you don't know what tone to say them in, you can't say them at all: they are not words. . . . 'The proposition', understood as a form of words expressing thought and not *emotion* . . . is a fictitious entity."[64]

Collingwood is obviously concerned to show that expressiveness is an ineliminable feature of all language. (An attempt to eliminate it is, indeed, part of the process whereby language becomes intellectualized— i.e., modified to serve the purposes of thinking—but while language can allow this attempt to introduce "a not altogether disruptive tension" into itself, it cannot allow it to succeed fully: "it retains its function as language only in so far as the intellectualization is incomplete."[65]) If this makes him oppose any ultimate distinction between expressive and non-expressive uses of language, the question arises as to whether he himself distinguishes significantly even between *degrees* to which language is expressive. And, if he does not, must he not then accept the conclusion that *all* language is artistic; and is this not a hopelessly undifferentiated position in which the *specificity* of art remains unaccounted for?

It must be said that in some respects Collingwood appears to find nothing unpalatable in this conclusion, and in fact to embrace it. Thus, near the end of the book, he dismisses with some gusto the bases on which philosophy and poetry have usually been distinguished from each other, and though he then puts forward a basis of his own which he considers stronger than any of these, he immediately declares it to be "arbitrary and precarious" and, indeed, a few lines later, "wholly illusory." "Good philosophy and good poetry," he concludes, "are not two different kinds of writing, but one; each is simply good writing. In so far as each is good, each converges, as regards style and literary form, with the other; and in the limiting case where each was as good as it ought to be, the distinction would disappear."[66] And what he is stating here about two forms of writing which have been seen as rivals since ancient times is only a special case of a truth about writing itself. "There can be no such thing as inartistic writing, unless that means merely bad writing. And there can be no such thing as artistic writing; there is only writing."[67] Moreover, his disregard for differentiation is not confined to the case of writing. Elsewhere it becomes clear that quite apart from the written word, his notion of art is in fact extraordinarily capacious. This may come as a surprise, given that the strictness with which he disqualifies as art such things as craft, representation, amusement, and magic can easily make his position seem purist (if indeed his casual dismissal of jazz, or his reserved attitude to the radio, the cinema, and the gramophone do not betray it as incorrigibly high-brow and elitist).[68] It transpires, however, that whatever his narrowness with regard to formally and self-consciously produced 'works', art for him, so far from being the preserve of great masters, is in fact an intrinsic element in the lives of everyone. For, as his theory allows him to say without embarrassment: "Every utterance and every gesture that each one of us makes is a work of art."[69]

Despite Collingwood's refusal to succumb to customary distinctions, he does not leave us in a night in which all cows are black. He has after all spoken of 'bad writing', and this must be different from something else (though his calling this something 'writing'—rather than 'good writing'—may disconcert us by seeming to imply that 'bad writing' is not writing at all). And again, though every utterance and every gesture may be a work of art, this does not imply that every use of speech is an utterance or that every bodily movement is a gesture. More significantly, however, he actually makes a distinction in an earlier part of the book between expression and *description* that, even though it does not recur in the later discussion of language (which emphasizes so much that an element of expressiveness is an inextinguishable feature of *all* language use), seems to imply that the act of expression as such *is* a specialization of language use.

Expression fastens on the individual and particular, while description—even of an individual—takes the form of generalizing: "to describe a thing is to call it a thing of such and such a kind; to bring it under a conception, to classify it."[70] Description fits with craft-work in that "the end which a craft sets out to realize is always conceived in general terms, never individualized. However accurately defined it may be, it is always defined as the production of a thing having characteristics that could be shared by other things"[71] (or, as we might illustrate this point in Aristotle's words, the doctor *qua* man of techne, does not cure Callias or Socrates *per se* but rather each insofar as he belongs with "all persons of a similar constitution, marked off in one class, suffering from this disease").[72] Now the artist differs from the craftsman in that he wants "to get *this* clear," and therefore "gets as far away as possible from merely labelling his emotions as instances of this or that general kind, and takes enormous pains to individualize them by expressing them in terms which reveal their difference from any other emotion of the same sort."[73]

Expression differs from description in that it is never a repetition or a rehearsal but always in itself a real actualization — both of a new meaning and of the person himself in a new way.[74] When we are in a position to describe something (in Collingwood's strict sense here) there is no work for the imagination to do; relationships are being formulated between ideas which are already clear to the mind, and while Collingwood's later discussion seems to imply that the descriptive statement will express emotion, in the normal case this will be the emotion attendant precisely on performing an intellectual operation for which one has a routine competence.[75] (Perhaps what Collingwood is more aware of in his later discussion, however, is that there is *no* 'normal' case — so that 'description', as he conceives it here, is an analytic construct rather than something that occurs in actual speech.)[76] A good novelist's description of a scene or a face would presumably not count as 'description' in this sense, however. For what she would be trying to capture would be the 'thisness' of the scene or face as it impresses itself on her, and this 'capturing' would be her becoming conscious of, and at the same time expressing, both her impression and the emotion engendered in her by it. Whereas 'description' draws unproblematically on previous knowledge and is none the worse, *qua* description, if it is simply a repetition of it, 'expression', being creative, is in a relationship of tension both with its own products or outcomes and with the established abilities of the person whose act it is. "The act of expression," Collingwood writes, "creates a deposit of habits in the agent and of by-products in his world and these habits and by-products become things utilizable by himself and others for ulterior ends." But in itself expression "is not a utilizable thing but a pure activity" (or to use Aristotle's term, an *energeia*);[77] and so the artistic activity which "creates these habits and constructs these external records of itself supersedes and jettisons them as soon as they are formed . . . every genuine expression must be an original one."[78]

If art is expression, and expression involves exploration and discovery, then description is not art, since what one describes one already knows — it is something that one's previous knowledge can adequately meet, and so the latter is not challenged or extended through it. On the other hand, it can happen that one attempts expression in a case where there really is something for one to discover but where one is unable to allow the novelty of this thing to re-compose one's established knowledge. This is a case not of non-art (where expression is not even attempted) but of *bad* art (where it is attempted but fails). In fact, however, what Collingwood calls bad art can scarcely, on his own analysis, be considered art at all. For when he says: "To express it badly is not one way of expressing it, it is a failure to express it,"[79] he seems to imply that the kind of failure involved in 'bad art' is not failure *as* expression but rather failure *to be* an expression at all. Bad art does not express living (and therefore true) emotion; it is the counterfeit that results from disowning or sterilizing emotion and packaging (but not expressing) it in what Collingwood calls "clichés or corpses of language." The 'failure' involved in it is a failure of consciousness in its most basic task: it indicates the 'corrupt consciousness' that we have already met. This is "the true radix malorum": all kinds of intellectual and moral failings can be traced back to it as source, and what it is in itself is simply bad art: "corruption of consciousness is the same thing as bad art."[80]

4. Aesthetics and Ethics: Collingwood and Aristotle

We have already seen that Collingwood does not regard the 'corrupt consciousness' as a properly moral category; it is pre-moral in that it arises at a level below that at which moral deliberation and choice — be they good or bad — occur. Nor does he think that what is expressed in good art has, as such, any claim to moral commendation — any more than the depiction of what is morally laudable need have any claims to artistic merit. And the same nonconvertibility holds with respect to badness: "Bad art is never the result of expressing what is in itself evil. . . . Every one of us feels emotions which, if his neighbours became aware of them, would make them shrink from him with horror. . . . It is not the expression of these emotions that is bad art. . . . On the contrary, bad art arises when instead of expressing these emotions, we disown them, wishing to think ourselves innocent of the emotions that horrify us, or wishing to think of ourselves as too broad-minded to be horrified by them."[81] Nor, again, does he think that art can be co-opted for purposes of moral uplift or political propaganda. What *can* serve here is something which, as we saw earlier, Collingwood is careful to distinguish from art: "If we were talking about the moral regeneration of our world, I should urge the deliberate creation of a system of *magic,* using as its vehicles such things as the theatre and the profession of letters as . . . means to that end."[82] A person who has strong commitments and feelings, morally or politically, is, indeed, *ceteribus paribus,* in a better position to produce worthwhile art than someone who has not. But he will do so only so long as his work is exploring and discovering, for himself as well as for others, what these emotions are. On the other hand, "if he begins by knowing what they are, and uses his art for the purpose of converting others to them, he will not be feeding his art on his political emotions, he will be stifling it beneath them. . . . He may be doing good service to politics but he will be doing bad service to art."[83]

The points I have just made show that Collingwood is far from making any naive identification between art and morality. At the same time, however, he recognizes that there is an intimate connection between the two when he says that a person who has gained the kind of awareness that comes with being an artist (in his sense of this word which allows that we can all be artists) "has not yet, it is true, entered on the life of morality; but he has taken an indispensable step forward towards it."[84] Although he does not elaborate on this remark in *The Principles of Art* nor, for that matter, advert to aesthetic considerations when he explores ethical issues in his other writings,[85] I shall attempt to spell out in this section what is, I believe, the considerable significance for ethical reflection of some of the points made in his aesthetics. I may relate this attempt to a remark of Alasdair MacIntyre's. In including an essay by Quentin Bell, called "Bad Art," in an *ethical* anthology, MacIntyre suggests that despite the fact that "the parallels between or the relationship of morality and art" are not illuminated by most philosophical writing on art, Bell's essay, "with its thesis that 'bad art' arises from a failure of sentiment . . . should be on every moral philosopher's bookshelf." Now Bell's "failure of sentiment that is caused by some form of insincerity" seems very close to Collingwood's "corruption of consciousness"—which is also related to "insincerity"; and so MacIntyre's claim on behalf of Bell's essay encourages me to make a similar, though more circumscribed, claim for Collingwood's book.[86]

From the point of view of a rationalistic ethic, which construes moral problems as ones that are to be tackled in the light of rules and principles that can be discussed and agreed by all rational agents, what Collingwood has to say would not be considered very illuminating. It is illuminating, however, if we see the moral life as (a) deeply affected by passions and emotions with respect to which it requires a kind of knowledge (or self-knowledge) that is as much a matter of character as it is of reason, and as (b) actualized in particular situations, an adequate knowledge of which requires a finely discriminating sensitivity to what is unique in them.

Now this view of the moral life was certainly Collingwood's. With respect to (a), his emphasis on the role of *character* in moral reflection is evident at *P.A.*, pp. 289–290. With respect to (b), his acute sense of the uniqueness of moral situations, and of the moral agent's need for a corresponding discernment, is best evidenced in the *Autobiography*. Here he speaks of the need for "something altogether different from rules, namely insight," which involves an ability to "extemporize" or "improvise."[87] Insight will be needed in cases where, through inexperience, one does not know the rules for the situation with which one has to deal and also in cases where one knows the rules but is sensitive to the mismatch between the standard type of situation covered by them and the actual situation in which one finds oneself. With regard to cases of the first type it is right to recognize the significance of rules and to value the accumulated experience and insight that is formulated and made available in them — thereby freeing one, as it were, from the burdens and hazards of personal insight. It was with regard to cases of the second kind, however, that Collingwood came to see that rules of conduct "kept action at a low level because they involved a certain blindness to the realities of the situation."[88] The knowledge required in such cases, it should be recognized, is not without rules (for it goes with rules so far as they can take it), nor below rules (for it is not necessarily the case that it can or will be superseded by rules yet to be discovered) but rather *beyond* rules. It arises "only for people of experience and intelligence, and even then . . . only when they take a situation very seriously; so seriously as to reject not only the claims of that almost undisguised tempter Desire, and that thinly disguised one Self-Interest, but (a tempter whose disguise is so good that most people hardly ever penetrate it at all and, if they do, suffer the sincerest remorse afterwards) Right Conduct, or action according to the recognized rules."[89]

It is more to the point here, however, that the nonrationalist view of the moral life, summarized in the two points in the paragraph before the last one, was Aristotle's view; and what I want to bring out is the close connection between the latter and some key points in Collingwood's aesthetics. It was a cardinal point for Aristotle that moral knowledge or insight, even though it be intellectual, is still very significantly conditioned by pre-intellectual factors. One's emotional disposition affects not just one's ability to *act* well but even one's ability to *know* or to *see* what acting well in each case would be. One's reading of a situation will be a function of the person one is, and the kind of insights one will need in order to act well simply will not occur, will be blocked, unless one has become at a pre-rational level a person of a certain kind. Collingwood's notion of 'corrupt consciousness', then, is very comprehensible from the viewpoint of Aristotle's moral psychology. For even though in a strict sense the corrupt consciousness might be regarded as pre-moral (in the sense that it puts one in a state of falsehood before one begins to exercise choice at all) what Aristotle shows us is precisely the extent to which the moral is built up on the 'pre-moral'—or, put more coherently, how our notion of the 'moral' is not large enough if it does not include the pre-rational.

Neither Collingwood in his aesthetics nor Aristotle in his ethical theory succumbs to irrationalism. Neither wants to dispense with knowledge but rather to highlight a particular type of knowledge which, given the dominance of the technical paradigm, has been undervalued or ignored. It is a peculiarly *engaged* knowledge, intimate to the action itself (be it artistic creation or moral conduct). Let us look at how Collingwood illustrates this intimacy in the case of painting—and notice how entirely supplanted here is the technical model in which 'knowing' is related to 'acting' as 'planning' to 'execution':

> One paints a thing in order to see it. People who don't paint . . . like to fancy that everybody . . . sees just as much as an artist sees, and that the artist only differs in having the technical accomplishment of painting what he sees. But that is nonsense. You see something in your subject, of course, before you begin to paint it . . . but only a person with experience of painting, and of painting well, can realize how little that is, compared with what you come to see in it as your painting progresses . . . a good painter . . . paints things because until he has painted them he doesn't know what they are like.[90]

Collingwood does not deny that there are two aspects here, 'knowing' or 'seeing' (cognition) and 'painting' (activity). What he is drawing attention to, however, is just how closely connected to each other they are. "The two activities are not identical . . . but they are connected in such a way . . . that each is conditional upon the other. Only a person who paints well can see well; and conversely . . . only a person who sees well can paint well."[91] To a person set in a technical way of thinking there is nothing odd about the active side being conditioned by the cognitive side, but the converse point—that it is only in and through doing that we come to know—seems distinctly odd. It is just this oddity, however, that we shall meet later in our reading of Aristotle when we shall explore in some detail the close reciprocal relationship that he posits between acting virtuously and seeing what a virtuous act is.[92]

What both kinds of seeing have in common is a focus on the individual or concrete particular (what Aristotle calls *to eschaton* and what Collingwood means by "get *this* clear"). Both of them are in sharp contrast with general knowledge—a contrast which we have already met in Collingwood's distinction between 'expression' and 'description', and which will loom large again in our examination of phronesis in Part 2. Moreover the individual with which the artist is concerned is, we ought to notice, very close to that with which the moral agent, too, is concerned. "The individual of which art is the knowledge," writes Collingwood, "is an individual situation in which we find ourselves";[93] and this situation includes very crucially, of course, our own emotional response in it. But is it not of this situation and response that the moral agent too must develop his awareness? (One of the most acute commentators on the *Ethics* has proposed "situational appreciation" as the best English equivalent of the moral *aisthēsis* that goes with phronesis.)[94] The individualizing activity of expression (which we do in order to see) is illustrated by Collingwood: "The anger which I feel here and now, with a certain person, for a certain cause, is no doubt an instance of anger, and in describing it as anger one is telling truth about it; but it is much more than mere anger: it is a peculiar anger, not quite like any anger that I ever felt before, and probably not quite like any anger I shall ever feel again. To become fully conscious of it means becoming conscious of it not merely as an instance of anger, but as this quite peculiar anger."[95] Is Collingwood's depiction of the artist's task here very different from Aristotle's comment on the task of the moral agent: "any one can get angry—that is easy . . . but to do this to the right person, to the right extent, at the right time, with the right aim, and in the right way, *that* is not for every one, nor is it easy"?[96]

We will want to hold back here from any facile equation of art and morality, if only because (as we have already noted) there are emotions which we should certainly not regard as good were we to meet them in a friend (or in ourselves) but which we might nonetheless find powerfully expressed in what we should be compelled to regard as a good work of art. We ought to notice, however, that to express emotion, which is the artistic task, is not the same as to 'betray' or 'cathart' it.[97] Unlike these, it is a normative activity, subject to evaluation as to whether it has been done well or badly. And the evaluative judgments that must be made here are like those that must be made in moral situations. In both cases judgment is integral to the first order performance: for it cannot be left entirely to critics in the one case, any more than it can be left to moral philosophers in the other. Here is how Collingwood emphasizes the internality of critical judgment to the artistic activity itself: an artist, in pursuing his artistic labor is able to tell whether he is pursuing it successfully or unsuccessfully . . . it is possible for him to say, 'I am not satisfied with that line; let us try it this way . . . and this way . . . and this way . . . there . . . there! that will do.' . . . [We must not suppose that] the artist in such cases is working not as an artist, but as a critic and even (if criticism of art is identified with philosophy of art) as a philosopher. . . . The watching of his own work with a vigilant and discriminating eye, which decides at every moment of the process whether it is being successful or not, is not a critical activity subsequent to, and reflective upon, the artistic work, it is an integral part of that work itself. . . . In point of fact, what a student learns in an art-school is . . . to watch himself painting. . . .[98]

Critical judgment as something exercised in the very activity, rather than as a higher type of knowledge that can be brought to bear on it, is exactly what we shall find in Aristotle's notion of phronesis. Moreover, Collingwood and Aristotle are also at one in refusing to allow that a person can possess this judgment unless he is rightly disposed or in a certain state of being. If he is not so disposed, it is not just that he will not be able to perform the action, but he will *not even be able to know* whether or not he has done so:

The corruption of consciousness in virtue of which a man fails to express a given emotion makes him at the same time unable to know whether he has expressed it or not. He is, therefore, for one and the same reason, a bad artist and a bad judge of his own art. A person who is capable of producing bad art cannot, so far as he is capable of producing it, recognize it for what it is. He cannot, on the other hand, really think it good art; he cannot think that he has expressed himself when he has not. To mistake bad art for good art would imply having in one's mind an idea of what good art is, and one has such an idea only so far as one knows what it is to have an uncorrupt consciousness; but no one can know this except a person who possesses one. An insincere mind, so far as it is insincere, has no conception of sincerity.[99]

There can be few, of course, whose consciousness is *entirely* corrupted and so the ability to recognize failure comes as the reward for previous successes. When an artist says, "this line won't do," what happens, Collingwood suggests, is that he "remembers what the experience of expressing himself is like, and in the light of that memory he realizes that the attempt embodied in this particular line has been a failure. Corruption of consciousness is not a recondite sin . . . which overcomes only an unfortunate . . . few, it is a constant experience in the life of every artist, and his life is a constant . . . warfare against it."[100] Knowledge like this which cannot be made accessible through general propositions or guaranteed by intellectual powers alone, knowledge that depends rather on the kind of person one is and is not won without an inner struggle, is not the kind of knowledge that receives recognition in a technocratic culture. We shall see later, however, that it is just the kind of knowledge which Aristotle — often taking the intellectualism of Socrates as a foil — tried to set out in his analysis of phronesis.[101]

5. Collingwood's Subjectivism and Anti-Individualism

In the previous section I have tried to assimilate Collingwood's voice into our overall conversation by accentuating the echoes in it of Aristotle. In this section and the next, final section, I shall examine a tendency in Collingwood's thought which has been alleged to be the source of a fundamental problem in his aesthetics[102] — and which also, we shall find, opens up to our wider conversation. The tendency in question is 'subjectivism' (or 'psychologism'); it manifests itself in his understanding of what might be called the ontological status of the work of art, and the problem it gives rise to comes into sharpest focus as it bears on the *audience's relationship* to the work. Collingwood calls a work of art an "imaginary thing" and says that it "may be completely created when it has been created as a thing whose only place is in the artist's mind."[103] Or, in the specific case of music, he says that when a person makes up a tune, the latter "is already complete and perfect when it exists merely as a tune in his head"[104] — so that although "he may and very often does at the same time hum it or sing it or play it on an instrument . . . all these things are accessories of the real work. . . . The actual making of the tune is something that goes on in his head and nowhere else."[105] Or, again: the "work of art in the proper sense of that phrase is not an artifact, not a bodily or perceptible thing fabricated by the artist, but something existing solely in the artist's head, a creature of his imagination."[106]

When Collingwood says things like this he may seem to be committing himself to the notion of the artist as an enclosed consciousness, a sovereign imagination, which creates an inner world of art, and only *per accidens* records or reveals this outwardly in the matter of stones, canvas, sound waves, etc. And his notion of expression may be taken to imply or assume an ego that has its own imaginings, thoughts, and feelings welling up from some mysterious source within the 'self' — so that their then taking form within the mind (and not even in the public world as one might have supposed) is their 'expression'. Now if he were committed to a position like this, then clearly his biggest problem would be to explain how

an audience ever comes to appreciate a work of art. For one can have access
to a work at all only through its material embodiment; but if this embodiment is, on the expressivist theory, quite extrinsic to the 'work of art
proper', then how can it be intrinsic to the audience's reception of the
latter? (This, it may be noted was *not* a problem for the technical theory.
For according to the latter a very direct relationship with the audience
is built into the artist's work: his task is precisely to arouse determinate
emotions in his audience — rather than to express emotions of his own —
and he does this through his technical mastery of the materials or 'medium' of his art.)

This problem is one to which Collingwood himself does not fail to
advert. And his attempt to answer it shows that what he envisaged as a
replacement for the 'objectivity' of the technical theory was a notion not
of radical subjectivity but rather of *intersubjectivity;* the emphasis which
he put on the consciousness of the artist did not prevent him from having
a very deep insight into the extent to which an individual is inconceivable
outside a *communicative nexus* of persons. His attempt to formulate this
insight, it is true, remained encumbered by very basic assumptions about
the priority of consciousness which he had inherited from the Cartesian
tradition; and so he never succeeded in disengaging it from a conceptual
framework that was in fact deeply inhospitable to it. His difficulty here,
it may be noticed, is of a kind which he himself had diagnosed in other
thinkers and to which — since he recognized it as the characteristic fault
of philosophers — he could hardly suppose that he himself was immune.
A mistaken philosophical theory, he says, "is based in the first instance
not on ignorance but on knowledge. The person who constructs it begins
by partially understanding the subject, and goes on to distort what he
knows by twisting it into conformity with some preconceived idea."[107] This
way of construing the difficulty dictates the appropriate response to it.
One's task — and this is what I shall now take up in relation to his own
thought —"consists in isolating the preconceived idea which has acted as
the distorting agent . . . so as to correct the distortion and thus find out
what it was that the people who invented or accepted the theory were trying to say."[108] With these words of his own as license, I shall try to identify what Collingwood is "trying to say"— and suggest that this is something that another philosopher (more liberated from the "preconceived
idea") has succeeded in saying better.

It is true that the 'technical theory' guarantees and offers a clear account of the bond between artist and audience. It sees this bond, however, as lacking any real reciprocity. Insofar as the artist's clear-cut goal
is a quite specific response in the audience (as the teacher's clear-cut goal
in the behavioral objectives model of teaching is a specific response—

evidenced in behavior—in the pupils) he is the 'agent' of the transaction and the audience is the 'patient' (the materials of his art are also 'patient' of course, but his mastery of these will count for nothing if it does not lead to the intended change in the audience as ultimate 'patient'). The artist will need to 'target' his audience (Collingwood does not say so, but advertising or the management of a modern political campaign are perfect exemplifications of his technical theory), i.e., to know which specific 'effects' will produce which specific responses in a specifically intended audience—and to possess the requisite skill to produce them. One may see the audience here as being manipulated by the artist for his ulterior purpose or, more benignly, as the consumer of something which the artist as servant has made for the audience's satisfaction and tailored to its desires; but in either case one can scarcely speak of an active partnership between artist and audience. Now, in Collingwood's theory, if the relationship between the two seems immediately more obscure, at least it cannot be construed in terms of agent/patient or producer/consumer; it reduces neither the role of audience to that of manipulated object nor the role of artist to that of panderer. But what then, in his view, is this relationship?

First of all, whereas the technical theory does not require that the artist himself experience the emotion which he seeks to 'arouse' in his audience, in Collingwood's theory the artist must in the first instance experience an emotion or rather an emotion-struggling-toward-expression. If I have any purpose as an artist with respect to my audience, it is simply that the latter should, through my expression, come to an awareness or an understanding of my emotions (and thoughts). But this purpose puts the audience in a position which, in a significant way, is no different from the position I am in myself. For through the same act of expression what *I* am doing is precisely becoming aware of my emotions: "A person arousing emotion sets out to affect his audience in a way in which he himself is not necessarily affected. . . . A person expressing emotion on the contrary is treating himself and his audience in the same kind of way; he is making his emotions clear to his audience, and that is what he is doing to himself."[109]

One may wonder whether Collingwood has got things right here at all. Is it the artist's intention to get an audience to understand *his* emotions or, quite apart from his intentions, is the audience really concerned with *him*, or his imaginative or emotional states at all? Is the work of art not an object in a public space, and do we not create all kinds of insoluble *aporiai* if we insist on referring it back to the privacy of its creator's consciousness? If *King Lear* is a great play, how can it matter, and in any case how could we ever possibly know, what really went on in Shakespeare's head when he wrote it? Given doubts such as these (which could be compounded further if we were to ask the question in relation to, let's say, the *Iliad*—who, after all, was Homer?—and which can feed on recent literary theories which annihilate the 'author' in favor of the 'text'), how can sense be made of Collingwood's position?

The concept which Collingwood himself introduces in his attempt to make sense here is that of "reconstruction" or "reproduction."[110] What we get out of a work of art "is something which we have to reconstruct in our own minds, and by our own efforts."[111] The process here is not, in fact, much different from what goes on in ordinary communication, which should be thought of "not as an imparting of thought by the speaker to the hearer, the speaker somehow planting his thought in the hearer's receptive mind, but as a 'reproduction' of the speaker's thought by the hearer, in virtue of his own active thinking."[112] Now it is surely unexceptionable to say that a person listening to a symphony or looking at a picture must—just like a person attending a lecture or reading a book—bring to it a quality of active attention. But what is the force of the prefix in *re*production? Does it imply that the artist has brought forth in himself (through the act of 'expression') an 'experience' and that the audience's task with respect to this experience is analogous to the task of a reproductive 'artist' with respect to an original work? The answer here seems to be, 'no'; for in the analogy what is striking about what the reproducer does—no matter how 'perfect' a 'copy' he may achieve—is precisely its *difference* from what the artist does. But what Collingwood is trying to stress is the similarity, if not identity, of the acts which must be performed by artist and audience. And, paradoxically, what this seems to point to is the fact that it is not the artist's so much as *its own* experience that the audience must create. Even though he speaks in one place of the "audience as understander, attempting an exact reconstruction in its own mind of the artist's imaginative experience,"[113] elsewhere we get a fuller picture of what is involved in this: "when some one reads and understands a poem, he is not merely understanding the poet's expression of his, the poet's, emotions, he is expressing emotions of his own in the poet's words, which have thus become his own words. As Coleridge put it, we know a man for a poet by the fact that he makes us poets. We know that he is expressing his emotions by the fact that he is enabling us to express ours."[114]

Now, to speak of me, *qua* audience or understander, as expressing *my* emotions, through the poet's words, may be no more helpful than to speak of me as reconstructing *his* emotions in myself—any more, indeed, than it was helpful to even suppose that it is *his* emotions, in the first place, that the poet has expressed in the work. What all this talk seems to suggest is that art is a subjective experience that occurs in two different consciousnesses that are as it were two quite separate territories; and that this territoriality enables, indeed requires, us to designate it as either 'mine' or 'yours' (or 'his' or 'hers'). In fact, however, there is much in Collingwood's discussion that explicitly combats any view of art as something individual or private — and thereby undercuts the whole problem of the relationship between artist and audience as we have been conceiving it. He expressly repudiates what he calls "aesthetic individualism" (i.e., the idea of the "artist as a self-contained personality, sole author of everything he does"), pouring scorn on the "nonsense about self-expression" (especially when this self is considered a 'genius' or 'great personality') which has "confused art with exhibitionism."[115] As a matter of fact, he points out, publication is a necessity for every artist,[116] if only because on his own he can never be an adequate judge of his work: "Unless he sees his own proclamation, 'This is good,' echoed on the faces of his audience —'Yes that is good'— he wonders whether he was speaking the truth or not. He thought he had enjoyed and recorded a genuine aesthetic experience, but has he? Was he suffering from a corruption of consciousness?"[117] But it is not only that, unable to answer these questions on his own, the artist is helped to do so in the confirming or critical gaze of an audience. For the latter relates to him not only *post factum* as spectator or judge but as actually "defining what the problem is which as an artist he is trying to solve—what emotions he is to express—and what constitutes a solution of it."[118] In other words, whereas if these emotions "are his own and no one else's there is no one except himself who can judge whether he has expressed them or not,"[119] the fact of a partnership in judgment is evidence of a deeper collaboration: "he understands his artistic labour not as a personal effort on his own private behalf, but as a public labour on behalf of the community to which he belongs. Whatever statement of emotion he utters is prefaced by the implicit rubric, not 'I feel' but 'we feel'."[120]

Collingwood is quite prepared to draw practical conclusions from his position here. For example, he canvasses the desirability of genuine participation in the performing arts (where the work of writers and composers is open to enrichment from the side of players), favors 'live art' in which the audience can participate (as where, e.g., a theater group builds up a faithful audience, creating ways in which the latter can really contribute to the artistic development of the company), and shows a corresponding antipathy to the growing mechanization of art (films, radio, gramophone — television had not yet appeared — and even the printing press), which tends to make the audience "merely receptive and not concreative," or "a licensed eavesdropper overhearing something which would be complete without him."[121] More radically, he recommends the abolition of the whole institution of "artistic ownership," suggesting that "every artist make a vow . . . never to prosecute or lend himself to a prosecution under the law of copyright" but, on the contrary, "to plagiarize each other's work like men,"[122] "to steal with both hands whatever they can use wherever they can find it."[123] One might still wonder, however, whether all this is not evidence of Collingwood's simply having, as a cultivated lay person, a robust conception of the arts—a conception which he is not entitled to, however, as the philosopher that he is. Do we find in *The Principles of Art*, in other words, an unintegrated hybrid: interesting ideas about the arts at the end of the book, hanging loose, however, from the whole philosophical apparatus that had been so laboriously constructed to support them?

In responding to this question, we may first of all observe that Collingwood himself sees his attack on the sovereignty of the artist, and his vindication of the active and intrinsic role of the audience, in the context of a wider viewpoint. He speaks of "traditional individualistic psychology through which, as through distorting glasses, we are in the habit of looking at artistic work."[124] And in squaring up to this, he lays down what must be considered a fundamental position in philosophical anthropology: "Individualism conceives a man as if he were a God, a self-contained and self-sufficient creative power whose only task is to be himself and to exhibit his nature in whatever works are appropriate to it. But a man, in his art as in everything else, is a *finite* being. Everything that he does is done in relation to others like himself."[125] We can understand art, then, only within the context of this fundamental intersubjectivity. People "become poets or painters or musicians not by some process of development from within . . . but by living in a society where these languages are current."[126] As an artist, as indeed also as a thinker, one is essentially dependent on, or rather interdependent with, others. Thought and feeling can never be merely private acts; a normativity which is constitutive of them carries with it an inherent reference to other persons. "If he has a new thought he must explain it to others, in order that, finding others able to understand it, he may be sure it is a good one. If he has a new emotion, he must express it to others, in order that, finding them able to share it, he may be sure his consciousness of it is not corrupt."[127] The 'must' here is not external or conditional: it does not have to do merely with 'communication' as if this were an optional addition to thinking and feeling, nor with 'self-assurance' as if this were merely a variable psychological state. It is rather an existential or ontological imperative, having to do with our fundamental constitution as persons: "As a finite being, man becomes aware of himself as a person only so far as he finds himself standing in relation to others of whom he simultaneously becomes aware as persons."[128]

6. Intersubjectivity and Language:
What Collingwood Is 'Trying to Say'

The theme of finitude that we meet here in Collingwood is one that will be developed and amplified in our remaining chapters on Arendt, Gadamer, and (with a different emphasis) Habermas. For it is not at all a diversion from our central concern with the limits of technical rationality and the need for an alternative kind of reasonableness such as Aristotle worked out with his notion of phronesis. To the contrary, what we shall find in subsequent chapters is that a critique of technical reason deepens into a questioning of the solitariness and sovereignty that have been taken to be definitive of the modern self. And phronesis will appear as the characteristic mode of knowledge of a being who has no escape from contingency and is forever deprived of an absolute standpoint.

Here, however, we may still wonder whether our question about the coherence of Collingwood's book has been answered. Even if his concluding remarks on art are coupled, as we have just seen, with remarks on intersubjectivity and finitude, the question still remains, perhaps, as to whether these latter remarks themselves can be adequately articulated through, or are indeed reconcilable with, the whole philosophy which forms the substantial core of his book (and which we have already met in §2 and §3 above). To answer this question we need to look again at Collingwood's consideration of language. *The Principles of Art* contains a very decisive 'linguistic turn'—despite its being published some time before the latter phenomenon is generally supposed to have become the distinguishing feature of twentieth-century English philosophy.[129] That it (*P.A.*) marks a watershed is reflected, perhaps, in the fact that it works out, at the same time, a philosophy of consciousness *and* a philosophy of language. In subsequent work—in what we might call full-blown linguistic philosophy, as well as in the continental European philosophy (especially in the Heideggerian tradition) which will be our own concern later on—'consciousness' as the central theme of philosophical reflection has been eclipsed; having been installed by Descartes as the foundation of modern philosophy, it has been the main casualty of the sustained critique to which this philosophy has been subjected in recent decades. Now, the fact that Collingwood retains and gives such a cardinal role to 'consciousness' might be taken to reveal that his theory of language must be a hopelessly subjectivistic one: a judgment which might be taken to be suitably corroborated by the weight which this theory puts on the notion of 'expression'. What I shall try to show, however, is something like the converse of this: that rather than his understanding of language being vitiated by its complicity with his notion of consciousness, this latter notion is itself shown to be in need of reconsideration, given the theory of language to which it is yoked, and that 'expression', as used by him, means in fact almost the opposite of what it most often means in 'expressivist' theories.[130]

We have already seen that, for Collingwood, it is only through expressing something that I become conscious of it: "The expression is not an afterthought to the idea; the two are inseparably united, so that the idea is had as an idea only insofar as it is expressed."[131] Now this understanding of the coincidence of consciousness and expression makes it impossible for him to entertain a notion of consciousness as private. For expression always occurs within language, and language, no matter how creative or original the shapes even a poet may pull it into, is always public; it is always there before one, and what even the poem achieves is only something that language was already capable of yielding. And not only is thought always linguistic but, conversely, language is already thoughtful. Language, in other words, is not something that we learn separately, in order subsequently to have the equipment, as it were, to think or feel: "One does not first acquire a language and then use it. To possess it and to use it are the same. We only come to possess it by repeatedly and progressively attempting to use it."[132] (What we are trying to grasp here—the fact that one can have something to say only when one is already active within language—is analogous with, and is perhaps more perspicuous in the case of, something we have already noted about painting: that it is only when he is active with his hand, brush, canvas, and paints, only when he is already immersed in the *medium* of his art, that a painter discovers 'what' it is he is trying to paint.)[133]

The nonprivacy of thought and feeling, their being public by virtue of their being inherently linguistic, introduces the notion of *intersubjectivity*. This notion is formulated very clearly by Collingwood in his pivotal chapter on language: "Consciousness does not begin as mere self-consciousness, establishing in each one of us the idea of himself, as a person or center of experience, and then proceed by some process, whether of projection or of argument by analogy, to construct or infer other persons. Each one of us is a finite being, surrounded by others of the same kind; and the consciousness of our own existence is also the consciousness of the existence of these others."[134] Now this consciousness (of self *and* others) exists and develops through language—through what might be called a dialectic of speaking and hearing. While, as organisms, human beings are already related through instinctive sympathies,

> as persons, they construct a new set of relations between themselves, arising out of their consciousness of themselves and one another; these are linguistic relations. The discovery of myself as a person is the discovery that I can speak, and am thus a *persona* or speaker; in speaking, I am both speaker

and hearer; and since the discovery of myself as a person is also the discovery of other persons around me, it is the discovery of speakers and hearers other than myself. Thus, from the first, the experience of speech contains in itself in principle the experiences of speaking to others and of hearing others speak to me.[135]

Here Collingwood is affirming intersubjectivity if not as prior to then at least as co-ultimate with subjectivity. His development of this position, however, is not free from, and is I believe damaged by, elements of a residual, unreconstructed subjectivism. Thus, he models the dialectic of speaking and hearing between two persons on what he seems to think of as a more primary dialectic of speaking and hearing within each person singly. He grafts the distinction between speaking and hearing on to the distinction between expressing and becoming conscious: in expressing *I speak to myself* and my becoming conscious of what I express is then *my hearing myself speak*. (Thus he writes: "1) it is only because we know what we feel that we can express it in words; 2) it is only because we express them in words that we know what our emotions are. In the first, we describe our situation as speakers; in the second, our situation as hearers of what we ourselves say.")[136] Then he brings a speech-situation between me and another person back within the orbit of a conversation within myself: "The hearer, therefore, conscious that he is being addressed by another person like himself . . . takes what he hears exactly as if it were speech of his own: he speaks to himself with the words that he hears addressed to him, and thus constructs in himself the idea which those words express."[137] Moreover, he then compounds what he says here by what he goes on to lay down as a necessary condition for the accomplishment of this act of constructing the idea in oneself (the idea expressed in the words that one has somehow taken over as one's own): "no idea can be formed as such in consciousness except by a mind whose sensuous-emotional experience contains the corresponding impression, at least in a faint and submerged shape, at that very moment."[138]

Now the potential that was opened up by Collingwood's emphasis — evident in our earlier quotation — on intersubjectivity and language is seriously compromised here. The dialectic of speaking and hearing is derailed when we suppose that its primary locus is *within* myself and not *between* myself and others. If I can think of myself as speaking to and hearing myself, it is only by analogy with, or by extrapolation from, the more primordial experience of speaking to and hearing another. And this latter experience, itself, is essentially and irreducibly ek-static — a fact which is lost sight of if it is construed as an activity (whether of [re-]construction, production, or enactment) that goes on within myself.

"[H]e speaks to himself with the words he hears addressed to him, and thus constructs in himself the idea which those words express." What I have been adverting to with regard to this formulation is that it takes the activity of my understanding (or reading) another person's words (or text) to be something that goes on within me. This something is the reconstruction of the speaker's (or author's) thought and it is in aid of this that I speak his words to myself as if they were my own—and then, activated as it were by them, try to find experiences (even at a psychic, i.e., nonconscious, level) from which I will be able to draw forth the meaning expressed in them. What is unfortunate about this whole way of looking at things, I believe, is that in it Collingwood does not follow out his own best insights; for the dynamism of speaking and hearing is severely curtailed here, and language is not allowed as it were to do its work.

Collingwood is right, surely, when he takes understanding to include hearing *and speaking*. Let us suppose, however, that rather than speaking the author's words to myself, *I speak back words of my own to him*. Rather than taking what he says as the only expression here—which sets me the task of simply laying hold of the meaning that he had in his mind when he made it—let us suppose that I really express what I (take myself to) hear in his words and do so—as, if it is a genuine expression, I must—*in my own words*. What I am suggesting here is that if the author is involved in a process of thinking and expressing—where these acts are distinguishable from, but still indissolubly intimate with, each other—so we should see the reader as involved not just in understanding but in *understanding-and-interpreting*—where the interpretation is as intimate to the understanding as the author's expression is to his (the author's) thought. Now, in interpreting, the reader is really speaking, not merely rehearsing in himself the author's speech—is, in fact, *speaking back*. He is, indeed, trying to understand what is meant by the author's words; but what this involves is not trying to get behind the words to the meaning (or 'intention') in the mind that uttered them (so that one 'repeats' this 'identical' meaning in one's own mind) but rather letting the words sow their meaning *in other words*. When I say that these latter words are then spoken back to the author's text, I mean that the interpretation that comes into being in them is tentative and provisional: one goes on listening and reading and if, in doing so, one comes to hear differently or better, this is expressed in a new, amended interpretation—one that is prompted, as it were, by the way that the *text speaks back* to it.

What has been emerging here, in place of 'reconstruction' is the notion of '*conversation*'. I do not try so much to recreate the author's monologue in myself as to enter into dialogue with his work. And this dialogue, or conversation, is not something that happens *after* I have first understood the text—when, secure in my understanding of it, I then confront it with my own thought. Rather, my own thought has been in a kind of inter-play with it all along, and only within this inter-play do I come to understand it at all. The underlying point here is that understanding is always *interpretation* — i.e., not just a 'mental act' but an articulation in language of what is understood. This is the point that seems to be crucially missing from Collingwood's analysis — though making it is no more than making explicit, on the side of the reader, what he himself makes very explicit, on the side of the author, with his notion of 'expression'. If one accepts the inevitability of interpretation then one gives up the hope of ever copying the author's idea in one's own mind. This does not imply, however, that one gives up the hope of understanding, or that one must remain forever estranged from the meaning of the text. It implies, rather, that one joins up with this meaning only on the sea of language. Trusting oneself to words, one relies not so much on contents stored in one's consciousness or on some "sensuous-emotional experience" that is still nonconscious. One relies, rather, on language itself to bring about understanding through the interpretation that unfolds, with cumulative correction and refinement, in the conversation — the passing back and forth of words — between oneself as reader and the text.

The notion of conversation — with its hypostatizing appeal to language as something in itself active and effective — may seem to be no more than a metaphor which skirts around or obscures the hard problems it is supposed to address. If I have been arguing against the notion of 'reconstruction' as a solution to this problem, I have not yet, I should acknowledge, done nearly enough to argue for conversation as an alternative to it. Now in fact this latter notion, with the perspective on language that it opens up, is one that we shall be exploring in depth later on in our reading of Gadamer.[139] Lest my introduction of it here should seem premature, however, I want to point out that conversation is a notion that we already find in Collingwood.[140] Responding to the charge that if language is something that does not have a firm shape that we can securely lay hold of independently of our successive essays at thinking — but rather (like the Lesbian rule)[141] must bend on each occasion to the shape of our thinking-speaking — then "there could never be any absolute assurance, either for the hearer or the speaker, that the one had understood the other," he writes:

> That is so; but in fact there is no such assurance. The only assurance we possess is an empirical and relative assurance, becoming progressively stronger as conversation proceeds, and based on the fact that neither party seems to the other to be talking nonsense. The question whether they understand each other *solvitur interloquendo*. If they understand each other well enough

to go on talking, they understand each other as well as they need; and there is no better kind of understanding which they can regret not having attained.[142]

"[S]olvitur *inter*loquendo," he says—and not *re*loquendo. Here Collingwood is true, I believe, to his best insights (though even this passage occurs in a context where these insights have by no means been released, as I believe they can and ought to be, from the shackles of 'reconstruction'). More remarkable, however, than this passage in itself—which refers quite clearly to the oral exchange between two partners that we are accustomed to designate as a 'conversation'—is the fact that later in the book Collingwood explicitly refers back to it and makes it clear that the structure which he had identified in it holds not just for the case where two persons engage in face-to-face dialogue but also in the case where one looks at a painting and, indeed, quite *generally,* i.e., in every relationship between a work and its audience. Here, again, his construal of the problem is dogged by the notion of reconstruction: "How is one to know that the imaginative experience which the spectator, by the work of his consciousness, makes out of the sensations he receives from a painting 're-peats', or is 'identical' with, the experience which the artist had in painting it?"[143] The fact that he puts the two crucially problematical words in this question in quotation marks indicates, perhaps, an unease with the whole conceptual machinery of 'reconstruction'. But however this may be, his answer to the question is one which seems to me to burst through this machinery altogether. He first invokes, repeating it verbatim, the key sentence from the passage cited above and then, a little later, goes on to give this illuminating gloss on it:

> The imaginative experience contained in a work of art is not a closed whole. There is no sense in putting the dilemma that a man either understands it (that is, has made that entire experience his own) or does not. Understanding it is always a complex business, consisting of many phases, each complete in itself but each leading on to the next. A determined and intelligent audience will penetrate into this complex far enough . . . to get something of value; but it need not on that account think it has extracted 'the' meaning of the work, for there is no such thing. The doctrine of a plurality of meanings, expounded for the case of holy scripture by St. Thomas Aquinas, is in principle perfectly sound: as he states it, the only trouble is that it does not go far enough. In some shape or other, it is true of all language.[144]

What Collingwood says here seems to me both to explode the paradigm of 'reconstruction' and to be, in essence, true. It raises issues, however, which he has scarcely touched (what becomes of 'objectivity', or are there any criteria of truth or correctness if the dike is opened to a 'plurality of meanings'? If one is cast out on the high sea of language, has one any craft, rudder or compass?) and seems to call for an elaboration that he does not supply. To find a context in which what he says here can be developed more fully, and in which these issues can be more justly met, I shall turn to the hermeneutical philosophy of Hans-Georg Gadamer. Before doing so, however, I want to further illustrate the range of our overall theme by looking at a work of another philosopher who, in a context quite different from Collingwood's, develops an argument which is structurally very similar to his and who, in doing so, manages more successfully to fly the nets of subjectivism.

3. Hannah Arendt's Distinction between Action and Making in *The Human Condition*

The Principles of Art is notable because of its thematic treatment of the notion of techne ('craft' or 'technique') and its explicit attempt to develop other concepts that are neither dependent on, nor assimilable to, a technicist mold. The critique of technique is, however, confined to the aesthetic field and moreover, as we have seen, the alternative conceptualization that is developed does *not* appeal to phronesis/praxis. I turn now, however, to another book that confronts the technicist phenomenon (or the entrenchment of fabrication or poiesis) on a broader front and which, moreover, in trying to retrieve an alternative mode of activity that is threatened with disappearance under the growing mass of fabrication, *does* appeal to the other pole of the Aristotelian distinction, namely, to the notion of action or praxis. Hannah Arendt's book *The Human Condition* is an attempt to bring out the distinctions and articulations *within* the *vita activa* which, in her view, were occluded by the Greek (and medieval) concern for the priority of the *vita contemplativa* over the *vita activa* — and were not properly restored in the modern reversal of this priority which found its most vehement (albeit very different) expressions in the works of Marx and Nietzsche.

It must be acknowledged that there are strong grounds for including Aristotle's voice in a general Socratic consensus on the primacy of the life of contemplation — the most notorious text here being a few chapters in the tenth book of the Nicomachean Ethics.[1] And it is also true, perhaps, that Aristotelian commentators have been more exercised by this latter text than by the analysis, in book six of the *Ethics,* of the distinction *within* the practical life between praxis/phronesis and poiesis/techne. Our own attention throughout this study, however, is precisely on this latter distinction; and so Arendt's book — with its quite systematic argument for a distinction between action and making, and its (admittedly ambivalent)[2] advertence to the Aristotelian precedent for such an argument — is of particular significance to us.

1. Action and Behavior

Through Arendt's eyes, much of the social and political history of
the West can be read as the story of the fall from 'action' into 'making'.
'Making' here connotes activity which establishes a durable world of artefacts and utilities—and thereby rises out of the cycles of *labor* which are
tied to the sheer necessity of biological survival.[3] 'Action', on the other
hand, brings into being a higher freedom in which persons realize and
reveal themselves as distinct, and indeed unique, persons. It is grounded
in two primordial facts of the human condition: plurality and natality.
Human existence is given to persons who are equal with, but unexchange-
able for, each other—since they are not mere replicas of one determinate
prototype, but unrepeatable individuals—and it is given to them in birth,
a miracle of beginning which can be renewed throughout their lives precisely if they continue to take upon themselves the initiatives of action.
'Action', in this sense, is to be distinguished from 'behavior', which
is the activity that can be reliably expected from people who have forfeited
their distinctness to the all-consuming sameness of 'society'.[4] It is an unfortunate truth, in Arendt's view, that "the more people there are the
more likely they are to behave and the less likely to tolerate non-behavior.
Statistically, this will be shown in the leveling out of fluctuation. In reality, deeds will have less and less chance to stem the tide of behavior. . . .
Statistical uniformity is by no means a harmless scientific ideal; it is the
no longer secret political ideal of a society which, entirely submerged in
the routine of everyday living, is at peace with the scientific outlook inherent in its very existence."[5] The real power of behaviorism (which, for
Arendt, need not be confined to the strict doctrine of a Skinner but is
implicit in all the modern behavioral sciences of which economics was
the first) stems from this fact: that it represents not only a methodological
option in science but also a real tendency in modern societies themselves—
a tendency to suppress action, or at least to greatly weaken it by banishing
it into "the sphere of the intimate and the private." Or, as Arendt puts
this near the end of her book: "the trouble with modern theories of be-
havorism is not that they are wrong but that they could become true, that
they actually are the best possible conceptualization of certain obvious
trends in modern society."[6]
Although 'action' may be distinguished from 'behavior', the distinction which is highlighted in Arendt's book is that between 'action' and
'making'. 'Behavior' may be taken to be correlative with, but in fact conceptually subordinate to, 'making'; it is the passive adaptation of citizens
in a society whose affairs are increasingly administered according to the
standard of technocratic efficiency, i.e., the most modern version of the

logic of 'making'. Our task will be to clarify the notion of action, and—although it is the currency of the term 'behavior' (as in the 'behavioral objectives model of teaching') which most alerts us to the decline of this notion—to bring out the implications of its distinction from the concept of 'making'.

It is through action that a person discloses 'who'—rather than 'what' —she is. This 'who', or fugitive thisness of a person, which has "a curious intangibility that confounds all efforts toward unequivocal verbal expression,"[7] and which is not captured in the sum total of a person's achievements or even in a full listing of her personal qualities—for all of these hint only at *what* she is—is revealed, obliquely, through the person's actions and speech. Genuine speech, indeed, ought not to be understood, as it often now is, as something separate from, or even as a substitute for, action. "No other human performance requires speech to the same extent as action"—though "from the viewpoint of sheer utility [it] seems an awkward substitute for sign language."[8] Indeed, not only is speech invariably an intimate accompaniment to action but, as the Greeks were aware, "finding the right words at the right moment, quite apart from the information or communication they may convey, *is* action."[9] (Speech here, we may remark, clearly has the same originative quality that we have already seen in Collingwood—the "clichés" which he wants to ban from true speech belong, we might say, with 'behavior' and not with 'action'.)

While it is through action, and speech, that people "reveal actively their unique personal identities and thus make their appearance in the human world"[10]—or, in other words, provide an implicit answer to the question "who are you?"—still this always happens obliquely; in Arendt's words, it "can almost never be achieved as a wilful purpose, as though one possessed and could dispose of this 'who' in the same manner he has and can dispose of his qualities."[11] The reason one cannot preside over or control this revelation of oneself (and this is similar to the reason why Collingwood maintains that one cannot really know what one's emotion is until one has expressed it) is that what is going on here is a full actualization of oneself—in the sense, as we shall see presently, of Aristotle's notion of *energeia*—in which any possibility of spectatorship on one's part is swept away. Action cannot merely reveal one as one would be without action; rather one is constituted as the person one is through the same actions which simultaneously reveal one as thus constituted. Moreover, this revelation is always clearer to others than it is to oneself. Since it is always going on behind the agent's back, as it were, and is as elusive to him as his own shadow, what is going on in human affairs is always more than the agents can intend or encompass; and it is this 'more' that gives these affairs their specific character and ensures, for instance, that they are never "a mere productive activity which . . . has no more meaning than is revealed in the finished product and does not . . . show more than is plainly visible at the end of the productive process."[12] Action and speech go on, of course, in the midst of a world of objects which are themselves the outcomes of production; even when they are directly taken up with these however—as indeed they most often are—the 'more' makes its appearance. Since the disclosure of the agent is an "integral part of all, even the most 'objective' intercourse, the physical, worldy in-between along with its interests is overlaid and, as it were, overgrown with an altogether different in-between which . . . owes its origins exclusively to men's acting and speaking directly *to* one another."[13]

This second "in-between"—called the "web of relationships" by Arendt —which is constituted by deeds and words but which "is not tangible, since there are no tangible objects into which it could solidify"[14] makes up the very substance of human affairs ("the realm of human affairs, strictly speaking, consists of the web of human relationships which exists whenever men live together").[15] And yet it is the very reality which is most consistently ignored or underestimated in all reductionist accounts of these affairs: "the very basic error of all materialism in politics . . . is to overlook the inevitability with which men disclose themselves as subjects, as distinct and unique persons, even when they wholly concentrate upon reaching an altogether worldly material object. To dispense with this disclosure, if indeed it could ever be done, would mean to transform men into something they are not; to deny, on the other hand, that this disclosure is real and has consequences of its own is simply unrealistic."[16]

2. Uncertain Stories and the Limits of Practical Knowledge

What are these consequences? They will be worth making explicit since it is from them that human affairs, properly understood, derive their characteristic qualities. The overall consequence is an uncertainty which attaches to action and gives to human affairs their irremediable frailty. This uncertainty which takes the form both of unpredictability and irreversibility, derives from the fact that the person as agent is never the maker of his life but rather the subject of his life-story; and he is "subject" not in the sense of being author of the story but rather in the sense of being actor and sufferer in it. A person's actions and speech cumulate into the story of his life, and we can come closest to knowing 'who' he is when we know this story. He is not its author or producer, however: "the real story in which we are engaged as long as we live has no visible or invisible maker because it it not made."[17] It is not made because its plot is never under our control; and this is so because we never act and speak in isolation; rather, through speech and action we insert ourselves into the web of human relationships which is "a medium where every reaction becomes a chain reaction and every process is the cause of new processes."[18] This medium or web is the only home of action, and within it every action is boundless. This is what Arendt has in mind when she points to the fact "that he who acts never quite knows what he is doing, that he is always 'guilty' of consequences he never intended or even foresaw [and] can never undo [and] that the process he starts is never consummated unequivocally in one single deed or event."[19] Nor is this a fact only about overtly political activities in which large numbers of people are involved. It is no less inescapable even if we should try to confine ourselves to "a limited, graspable framework of circumstances"; for all action, if only in virtue of its capacity to establish relationships—which is its "specific productivity"—has "an inherent tendency to force open all limitations and cut across all boundaries."[20]

This boundlessness of action which is the root of its uncertainty and which makes it, from the point of view of those who are engaged in it, both unpredictable and irreversible, forces on our attention one very significant structural fact that obtains in the relationship between action and *knowledge*. It is a fact which is well expressed in these words of Arendt:

> In contradistinction to fabrication, where the light by which to judge the finished product is provided by the image or model perceived beforehand by the craftsman's eye, the light that illuminates processes of action, and therefore all historical processes, appears only at their end. . . . Action reveals itself fully only to the storyteller, that is, to the backward glance of the historian, who indeed always knows better what it was all about than the participants. All accounts told by the actors themselves, though they may in rare cases give an entirely trustworthy statement of intentions, aims, and motives, become mere useful source material in the historian's hands and can never match his story in significance and truthfulness. What the storyteller narrates must necessarily be hidden from the actor himself, at least as long as he is in the act or caught in its consequences. . . .[21]

The essential non-transparency of action to the agent, which Arendt here draws attention to, implies an in-built limitation on our practical knowledge and on our power of intention (since we always do more than we can know, and can never be sure of doing just what we intend), a limitation, moreover, which must be a source of scandal to those (e.g., proponents of the behavioral objectives model) whose foremost priority is that action should have definite prespecified outcomes. This limitation can be spelled out further by adverting to the peculiar kind of power which infuses action, and to the lack of sovereignty on the part of the agent which it entails.

The resourcefulness of a person's action depends on the resonance which it finds in the medium of relationships and "innumerable conflicting wills and intentions"[22] into which it is inserted. From the point of view of the one who acts, this resonance—or the degree to which his action strikes a responsive chord in others who will co-operate with it and carry it along toward some completion—is always a happening as well as an achievement. It may well be forthcoming but it is not something that can be reliably counted on or guaranteed; even if it has happened for him with some regularity in the past, there still remains an element of hazard about each new occasion on which it is actualized. The power or *dunamis* of action, then, is not so much a property of the agent as of the whole constellation in which he acts; it is "dependent upon the unreliable and only temporary agreement of many wills and intentions," and so cannot "be possessed like strength or applied like force."[23] There is, in fact, a very marked contrast, for Arendt, between power, in this sense, and violence. Power, which "springs up between men" and is a "potentiality in being together," is not "an unchangeable, measurable, and reliable entity like force or strength," and so cannot "be stored up and kept in reserve for emergencies, like the instruments of violence, but exists only in its actualization."[24]

The evanescence and riskiness which characterize genuine power derive from the basic condition of action which we have already seen, namely, plurality. This plurality excludes the possibility of anyone's ever exercising real sovereignty either over his own life or over the lives of others: "sovereignty, the ideal of uncompromising self-sufficiency and mastership, is contradictory to the very condition of plurality."[25] It is the refusal to renounce the aspiration to sovereignty—or, in other words, to abide by the reality of plurality—that leads to tyranny; and tyranny is still a form of violence (i.e., a way of depriving others of the power of action) even when it is "benevolent and enlightened." A tyrant, in fact, can never achieve by means of his tyranny what he would have achieved by action if only his subjects had been more responsive. In an attempt to compensate for the "intrinsic weakness of plurality," he can eliminate power, but what he puts in its place—however great the degree of force he exerts—is literally a form of impotence.

3. Tyranny and the Flight from Action into Making

It seems to run like a refrain throughout Arendt's whole discussion that tyranny (i.e., "the always abortive attempt to substitute violence for power"),[26] far from being alien to, or an aberration from, the whole Western tradition, is in fact deeply inscribed in it. It is to be discerned especially in what Arendt sees as a distrust and even "contempt" for action, which has inspired a persistent attempt to eliminate it (action) "because of its uncertainty and to save human affairs from their frailty by dealing with them as though they were or could become the planned products of human making."[27] This attempt to replace action by making seems especially manifest in the modern age with "its early concern with tangible products and demonstrable profits or its later obsession with smooth functioning and sociability."[28] Although it is now commonplace to see a new notion of politics foreshadowed and legitimized by Hobbes and Machiavelli in the sixteenth and seventeenth centuries,[29] and helped toward methodical implementation by the rise of the social sciences, Arendt's own diagnosis is more radical. The "authentic perplexities of action" are so deep, in her view, that (like Collingwood) she sees the real root of the tendency she is trying to expose already there in Greek, or at least Socratic, thought: the Socratic philosophers had already succumbed to "the temptation [the same word we have already seen in Collingwood] to eliminate [action's] risks and dangers by introducing into the web of human relationships the much more solid and reliable categories inherent in activities [i.e., those of making] with which we confront nature and build the world of the human artifice."[30]

The great culprit here, of course, is Plato. His realignment of the meanings of the two Greek verbs *archein* and *prattein* (the verb of which *praxis* is the noun) is the most telling sign, for Arendt, of the early disintegration of the notion of action which she is trying to salvage and which had been gloriously exemplified by the Homeric characters and still clearly understood by Pericles. In Arendt's view *archein* and *prattein* had both been used to express different aspects of action—*archein* bringing out the element of beginning or opening up and *prattein* the element of carrying through or accomplishing (which is, at the same time, an undergoing or bearing of the consequences that unfold from this beginning); both of these together had been intrinsic in the actions of everyone within the plurality of free agents. In Plato, however, we get a separation and specialization: *archein* comes to mean not the beginning by someone who will himself continue to be engaged in the *prattein*, but rather the *rule* by one who will now be aloof from the *prattein*—which thus becomes merely the execution by others of commands laid down through an *archein* in which they themselves have no part. Through this linguistic transformation, Plato was, in Arendt's view, "the first to introduce the division between those who know and do not act and those who act and do not know, instead of the old articulation of action into beginning and achieving, so that knowing what to do and doing it become two altogether different performances."[31] Moreover, the political implications of this division were immediate: knowledge coincided with rulership and command, and action with obedience and execution, and so a move was made here which "became authoritative for the whole tradition of political thought," and which, in fact, "has remained at the root of all theories of domination."[32]

What has brought the concept of rule (i.e., "the notion that men can lawfully and politically live together only when some are entitled to command and the others are forced to obey")[33] to the forefront of political philosophy—and thereby made this philosophy consist in large part of a "whole body of argument against 'democracy'"—has been not only the sundering of the old notion of action but its *replacement by the notion of making*. For, as Arendt points out, "the division between knowing and doing, so alien to the realm of action, whose validity and meaningfulness are destroyed the moment thought and action part company, is an everyday experience in fabrication, whose processes obviously fall into two parts: first, perceiving the image or shape (*eidos*) of the product-to-be, and then organizing the means and starting the execution."[34] And what motivates this replacement, "consciously or unconsciously," is, as we have already seen, an attempt to escape from "the threefold frustration of action—the unpredictability of its outcome, the irreversibility of the process, and the anonymity of its authors," by "seeking shelter . . . in an activity where one man, isolated from all others, remains master of his doings [or the doings of his subordinates] from beginning to end."[35]

The primacy of the paradigm of fabrication or craft, for Arendt, is as endemic in the whole conceptual apparatus of politics as, for Collingwood, it is in that of aesthetics: "How persistent and successful the transformation of action into a mode of making has been is easily attested by the whole terminology of political theory and political thought, which indeed makes it almost impossible to discuss these matters without using the category of means and ends and thinking in terms of instrumentality."[36] The close structural similarity between Arendt's whole diagnosis and that of Collingwood may be highlighted here. Both are trying to argue that the domains which they analyze (politics, art) have been distorted by the systematic importation of alien categories. For both of them these categories come from the same source, i.e., the realm of fabrication and had already been not only definitively articulated but inappropriately extended by the Socratic philosophers. For both of them the distortions caused by these extensions are so deep as to amount almost to the elimination of the two domains which are the objects of their analyses, and in trying to recover the integrity of these domains, they each appeal to a basic concept in whose elaboration a systematic contrast with "fabrication" plays a crucial role.

"Action," for Arendt, is to politics what "expression," for Collingwood, is to art; and just as Collingwood is continually trying to protect the concept of art against the counterfeits which he calls "non-art" (and whose most fertile origins lie in the fabrications of craft as conceived by the Greeks), Arendt is involved in a similarly post-lapsarian attempt to rescue a notion of politics not so much from "bad politics" as from what she sees as the demise of politics altogether—a demise caused by essentially the same flight into fabrication. Close as this comparison between them is, however, Collingwood might be said to find himself in a somewhat happier position than Arendt; for he at least can point, near the end of his book, to contemporary exponents of a genuine and indeed great art (Eliot's *Wasteland* is his paradigm example), whereas politics seems more totally vulnerable to the encroachments of making and so Arendt can hardly do more than point to the wasteland itself.[37] Whereas the failure of politics is virtually complete, art can survive if only by expressing the emotions engendered by this very failure.[38]

That there has been a significant shift in the mode through which the primacy of making asserts itself in the political field seems to be implicit in Arendt's discussion. The classic mode is exemplified in all those utopian frames (of which Plato's *Republic* was the first and perhaps the greatest) that very deliberately set out to make politics a means to attain "an allegedly higher end," be it "the protection of the good men from the rule of the bad in general, and the safety of the philosopher in particular"[39] (a somewhat sardonic formulation of the aim of classical political thought), or the "salvation of souls" as envisaged in the Middle Ages, or the modern conception of a society of unalienated labor. What all of these schemes have in common—however noble or disparate from each other their respective ends may be—is that each of them *has* an end which is, in a sense, suprapolitical—albeit that the whole function of politics is to achieve it. In this way they imitate the work of the craftsman, which is guided by a form or specification which precedes it and to which it always remains strictly instrumental.

While constituting political activity as a species of craft, these utopian programs contain some "vision of the good" or theory of optimal human functioning which—even though it sets up a blueprint for the craft of politics —is itself supplied not by craft but by some other type of knowledge. In advanced industrial societies, however, such ambitious utopian projects do not figure, precisely because modern intellect no longer has the confidence to hold up any definite picture of the good life that is worth striving for, and so political activity cannot in this way be regarded as the exercise of a craft. Although, in the absence of any guiding and to some extent transcendent idea, modern political and social activity cannot be regarded as a craft, still, in another way, it is infused even more fully than utopian programs by the idea of craft. For this idea — in its abstract form, we might say, and without any independently grounded content— has come to be the governing idea of modern societies. Lacking the power to generate a substantive form which would provide a *telos* for a craftlike process of political activity, modern societies, by a curious inversion and at the cost of a drastic loss of meaning, have made craftlike process itself their one, overriding form or *telos*.[40]

This, at any rate, is how I interpret remarks of Arendt's about "the generalization of the fabrication experience in which usefulness and utility are established as the ultimate standards for life and the world of men."[41] This generalization, which is the core of utilitarianism —"the philosophy of *homo faber* par excellence"[42] —works in such a way that a criterion which is proper within the world of *making* remains as a criterion of the *made*, and lived-in, world. What disappears in utilitarianism is the distinction (expressed idiomatically in the distinction between "in order to" and "for the sake of") between utility and meaning; or rather utility itself becomes the criterion of meaning, and this, in the end, leads to meaninglessness.

> The ideal of usefulness . . . is actually no longer a matter of utility but of meaning. . . . [It] can no longer be conceived as something needed in order to have something else; it simply defies questioning about its use. . . . The perplexity of utilitarianism is that it gets caught in the unending chain of means and ends without ever arriving at some principle which could justify the category of means and end, that is, of utility itself. The "in order to" has become the content of the "for the sake of"; in other words, utility established as meaning generates meaninglessness.[43]

4. Promising, Forgiving, and the Condition of Plurality

Our attention has been on the attempt to "escape" from the "frailty of human affairs," or from "the haphazardness and moral irresponsibility inherent in a plurality of agents"[44] which Arendt sees as the motive, almost from the beginning of the Western tradition, for a wholesale desertion of action in favor of making. The intended "escape" has been into "the solidity of quiet and order,"[45] but Arendt's analysis, as we have just seen, tries to show that this attempt has always been marked, necessarily, by a deep impulse toward tyranny and domination. In a final clarification now both of the distinction between making and action and of the positive nature of action itself, I want to briefly advert to the way in which making is inherently committed to force, while action, in virtue of two particular possibilities which it keeps open, avoids or rises above this commitment. In the process of fabrication the material is always subjected to violence, not only by being ripped from its natural home (e.g., wood in trees), but also by being entirely subordinated to the dictates of the form in the mind of the fabricator, who, so long as he is a proficient craftsman, always remains 'sovereign' over it. Moreover, while there is always a reversibility in the order of making, nonetheless just as one *does* here "with the means of violence necessary for all fabrication" so too one also has to "*undo* what he has done as he undoes an unsuccessful object, by means of destruction."[46] On this analysis, when political or social activity is conducted in the mode of making, whether by being successful or in attempting to overcome its lack of success, it cannot avoid being implicated in violence.

If this inner propensity to violence is related essentially to the 'solidity', reliability, and reversibility of making, then the evanescence, unreliability, and irreversibility of action may appear as the price that action has to pay for its non-violence. In Arendt's view, however, action is not reduced by its non-violence to total vulnerability; for it contains within itself two potentialities which, even though they are neither coercive nor subject to coercion, still provide "compensation for the intrinsic 'weakness' of plurality,"[47] or which "enable it to survive the disabilities of nonsovereignty."[48] These are the potentialities for *forgiving* and *promising*.

Through their capacity to make and keep promises people can secure some measure of protection against the encompassing uncertainty that arises both from their inability to foretell the consequences of their acts and, more particularly, from the fickleness and unreliability over time to which they themselves are prone. Promises — be they the commitments to which people bind themselves in their personal relationships, or covenants and treaties which are enshrined in law — have the power to create, as Arendt puts it, "islands of certainty in an ocean of uncertainty."[49] The security they provide is the only kind of security that is available in human affairs. It is limited, however, in the sense both that it must tolerate a wide area of uncertainty around it — we can never hope, as it were, to reclaim the whole ocean — and that it can never be *guaranteed*: for it is always possible that those who make promises will not keep them. And yet, in spite of these limitations, the power of promising is real: people may show the kind of trustworthiness that will introduce into their actions an element of constancy on which others involved with them in the "web of relations" may rely. This power, which is always different from

the total control aimed at in the operations of a craftsman—or in the dreams
of a tyrant—is commensurate with the nature of action itself. While it
is a way of dealing with the hazardousness of human existence, still it
cannot be other than a hazardous way of doing so: since it is itself a way
of acting, it can arise only within the elemental hazard that belongs to
the very structure of action as such. Or, as Arendt put it, it "corresponds
exactly to the existence of a freedom which was given under the condition
of non-sovereignty."[50]

If promising is the only resource against the perils of an uncertain
future, the burden of an irreversible past is relieved only by forgiveness.
What is past remains in the strict sense irreversible, of course, but what
can be remedied, or at least ameliorated, by forgiveness—and only by
forgiveness— is the chain of consequences unleashed by past actions. Since,
as we have already seen, actions are always carried out within a web of
relationships with others and always entail a very limited foresight or control on the part of the agent, trespassing (to use the gospel word favored
by Arendt) is a constant feature of human life. A life in which the consequences of one's trespassing always rebounded on one would be intolerable,
and such would be a life where there was no alternative to vengeance, which
"acts in the form of re-acting against an original trespassing, whereby far
from putting an end to the consequences of the first misdeed, everybody
remains bound to the process, permitting the chain reaction contained
in every action to take its unhindered course."[51] The only power which
can break this chain, and thereby provide a release from the "relentless
automatism" which would otherwise be inseparable from a life of action,
is forgiveness—which is the "only reaction which does not merely re-act
but acts anew and unexpectedly, unconditioned by the act which provoked
it and therefore freeing from its consequences both the one who forgives
and the one who is forgiven."[52]

The act of forgiveness meets a trespasser at the level of disclosure
which most deeply characterizes him as an agent; it is inalienably personal in that "*what* was done is forgiven for the sake of *who* did it."[53] And
the healing power of forgiveness (which for Arendt is indispensable in the
political sphere no less than in that of intimate relationships) can happen
only in a society founded on *respect* between its members. Respect is not
the same as 'love', though it might be regarded as a form of 'friendship',
"not unlike the Aristotelian *philia politikē*."[54] Although it is "without
intimacy and without closeness" it does not depend, either, on self-in-
terested or even objective judgment of a person's worth. It is simply "a
regard for the person from the distance which the space of the world puts
between us, and this regard is independent of qualities which we may
admire or of achievements which we may highly esteem."[55]

It is significant for Arendt that the personal nature of forgiving—
and this is true also of promising—is inherently *inter*-personal and not
intra-personal. Here again, the 'logic' of action (in which forgiveness is
the only available move against the irreversibility of what has been done)
differs radically from that which prevails in the universe of Platonic rulership. As a Platonic ruler, my power is justified and limited in the first
place by my mastery of *myself.* It stems from "a relationship established
between me and myself, so that the right and wrong of relationships with
others are determined by attitudes toward one's self, until the whole public realm is seen in the image of 'man writ large,' of the right order between man's individual capacities of mind, soul, and body."[56] If the notions of rule and domination make some sense, and are indeed to be established in the first place, in relation to oneself, this is impossible in
the case of forgiving, which "rests on experiences which nobody could ever
have with himself, which, on the contrary, are entirely based on the presence of others."[57] Indeed there is a complete inversion of the two orders:
"just as the extent and modes of self-rule justify and determine rule over
others—how one rules himself, he will rule others—thus the extent and
modes of being forgiven and being promised determine the extent and
modes in which one may be able to forgive himself or keep promises concerned only with himself."[58] The central point that emerges here again
is the non-equivalence of freedom with sovereignty and the essential determination of action by the inextinguishable condition of *plurality*.

5. Arendt and Aristotle

Our own overall theme makes us more concerned about Aristotle's
role in Arendt's account of action than with Plato's, and it is with a consideration of this that I shall now bring the present chapter to a close.
If Plato emerges, as I have already intimated, as chief 'villain' in her book—
insofar as he was the first and most consequential to provide a conceptual
basis for "handling political matters and ruling political bodies in the mode
of fabrication"[59]—it has to be admitted that Aristotle is by no means its
unambiguous 'hero'.[60] For he too belonged to the 'Socratic school' which
was turning to the "reliability" of making as a refuge from the "futility,
boundlessness, and uncertainty" of action; and so Arendt is not inclined
to credit him with providing any more than the "feeble echo"[61] which,
in general, this philosophy gives of the pristine experience of action which
she supposes to have been that of the earlier, pre-philosophical Greeks.
If this goes onto the scales against any claim for a strongly Aristotelian

strand in Arendt's thinking, I should like to show the counterweight of this latter claim by making three points.

In the first place, Arendt recognizes very clearly that the whole paradigm of 'fabrication' or 'making', which provides both the conceptual foil and the real alternative[62] to 'action' in her sense, was already definitively established in the concepts of *technē* and *poiēsis,* which were (in the formulation of Collingwood that we have already met and with which she would entirely concur) "one of the greatest and most solid achievements of the Greek mind or at any rate of that school from Socrates to Aristotle."[63] And so, by demonstrating that this paradigm dominates our conception and organization of society (in business, communications, education, etc.), Arendt's analysis testifies to the decisive significance which these 'Socratic' (in a sense which includes 'Aristotelian') concepts still possess. If only negatively, they are shown as important diagnostic tools for any analysis of contemporary society that seeks even a minimum depth of historical perspective.

In the second place, and more positively, while Arendt does not exempt Aristotle from complicity in the general Socratic project of conceptualizing, *and generalizing,* the model of the craftsman—for like Socrates and Plato, he too speaks of politics as a techne—still she recognizes that he was implicated in it "to a lesser degree."[64] She cannot help conceding his "emphatic attempts to distinguish between action and fabrication, *praxis* and *poiēsis*"[65] and so acknowledging, at least implicitly, the groundwork he had laid for her own project itself. If, as a Socratic, Aristotle helped to provide the conceptual elaboration of the idea of fabrication or craft, he also worked out beyond this, and in his own very distinctive idiom, basic notions for articulating the *alternative* idea of praxis. Arendt's awareness of this comes out most fully in the following passage:

> It is this insistence on the living deed and the spoken word as the greatest achievements of which human beings are capable that was conceptualized in Aristotle's notion of *energeia* ("actuality"), with which he designated all activities that do not pursue an end (are *ateleis*) and leave no work behind (no *par'autas erga*), but exhaust their full meaning in the performance itself. ... in these instances of action and speech the end (*telos*) is not pursued but lies in the activity itself which therefore becomes an *entelecheia,* and the work is not what follows and extinguishes the process but is imbedded in it; the performance is the work, is *energeia.* Aristotle, in his political philosophy, is still well aware of what is at stake in politics, namely, no less than the *ergon tou anthrōpou* (the "work of man" *qua* man), and if he defined this "work" as "to live well" (*eu zēn*), he clearly meant that "work"

here is no product but exists only in sheer actuality. This specifically human achievement lies altogether outside the category of means and ends; the "work of man" is no end because the means to achieve it—the virtues, or *aretai*—are not qualities which may or may not be actualized, but are themselves "actualities." In other words, the means to achieve the end would already be the end; and this "end," conversely, cannot be considered a means in some other respect, because there is nothing higher to attain than this actuality itself.[66]

If this passage goes a long way toward showing an appreciation on Arendt's part of the Aristotelian provenance of much of what she wants to say about action, my third and final point is that a more thorough and sympathetic reading of Aristotle might have allowed her to make her case under a more boldly Aristotelian banner. I shall make this point very briefly by adverting to a recent book which is explicitly and unabashedly Aristotelian —but which might also be regarded as *Arendtian* in its overall preoccupation and spirit. Martha Nussbaum's *The Fragility of Goodness* neither refers to Arendt's work nor shows any sign of being susceptible to the particular tradition of European philosophy that nourished it. It is, however, a critical "examination of the aspiration to rational self-sufficiency in Greek ethical thought"[67] which bears a striking resemblance to Arendt's examination, in *The Human Condition,* of "sovereignty, the ideal of uncompromising self-sufficiency and mastership."[68] Like Arendt, Nussbaum depicts Plato as the great advocate of this aspiration or ideal, but she goes beyond Arendt in her reliance on Aristotle for her exposition of everything in the ethical life which frustrates it and leaves human beings exposed to "ungoverned contingency." As Arendt wants to argue for the "always utterly fragile meaning" of action—or for the irremediable "frailty of human affairs" with their "futility, boundlessness and uncertainty of outcome"[69]—and for the consequently very severe limits on self-knowledge or fore-knowledge in situations in which one genuinely *acts,* so Nussbaum (with Aristotle as mentor) argues for the fragility of a life which is lived in a properly human way, "situated between beast and god,"[70] which is caught up in relationships and attachments that always put it at risk, and which, beyond "motives having to do with closedness, safety and power,"[71] must settle for a type of knowledge that is characterized by flexibility, improvisation, and "refined perception of the contingencies of a particular situation."[72]

In saying all this I do not intend to claim an identity of viewpoint between Nussbaum and Arendt in relation to action.[73] Rather, I want to suggest, first, that Nussbaum's picture of Aristotle's view of the ethical life—largely because of the success of her strategy of trying to bring out the affinities between this view and the vision of the tragic poets ("after Plato, tragedy needs Aristotle")[74] — reveals him not as the cautious middle-of-the-roader of most profiles contrasting him and Plato, but rather as a philosopher whose sense of the precariousness of virtue and the limits of ethical knowledge gave him a profound sense of human finitude; and, second, that this picture of Aristotle allows us to claim that the whole thrust of Arendt's analysis is even more Aristotelian than she herself, with her rather more conventional picture of Aristotle, cared to claim. But this point will become clearer if we turn now, in our next chapter, to another philosopher, whose main concern has been to expose the nature and implications of human finitude and who, with less circumspection as well as more attention to Aristotle's own texts than we find in Arendt, has laid claim to the legacy of Aristotle's practical philosophy.

4. The Play of Phronesis and Techne in Hans-Georg Gadamer's *Truth and Method*

The philosopher of 'finitude' to whom I now turn, in this chapter and the next, is Hans-Georg Gadamer. He and Jürgen Habermas—whose work will concern me in the following two chapters—have been the dominant figures in German philosophy over the past few decades. In the density of their appropriation of the whole Western philosophical tradition, in the ambition and scope of their thinking, and in the pervasive influence that each of them has exercised across virtually the whole range of human studies, Gadamer and Habermas can find few rivals among contemporary thinkers. They are by no means in accord in their basic philosophical outlooks; their differences, in fact, have been amply aired in a celebrated and protracted debate between them in the late 1960s and 1970s. I do not wish to underestimate the significance of these differences, which are still unresolved; later on I shall have to address them and take stock of their implications for my overall theme. At this point, however, in introducing Gadamer and Habermas, what I want to emphasize is the extent of the common ground which they share (and which in any case has made possible the strength of focus and the fruitfulness of their polemics). What most unites them is their common opposition to the 'objectivism' of a positivist view of knowledge, and its corollary that a technical mastery of human action through 'objective' knowledge is a viable project. It is the strategy that both of them adopt in working out this opposition that makes them significant in the present work. For, in contesting the positivist—and, more radically, the Cartesian—domination of modern epistemology they have both rehabilitated, in quite systematic and explicit (albeit in Habermas's case, it must be admitted, in highly 'mediated')[1] terms, the Aristotelian distinction between the concepts of *poiēsis/technē* and *praxis/phronēsis*. The context and the manner in which they have done this will be the object of inquiry in this chapter and the next (on Gadamer), and in chapters 6 and 7 on Habermas.

Gadamer's great achievement has been the way in which, exploiting and developing some fundamental insights of Heidegger, he has radically reconstructed the nineteenth-century German attempt to found a systematic discipline of hermeneutics (i.e., the study of interpretation) and, through the combustive power of his *magnum opus, Truth and Method*,[2] has brought hermeneutics to the very center of philosophy and of the debate about the nature of the 'human sciences' over the past few decades. His other great achievement has been the way in which, more compellingly and far-reachingly than anyone else, he has recovered and confirmed the power of Aristotle's practical philosophy, so that mainly through his influence 'phronesis' may be said to have become naturalized in the discourse of contemporary philosophy.[3] This latter achievement has not indeed been 'other' in the sense of being separate from his achievement as the doyen of twentieth-century hermeneutics; on the contrary, in the elaboration of his hermeneutical philosophy the distinction between techne and phronesis has played a crucially important strategic role.[4] Nor has Gadamer simply pressed Aristotelian ideas into service in his own philosophical investigation as if we already knew what these ideas were. Rather, in the very midst of his own preoccupation with the nature of understanding and interpretation, he has turned to Aristotle's texts themselves (and in this he differs from all the other philosophers whom I deal with in these chapters) and succeeded in finding there a meaning which both illuminates his own problem and is at the same time fresh light on Aristotle. Within the most fitting hermeneutical circles, the nature of hermeneutical experience and Aristotle's practical philosophy are both elucidated.

In *Truth and Method,* Gadamer removes any secure vantage point outside or over against his text that an objectivizing interpreter might have supposed himself to be in possession of. He shows that understanding is an event that happens within a relationship of vulnerability to the text, that it arises out of a fusion of the contexts of both interpreter and text in the one fluid medium of an effective tradition and that it contains within itself an application of the possibilities of the text to the interpreter's own position—an application that is not at all subsequent or extraneous to it but is already unavoidably contained in it as an act of understanding. When Gadamer has shown all this and wants then to shed further light on the peculiar structure of this always already implicated and prejudiced act of understanding, at this point in his book he turns to Aristotle. Specifically, he turns to the analysis of phronesis in the sixth book of the *Nicomachean Ethics,* where, as he puts it, Aristotle "is concerned with reason and with knowledge, not detached from a being that is becoming, but determined by it and determinative of it."[5] Gadamer is interested in phronesis because he sees that with this unique concept

Aristotle was addressing a problem very similar to his own: he was trying to overcome the abstractness of the *logos* with which *aretē* had been identified by Socrates and Plato, and to reveal instead the more complicated texture of a *logos* that can never be finally disembedded from the *ēthos* within which it arises.

In the rest of this chapter my purpose will be to explain and discuss what I have tried to convey in a comprehensive but very compressed manner in the preceding paragraph. Then, in the next chapter, when we shall already have met Gadamer's basic themes and seen how integral the analysis of phronesis is to his unfolding of them, I shall try to disclose the very general philosophical implications of his hermeneutics. For the problems raised by the activity of interpreting texts — as, from another direction, the problems raised by works of art[6] — open onto the most basic questions of philosophy and indeed, in Gadamer's handling of them, might be said to lead to a bold reconception of philosophy itself. Moreover, Aristotle's significance is fully coextensive with these more generic concerns: when we examine in the next chapter the conception of philosophy which emerges from Gadamer's reflection on language in the third and final part of *Truth and Method* — and which becomes fully explicit only in the later essays which as it were take stock of the book[7] — we shall see that this conception involves a very ambitious rehabilitation of the Aristotelian idea of "practical philosophy."[8]

1. Nineteenth-Century Hermeneutics

What might be taken to be the root cause of all the distortions which beset interpretations of ancient texts was a failure on the part of the interpreter to appreciate the discrepancy between his own context and that of the author whom he was attempting to understand. This primary naïveté would have led him to import into his reading of the text all kinds of significances and assumptions which were his own but which, insofar as he had not critically appropriated them as such, could only falsify his account of the author whom he was purporting to understand. It was only with the rise of historical consciousness in the eighteenth and nineteenth centuries that a measured awareness of the *otherness* of previous ages and epochs became available. And hermeneutics, in its modern form,[9] arose, on foot of this deepened historical consciousness, as a methodological discipline charged with the responsibility of protecting the integrity of texts by exposing the pitfalls of interpretation and articulating critical exigences which would have to be met by any serious interpreter. What became normative in the conception of interpretation proposed in this new hermeneutics was the reproduction of the mind of the author.[10] The interpreter's task was essentially empathetic; its aim was accurate and exhaustive recreation of the original meaning and intention of his author. The fact that this meaning and intention had been delivered up, once for all and definitively, by the author himself strictly circumscribed the interpreter's work and at the same time provided a final and unambiguous criterion of its success.

Not that interpretation as thus conceived had an entirely closed horizon, or that it was committed only to a *modus demonstrandi* in which the subtleties of a *modus inveniendi* would have no part. For it could still be acknowledged that an author's intentions might have been several and varied and (throughout the course of his development as a writer, within a single text, and, *a fortiori*, in a complete life's work) changing and even conflicting—in ways, moreover, that might have remained veiled from himself. Within the setting of his time, and without the benefit of a god's eye view, he would have been caught up in a multiplicity of influences and concerns. And so it could be granted that the interpreter's task, even under the overall rubric of reproduction, still required a very considerable exercise of active intelligence. In part it could call for gifts that were in a kind of inverse correspondence with the gifts of the author he was interpreting. (For example, "corresponding, in hermeneutics, to the production of genius is divination, the immediate solution, which ultimately presupposes a kind of corresponding genius";[11] divination here connotes "an apprehension of the 'inner origin' of the composition of a work, a recreation of a creative act.")[12] But also it could bring into play a synthetic power and a capacity for insight and discriminating judgment, in reproducing, for instance, a theme or tendency that had not been the conscious production of any single individual. And in all this it could even make sense to suppose—this, in fact, was the sense of a celebrated dictum of Schleiermacher—that an interpreter could actually understand his author better than the author had understood himself.

In spite of these qualifications, however, a basic assumption of the new hermeneutics was that the object of interpretation had a "self-containedness of content in a totality of meaning," that this existed "in detachment from the person understanding it,"[13] and that it therefore presented the possibility as well as the challenge of reaching the one valid and objective interpretation. With this assumption in place, the primary focus of hermeneutical discipline came to be less the object to be interpreted than the whole cluster of anticipations and prejudices that formed the interpreter's orientation to the text and that could only encumber his attempts to understand it. Another way of saying this is that the emphasis shifted from understanding as a 'natural' achievement to the avoidance

of misunderstanding as a methodically pursued task. And the prolific source
of all misunderstanding, it was supposed, was the context of the interpreter's own intellectual world insofar as this differed from the world he
was trying to understand. Abolishing this difference or distance (this was
the "self-extinction" proposed by Ranke as a desideratum for the interpreter) through systematically divesting oneself of one's prejudices, and
thereby establishing 'contemporaneity' with one's author, became the crux
of interpretation. What made this overcoming of 'temporal distance' theoretically possible was the assumption that the interpreter could cleanly
extricate himself from the limitations of his own historical conditioning.
But this critical assumption was usually buttressed by another more affirmative one which provided an escape from the flux of history onto the
terra firma of a kind of metaphysical psychology. This psychological element in nineteenth-century hermeneutics postulated "human nature as
the unhistorical substratum of its theory of understanding."[14] 'Empathy'
was possible because in the end the adequate interpreter was 'connatural'
with his author, and real historical understanding, paradoxically, consisted
in tearing away the veil of history so that this elemental connaturality could
assert itself.

This nineteenth-century hermeneutics (which culminated in the work
of Dilthey) had its home in the romantic protest against the Enlightenment. The scrupulosity of its attempt to recreate the meaning of ancient
and, especially, classical texts (and through its extension into disciplines
such as cultural anthropology, 'text' came to have a wider connotation than
simply what was written down) was a manifestation of its commitment
to reassert the value of tradition against the hubris of the new Reason.
And it was, at the same time, an assertion of the existence and legitimacy
of a mode of knowledge (the *Verstehen* of the *Geisteswissenschaften*) that
was irreducible to—and in fact, in the investigation of the cultural world,
the necessary counterpart of—the increasingly dominant knowledge of the
natural sciences.

Gadamer's criticism of this whole hermeneutics, however, is that,
in spite of itself, it remained impaled on that against which it sought to
protest. Its anxiety to assert the 'objectivity' of its grasp of the past through
increasingly methodical 'research' showed that it was already under tribute
to the notions of detachment, objectivity, and control that prevailed in
the natural sciences. While the recovery of tradition was its ostensible concern, still what it succeeded in empowering, in Gadamer's view, was not
tradition but rather the method which made tradition its leveled-off object; what it furthered was not the voice of a tradition but rather the steril-
ized vantage point from which it supposed that all traditions could equally
be surveyed. From this perspective, the historicism of Dilthey—which was

the ultimate attempt to establish the objectivity of *Verstehen* — only seemed to stake out an *alternative* mode of knowledge to that which prevailed in the positive sciences; actually it created a new outpost for positivism. Or, in Gadamer's formulation, the "unresolved Cartesianism"[15] in Dilthey's thought ensures that through him "the Enlightenment is completed as an historical Enlightenment."[16]

But what, after all, was wrong with the Enlightenment — and why should entanglement in its ambitions be enough, in itself, to vitiate these attempts to found hermeneutics as a distinct discipline? Gadamer's answer to this large question is the vital hinge in his thinking: "historicism . . . is based on the modern Enlightenment and unknowingly shares its prejudices. And there is one prejudice of the Enlightenment that is essential to it; the fundamental prejudice of the Enlightenment is its prejudice against prejudice itself, which deprives tradition of its power."[17] Gadamer's own hermeneutical theory is a sustained attempt, against the demystifying intention of the Enlightenment, to rehabilitate the role of prejudice (*Vorurteil*) in knowledge, by showing that prejudices not only need not distort but can actually be fruitful — as well as being, in any case, simply unavoidable — in all understanding.

2. The Heideggerian Background

Here Gadamer sees himself as developing and making explicit the implications of fundamental insights of Husserl and especially of Heidegger. These were insights that subverted the subject/object polarity which was deeply entrenched in the whole metaphysical tradition and which provided modern science with the framework for its predominant understanding of itself.[18] Husserl's conception of the 'life-world' (*Lebenswelt*) (or "the anonymous creation of meaning that forms the ground of all experience")[19] had already challenged the notion of a detached ego impartially and methodically oriented to the 'object' as the center of a privileged and irreducible 'subjectivity'; rather than this notion setting a norm against which other types of subjectivity might be deemed to be wayward or deficient, it itself was shown to be only one particular precipitate out of the primordial 'worlding' of human existence. In Husserl this idea was never quite released from the impasses of the transcendental idealism out of which he was tortuously trying to extricate himself. It became more secure, however, in Heidegger's reflection on temporality as the basic existential structure of *Dasein* (There Being, i.e, human being). A human being is already 'thrown' into existence and, as thrown, exists only as always projecting into possibilities of being.

For Heidegger, understanding is not a particular kind of act which arises episodically, and alongside other kinds of acts, within this existential structure of thrown projectedness. It is, rather, coincident with this structure itself; as such it is "a fundamental existentiale," a "basic mode of Dasein's Being," "the original character of human life itself." This is the "primordial understanding," of which "understanding in the sense of *one* possible kind of cognizing among others (as distinguished, for instance, from explaining) must, like explaining, be interpreted as an existential *derivative*."[20] Understanding, in the primordial sense, is not something that one performs on the basis of one's having already achieved substantial selfhood or subjectivity. On the contrary, understanding in this sense is constitutive of one's being as a self:

> as thrown, Dasein is thrown into the kind of Being which we call "projecting." Projecting has nothing to do with comporting oneself towards a plan that has been thought out, and in accordance with which Dasein arranges its Being. On the contrary, any Dasein has, as Dasein, already projected itself; and as long as it is, it is projecting. As long as it is, Dasein always has understood itself and always will understand itself in terms of possibilities. . . . As projecting, understanding is the kind of Being of Dasein in which it is its possibilities as possibilities.[21]

In analyzing understanding as a projecting within thrownness, Heidegger draws particular attention to its 'fore-structure', i.e., to the fact that "an interpretation is never a presuppositionless apprehending of something presented to us,"[22] but always arises within an ineradicable 'forehaving', 'foresight', and 'foreconception'. This fact makes of understanding a circular process: our foreknowledge must be open to modification by what we are trying to understand; but this 'what' is not available to us at all outside our foreknowledge. For Heidegger, this circular movement of understanding is unavoidable and definitive: "if we see this circle as a vicious one and look for ways of avoiding it . . . then the act of understanding has been misunderstood from the ground up."[23] This is because it is "the expression of the existential forestructure of Dasein itself." Far from reducing it "to the level of a vicious circle, or even of a circle which is merely tolerated," we need to recognize that in it "is hidden a positive possibility of the most primordial kind of knowing."[24]

This is the recognition whose implications Gadamer tries to elaborate in *Truth and Method*. In doing so, he works within the context of a fundamental Heideggerian motif, while developing very considerably a specific aspect of this motif which Heidegger himself had raised toward the end of *Being and Time*. The motif is the *historicality* of human existence—a historicality which is to be understood in terms of the basic mode of *temporality*. What Heidegger most strenuously wants to avoid here is any view of history which sees time simply as a kind of casing within which an already essentially constituted subjectivity is inserted and by which — from the outside, as it were — it may be shaped. Rather: "in analysing the historicality of Dasein, we shall try to show that this entity is not 'temporal' because it 'stands in history', but that on the contrary it exists historically and can so exist only because it is temporal in the very basis of its Being."[25]

The particular aspect of this theme which Heidegger touches on (with specific reference to Dilthey) in the penultimate chapter of his book is the fact that the specialized understanding of the historian remains conditioned from within by the structure of temporality and, no matter how exacting its methodological restraints, does not succeed in removing itself from the orbit of the primordial understanding which makes us what we are. This point is taken up by Gadamer into the center of his hermeneutics. He writes: "that we understand history only insofar as we are ourselves 'historical' means that the historicalness of human There Being in its expectancy and its forgetting is the condition of our being able to represent the past. What appeared first to be simply a barrier that cut across the traditional concept of science and method, or a subjective condition of access to historical knowledge, now becomes the centre of a fundamental enquiry."[26] We shall now consider the key points in Gadamer's own exemplary conduct of this inquiry.

3. Finitude, Tradition, and the Hermeneutical Circle

We have seen Gadamer's concern to rescue the notion of 'prejudice' from the altogether pejorative connotations that were put upon it by the Enlightenment. (We turned to Heidegger only to notice that his disclosure of a forestructure of understanding, rooted in the historicality of an entity which is temporal through and through in its mode of being, provides an ontological matrix for Gadamer's whole elaboration of the notion of prejudice.) What Gadamer especially wants to show here is how effectively the romantic movement, which spawned the whole hermeneutical and historical movement of the nineteenth century, remained tied, even when it tried to oppose it, to the presupposition of the Enlightenment. This presupposition was the tenability of a clean dichotomy between reason and tradition (or myth). While the romantic project of restoring tradition was the opposite of the Enlightenment project of canonizing reason, still "it is the same break with the *continuity* of meaning in tradition that lies behind both."[27] The problem with the project of restoration is that it is attempted on the assumption that we are now out of a living connection with tradition, that we inhabit some unprejudiced neutral ground (which is precisely what is postulated by Enlightenment reason) so that what will be 'restored' (when restoration is always attempted only on the other side of a disenchantment which has already occurred) will have only the devitalized reality, the 'discreet charm', of the museum object.[28] What is blocked in this whole perspective is "an appropriate understanding of our finitude, which dominates not only our humanity, but also our historical consciousness."[29] Gadamer offers a provocatively strong formulation of this finitude and at the same time seems to box himself into a very tight corner for any subsequent attempt to show that there can be such a thing as a *reasonable* understanding:

> In fact history does not belong to us, but we belong to it. Long before we understand ourselves through the process of self-examination, we understand ourselves in a self-evident way in the family, society and state in which we live. The focus of subjectivity is a distorting mirror. The self-awareness of the individual is only a flickering in the closed circuits of historical life. That is why the prejudices of the individual, far more than his judgments, constitute the historical reality of his being.[30]

Gadamer in fact tries to show that our 'judgments,' which contain our most self-consciously methodical efforts to 'understand', do not break free of our 'prejudices'; our 'knowledge' always remains part of our 'being'. What he needs to establish here, however—if he is not only to "do justice to man's finite, historical mode of being" but also to satisfy the claims of reasonableness—is that there are "legitimate prejudices," or *justified* prejudices, productive of knowledge."[31]

In doing this, the mediating concept which Gadamer finds it necessary to vindicate (for it, too, had been debased by the Enlightenment) is the concept of authority. If validity can be ascribed to authority then the suspension or abatement of the full use of one's own critical reason, which resting in a prejudice implies, can itself be valid. Gadamer is concerned to show, however, that the validity of authority can be secured only if we reject the outright polarization set up by the Enlightenment between authority on the one hand and freedom and reason on the other. Authority, for him, is something that can never be arbitrarily asserted or blindly accepted. If my acknowledgment of its presence in another person permits me, within my relationship with him, to take some things on trust, still the decisive thing is that the prior acknowledgment, on which the trust is always founded, is itself a *free* act in which I *reasonably* assent to the superiority—in this particular field—of the other.

The primary locus of the concept of authority is a defined relationship, within a circumscribed sphere, to one whom one acknowledges as one's superior (the educative relationship might be taken as the paradigm case here). It is worth noticing, however, that if, *within* this circumscribed setting, the subordinate's knowledge depends on the authority with which he invests the one from whom he accepts it, still there is a further grounding available, *outside* this relationship, in the superior's own *warranted* (i.e., evidentially based) way of possessing the knowledge. Gadamer's deployment of the concept of authority, however, extends its range beyond this primary locus and in doing so, we ought to note, implicitly forfeits the possibility of an 'external' (or 'objective') endorsement of authority. What he wants to do, it seems, is to ascribe a kind of primordial authority to *tradition* as something within which we are *all* circumscribed — and for which, therefore, there can never, in principle, be any validation from 'outside': "That which has been sanctioned by tradition and custom has an authority that is nameless, and our finite historical being is marked by the fact that always the authority of what has been transmitted — and not only what is clearly grounded — has power over our attitudes and behaviour . . . tradition has a justification that is outside the arguments of reason and in large measure determines our institutions and our attitudes."[32]

When Gadamer says here that tradition has a justification that is "outside the arguments of reason," he does not mean that it is, on that account, irrational or nonrational. If reason on its own cannot provide an independent ground for tradition this is not because tradition is outside reason but rather because reason itself is not outside tradition; to the contrary we might say that tradition is a condition of its possibility as human reason. And yet it is not a matter here, either, of setting up tradition in any kind of absolute priority to reason; for it is no less the case that tradition itself can live only with the help of reason: "Even the most genuine and solid tradition does not persist by nature because of the inertia of what once existed. It needs to be affirmed, embraced, cultivated. It is essentially preservation, such as is active in all historical change. But preservation is an act of reason, though an inconspicuous one. . . ."[33] And indeed it becomes particularly inconspicuous — to the point almost of invisibility — in an age dominated by the image of reason as an agent of planning, mastery, and control. The whole of *Truth and Method* is an unceasing effort, against the self-image of the age, to bring forward a kind of reflection in which this act will become more conspicuous. Gadamer's desire is to show that there is no "unconditional antithesis between tradition and reason";[34] or, as he later puts it: "the abstract antithesis between . . . history and knowledge must be discarded. The effect of a living tradition and the effect of historical study must constitute a unity, the analysis of which would reveal only a texture of reciprocal relationships."[35]

The unity or reciprocity that Gadamer is drawing attention to here brings us back to the "hermeneutical circle" which, as we have seen, Heidegger had already clearly recognized as implicit in his conception of the 'fore-structure' of understanding. Later on I shall have occasion to dwell on a closely corresponding circle which we find in Aristotle's ethical-political thought. But here we must ask how Gadamer elaborates his understanding of this circle between knowledge and tradition in the hermeneutical act. That there is a circle involved in coming to understand a text had, of course, long been recognized—in ancient rhetoric no less than in nineteenth-century hermeneutics. This circle, though, was thought of as merely methodological: as having to do with the ongoing interdependence between one's contextual construal of the whole and one's particular understanding of the parts, as one read one's way more deeply into a text. As such it was a necessary element in the heuristics of the reading process; but it was still only temporary insofar as the *telos* of this process was to reach a complete understanding of the text in which the circular movement would be superseded, or would come to rest in a perfectly worked out harmony between whole and parts. Where Gadamer follows Heidegger is in no longer seeing the interpreter's structure of precognitions simply as strategic projections which, through the circular movement, can be either cancelled out or else completely absorbed into the correct understanding which is the consummation of this movement and in which the interpreter's mentality has become, as it were, a fully transparent screen displaying nothing but the actual meaning of the text itself. Rather, for Gadamer, the important precognitions or anticipations of the interpreter have a more stubborn and involved existence. They will not obligingly dissolve themselves into the otherness of the text; and yet neither do they subsist in an otherness of their own which is simply alien to the life of the text. It is here, in fact, that we must recognize the permanence of the circle, beyond the level of methodology, as "an ontological structural element in understanding."[36]

What closes us into this circle—so that we can never get outside it, but can only try, in surrendering to it, to become more aware of it—is the fact that both our own anticipation of meaning and the meaning of the text already participate in the being of tradition. 'Anticipation' (as the 'foreconception' or prejudice in our understanding), 'text,' and 'tradition' itself must all be understood in the light of this participation. We must avoid thinking of tradition as that which lies in the old text and which the act of interpretation makes available for contemporary inspection. For the act of interpretation itself is governed by an anticipation which is "not an act of subjectivity, but proceeds from the communality which binds us to the tradition."[37] If this anticipation really were an "act of subjectivity" then tradition would simply be the domesticated object of our scholarly custody. But Gadamer's point is that tradition always overspills the text as the object of our attempted understanding and already has us in its tow as we make this attempt. Our questions and priorities as we approach the text are determined by our sense of what is relevant or important or likely to be true; but we have this sense only because of our own previous, unavoidable involvement in 'tradition'. The corollary, however, is that we must not only see ourselves as tradition-bound seekers after significance and truth but must equally see the texts that speak to us out of the tradition as really *speaking* to us — and therefore as making their own claim to significance and truth.

This last point is crucial to Gadamer's transformation of nineteenth-century hermeneutics. It carries him right outside the psychologistic framework in which the whole question of the validity or truth of a text had been bracketed so that the interpreter's task was simply to establish its meaning as an expression of the author, or of the age, which had produced it. For Gadamer, there is "no reason to go back to the subjectivity of the author." Attention remains on the subject matter or 'thing'[38] with which the text is concerned and the truth of which it tries to disclose. This is a thing which the interpreter, too, is attempting to understand truly, so that in his attempt he is fully open to what the text may be able to reveal to him. What joins the interpreter to the text, now, is not any putative 'connaturality' between his subjectivity and that of the author but rather the thing which is at issue in the text *and* continues to be an issue for the interpreter. This community of concern about the 'thing' gives hermeneutical activity its real character; it restores potency to the traditional text by putting the interpreter in the position of being 'addressed' by it; and it underlies Gadamer's favorite image of conversation (rather than the more monologic 'research' — with its correlative 'results' — which was so favored by Dilthey)[39] as the model of what transpires in coming to understand a text.

We have not yet answered the question of how, on Gadamer's account, prejudices can be justified or shown to be reasonable (how legitimate prejudices are to be distinguished from illegitimate ones); we have only seen that no answer will release us from the hermeneutical circle within which we inescapably find ourselves. Granted this, however, the task remains of establishing that this circle is not a vicious one. In doing this, Gadamer appeals to the idea of conversation, complemented by the idea of 'temporal distance'. What can never be available to us, he insists, is a technique which would make our prejudices transparent to us. They are not "at our disposal" and so there is no way of separating "in advance" the prejudices which lead to understanding from those which bring about misunderstanding.

It is this fundamental point, we may note in passing, which makes Gadamer integral to our overall study and bonds him with the other thinkers who figure in it. We have already seen Collingwood's argument that in genuine artistic endeavor there can never be a way of putting together what is to be expressed in advance of actually expressing it. When Gadamer writes that "it may be asked whether there is such a thing as this art or technique of understanding" and goes on to argue very crucially that there is not, we may recall a very closely corresponding remark of Collingwood's which we have already met: "Expression is an activity of which there can be no technique." Indeed both these cases of the unavailability of technique might be seen as closely related. Gadamer's whole point is that when I set out to *understand* an author's text, I do not have to hand any method that will guarantee my success; and Collingwood's point is that the author himself was similarly exposed when he set out to *write* it. The affinity which I suggest here between the approaches of Collingwood and Gadamer—so that one is, as it were, the obverse of the other—is borne out, I believe, by their similar views of language, which is after all the medium in which both writer and reader exist. It is a fact well noted by readers of *Truth and Method* that when Gadamer attempts to undercut the fixity of "statements" and to reveal the whole dynamic field which generates them, gives them point and substance, and conditions their waxing and waning, he relies very heavily on the "logic of question and answer" which Collingwood outlines in his *Autobiography*. The point in his book where Gadamer does this is in fact at the point of transition into his extended reflection on language; when we look at this reflection later on we shall find echoes, I believe, of what we have already seen of Collingwood's conception of language in *The Principles of Art*.[40]

It is not only Collingwood who comes to mind at this point in our elucidation of Gadamer's thought. We may also recall that Newman's whole point in giving such centrality to the 'Illative Sense' was precisely his awareness of how deeply we must rely on "previous notices, prepossessions, and (in a good sense of the word) prejudices"[41] that cannot be regulated by "any technical apparatus of words and propositions."[42] And we may also recall how for Arendt the elusive 'who' at the core of one's identity is never at one's disposal but makes its appearance, beyond one's reach as it were, only in the actions and speech in which one is already committed. And later on I shall try to bring out, as a major theme in my analysis of Aristotle, the way in which a similar nondisposability operates in phronesis—how the latter is a kind of knowledge that remains conditioned by, and so can never give us an independent purchase on, the character that has already been formed in us. Finally, we may remember that what launched us on this whole investigation in the first place was our uneasiness with the ambition of the behavioral objectives authors to make teaching a comprehensively rationalized activity on the basis of objectives which could be specified in advance. What the behavioral objectives authors seek to avoid — and what our other authors, in their different contexts, insist on as unavoidable — is the necessity of surrendering to an interaction in which one's lack of sovereignty always puts one at some kind of hazard and in which there is always a need for a *situated reflection* for which no indemnity can be provided by a method or technique with an independent security outside this interaction itself.

4. Conversation as the Medium of 'Effective-Historical Consciousness'

For Gadamer, the interaction to which we must surrender — and which therefore has the character of an 'event' (literally a 'coming out' to us) as much as of an 'action' — is conversation. It is only in conversation with the text that understanding occurs — and that, as it occurs, one becomes able to distinguish 'productive' from unproductive prejudices. Such distinguishing is completely necessary — Gadamer's "fundamental rehabilitation of the concept of prejudice" is not an indiscriminate licensing of *all* prejudices — but the point is that it cannot be carried out as a propaedeutic. There is no antechamber, as it were, where one's prejudices can be checked to ensure that one will already have discarded unaccredited ones when one is admitted to an actual encounter with the text. Rather, *in* this encounter such checking can take place if the encounter really has the structure of a *conversation.* It would be a poor conversation, indeed it would scarcely be a conversation at all, if I were already able to withhold from it everything in my own thinking, with all its partiality and particularity, which was not *ad rem* and true. (Indeed the more basic point, for Gadamer, is that ultimately I do not have any other way of establishing the *res* [the 'thing itself'] or the truth about it, except through conversation. Conversation is not just an optional way — a rather roundabout and desultory one it might even be considered — of reaching truth but rather reveals the essential structure of this reaching itself: the *dialectical* structure which was "unforgettably"[43] displayed by Plato and which, as Gadamer very powerfully shows, gives to his Dialogues their "unique and continuing relevance.")[44] The whole point of conversation is that I both allow some play to my own thinking and, in doing so, expose it to the counterweight of the other's contribution, which may confirm me in it or force me to amend or abandon it. (And the same is true, conversely, for my partner in the conversation, for whom I am the 'other'.) It is not through any attempt at selective sedation, then, but on the contrary through activating them in a context in which they are put at risk, that we deal effectively with our prejudices. The basic requirement here — what constitutes the conversational attitude — is *openness:* a readiness to allow the *questionableness* of one's own contribution or to be persuaded that the other's contribution may enrich it or even have to prevail over it.

In appealing to the notion of 'conversation', Gadamer gives a positive sense to 'temporal distance'. We have already seen that for nineteenth-century hermeneutics temporal distance was something that needed to be overcome; if the interpreter could somehow leap over it then he could seize hold of the fixed meaning of the text itself. For Gadamer, on the contrary, this distance is to be welcomed as a productive source of understanding; there is no such meaning — securely tied down, as it were, by the actual thought or 'life' of the author — that the text expresses. To the contrary, a text is always released into a semantic field, beyond the reach of its author, and is charged with possibilities of meaning that become actual only in virtue of movements in the rest of the field. It is the dynamism of history itself that constitutes this field and within it there is the never fully completed process of bringing to light different aspects of the meaning of the text. It is in this sense that Gadamer speaks of time (i.e., the time elapsed between the production of a text and its subsequent interpretation) not as a "gulf" but as a "supportive ground." Negatively, it provides a secure ground for understanding by having allowed the often peculiarly unreliable prejudices operative in contemporaneous judgments (i.e., those contemporaneous with the author) to fade away; positively it will have allowed for the emergence of other prejudices that have the power to disclose hitherto undisclosed meanings in the text. It is just because there is a distance between the interpreter and his text that we can conceive of him as being in conversation with it. Elements of his perspective that are not in the text are not necessarily, for that reason, to be suppressed; for they may have the power to bring forward a significance that is in the text but which, without their pressure, would have remained unrevealed.[45] We have even to be careful here, in speaking of what is in the text, not to imagine that its meaning is somehow always lying there in it from the beginning and that what consecutive interpreters do is to pull back from different directions the veils which cover it, or to shine a light from different angles through the darkness which obscures it. More dynamically, we need to see that the meaning of the text has its *being* in the conversations in which it is brought into partnership. It will not, of course, be a promiscuous partner in just any conversation. The other partner (the interpreter), as we have already seen, must be sensitive to what the text is saying and so be prepared to acknowledge that some of his own prejudices may have to be laid aside; while he can join the text in a conversation in which the latter's meaning is brought into being he can also lead it into a conversation in which it only loses its own voice. The constraints of responsible conversation itself are the only safeguards that the text can have when it is only in conversation that its fecundity of meaning can be realized.[46]

I have focused on temporal distance as the factor which creates enough 'otherness' between interpreter and text to make a conversation between them possible — and productive. But here as everywhere in the circular ambit of Gadamer's reflection we need to be vigilant; as soon as we seem to have established a point we must immediately begin to qualify — even, we might say, to dissolve — it. (It is this necessity which can make hermeneutics in contrast with the 'objective knowledge' of traditional epistemology, appear as in Richard Rorty's colorful phrase, "something squishier and more dubious.")[47] We have to avoid thinking of the perspectives of the interpreter and of the text as given separately, prior to the conversation itself. The interpreter is already formed by influences from the past, including the influence of the text itself perhaps, if it happens to be one that has significantly entered the tradition. He is under the sway of what Gadamer calls "effective history" (*Wirkungsgeschichte*), i.e., the past as still active in present thought. He cannot avoid being so influenced, whether or not he is *conscious* of it: ("the power of effective-history does not depend on its being recognised. This precisely is the power of history over finite human consciousness, namely that it prevails even where faith in method leads one to deny one's own historicality.")[48] For the interpreter, however, it is a requirement that he should become conscious of it, that he should attain what Gadamer calls "effective-historical consciousness" (*Wirkungsgeschichtliches Bewusstsein*).[49] The nub here, however, is that he can never become fully conscious of it and that he cannot become conscious of it at all outside the conversations in which it is already operative.

'Effective-historical consciousness' strives toward a reflective appropriation of the effect of tradition on and in one — an 'effect' which becomes 'effective', in fact, in those 'prejudices' with which we have all along been concerned. We must be careful with the idea of 'appropriation' here, however. In this part of his discussion Gadamer introduces the concepts of 'situation' and of 'horizon' (concepts that had already been introduced by Jaspers and Husserl, respectively).[50] What we strive to become conscious of is the situation or horizon within which we begin to see things in the text. This is always a peculiarly vexed consciousness, however; for "the very idea of a situation means that we are not standing outside it and hence are unable to have any objective knowledge of it. We are always within the situation, and to throw light on it is a task that is never entirely completed."[51] Similarly, having a horizon makes it possible for us to see things in perspective within it; hence our difficulty in putting this horizon itself in perspective. It is in this sense that to use a word like 'appropriation' for the type of coming into consciousness that is involved here is to run the risk of saying too much—or rather of saying the wrong sort of thing.

How then does Gadamer characterize this type of consciousness? We must return to the notion of conversation, resigned now to the fact—and perhaps in a better position to understand it—that if separateness seems to be required as a condition of conversation, still this separateness cannot be established in advance of, and appears, in fact, only at moments within, the deeper unity of the conversation itself. We saw earlier how Gadamer wants to acknowledge the authority of tradition. It is primarily for this that he has been regarded, and often attacked—especially, as we shall see presently, by Habermas—as a 'conservative'. I pointed out—more explicitly, I think, than Gadamer himself does—that the kind of authority with which he invests tradition cannot be the same as the normal authority which, being exercised within a circumscribed sphere, can have an independent ground—pedagogic authority being the prime example. Calling the authority of tradition 'primordial'—as we did at the time—suggested, perhaps, that it was greater than 'normal' authority. Perhaps it would be truer, however, to see it as in an important sense *less* than normal authority and to see a correspondence between this and what we are now exploring, i.e., the fact that the interpreter too lacks a really authoritative stance. It is this correspondence, or the lack on *both* sides, that makes *conversation* possible, for conversation cannot occur between unequal partners. Developing the implications of this point is in fact quite crucial to Gadamer's elaboration of 'effective-historical consciousness'—i.e., consciousness of one's hermeneutical situation with the prejudices that are embedded in it. The interpreter's situation is *not* comparable to that of an oral examiner who engages in 'discussion' with a candidate but only in order to elicit and assess the latter's perspective on the topic at hand. In such a discussion, the examiner has already reflected himself out of a symmetrical relationship, thereby both putting his own standpoint safely out of court and at the same time sidestepping any real claim to truth on the part of the examinee. Such an authoritative posture on the examiner's part aborts conversation, since it precludes a genuine mutual search for agreement on the topic. And at the root of it is the presupposition on the examiner's part that he can know and be confident of his own perspective and on this basis can evince the perspective of the examinee as something discrete over which he can preside. It is over against this kind of situation that Gadamer insists on the unity of partners who are committed to a conversation, as in his view interpreter and text are in any genuine attempt at understanding.

5. The 'Fusion of Horizons' in the Act of 'Application'

Gadamer's conception of this unity is quite radical, as will already have been evident from my characterization of the separateness of the two perspectives (i.e., of interpreter and text) as being only a momentary phenomenon within the unfolding of the conversation itself. He not only denies the existence of two *closed* horizons but even raises the question of whether there are actually *two* horizons here at all. What emerges in the openness and the flow of the hermeneutic conversation, he believes, is one horizon in which the two are already fused. This unity, which absorbs duality without altogether abolishing it, is difficult to formulate unequivocally because it is realized as a *movement*.[52] In the conversation with the text through which understanding emerges, the interpreter's horizon is already being stretched beyond itself, so that it is no longer the same horizon that it was independently of this encounter. And similarly the horizon of the text has been caught up in this movement and only through it becomes accessible. One simply does not possess one's present position as static so that the otherness of the text that speaks from the past "can be distinguished from it as from a fixed ground"; rather, as Gadamer goes on to put it, "the horizon of the present cannot be formed without the past. There is no more an isolated horizon of the present than there are historical [in the sense of past] horizons. Understanding, rather, is always the fusion of these horizons which we imagine to exist by themselves."[53]

". . . which we imagine to exist by themselves"—and yet there is a sense in which they *do* have some kind of distinct existence. Or rather the task of 'effective-historical consciousness' is precisely to make conscious a distinction or a tension that is otherwise lost in the automatic assimilation of the past and the present, which is a 'natural' accomplishment of naive consciousness. This tension is brought out through the alienation from the "familiarity" of an "unbroken stream of tradition" that is implicit in the act of *studying* a past text. And yet this distancing, which is an unavoidable element in "the situation in which understanding becomes a scientific task," never becomes an experience of total strangeness. The place of the text, and therefore the "true home of hermeneutics," is rather an "intermediate place between being an historically intended separate object and being part of a tradition."[54] Through the act of "intending" or "projecting," the horizon of the text is made to stand out as 'historical' and thus as distinct from our 'present' horizon, but this is "only a phase in the process of understanding and does not become solidified into the self-alienation of a past consciousness, but is overtaken by our own present horizon of understanding."[55] And so while effective-historical consciousness tries to bring out a distinction, it nonetheless "immediately recombines what it has distinguished in order, in the unity of the historical horizon that it thus acquires, to become again one with itself."[56]

The act of 'overtaking' or 'recombining' what is thus only momentarily 'intended' or 'projected' is what Gadamer calls the "fusing of horizons." This fusing is not subsequent to, but rather has already occurred in, an adequate understanding of the text. What this implies for the nature of understanding is brought out by Gadamer with the help of the notion of 'application'.[57] This is a notion which he retrieves from what he calls the "forgotten history of hermeneutics," i.e., from the theological and legal hermeneutics which had been largely eclipsed by the literary and historical preoccupations that came to the fore in the great revival of hermeneutics in the nineteenth century. The context within which documents of legal and religious tradition are interpreted is quite manifestly a context of *practice*. (And so, appropriately, as we are about to see, this point in Gadamer's discussion is the occasion for his introducing a close analysis of Aristotle's concept of practice — and its correlative, phronesis — not as a mere scholarly flourish but as an integral and furthering element in the overall discussion.) One is no longer within a religious or legal horizon if one is concerned simply to establish the meaning that a text has in itself — supposing oneself able, in doing this, to prescind from the import which this meaning has for oneself now. Rather the religious or legal horizon is constituted by the assumption that as an interpreter one is involved in a living relationship with this text — as are those to whom one's interpretation is of concern (one's congregation or clients) — so that to understand it is already to grasp and acknowledge its edifying or enjoining import or, in other words, to *apply* it, in the present situation. Clearly one must have some understanding here of one's situation coming into the encounter with the text; and one must also have some understanding of the text as something that has a transcendent power to address one. But neither of these understandings maintains itself separately; each is already passed out in the "fusion" of both which is the real achievement of understanding.

Gadamer introduces the perspectives of religious and legal hermeneutics not simply in order to correct an undue narrowness in the *extension* of hermeneutical theory but rather because he wants to argue that what is transparently true in the religious and legal spheres ought to be generalized and recognized in the *intention* of *all* hermeneutical activity. Two points carried over in this generalization deserve special mention. First is the dogmatic or normative element of scripture or law: the fact that they are acknowledged as having a saving or binding character in relation to those whom they address. Readers of *any* transmitted text must, in Gadamer's view, be open to the possibility of its having a similar validity or truth in relation to themselves — must, in other words, treat it not simply as an object of historical research but rather as something that may be able to speak compellingly to them in their own situation. The second point follows from this: the binding character of gospel or law can never be fully specified by textual explication in itself. It becomes determinate only through the ongoing juridical and pastoral applications which relate it to particular situations. And it is not just the particular situations that are illuminated by these applications. Rather, through the latter — and not without them — the meaning-potential of the text itself is realized. A similarly creative dialectic of universal and particular must be seen to operate, then, in *all* interpretation: it is true of any text that it simply does not have a universal meaning which could be grasped in one transcendent act of interpretation. Rather, since an application to one's self-understanding is always an intrinsic element in understanding, it follows that in all cases "the text must be understood at every moment, in every particular situation in a new and different way."

6. Aristotle as Mentor: The Centrality of the Appeal to Phronesis

At this point in his discussion (about two-thirds of the way through *Truth and Method*), where he invokes the precedents of legal and theological hermeneutics as exemplary disclosures of a kind of interpretation that edifies the reader at the same time that it "serves" the text, Gadamer has introduced the key ideas that give substance to his refashioning of hermeneutics. The remainder of the work does not add to the stock of hermeneutical ideas so much as develop (in the form of a "moving meditation")[58] the general philosophical context required to clarify and expose the full implications of the ideas that have already been introduced. Here, we may note, Gadamer is far from calling on an already secure philosophical framework which he now needs simply to push into place, as it were, in order to support the particular conclusions of his hermeneutical inquiry. To the contrary, the 'universal' issues that now engage him (primarily the nature of 'practice', 'experience', and 'language') are mediated through the 'particular' hermeneutical concerns that have brought him to them. The hermeneutical perspective — i.e., a concern to understand the nature and conditions of understanding itself—shows itself not only to stand in need of clarification by a more general philosophical context but also, and essentially, to be capable of entering transformatively into this context—to such an extent, indeed, that philosophy now becomes 'philosophical hermeneutics'. Moreover it does not require a very perceptive reading of *Truth and Method* to notice that Gadamer is not only providing a further theoretical elaboration of his hermeneutical insights but also, in doing this, is actually modeling or exemplifying them in practice. If he has already introduced these ideas *in actu signato*—how an element of "effective history" ensures the continuing vitality of tradition within understanding, and how an act of "application" brings about a "fusion of horizons" in which universal and particular enter each time into a unique reciprocal determination—he now goes on, not only to explain them but also to *show* them, *in actu exercitu,* in his own encounters with Aristotle, Plato, and Hegel.

Aristotle comes first. Although it would not be unreasonable to think that Plato's insights into the dialectical structure of thought as well as the metaphysics of beauty, or Hegel's insights into 'speculative' thought—or indeed Collingwood's insights into the 'logic of question and answer'—get more intimately to the heart of hermeneutical experience, still it is to *Aristotle* that he turns first,[59] as the philosopher who has most conspicuously provided, in his analysis of *phronēsis,* "a kind of model of the problems of hermeneutics."[60] In a supplement to *Truth and Method,* Aristotle is still regarded as "the supreme witness,"[61] one, moreover, who is so far from being merely 'historical' that Gadamer can state roundly near the end of the piece: "I do not regard the problem raised by Aristotle as in any way disposed of."[62] And since the publication of *Truth and Method,* in the prolific series of essays[63] in which he has offered further clarification of his enterprise in the book and responded magisterially to the growing interest in his work that has brought hermeneutics to the center of philosophy—as well as debates in theology, literary criticism and the human sciences—more and more it is the "neighbourly affinity of hermeneutics with practical philosophy"[64] (i.e., with the tradition of Aristotle's *Ethics* and *Politics*) that he has brought to the fore.

What is the basis of this affinity? Why should Gadamer be drawn to Aristotle as his special mentor from the tradition? The answer is that he sees Aristotle as having confronted a problem that was very similar to his own. In "the curious relation between moral being and moral consciousness that Aristotle sets out in his Ethics,"[65] he (Aristotle) very deliberately deconstructs the Socratic intellectualism (still shared by Plato, at least in the early Dialogues) which had accorded to moral knowledge an uncompromised sovereignty over moral being—a sovereignty whose prototype could be seen in the craftsman's masterly exercise of his knowledge and whose theoretical articulation, therefore, was anchored in the concept of *technē*. In his own reflection on the no less curious relation between the "hermeneutical situation" of the interpreter and his conscious act of interpretation, Gadamer is challenging, with equal deliberation, the objectivist claims for a reliably controlled interpretation whose proto-type — even if unacknowledged — is the methodically achieved knowledge of the empirical scientist and whose theoretical guarantee is to be found in the modern concept of 'method' itself. What mainly gets in the way of a proper recognition of the conditionedness and finitude of human understanding — which it is Gadamer's chief aim to bring about — is "the alienation by the objectifying methods of modern science" which deeply infiltrated nineteenth-century hermeneutics. When Gadamer writes that "the return to the example of Aristotelian ethics is made to help us realize and avoid this",[66] he is acknowledging one aspect of the illumination that comes about in the fusion of hermeneutics and practical philosophy: prac-tical philosophy throws a helpful light on hermeneutics, because in the context of his age's supreme attempt to give reason an independent footing, Aristotle had met and resisted a very similar attempt to deny the condi-tioned and finite nature of our understanding of human affairs. It may also be noted, however, that Gadamer's own acute identification of the core problem of hermeneutics puts him in a very strong position, in re-turning to Aristotle, not only to learn from him but also to reveal him, i.e., to bring to light a hitherto insufficiently appreciated richness in his analysis of phronesis.

Running like a refrain through Gadamer's book — and already high-lighted, of course, in its very title — is a repudiation of the idea that her-meneutics could ever serve as "an organon of the human sciences," i.e., provide a 'method' whereby interpretation in various fields could be reli-ably protected from whatever snares or obstacles might beset it and thus put on a sound objective footing. Nineteenth-century hermeneuticists had entertained such an ambition, that is, to found a discipline which would have therapeutic or instructional import for the actual practice of inter-pretation, so that this practice could now be carried on respectably, or 'scientifically', under its direct supervision. Such respectability appears to Gadamer to be only a cloak to cover a real impoverishment which is suf-fered by practice in this model. In his view practice must both remain rooted in the 'being' of the person — and, therefore, in the communal and historical matrix of this being — *and* incorporate within itself the knowl-edge which guides it. What he will not at all concede is that this knowl-edge can be evacuated to a supervening 'method' which, insulated from the contingencies of the person's being, would provide a secure vantage point from which directives could be issued to his 'practice'.

It is here exactly that Gadamer experiences the fascination of Aristotle. For there was a form of activity with which Aristotle was familiar and which was under the firm control of an objective and impersonal 'method'. And yet when he came to formulate his concept of praxis his crucial move was precisely to distinguish it from this form of activity—which was called poiesis. The activity of poiesis yielded a product or result which was quite separable from the one who produced it; and also separable—in the sense of being formulable and therefore at the disposal of anyone who might care to learn and use it—was the methodical knowledge or techne which governed this activity. Praxis, on the other hand, was always a realization of the person himself, and the knowledge which guides it, i.e., phronesis, was inseparable from the kind of person he had become.

Phronesis is the concept that attracts Gadamer's special interest. With it he believes Aristotle has disclosed in a subtle and profound manner the structure of a kind of understanding which, even though it is the conscious source of order in a person's dispositions and actions, nonetheless always remains indebted to these dispositions and to the history of actions which lives on in them. Gadamer is interested in phronesis because the kind of problems and tensions which Aristotle had to sort through in analyzing it seem so suggestively similar to the ones he himself faces in trying to articulate the kind of understanding which occurs in the interpretation of texts. We would be paying no compliment to Gadamer, of course, if we did not notice that as an interpreter of Aristotle he himself does not escape the influence of his own hermeneutical situation. What he is primarily at grips with in his own inquiry and what therefore shapes the 'anticipations' which he brings to Aristotle is the entrenchment of objectivism and therefore of method in post-Enlightenment theories of hermeneutics. In his interpretation of phronesis, then, what he fastens on, and renders quite thematic, is the way in which phronesis, for all its seeming kinship with techne as a mode of knowledge (an *eidos gnōseōs*), is nonetheless crucially distinct from and irreducible to it. Here Gadamer, stimulated by his own problematic, focuses on something which Aristotle himself had not taken pains to bring into profile. A distinction which Aristotle had made very succinctly in a brief formula, and then elaborated only in one or two fragmentary and quite cryptic remarks, becomes, in Gadamer's reflection, the basis of a full-scale *via negativa* which is at the same time the royal road to an understanding of phronesis.

Here I will just briefly indicate the main features which emerge from Gadamer's systematic focus on the nontechnical nature of phronesis. There is first of all the nondisposability of phronesis—the fact that one is never sufficiently at a distance from it to be able simply to use it, or the fact that it gives one a peculiarly intimate kind of self-knowledge without however making this self fully transparent or available. Again, there is the fact that it breaks out of an instrumentalist framework and cannot therefore be understood in terms of the categories of ends and means (and can never be reduced to a power of calculating means since in its sphere 'ends' are never separable from the 'means' through which they are realized). Again there is the fact that it is realized always in concrete applications and never resolves itself into formulated knowledge that can be possessed apart from these applications (in an application we are never simply subsuming a particular with which we are now confronted under a universal which we already possess; rather, the understanding we reach through it contains a unique determination of the universal and particular together). The undermining of various separations—between being and knowing, matter and form, means and end, particular and universal, 'possession' and 'application'—which is inherent in the above characteristics makes of phronesis a very fluid reality. Gadamer gives positive expression to this fact by relating phronesis to *experience,* and insisting in fact that phronesis is so intimate to experience that in the end we must say that phronesis *is* a form of experience. Indeed Gadamer goes so far as to suggest that it is "perhaps the fundamental form of experience compared with which all other experience represents a denaturing."[67]

Here I have only very briefly adverted to the main points in Gadamer's reading of book 6 of the *Ethics*—without any concern for the detail or even the validity of this reading. This is because my purpose in this part of the study is not to engage directly with Aristotle's thought but rather to demonstrate its continuing fruitfulness and versatility in the work of leading philosophers of our own age. In Part 2, however, I shall be involved in detailed exegesis of Aristotle, and it is opportune to point out now that Gadamer will be of quite special significance to me then. Three distinct aspects of this significance may be noted here. First, like all the other thinkers whom I discuss in Part 1, he will have shaped the anticipations and the questions that I shall bring to my reading of Aristotle. My appropriation of his thought, fused with that of those other philosophers who appear in these pages, will, in large measure, have formed my own 'hermeneutical situation' or 'horizon of interest' as I approach Aristotle's texts. Second—and here Gadamer *differs* from the others—he is the philosopher who provides an explicit account and justification of the kind of inquiry which I conduct into Aristotle. It is his hermeneutical theory that legitimizes my practice in Part 2 by showing that any scholarly approach to the tradition cannot avoid bringing contemporary concerns into play with it and that this therefore may as well be done with as much focal awareness as one can manage. "It will always be the case," Gadamer writes in one of his essays, "that we have to ask ourselves why a text stirs our interest."[68] To attempt some answer to this question is for him "the first, basic and infinitely far-reaching demand called for in any hermeneutical undertaking."[69] He goes on:

> Not only in philosophy or theology but in any research project it is required that we elaborate an awareness of the hermeneutical situation. That has to be our initial aim when we approach what the question is. . . . To imagine that one might ever attain full illumination as to his motives or his interests in questions is to imagine something impossible. In spite of this it remains a legitimate task to clarify what lies at the basis of our interests as far as possible. Only then are we in a position to understand the statements with which we are concerned [i.e., in the text], precisely insofar as we recognize our own questions in them.[70]

I try to meet the 'demand' or to carry out the 'legitimate task' which Gadamer indicates here by presenting (in the Introduction) my encounter with the behavioral objectives model of teaching as the original stimulant of my questions, and by presenting (here in Part 1) my research into the more recent thinkers who make a bridge between these questions and Aristotle. The third aspect of Gadamer's significance for the work in Part 2 — and here again he stands apart from my other interlocutors — is more substantive: it concerns the actual interpretation of Aristotle which he presents in quite considerable detail in *Truth and Method*[71] and the main points of which I have just summarized. My interpretation of phronesis will not set out to corroborate Gadamer's reading, nor will it refer to it much as a secondary source; still the 'spirit' of his interpretation has, I believe, entered my own; and so the themes which we have just seen in his interpretation are very close to ones which will emerge as significant and be analyzed in detail in my own interpretation later on.

7. Gadamer's Account of Experience, in Relation to Aristotle

A question which may indeed occur to a reader later on is whether I do not, in the end, make Aristotle a good deal more 'Gadamerian' than Gadamer himself has done! A major theme in Part 2 will be the intimate connection between phronesis and experience — a theme which, as we have just seen, is strongly emphasized by Gadamer. The section on phronesis occupies a peculiarly intermediate position in *Truth and Method*, however, and Gadamer's piety toward Aristotle does not leave him entirely unreserved in his attitude to him. His recourse to Aristotle occurs at a point where the concept of 'application' has brought 'practice' into focus and where he wants to elucidate a knowledge that remains embedded in practice, over against a knowledge that can be guaranteed by method. Aristotle furnishes him with a concept of practical knowledge (i.e., phronesis) whose irreducibility to method is bound up with the fact that it always remains *experiential*— to such an extent indeed that "it is pointless to distinguish here between knowledge and experience, as can be done in the case of a techne."[72] While Gadamer suggests that the key to phronesis is its relation to experience, he does not develop this in his section on Aristotle however; and, more importantly, it subsequently becomes clear that the notion of experience (*Erfahrung*) that he has in mind here is much richer than Aristotle's rather limited notion of experience (*empeiria*).

When he sets out, some pages *after* his *ex professo* treatment of Aristotle, to examine 'experience' (a concept which, as he confesses, is "one of the most obscure we have")[73] he is concerned to rescue it from the "epistemological schematization" to which it has been subjected in the tradition of British empiricism. Although this tradition put a premium on experience as the source and ultimate touchstone of knowledge, still its critical concern with validated (ultimately with *scientific* knowledge) led to a standardization of experience, to a preoccupation with methods (*empirical* methods) which "attempt to guarantee, through the objectivity of their approach, that these basic experiences can be repeated by anyone." What is lost in the attenuated conception of experience spawned by this epistemological preoccupation is "the inner historicality of experience." Gadamer acknowledges that when science sets out "to so objectify experience that it no longer contains any historical element" it is no more than conspiring with experience itself, which "by its very nature, abolishes its history"[74] in that it preserves only what is reliably confirmed by subsequent experience (and so attains the status of 'knowledge'), while at the same time allowing what is not so confirmed to simply slip away. But he still insists that this tendency, for which Aristotle remains the best witness, is only *one* feature of experience and that an overexclusive emphasis on it needs to be combatted by drawing attention to other aspects of experience that are in fact neglected in Aristotle's account. When he himself draws attention to two other such features he therefore sees himself as going quite explicitly beyond Aristotle.

Aristotle's view of experience was what might be called a retrospective view from the vantage point of the concepts that had been generated out of it. His famous battleground image (in *Posterior Analytics* 2.19) for explaining the formation of concepts was a masterly one which Gadamer admiringly refers to not only in *Truth and Method* but also in several of his later essays. This image likens the emergence of a coherent experience out of a succession of perceptions, and the gradual consolidation of this experience into universal concepts, to the process whereby a fleeing army brings itself into array when first one man and then another makes a stand—until eventually it comes together again in a united front, amenable to a single *archē* (which in Greek means both 'command' and 'principle'). What Gadamer especially likes about this image is its nonrationalist import, the fact that it shows that "the birth of experience is an event over which no one has control and . . . in which everything is coordinated in a way that is ultimately incomprehensible,"[75] so that rational concepts arise ultimately from an "unprincipled universality of experience,"[76] rather than being guaranteed by a sovereign, self-disposing reason. Despite this, however, Gadamer sees it as a limitation of Aristotle's account that he is interested in experience only from the point of view of its role in the formation of concepts. This gives him what Gadamer calls a "teleological" notion of experience: concepts are regarded as the *telos,* or proper outcome, of experience. But the one-sidedness of this notion lies in the fact that "if we look at experience in this way in terms of its result, its real character as a process is overlooked."[77] (The critical relevance of this analysis of experience to the behavioral objectives model of teaching should be apparent. The latter model, we might say here, mistakenly supposes that a detailed preoccupation with *outcomes* will somehow protect the teacher from the 'unprincipled' demands of a *process.*)

The historical character of experience—i.e., the fact that it is a process—is the first of the two features overlooked by Aristotle to which Gadamer draws attention. What is significant in experience as a process is the negative element which gives it a dialectical structure and which was most successfully articulated by Hegel. As against the smooth conglomeration of experience out of an uninterrupted succession of particular impressions suggested by Aristotle's account, we see under Hegel's guidance the tension between our established or routinized experience and a new experience that impresses itself on us (and finds expression in a phrase like "that really was an *experience*") precisely by interrupting or contradicting our previous experience and thereby enriching it. There is a "reversal of consciousness" in the process of experience in that new experiences (if they are really new and not simply repetitions of 'old' ones) not only give us access to a new reality but also involve us in amending and reshaping our previous apprehensions of reality. And the experience of recurrently carrying through this reversal (i.e., the experience of experience itself) leads to a deepened self-awareness or self-presence in the truly experienced person; in becoming experienced, he has been involved not only in acquiring information but also, through this very acquiring, in a process of self-formation.

Although Gadamer appeals to Hegel as his "important witness for the dialectical element of experience"[78] he nonetheless balks at Hegel's conclusion that "the dialectic of experience must end with the overcoming of all experience"—in the achievement of an absolute knowledge that will abolish the disunity of self and object which gives experience its whole momentum. Gadamer's taking leave of Hegel here is similar to his earlier parting company from Aristotle. Absolute self-knowledge might be taken as a more extreme version of the concept in Aristotle, or at least as having this much in common with it, that in both cases "the nature of experience is conceived in terms of that which goes beyond it." What Gadamer himself wants to argue is that if experience has a *telos* it is not one that carries us beyond experience to 'science', or to the possibility of "that kind of instruction that follows from general theoretical or technical knowledge." We never really graduate from the school of experience to a university of higher knowledge: "the perfect form of what we call 'experienced' does not consist in the fact that someone already knows everything and knows better than anyone else . . . the dialectic of experience has its own fulfilment not in definitive knowledge, but in that openness to experience that is encouraged by experience itself."

Gadamer's point here is more than a Popperian one to the effect that experience is always refutable and hence provisional, so that the experienced person always remains something of a skeptic. It is more an existential than an epistemological point. The truly experienced person is one who, in acknowledging the ineluctability of experience and the limits of "definitive knowledge," has gained insight into the *finite* nature of his own existence. The best witness to this insight—which is the second of the two features not found in Aristotle's account of experience—is Aeschylus. His tragedies show that no one can be exempted from the trials of experience and that the highest lesson to be learned from this experience—and it is always a hard learning through suffering (*pathei mathein*)—is "the absoluteness of the barrier that separates him from the divine." The truly experienced person is the one who has learned this lesson, "who knows that he is master neither of time nor the future," who has discovered "the limits of the power and the self-knowledge of his planning reason," and who has come to see that "all the expectations and planning of finite beings is finite and limited." (What Gadamer is saying here is closely akin to something we have already seen in Arendt. The uncertainty and irreversibility which were so central in her account of action—and which underlay the need for promising and forgiving as remedies against an otherwise overwhelming hazardousness—find an exact parallel in Gadamer's insistence on "the limitedness of all prediction and the uncertainty of all plans" and on the fact that the experienced person has learned that "it proves to be an illusion that everything can be reversed." It is noteworthy also that just as Gadamer appeals at this point to the first of the great tragedians who preceded the birth of Socratic philosophy, so Arendt, too, was appealing back beyond the Socratics to "the pre-philosophical Greek experience of action and speech.")[79]

I have gone into Gadamer's conception of experience because even though it goes well beyond what is found in Aristotle's concept of experience, what my own work in Part 2 goes a long way toward showing, I believe, is that it is very close to Aristotle's concept of phronesis. Gadamer himself does not articulate or develop this closeness, but rather presents his analyses of Aristotelian phronesis and of experience as two successive increments in his evolving and deepening reflection on hermeneutical understanding as an inextinguishably nontechnical process. Because of this I said earlier that my own interpretation of Aristotle may make him more 'Gadamerian' that the *ipsa verba* of Gadamer himself might seem to warrant. But if it does, the only decisive issue is whether Aristotle's texts give it warrant. I hope to show later that they do.

8. Experience as Being-in-Play

I shall continue my account of Gadamer by adverting to the way in which this notion of experience is absorbed into his hermeneutics and, in being thus absorbed, is connected with other basic concepts, one or two of which we have not met so far. Gadamer's case in relation to hermeneutical experience (or understanding as the achievement of "effective-historical consciousness") is that it *is* just that (i.e., experience) and not, therefore, a knowledge that has managed to overcome the vulnerability which belongs to experience. "The dialectical illusion of experience perfected and replaced by knowledge"[80] is what he steadfastly tries to unmask. In doing this he makes a crucial comparison between the hermeneutical experience of the tradition and the experience that one has of another person as a 'thou'. (His appeal to phronesis, it may be noted, is of a piece with this deployment of an interpersonal model as the basic hermeneutical paradigm. For, in Aristotle's many-faceted account of it, phronesis has as cognate virtues understanding (*sunesis*) and judgment (*gnōmē*);[81] these are virtues which are exercised in one's counsel of *others*, and which, as Gadamer himself points out in his section on Aristotle, require of one a friendly spirit so that one "does not know and judge as one who stands apart and unaffected; but rather, as one united by a specific bond with the other.")[82] One does *not* experience the other as a thou when one tries to isolate what is typical or predictable in his behavior and thus to understand him in terms of some general taxonomic or explanatory schemes. Neither does one have genuine experience of the thou when one tries to intercept and, as it were, to disarm his address to one, by withdrawing from a direct relationship and presuming to 'understand' him from some superior vantage point which somehow 'explains' his position and thus neutralizes its claim on oneself. The first of these distortions of genuine encounter finds its hermeneutical equivalent in "the naive faith in method and in the objectivity that can be attained through it" which "flattens out the nature of hermeneutical experience precisely as we have seen in the teleological interpretation of experience since Aristotle."[83] The second distortion of interpersonal relationship, which "destroys its moral bond,"[84] has, as its equivalent in the hermeneutical sphere, the kind of 'historical consciousness' that tries to transcend its own historical conditionedness and, supposedly outside of a living relationship with the tradition, claims to be in a position to "understand" it.

Adequate hermeneutical experience corresponds with a third form of relationship in which there is genuine experience of the 'thou'. Here one is involved and belongs with the other—be it person or text; one listens to it and not only acknowledges its otherness but remains *open* to the possibility of being affected by it oneself. This openness or receptivity to the other, a kind of *docta ignorantia* in which one is unsuspicious[85] without being gullible, is the most essential requirement for fruitful interaction with a person or tradition. It is also, in Gadamer's view, the most inward achievement of the experienced person, so that hermeneutical accomplishment and a real depth of experience come to the same thing: "The hermeneutical consciousness has its fulfilment, not in the methodological awareness of itself, but in the same readiness for experience that distinguishes the experienced man by comparison with the man captivated by dogma."[86] The fact that the word 'experienced' is grammatically a past participle should not obscure the meaning that Gadamer has for it here. In its primary sense an experience is something that brings with it an element of surprise, and to be experienced does not mean to have had one's surprises so that one is now proof against any new ones but, on the contrary, to have learned to be at home with the possibility of surprise as a permanent possibility inseparable from historical existence itself. Nor, finally, should the significance of this capacity to discover new things in the old be obscured by Gadamer's unceasing criticism of all Promethean urges to create something radically new: his deep skepticism about the ambitions of "utopian or eschatological consciousness"[87] does not block out for him the possibilities of bringing forth new or forgotten meanings in our encounters with tradition.

The openness which is characteristic of experience in Gadamer's conception of it is elaborated further in terms of the priority of *questioning* and of *conversation* as the natural home of questioning. We have already noted these themes, but I shall advert to them briefly again in order to show how they open on to others which we have not so far explicitly considered but which are perhaps the most quintessentially Gadamerian themes of all, namely, *play* and *language*. Play is introduced as the concept which can most deeply subvert the instrumentalist bias of modern thought, i.e., the tendency to think of unimpeded 'subjects' achieving their pre-planned 'ends' through the efficacy of methodical 'means' which they are able to put at their disposal. And language is the all-encompassing reality which, to the extent that we succeed in reflecting on it,[88] shows more deeply and with more universal import than anything else the limits of instrumentalist or method-based rationality. Language and especially play may not seem to be centrally at issue in Aristotle's work.[89] But the perspective which Gadamer develops through his reflection on them has a great deal of affinity with what, on my interpretation, Aristotle is trying to bring out in his analysis of *phronēsis*.

First, then, a brief advertence, once again, to questioning and conversation as themes that have been reopened by our consideration of experience and that in turn lead us into a discussion of play and of language. Questioning is the power which keeps experience open, and all the 'knowledge' that the experienced person achieves is best understood as answers that respond to and remain in lively relation with questions that have arisen. The questioning that is alive in hermeneutical experience has, as it were, a double layer. In the first place we begin to get into the text only when we get behind what it says to the questions which (however implicitly) it is attempting to answer. We are permanently on the outside, we have no way of really joining issue with the text, until we have identified the generative questions that have stirred it into being.[90] When Gadamer writes of the "hermeneutical priority of the question,"[91] however, he means more than this. In genuine hermeneutical experience the question to which the text is an answer is not only reconstructed as a meaningful question that could be, and in fact was, raised by someone (in a perhaps far distant age), but it "passes into our own questioning."[92] We do not understand it *as a question* at all unless the issue which it brings before us is still really open for us. Or, as Gadamer very simply puts it: "To understand a question means to ask it."[93]

To be able to ask a question, however, in the sense of being gripped by its unsettledness is itself the high gift of the experienced person. The fact that one may have a dearth of questions—or, more vexingly, have a facility for asking the *wrong* questions (so that, in a witty formulation, one is like a man trying to milk a bull while holding a sieve underneath) —bears out this "true superiority of questioning."[94] (Gadamer points to Plato's depiction of Socrates as the classic revelation of the fact that "it is more difficult to ask questions than to answer them.")[95] Most essentially, a question opens something up and places it in a kind of indeterminacy; if it does not do this it is not a question at all. At the same time in doing so it is not vacuous. It already has sense and so anticipates and limits what can qualify as an answer. It gets this sense only against a background of established meanings which it presupposes. And yet the art of questioning never allows itself to be entirely dependent on particular presuppositions; it may always prove capable of releasing itself from them and of bringing even them into question (admittedly, in doing this it will have incurred a debt to *other* presuppositions; but the hold of these latter is not guaranteed any greater permanency). 'Public opinion' is the force which makes many assumptions appear to be invulnerable that are not in fact so. It is therefore the great enemy of questioning (to which the death of Socrates bears dramatic witness).

Although maintaining the poise between openness and determination which characterizes genuine and fruitful questioning may be described as an art, Gadamer very characteristically insists that "it is not an art in the sense in which the Greeks speak of techne, not a craft that can be taught and by means of which we would master the knowledge of truth."[96] Not only, in fact, is it not a techne to regulate an activity but, properly understood, it is not even an activity: "questioning too is more a 'passion' than an action."[97] Not being under our control, it is the kind of 'event' which, as we have already seen, cannot be guaranteed through method. There is often a *suddenness* about it that makes us say that a question "'comes' to us, that it 'arises' or 'presents itself' more than that we raise it or present it."[98] It comes to us above all in conversation and it is by understanding the structure of conversation that we can best understand the adventitious but still not arbitrary nature of questioning. We do not preside over conversation—as we have already seen—any more than we do over questions. Activity here again turns out to be passivity: "To conduct a conversation means to allow oneself to be conducted by the object to which the partners in the conversation are directed."[99] This 'object' (*die Sache;* see note 38 above) is not an object in the sense of something that stands over against me and that I, as a 'subject' can survey. To the contrary, the whole point of this activity which is also a passivity is that in it the polarity of subject and object is undercut.

The concept which for Gadamer best articulates this nonobjectivistic, and equally nonsubjectivistic, structure is the concept of play, or game (*Spiel*). This concept had been introduced in the first part of *Truth and Method*,[100] in order to disclose the ontological structure of the work of art—and in particular to combat the radical subjectivism that had dominated accounts of aesthetic experience since Kant's *Critique of Judgment.*

Although 'play' is formally treated only in the discussion of art—where art is shown to be best understood as a "transformation" of play and play is claimed to reach its highest perfection in art—it still lingers influentially through the rest of the book. Its most concentrated realization may be in art, but it is also present in all genuine experience; and in fact conversation, which is such a basic medium in which experience articulates itself, can best be understood as a mode of play. What is crucial in relation to play for Gadamer is "the primacy of play over the consciousness of the player."[101] If a player becomes a master he does so only by surrendering to the spirit of the game itself. It is in this sense that "play is not to be understood as a kind of activity."[102] For one cannot maintain the stance of 'subject' or 'agent' in relation to the game—apart perhaps from having the power to make an initial decision whether to enter or withhold oneself from *particular* games. But when one *has* entered, then "all playing is a being played. . . . The real subject of the game . . . is not the player but instead the game itself. The game is what holds the player in its spell, draws him into play and keeps him there."[103] Or the same thought once again: "Play does not have its being in the consciousness or the attitude of the player but on the contrary draws the latter into its area and fills him with its spirit. The player experiences the game as a reality that surpasses him."[104]

When two people join together in the mutual questioning and answering of a conversation what emerges is not a product which can be ascribed to either—or even to both of them—as producers; it is always something other and more than they could have envisaged. Here in fact is the element of play: each has become a medium in and through which the conversation plays itself out. This playfulness is the secret of fecundity. A conversation really has a life of its own and is most fruitful when the partners surrender to this life—a surrender that is accomplished, of course, only through the intense 'activity' of remaining open and responsive to the to and fro movement of the questioning. To understand conversation as a form of play is not to imply any frivolousness or lack of seriousness on the part of the participants but rather to suggest that only through a certain kind of suspension of their 'projecting' subjectivity can the matter-at-issue (*die Sache*) come to disclose itself to them. Gadamer believes that Plato and Aristotle, as well as Hegel,[105] understood dialectic in this way as the process in which two people allowed themselves to be led by the thing itself to a true comprehension of it. (The solitary thinker could accomplish this with the help of an internalized interlocutor in what Plato called the "dialogue of the soul with itself" [*Sophist* 263e].) And he further believes that this dialectical process can be best understood on the model of the game. As we have just seen, "the game is not so much the subjective attitude of the two men confronting each other as it is the formation of the movement as such, which, as in an unconscious teleology, subordinates the attitudes of the individuals to itself . . . neither partner alone constitutes the real determining factor; rather it is the unified form of movement as a whole that unifies the fluid activity of both."[106] The loss of sovereignty that one experiences by giving oneself to this movement is not really a *loss:* "absorption into the game is an ecstatic self-forgetting that is experienced not as a *loss* of self-possession, but as the free buoyancy of an elevation above oneself."[107] And all of this that pertains to a game pertains no less to a conversation: "it cannot be denied that in an actual dialogue . . . something of the character of accident, favor and surprise — and in the end of buoyancy, indeed of elevation — that belong to the game is present."[108]

It will help us to understand how fully intimate to Gadamer's whole conception of hermeneutical experience the notion of conversation is, and to be less disconcerted, perhaps, by the 'playfulness' which he sees as constitutive of it, if we turn next to a consideration of *language.* The major themes of his hermeneutics, which, as we have seen throughout this chapter, flow so easily into one another, all flow together finally into this one all-encompassing theme of language. As a 'moving meditation', *Truth and Method* brings us closer to an understanding of understanding itself through a kind of spiral in which we retrace our way over the same points again and again — finding ourselves, at each turn, in a better position to appreciate them. This movement takes us eventually toward the "center of language." This center or medium (*mitte*), at which we arrive in the third and final part of the book, is not still but moving; it is in fact the source of the movement that we have all the time been glimpsing in understanding itself and which has, moreover, all the time been making itself felt in our own attempt to understand it. In the next chapter we shall attempt to follow Gadamer to this center; it is there that we shall get our most inward understanding of hermeneutical experience and of the unity into which all the points that we have seen so far are gathered.

5. Language, Hermeneutics, and Practical Philosophy

1. The Unity of Thought and Language

Gadamer's whole inquiry in *Truth and Method* culminates in an abandonment to language. By not trying to protect thought from its fate of always being already delivered over to language he seals his opposition to all the forms of objectivism that he has been confronting throughout the book and, at the same time, reveals the ultimate context within which all his own hermeneutical (i.e., nonobjectivistic) concepts find their place together. He does not deny that the linguistic nature of our experience of the world implies a distance or a freedom which gives us a *world*— and not simply the habitat within which the animal always remains enclosed; and he admits, moreover, that with language we have a way of 'coping' in which "threatening, even annihilating immediacy is removed, brought within proportions, made communicable and hence dealt with."[1] What is important here, however, is that whenever there is some degree of understanding in our experience this distancing and coping, such as they are, have already occurred. To be sure, we cannot rule out "prelinguistic and metalinguistic dawnings, dumbnesses, and silences in which the immediate meeting with the world expresses itself,"[2] but these experiences happen only against a background of language toward which, in some way or another, they are always being drawn. And searching hard, as we often have to do, for just the right word or words to say what needs to be said, much more often occurs *within* words; what we experience is the unsatisfactoriness of the present formulation and the push that this gives us to look for a better one ("stitching and unstitching" Yeats called this) rather than a pristine, prelinguistic thing-in-itself. Neither the world of our experience and understanding nor our language are available to us independently of each other; they belong together in an indissoluble unity: "not only is the world 'world' only insofar as it comes into language, but language too has its real being only in the fact that the world is represented within it."[3]

138

While Gadamer's chief concern is to develop the implications of this unity for the nature of understanding, he cannot do this without at the same time pointing out certain views of language which are immediately excluded once that unity is taken seriously. Any attempt to treat language as a formal apparatus which can be studied in itself will be seen to have severe limitations. More important here than the inability of such disciplines as grammar or linguistics to do justice to the inner life of a language, is the ill-foundedness of all attempts to discover or invent a fundamental 'language' that could be regarded as prior to, or as a desirable substitute for, the whole variety of natural languages with which history has made us familiar. Babel, in the sense of many different languages, each with its own measure of the haphazard and ramshackle, is an essential feature of our humanity and not a curse from which we should be trying to release ourselves. And yet, the desire and the search for just such a release has been endemic in the whole Western tradition. It is to be found in the commitment of modern sciences to forge a technical vocabulary in which a term is an entirely artificial construct or, if it is borrowed from ordinary usage, "has the variety and breadth of its meaning excised and is assigned only one particular conceptual meaning."[4] We find it no less in the ambition (most classically expressed in Leibniz's ideal of a *characteristica universala*) to found a system of signs which, being entirely unambiguous and without any attendant chains of association, would facilitate a type of rigorous rationality that has never been possible within the folds of natural language. And we find it too, Gadamer believes, at the beginning of the tradition in Plato's highly partisan stance in the great battle between dialectic and rhetoric for the soul of Greek youth; Plato's dialectic "claims to make thought dependent on itself alone and to open it to its true objects, the 'ideas', so that the power of words (*dunamis tōn onamatōn*) and its demonic technicization in the sophistical art of argument are overcome."[5] For all Plato's own wonderful way with words, language appears within his philosophy as a source of bewitchment or seduction which must be strenuously resisted if we are to reach the true *logos*—a pure thought which thinks its ideal object without words (*aneu onomatōn*).

Gadamer's objections to these different approaches to language remain the same: for all of them, "language is taken to be something wholly detached from the matter under consideration and to be, rather, an instrument of subjectivity"[6]—an instrument which Plato would discard and which more aggressive moderns would artifically perfect. As against these views, there is positive value in the new interest in comparative linguistics deriving from Herder's and Humboldt's insistence on the determination (and not simply the expression) of thought by language, so that the limits

of language are the limits of the world—in the sense not just that a person
without a language would be a person without a world but also that a
person's world bears the stamp of the particular language through which
it comes to be for him. At the point where this insight of romanticism
is pressed to relativistic conclusions, however, Gadamer opposes it. An
acceptance of the contingency and sheer particularity of natural languages,
and of the fact that thought, if it is to happen at all, must dwell in some
one of them, does not imply an "exclusiveness of perspectives."[7] Gadamer
does indeed repudiate rationalism, but he still holds that it is always the
case that "language is the language of reason itself."[8] The universality of
reason, whose defense was the chief concern of the whole tradition from
Plato to Hegel, does not simply splinter through the exposure to particular languages. Rather, Gadamer is concerned to show (*contra* Plato and
Hegel, who had the deepest sense of this problem and who are therefore
the ones with whom it is still most worth debating it)[9] that the universality of reason must now be reconceived, and can in fact be preserved,
as the universality of the hermeneutical phenomenon, or, in other words,
as the universality of language itself. For "our capacity for saying keeps
pace untiringly with the universality of reason."[10]

Before exploring this universality of language, we must show how
it is not compromised by the plurality of languages that became apparent
with the decline of Latin and the emergence of an educated laity during
the Renaissance. The later assimilation of this plurality into romantic theory was, as we have just seen, a significant advance in our understanding
of language and of its inextinguishable intimacy with thought. In Gadamer's view, no language stands completely outside other languages; each
one, by its very nature as language, stretches and opens itself toward every
other one: "each one contains potentially within it every other one, i.e.,
every one is able to be extended into every other one. It is able to understand, from within itself, the 'view' of the world that is presented in another language."[11] This ultimate affinity between even the most heterogeneous languages is grounded in the fact that each of them is a mode
of presenting what, in the end, remains a common world. If there is a
common world, which, in pulling languages toward itself, pulls them toward each other, this is not, however, a prelinguistic world-in-itself, any
more than it is a world which resides definitively in some original "language of Adam," or in some privileged metalanguage below or above the
actual historical languages. Rather, the world is presented—or, better, presents itself—in each language, and there is, then, in each one a kind of
inner inexhaustibility which matches the inexhaustibility of the world itself. Different languages do *not* give us different worlds. At most, a given
language may have developed a facility or genius for disclosing particular

facets or nuances of the world; but a person from a different linguistic community, even though he may at first be tantalized by the seemingly overwhelming difference or even superiority in certain respects which he experiences in this new language, still finds that his own language has been quickened and stirred through the encounter with it. "By learning foreign languages men do not alter their relationship to the world, like an aquatic animal that becomes a land animal but, while preserving their own relationship to the world, they extend and enrich it by the world of the foreign language. Whoever has language [i.e., *any* language and the endless virtuality that comes with it] 'has' the world."[12]

This is not to deny that really entering into the life of another language requires one to let one's thinking be borne along by it—so that one stops the business of translating backwards and forwards between it and one's own. Nor is it to deny the disconcerting fact that when two people conduct a conversation, with each speaking his own language while following that of the other, one of the languages, "as if impelled by a higher force,"[13] will strive to establish itself as the dominant medium of communication (almost like the way in which a person listening to different messages, even in the same language, through two earphones, will hardly be able to avoid giving a preferential hearing to one of them). Nor, finally, is it to deny that when translation *is* attempted, the translator will always have to make difficult decisions and may indeed often feel defeated by the "unsurpassable appropriateness" of the original. Gadamer's response to these undeniable facts about the negotiations between different languages is not to dismiss them so much as to insist that they do not confront us with the basic problem—or rather that the problem that they do confront us with is only a more acute version of the basic problem that we already face in any linguistic communication (even in the same natural language). For translation, however formidable the difficulties that confront it, is essentially a process of *interpretation* and it is not therefore fundamentally different from what transpires in *any* hermeneutical situation. It is, in Gadamer's words, "simply an extreme case of hermeneutical difficulty, i.e., of alienness and its overcoming. . . . The translator's task of recreation differs only in degree, not qualitatively, from the general hermeneutical task presented by any text."[14]

What, then, is this general hermeneutical issue, and how does it bring into focus the essential issue about language? This question brings us back to the unity between language and thought which we had just introduced when we were diverted somewhat by the need to close off certain approaches to language that prevent this unity from coming into view. The unity of thought and language can in fact be reformulated as the unity of understanding (*Verstehen*) and interpretation (*Auslegung*), and the way in which hermeneutics brings up the question of language will be clearer if we focus more closely now on *interpretation*. I have, in fact, been using the two terms "understanding" and "interpretation" interchangeably up to now, and we might say that it was because of this that the question of language has not so far become thematic. In this I have been following Gadamer's own path in *Truth and Method*. Before the third part of the book, the part on language, the difference between understanding and interpretation is not dwelt on.[15] It is only when the linguistic dimension of understanding becomes more explicit that we begin to see that understanding and interpretation can in fact be distinguished: interpretation is always the articulation in language of what we have understood. While this distinction becomes explicit through Gadamer's reflection on language, the real point of this reflection is to confirm what had been present implicitly in the earlier parts of the book: the distinction between understanding and interpretation is not a *separation* and we learn to see the two as distinct only by coming to see them, at the same time, as 'belonging' together in a peculiarly intimate unity. It is this unity that we must now explore.

To interpret a text is to make it speak, and to do this one must be able to make it available in the language of the situation into which it is to speak. Interpretation is, then, a process of assimilation through which what is to be understood is drawn into the living discourse of the interpreter, so that, to use words of Gadamer which we have already met, its 'alienness' is 'overcome'. What Gadamer wants to get away from, however, is the idea of interpretation as a pedagogical device, i.e., as something that is undertaken by a resourceful teacher when faced with something particularly obscure in the text. Here, with one eye on one's audience and the other on the difficult passage, one 'interprets' the latter by finding an apt correspondence or analogy between it and some concept or theme with which the former is already familiar. In this kind of 'interpretation', one already understands the text and, secure in this possession, has merely to find an adroit way of mediating it to one's audience. Interpretation, in its primary sense, however, does not afford one the luxury of this distance; it is already at work in one's very act of understanding. One does not understand at all, in other words, without at the same time interpreting. For to understand something is to make it one's own. And there is no other way of making it one's own except by finding a home for it in the language in which one lives. The crucial point here is the simultaneity and inextricability of understanding and interpretation. The language of the interpretation does not merely offer what is understood a means of presenting itself. Rather the presenting *is* the understanding, and the words have, as it were, no being of their own but, in a kind of complete self-effacement, lose it to that which they say: "The linguistic explicitness that the process of understanding gains through interpretation does not create a second sense apart from that which is understood . . . the interpretative concepts are not as such thematic in understanding. Rather it is their nature to disappear behind what they bring, in interpretation, into speech. . . . The possibility of understanding is dependent on this kind of mediating interpretation."[16] Here language is not as it appears in those instrumentalist (or, as Collingwood would say, "technical") theories of language which we have already rejected: "The interpreter does not use words and concepts like an artisan who takes his tools in his hands and then puts them away."[17] Not the least reason, from my point of view, why it is worth following Gadamer through his reflections on language is that we see very clearly here the limitations of techne. But I shall return to this presently.

Whether one speaks, as I have just done, of language putting itself out for thought or, as I did earlier in an apparently contrary formulation, of the way in which thought is delivered over to language, both of these ways of putting things gesture toward the same reality: "the intimate unity of thought and language."[18] We have already seen that this unity was resisted by Plato, and we might not expect it to fare any better with Aristotle, who, as the self-professed founder of logic, was, after all, the most successful of the *logos* philosophers in laying down paths of thought that were invulnerable to "the prejudice of language and its naive teleology."[19] Gadamer believes, however, that Aristotle gives us a very good account of how our experience of the world assembles and articulates itself according to the "natural logic of language"—albeit not his own explicit intention. Gadamer refers to his favorite image (from *Posterior Analytics* 2.19) of the troops in battle regrouping themselves, which serves for Aristotle as a depiction of the way in which our experiences gradually come to assume the universality of 'experience' (*empeiria*) and of concepts, but which also provides, in Gadamer's view, the perfect way of understanding how a child learns to speak: by a kind of natural expansion and assimilation, with no conscious master plan, but with new words miraculously finding their place in relation to 'old' ones which they subtly modify, all growing together into a unity which contains ever finer differentiations.

What Gadamer sees here is not the happy coincidence that one brilliant image can capture two different processes; rather, the process of growing into our language *is* at the same time the process of introducing differentiation and order into our world: "experience is not wordless to begin with and then an object of reflection by being named, by being subsumed under the universality of the word. Rather, it is of the nature of experience itself that it seeks and finds words that express it."[20] This seeking and finding is, in fact, the primary process of concept formation which keeps pace with the growing complexity of the way in which we experience the world. It is a very inadequate account of the nature and role of concepts, then, to suppose that we learn a concept through a process of abstracting what is common to different things (this commonality becoming the bearer of the name) and that we then use it to cover the particulars which we recognize as included in its universality. This "logic of definition" fails to account for the continual improvization within "the free universality of language"[21] whereby, very often through the untrammeled expansiveness of *metaphor*, "what emerges is a new, more specific word-formation which does more justice to the particular features of the subject matter."[22]

Gadamer is well aware that this "living metaphoric nature of language" (or "the natural formation of concepts that takes place in language") was overshadowed by Aristotle's concern to establish the lineaments of a new, well-founded *epistēmē*, based on strict classification according to genus and species, and governed by explicitly formulated logical procedures. From the vantage point of such a superior science this essential metaphoric nature "is pushed to the side and instrumentalized into a rhetorical figure called metaphor";[23] its truly constitutive and productive role in thought (even as a kind of "advance work" for logic itself) is no longer recognized. And yet my point here is that, despite this, Gadamer still calls attention to the fact that in the brief treatment of induction (*epagōgē*) at the very end of his treatise on scientific method,[24] Aristotle "left open in the most intelligent way, the question of how universal concepts are formed"; and this, for Gadamer, is enough to suggest that Aristotle, even if only implicitly, "was taking account of . . . the natural formation of concepts by language."[25]

2. Finitude and the 'Infinity' of Language

While Gadamer can, as it were, sweep from behind the imposing structure of Aristotle's logic some undeveloped insights into the nature of language, the full significance that language comes to assume for him can be comprehended only in the context of his recapitulation of the whole philosophical tradition, a recapitulation which, put very schematically, leads him to the following "reckoning of profits and losses."[26] The notion of 'subjectivity' and the correlative notion of scientific 'objectivity,' which are so deeply entrenched in modern consciousness, and provide the basis for our wholesale projects of domination and control, must be deconstructed. In trying to do this, much can be gained by going back to the Greek con-

ception of a harmony or 'belongingness' between the human mind and
being—so that the 'subject' no longer stands in sovereign detachment but
recognizes itself as constituted through its participation in a divinely pre-
established order. This belongingness is the deepest truth of our existence.
Classical thought, however, for all its admirable qualities, provides a way
of formulating it which no longer suffices. With Heidegger, we must be
prepared to convict Socratic philosophy, with its dominant concept of substance as 'what-is-to-hand', of already secreting that "ontological prejudice"
which modern positivism does no more than exploit and make fully explicit. Moreover, we are constrained (especially "in the face of an experience of history that is no longer dominated by the knowledge of salvation")[27] to make no claims on the idea of an Infinite Mind, which in Greek
(and more explicitly in medieval) metaphysics was the ultimate basis of
the transcendental correspondence between intellect and being (or the
'ontological truth') that was the precondition of the truth of human cognition. But if we want to retrieve this correspondence, while at the same
time being constrained to let go of what held it together in the whole
tradition of classical metaphysics (right up to Hegel), where can we turn?
Here is a passage in which Gadamer very concisely formulates this problem and suggests his answer:

> the task of metaphysics continues, though certainly as a task that cannot
> again be solved by metaphysics, that is by going back to an infinite intel-
> lect. Hence we must ask: are there finite possibilities of doing justice to
> this correspondence? Is there a grounding of this correspondence that does
> not venture to affirm the infinity of the divine mind and yet is able to do
> justice to the infinite correspondence of the soul and being? I contend that
> there is. There is a way that attests to this correspondence, one towards which
> philosophy is ever more clearly directed—the way of language.[28]

While this 'way of language' is only being cleared in twentieth-century
philosophy (and in the tradition of Wittgenstein and Austin as well as
in that of Heidegger),[29] still the appropriation of *logos* philosophy by a
Christian theology burdened with the task of conceptualizing the Divine
Incarnation in history had already made important gains in this direction. The very unGreek ideas of Trinity (a God as not only personal but
tri-personal), Creation (a gratuitous act of this God), and Incarnation
(the 'folly' of His becoming a human mortal)[30] had given a force to contingency and history that would have been unthinkable in a Greek theology of timeless, changeless self-thinking thought. And in trying to make
sense of these ideas, while at the same time taking over some of the basic
categories of Greek thought (and of course *logos* is already inscribed in
the prologue to St. John's Gospel), a whole tradition of reflection from

Augustine and neo-Platonism through high scholasticism in St. Thomas up to the nominalism of Nicholas of Cusa was driven to give a central role to language; in doing so it went a fair distance toward recognizing the intimacy of thought and word and in particular how intrinsic linguistic utterance is to the peculiar discursiveness of human thought itself. In attempting to find within the natural order some analogical basis for understanding the mysterious unity and distinctness of the Father and the Incarnate Son, this theological reflection had turned to the relationship between understanding and its expression in the *verbum*. The Son was likened to the perfect Word which 'proceeds' or 'emanates' from the act of understanding and has its whole being simply in uttering it. The great contribution of this tradition of reflection, however, lay not so much in opening up a distinction between thought and word and then conceiving the two as belonging together in an indissoluble union; it lay rather in working out the negative moment in this analogy, i.e., in its clarification of the *difference* between the complete utterance that is the one infinite Word of God and the piecemeal articulation, in a multiplicity of words, of finite human thought.

Gadamer himself transforms the insight into finitude contained in this tradition of Trinitarian speculation into a more radical reflection which sees the finite nature of the human mind not as a limitation on its powers of apprehension—which is to be pointed up by reference to the perfect act of knowledge through which God, in self-knowledge, knows all being —but, rather, as pertaining to its profound 'belongingness' with being itself. This is his nonmetaphysical retrieval of the "infinite correspondence of the human soul and being." It is an ontology of finitude: of *finitude*, because the infinity here lies not in a perfect self-presence of soul or in an indivisible totality of being but, on the contrary, in the endlessly ramifying movement through which a 'complicated' soul and a multifarious world seek each other out; and an *ontology*, because through this movement the 'world' is not just re-presented *per modum recipientis* but actually presents itself. The movement we speak of here is language itself, a movement of the soul which is at the same time a movement of being. The language that comes into being with understanding has what Gadamer calls an "eventual" character; it is "the coming-into-language of the thing itself."[31] If man is, as Heidegger says, the shepherd of being, this is because, in Gadamer's words, "language [is] more the language of things than the language of man."[32]

I want to examine now the peculiar kind of 'infinity' that unfolds in our language—without at all preventing this language from being the 'record' of our finitude.[33] I have been speaking of language as a 'movement' because it is impossible for any word or set of words to contain in itself all that it says. A word is never merely itself but is always silently invoking other words that qualify, restrict, enhance, or explain it: "nothing that is said has truth simply in itself but refers instead backwards and forwards to what is unsaid."[34] Words never allow us to lay hold of their meaning in a clean snatch; they entangle us in the countless connections that bind them to other words. Indeed each modest combination of words that essays a sense is charged with the energy of the whole language, so that we cannot understand what it actually says without at the same time having some sense of the 'world' that is virtually present in it. What I said earlier about words doing their work by disappearing in favor of what they present must not be taken to imply that they, as it were, release us from themselves into meaning; to the contrary they deliver their meaning only by drawing us further into words. This is the "linguistic nature [*Sprachlichkeit*] of human experience of the world"[35] which, in Gadamer's view, the dialectics of Plato and of Hegel, for all their deep riddling out of the one and the many, fell short of. It is, in Gadamer's vivid formulation, a

> dialectic of the word, which assigns to every word an inner dimension of multiplication: every word breaks forth as if from a centre and is related to a whole, through which alone it is a word. Every word causes the whole of the language to which it belongs to resonate and the whole of the view of the world which lies behind it to appear. Thus every word, in its momentariness, carries with it the unsaid, to which it is related by responding and indicating. The occasionality of human speech is not a casual imperfection of its expressive power; it is, rather, the logical expression of the living virtuality of speech, that brings a totality of meaning into play, without being able to express it totally. All human speaking is finite in such a way that there is within it an infinity of meaning to be elaborated and interpreted.[36]

3. Limitations of the 'Statement' and the Synthesis of Hermeneutical Ideas in Reflection on Language

Gadamer develops the implications of this dialectic of language by way of a deepened critique of the 'statement';[37] if we look briefly now at this critique we will see that the various themes of his hermeneutics which we met in the previous chapter are encompassed in it. It is perhaps inevitable that we should assert ourselves against the centrifugal and dispersing tendencies of language by attempting to encapsulate a clear and definite meaning in a precise and totally explicit statement. And certainly Gadamer is not issuing any dispensation from the obligation to exercise a fastidious care in one's writing and speech. But he wants us to be under no illusion about what this means. It does *not* mean that one can ever succeed in prizing what one has to say out of the virtuality of its supporting context; it means rather that one does one's best to make the strength of this virtuality present in it. One tries to learn "the art of writing in such a way that the thoughts of the reader are stimulated and held in productive movement"—which is not at all an art in the sense of a rhetorical skill or style, a kind of virtuosity with language as if the latter were something extrinsic to thought, but rather "consists entirely in one's being led to think the material through."[38] Or we find the same exigence expressed elsewhere in *Truth and Method* thus: "To say what one means . . . to make oneself understood means to hold what is said together with an infinity of what is not said in the unity of one meaning and to ensure that it be understood in this way."[39]

One can never fully ensure this, of course, and it is here precisely that one depends on the hermeneutical sensitivity of one's audience. One's dependence is greater, we may immediately note, when one is writing rather than speaking. The paradigm object of all hermeneutical activity, clearly, is the written word deposited and transmitted in texts. This written word has overcome the evanescence and occasionality of the speaking voice: "its detachment from a specifically addressed recipient or reader has given it a life of its own. What is fixed in writing has raised itself publicly into a sphere of meaning in which everyone who can read has an equal share."[40] And yet this conquest of speech by writing is secured at a high cost—and has been worthwhile at all only if it proves to be temporary. At the root of Gadamer's whole hermeneutics, indeed, is a kind of holy dissatisfaction with the state of the written word. It is a weak, one might say a helpless, state that language falls into when it is written down —unless, that is, it has the good fortune to be rescued by an able interpreter.[41] And such rescuing always takes the form of restoring it to a kind of speech. This was the whole point of Gadamer's appeal to the model of conversation (which, we may remember, was the point of departure for his extensive inquiry into the mysterious nature of language). For the interpreter rescues his text from "the alienation in which it finds itself" (i.e., just by being written down) precisely by bringing it back into "the living presence of conversation."[42] The full, and entirely nonfigurative, import of Gadamer's appeal to conversation is brought out most clearly, I believe, in the following passage:

> Precisely this is what characterises a dialogue, in contrast with the rigid form of the statement that demands to be set down in writing: that here language, in the process of question and answer, giving and taking, talking at cross purposes and seeing each other's point, performs that communica-

tion of meaning which, with respect to the written tradition, is the task of hermeneutics. Hence it is more than a metaphor, it is a memory of what originally was the case, to describe the work of hermeneutics as a conversation with the text.[43]

In this work of conversation one tries to bring the text back to the virtuality from which it issues (as one might restore to the open ground a plant whose roots have been potted); and since this is the 'infinite' virtuality of language itself one finds oneself in an openness where the intentions of the author and the intentions that one may have brought to one's reading can be brought toward each other and surpassed in a new concretion of meaning. This is, I think, what Gadamer means when he says: "the fusion of horizons that takes place in understanding is the proper achievement of language."[44] This virtuality of language is, of course, proportionate to the inexhaustibility of the thing itself on which the interpreter and text are co-intent—or, better, which is at the center of their conversation. It was this thing which presented itself in the first place in the text and which now, through the interpretation and the entry into the whole virtuality of language that is instinct with it, has the opportunity of, as it were, reimmersing itself in its field of possibilities in order to emerge again in a new presentation of itself.

The fact that we can speak with such apparent ease about the 'virtuality' of language should not lull us into thinking that it is something over which we preside. We may be supported by it, but we cannot summon it or make it available. And yet it is our element and its containing us is far from being a containment. It reveals our finiteness but does not define it. The fact that we cannot fully comprehend it or make it exhaustively our own turns out to be a favor: for we get to participate in its very inexhaustibility. The 'I-lessness' of language means that it is never 'mine', and yet this very fact allows me to share in the boundless expansiveness of this 'we' to whom the world, in language, is ever disclosing itself.[45]

Nor is this 'we' confined to my contemporaries, for it includes, just insofar as there is an unbrokenness of language, men and women of all history: "the mode of being of tradition . . . is language."[46] And it is because of the peculiar availability and unavailability of language to us that our 'effective-historical consciousness' is such as it is. If the tradition has lived on in language, it is only by having lived on into our language and so become part of us. This is its being as 'effective history'. But even when we seem to rise, through disciplined study, to an *interpretation* of tradition, the 'effective-historical consciousness' that we thus acquire does not succeed in objectifying the tradition or, in other words, in canceling out its effects in ourselves. This is so quite simply because this consciousness is realized only in language, and language *never* releases a world as 'object': "As little as 'world' is made objective in language so little is effective-history the object of hermeneutical consciousness."[47]

The fact that language never gives us the thing in an enclosed space as 'object' does not abrogate the possibility of truth. Rather, truth is to be found precisely by entering on the path which the thing itself continually opens up within language. Our finitude is such that it allows us into the inner infinity of language, and truth arises here when we allow ourselves to be led on by the movement of the thing itself in language. A true interpretation, then, is reached not by any intuitive leap into the mind of the author but rather by going with what the text has to say about the thing, on a movement of thought where one comes to understand the thing better and to understand the text better in the light of this understanding of the thing to which it contributes. This movement of thought is always progressive only in a piecemeal way, advancing and doubling back on itself, confirming here, entering a reservation there, never providing short cuts to an understanding of the thing which would allow one superiority over the text but always insisting rather on the courtesy that is due to the latter as a partner on the search. What we are talking about here again, of course, is conversation. It is in conversation that language really comes into its own: "language has its true being only in conversation."[48] And to say that interpretation *is* conversation is simply to point out that "interpretation shares in the discursiveness of the human mind, which is able to conceive the unity of the object only in successiveness."[49]

This discursiveness that unfolds in language is not, in fact, properly understood simply as a function of 'the human mind'. It is 'the things themselves' that take the initiative and reveal themselves in this way in language: "Being that can be understood is language."[50] The human mind partakes of this as play—as a playing that is really a being played. For, in the end, the play here is "the play of language itself, which addresses us, proposes and withdraws, asks and fulfils itself in the answer."[51] Moreover the playfulness here resides not only in the way in which our minds are carried along in particular conversations. For we learn the language in the first place by being irresistibly drawn into it as into a game (in Merleau-Ponty's words, "the whole of the spoken language surrounding the child snaps him up like a whirlwind, tempts him by its internal articulations"[52]); and it is as an extension of this same game that the language itself develops over history: "the life of language consists in the constant playing further of the game that we began when we first learned to speak."[53]

If we ask how it is that our human mode of being is such that we

are carried up in this playful movement, this *event,* of language, Gadamer suggests that the best answer to this limit-question is through a retrieval of the Platonic idea of the beautiful. (Here, we may note, he has
come full circle; for his book had opened with a discussion of art and now
we discover that the mode of being of an artwork is not confined to a special 'aesthetic' sphere but is in the end simply the fundamental mode of
being itself. There is, I suggest, a close correspondence between Gadamer's conclusion here and the way in which Collingwood too, precisely
in the reflection on language to which his whole inquiry leads him, ends
up suggesting that art does not belong in any special sphere, since *all speech,*
simply *qua* expression, is an artistic activity.) The beautiful (*to kalon*) is
that to which the soul has no more resistance than the healthy eye has
to light. Its appeal, unlike that of the useful (*to chrēsimon*), does not depend on something else but rather by its own sheer radiance "it draws
directly towards itself the desire of the human soul."[54] For Plato the beautiful was that which appeared in total transparency as itself, so that there
was full *alētheia* or truthful disclosure, with no loss at all between its idea
and its appearance. It simply irrupted, as it were, into our human world
so as to disable, even before they could begin, any strategies we might
have had for a defensive reception of it. This idea of the beautiful was
a kind of Platonic "undercurrent" in scholastic metaphysics, where it was
assigned an intermediate position between the true and the good as one
of the 'transcendental' ideas that were coterminous with being itself. In
Gadamer's retrieval, the shining forth of the beautiful is assimilated to
being's manifestation of itself as comprehensible in language. In language,
being does not fall short of itself. This is because of what Gadamer (following Hegel) calls the 'speculative' character of language, i.e., the fact
that it is not a tool which man can interpose between himself and being
but rather, like light, is something which has no way of being present
except through those things which it presents.

When we speak of language like this we must always remind ourselves, however, that we do not refer to the lifeless cliches or the frantic
propagandese that pass themselves off as language. If language is a game,
this also means that it can go slack, and then it is no longer a disclosure
of being; it has become a possession but it is no longer an event. This
event is understanding, and language has its proper tension when it is
bearing the strain of understanding coming forth in it. Language, in its
speculative self, can become so available to understanding that it disappears as 'language' and simply *is* the realization of understanding; but
it never does this at the bidding, nor is it ever a secure achievement, of
the one who through it comes to understand. Rather this person has given
herself to the movement of language in which she can never quite steady

herself, when the game, as it were, takes over and she is "suddenly the catcher of a ball:"[55] understanding happens and being is present — in the sense both of self-revelation and of gift.

4. Beyond 'Substance Metaphysics': Reflection on Language as a Way of Profiling Techne and Phronesis

Our excursus on language has given us an opportunity for a final resumé of all Gadamer's major themes. But the question surely arises as to whether in bringing us into ontology — if not, indeed, dangerously close to poetry — it has not brought us far afield from the philosophy of practice and from our own overall theme of phronesis and techne in Aristotle. It is this question that we must now take up.

We have already seen that according to Gadamer "Aristotle's account of experience left open in the most intelligent way the question of how concepts are formed";[56] and that Gadamer is able to see in this Aristotelian account a very good reflection of the way language, "with a quite undogmatic freedom,"[57] acts as a force for order in our experience. The seriousness or degree of explicitness with which Aristotle himself reflected on language is not the decisive factor here, however. More important for my purpose is the fact that Gadamer, in his reflection on language (which is simply the culmination of his whole reflection on understanding and not at all a treatment of language *per se* — whatever that might be) is all the time showing the uncongeniality between language and techne (so that, in Heidegger's words, it is only when language or thinking "slips out of its element" that it "replaces this loss by procuring a validity for itself as *technē*").[58] Moreover Gadamer is doing this in the most radical way by pitting himself against the whole metaphysical framework which, as I shall attempt to show in Part 2, provided a conceptual matrix for the articulation of techne and was at the same time most perspicuously illustrated by it (techne). Gadamer's approach to the tradition is certainly less violent than Heidegger's, but neither the piety nor the urbanity[59] of his discourse should obscure the fact that "the first and last insight" which he is always trying to work out is one that "transcends the horizon of substance metaphysics."[60] (Nor, incidentally, should we miss this fact simply because Gadamer's more obvious and immediate target is the modern framework built around the concepts of subjectivity and scientific objectivity; for, following Heidegger, he sees these concepts themselves as "a metamorphosis of the concept of substance"[61] bequeathed by classical metaphysics.)

This sustained act of 'distancing' with respect to the dualisms of matter and form, and end and means, that the overwhelming influence of Aristotelian metaphysics had made so ready to hand for all subsequent thought, releases our thinking into a new and unaccustomed medium. But in doing so it introduces us to a perspective (or a 'prejudice') that can help us, in turning back to a reinterpretation of Aristotle, to bring into sharper focus some basic tendencies and tensions in his thought. This attempt by Gadamer to think beyond method or technique puts us in a position to search out with greater clarity the nature and limits of the great original attempt, by both Plato and Aristotle, to encapsulate in the concept of techne a kind of knowledge that would provide a bulwark against contingency in our worldly projects, including thinking itself. And, in particular, it enables us to look back with heightened interest at the way in which Aristotle, while he was consolidating the Platonic notion of techne within a more developed conceptual framework, at the same time — without any very ostentatious declaration of intent and not always, it must be said, with total consistency — contrived to remove the whole domain of worthwhile human practice (*eupraxia*) from the jurisdiction of techne, and to assign it instead to a type of knowledge which was itself wedded to contingency and which — radically altering Platonic usage — he called phronesis.

If we are now in an advantaged 'hermeneutical situation' with respect to these Aristotelian concepts, perhaps we can say that this is because of an extreme but peculiarly symmetrical difference between the Greek 'condition' and our own. The Greek *ēthos* (as depicted in the great tragedies and illuminated somewhat for us in chapter 3 by Arendt) was one in which ordinary experience remained fragile, exposed to the vicissitudes of fortune (*tuchē*) by one's dependence on others, by the chronic possibility of conflict inherent in the plurality of one's engagements, and by the unruly depths within oneself which gave to one's actions (especially from one's own point of view as agent) a profound inscrutability.[62] Given the strength of this *ēthos,* what was heroic in Greek philosophy, we might say, was precisely its attempt, centered on the concept of techne, to wrest from all this contingency some measure of reliability and control. But if it is the case (as Collingwood and Arendt have wanted to persuade us) that the very *success* of the Socratic philosophers in this attempt has led to *our* inhabiting an *ēthos* in whch vulnerability, as it were, loses all official recognition, then the heroic attempt in contemporary philosophy is one that leads precisely in the opposite direction to the Greek one. And it is for this reason, pointed in the direction in which it is pointed, that contemporary philosophy all the more keenly recognizes an affinity between itself and the unheroic ethics of Aristotle, which never aspired to a loftier task than that of "saving the appearances" — i.e., vindicating the

intuitions that were contained in an always more or less haphazard practice of life and which, significantly in the present context, were expressed
in the language of ordinary speech.[63]

There is something about the weight which Gadamer puts on language which we have not yet attended to sufficiently. If we advert to it
now, it will bring into clearer relief the deep affinity between his whole
approach and Aristotle's ethical-political philosophy. At the same time
it will show that although the appeal to phronesis (which we met in the
previous chapter) occurs before the 'linguistic turn' in the final part of
Truth and Method and although Aristotle himself does not elaborate on
the connection between phronesis and language,[64] still this appeal is not
displaced from the center nor made less congruous when language emerges
in the foreground. What I am referring to here can be brought out obliquely
and perhaps surprisingly by showing how it puts Gadamer at a distance
from his mentor, Heidegger, while at the same time it brings him close
to our first interlocutor, Newman.

Gadamer himself tells us that when he brought language to the foreground of his hermeneutical reflection he was trying "to support the struggle
led by Heidegger in his almost tragic grappling against a fall back into
the language of metaphysics."[65] And yet it is precisely the *difference* here
between Gadamer and Heidegger that is instructive. For Heidegger, being is, through thinking, "on the way to language." But he laid overwhelming stress on the corruption of current languages: in their very grammar
is the worm of metaphysics. And so, little wonder if all around us language "surrenders itself to our mere willing and trafficking as an instrument of domination over beings."[66] It is this dark diagnosis of the present
state of language that makes Heidegger go to such desperate lengths in
his own linguistic usage. So tarnished is the state of language that being
has become almost ineffable. Hence his own oracular style: his rude shaking up of old words, his shocking neologisms and "half-poetic attempts
at discourse." Hence too his preoccupation with the poet Hölderlin as well
as his strenuous attempts to recover something of the original simplicity
of the pre-Socratics.

Now Gadamer shares Heidegger's sense of the ubiquitous menace
of the technocratic consciousness, and he does not deny that in poetry
there is a uniquely immediate disclosure, an epiphany, of being. What
sets him apart from Heidegger is his refusal to believe in the ultimate
corruption of ordinary language, his steadfast attempt, we might say, to
"save the appearances" of our everyday speech. However deep the inden-
tations made in it by an obsessional tendency to objectification, ordinary
language still has not lost its affinity with being. In the unesoteric medium of conversation, "objectification—the uniform accessibility of every-

thing to everyone" (Heidegger)[67] — can be undercut and, beyond the capacity of any individual subjectivity, being can come to presence. In an essay written some years after *Truth and Method* Gadamer has this to say about what he had done in the book: "I have pointed towards the interchange of dialogue and to the dialogical structure of language in which an entirely undogmatic dialectic is enacted, and I have shown the way a communal language is shaped in it beyond the explicit awareness of the individual speaker and how a step-by-step unveiling of being comes about in this way."[68] And he goes on to underscore the essential sobriety of this undertaking when he points out (later in the same piece) that through it "the extreme consequences of thought heightened by Nietzsche with anguished enthusiasm and by Heidegger with eschatological pathos found a counter-poise in the continuity of a linguistically interpreted order of life that is constantly being built up and renewed in family, society and state."[69]

Here we see the full appropriateness of Gadamer's appeal to Aristotle (which corresponds, we might say, to Heidegger's appeal to the pre-Socratics) and his kinship with Newman. A greater contrast in philosophical styles can scarcely be imagined than that which exists between Newman and Gadamer: the English priest who engages the reader directly in concerns which he takes to be shared by both of them and who is disinclined to tangle with other philosophers except insofar as they speak very immediately to these concerns, and the German professor, available, it seems, only in a discourse which is always heavily laden with other discourses, the philosopher's philosopher who summons with consummate ease onto his every page all the great (as well as many of the obscure) figures from the philosophical tradition.[70] Still, at this point, the resemblance between them can be brought out by showing how Aristotle, as it were, reflects them back to each other. We have already seen that according to Newman the integrity of the faith of 'ordinary believers' could not be undermined by the most theoretical inquiries, whether of theologians or of thoroughly secularized scientists, and that his own 'theory' (centered on the Illative Sense) was intended precisely to show this, by not only vindicating the implicit motives of belief but by showing that the most rigorously and explicitly derived propositions of theory had their own roots in a hidden subsoil of the mind. We can now set beside this Gadamer's reliance on the resourcefulness of an always tentative and precarious conversation, so that even if this reliance should seem like "blind optimism in an age of faith in science and of the flattening technological destruction of all that has flourished,"[71] still the more elevated resources of theory provide no greater prospect of deliverance. Gadamer frankly confesses that the place of 'conversation' in his own thought is linked to "a profound skepticism regarding the role of intellectuals and especially of philosophy in humanity's household of life."[72] This skepticism endures, we may suppose, unless, like Aristotle and Newman — and Gadamer himself — the 'intellectual' makes it his task to appropriate into thought what is nourishing and enabling in our ordinary practice of life. For, as Gadamer roundly asserts: "the great equilibrium of what is living, which sustains and permeates the individual in his privacy as well as in his social constitution and in his view of life, also encompasses those who think."[73]

5. Theory and Practice: The Extent of Gadamer's Appeal to Aristotelian Practical Philosophy and Phronesis

Here we have come upon an issue which we have not addressed so far and which will allow us now to bring out one final and very prominent strand in Gadamer's Aristotelianism: the relationship between theory and practice. That Gadamer sees understanding or interpretation as in some sense a practice is already familiar to us: we saw that religious and legal interpretations, which have manifestly practical import, are not so much special cases as paradigm examples of the practical dimension of *all* interpretation. It is not that interpretations may become practical by being applied in some "really practical" context, but rather that they are practical anyhow since they arise within a prior engagement which is never detached and they are already an "application" in the sense of a modification of the stand that one takes in the world. This, we will remember, was the basis for Gadamer's appeal to Aristotle's concept of phronesis — which is after all *practical* knowledge — as an exemplary model of the kind of knowledge which he himself wants to disclose in the act of interpretation. (Within the *linguistic* dimension that has since become explicit, this practical structure continues to be reflected in the way in which language is already there around us as an ethos so that "doing things with words"[74] is never the masterful execution of a technique but calls for the kind of traits — responsiveness, flexibility, and perceptiveness in discerning what is needed — that are the hallmarks of phronesis.)[75] Given all this, however, we are now led by our immediately preceding discussion to ask: what is the nature and status of Gadamer's own theory of hermeneutical experience, i.e., the theory that he himself elaborates in *Truth and Method*? This question is only lightly touched on in the book itself, but it is expressly raised in several later essays where Gadamer provides a thoroughly Aristotelian answer.

This answer can be put very schematically: just as understanding is modeled on phronesis so hermeneutics (i.e., the theory of understanding)

is modeled on practical philosophy—or, put somewhat differently: hermeneutics is to understanding as practical philosophy is to phronesis. To gain
enlightenment from this we now have to ask: what is this relationship
between practical philosophy and phronesis, and why does Gadamer find
it an attractive exemplar of the relationship that exists between his own
reflective (second-order) work and what transpires in the (first-order) labors
of interpreters, including his own? Here we are squarely back with Aristotle. For him phronesis was practical knowledge. Not only was it not itself theory but neither was it the *application* of theory to particular cases.
Aristotle's schema appeals to Gadamer in the first instance because it gets
us away from the modern conception of theory as generalized lawlike
knowledge and of practice, then, as the domain where this theory is exploited or applied. Insofar as there was a parallel to this in the Greek
framework it lay not in theory but rather in techne, a systematic body
of knowledge, in a specific field, which the good maker could call upon
for guidance in his actual projects in that field (e.g., house building or
medicine).[76] Theory in the sense that it had for the Socratic philosophers
(as *theoria, sophia* or *epistēmē*) lay askew of our modern framework because it had no application and also because it could be conceived as itself
a kind of practice (*praxis tis*) in that it not only answered to the criterion
that its *ergon* should not be external to it (that it should, in other words,
be an *energeia*) but also in that it represented, on the part of the person
"practicing" it, a commitment (*prohairesis,* which, as Gadamer points
out, means "preference and prior choice") to a certain way of life (*bios*).
While theory could legitimately be considered as praxis, praxis in its more
specific sense, of course (and especially when it went by the name of *eupraxia*
and so had approbation written into it), referred to a life of engagement
with one's fellow citizens in the affairs of the polis, a life which, presup-
posing the prior fulfilment of the needs of survival, could exemplify various excellences of character (*ēthos*) such as justice, courage, self-control,
and magnanimity.

   Now, in his ethical-political writings Aristotle made this latter life
the object of theory. In doing so he was following the anthropological turn
of Socrates—the turn from cosmological to moral/psychological/political
concerns—but with a heightened sense of the methodological difficulties
involved in this turn. Clearly this was not theory in the strict sense (of
mathematics, theology, and physics) if for no other reason than that its
object was a highly fluid and changeable reality. Could it then be accorded
what we might call the quasi-theoretical status of techne—i.e., a treatiselike systematization of the principles (*archai*) and explanatory factors (*aitiai*)
that account for competent performance in specific areas of endeavor? It
will be an upshot of my own argument in Part 2 that there was a looseness

in Aristotle's own reflection on techne which does not make it easy for us to answer this question in his name. Here of course we are concerned with Gadamer's response to Aristotle. There is, I believe, a certain ambivalence in this response which may be taken to reflect something that remained unresolved in Aristotle's own treatment. In one essay he tells us that "Aristotle thought this issue through [i.e., "the mutual implication between theoretical interest and practical action"] with complete lucidity."[77] Yet in another closely related essay, referring to "the specific condition of the scientific quality which holds sway in these areas" (i.e., areas where there is a second-order attempt to systematize first-order performance) he maintains that "Aristotle himself characterizes them only with the vague indication that they are less exact"[78] and that he did not reflect, as we think that we must, on the distinction between the "knowledge of a physician or a craftsman or a politician that is always to be found in application" and on the other hand "knowledge about what may be said and taught in general about such knowing."[79]

Despite these reservations, however, Gadamer still feels that the specific case of the relationship between ethical systematization and ethical practice "called forth a certain methodological reflection on Aristotle's part."[80] He saw that practical philosophy needs "a unique kind of legitimation"[81] — and was successful enough in formulating it to have made available what Gadamer has come to recognize as the best "exemplar" of the kind of "legitimacy" to which his own hermeneutics (set as it is in the inhospitable milieu created by the dominance of *modern* analytic-inductive sciences) can now lay claim. Two things in Aristotle's treatment of this matter stand out for Gadamer.

The first is his sensitivity to the uniqueness of the object-domain of practical philosophy — i.e., human practice itself. We might say that it was his conception of the peculiar texture of this object-domain that determined for Aristotle the nature of the theoretical reflection that supervened on it; this would be in accord with his general habit of granting priority to 'ontological' considerations in his reflections on the methodology of knowledge. We ought to notice, however, that there is a certain unavoidable circularity here. For we cannot really talk about the object domain independently of Aristotle's theoretical construal of it. It was, in other words, precisely in his ethical theory that the specificity of ethical practice emerged into more or less clear recognition. I say "more or less" because techne-activities recur most vexingly throughout all Aristotle's own writings on these matters — and by no means always in contexts where ethical activity is being set off against them.[82] Still, it seems clear that Aristotle's overall intention was to stress the fact that ethical practice is unique because of its not being confined to one easily circumscribable domain (where the principles and criteria of competence might be rigorously and exhaustively specifiable). Exertions in other fields are subordinate to purposes set by nature (e.g., gardening) or by another field which it serves (e.g., saddle making). To be sure, we cannot set over against these a kind of ethical practice into which we have imported the radical indeterminacy of Sartrian freedom: the recognition that Aristotle gives to the established ethos, and indeed to this ethos as an expression of nature (*phusis*), precludes this.[83] At the same time, however, bringing into play "the all-embracing problem of the good in human life," praxis involved free choice in situations which are complex and changing and therefore always calling for a flexible response. The stress which Aristotle puts on *prohairesis* (choice) in book 3 of the *Ethics* and especially the distinction which he makes between 'phronesis' and 'techne' in book 6—where he explicitly correlates phronesis with praxis and limits techne to poiesis or productive activity in specific fields—ensure that praxis is a unique kind of engagement, irreducibly different from any other.

Even if ethical practice is already, in the way I have suggested, within the embrace of ethical theory, we can still go on to ask what status this theory has and how, more precisely, it relates to the practice that is the object of its study. What can be reconstructed as Aristotle's answer to this question is the second factor which takes Gadamer's attention. It will be helpful to begin with negative indications. In the first place, Aristotle did not see himself as working out, on the smooth ground of 'theory', either a method or a set of laws which were then, through their application by practical reason, to bring order and system into an otherwise messy and irrational practice. But if it is not constructive in this sense, neither is it a kind of sifting of, and drawing ethical implications from, other unambiguously theoretical domains: "the expression 'practical philosophy' intends precisely to say that it makes no determinate use of arguments of a cosmological, ontological, or metaphysical sort for practical problems."[84] Nor again is ethical theory simply coincident with phronesis. This needs to be said if only because some Aristotelian commentators have claimed that it is[85]—that Aristotle's spelling out of the contours of the practical moral life is not essentially different from what any *phronimos*, if he cared to try, could accomplish. Gadamer is firmly against this interpretation. But what then, he has to ask, *is* the status of Aristotle's ethical-political theory? What purpose can it serve, especially when Aristotle, not unlike Rousseau,[86] goes out of his way to pour scorn on theoretical pretensions in this area and complements this by building into the well-developed moral consciousness itself (i.e., phronesis) an ability to "recognize the good and duty, with unsurpassable exactitude and most delicate sensitivity"?[87]

What we have just seen is the impossibility of giving any priority to theory over practice in the case of practical philosophy. What Aristotle gives us instead, Gadamer believes, is "an idea of knowledge that has taken the opposite path leading from practice towards making it aware of itself theoretically."[88] Aristotle's practical philosophy is, one might say, a theory which, designed precisely to protect practice against unwarranted theoretical incursions, bolsters it by showing how and why it must stand fast in its own peculiar strengths and modes of procedure. Theory here contributes to a heightened awareness on the part of the practiced moral agent of what is already implicit in his way of life. A person is not in a position to benefit from it, then—nor is Aristotle himself, or any other teacher, in a position to expound it—unless he is already a *spoudaios* or *phronimos*. (Phronesis is, then, if not identical with this theory, at least a necessary precondition of it; it is, we may say, the most important of the "special preconditions which are set for a student who can meaningfully receive instruction about the 'practical good'.")[89] The priority here clearly lies on the side of practice. In Gadamer's blunt statement of it: "*ēthos* for [Aristotle] is the *archē*, the 'that' from which all practical-political enlightenment has to set out."[90] And yet, while setting out from the already established ethos, this theory does intend to contribute to or benefit those engaged in the life of practice. Just because it does not, of itself, propose anything for application, this does not mean that it is 'pure theory'. On the contrary, "it cannot renounce the claim not merely to know but even to have a practical effect. In other words, as the science of the good in human life, it promotes that good itself."[91]

But given its thoroughly *a posteriori* approach, how can practical philosophy actually be *practical*—in the sense of contributing anything that is not already within the compass of concrete practical judgment itself? The answer is not through providing specific guidance—hence it only "clarifies the good in sketchy universality"—but rather through a kind of reinforcement which helps practical judgment to be more alert regarding the nature of its own task. Practical philosophy's apparently empty formulations such as '*hōs dei*', and '*hōs ho orthos logos*' are not "evasions relative to a more stringent terminological exigency but pointers to the concretization in which *aretē* alone can reach its determinacy." Aristotle's own analogy of making the target more perspicuous for the archer is one that appeals to Gadamer. This does not at all replace actual skillfulness with the bow, but it helps "to make aiming easier and to make the steadfastness of the direction of one's shooting more exact and better."[92] Similarly "it can be a kind of assistance in the conscious avoidance of certain deviations that ethically pragmatic instruction is capable of affording inasmuch as it aids in making present for rational consideration the ultimate purposes of one's actions."[93] And it is crucial here that the instructor does not see himself as purveying the "neutral specialized knowledge of the expert": with his students he is himself committed to a pursuit of the good, and so realizes that the kind of knowledge with which he deals "does not allow for the ideal of the non-participating observer but endeavors instead to bring to our reflective awareness the communality that binds everyone together."[94] As *philosophy*, practical philosophy is an articulation of what Gadamer calls the "universal desire to know"; and it is *practical* because this desire "does not break off at the point where concrete practical discernment is the decisive issue. The connection between the universal desire to know and concrete practical discernment is a reciprocal one."[95]

At this point the exemplary value to Gadamer of the Aristotelian precedent should be apparent. We have seen all along how in his own hermeneutics he has been rejecting "the ideal of the non-participating observer" and has been attempting "to bring to reflective awareness the communality that binds everyone together." And the reciprocity that we have just seen in Aristotle's schema is also likely to attract him. For while hermeneutics tries to reconstruct what actually happens in understanding, rather than to dictate from a supposedly superior vantage point what should happen ("it is not my intention to make prescriptions for the sciences or the conduct of life, but to try to correct false thinking about what they are"),[96] this reconstruction (or correction) must surely be capable of some edifying effect on the practice of understanding itself. 'Edification' is probably a good word to use here.[97] For it indicates a really internal relationship to the practitioner—it indicates, in fact, a change *in himself*—rather than the kind of external guidance that he might derive from 'method'. It is precisely the externality of method to the one using it that lies at the base of all Gadamer's skepticism about it. From the point of view of method itself, things are much too unreliable if a settled accomplishment on the part of the practitioner must be presupposed; but for Gadamer, no methodological sophistication can compensate for a lack of such accomplishment. (Here we may recall Newman's defense of what he called "the unsupersedable mental faculty" against the usurpations of a "technical apparatus.")

It is appropriate here to mention briefly Gadamer's appeal to ancient *rhetoric*. It seems clear to him that no amount of refinement in the theory of rhetoric can be of any avail if "natural giftedness for speaking is lacking."[98] And so rhetoric, too, offers a model which is fundamentally different to modern method insofar as "it presents itself more as a cultivation of a natural gift and as a theoretically heightened awareness of it."[99] We might indeed say that rhetoric exists in an even more 'neighborly' relationship, or offers a more proximate source of illumination, to hermeneutics, than practical philosophy does. For if rhetoric is the art of speech, hermeneutics, as we already know, "may be precisely defined as the art of bringing what is said or written to speech again."[100] The point here, however, is not to set rhetoric over against practical philosophy. For Gadamer sees rhetoric not as the sophistical art which was castigated by Plato in the *Gorgias,* and the *Sophist,* but rather as a reflection on speech which, because of the universality of speech, could rival philosophy in its claims and which for that very reason had to be taken up into philosophy itself. In fact it is so taken up by Plato in the *Phaedrus* and also by Aristotle in the *Rhetoric,* which presents "more a philosophy of human life as determined by speech than a technical doctrine about the art of speaking,"[101] and, therefore, despite its title (*Technē Rhētorikē*), is itself a modality of practical philosophy.

It is in relation to rhetoric that I may say something about Gadamer's balance of accounts between Plato and Aristotle. He is well aware that the decisive impulse for 'practical philosophy' was Aristotle's critique of "the Platonic idea of the good as an empty generality,"[102] and that the whole thrust of this philosophy may be seen as an attempt to undercut the 'intellectualism' of Socrates and Plato. And yet (a good example of his fidelity to his own quintessential dictum that "one has to make distinctions, to be sure, but even more one has to see things in their relatedness"),[103] far from casting Plato as the fall guy here, he brings out the neglected Plato — the one who "was no Platonist"[104] — and shows the essential continuity between him and Aristotle.

In the *Phaedrus,* Plato showed that genuine rhetoric is much more than the mere skill in argumentation and flattery represented by the sophists and that it is in fact "indissoluble from dialectic: persuasion that is really convincing is indissoluble from knowledge of the true."[105] Now this move on Plato's part might be seen not so much as a vindication of rhetoric as an annexation of it[106] if it were to turn out that he takes dialectic itself to be a techne. But it is just this "widely accepted view" of Plato that Gadamer challenges. Although 'techne' functioned as a leading paradigm of knowledge for Plato and although dialectical (i.e., philosophical) knowledge of the good might be seen as "the utmost fulfillment" of this paradigm, nonetheless this knowledge really explodes the paradigm insofar as it cannot be considered simply as the "highest learnable science."[107] Gadamer points to the dominance of the negative moment in Socrates's inquiries concerning the good:

> his own knowledge is *docta ignorantia,* and it is not called dialectic for nothing; only that individual knows who is capable of standing his ground right down to the final speech and response. . . . Only he is truly capable

of speaking who has acknowledged that to which he knows how to persuade people as something good and right and thereby is able to stand up for it. This knowledge of the good and this capability in the art of speaking does not mean a universal knowledge of 'the good'; rather it means a knowledge of that to which one has to persuade people here and now and how one is to go about doing this and in respect to whom one is to do it.[108]

Gadamer thus brings out the concreteness, flexibility, and attunement to the *kairos* of the knowledge possessed by the dialectical rhetorician. The latter "does not possess a special knowledge, but in his person he is the embodiment of dialectics or of philosophy."[109] He is, in fact, in being a dialectically endowed speaker, already a *phronimos*—even if this is a concept whose formal elaboration, and fuller disengagement from techne, we owe to Aristotle. And Plato's retrieval of rhetoric as dialectic in the *Phaedrus* can be seen, then, as having laid down the lines for Aristotle's own elaboration of rhetoric as an aspect of practical philosophy. For both of them, using these terms with their full Aristotelian resonance, "what is at issue for the dialectical rhetorician as well as for the statesman and in the leading of one's own life is the good. And this does not present itself as the *ergon*, which is produced by making, but rather as *praxis* and *eupraxis* (and that means as *energeia*)."[110]

But we must now come back and ask what all this has to do with hermeneutics. Gadamer uses a variety of expressions for the connection here: he speaks of practical philosophy as having a "neighborly affinity" with hermeneutics, or as providing it with an "example," a "readymade point of orientation," "a stronger clarification" (i.e., than anything deriving from the methodology of modern science) or "the only scholarly model." More helpful than any of these indications, however, is his perhaps most explicit statement: "practical philosophy is more than a mere methodological model for the hermeneutic sciences. It is also something like its substantive foundation."[111] Here, I believe, we are being invited to distinguish *two* claims. One is that hermeneutics is to understanding as practical philosophy is to phronesis (and praxis). Now so far this might be a merely formal claim, implying no very close relationship between the two sides—just as the proposition "an adult human is to a child as a cat is to a kitten" implies no great affinity between human and feline being. But, taking this as a 'vertical' claim, it becomes a great deal more substantial if we build onto it the horizontal claim which Gadamer is *also* making (and which we met in the previous chapter), namely, that understanding is modeled on phronesis/praxis. I want now to conclude with some brief remarks on the nature and scale of Gadamer's enterprise as it appears through this double reference to the Aristotelian precedent.

6. The Scope of Gadamer's Thought: Concluding Questions

Gadamer's overall claim is very large. It is true that he has all the time been exposing the inability of reason either to shed full light on our situation or to provide us with an instrument of unambiguous control over it; reason always remains within the "relentless inner tension between illumination and concealment" which is at the core of our finitude. And yet, if the claims of all self-inflated sciences and philosophies are to be rejected, hermeneutics, as the philosophy which both does this rejecting and at the same time brings our finitude into the clearest relief, itself comes to embody the highest aspirations of reason — a reason which now recognizes itself as irredeemably *practical*. Gadamer is not just looking to practical philosophy as a "scholarly model." He is doing nothing less than attempting to establish hermeneutics as the discipline that can serve the same function in contemporary culture that Aristotle envisaged for practical philosophy in the ancient world. The scale of Gadamer's ambition becomes apparent if we bear in mind that, for Aristotle, *politikē* was the most universal — in the sense of the most architectonic — of all knowledge, which assigned to other pursuits their proper roles in subordination to itself. Indeed, in Gadamer's deconstruction, hermeneutics must carry an even greater weight than Aristotle's practical philosophy did. For the latter was always to some degree overshadowed by the transcendent status of *theoria* or *sophia* (an overshadowing which we find not just in *E.N.* book 10 but even in book 6, where Aristotle brusquely remarks that "it is extraordinary that anyone should conceive *politikē* or *phronēsis* as most important unless man is the highest being in the world"[112] — something which, for him, is almost a self-evident nonsense).[113] For us now, on the other hand, with "the getting over of metaphysics,"[114] no such *theoria* is any longer possible. And so hermeneutics must assume the role not only of practical philosophy but of a practical philosophy which itself has to "take the place of a *theoria* whose ontological legitimation may be found only in an *intellectus infinitus* that is unknown to an existential experience unsupported by revelation."[115]

Gadamer's overarching claims are based on a particular conception of understanding and on the position of hermeneutics as the discipline that reflects on the conditions in which this understanding comes to fruition (though we must note here the same circularity that we noted in Aristotle — insofar as it is only within hermeneutical theory itself that we get to recognize this understanding for what it is). Now the conception of understanding that emerges — as we have already seen in relation to 'application' — is practical: "understanding, like action, always remains a risk . . . [it] is an adventure and like any other adventure is dangerous

. . . [and] affords unique opportunities as well. It is capable of contributing in a special way to the broadening of our human experiences, our self-knowledge, and our horizon, for everything understanding mediates is mediated along with ourselves."[116] The primary locus of such understanding, in Gadamer's treatment of it, is to be found in such disciplines as literary criticism, philology and history; but it need not be focused exclusively on written texts and so it embraces not only other disciplines such as interpretative sociology and anthropology but also everyday practical understanding among people in the life-world. Indeed when Gadamer gets to work on understanding, one of the things that he is chiefly concerned to show is the permeability to each other of disciplined scientific study and the perspective of the life-world: hermeneutics helps us "to see through the dogmatism of asserting an opposition and separation between the ongoing natural 'tradition' and the reflective appropriation of it."[117] (Or as he puts the same point in another piece: "the calm distance from which a middle-class educated consciousness takes satisfaction in its educational achievements misunderstands how much we are ourselves immersed in the game and are the stake in the game.")[118]

Moreover, it is not just the interpretative sciences and their relation to our 'common sense' understanding (which is also a self-understanding) that come within the scope of hermeneutical reflection, for this scope is truly universal and so includes also the natural or 'hard' sciences. Gadamer is well aware that there is "something comical" about "making prescriptions for science and recommending that it toe the line."[119] And yet he wants to show that, for all the methodological self-enclosure of these sciences, the *questions* that motivate them are not altogether immanently generated and that certainly their *effects* in terms of a whole technological reordering of the environment, have to be reabsorbed into the world of intersubjectively lived-out practice. And so in science and technology, too, understanding 'happens', and there may be something to be gained from a 'heightened awareness' of the peculiar prejudices that are operative in it; for if "the presuppositions of these possibilities of knowing and making remain half in the dark, cannot the result be that the hand applying the knowledge will be destructive?"[120] Such destructiveness need not be due to any malign subjective intent on the part of scientists, industrialists, administrators, or politicians. But it can scarcely be avoided if the sciences and technologies are allowed to harden into autonomous enclaves within the life-world, or much more so if—as their self-propelling force seems to make them ever more capable of doing—they lead to the colonization of the entire life-world itself. Even these apparently least hermeneutical of endeavors present a task which is at once hermeneutical and political: that of bringing them into a communal conversation, where their relatedness with everything else can be experienced and understood. "The hermeneutic task of integrating the monologic of the sciences into the communicative consciousness includes the task of exercising practical, social, and political reasonableness."[121]

Our predicament, much more acute surely than that of Aristotle's contemporaries or even of Hegel's, is to maintain in the midst of all our fragmenting and proliferating areas of endeavor some sense of a common world, or to find in language—"the most communal and communicative factor"—a way of presenting conflicts and differences of all kinds, and of still reaching for an agreement in which human solidarity is preserved and enhanced. This is primarily a practical task. But Gadamer believes that in dealing with it we can still look to philosophy—in the form of a hermeneutics in which the heritage of practical philosophy lives on. He does not minimize the task of this hermeneutics: "it has to bring everything knowable by the sciences into the context of mutual agreement in which we ourselves exist . . . [and] that links us with the tradition that comes down to us in a unity that is efficacious in our lives."[122]

If we began with a sense that hermeneutics was "a secondary and derivative concern, a modest chapter from the heritage of German idealism,"[123] its full scope as well as its practical intent cannot now escape us. Despite the restriction of his focus in *Truth and Method* to the areas of art and historiography, and despite the rootedness of the whole inquiry in an extraordinarily rich soil of humanistic learning or *Bildung*, Gadamer tells us in a later essay that his "only concern there was to secure a theoretical basis that would enable us to deal with the basic factor of contemporary culture, namely science and its industrial, technological utilization."[124] This "theoretical basis" is not to be established through any kind of primordial thinking that would deliver us from a cosmic night into which we are supposed to have fallen; Gadamer's nonlapsarian vision, as he readily acknowledges, means that his "divergence from Heidegger is fundamental."[125] As we are by now well aware, the theoretical basis to which he looks has its own basis in the ethos and language of an existing practice: "the displacement of human reality never goes so far that no forms of solidarity exist any longer . . . ; this is what in my opinion is the basis for the possibility of practical philosophy."[126]

But is this enough? Or has practice not been so debased in modern society that it needs a more resourceful theory—and one that is less parasitic on it itself—to come to its aid? And has Gadamer—whose masterly exposure of the unavoidability of prejudices does not free him from *his own* prejudices and who has indeed confessed to being "acutely aware of just how much I am caught up, one might say, in the tradition of German Romantic and post-Romantic philosophy"[127]—engaged at close enough quarters with the density of the scientific-technical reality in our world, or with the powerfully entrenched forces that act against all forms of human solidarity?

If these are the right questions that we should ask of Gadamer at this point, there is hardly a better way of following them up than by turning now to another philosopher with whose help they can be considerably sharpened. I want to extend the conversation now to include the voice of Jürgen Habermas. Doing so may not only help us to reach some judgment on the adequacy of Gadamer's — and hence of Aristotle's — contribution to our contemporary predicament; it may also offer the best way of judging the adequacy of Habermas's own philosophy — by revealing how successfully he manages to answer the above questions *against* Gadamer.

6. The Distinction between Praxis and Technique in the Early Philosophy of Jürgen Habermas

1. Situating Habermas

The protagonists in the three preceding chapters, Arendt and Gadamer, may be regarded as coevals; both of them were students of Heidegger in the 1920s and for both, indeed, this was a crucial formative experience. The philosopher to whom I turn now (in this chapter and the next) represents a later generation of German thinkers—a generation that was coming to self-consciousness in the immediate aftermath of the Second World War, faced not just with the reality of German defeat but with the deepening realization of the immensity of the Nazi horror.[1] Jürgen Habermas's work is of a different tenor from that of both Gadamer and Arendt. This difference might be expressed by saying that he stands nearer the Enlightenment than either of the two older thinkers. Habermas's relationship to the Enlightenment, however, as well as to the later tradition of German Idealism—with all its romantic proclivities—is by no means straightforward. He is far from believing that the eighteenth century had succeeded in releasing a Reason that was as securely yoked to Progress as it itself had supposed; and on the other hand he does not share the vehement hostility to German Idealism that one finds, for instance, in such a conspicuous heir of the Enlightenment as Karl Popper.[2]

In fact, Habermas takes up a line of reflection that had been developed by a group of thinkers (of the same generation as Arendt and Gadamer) who reacted against what they saw as the dangerous obscurantism of Heidegger[3] while at the same time refusing to regard the exact sciences as an adequate realization of the potential—especially the critical and liberating potential—of reason. These were the "critical theorists" of the Frankfurt School[4] (especially Max Horkheimer, Theodor Adorno, and Herbert Marcuse), who tried to show that the emancipatory ideals of the Enlightenment could be vindicated only by a reason which had deepened

Enlightenment reason's suspicion of tradition into a suspicion of Enlightenment reason itself. This suspicion, for them, had been developed most powerfully—and without any concessions to irrationality—in historical materialism and psychoanalysis, and in turning to both of these they founded, in Habermas's own words, "a tradition of thought that unites Marx and Freud."[5]

The finest fruit of the Enlightenment had been its conception of science, which put rational inquiry on a new footing and made possible an unprecedented control over the whole environment of human life. The critique of the Frankfurt thinkers sought to show that this new program of control based on the predictive knowledge of science did not, of itself, guarantee an enhancement of human life with respect either to justice or to happiness, but that it was locked into a whole economic and psychological matrix which, on the contrary, made it an instrument for the domination not only of nature but also of human beings themselves.[6] In Habermas's own formulation of what he calls "the core argument" of Horkheimer's and Adorno's *Dialectic of Enlightenment*, "with each conquest over external nature the internal nature of those who gain ever new triumphs is more deeply enslaved."

In taking over this tradition of thought, whose concerns had been at once epistemological and political, Habermas's central preoccupation is with the nature of the relationship between knowledge and action. Within the terms of the Frankfurt School itself, his philosophical undertaking might be seen as an attempt to undercut Adorno's and Horkheimer's pessimistic conclusions about the possibility of *action* (which in the end seemed only to confirm the gloomy diagnosis of Max Weber which they had been so anxious to contest) while at the same time not succumbing to the loose and rather 'romantic' conception of *knowledge* that seemed to go with Marcuse's irrepressible utopianism.[7]

If Critical Theory is the nearest thing to Habermas's intellectual home, in that the Frankfurt thinkers most deeply share his fundamental intuitions, the full sweep of his project has carried him far beyond the discourse of this school. True to the greatest philosopher of the Enlightenment, he has been stubbornly committed to the formulation of a (quasi-)transcendental framework.[8] At the same time, anxious to avoid the empty formalism which has resulted from the usual apriorism of such attempts, he has tried to give historical depth to this framework—in a series of brilliant essays which have taken him over "abandoned stages of reflection"—as well as to build into it a great deal of fallibilist material drawn from developmental psychology, linguistics, economics, and other disciplines. Habermas's ideas, then, have evolved in dialogue with a disconcerting array of other thinkers, without squeamishness about the proper matter of 'philosophy', and in a prolific, seemingly unceasing series of books and articles. The sheer scale of his enterprise is what I am calling attention to here, but also the difficulties that it presents to any commentator. Given the range as well as the bulk of his writings and the fact that he is still in his intellectual prime, trying to give an account of his views can seem like trying to record a city-scape as one travels on a very fast train.

My response to this difficulty will obviously be conditioned by the fact that the primary interest here is not Habermas's work *per se* but rather our central Aristotelian distinction as it is brought to life in his work. This selectivity of focus scarcely eases our difficulty, however, as can be illustrated by reference back to Gadamer. In the latter's case we were not just dealing with an achieved work (he was sixty when *Wahrheit und Methode* was published, and while his later writings clarify and expand, they do not significantly recast, its basic thesis); we also found (even though our interest was not in his work *per se,* either) that the integrality of Aristotle to his whole hermeneutical philosophy made it easy to expound this philosophy and *at the same time* to reveal Aristotle's profile in it. Now in Habermas's case there is certainly a recognizably Aristotelian strand in his thinking; but there are also other important strands that, as it were, pull across and, indeed, against, it—thereby making it more difficult to extricate. And this, then, is further compounded by the developmental factor: as Habermas's thought has evolved and also, it should be said, as Aristotle himself has come to be cast in an increasingly polemical role in contemporary debates, Habermas's relationship to the latter has become more mediated and 'suspicious'. While the early Habermas could turn Aristotle to handsome account in attempting to defend the Enlightenment from itself, for the later Habermas a clear implication of any such defense is a sharp rejection of neo-Aristotelianism and the antimodernist, neoconservative animus which he takes it to represent.[9]

Given this complexity in our materials and the maze that it might lead us into, I want to clearly delimit what I shall be trying to accomplish in my treatment of Habermas. (Here, too, however, the same caveat which I entered at the beginning of my account of Gadamer still holds: things can become really comprehensible—especially in the light of so much jargon carried over from the German—only *ambulando*.) In this chapter, I shall first outline the strategic importance of the Aristotelian distinction between 'technique' and 'praxis' in his earlier philosophy (section 2).[10] Next, I shall show the way in which the notion of 'praxis' which he took over from Aristotle was gradually reworked through his encounters with a series of other, specifically modern, thinkers, including Gadamer (sections 3 and 4). And I shall then present his analysis of the modern *loss* of the distinction between 'technique' and 'praxis' and show how central this analysis has been to his diagnosis of the ills of modernity (section 5). In doing all this, I shall be confining attention to Habermas's writings *prior* to the major reformulation of his position which went on throughout the 1970s and culminated in the publication of his *magnum opus* in 1981.[11] My approach will be primarily expository and I shall be trying to emphasize everything in his work that puts him in some kind of continuity with the other thinkers whom we have already studied. (He himself acknowledged the influence of both Arendt and Gadamer on the early historical essays in which, as he would later put it, "the Aristotelian distinction between praxis and techne serves as the connecting thread.")[12]

In the next chapter, there will be a change of focus. I shall be concentrating on Habermas's later work, the *dis*continuity between him and our other thinkers will come more into relief, and my purpose will be appraisal as well as exposition. What makes Habermas's a discordant or, as I prefer to see it, a challenging voice in our overall conversation is the strength of the *critical* impulse that drives his thinking. Although this emphasis on critique will be apparent in my account of his notion of praxis in this present chapter, only in the next chapter shall I fasten on it and consider its implications for our overall theme. Does Habermas's espousal of critique not bring him in the end right outside the Aristotelian tradition? And if critique is indeed what is called for by our modern predicaments, does this fact not undermine this tradition anyhow—and thereby render implausible any contemporary attempt to retrieve the notion of phronesis?

These are the main questions which will concern me in the next chapter. I shall first outline there the shift in Habermas's later writings to what he calls a "communicative" notion of rationality and, in doing so, shall focus in particular on the changed relationship between praxis and critique which emerges in the central concept of "communicative action" (section 1). I shall then look briefly at his new formulation, in terms of "system" and "life-world," of what he had earlier conceptualized in terms of the distinction between "technique" and "praxis." I shall suggest that although the new conceptual framework has lost in Aristotelian resonance —and gained in sophistication—it does not significantly alter the burden of what he had been able to express with the earlier distinction (section 2). The really significant, and problematical, element in his later work, I shall argue, is not what he has to say in terms of system and life-world but rather his distinct, though complementary, thesis about the "rationalization of the life-world." I shall first advert to two problems which he raises in relation to this rationalization process and consider critically his response to these problems, which sees them as being ultimately tractable to a resourceful critical theory (section 3). I shall then try to bring out what are,

I believe, deeper reservations on his part about rationalization, which seem to indicate inherent, and therefore unsupersedable, limitations on it (section 4). These reservations are not much stressed by Habermas himself, but they are nonetheless present as a kind of undertow in his thought — pulling it back, in fact, in the direction both of Aristotle and of our other thinkers. The final question which is left for consideration then (in section 5) is whether the main current in Habermas's thought (i.e., the more obvious one toward "rationalization," "critique," and "emancipation") can carry him, against the undertow, to where he wants to get; or whether the contrary directions of both currents do not leave him, for all his extraordinary virtuosity as a helmsman, ultimately adrift.

In our overall conversation, Habermas's role is primarily adversarial: by his herculean attempt to support and redirect what he sees as the deepest impulses of modernity, he presents a very sharp challenge to the whole tradition of thought from Newman to Gadamer which I have already recapitulated. Moreover, he can all the better fill this role precisely because his awareness and indeed appropriation of a good deal of what we have already met in these other thinkers makes it impossible to regard him — as we might for instance regard an unabashed positivist — as a hopelessly uncomprehending or even unsympathetic adversary. He himself is an eminently "conversational" thinker — in the sense that his systematic analysis of issues is most often pursued through drawing other thinkers into dialogue about them. In these dialogues (as will be particularly evident in sections 3 and 4 of the present chapter), his tendency is to selectively assimilate or "reconstruct" the other thinker; and in such reconstruction his particular skill is to show that the thinker was actually at odds with himself, that what was valuable (and is thus still assimilable) in his thought needs to be extricated from other elements or tendencies by which — usually without his advertence — it was compromised (and which are therefore to be discarded).[13] Now in all these many conversations Habermas has shown himself to be so endlessly learned, so much the master at unconcealing others, and at the same time so *knowing* in his own moves, that one could hardly hope to find him out by a maneuver similar to his own. By including him in this present conversation I do not, in fact, presume to bring to light any particular element of his thought which might be claimed to have escaped his own notice. But the issue I do hope to raise, nonetheless, is whether, for all his fine circumspections, he is really entitled to say *all* the things that he wants to say: in particular, if full weight is given to the concessions he makes to the tradition which is explored in *this* conversation, whether his ultimate opposition to this tradition from the vantage-point of "cultural modernism" can really be sustained. But all this is anticipation. We must now go back and take up the story nearer the beginning.

2. The Aristotelian Background

The focus of Habermas's attention since the early 1960s has been on the contemporary state of knowledge and action—where the primary determinant, in his view, has been the development of science in a capitalist society. In formulating his understanding of the contemporary position, however, he found it decisively important to determine the manner and the consequences of the latter's departure from the classical position which had been most effectively expressed in Aristotle's categories and which had survived, in his view, in the dominant European tradition, in more or less recognizable form, until the seventeenth century. This historical reading is not at all extraneous to Habermas's systematic intentions: phronesis/praxis and techne/poiesis interest him not simply because they conceptualize a position that has been historically superseded—that is, as it were, the ruin on which the modern edifice is built. To the contrary, he believes that the collapse of the older tradition, which began with Machiavelli and Hobbes and which has been deepened and extended through the subsequent development of the 'human sciences', has had some very damaging consequences; and he further believes that the Aristotelian categories, even if they cannot be simply reinstated in the face of modern developments, still possess an irreplaceable critical power in that they contain suppressed elements of truth about the investment of knowledge in action that can help us to grasp just what these consequences are.

Like Vico before him, then, Habermas, undertakes "a reckoning of profits and losses" in regard to the transition from classical to modern politics. In doing this he is well aware of the merits of Aristotelian phronesis, "its hermeneutic power in the theoretical penetration of situations which were to be mastered practically,"[14] its ability "to provide practical orientation about what is right and just in a given situation."[15] He *also* realizes that these merits have been sacrificed in the transition to the modern study of society, which, "having taken on monologic form, is no longer capable of essentially relating to praxis" and which has therefore been bought at "the cost of a separation from that connection with experience which practical philosophy maintains."[16]

At the same time, however, Habermas believes that the sciences have inaugurated a more exacting notion of theoretical rigor, against which the older practical philosophy must be seen to be at a disadvantage and which modern social philosophy, therefore, must now incorporate. And so he himself desires to take up a high ground where the key question becomes: "how can the promise of practical politics . . . be redeemed without relinquishing, on the one hand, the rigor of scientific knowledge, which modern social philosophy demands in contrast to the practical philosophy of classicism? And on the other, how can the promise of social philosophy, to furnish an analysis of the interrelationships of social life, be redeemed without relinquishing the practical orientation of classical politics?"[17] Habermas's own philosophy is a supremely ambitious attempt to provide an answer to this question, or in other words, to construct "a theory of society conceived with a practical intent, which avoids the complementary weaknesses both of traditional politics and of modern social philosophy; and which thus unites the claim to a scientific character with a theoretical structure referring to practice."[18]

The Aristotelian scheme of knowledge and action sets up a threefold distinction between theory (*epistēmē*) and two forms of practical knowledge (techne and phronesis). Habermas's approach to the relationship of knowledge and action can be seen, without too much strain, as an elaborate commentary on the disintegration of this schema and at the same time as an attempt to reconstruct important elements of it within a very formidable conceptual framework of his own. Theory for the Greeks arose within a life of contemplation, a *bios theoretikos* which, as Plato's *Seventh Letter* and the tenth book of Aristotle's *Ethics* make clear, was quite separate from, and superior to, the practical and productive life of the *polis*. Both phronesis and techne, therefore, as forms of practical knowledge, were to be strictly distinguished from *epistēmē* or theoretical knowledge: "the life-world (*Lebenswelt*) of human beings and citizens concerned for their preservation [through poiesis] or for their communal life [through praxis] was, in the strict sense, theory-free."[19] This was because, being changeable and uncertain, it could never yield knowledge of the eternal and necessary realities whose ontological primacy gave to theory its overridingly superior status.

The disintegration of the Aristotelian schema stems mainly from the fact that with the rise of the natural sciences in the seventeenth century this Greek notion of theory has been entirely superseded. The major change that ushered in the new science was the adoption of boldly experimental methods and the simultaneous exploitation of mathematics.[20] In Habermas's view, this change signified, at its core, a complete displacement of the contemplative ideal in favor of a *technical* one — or, in Aristotelian terms, the collapse of *epistēmē* and its absorption into a new, powerful, and expanded form of techne: "the modern scientific investigation of nature set about to pursue theory with the attitude of the technician."[21] This does not mean that the subjective intention of scientists was to construct knowledge that would have a technical application. More profoundly, it means that they invented a new type of knowledge whose method — based on ingeniously controlled interventions in the course of natural events — is *inherently* technical even as a mode of *knowledge:* "Theory is measured by its capacity for artificially reproducing natural processes. In contrast to *epistēmē*, it is designed for application in its very structure. Thereby theory gains a new criterion of its truth . . . we *know* an object insofar as we can *make* it."[22]

What Habermas is hinting at here in an early essay (1963), he was soon to develop in terms of the fundamental category of *"knowledge-constitutive interest."*[23] He came to see the natural sciences as being founded on a *technical* interest: in other words, technical control is the defining perspective or framework within which all scientific knowledge is assembled. Science objectifies the world of experience precisely from the viewpoint of possible technical control. Control through prediction is inscribed in its whole methodology, and the fact that it produces technically exploitable knowledge is therefore essential and not merely accidental to it. Modern technology, we might say, is written into the "quasi-transcendental" script of modern science.

We see here the first and most immediate of the two hugely significant moves through which the Aristotelian constellation of knowledge (and action) was overthrown. Technique, that is, productive know-how which previously had constituted a specific form of practical and therefore *non*-theoretical knowledge (techne), is now brought into alignment with the new science, which therefore no longer retains the contemplative aspiration of the old theory. Henceforth the only type of knowledge that really counts, both as theory and as source (or *archē,* in Aristotle's term) of production, is precisely that which is given to us by science. Scientific information about the world contains technical imperatives: the formulae for the new technology and modes of production no longer reside in the rules of craftsmen but rather in the corroborated findings of scientists. And so the gulf which had separated theory and production for the Greeks is now eliminated.[24]

If the assimilation to each other of theory and technique represents the first collapse in the classical constellation, its complete obsolescence is presaged in the *second* collapse whereby, more and more, *praxis is assimilated to technique.* And while Habermas can accept the first of these shifts, i.e., the emergence of the technical orientation of modern natural science and its unleashing of undreamed-of productive forces as historical progress[25] — provided that it is correctly understood and not distorted by a positivistic self-understanding — he has the greatest reservations about the further movement which sees hitherto practical domains (in the conduct of personal and communal affairs) penetrated by a technical logic: "But of course the real difficulty in the relation of theory to praxis does not arise from this new function of science as a technological force, but rather from the fact that we are no longer able to distinguish between practical and technical power."[26]

The seemingly inexorable loss of this distinction, both as a conscious articulation and as a reality in the objective organization of social life, is, for Habermas, the defining feature of modernization. He wants to argue, however, that it is a loss which can be sustained only at the cost of a radical, and demonstrably incoherent, revision of what it means to live a human life. At the core of his critical philosophy is an attempt to reassert the distinction between technique and practice, and even to provide it with some kind of transcendental grounding—by showing that it derives from two ineluctable interests of human living,[27] or from "the imperatives of a sociocultural life-form dependent on labor and language."[28] Since the ascendancy of technique can function, therefore, only by suppressing a fundamental interest of human beings (i.e., the practical interest which is "grounded in one of the two fundamental conditions of our cultural existence: in language or more precisely in the form of socialization and individuation determined by communication in ordinary language,")[29] the positivistic articulations of this ascendancy have the hallmarks of all beliefs which rationalize a suppression, i.e., they are a form of ideology.

If Habermas is to reaffirm some version of the distinction between technique and praxis, as well as to demonstrate the destructive consequences of its modern loss, clearly his biggest task is to recover some sense of the suppressed sphere of *praxis*. By "praxis," he intends a type of human engagement that is embedded within a tradition of communally shared understandings and values, that remains vitally connected to peoples' life-experience, that finds expression in their ordinary linguistic usage, and that, rather than being a means through which they achieve outcomes separate from themselves, is a kind of enactment through which they constitute themselves as persons in a historical community. It is through praxis that a person comes to have an individual identity, but at the same time it always transpires within an intersubjective medium. Through it a person's life becomes meaningful but the meanings always depend on the establishment of mutual understanding and reciprocity with others. The essential processes of individuation and socialization are therefore intimately bound up with it. And these are really aspects of the same process "for individuation can be comprehended only as a process of socialization. The moral subject, the subject of praxis, is inconceivable in abstraction from communicative relations with others."[30]

The Aristotelian provenance of 'praxis' still resonates in the Habermasian conception of it which I have just briefly outlined. We can still pick up the emphasis on the established ethos of the *polis* as the primary determinant of the person's identity-formation, the authoritativeness of the *endoxa* enshrined in the vernacular of the community, and the non-

separation of 'moral psychology' and 'political science', so that a subjectivist framework for the former is as inappropriate as an objectivist one
is for the latter. Still, even if we can identify a strong Aristotelian influence on Habermas's concept of praxis, we need to follow the way in which
this concept is transmuted through his encounters with a succession of
modern thinkers. In the next section (3), I shall review the import of some
of the most significant of these encounters, while, in the following section
(4), I shall focus specifically on his encounter with the hermeneutical tradition, especially in its preeminent embodiment in Gadamer's work.

3. 'Praxis' Mediated through Modern Thought

'Praxis' is deployed on a broad, 'macro' level in Habermas's response
to Max Weber's thesis of the progressive rationalization of society. According to Weber, modern societies are coming to be regulated by purely purposive or *formal* rationality, i.e., by an increasingly sophisticated calculus
of efficiency and economy in assembling means toward ends—where the
ends, themselves, however, are no longer capable of being justified by any
substantive rationality. Habermas concedes the force of this thesis, which
correctly discerns the fact that "measured against the new standards of
purposive rationality, the power-legitimating and action-orienting traditions—especially mythological interpretations and religious worldviews—
lose their cogency."[31] Nevertheless, he wants to reformulate this thesis by
articulating clearly the frame of reference of another mode of action that
is different from Weber's purposive-rational action and whose replacement
by the latter may not after all be quite so inevitable as Weber seems to
imply. This mode of action is praxis or, as he puts it in the language of
sociology, 'symbolic interaction' (elsewhere he calls it "communicative action," a concept which, immensely elaborated later on, was to become
the central category of his mature work). It has to do not with technical
rules but with social norms; it is expressed not in context-free language
but in an intersubjectively shared ordinary language; it sets up not conditional predictions but rather reciprocal expectations; its function is not
the solution of problems or the attainment of goals but rather the maintenance of human institutions (and through them of coherent personal
identities).

Praxis, as we saw, involves a mediation of the social and the individual, and if his response to Weber leads Habermas to accentuate its role
on the "macro" level of objective social processes and institutions, his appropriation of Hegel leads him to stress also its role in the drama of a
person's self-constitution as an individual. And whereas in his response

to Weber praxis as symbolic interaction tends to be formulated in functionalist language and to assume a somewhat static aspect, Hegel helps him to build into his notion of praxis an understanding of the dialectic of interaction—i.e., of the fact that a self is not posited from an original a priori unity of consciousness (à la Kant) but rather emerges in a formative process of working through conflict and struggle toward mutual recognition with others.

In his later philosophy, as we shall see presently, Habermas has developed the notion of an "ideal speech situation," or a fully achieved dialogical relationship, as a kind of ideal limit, the anticipation of which can be reconstructively analyzed in all human communication. At the same time, however, his reading of the early Hegel makes him well aware that in the actual communication which our lived history makes us familiar with, this anticipation is invariably frustrated. Communication is bedeviled by competing interests and unequal distributions of power; it is, in other words, "systematically distorted communication." And so here under Hegel's tutelage, life-practice is seen as thoroughly post-lapsarian. In what, for my purposes, is a significant shift from the Aristotelian emphasis, it is no longer seen as securely established within the favorable ethos of a *polis* where good character will develop smoothly by habituation and simply as a function of a good natural temperament and the supervention on it of phronesis. To the contrary, it is now definitive in the Hegelian tradition, which Habermas so constructively appropriates, that praxis is already subverted by, or at best always reasserting itself against, conditions that are deeply inimical to its genuine accomplishment; or, in the words of one of Habermas's commentators: "interaction, as a category . . . does not refer immediately to unconstrained intersubjectivity but to the history of its repression and reconstitution: the dialectic of the moral life."[32]

Habermas follows Marx's de-spiritualizing of the later Hegel by making the sphere of work the primary arena for the playing out of this drama of self-constitution, for individuals, classes, and the human race itself. He goes along with Marx's insistence, against Hegel, that the achievement of a reconstituted and fully human praxis cannot be left to the immanent unfolding of a world-spirit. It calls, rather, for a critical theory which will expose systematically the causes of alienation in human praxis and at the same time provide the basis of an agenda for overcoming this alienation. If Habermas makes these two moves with Marx, however, in doing so he subjects Marx himself to substantial reconstruction. A serious weakness in Marx's theory, he believes, was precisely his failure to make the distinction with which we have all along been concerned between production (poiesis) and human interaction (praxis):

Marx does not actually explicate the interrelationship of interaction and labor, but instead, under the unspecific title of social praxis, reduces the one to the other, namely: communicative action to instrumental action . . . the productive activity which regulates the material interchange of the human species with its natural environment becomes the paradigm for the generation of all the categories; everything is resolved into the self-movement of production. Because of this, Marx's brilliant insight into the dialectical relationship between the forces of production and the relationships of production could very quickly be misinterpreted in a mechanistic manner.[33]

Here Habermas, himself a "neo-Marxist" thinker, directs his critique right at Marx's most central concept, i.e., the notion of praxis, and it is worth noting that his own revision of this concept takes him back in the direction of Aristotle. Marx's advance on Aristotle, we might say, lay in his insight into the dialectical interdependence of the spheres of production and of cultural/moral interaction. (Aristotle had maintained in book 6 of the *Nicomachean Ethics* that "practical intellect" should govern "productive intellect," but he did not admit the extent of the converse conditioning of practical life by the existing mode of production.) The implicit gains in Marx's insight into this interdependence were compromised, however, by his simultaneous failure to maintain the distinctness of its two elements, or in other words, by his understanding of practical-moral life as a mere reflection of processes of material production and his consequently highly reductionist concept of praxis.

This concept led Marx not only to oversimplify his account of bourgeois culture but also, and despite the great critical force of his own thinking, to misconstrue the nature of critique itself and of the revolutionary action that should be bound up with it. Because of his failure to grasp the specific difference—which does not cancel out the intimate connection—between *"self-generation through productive activity* and *self-formation through critical-revolutionary activity,"*[34] (or what comes to much the same thing, his failure to see that "liberation from hunger and misery does not necessarily converge with liberation from servitude and degradation")[35] Marx could suppose that his own intended science of society was all of a piece with the established natural sciences and that the project of gaining conscious mastery of history could, with the sweeping away of ideological mystification, be modeled on the rational penetration and control of nature. This is the unreconstructed positivism which seriously flawed Marx's formulation of his own project and which is the primary source of all the defacements to which it has led—and this notwithstanding his trenchant polemics against 'empiricists', as well as the fact that his own actual social and historical inquiries often assumed a wider viewpoint.

In his response to Marx, Habermas — like the earlier Frankfurt School before him — turns to Freud. A crucial and highly controversial[36] component in his reconstruction of Marxism has been his assimilation of enlightening political action to psychoanalytic intervention. But here again we see the relentlessness of Habermas's purgative reading of his protagonists from the tradition. For psychoanalysis furnishes him with a suggestive model only after he has reinterpreted it in such a way that, behind the back, as it were, of the scientistic *Weltanschauung* of Freud's own formulation of it, it appears as a *hermeneutical* procedure, "moving irretrievably in the medium of self-reflection." Freud himself was hardly less naïvely positivistic than Marx in his assumption that his new discipline could achieve intellectual respectability only if it were formulated in terms of the established empirical sciences. What he failed to recognize with sufficient clarity — and what Habermas tries to make explicit — is the fact that the novel procedure of interaction which he developed in the uniquely sheltered setting of the psychoanalytic session implies an essentially different type of knowledge, one that is irreducible, and by no means inferior, to the standard nomological sciences.

In actu exercitu what Freud had devised, even if *in actu signato* he misrepresented its nature, was a theory of systematically distorted communication which closely paralleled Hegel's developmental sketch of the loss and regaining of self-consciousness but which went beyond Hegel by providing the basis for a practice in which the drama of an individual subject's life-history could be not only conceptually analyzed but concretely reconstructed. And Freud's concretization of Hegel's dialectic of self-constitution was not flawed, as Marx's materialization of it had been, by confinement to "the categorical framework of production." This confinement had prevented Marx from developing his cardinal insight into the role of ideology. Although 'power' was of central concern to him, the more it departed from naked force and was mediated symbolically in entrenched patterns of social as well as intrapsychic communication, the more it overdrew the resources of his conceptual framework.

> This framework could account for productive knowledge but not reflective knowledge. Nor was the model of productive activity suited for the reconstruction of power and ideology. In contrast, Freud has acquired in metapsychology a framework for distorted communicative action that allows the conceptualization of institutions and the role and function of illusions, that is of power and ideology. Freud's theory can represent a structure that Marx did not fathom.[37]

In fact, Freud's theory offered, in Habermas's view, the best "example" of a kind of knowledge which is interactive—and therefore practical— at its very core, which remains immediately linked to experience, and which at the same time has a critical purchase on the unfolding of this experience by releasing it from the causality of naturelike fixations and thereby transforming it into a reflective process of self-constitution. Psychoanalytic knowledge is generated in the first instance by the analyst, but he cannot simply 'apply' it to the analysand in order to 'make' him well-adjusted. Rather it is confirmed only when it is communicated to the latter in such a way that he appropriates it into a process of self-reflection—which will be released in him only if the communication manages to outwit his resistances and which, once it is released, dissolves—by integrating them into an enlarged consciousness—the previously unconscious repressions which were the source of these resistances. This is how Habermas contrasts the psychoanalyst searching for the applicability of an interpretation with an empirical scientist testing an explanatory theory:

> In the case of testing theories through observation (that is in the behavioural system of instrumental action), the application of assumptions to reality is a matter for the inquiring subject. In the case of testing general interpretations through self-reflection (that is in the framework of communication between physician and patient), this application becomes *self-application* by the object of inquiry. The process of inquiry can lead to valid information only via a transformation in the patient's self-inquiry. When valid, theories hold for all who can adopt the position of the inquiring subject. When valid, general interpretations hold for the inquiring subject and all who can adopt its [i.e., his or her] position only to the degree that those who are made the object of individual interpretations *know and recognize themselves* in these interpretations. The subject cannot obtain knowledge of the object unless it becomes knowledge for the object—and unless the latter thereby emancipates itself by becoming a subject.[38]

Clearly a dynamic form of knowledge and communication is involved here: to achieve this kind of insight is not to gain knowledge that can *then* be applied in order to implement some process of change. Rather, to achieve the insight is *ipso facto* to change, or to gain "emancipation from pseudo-natural constraints whose power resides in their non-transparency."

Powerful as this therapeutic insight is when it occurs, psychoanalysis can provide no guarantee that it *will* occur—either in the conduct of an individual analysis or, phylogenetically, in the attainment of some future state of enlightenment by the human race itself. Freud is aware that advances in the material modes of production create opportunities for weakening the force of institutionally backed sources of repression in a society. But he also remains aware that the stubbornness, and ingenious powers of regrouping, of systems of distorted communication ensure that these systems will not simply wither from below, no matter what transformations may take place in the material base. Psychoanalytic intervention does not possess anything superior to "a logic of trial and error,"[39] and it remains "committed . . . to the practical-hypothetical consciousness of carrying out an experiment that can *fail.*"[40] Habermas believes that in this, psychoanalysis reflects what is the case for any critical theory directed to practice. It must travel in the knowledge that it may never arrive; neither transcendental argument nor History provides it with any assurance of success.

I have been outlining Habermas's conception of praxis or communicative interaction and stressing, in particular, his efforts to move toward a notion of *critical* practice, i.e., one that would be self-consciously directed by an emancipatory interest. He is drawn to psychoanalysis because he considers it to be the best existing attempt at the formulation of such a practice. Moreover he believes that the psychoanalytic engagement (which goes on between individuals) can be transposed to the social level to become the model for processes of enlightening political action—or education (*Bildung*) as he calls it. He believes, further, that the paradigm examples of psychoanalysis and historical materialism, when taken together, provide valuable elements from which the lineaments of a generalized theory of society with a critical intent can be constructed. Habermas's own later work, especially *The Theory of Communicative Action*, has been almost entirely taken up with the attempt to work out such a theory— though the profiles of both Marx and Freud, it must be said, have diminished in it—by developing what he has come to call "universal pragmatics" and the notion of "communicative competence." This work will be our concern in the next chapter but, more immediately, I want to complete my outline of Habermas's notion of praxis by making good an omission— occasioned by my concentration on a *critical* exigence—in my review of the succession of modern thinkers who have helped him to fill out this notion. I need to say something about his appropriation of hermeneutical thought, in Dilthey and especially in Gadamer.

4. Habermas and Hermeneutics

In two acute essays on Dilthey,[41] Habermas shows how the latter, on the basis of the achievements of the German Historical School, made secure for thematic reflection epistemological issues that pointed beyond the positivism which was already well established in the self-understanding of the natural sciences. He does not believe, however, that Dilthey's own reflection on these issues brought their true nature to light: the latter's adherence to the notions of empathy and reproduction as the central acts of hermeneutical endeavor left him "caught in a covert positivism." Having done so much to recognize, Dilthey ends up repudiating—rather than adequately accounting for—all that is most characteristic in hermeneutical experience. He is vividly aware of life-practice as both object and context of *Verstehen;* but he still sees a conflict between "life" and "science" which he cannot help trying to resolve in favor of the latter. He remains "in the last analysis so much subject to the force of positivism that he leaves off the self-reflection of the cultural sciences just at the point where the practical interest is comprehended as the foundation of possible hermeneutic knowledge and not as its corruption. In so doing, he falls back into objectivism."[42]

This verdict on Dilthey is, in fact (as we are aware from chapter 4, section 1 above), very close to Gadamer's. And so, if we now ask about Habermas's relation to Gadamer, we should not expect to find them completely at odds. It is true that hermeneutics has never been at ease with the tradition of critique[43] and that Habermas's own undeviating allegiance to the latter makes him a stern critic of what he sees as the conservative implications of Gadamer's work. Still, while resisting these implications, Habermas wants to incorporate what he acknowledges as valid insights of philosophical hermeneutics and this incorporation has, in fact, been of central importance in the development of his thought. This is hardly surprising, indeed, since a hermeneutical element may be taken to be more essentially constitutive of praxis than critique is. Whereas a praxis that is not mediated through critique—and which, for that reason, may or may not be 'distorted'—still remains a praxis, a praxis without a hermeneutical dimension is simply inconceivable. And so, however necessary critique may be from the point of view of reforming a particular praxis, when it is a matter of simply defining the *concept* of praxis, hermeneutics has a more intrinsic role.[44] This is so, simply in virtue of the fact that in their practical lives people have to continually understand or interpret each other's language in gestures and speech and that without the reliable background of such understanding, action or praxis would be impossible. Nor is praxis an external adjunct to understanding, for in understanding itself there is already an element of praxis. This is why Gadamer's disclosure of the nature of understanding is at the same time an opening into a more adequate conception of praxis. Or, contrariwise, it is why his reopening of what had been an adequate conception of praxis, i.e., Aristotle's practical philosophy, plays such a crucial role in his own disclosure of the nature of understanding. The medium in which understanding goes on is always "the medium of practical reason (and unreason)."

Gadamer himself has already occupied us at length. Here I shall just briefly mention the points which Habermas wants to assimilate from him (what I called above his "valid insights"), as well as the points on which he very decisively disagrees with him. These latter points will be the matter of substantive discussion when I return to them in the next chapter.

The nub of Habermas's agreement with Gadamer concerns the latter's attack on subjectivism, particularly in its historicist version. Habermas accepts the view that our powers of objectification are not such that we can constitute ourselves as subjects entirely over against the object (be it a text, a person, or a tradition) that we seek to understand. Rather, we already inhabit (or are inhabited by) a whole complex of prejudices or anticipations that unavoidably structure our understanding. Far from having any transcendental source (which was still the case with Kant's *a priori* categories) these prejudices enclose us within a tradition, and especially within language as the bearer of tradition. It is only through prejudices, and the standing within tradition which they give us, that we have any access at all to the 'object'. And so the object, too, far from being outside tradition, or even securely deposited in one fixed 'layer' of it, appears only in the "fusion of horizons"—which is an event in which, simultaneously, understanding is attempted and the tradition breathes with new life. Habermas is particularly keen to embrace this insight because of the critique of the "predominant view" of social science which it implies. This is the view that

> the social sciences have escaped from the hermeneutic limitations of the *Geisteswissenschaften* and attained an unproblematic relationship to history in which general theories of social action are on a different plane than the historical context of tradition. . . . Sociology is indifferent to history . . . the historical standing of the data is thus neutralized from the outset. For sociology, all history is made present . . . projected onto a screen of universal simultaneity and is thus robbed of its authentic spirit.[45]

What is concealed by the "objectivist illusion" of this view is the irrepressible vitality of tradition (*Wirkungsgeschichte*) manifested here in the fact that historically conditioned precognitions already operate tacitly in the conceptual apparatus of scientists, and thus in the way in which their data are able to speak to them. If the untenability of a privileged standpoint *outside* their data is exposed, then hermeneutically aware students of human practices—like 'practical persons' who are more obviously implicated in them—are learning about themselves at the same time that they are acquiring knowledge about their 'data'. Human science in this sense — i.e., if pursued with hermeneutical consciousness — has itself a *practical interest;* it is, in Habermas's words, "linked . . . to the articulation of an action-orienting self-understanding." (And precisely to have shown this is, for Habermas, "Gadamer's real achievement".) Rather than being conducted in what Habermas calls the "monologic" mode, its whole point is to enact and extend a *dialogue* in which our self-understanding is enriched through the actualization of tradition: in a formulation whose strength is justified by the practical dimension implied here, Gadamer speaks of this as "the conversation that we ourselves *are.*"[46]

This last phrase may serve as a point of departure for bringing out Habermas's *dis*agreements with Gadamer. First, he rejects Gadamer's universalization of the hermeneutic situation. He wants to say that we are *more* than this dialogue; we are also beings who are tied to structures of production and power. Second, and put paradoxically, he believes that what Gadamer proposes is *not sufficiently* dialogical. In the Gadamerian scenario tradition speaks (or, in Heidegger's famous phrase, "language speaks"), but so all-encompassingly that there seems to be nobody or nothing left to *speak back.* While releasing us from objectivism, Gadamer ends up imprisoning us within a monologic tradition. These two points are closely related. The second refers to what Habermas sees as Gadamer's interdict on *critical reflection,* and the first refers to a major reason for this interdict: Gadamer's refusal to admit that production and power are two intransigent realities that cannot be simply dissolved into the hermeneutical or dialogical medium.

Habermas grants that "the hermeneutic insight is certainly correct, the insight that understanding — no matter how controlled it may be — cannot simply leap over the interpreter's relationship to tradition." But he goes on:

> But from the fact that understanding is structurally a part of the traditions that it further develops through appropriation, it does not follow that the medium of tradition is not profoundly altered by scientific [i.e., disciplined] reflection. . . . Gadamer fails to appreciate the power of reflection that is developed in understanding. This type of reflection . . . does not detach itself from the soil of contingency on which it finds itself. But in grasping the genesis of the tradition from which it proceeds and on which it turns back, reflection shakes the dogmatism of life-practices.[47]

Gadamer's tendency to lock up critique inside the walls of tradition, Habermas might say, stems from a mistake which is in a sense the opposite of the mistake which we have already seen him attribute to Marx. For whereas the latter, by absolutizing productive categories, failed to recognize the specificity of communicative relationships, Gadamer's absolutization of language and communication fails to do justice to the opacity of productive processes. Habermas concedes to Gadamer that, in practical life, institutions of power and processes of production can be expressed in no other way than by ordinary language. But he goes on:

> But . . . language as tradition is evidently dependent in turn on social processes that are not reducible to normative relationships. Language is *also* a medium of domination and social power; it serves to legitimate relations of organized force. Insofar as the legitimations do not articulate the power relations whose institutionalization they make possible, insofar as these relations merely manifest themselves in the legitimations, language is *also* ideological. Here it is a question not of deceptions within a language but of deception with language as such. Hermeneutic experience that encounters this dependency of the symbolic framework on actual conditions changes into critique of ideology.[48]

I conclude here—without going into Gadamer's spirited defense of his position[49]—my account of Habermas's many-layered notion of praxis. Within the context of my overall study, this notion raises serious questions to which I shall have to return. My more immediate task, however, is to outline Habermas's understanding of the ubiquitous threat to praxis that is contained in the modern fascination with technique.

5. The Modern Loss of the Distinction between Praxis and Technique

We have seen how hard Habermas has had to work, in his recapitulation of modern philosophy, to preserve a notion of praxis against the positivist secretions in the work of even the most critical (or 'suspicious') of modern thinkers. It is hardly surprising then, if in the development of modern culture—which has been vastly more exposed to science than to philosophy—practice has been virtually eclipsed. Habermas believes that this has occurred as the "expansion of the rational form of science and technology" has been not merely a quantitative phenomenon but rather a qualitative change to "the proportions of a life-form, to the historical totality of a life-world." Advanced industrial society is one in which the regulation of action falls more and more to technical prescriptions emanating from sciences whose own defining 'interest' is inherently 'technical'. The only adequate analysis of this change is one that retains explicit reference to the *concept* of praxis; but this reference becomes increasingly difficult as the growing scale of the change makes praxis *as a reality* more and more obsolete. Habermas's strategy, nonetheless, is to describe the massive presence of technique only by acknowledging the

absence which it obscures. He shows how "from the outset all practical
questions which cannot be answered adequately by technical prescriptions
but which instead also require a self-understanding within their concrete
situation go beyond the cognitive interest invested in empirical science."[50]
And so

> the empirical, analytical sciences produce technical recommendations, but
> they furnish no answer to practical questions. . . . Emancipation by means
> of enlightenment is replaced by instruction in control over objective or ob-
> jectified processes. Socially effective theory is no longer directed toward the
> consciousness of human beings who live together and discuss matters with
> each other, but to the behavior of human beings who manipulate.[51]

The hegemony of technique has been the central concern of all the
thinkers who figured in our previous chapters. In making it so much his
concern, Habermas, therefore, joins their company. More particularly, in
invoking the concept of praxis, and thereby setting limits to the jurisdiction of technique, he is in clear continuity with Arendt and Gadamer.
There is, nonetheless, something quite distinctive about Habermas's analysis of modern technicism. One might speak of a recoil from technique
in both Arendt and Gadamer, a recoil that easily gives the impression
of a yearning for what is taken to be the relative integrity of earlier times.
In Habermas, the impression is quite different. His analysis brings us up
much harder against the complexity and opaqueness of advanced industrial societies and, in doing so, is much keener to deploy the resources
of specifically modern thought — albeit that much of this thought, as we
have already seen, has first to be subjected to his own 'reconstructive' at-
tentions. If I go on now to outline Habermas's analysis and critique of
technicism, this difference of tone and outlook will, I believe, be apparent. Moreover, it will carry on into his later work and will be one of the
factors which we shall have to take into account, in the next chapter, in
deciding where Habermas stands in relation to our other thinkers as well
as to Aristotle himself.

The extension of the technical form of rationality has been pursued
on the basis of a claim to value-neutrality. This has involved a discrediting
of, or a withdrawal of the status of *rationality* from, ways of deciding issues or of working out policies that were located within contexts of practical interaction and discussion. In the new dispensation there are no rational resources for settling substantive questions of policy; such questions
are swept into the area of 'decision' or 'commitment' in which, it is supposed, reason can play no part. And so 'reason', defined as coextensive
with technical rationality, "has lost together with its critical sting, its commitment, its moral decisiveness and has been separated from such de-

cision as from an alien element."[52] Or, as he expresses this later in the same essay:

> Interest and inclination are banished from the court of knowledge as subjective factors. The spontaneity of hope, the act of taking a position, the experience of relevance or indifference, and above all the response to suffering and oppression, the desire for adult autonomy, the will to emancipation, and the happiness of discovering one's identity—all these are dismissed for all time from the obligating interest of reason.[53]

And yet the newly "disinfected reason" which seems bent on separating itself from decision as from an "alien element" is itself, *nolens volens,* founded on a *decision.* For it remains the case that "even a civilization that has been rendered scientific is not granted dispensation from practical questions."[54] And so technique itself performs—albeit in a latent or disguised form—the humanly indispensable functions previously carried out through practical discourse. An orientation to efficiency and economy in the organization of means, which is the core of technique, does not in fact, as is often claimed (e.g., by exponents of the behavioral objectives model), stand ready to serve any set of values which is otherwise (non-rationally) decided upon. Rather, by a deeper, though unacknowledged, decision, this orientation is imposed on the organization of practical life as itself the *only* value—even though it is not conceived as a value at all but is granted a privileged status because of its seeming coincidence with the structure of rationality itself. And so what needs to be recognized about the new ascendancy of technique is that it is *not merely technical.* On the contrary, "the concept of rationality which it seeks to make prevail in its commitment ultimately implies an entire organization of society: one in which a technology become autonomous dictates a value system—namely, its own—to the domains of praxis it has usurped —and all in the name of value-freedom."[55] Or, as we find the same point elsewhere: "The substantive rationality suppressed in the innocent partisanship for formal rationality reveals, in the anticipated concept of a cybernetically regulated organization of society, a tacit philosophy of history."[56]

The particular thrust of Habermas's analysis of positivism—as an explicit philosophy, and even more as a 'technocratic consciousness' that is now simply the naturalized attitude of contemporary administrators—extends beyond epistemological critique to its ethical-political consequences. It is here that he most conspicuously takes up and develops the legacy of the earlier thinkers of the Frankfurt School. His recasting of Marx, which we have already met, here takes on a more developed form: beyond a conceptual analysis and reconstruction of the Marxian canon, he is taking account of specific features of advanced capitalism which Marx himself, as a critic of capitalism in its early liberal phase, had not anticipated. Marx believed that, with the emergence of capitalism, the legitimation of political power and the sanction for institutional values had, for the first time in history, come to be detached from a traditional basis and become *immediately* economic—albeit that the economic basis was dressed up, in capitalist ideology, in terms that preserved some resonance of the traditional morality of justice (e.g., in concepts such as 'equivalence', 'reciprocity', and 'fair exchange'). Marx also believed that his own critique of ideology had exposed the thread-bareness of these concepts and that, in reality, political systems and institutions would, from now on, be exposed—without the protection of any effectively mediating factors—to the logic of the development of the productive forces which capitalism had unleashed for the first time. And, of course, he further assumed that the development of these productive forces would itself inevitably lead to emancipation. The proletariat, as the main productive force, would, so long as it was exploited, be the unfailing source of a chronic and ultimately unsustainable tension. This diagnosis of capitalism as a system which contains both its own grave-digger and the harbinger of universal liberation has come unstuck, however, because of two major interrelated developments which Habermas highlights.

The first of these is the vigorous role of the state which, far from withering away, has in fact intervened hugely in the organization of the economic base, correcting the dysfunctional tendencies of free exchange by stabilizing the business cycle, maintaining scope for 'achievement' (with the state-sponsored school system becoming the major source of status-assignment) and at the same time providing a welfare system as a safety net for "low achievers"—or as a safety valve for itself. This recrudescence of politics in the form of state interventionism has had an inherently *negative* character; its primary, indeed sole, function is "the elimination of dysfunctions and the avoidance of risks that threaten the system." In contrast to the old politics which had to generate legitimations through projecting some notion of the "good life" and had to engage and placate people through the medium of practical discourse and interaction, this new politics has as its natural orientation "the solution of technical problems"; for it is aimed exclusively at "the functioning of a manipulated system."[57]

It is here that this first major feature of advanced capitalism is joined by the second major feature—i.e., the emergence of science/technology—as a primary determining force. This second feature, like the first, undermines Marx's thesis of the autonomy of the economic base, by invalidating his labor theory of value;[58] but in fact it achieves even greater significance by the way in which it *complements* the first feature. For what has happened, in fact, is that the form of scientific-technical rationality has meshed in with the overall state-regulated system, with the function of providing the latter with the technical solutions that serve simply to maintain it. With the elimination of "practical substance" from politics,

> the quasi-autonomous progress of science and technology then appears as an independent variable on which the most important single system variable, namely economic growth, depends. Thus arises a perspective in which the development of the social system *seems* to be determined by the logic of scientific-technical progress. The immanent law of this progress seems to produce objective exigences, which must be obeyed by any politics oriented toward functional needs.[59]

This new mode of politics, anchored in the two major structural readjustments within capitalism that we have just seen, has taken the wind out of the older politics, including unreconstructed Marxist politics. For by its various corrective and compensatory measures, it has softened up the class structure; the mass of wage-earners have been absorbed into the system through rewards that meet what are increasingly privatized needs; and such residual disaffection as still exists is now located on the 'margins', in 'underprivileged' groups who are not, however, *exploited*—in that the system does not live off their labor—and who do not, therefore, through the possibility of withdrawing their cooperation, possess any real revolutionary potential. In this new system the kind of *confrontation* expressed in "Hegel's concept of the ethical totality of a living relationship which is sundered because one subject does not reciprocally satisfy the needs of the other"[60]—a concept which remained implicit in Marx's concept of class—no longer occurs. What we have now is "not the sundering of an ethical situation but the repression of 'ethics' as such as a category of life."[61] And with this, we witness not so much the replacement of one mode of politics by another as the suppression of politics itself through the systematic *depoliticization* of the citizenry, i.e., the evacuation of the public sphere as a sphere in which—however great might be the distortions—relevant discussion, enlightened decision, and efficacious action might still be attempted.

Habermas believes that the scientific-technical mode of rationality has not only decisively helped to bring about this state of affairs but has also, *qua* ideology, served to *legitimate* it. It is a radically new kind of ideology, however, which in fact destroys the very framework within which older forms of ideology could arise—*and be challenged.* "The common positivist way of thinking renders inert the frame of reference of interaction in ordinary language in which domination and ideology both arise under conditions of distorted communication and can be reflectively detected and broken down."[62] It functions as an ideology insofar as it is internalized by members of society who are subjected to it and becomes the substance of their self-understandings as citizens. They come to see their social being as constituted through processes of "purposive-rational action"—when they are "agents"—and "adaptive behavior"—in the much more frequent cases of their being "patients," i.e., objects of purposive-rational organization by planners, administrators, and "leaders" in different domains of life. (Teachers and pupils would fall into such a pattern of agency and patients in an educational system organized around "behavioral objectives"—though ideally even teachers would be patient in the sense of receiving their 'objectives' from some accredited agency.) What is going on here is described by Habermas as a process in which "the reified models of the sciences migrate into the socio-cultural life-world and gain objective power over the latter's self-understanding".[63]

An ideology in the old sense—inaugurated by Marx—which justified one "interest" while concealing the suppression of another, always remained vulnerable to advances in the productive forces. But the new ideology of technique is not vulnerable in this way and hence gives rise to "the peculiar semblance of *post-histoire*," precisely because it is *itself* a major productive force. Moreover, it does not affect the interests of specific classes so much as "the human race's emancipatory interest as such." It occludes the interest in emancipation by the really radical step of suppressing the very sphere of *practice*, which is the only medium within which a concern for emancipation can, in principle, arise. The "nucleus" of this ideology is precisely its "*elimination of the distinction between the practical and the technical*";[64] and its potency as ideology resides in the fact that this elimination has been accomplished not only in the sciences but also in a 'life-world' which is increasingly just the congealed working out of the technical interest which constitutes these sciences.

The fact that the expansion of technique is not the product of political will exercised within an enduringly vital sphere of praxis but, on the contrary, is a self-propelling force whose own product is a state of depoliticization and an annulment of practice, leads to a "paradox" which cannot at all be resolved within the frame of technical logic. This paradox resides in the peculiarity of our relationship, "at the same time intimate and yet estranged," to the interlocking system of "research, technology, production, and administration . . . which has literally become the basis of our life": "On the one hand we are bound externally to this basis by a network of organization and a chain of consumer goods; on the other hand this basis is shut off from our knowledge and even more from our reflection."

For Habermas there is only one force which can help us out of this impasse into which we have been brought by the technicist monopoly, i.e., *critique:*

> The paradox of this state of affairs will, of course, only be recognized by a theory oriented toward praxis, even though this paradox is so evident: the more the growth and change of society are determined by the most extreme rationality of processes of research, subject to a division of labor, the less rooted is this civilization, now rendered scientific, in the knowledge and conscience of its citizens. In this discrepancy, scientifically guided techniques . . . encounter a limitation which they cannot overcome; this can only be altered by a change in the state of consciousness itself, by the practical effect of a theory which does not improve the manipulation of things and of reifications, but which instead advances the interest of reason in human adulthood, in the autonomy of action and in the liberation from dogmatism. This it achieves by means of the penetrating ideas of a persistent critique.[65]

What is the nature of this critique for which Habermas clearly entertains such large ambitions? What, more precisely, is its relationship to praxis? And how reconcilable is it with the notion of phronesis which has been at the center of our attempt, throughout the previous chapters, to understand the limits of technique? To tackle these questions properly we need to turn to Habermas's more recent work.

7. Habermas's Later Philosophy: Ambiguities of Rationalization

1. Critique and Praxis: The Shift to the Notion of Communicative Action

In the previous chapter, we have seen how Habermas developed his critique of contemporary society by exposing the unsupersedable human need for 'praxis' and the consequently dehumanizing effects of the attempt to absorb praxis into a newly expanded, omnicompetent sphere of technique. Habermas's espousal of 'critique' as well as the sense in which he is to be considered a 'critical' thinker involves much more than this, however. Indeed, if it did not, he would hardly differ significantly from Arendt or Gadamer. For the latter, even if they should be deemed 'conservative', are, after all, no less critical of contemporary society than he is — and, in developing this criticism, no less anxious to argue for the irreducibility of praxis to technique. What we need to notice, then, is that Habermas is not just offering a critique of contemporary society which inveighs against the suppression of praxis and argues for its restoration; rather, the *kind* of praxis he argues for — and it is this that sets him apart from our other interlocutors — is one which would *itself* be deeply *informed by critique*. It is the precise manner in which critique is meant to thus 'inform' praxis that we must now examine.

We have already seen the drive toward critique in Habermas's assertion, against Gadamer, of the need to "shake the dogmatism of life-practices"; and we also saw how he has looked to Marx and Freud as the pioneers of such critique, while at the same time finding it necessary to 'reconstruct' the implicit epistemology of both of them. Now this reconstruction of historical materialism and of psychoanalysis has gradually given way in Habermas's later writings to what might be considered a thorough reconstruction of his own earlier thought — a reconstruction in which these two traditions have, in fact, been relegated to a much less conspicuous place. So long as they featured as the paradigm cases of critique, Habermas's problem was to understand the manner in which, *qua theory,* they

193

were to be translated into life-practice—it being already established, of course, that such translation could not be any form of *technical* application, but must rather be some form of enlightenment. Formulating the precise nature of this enlightenment, however, proved very vexing, leading to a number of consecutive corrections and amendments.[1] The difficulties arose from the supposition that critique is a special type of theory, with its own distinctive 'interest' (i.e., the 'emancipatory' one) and therefore with its own unique mode of application. The attempt to resolve them, however, has eventually led Habermas, beyond reformulations of the emancipatory interest, to a virtual abandonment of the basic category of 'knowledge-constitutive interest' itself. There has been a 'turn' in his thinking which, whatever the degree of substantive change involved in it, has certainly opened up a different strategic approach to critique.[2] It is to this approach—with its assimilation of conceptual materials quite different from those of Marxism or psychoanalysis—that I now turn.

As we have seen from the beginning, the distinctions and relations between theory and practice have always been Habermas's central concern; what has particularly characterized his philosophy—and introduced the biggest strains into it—has been an attempt to protect the integrity of practice and *at the same time* not to foreshorten or dilute the claims of theory. If I now speak of a change of 'approach' in his later philosophy, it is, therefore, his approach to the relation between theory and practice that is primarily in question. His earlier philosophy envisaged a kind of theory which would strip away the semblance of necessity or naturalness attaching to given historical processes and thus (it was this 'thus' that was never quite clarified) open up a new field of possibilities into which a liberated practice could expand. Real gains were first achieved in theoretical reflection and the task then was to make good these gains in practice. It was as if practice in itself was deficient but was nonetheless remediable insofar as it was susceptible to therapeutic interventions from the side of theory. In Habermas's later work, however, practice is shown not so much to be instructed or 'enlightened' by theory as to contain within itself a rational structure which drives it immanently (though not inevitably) toward self-transparency.

This kind of practice is what Habermas now calls "communicative action." As in his earlier formulations of praxis, the emphasis is on the intersubjective medium through which persons regulate their actions toward each other and, at the same time, form their own personal identities. 'Communicative action', however, introduces a rather more specialized type of interaction and, in particular, one that is more explicitly *rational*, than that suggested by the earlier concept of 'praxis'. This is brought out clearly by Habermas' distinguishing communicative action not just from "teleological action" (a distinction which parallels the earlier one between praxis and technique) but also from "normatively regulated action."[3] The earlier notion of praxis was more or less coextensive with action guided by inter-subjectively agreed norms; the new notion of communicative action, how-ever, picks out a specific, more fully and explicitly rational *procedure* whereby the norms governing the action are in fact agreed. Whereas nor-matively regulated action functions within the stable context of a social world where norms are securely established — i.e., are unproblematically internalized by the members of that world and coordinate their actions in ways that can ground reliable expectations on the part of other mem-bers — communicative action comes into its own when norms are exposed to challenge, when agreement can no longer be relied on as a product of a previous process of socialization but must be *reached* in a situation whose own proper definition may even have to be negotiated. Moreover it is important to notice that, in Habermas's understanding of it, com-municative action is not just an occasional or exceptional undertaking that projects people out of the routine pattern established by their socializa-tion; more substantially, it is itself the pervasive medium through which, *in specifically modern societies,* the socialization (in the sense of the per-sonality formation) of individuals — as well as the transmission of cultural understandings and the stabilization and cohesion of social groups — can be achieved.

It is clear here that the broad context for Habermas's deployment of the concept of "communicative action" is reflection on the process of modernization; he is in fact still grappling with the fatalistic diagnosis of Max Weber,[4] which had, in his view, overpowered the first generation of Frankfurt thinkers, and a constructive response to which has, almost from the beginning, been the supreme motivation of his own work.[5] Weber had tried to show that the wholesale *rationalization* of society (according to the standards of a mere *Zweckrationalität,* i.e., formal or ends-means rationality) — in the spheres of morality and law as much as in economics and politics — was not just a process of *disenchantment* (or "loss of mean-ing") but also a *disabling* (or "loss of freedom"); it resulted in *anomie* and in a loss of any sense of rational participation in the conduct of affairs on the part of social agents. Habermas accepts of course that the process of rationalization afoot since the Enlightenment has been a solvent of tra-ditional values and legitimations; with the concept of communicative ac-tion, however, he wants to show, against Weber, that it *need* not entail an unbridled pursuit of bureaucratic efficiency or a voiding of all values. Moreover, he *also* wants to show that avoiding this entailment requires neither the restoration (often under a neo-Aristotelian banner) of tradi-tional values nor — and this has been the major preoccupation of his most recent work[6]—the espousal of a style of thinking which (in Nietzschean spirit) frankly, even gladly, disclaims a rational warrant.[7] Against sociological pessimism, then, as well as against pre-modernist or post-modernist responses to it, Habermas wants to show that the development of modern consciousness contains a potential to ground values universally as well as to facilitate a deeper autonomy on the part of individuals.

The scale of his project, clearly, is very formidable. "The theory of language and action has not (despite Humboldt) found its Kant";[8] when Habermas wrote these words (in a long programmatic essay which decisively marked the transition from his "early" to his "later" philosophy) he was, one is tempted to say, busily engaged in falsifying them—by becoming, himself, this Kant. His attempt to defend reason is hardly less grand or comprehensive than Kant's; but it shifts the ground of this defense from the thinking ego to the person involved in communication with others. Here I can attempt only the most schematic outline of his project. Building mainly, though by no means exclusively, on the 'speech act' theories of Austin and Searle, the reconstructive linguistics of Chomsky, the developmental psychology/epistemology of Piaget and Kohlberg, and the symbolic interactionism of George Herbert Mead, he has tried to show that through the pragmatics of speech—through our *use* of language or the ways in which we 'do things with words'— we are already committed to kinds of validity, or to ways of being reasonable. When language is not just a decontextualized specimen for analysis (e.g., within the confines of a narrowly conceived science of grammar, logic, or linguistics) nor an instrument that I use strategically in order to achieve my own purposes (to which the viewpoints of others are in the end subordinate), nor a freewheeling vehicle of world-creation (this must be said against deconstructionist tendencies to level all differences between types of linguistic utterance from the viewpoint of an all-encompassing poetics[9]); when it is, rather, the medium of communication through which people reach for mutual understanding and agreement with each other, then all the participants in this language are already operating a structure which binds them to the making, and proper meeting, of claims. This claiming, which is implicitly or intuitively present in the communicative action of everyday life, is the ultimate locus of rationality. Habermas wants to reconstruct it systematically through the formal analysis which he calls "universal pragmatics," and which is his proposed substitute for the philosophy of consciousness whose insoluble *aporiai* he has been relentlessly exposing— even in thinkers such as Marx and Heidegger, who, for all their revolutionary or 'destructive' intentions, only *supposed* they had transcended it.[10]

Habermas tries to show that there are four "validity-claims," built into communicative action, which are universal in the sense that they are implicitly posited on all occasions—irrespective of particular contents or contexts—on which such action takes place. Every speaker engaged in communicative action cannot help claiming that her utterance is (i) *true* in what it proposes; (ii) *right* in the sense of congruent with appropriate background norms; (iii) *truthful* as a revelation of her meaning or intent; and (iv) *comprehensible* according to the syntactical and semantic rules of the particular language being used.[11] I shall skip over Habermas's way of showing that all these claims come into play in every communicative situation—though different types of situation evince, in a more specific way, one or other of them—and shall focus instead on the second type of validity, normative rightness; for it is this that is more specifically linked to the coordination of action and thus joins up with our discussion of praxis and critique.

When two speakers discuss what is to be done in a given situation, or the rightness of a possible course of action, they do so against the background of each one's already established set of norms. Very often the two sets of norms will harmonize or overlap, and agreement will be reached while much that guides their discussion remains in the background, unthematized. Any speaker/agent, then, operates on the basis of a great deal of habitual, tacit knowledge that seldom if ever comes above the threshold of explicit reflection or discussion; and what keeps it below, as part of the life-world, is the fact that it is shared among a group of people, making for ready if not routine agreement between them. Even routine agreement, however, is agreement only if, however remotely, it acknowledges the *possibility of disagreement;* there must always be a subliminal recognition that what is actually agreed is not unconditioned but rather something conditioned that has its conditions *satisfied.*[12] A consensus, then, even if, in the taken-for-grantedness of a stable life-world, it is actually closed is, nonetheless, always potentially *open*—open, that is, to challenge—to demonstration that its conditions are in fact satisfied or else to revision or rejection. Now Habermas believes that this openness which belongs in principle to the very structure of communicative action, however latent it may have been in all traditional cultures, has as it were been released by the process of modernization. The modern age is precisely one in which the pressure for *justification* of validity claims has been intensified or in which the worthiness of norms to be complied with has more and more been put at issue; a modern society is one in which norms are more likely to be recognized as *hypothetical,* so that the reasons or grounds that support them must be brought into the open and argued for.

When communicative action is opened up in this way—so that the pressure of criticism is allowed, and the whole process is not aborted by recourse to force or strategy—it assumes the character of what Habermas calls "discourse"; hypothetical validity claims must now be "discursively redeemed." Moreover, the especially characteristic achievement of modernity—and a particular target of post-modernist critics—is the establishment of specialized domains of discourse which, through the consolidation of cumulative learning processes, are available as institutionalized cultural traditions (e.g., in the *scientific* discourse of research-programs, in the *practical* discourse of law, jurisprudence, and philosophical ethics, or in the *aesthetic* discourse of art criticism)[13] to support the clarification and resolution of problematic or contested validity claims. Habermas variously characterizes this process whereby the power of prejudgmental attitudes is diminished, through the discursive breaking down of their dogmatic fixity, as a process of "communicative liquefaction," the "linguistification of the sacred," or the "rationalization of the life-world." It involves "the increasing reflexivity of the cultural tradition, the universalization of values and norms, the freeing of communicative action from tightly circumscribed normative contexts, the diffusion of models of socialization which promote processes of individuation and the formation of abstract ego-identities, and so on."[14] It also involves increasing *differentiation,* on many levels: within the life-world, vertically, between action and discourse, and horizontally between different domains of action as well as between correspondingly different domains of discourse; and then the further differentiation between (or "uncoupling" of) the life-world itself and the subsystems of economy and governmental administration (which he sees as regulated by the semi-autonomous, noncommunicative "steering media" of money and power).[15]

2. The 'Uncoupling of System and Life-World': Progress and Deformation

When Habermas outlines this whole scenario of growing complexity, reflectiveness, and differentiation, in one sense he is only being a good sociologist: largely following Weber, he is simply assembling a categorial framework which helps to describe what is, whether one likes it or not, "a world-historical process."[16] But does Habermas himself like it? As a thinker who has always vigorously contested the idea of a value-free social science, what is his critical response to this whole development? All that I have said so far about his stance as a defender of modernity makes it clear that, in the main, and of course with reservations, he supports it. As he put it in a revealing interview:

> I do not know how one could renew the cushion of tradition that supported capitalist societies for centuries, which was consumed without being regen-

erated, indeed how traditionalism in any sense could be renewed by a historically enlightened consciousness. The only resource we can still creatively
draw on [is] cultural modernism. . . . Modern life-worlds are differentiated
and should remain so in order that the reflexivity of traditions, the individuation of the social subject, the universalistic foundations of justice and
morality do not all go to hell.[17]

I said "in the main, and of course with reservations," however, because
Habermas's support for the project of modernity, as we are already well
aware, is itself differentiated; what never escapes him is "the highly *ambivalent* content of cultural and social modernity."[18] In his earlier writing,
as we have already seen, he was not embarrassed to invoke Vico's example
in drawing up a balance sheet of profits and losses with respect to the
transitions from classical to modern politics, and in all his writings since,
he has never ceased to be aware of the debit side of these accounts.

His main reservations focus on what he now calls the "uncoupling
of system and life-world." Progress in technology and economics in the
Occident became possible only when two complementary and interlocking subsystems (i.e., the market-based economic system and the bureaucratic apparatus of the modern state) were firmly unyoked from traditionalist frameworks and allowed to develop autonomously—by being given
over to the "steering media" of money and power.[19] Habermas is not opposed to the differentiation and "mediatization" of these subsystems *per
se*. He is prepared, for instance, to convict even Marx of naive anti-
modernism on account of his not recognizing that growing system complexity *can* represent "a higher and evolutionarily advantageous level of
integration by comparison to traditional societies" and that it ought not,
therefore, *as such*, be seen as a symptom of alienation. Marx's failure here,
according to Habermas, lay in his not making "a sufficiently sharp separation between the *level of system differentiation* attained in the modern
period and the *class-specific forms* in which it has been institutionalized."
However, even if the devolution of action-coordination to media must,
in itself, be accounted as one of the "normal components of modernization," the critical task still remains of identifying "the threshold at which
the mediatization of the lifeworld turns into its colonization"—or, in other
words, the point at which the "intrinsic evolutionary value" of structural
differentiation becomes forfeit to the distortions of capitalist modernization.[20] And here Marx remains indispensable. "Too much Weber! Too little Marx!"[21] is an understandable and not uncommon response to *The
Theory of Communicative Action*. But the book's admittedly heavier reliance on Weber for an analytic description of modern society should not
obscure the fact that it is still Marx (even if only as "reconstructed") who
provides the best explanation of why modernization has assumed the one-

sided character which it has: the continuing "theoretical superiority" of the Marxian approach, Habermas believes, derives from its "ingenious *coup de main* in the analysis of the commodity form."[22]

What takes Habermas's attention, then — in the light of a correction of Marx which is intended to salvage rather than abandon his main insight — is the power of the subsystems, once released from the constraints of normative or communicative contexts within the lifeworld and at the same time given over to the "irresistible inner dynamics" of capitalism, to *turn back* against this life-world itself and subject it to "internal colonization." This is indeed the major theme of volume two of *The Theory of Communicative Action:* the deepest dehumanization is caused by the subjection of the life-world to systemic imperatives, the deepest crises spring from the inherent impossibility of dealing with this dehumanization through compensatory mechanisms based in the subsystems themselves ("money and power can neither buy nor compel solidarity and meaning"),[23] and the deepest protests, therefore, emerge along "the seams between system and life-world" and are concerned ultimately with the "grammar of forms of life."[24]

I shall not dwell on this aspect of Habermas's thought: not because it is unimportant but rather because the points he is making here are, I believe, the same points, differently formulated, that we have already (previous chapter, section 5) seen him make in terms of our central distinction between praxis and technique and of the modern attempt — with all its attendant consequences — to ignore or suppress it. The new conceptual framework scores in terms of sophistication, but I am not sure to what extent, in the end, it enables Habermas to say anything substantially different from what he had already said about the *thing itself.* He himself believes that it helps us to distinguish, more clearly than either Weber (with his notion of "purposive rationality") or Adorno and Horkheimer (with their notion of "instrumental reason") were able to do, between *system* and *action* rationality. Both Weber's gloomy diagnosis and Adorno's and Horkheimer's scarcely less bleak response to it were formulated in terms of a totalization of one kind of action orientation, whereas what needs to be criticized, in Habermas's view (and what he now calls *functionalist* reason), is the subordination of communicative or consensus guided action to systemic considerations. It seems to me, however, that Habermas's own earlier notion of technique did embrace a systems dimension, and in his analysis of the latter subordination in *T.C.A.* it is worth noting how frequently and casually the word 'technicist', or some variant of it, still occurs.[25]

What I do want to explore further, however, is his more recent understanding of the "rationalization of the life-world" in the *narrow sense* —

i.e., as deriving not from the alien imposition of systems-rationality but rather from the release of a communicative rationality which requires that norms and values be tested and validated consensually. It is this rationality which, according to Habermas, escaped the notice both of Weber and of Adorno and Horkheimer—so that in the end they had nothing left to oppose to a totalized (and, for Habermas, "demonized") ends-means rationality except in the one case an elevated stoicism and, in the other, "the mimetic power of art and love" or, *in extremis,* "the impotent rage of nature in revolt." But if Habermas sees his own main achievement as being precisely the recognition and articulation of this other mode of rationality and the possibility thereby gained of outlining a *different* process of rationalization to the one so deprecated by Weber, what I now want to ask is whether Habermas has any reservations at all about *this* process, which is essentially one of making the lifeworld more transparent to itself?

3. Habermas's Defense of the 'Rationalization of the Life-World': Technicism in a New Guise?

This question raises our central issue about Habermas's understanding of the nature and limits of *critique;* for it seems clear that he now sees critique as exercising its influence in society precisely through the deepening and expansion of this rationalization process. We have been aware all along that it is his belief in the power of critique to gain a purchase on and to substantially transform life-practice that most significantly sets him apart from the philosophers whom we have met in previous chapters. What has become apparent in this chapter, however, is that 'critique' has lost some of the strong charge which it had in his earlier writings—when Marx and Freud (their meta-theoretical shortcomings notwithstanding) were still exemplary for it—and has come to coincide with a search for consensus, informed by the differentiated theoretical endeavors which are more or less securely established by enlightened modernity and institutionalized in its universities and research institutes. "Rather than hunting after the scattered traces of revolutionary consciousness," we are told in *A Theory of Communicative Action,* a critical theory "would have to examine the conditions for re-coupling a rationalized culture with an everyday communication dependent on vital traditions."[26] It seems clear that the radicalism of his thought is now confined to a reinterpretation and vindication of the kind of enlightened reason which has always been internal to the project of modernity.

If what we see here is Habermas's deeply liberal instincts gaining over the Marxist ones ("my Marxist friends are not entirely unjustified in accusing me of being a radical liberal")[27] this still, of course, leaves him at quite a distance from Aristotle as well as from the recent philosophers in whose work I have been retrieving a central Aristotelian distinction. Indeed it may be that this distance is now *greater*, given that the Kantian perspective to which he has been retreating is, in fact, a less resonant echo-chamber for Aristotelian thought than the more pronouncedly Hegelian-Marxist one of his earlier thought. In the previous chapter, I was able to show that the early Habermas had a viewpoint on modern society which he could formulate in terms of the Aristotelian distinction. The question which presses itself in the light of what we have seen in the present chapter, however, is this: Has Habermas rescued praxis from the rationalist encroachments of technique only to deliver it over to another kind of rationalism—that which is at work in what he now unabashedly, and "in a thoroughly positive sense,"[28] calls the "rationalization of the life-world"? The central motif of our previous chapters, one shared by all our featured philosophers—notwithstanding the different contexts and idioms in which it was worked out by each of them—was the manifold ways in which practice eludes or resists the designs of a sovereign reason. Is this same motif at all recognizable in a philosopher who emphasizes so much the transparency of life-practice and, as its correlative, the autonomy of those who engage in it, so that consensus cannot be taken to pre-exist as a *condition* of right reason but must, rather, be *achieved* by an unencumbered reason itself?

Before being able to answer this central question about Habermas's profile in our inquiry, we need first to go back and take up the question (raised at the end of the previous section) which immediately prompted it: How unreserved is his attitude to what he calls the rationalization of the life-world? I shall answer this by identifying what are, I believe, two significantly different levels at which he has reservations in relation to it. In the rest of this section I shall consider his reservations at the first level and show how his response to them suggests one particular answer to the central question posed above. In the next section (4), however, I shall look at reservations which he has at what seems to be a deeper level. Then, having taken these into account, I shall attempt (in section 5) a fuller, more complex answer to our question—one which will involve a final "reckoning of profits and losses" in relation to Habermas's philosophy.

Habermas's first level of reservation concerns the discourses which are differentiated out in the process of rationalization. Although *per se* these discourses (i.e., the cognitive-instrumental, the moral-practical, and the aesthetic-expressive) represent a higher level of reflexivity and so—like system complexity *per se*—meet with Habermas's approval, their inherent potential has not been realized. This is because they have been

dammed up in "expert cultures" which are split off from the ordinary practice of life. Thus we get, on the one side, a hermetic professionalization
and, on the other, "cultural impoverishment." The impoverishment stems
from the fact that while capitalist modernization has had an open field
for the destruction of traditional life-forms, the potential of cultural modernity for "salvaging" the "communicative substance" of these life-forms
and renewing it "at a higher level of differentiation" has not been exploited.
Thus "the explosive contents of cultural modernity have been defused"
and, as a result, "everyday practice is impoverished with traditionalist left-
overs."[29]

At this first level of reservation, then, Habermas's point is that "the
space opened up by the rationalization of the lifeworld does not get utilized."[30] What we need to notice, however, is that in his view this space
has got opened up — and *could* get utilized. He seems to believe that
(i) the process of modernization contained within itself both the potential for enormously increased productivity and efficiency *and* the utopian
promise of a "post-traditional life-world"; (ii) as this process has unfolded
the utopian promise has been made void by the ruthless exploitation of
the economic/bureaucratic potential, to such an extent that it might be
interpreted as a mere ideology obscuring just how ruthless this exploitation has actually been; and (iii) this promise is *more* than mere ideology,
however, insofar as it has accumulated into cognitive resources which, even
though they have as it were been shunted into a cultural siding, nonetheless really do have the power to facilitate "moral-practical will-formation,
expressive self-presentation, and aesthetic satisfaction." Habermas seems
to be asserting here, that cultural modernism has created a virtual space
over against the actual space of capitalist modernization and that we can
at least envisage some kind of "mediation" or "recoupling" through which
the virtuality (of high culture enclaves) could itself be actualized (in a
rationalized life-world).

It is worth noting that even though it is a reorientation of everyday
practice that Habermas has in mind here, the cultural resources which
he is looking to for this task are by no means limited to practical/moral
discourse. He believes that the sciences also (whose horizons, therefore,
need not be entirely confined to "technical progress, capitalist growth,
and rational administration") can contribute to "the understanding that
communicating citizens have of themselves and of their world" — of themselves in terms of their real interests and needs, and of the world in terms
of ways in which these may be met. And he believes that the arts, too —
more immediately than the sciences insofar as they stay closer to ordinary
language — can "penetrate in a transforming, illuminating, and liberating
way" into the "communicative practice of everyday life." The aesthetic sphere,

which was largely absent from Habermas's earlier work — even though it had been a central concern of the earlier critical theorists, especially Benjamin and Adorno — has come to assume increasing significance in his later writings.[31] Although he still does not offer a developed aesthetics — and one can get the impression that this sphere interests him mainly because it affords a plausible way of filling out one of the "blanks" in his overall schema — his main idea seems to be that artists and writers have unique access to the innards of modern experience: they expose experiences which have been sapped in the transitions to modernity and they reveal — or give "illuminating, suggestive, and visible expression" to — diffuse new experiences secreted by these same transitions. The artistic posture is that of a "subjectivity that is decentered and removed from the spatiotemporal structures of everyday life . . . from the conventions of daily perception and of purposive activity, from the imperatives of work and of what is merely useful."[32] With this posture, artists are a kind of *avant garde* whose imaginative projections — if they can be released from high-cultural encapsulation — can enter transformatively into our "world-disclosing and need-interpreting languages," and thus inform us of "what we really want, and above all: what we *cannot* want."[33]

Habermas is of course aware (and this is a second reservation about the "rationalization of the life-world" though still at what I called above the first level) that even if the life-world could be made properly porous to expert cultures, given that these cultures now reside in *three* autonomous value spheres, it would be threatened with a kind of fragmentation to which an earlier lifeworld — despite, or rather because of, what Habermas would regard as its lower level of reflectiveness — was not exposed. Moreover this threat can all too easily be answered in a way that does violence to the differentiations that have been painfully achieved in modernity. Knowledge specialized along one dimension of validity can bid for influence in the lifeworld in too unmediated a manner and without due regard for other types of knowledge; examples of "insufficiently complex incursions" of this sort — which disturb "the equilibrium of the lifeworld's communicative infrastructure" — are furnished not just by technocratic undertakings but also by "the aestheticizing . . . or the moralizing of particular domains of life" that is to be found in "expressivist countercultures . . . or fundamentalist movements."[34] The question then arises whether the "magnificent 'one-sidednesses' which are the signature of modernity" can be reconciled, or whether there is any way in which "the intermeshing of cognitive-instrumental with moral-practical and expressive moments, which had obtained in everyday practice prior to its rationalization, could be retained at a higher level of differentiation."[35]

We have been considering Habermas's reservation about a culture split by differentiated but mutually uncomprehending specialisms, and his rejection — as unsatisfactory reactions to this — of premature and one-sided attempts at unification which he associates with the counterculture. It is interesting, however, that insofar as he himself has any answer to this problem of fragmentation, he seems to find it precisely in what (near the end of *T.C.A.*) he calls "countermovements" which "under the primacy of one dominant aspect of validity, bring back in again the two aspects of validity that were at first excluded." He mentions here "non-objectivistic approaches to research within the human sciences that bring viewpoints of moral and aesthetic critique to bear"; the insinuation of the cognitive and the expressive into ethics through "the stronger consideration given to hedonistic motives . . . the calculation of consequences and the inter-pretation of needs"; and "tendencies toward realism and engagement" in an art which still moves at "the level of the wealth of forms that the *avant garde* set free." Apart from these suggestions, Habermas does not pursue any further "the tortuous routes along which science, morality and art com-municate with one another." But the tentativeness of what he offers here is evident in the final sentence of the paragraph from which I have been quoting: "It seems as if the radically differentiated moments of reason want in such countermovements to point toward a unity — not a unity that could be had at the level of worldviews, but one that might be estab-lished *this side* of expert cultures, in a nonreified communicative everyday practice."[36] But beyond the imputation to reason itself of some kind of inner aspiration — an imputation which seems incongruous when world-views are simultaneously being abjured — what is not evident at all, or even broached, is just *how* these countermovements — which even if, benignly interpreted, they betoken attempts at rapprochement, are still *refinements within esoteric discourses* — are to be translated into our everyday practice "*this side* of expert cultures."

There are other places in *T.C.A.* where we encounter this same issue and, despite the length and indeed the frequent repetitiveness of the work, a similar silence on Habermas's part. In his critique of the "violent abstrac-tions" of bureaucratized welfarism, we see his opposition to experts, not just tough-minded administrators but even tender-minded social workers and therapists, and then, a little later, his cautious endorsement of "youth and alternative movements."[37] It is not made clear, however, whether these "experts" are to be credited with possessing some genuinely worthwhile discursive or critical knowledge and, if so, how this knowledge is to be disengaged from its shell of professionalism and made available to an "alter-native practice" in such a way that the latter does not thereby forfeit the grass-roots character which seems to have made it commendable in the first place. "Communication . . . standing on its own feet . . . bursting encapsulated expert cultures . . ."[38]—what Habermas conveys in these phrases has a powerful rhetorical ring, but we are still left curious about how, with beneficent effect, it could be accomplished.

Again, near the end of the book, Habermas acknowledges that in responding to *non*-modern societies, we moderns should "not only comprehend the learning process that separates 'us' from 'them' but also become aware of what we have *unlearned* in the course of this learning."[39] In fact he is echoing here a question he had raised near the beginning of the book in his recapitulation of the debate about rationality sparked off in the 1960s by Peter Winch's discussion of Evans-Prichard's anthropological research: "Shouldn't we, beyond all romanticizing of superseded stages of development, beyond exotic stimulation from the contents of alien cultures, recall the losses required by our own path to the modern world?"[40] And this question is pursued throughout the work, which analyzes these losses as "deformations" caused (as we have already seen) by the subordination of communicative rationality to systems rationalization —while at the same time recurrently disabusing us of any wish to reinstate "the nostalgically loaded, frequently romanticized past of pre-modern forms of life."[41] I cannot see, however, that Habermas has succeeded in showing us the possibility of our relearning what (to his dismay) we have unlearned without our having to unlearn some of what (with his approval) we have learned. What I am hitting at, in other words, is not just the tension between Habermas's high esteem for the achievements of modernity and his keen sense of its losses but, more particularly, the difficulty which he experiences in trying to show that these losses can in fact be made good. He himself has taken other theorists (even his close collaborator McCarthy) to task for hankering after a "substantive worldview" (anchored in some notion of *nature*) and therefore "dedifferentiating forms of knowledge behind whose categorial distinctions we can no longer retreat in good conscience." He suggests that any attempt to appropriate his own theory and at the same time to satisfy this hankering will only add to the "many failed attempts to have one's cake and eat it too: to retain both Kant's insights and, at the same time, to return to the 'home' (*Behausung*) from which these same insights have driven us."[42] But I am raising the question of whether Habermas himself, in postulating a unity at the level not of worldviews but of everyday practice, is not trying to have *his* (even bigger) cake and eat it too.

What I am expressing here is a reservation about the adequacy of Habermas's response to his own reservations about the "rationalization of the life-world." Its basis will become clearer, perhaps, if we look again, a little closer, at these reservations. Clearly they concern deformations of the rationalization process which have marked it as a matter of historical fact but which Habermas nonetheless wants to see as, in principle, re-mediable. For him, the deformations are failures to realize the potential of rationalization rather than inherent limitations on this potential itself. None of the problems of mediation or of fragmentation really shakes his positive conception of the enlightened and enlightening discourses of modernity. So positive, indeed, is this conception that it might, ironically, be regarded as *positivistic*. In a familiar version, positivism is a canonization of science and a consequent withdrawal of the status of rationality from the ethical and the aesthetic; but Habermas's position might be seen as having positivistic implications insofar as his endorsement of ethical and aesthetic validity claims seems not so much to contest the requirement in the positivist major premise (i.e., that all real knowledge is modeled on or meets the criteria of modern science) as to suggest that in important respects it is *met*.

Insofar as this attributes to Habermas something that is so manifestly contrary to his intentions, it is a provocative line to press against him. What suggests it, however, is the fact that his differentiation between the three "cultural value spheres" (Weber's term) of science, morality, and art does not prevent him from putting the three of them on the same kind of footing—all equally to be endorsed, it seems, as the products of modernity, and equally to be disinfected of, or made proof against, "worldviews." "It is no different with modern culture as a whole than it was with the physics of Newton and his heirs: modern culture is as little in need of philosophical grounding as science. . . . With modern science, with positive law and secular ethics, with autonomous art and institutionalized art criticism, three moments of reason crystalized without help from philosophy."[43] Even if this is correct—as in a sense it surely is—does it imply that, *post factum*, philosophy must find itself equally chastened in the face of all three developments? Habermas gives the impression that it does—when, for instance, he writes, characteristically: "Professionalized treatment of cultural tradition under only *one* abstract aspect of validity *at a time* permits the inner logics of cognitive-instrumental, moral-practical and aesthetic-expressive complexes of knowledge to manifest themselves. From this point on there are *internal histories* of science, of moral and legal theory, of art—not linear developments, to be sure, but learning processes nonetheless."[44]

Just what kind of "learning processes" are involved here, Habermas himself does not find it easy to clarify.[45] It seems clear, however, that he sees a basic approach underlying developments in all three spheres. The "modern understanding of the world," he tells us, "makes possible a *hypothetical* approach to phenomena and experiences, which are isolated from the complexity of life-world contexts and analyzed under *experimentally*

varied conditions. This is *equally* true for the states of an objectified nature, for norms and modes of acting, and for the reflective experiences
of an 'unbound' subjectivity (set free from the practical constraints of everyday life)."[46] The emphases in this quotation are my own and are intended
to highlight the way in which ethical and aesthetic experiences are made
to bear what are normally considered the characteristic marks of *scientific*
experience. Habermas himself cannot but entertain doubts about just how
progressively cumulative the results of "learning" might be, particularly
in the aesthetic sphere,[47] but clearly the "decentered" approach which he
has in mind is intended to generate, in all three spheres, distance, generalized knowledge,[48] and reliable control. And it is the unfavorable contrast
with this control that ultimately sanctions Habermas's poor opinion of
traditions that have not been modernized: "having lost their credibility,
these traditions continue along on the basis of everyday hermeneutics as
a kind of second nature that has lost its force."[49]

At this point it is hard to resist the impression that what Habermas
is driving at here—even though he would surely be sensitive about the
term—is 'techne'. For Aristotle (as for Plato and indeed the sophists) techne
came into being only with the differentiation and specialization of domains, and it too was an attempt to improve on nature that was intimately
related to learning: one could speak of a techne only if there was sufficient
formalization in an area to underpin professional expertise and the possibility of instruction, which was but an orderly way of initiating an individual into the fruits of a cumulative, communal learning process. What
was learned was the reasons or causes (*aitiai*) which accounted for competent performance in an area and thus made this performance amenable
to a discourse (*logos*) which was generalized, public, and rational. It might
be expected that a contemporary philosopher of such immense sophistication as Habermas would be beyond reach of the Greek philosophers. But
what I am nonetheless proposing is that the driving intention which was
captured in the concept of techne is very close indeed to the intention
behind Habermas's whole philosophical enterprise.

Here I seem to have answered in the affirmative the central question
which I raised at the beginning of this section: Even if Habermas's early
philosophy painstakingly and explicitly distinguished the practical from
the technical sphere, has he gone on in his later work to develop a notion
of the practical (now called communicative action) which gives it (in the
sense which I have just explained) an inherently technical slant? When
I raised this question, I said that we would not be in a position to answer
it until we had considered the reservations that Habermas has with regard
to the rationalization of the life-world, reservations which, I suggested,
arise at two significantly different levels. Now at this stage we have ex-

amined only his first-level reservations, and it is his way of handling these which points us toward the conclusion that in the end his project may secrete its own form of technicism.

We should not regard this as the complete answer to our question, however. A more complex picture may emerge when we consider, as I now propose to do, other reservations about rationalization which can be found in his work and which, I want to suggest, belong at a different, and in fact deeper, level than the ones we have just seen. The latter are ones which he feels his own critical theory is able to deal with—by showing that the problems adduced at this level come from *distortions* of the rationalization process, or from a failure to realize what can nonetheless be demonstrated to be its proper *telos*. So long as this failure persists, critical theory can relentlessly expose it and, with a respectable (because not ungrounded) utopianism, point beyond it. The reservations which we shall now consider are at a different level in that they raise the issue of *inherent limits* to rationalization—and indicate, therefore, an unavoidable modesty which critical theory itself must adopt. Within the context of our study, in fact, they reveal that even while Habermas is imbued with, and attempting to give a more adequate account of, the spirit of modern reason, he still cannot avoid making concessions which keep him from entirely parting company with our other thinkers.

4. The Life-World and the Limits of Rationalization: The Shadow Side of Habermas's Thought

What I shall be trying to bring into relief now is what might be called the shadow side of Habermas's thought. This is something that is always in shadow in the actual texture of (pre-philosophical) experience but the point here is that it tends to *remain* shaded in a philosophy such as Habermas's whose overwhelming commitment is to enlightenment and transparency. Despite this commitment, however, Habermas is not unaware of its existence. His most explicit acknowledgements of it are to be found in the published interviews where a more relaxed posture on his own part, combined with the pressure of questioning from (on the whole friendly) interlocutors, tends to bring it more into the open. These interviews will now be my primary source.

> The life-world is that remarkable thing which dissolves and disappears before our eyes as soon as we try to take it up piece by piece . . . the moment this background knowledge enters communicative expression, where it becomes explicit knowledge and thereby subject to criticism, it loses pre-

cisely those characteristics which life-world structures have for those who belong to them: certainty, background character, impossibility of being gone behind.[50]

The whole point of communicative action which has taken on a discursive form is that through it the horizon of the life-world is, as it were, progressively pushed back (this pushing back is what Habermas means by "rationalization"). Still, no matter how much it may be pushed back, this horizon cannot be made to disappear. However incongruous the image of Sisyphus may seem in connection with Habermas's philosophy, there still seems to be something inherently Sisyphean about the project of critical enlightenment:

> One thing you must not forget in any case: for every element of the most explored, well-worn and well-tried life-world that is changed or even consciously accepted, there are untold masses of elements that, even in the course of the most radical weighing of alternatives, never even crossed the threshold of thematization. The life-world is so unproblematic that we are simply incapable of making ourselves conscious of this or that part of it at will. The fact that certain elements of the life-world become problematic is an objective process. It depends on the problems that press in on us from outside in an objective way, by virtue of the fact that something has *become* problematic behind our backs.[51]

Here, surely, we are on ground that is familiar to us from previous chapters. If Marx's materialism ("consciousness is determined by environment") is still detectable, it is so only as refracted through the same phenomenological ideas (of life-world and horizon) that we have already seen reworked by Gadamer into his concept of prejudice. And the limitation on "will" here—which is also to be found in *The Theory of Communicative Action*, where we are told that the life-world is something "over which no one can dispose at will"[52]—echoes Arendt's point about the nondisposability of the 'who' that is disclosed in our acting and speaking. Such disclosure, Arendt tells us, "can almost never be achieved as willful purpose, as though one possessed and could dispose of this 'who' in the same manner he has and can dispose of his qualities." And as, for Arendt, the 'who' is like a *daimōn* which "accompanies each man throughout his life, always looking over his shoulder from behind,"[53] so, for Habermas, the life-world is a "background of implicit knowledge which enters *a tergo* into cooperative processes of interpretation. Communicative action takes place within a lifeworld that remains at the backs of participants."[54]

Moreover what we are faced with here is not simply that the life-world does not become available for thematic reflection at our discretion (but only through the force of "problems that press in on us from outside in an objective way,") or that the process of thematization can never be complete (since even if the horizon is made to recede "untold masses of elements" will always remain on the *other* side of it). We might take both of these facts and still suppose that however, and insofar as, elements *do* come *this* side of the horizon – or above the threshold, to use Habermas's own metaphor – then they at least have, as it were, been cleanly won from the life-world and so are now fully within the ambit of discursive reason. But this is to ignore another fact which Habermas does not lose sight of: i.e., the fact that there is not a *clear line of demarcation* between an explicit communicative action and an implicit life-world. Rationalization occurs on a messy front and the forces of reason are never quite uncompromised or able to conduct the campaign on their own terms. This fact – which we might almost say makes "rationalization of the life-world" an inherently paradoxical expression – is not one which Habermas's priorities lead him to emphasize; but there are one or two places in his writings where it does come through and where, in fact, the tone may strike us as more characteristic of Newman than of Habermas himself: "Stability and absence of ambiguity are rather the exception in the communicative practice of everyday life. A more realistic picture is that . . . of a diffuse, fragile, continuously revised and only momentarily successful communication in which participants rely on problematic and unclarified presuppositions and feel their way from one occasional commonality to the next."[55] And even when commonality or agreement *does* occur, we must recognize that it is seldom reached through the kind of unequivocal verification/falsification procedures that may be available with regard to hypotheses generated in experimentally controlled settings: "When claims to truth or justice become really obstinately problematic, there are no neat deductions or decisive pieces of evidence which could *enforce* an immediate decision for or against. Rather a play of argumentation is required, in which motivating reasons take the place of the unavailable knockdown arguments."[56]

The "motivating reasons" that Habermas refers to come into play not only in the exchanges that are generated by situations for which the life-world obviously provides the backdrop; they also function even in the more theoretically rarefied domain of philosophy itself. We have seen how much Habermas's own philosophy is directed against the "dogmatism of life-practices"; but when he is challenged about the "basic intuition" or impulse which animates his own work – giving him "the impression that something is deeply amiss in the rational society in which I was brought up and in which I now live"[57] – he frankly confesses:

There is also a dogmatic core to my convictions, of course. I would rather abandon scholarship than allow this core to soften, for those are intuitions which I did not acquire through science, that no person ever acquires that way, but rather through the fact that one grows up in an environment with people with whom one must come to terms, and in whom one recognizes oneself.[58]

Habermas is an uncompromisingly difficult philosopher who has more than honored the requirement of "bringing one's work up to the standards set by institutionalized research"—to the chagrin, indeed, of certain countercultural elements who would like an endorsement of more 'immediate' action and critique; yet here he is acknowledging the pre-philosophical roots of his deepest intuitions. And in fact the relationship of his philosophy to pre-philosophical experience (in the 'life-world') is even stronger than this acknowledgement on its own might suggest. *Every* philosophical position may be taken to reflect certain determining experiences or impressions of life—so that it is always true even of *philosophical* thought that "its sources are too remote and hidden" (Newman) or, in Habermas's own words, "one never really knows what one is up to."[59] Beyond this tacit and unavoidable infiltration of the life-world into it, however, Habermas's philosophy expressly and formally assigns a surprisingly big role to negotiations within the life-world. Moreover, it does this precisely by scaling down its own claims as philosophy. For all its seeming ambitiousness, and notwithstanding the fact that it started out as an attempt to formulate "a critical theory with a practical intent," it is in the end self-consciously modest, not to say minimalist, in its own claims to practical efficacy. This stems from the highly formal or procedural nature of what it reconstructs as the "rationalization of the life-world." The push toward universalization, abstraction, and explicit justification which Habermas sees as a world-historical tendency and which he tries both to articulate and to vindicate in his philosophy does not provide any *substantive* criteria which could be deployed in actual discussions about practical affairs. Habermas himself is well aware of this, but he seems more comfortable to leave his philosophy open to the charge of vacuity (for its self-imposed abstemiousness) rather than to that of *hubris* (for its architectonic ambitions): "Nothing makes me more nervous than the imputation . . . that because the theory of communicative action focuses attention on the social facticity of recognized validity-claims, it proposes, or at least suggests, a rationalistic utopian society. I do not regard the fully transparent society as an ideal, nor do I wish to suggest *any* other ideal."[60]

Habermas's espousal of this "weak" or "restrictive" conception of philosophical theory is primarily motivated by a desire not so much to clip the wings of philosophers as to enhance the status of what can be accomplished only by the participants themselves in practical affairs:

> According to my conception, the philosopher ought to explain the moral point of view. . . . Anything further than that is a matter for discourse between participants. Insofar as the philosopher would like to justify specific principles of a normative theory of morality and politics, he should consider this as a proposal for the discourse between citizens. In other words: the moral philosopher must leave the substantive questions which go beyond a fundamental critique of value-scepticism and value-relativism to the participants in moral discourse.[61]

Now Habermas grants that the philosopher may himself participate in this discourse, may indeed have a special competence to bring to it.[62] But if he does, this competence resides not in any capacity to introduce novel theories or arguments but rather in his greater ability to clarify and formulate moral intuitions which are already operative in a way of life. And of course it is Aristotle and not Kant who comes to mind here: "Moral theory proceeds reconstructively, in other words after the event. Aristotle was right in his opinion that the moral intuitions which theory clarifies must have been acquired elsewhere, in more or less successful socialization processes."[63] Or we find this same point expressed in a passage where Habermas again invokes Aristotle, albeit with scarcely concealed reluctance:

> There is also . . . the Aristotelian argument in the Nicomachean Ethics, that nobody can deal with ethical questions who has not been raised properly. I do not think that this is quite true. I feel inhibitions about saying that. But it is fair to ask: how could anyone focus on moral intuitions and reconstruct them, before having them — and how do we get them? Not from philosophy and not by reading books. We acquire them just by growing up in a family. This is the experience of everyone except perhaps psychopaths with no moral sensibility whatsoever. There can't be anyone who ever grew up in any kind of family who did not acquire moral intuitions. . . . I don't believe that we can change moral intuitions except as educators — that is not as theoreticians and not as writers.[64]

The priority of practice over theory which Habermas grants here is binding on the philosopher not only when he is 'engaged' as a citizen in argumentative discourse — taking up a position of advocacy on particular issues such as economic or environmental policies, nuclear weapons, abortion — but also, in fact, when he sticks to his own last as a philosopher. His business, strictly as a philosopher, is simply to explain "the moral point of view," which for Habermas means making explicit what is, beyond all differences of culture, race, or epoch, "a universal core of moral intuition in all times and in all societies." The intuition to which Habermas refers is one that is operative for all participants in language; it is implicit in the "conditions of symmetry and reciprocal recognition which are unavoidable presuppositions of communicative action." And so the *a posteriori* nature of Habermas's own philosophical task in relation to it is clear: in Rylean terminology, this task is to "transform a practically mastered pretheoretical knowledge (know-how) of competent subjects into an objective and explicit knowledge (know-that)."[65]

I tried to bring out in the previous chapter (section 4) the differences between Habermas and Gadamer — differences which are, indeed, in some respects, as I have since intimated, only accentuated by Habermas's later work. At the same time, however, we should not fail to notice that this later work brings his approach into a kind of alignment with the approach of Gadamer, which (as we saw in chapter 5, section 5) self-consciously invokes the model of Aristotelian practical philosophy. It may be that Habermas's critical and utopian intent still commits him to a radical reform of life-practice; but if this is so, what is now much clearer is that his theoretical articulation of this intent appeals crucially to resources which are embedded in life-practice itself. We may recall that in highlighting the extent to which Gadamer's hermeneutics is an attempt "to bring to reflective awareness the communality that binds everyone together," we noted that it is, in this respect, a move toward Aristotle and a move away from Heidegger; by his own admission, Gadamer wanted to gain, in relation to "the extreme consequences of thought heightened . . . by Heidegger with eschatological pathos," "a counter-poise in the continuity of a linguistically interpreted order of life that is constantly being built up and renewed in family, society and state."[66] Now Gadamer's relation to Heidegger finds a close parallel in Habermas's relation to his own mentor, Adorno. Gadamer's hermeneutics could refuse to go down the dark path of Heidegger's esoteric discourse, and take instead the "path leading from practice towards making it aware of itself theoretically,"[67] only because — despite all the encroachments of technique — it could still count on something ultimately intact in this practice itself. In Habermas we see a similar balking at the "extreme consequences" or "pathos" to which Adorno was reduced when he "found political institutions, all social institutions and daily practice as well, completely void of all traces of reason."[68] Like Adorno, Habermas, too, wants a critical theory of society, but for him "it makes a difference whether you see *any* kind of communicative rationality built into daily practice or the life-world."[69] The difference here is precisely what separates Adorno — who "cannot appeal to any structure heterogeneous to instrumental reason, against which the force of totalized purposive rationality must collide"—from Habermas himself, who finds a way of "pinning down such a resistant structure, namely the structure of a rationality which is immanent in everyday communicative practice, and which brings the stubbornness of life-forms into play against the functional demands of autonomized economic and administrative systems."[70]

What we have just seen is that the rational capacities which Habermas must rely on for a critical opening up of life-practice—through a pressure toward universalization, individuation, and "abstract ego-formation"—are themselves based in life-practice. Beyond recognizing this dependence on rational structures which must be *given* in life-practice before they can be reconstructed in theory, however, Habermas is also aware that the integrity of a way of life cannot be sustained by critical or discursive reason alone. Even if the whole stress in his writing is on such a reason, we find occasional but very telling advertences to the need for something else, i.e., *remembrance* or *preservation*—which Gadamer, we may recall, emphasizes as "an act of reason, though an inconspicuous one." The critical and the technical uses of reason can release us from the tyranny of a bad past, but in doing so they can also induce a kind of historical weightlessness in which our identity becomes all too abstract: "Material improvements . . . bear so to speak a loss of historical memory on their brow . . . a level of satisfaction, once attained, eliminates, as it were, the traces of the history of its own appearance."[71] Here is a passage that brings us as close as we ever get in Habermas to an apprehension of what drove Gadamer's analysis of experience back behind the too-easy annulment of process in Aristotle's account of concept-formation to an insistence, with Aeschylus, on the need for "learning through suffering":[72]

> Utopias are important . . . but memory is just as important. . . . What is terrifying about material progress, even about political and constitutional progress among people who have not fought through a revolution, is this traceless disappearance of the historical path. It is terrifying both for past suffering and past sacrifice, which, without the possibility of a reconciling rememoration, is as good as lost, and for the identity of those who come later, who, without an awareness of the heritage which they have entered into can have no idea of who they are.[73]

Habermas seems to be recognizing here that peoples' identity, their "idea of who they are," is not to be formed simply by a process of critical distancing (or the "post-conventional" decentering which he appropriates from Kohlberg's theory of moral development); rather it must also depend on their continuing to experience solidarity—at a pre-discursive level and through the crucial mediation, one assumes, of custom and ritual—with significant elements of their own, or their community's, past.

And here, again, finally, what is true at the level of practice finds its reflection at the level of theory: *anamnesis,* or "awareness of the heritage which they have entered into," is important not only for everyone engaged in the life-world but also for philosophers. Habermas's own work, he does not mind admitting, is driven by the "fear" that much advanced contemporary thought is "racing toward the destruction of all that I consider *deserves to be saved* in the substance of Western traditions and inspirations."[74] This is a very plain reminder of what is perhaps too easily forgotten: even if critical theory sets itself against tradition (and canvasses a "post-traditional everyday practice"), it cannot help now being, for a latecomer like Habermas, itself a tradition.[75] The tireless "reconstruction" to which he has subjected a whole succession of modern thinkers—from his earliest writings right up to the present—has really been an attempt to preserve or to "save" what, behind their own often inadequate formulations of it, he has been able to recognize as their genuine striving toward emancipation. And, equally, his passionate opposition to fashionable post-modernist thinkers such as Derrida, Foucault, and Lyotard stems precisely from his sense of their having so lightly discarded what for him (despite, or rather partly because of, what remains of his Marxism) is the hard-won, fragile, and unrelinquishable gains of the liberal, Enlightenment heritage.[76]

5. Conclusion: *Aporiai* in Habermas's Thought and the Point of a Return to Aristotle

We have just been looking at elements in Habermas's thought which are least congruent with his overall thrust and which keep him, in fact, in some neighborly closeness to the thinkers who featured in our earlier chapters. On the other hand, in the previous section (3) we looked at, and raised critical questions against, those elements in his thought which make him—as a resolute apologist for modernity—dissatisfied with the acceptance by our other thinkers of *givens* which define (in the strict sense of setting limits to) human reason and so cannot be dissolved or transcended by it. It is time now to bring my account of Habermas's work to a close and in the light of everything we have seen—but especially the two previous sections—to attempt some final "reckoning of profits and losses" in relation to it.

We may begin by taking our cue from Habermas himself. In *The Theory of Communicative Action* he appropriates a good deal from George Herbert Mead's reflections on communication or consensus-seeking as the defining characteristic of human reason, but he ends his discussion of Mead by pointing out a significant weakness in the latter's whole approach. This weakness has to do with "Mead's fixation on the *formal* features of modern legal and moral development, and on the formal features of individualism in the domain of personality development." Because of this fixation, Mead "neglects the other side of this formalism and does not consider the price that communicative reason has to pay for its victory in the coin of concrete ethical life (*Sittlichkeit*)."[77] Formal morality limits itself to considerations of abstract *justice,* whereas "concrete ethical life" cannot renounce a broader concern with *happiness.* And Habermas goes on, a few pages later: "Ever since Aristotle the philosophical tradition has dealt with this difficult-to-grasp connection between happiness and justice under the title of 'the good.' Life-forms no less than life histories crystallize around particular identities. If it is to be a good life these identities may not contradict moral demands, but their substance cannot itself be justified from universalistic points of view."[78] Although, in urging this case against Mead, Habermas does not mention Hegel, he is in fact echoing Hegel's famous complaint against Kant: the concepts of autonomy, duty, good will, and the categorical imperative are the highest achievements of moral philosophy—but, devoid of the "determinate particular," they are contentless and empty, and, separated from passion and desire, they cannot deal with the problem of motivation.[79]

Now this charge which Habermas brings in the clearest terms against Mead is precisely the same charge to which he himself is most vulnerable. He believes that the shift in his later work to a "communicative paradigm" is a major advance on the 'monologism' of the subject-centered paradigm which Kant still preserved from the legacy of Descartes. It might be argued, however, that the long detours which he has taken through, for example, Mead's own concept of "taking the attitude of the other" as well as Piaget's "decentering" and Kohlberg's "ideal role-taking" (all capacities for entering into reciprocity which carry a person beyond the projections of a naive egocentrism and thereby underpin the objectivity of the consensual search for truth) serve only to confirm what was already implicit in Kant's categorical imperative: "Act only on that maxim through which you can at the same time will that it should become a universal law."[80] The later Habermas tends to speak of "undamaged intersubjectivity" where the early Habermas would more likely have spoken of "mature autonomy" (*Mündigkeit*). But "intersubjectivity" was already implicit in "autonomy" (even in Kant's notion of the latter, which included, after all, a concern for "humanity whether in one's own person *or in the person of any other*")[81] and, as explicated in the later work, intersubjectivity does not relativize autonomy but, on the contrary, provides the medium through which it is to be achieved. Autonomy remains the cherished ideal which "undistorted communication" serves and manifests; and both of them stand under the *universal* and *abstract* features which Habermas tries to delineate. And so the upshot here is that if Habermas has gone beyond Kant, in doing so he has *not* extricated himself from Kant's incorrigible formalism.

Now what I have just said is something which would not, I believe, be denied by Habermas himself. He recognizes very clearly the vulnerability of his own philosophy to the case which he brings against Mead. The interesting thing, however, is that he does not so much try to rebut this case as simply concede it — and in the light of this concession, deliberately scale down the claims of his own theory. This brings us back to the self-effacing character of his philosophy which we saw in the previous section and which we must now examine a little further. We saw that Habermas declines to offer a utopian blueprint; he is not recommending a transparent or "rationalized" society as an ideal — indeed, he is not recommending *any* ideal. We should notice that what he wants to put aside here is not just eschatology, or the presumption of dictating to, or even anticipating, the future from the standpoint of the present; more radically, he is renouncing any claim to judge — or even to be providing criteria that might help in judging — the overall integrity or well-being, *in the present,* of a life, be it the life of an individual or the way of life of a community. He warns us against "inferring an idea of the good life from the formal concept of reason with which the decentered understanding of the world in the modern age has left us."[82] This "formal concept of reason," which he himself has gone to such pains to reconstruct, refers only to "single dimensions and universal structures" and it therefore can say "nothing about the value of a concrete way of life."[83]

What puts concrete lives and ways of life out of court is their *totality* and *plurality.* As total — i.e., as relatively seamless weaves of all three dimensions that have been differentiated out by modern reason — they resist judgment from the perspective of any single dimension; and as plural — i.e., as inextinguishably different from each other — they cannot be adequately judged against universal structures. What asserts itself here as totality and plurality is in fact the stubborn opacity of the life-world (or rather life-worlds) which we also met in the previous section. If truth, utility, justice, and beauty (or authenticity) are standards which crystallize out of life-worlds along single dimensions, what can be meaningfully attributed to life-worlds *qua* totalities, as we just saw, is *happiness:* "Happiness, unlike justice, or knowledge is not a concept that relates only to one of these dimensions and to general structures of the life-world. It is related to particular constellations of lived practices, value orientations, traditions, and competences as a whole. Its object is always a historically unique configuration."[84] Habermas grants that we may want to make judgments about such configurations (we do, after all "have more or less definite feelings about the success of modes of life and—with less deception— about their failure")[85] but if we do, it is best to construe happiness in terms of *health* ("If we do not wish to renounce altogether standards for judging a form of life . . . if it is really necessary, the model of sickness and health presents itself")[86] and to see these judgments, then, as analogous with those of a clinician. While Habermas recognizes that making such judgements was "once the aim of classical ethics,"[87] his own attitude to them, however, is unashamedly agnostic: "So far I have no idea how the universal core of those merely clinical intuitions—if indeed they have one at all—can be theoretically grasped."[88]

What are we to make of this agnosticism? Can something which seemed to count against Mead as a culpable weakness be transformed in Habermas's own theory into a necessary privation? When he commits himself to "a domain of autonomous morality and moral universalism that distills a class of rationally solvable problems from the complexity of the contexts of ethical life under the single aspect of justice" can we be satisfied with what is *excluded*—albeit very self-consciously excluded—by this commitment? First let us be clear about what the commitment is to and what, in turn, is excluded by it. Essentially it is a commitment (as we are aware from section 1 above) to *justification*. Habermas makes much of the fact that his philosophical project is not a foundationalist one, in the sense that even if certain universal structures of rationality become perspicuous in his theory (as in Weber's also) they can do so (as Marx most keenly recognized) only on foot of an actual historical evolution—the *"ratio cognoscendi"* cannot outstrip the *"ratio essendi"*[89]—and moreover his formulations of them must always be undertaken in a fallibilist spirit. However, if Habermas's theory eschews the foundationalism of what might be called first philosophy, it more than compensates by the onus of justification which it places on agents in a modern life-world and by the exclusive concern for justification which it attributes to the moral theories that are supposed to help these agents. And what is excluded by this commitment to justification? Here is a passage in which the answer is, I think, clear: "They [i.e., moral theories of the type which enjoy Habermas's approval] are typically restricted to the question of the *justification* of norms and actions. They have no answer to the question of how justified norms can be *applied* to specific situations and how moral insights can be *realized*."[90]

I want to focus on the split here between justification (which would most properly occur within "decentered" discourse) and realization (which could only occur in the full concreteness and density of a particular life-world). If one is unhappy—as I am—with this split one might take the view that Habermas's position is simply *incomplete* and that what he has worked out so well on the level of justification (let us call it the cognitive side) needs to be supplemented by insights of comparable sophistication into the concrete realization of ethical norms (let us call this the affective or motivational side). In fact this is the view Habermas himself seems to take in a reappraisal of his work subsequent to the publication of his *magnum opus:*

> I have to point out that I have revised my earlier interpretation. . . . Previously I was not sufficiently clear about the fact that . . . cognitive capacity to justify moral actions and norms has to be supplemented if it is to become effective in the context of ethical life. Only a capacity for judgment (informed by practical reason) makes possible an application of abstract and general norms that is appropriate to particular situations; only motivational resources and structures of inner control make possible actions that are in accord with moral insight. Without the capacity for judgment and motivation, the psychological conditions for translating morality into ethical life are missing; without the corresponding patterns of socialization and institutions, i.e., without "fitting" forms of life to embodied moral principles, the social conditions for their concrete existence are missing.[91]

Here Habermas is trying to make good the cognitivist theory of moral development which he had appropriated from Kohlberg.[92] In this appropriation he had in fact already made what we might regard as a first attempt to improve on Kohlberg, not at all by calling in question the latter's framework of six stages of moral consciousness, but rather by reinterpreting it in terms of "interactive competence" and, at the same time (since an "unexpected result" of this reinterpretation was "the demonstration that Kohlberg's schema of stages is incomplete"), proposing the addition of a *seventh* stage! Even Kohlberg's highest stage of moral development, Habermas had argued, albeit that it is conceived as "post-conventional" and operates at the level of "universal ethical principle," still does not break through to a truly utopian perspective. This is because, for all its higher level rationality, it still does not provide any potentially transformative access to instinctual needs; only as "stencilled" according to convention and tradition do these needs get interpreted and then taken up into a concern for consistency, generalizability, etc. Habermas himself therefore proposed a higher level at which "[i]nner nature is rendered communicatively fluid and transparent to the extent that needs can, through aesthetic forms of expression, be kept articulable [*sprachfähig*]." Through hypothesizing such a level, Habermas believed he had introduced a "model of an unconstrained ego identity [which] is richer and more ambitious than a model of autonomy developed exclusively from perspectives of morality."[93]

Now this earlier attempt to "complete" Kohlberg might be seen as a first attempt on Habermas's part to effect a rapprochement between the cognitive and the affective that would give the latter more of its due. From the passage quoted above, however, it seems he has come to recognize that this attempt was "more ambitious," not so much in expanding the possibilities of instinctual gratification, perhaps, as in inflating the cognitive self's power to make the instinctual life transparent and tractable. In a way that was left quite unclarified, the "aesthetic" was invoked as a medium in which the claims of reason and of instinct are smoothly reconciled; and what I am pointing out with respect to this rather *too* smooth reconciliation (in which responsible moral subjectivity seems to converge with "unbound" aesthetic subjectivity to yield an "unconstrained ego identity") is that if reason is put at the service of instinct here, through such service it seems only to extend its own mastery.[94] In his *second* attempt to correct the rationalist tendency in Kohlberg (and in himself), Habermas depicts the psyche, with all its instinctive and cultural loading, not as providing the discursive ego with materials on which to do its work of "justification" but rather as *setting conditions* which the latter must meet if it is to succeed in "translating morality into ethical life." It is as if Habermas has come to recognize that Kohlberg's theory, even as reconstructed by himself, had provided only a steering apparatus and if it is to be made roadworthy—or rather if it is to adequately model how moral agents actually get around—a drive-shaft must be added. And so, in his amended reconstruction, the cognitive or directional problems—i.e., the ones that involve "justification" or the "redemption of validity claims"—are still to be sorted out by a "decentered" and discursive ego (in communication of course with relevant *alter*); but if the *results* of this strictly cognitive transaction are to reach "application" or "realization" one must have, in addition to an argumentatively adept ego, a psychic disposition which will execute approved or justified decisions.

What is questionable about all this effort at correction and completion is the assumption from which it has proceeded. I want to ask, therefore, not so much whether Habermas has succeeded in connecting the two sides that were separated but rather whether he was right to conceive them as separated in a way that required and allowed the kind of connection he has proposed. This is a connection, we should notice, which preserves the essential separateness of both sides. For while the ego may have to deal with, and may even be dependent on, a "historically unique configuration" of culture and instinct, it cannot allow the latter any place in its own *constitution;* to do so would be to forfeit the *decenteredness* which for Habermas seems to be definitive of the modern ego. At this point the question arises whether this basically dualistic picture of the moral agent is a plausible picture of how people actually live their lives. A second question can also arise: if a person *did* conduct her affairs in this way are there grounds for thinking that, by so doing, she was a better person? On Habermas's self-interpretation, admittedly, this second question ought not to arise. For the formal picture he has drawn is one which supposedly prescinds from issues of the better or the good; such issues, we are to understand, arise only when, outside the parameters of his whole discussion, "substance" is given to ethical life from within the resources of some particular life-world. But this way of excluding our question holds up only if the separation to which we have been adverting is assumed. And of course it is precisely this assumption which is the target of our question. In any case and quite apart from logical points, if, in response to our first question, we can show that there is *another* picture of moral agency which is at least as plausible as Habermas's picture, then it may become clear that both of these pictures do not simply offer models of how people might "process" basically the same moral content but confront us, rather, with alternative and rival pictures of what it is to be a moral person.

   I raise the first question about the plausibility of Habermas's picture, I readily confess, from the standpoint of a very different picture. In this different picture, the cognitive self is dependent on certain culturally shaped passions not just for "translating," "applying," or "realizing" what, with justification, it knows, but rather for the very knowing itself. The "motivational resources" and "structures of inner control" which for Habermas (in the passage quoted in the text at note 91 above) simply "make possible actions that are in accord with moral insight," in this different picture also make one capable of having moral insight at all. And the "judgment" and "practical reason" to which he assigns the "application of abstract and general norms to particular situations" are intimately involved in the *formation* of such general norms in the first place. The further articulation of this alternative picture would lead us into a conceptual vocabulary very different from Habermas's. Rather than "flexible ego-identity," we would find ourselves speaking of "character," and rather than "norms" —which are agreed discursively and *then* applied—we would speak of 'virtues' which are embodied in a character and embrace rational capacities—including one (phronesis) that, among other things, makes us capable of flexibility in our ethical judgments. Moreover, in giving an account of character and reason as intimately united rather than as separate, we would

give a central place to '*experience*', a notion which is curiously inconspicuous in Habermas's picture.

I need hardly say that this other picture which I have just briefly
sketched is Aristotle's. To introduce it now, at the end of our consideration of Habermas, is not just to naively juxtapose a rival theory to the
latter's and, in so doing, to derail the process of immanent critique. For
Aristotle has from the beginning been internal to Habermas's own understanding of his project. His early, very clearly stated intention, we may
recall (from chapter 6, section 2), was not the repudiation of Aristotelian
practical philosophy but rather an ambitious *Aufhebung* that would both
preserve its merits and transcend its limitations by absorbing it into the
perspective of modern theory—a theory whose own tendencies to an arid
positivism would, moreover, be checked by this very absorption. The key
question Habermas formulated, and which we can see his whole subsequent philosophy as an attempt to answer, was: "How can the promise
of practical politics . . . be redeemed without relinquishing, on the one
hand, the rigour of scientific knowledge, which modern social philosophy
demands in contrast to the practical philosophy of classicism? And, on
the other, how can the promise of social philosophy, to furnish an analysis
of the interrelationships of social life, be redeemed without relinquishing
the practical orientation of practical philosophy?"[95]

Now in setting out, near the beginning of his career as a philosopher, to answer this question, Habermas was undertaking a task which
Aristotle, near the beginning of his *Ethics,* had assumed to be impossible.
Aristotle makes very little fuss of asking his readers to relinquish, at the
outset of his inquiry into conduct, nothing other than "the rigor [a pass-
able translation of his word, *akribeia*] of scientific knowledge." His whole
elaboration of a philosophy of practice throughout the rest of the treatise—
and in particular his presentation of the concept of phronesis—makes sense
only if it is seen as an attempt to work out the kind of knowledge and
the kind of orientation-in-action which we are left with when we draw
the full implications precisely of this relinquishing. And here, of course,
he is putting theoretical rigor not only beyond his own reach as a professor
of practical philosophy but, *a fortiori,* beyond the person whose actual
deliberations this philosophy tries to elucidate. And so if it should turn
out that Habermas has failed in his project—which is to enlist the advantages of theory not only for a study of action such as his own but, also,
through the diffusion of "expert cultures," for the life-world—from Aristotle's standpoint his failure must seem inevitable.

We should recognize that Aristotle's standpoint did not derive from
any generalized or deep-seated antagonism to "theory." To the contrary,

his concern for systematization and his desire not only to contribute to careful empirical inquiry (e.g., in biology) but also to explicate the structure of rational competencies (his logic is surely not a bad precursor of the kind of "reconstructive sciences" which Habermas sees as largely displacing traditional philosophy) show an enlightened respect for theory which, allowing for the huge differences in historical context, is not unlike what we find in Habermas himself. Nor indeed would Aristotle have any *a priori* objection to Habermas's attempt to "reconstruct" or make him *aufgehoben*. For this dialectical treatment was just what he administered to *his* predecessors. (His "peculiar achievement," writes Alasdair MacIntyre, "was first to provide a framework of thought within which both the achievements and the limitations of his predecessors could be identified and evaluated and, second, in so doing, to transcend those limitations.")[96] Finally we may note that Aristotle did have something to actually relinquish; in turning away from a theoretical approach to action, he was in fact turning away from the example of Plato's attempt, in the early and middle Dialogues, to lift the problems of action out of the realm of makeshift calculation and to redefine them as subject matter of a respectably rigorous science (techne). From these points we should conclude (and this is made plain in the *Ethics* anyhow) that Aristotle's position stems not from a grudging or weak conception of theory but from a very strong conception of practice. If practice resists theoretical penetration (of the kind envisaged—albeit in their very different ways—by Habermas and Plato) this is because it has an intrinsic, irreducible makeup to which agents cannot but submit and which any "theory" of action (in the sense of an inquiry like Aristotle's own in the *Ethics*) can do no more than bring to a just articulation.

I believe that Habermas has not, in fact, managed to bring about the synthesis of theory and practice that he envisaged. Instead, the separation we have just been considering (psychologically, between a discursive cognitive self and an instinctual self bound to a cultural life-world and, methodologically, between procedural rationality and the substance of historical ways of life) allows him to maintain a tantalizing ambiguity throughout his work. On the *one* hand, this work seems to get to grips with the really pressing issues of the day and, with its purported "practical intent," to encourage expectations of real orientation, indeed "emancipation," in our lives. On the *other* hand, these expectations are continually put on ice by repeated reminders of the merely procedural or formal status by what is being put forward. On the *one* hand, Habermas stands out as a defender of "cultural modernity," committed to the detonation of its "explosive potentials." On the *other* hand his own reconstruction of this modernity is hemmed in by such severe metatheoretical constraints that it is not clear how, if at all, particular practices of life are, or can be, enhanced by it.

What is at stake here, I believe, is not just that we may be disappointed by what, in the end, Habermas "delivers" and may come to agree with the sentiment in Freud's remark: "Methodologists remind me of people who clean their glasses so thoroughly that they never have time to look through them."[97] The more important issue is the one raised by my second question above, i.e., whether Habermas's self-interpretation is correct when he supposes that his whole reconstruction of rationality *is* purely procedural, or that he is *not* involved in "inferring an idea of the good life from the formal concept of reason with which the decentered understanding of the world in the modern age has left us." One of the very great strengths of Habermas's analysis of technicism in his early work — based of course on his distinction between technique and praxis — was his demonstration that modern technique is not the neutral instrumentality which its exponents present it as being. On the contrary, by its very denial of praxis it involves a substantial redefinition of just what it is to lead a human life. The question now is whether the formalism which has become such a pronounced feature in Habermas's own subsequent elaboration of "praxis" is not just a more refined version of the very technicism he had so successfully exposed in his earlier analysis. And if it is, then what has been going on in Habermas's work is not so much the sacrifice of "practical orientation" to "theoretical rigour" as an attempted redefinition of the very meaning of practice — and thereby of the nature of our common humanity.

If the attempt to bring about a higher synthesis of practice and theory has always been integral to Habermas's philosophy, the full extent of his transformation of "practice" cannot be grasped within the confines of this philosophy itself. For this reason, light should be reflected back on Habermas when we go on now, in the second part of our study, to explore the "strong" notion of practice that is to be found in Aristotle. To proceed to Aristotle is not to abort the conversation but rather to extend it. And this is especially the case since we will not simply be appealing to Aristotle as a master whose lessons Habermas has not sufficiently taken to heart. Rather we shall find that Aristotle's treatment of these issues is not without its own ambiguities. It is certainly true that in his analysis of praxis and phronesis he got away from any notion of practice as "merely an expression of embarrassment at the deplorable, but soon overcome, condition of incomplete theory."[98] And it is also true that a key element in his doing this was the contrast which he drew between these two concepts and those of poiesis and techne. Nonetheless, when we come to examine the latter two concepts, we shall find what is, I shall claim, a tension in his thought between "theoretical" and "experiential" tendencies. And it may be that this tension, which he did not resolve or perhaps even recognize, is continuous with the one which still dogs Habermas. And so if our other interlocutors have helped to shape our anticipations of what is to be gained from Aristotle's conception of phronesis, Habermas may have sharpened our sense of a problem which lies deep in his notion of techne.

Interlude

Part 2 of this book is devoted to an analysis of Aristotle's concepts of phronesis and techne, and of the related concepts of praxis and poiesis. Being the second part of an overall study, however, it does not approach these concepts without anticipations or 'precognitions.' For in Part 1, which was presented as a conversation with five modern thinkers, we have already come upon these Aristotelian concepts indirectly—through meeting people who had deeply appropriated them or had found it important to take the bearings of their own ideas in relation to them (the former being the case more with Newman and Gadamer, and the latter with Collingwood, Arendt, and Habermas). And so, in turning to these concepts now, back at source in Aristotle's own texts, I shall bring to them, from my encounters with the modern thinkers, a strong sense of their power to illuminate, in different contexts of thought and action, a major and quite pervasive problem in contemporary culture. This sense could not of course have been Aristotle's own, nor is it to be got from a reading of his texts alone. It does, however, open up a certain direction of interest or line of questioning that I shall bring to his texts, and my purpose in this interlude is to acknowledge and, I hope, to justify this fact.

The problem that motivated the conversation in Part 1, and that therefore is implicitly carried over into Part 2, is the extent to which, rationality having been defined in the modern world as coextensive with technique, nearly all domains of characteristically human engagement are under pressure to become fully 'rational' (the case of teaching was our own special concern), and the extent to which, as this pressure is yielded to, there is an essential loss of integrity in these domains. In the course of this conversation we became aware of Aristotle as the one who had (with Plato) first installed the technical paradigm—through the concept of techne which was its original and classic articulation—at the heart of the Western conception of rationality and who had at the same time (departing significantly here from Plato) keenly appreciated its limits and offered—through the concept of phronesis—a considered alternative to it. Now in taking up this theme of technical reason—its nature and limits, and the possibility of an alternative to it—in areas of practice that have been of particular interest to them,

227

our modern thinkers have been concerned about the respective purchases, in these areas, of what might be called 'theoretical' and 'experiential' approaches. For their reservations about technique can be seen as reservations about the extent to which practical problems can be made amenable to theoretical solutions; and, correspondingly, their arguments that practice is not reducible to technique can be understood as arguments about the inescapably experiential character of practice. As retrieved in their writings, then, techne represents theoretical ambitions in relation to practice, while phronesis represents resistance to these ambitions from the side of practice — or the assertion, as necessary to the latter, of a distinctively practical (in the sense of experiential and nontheoretical) type of knowledge.

My approach to Aristotle's own texts will be informed by the whole discussion in Part 1. The very selection of the concepts of phronesis and techne, and of the distinction between them, is itself a function of that discussion; for this distinction, while not entirely absent from recent scholarship on the *Ethics*, has not, to my knowledge, been subjected to very close analysis. And, indeed, although phronesis has attracted a great deal of attention, techne (which of course has a far greater role in Aristotle's writings than that of simply providing a foil for phronesis) has, I believe, been unduly neglected by Aristotelian scholars.

Not only the selection of my topic, however, but also what I emphasize and systematically pursue in dealing with it is influenced by the earlier discussion. For the relationship of 'experience' to 'theory' which we met in it — the manner in which theory builds on and yet transcends experience, but more particularly the manner in which, in certain practical engagements, experience remains stubbornly untranscendable — will be the dominant motif in the discussion here of phronesis and techne. I shall try to show how techne (although it was not theoretical in Aristotle's sense of theory, which was a form of purely contemplative activity) enshrined much of what we have come to think of as the hallmarks of a theoretical approach — a concern not so much with particular instances as with a knowledge that is explanatory, generalized, systematic, and transmissible, and is at the same time a source of reliable control over the facts that it brings within its ambit. And in exploring phronesis, I shall be emphasizing its experiential nature, the immediacy of its involvement in concrete situations, and the responsiveness and resourcefulness in these situations that come to it only from the character and dispositions of the person, formed in the course of his life-history, and not from any knowledge that can be made available in treatises or manuals.

When I turn to Aristotle's own texts at this point, then, the previous engagement with modern thinkers gives my work a particular preoccupation and a particular focus that distinguishes it from work whose orien-

tation is scholarly in a more straightforward sense. At the same time, however, though prompted by the five chosen modern philosophers, the work
on Aristotle in Part 2 opens up an understanding of his concepts that goes
beyond what we have learned about them from the work of these philosophers themselves. This is the case at two levels. First, there is the level
of intimacy with Aristotle's texts—with their language and with the whole
array of auxiliary concepts which provide the background to our profiled
ones and which, in their ways of playing into and off each other, make
possible the fine-texturedness, the subtlety and nuance of his analysis.
Of the philosophers in Part 1 only Gadamer takes much trouble to support his retrieval of phronesis and techne by reference to Aristotle's own
texts, and, while very much informed by his reading in *Truth and Method*
of book 6 of the *Ethics,* my own reading here will, of its nature, be closer
and more detailed. More particularly, my analysis of techne goes a great
deal further than Gadamer's—for whom techne really only figures as a
concept which, by force of contrast, sets off everything that is experiential,
flexible, and improvisatory in phronesis. I shall attempt to show (especially in the final chapter) that 'techne' is far from univocal in Aristotle's
usage of it and that the polarity between theoretical and experiential emphases, which we have so far taken to coincide with the distinction between 'techne' and 'phronesis', can in fact, on closer scrutiny, be discerned
within the concept of techne itself.

Second, there is the level of philosophical illumination. It is not merely
out of antiquarian interest, nor because of any piety inspired by Gadamer
and the others, that I now return to Aristotle's own texts. My intention
is not just to provide a historical background (though it is that *also*) to
the real philosophical work that has been done in Part 1; it is, rather, to
deepen and strengthen this philosophical work itself. What I see in Aristotle is something that I could not have seen without the help of the philosophers whom we have met in Part 1; at the same time, however, it is
something more than we have already seen in them. It is not the case
that whatever was salvageable from Aristotle has already been so constructively assimilated by them as to make work on him now redundant. Having made this point, I shall not patronize Aristotle by trying to argue it
any further here; its validity can be established—if one is not already disposed to accept it—only *ambulando,* in the course of the work itself. In
following this work, however, there is one respect, in particular, in which
a reader who has followed the discussion so far will be alert to what Aristotle has to offer. For I have just suggested at the end of Part 1 that the
difficulties which beset Habermas's very ambitious philosophy are ones
that stem from his unwillingness to accept the restrictions that Aristotle
puts on 'a theory with practical intent'. And I have also suggested that

the firmness of Aristotle's analysis of the nature, and of the unsupersedable role in life, of experience can still provide a salutary basis for avoiding
Habermas's kind of difficulties. And this claim—though I shall not encumber the discussion with references to Habermas—ought to be redeemed
now in Part 2.

One might of course have a different concern, in fact the converse
of the one to which I have just been responding. One might wonder not
so much whether scholarly work can really contribute to philosophical
enlightenment as whether the philosophical preoccupations and 'prejudices'
that I bring, quite avowedly, to the second part of the study must not
interfere with it as scholarship. Can the integrity of Aristotle's texts be
respected, after all, if their meaning is being filtered through the lens
of different modern thinkers, as they address a problem which I myself
first became aware of through encountering an influential movement in
contemporary education?

The full context for an affirmative answer to this question has already been provided (as I mentioned at the time)[1] in the work on Gadamer's hermeneutics in chapter 4. Since the question has been posed here,
however, out of a concern for scholarship, it can be happily responded
to in the words of an author who both presents his own book on Aristotle's view of practical knowledge as "a piece of scholarship" and, at the
same time, makes a very clear case for a more philosophically engaged
approach which he admits to be different from his own. In the preface
to *Aristotle's Theory of Moral Insight*, Troels Engberg-Pedersen writes:

> The best person to write on Aristotelian ethics is no doubt the philosopher
> who, in connection with independent work on problems in ethics and the
> philosophy of action, has become sufficiently attracted to Aristotle's work
> in the area to spend the required amount of time on the necessary pains-
> taking analysis of his arguments. Such a person will be able to use Aris-
> totle's works in such a way as to justify directly the amount of time spent
> on them, viz., in order to elucidate conceptual problems with which we
> are ourselves confronted. And secondly, he will be able to let his exegetical
> work be guided by a grasp of conceptual machinery that is sufficiently sub-
> tle to match that of the philosopher himself.[2]

These words articulate, I believe, the approach to Aristotle that is taken
here. The "conceptual problems with which we are ourselves confronted"
in the present instance are those involved in clarifying the nature of our
practical engagements (originally this was the problem of finding conceptual resources in terms of which to understand and criticize a particular
model of teaching); and the "conceptual machinery" that guides the work
is that which was built up in Part 1 through the encounters with our mod-

ern thinkers. In taking Engberg-Pedersen's words here as an accurate statement of what I attempt to do, my intention is to claim not that I succeed
in doing it but only that the attempt itself is valid.

Reading an ancient text in the light of contemporary 'prejudices'
is not an illegitimate exercise because, if it is done perceptively, it is never
a one-way interaction; both sides to it (the contemporary and the ancient)
are disclosed in a new light through the 'hermeneutical circle' that is established by their encounter with each other. Far from being subjected
to an alien influence, then, the ancient thought reveals itself more fully
when new demands are made on it; and the source of these demands—
the contemporary problem or prejudice which is brought to the reading—is
itself opened up to reappraisal by being brought into play in this way.
Such indeed, it may be argued, is the nature of *any* reading, so that the
deployment of prejudices is not only not an intellectually disreputable
exercise but is actually an unavoidable one. It becomes disreputable only
when one is unaware, or does not make a clean breast, of the prejudices
that one brings, or when one allows them to be so blaring that the text
has no chance to speak back. Part 1 will have brought into clear relief
my own prejudices—which helped me to construe the contemporary problem and which now influence my reading of Aristotle. And I hope it will
be evident in what follows that Aristotle is continually speaking back to
the questions that are put to him and in fact forcing me continually to
refine these questions or to see them in a new light. It may be that when
a person is dealing with Aristotle and wants to "let his exegetical work
be guided by a grasp of conceptual machinery that is sufficiently subtle
to match that of the philosopher himself," such subtlety is something he
can scarcely bring with him to the work but can only move toward in the
course of doing it.

I have been emphasizing the philosophical rather than the scholarly
intentions of my work on Aristotle, but in fact this is a distinction I do
not wish to push too far. For in the first place a philosophical approach
to an author (more especially an ancient one) runs the risk of being clumsy
and crude if it ignores the tradition of scholarship that has built up around
his work; and it will, I hope, be evident that I have profited much (though,
I know, not nearly enough) from the very fine Anglo-American scholarship which the *Ethics* has elicited, especially over the past few decades.
Second, and perhaps more important, is the converse of this: scholars of
Aristotle's work are themselves inevitably implicated *as philosophers*. This
is a point which is implicit in what I have already said, and which Engberg-
Pedersen, too, even though he wishes to stress the scholarly intentions
of his own work, acknowledges: ". . . no firm line can be drawn between
the philosophic and the scholarly approaches . . . no serious work on Aris-

totle can avoid becoming philosophical."³ This is so simply because Aristotle himself is a philosopher, a fact which makes it impossible to deal substantially with his concepts or arguments without bringing some philosophical equipment to the task; and this equipment will inevitably bear the stamp—however discreetly—of some particular philosophical tradition.

Most of the best work on the *Ethics* in English over the past few decades—and this is true not only of the contributions of distinguished philosophers such as Anscombe and Kenny but also of a more recent generation of scholars—is conducted in a climate which is very much animated by the insights of the later Wittgenstein. Indeed, a strong case could be made out to support the claim that the recent renaissance in the study of the *Ethics* could not have happened before Wittgenstein. For it was only when English philosophy was released by him from the classic obsessions of the modern tradition of epistemology that the power of Aristotle's ideas on practical knowledge could become apparent and stake a strong claim on the attention of scholars. And this is only an illustration of my general point that the thrust, and even the very existence, of a body of scholarship in the history of philosophy is determined by the prevailing philosophical climate—a fact which may be expected to become more apparent when there is a major *shift* in this climate.

The philosophical 'climate' or tradition in which my own work on Aristotle has taken shape, as will have been amply evidenced in the foregoing chapters, is that of post-Hegelian German philosophy, reinforced by the work of two English thinkers who, for all the distinctive Englishness of each of them, might be considered to be more 'continental' in the style and reach of their thinking.⁴ It was the discovery of a common theme (i.e., the significance, for a critique of rationalism, of a distinction between 'technique' and 'practice' as two specifically different types of action, to which correspond two quite distinct forms of knowledge) in five, in some ways quite disparate, thinkers and the discovery that they themselves traced its provenance back to Aristotle which prompted me to explore this theme at its source. This fact gives an overall thematic unity to my work on Aristotle, and this perhaps distinguishes it from mainstream work on Aristotle in English. The difference may be more of approach than of substance, however. Characteristically, work on Aristotle in English is piecemeal and self-consciously modest; its attention to detailed analysis does not encourage any tendency to large-scale synopsis; and it would, accordingly, be circumspect about reading two concepts such as techne and phronesis as representing two major paradigms in dramatic tension at the heart of Aristotle's work. Despite its disinclination to speculate largely, however, there are two factors which may show that this work is not, after all, at a great distance from what is presented here.

First—and this is a point which I can only assert here and not demonstrate—the insights of the later Wittgenstein which I claim to be at
work, in solution as it were, in the Aristotelian exegesis of the past few
decades, have a strong affinity with the insights contained in that body
of philosophy which inspires my own interpretation; and this is so, notwithstanding all the differences of idiom and style that have made Anglo-
American and Continental philosophers uncomprehending—when they
have not been outrightly contemptuous—of each other.[5] A consequence
of this is that much of what is to be found in the literature, although
perhaps less over-reaching in intention, is not uncongenial with the general drift of what is presented here.

The second factor to be mentioned by way of lessening the distance
between the present work and more orthodox commentary on Aristotle
is that the kind of macro-reading essayed here has not rendered unnecessary—but, to the contrary, has actually required—close attention to Aristotle's texts and, indeed, detailed analysis of crucial passages in them. Here,
a comment comes to mind that Wilfrid Sellars made about an interpretation of Plato which he acknowledged to be "decidedly in the synoptic
mood—perhaps outrageously so," but which, as he nonetheless wanted
to claim, "finer-grained analysis . . . both illuminates and confirms":

> In the history of philosophy, as in philosophy itself, we must continually
> shift between analysis and synopsis, embracing the extremes of both. To
> stay at or near the middle is to be safe but uninspired. To give Kant's dic-
> tum one more twist: analysis without synopsis is blind, synopsis without
> analysis is empty.[6]

I hope that in what follows the synoptic intention gives overall perspective, while the analytic care protects against vacuousness.

Finally, while I have sought to bring out quite explicitly in this Interlude the connection between the two parts of my study, my main purpose in doing so has been to enable the work on Aristotle here to stand
on its own feet. Having acknowledged the background influences on my
interpretation, I shall now leave them in the background. The work that
follows is to be judged not primarily on whatever light it may take from
or reflect back on our earlier interlocutors, but rather on how much sense
it makes of our central concepts in Aristotle. In the Epilogue, then, I shall
return more directly to our overall theme and consider Aristotle's contribution to it.

PART 2

Phronesis and Techne
in Aristotle

I do not regard the problem raised by Aristotle as in any
way disposed of.

Hans-Georg Gadamer, "Hermeneutics
and Historicism"

Political thought . . . is always the elucidation of an historical perception in which all our understandings, all our experiences, and all our values simultaneously come into play
—and of which our theses are only the schematic formulation. All action and knowledge which do not go through
this elaboration, and which seek to set up values which have
not been embodied in our individual or collective history
(*or*—what comes down to the same thing—which seek to
choose means by a calculus and a wholly technical process),
fall short of the problems they are trying to solve.

Maurice Merleau-Ponty, "Indirect Language
and the Voices of Silence"

8. Theory, Techne, and Phronesis: Distinctions and Relations

Phronesis and techne are two modes of what we would call *practical*, as distinct from theoretical, knowledge. When Aristotle is being strict in his usage, he does not in fact give 'practical' (*praktikos*) this wide sense which is coterminous with 'nontheoretical'; he restricts it to phronesis and refers to techne as 'productive' (*poiētikē*) knowledge. He thus works with a threefold distinction between theoretical, practical, and productive modes of knowledge with no generic term to cover the two nontheoretical modes.[1] It is the latter two modes and the distinction between them which will be the object of attention throughout this second part of the book. It will be helpful at the outset, however, to outline briefly the conception of theoretical knowledge over against which both of them are conceived by Aristotle. This outline will delimit the area of our inquiry—by identifying the kind of knowledge which will *not* be of explicit concern to us. At the same time, however, it will serve a more positive function by providing a kind of reference point for the two modes of knowledge which we will be investigating. For, as I shall try to show, phronesis is much more firmly distinguished from theory than techne is, and techne, indeed, for all its concern with producing concrete outcomes, still adheres quite closely to the theoretical ideal.

1. Aristotle's Conception of 'Theory'

Following Plato, Aristotle called the kind of knowledge that was theoretical—and therefore, for him, neither practical nor productive—*"epistēmē."* In its ordinary sense, *'epistēmē'* was simply a generic term for knowledge, but with Plato it had already acquired an honorific sense which picked out *real* knowledge over against mere opinion (*doxa*), and this sense was further developed by Aristotle into a logical ideal of demonstrability: one's knowledge of something qualified as *epistēmē* only if one could give an account of the thing which traced it back, or tied it down,

to certain principles (*archai*) or causes (*aitiai*); and the form of such tracing or tying (i.e., the syllogistic form) was made explicit by him with quite
novel precision in the *Analytics*.[2] This logical ideal reached its highest
fulfillment in philosophical wisdom (*sophia*), which combined the power
of apprehending first principles and causes (*nous*) with the demonstrative
power of tracing other knowledge back to them.[3] *Sophia* was the most
comprehensive and exact form of knowledge; it was of the greatest difficulty—in that it was furthest from the senses—and at the same time it
was the most perspicuous (and hence teachable)—in that it reached the
highest level of intelligibility in things.[4] Moreover its epistemological pre-
eminence had an ontological correlate: an object-domain which was limited to necessary and eternal being,[5] and which therefore encompassed
only mathematical entities, the heavenly bodies and the divine being or
first mover.

Theoretical knowledge, thus conceived, was emphatically distinguished from any knowledge which might have a practical import. In the
first chapter of the *Metaphysics* we learn that, emerging only after the
technai which cater for the necessities of life had already been established,
it presupposes leisure and detachment; and that this fact was very much
to its credit may be gleaned from the statement in the last book of the
Nicomachean Ethics that "*eudaimonia* is thought to depend on leisure;
for we are busy that we may have leisure."[6] Men come to love *sophia*—i.e.,
become philosophers—because of their wonder (*to thaumazein*) or because of their desire simply to escape from ignorance and to know, rather
than for the sake of anything useful.[7] And this viewpoint from the *Metaphysics* is echoed in the *E.N.*, where Aristotle speaks of the "self suffi-
ciency" of theory, and tells us that it is "loved for its own sake; for nothing
arises from it apart from the contemplating [*to theoresai*] while from practical activities we gain more or less apart from the action."[8]

From all this it is clear that through theory we do not acquire a
knowledge-content which can then be exploited in the practical business
of life; the spheres of theory and of practice are incommensurable. Through
theory, we are made receptive to being—which is beyond time—and to
an order and harmony which are quite beyond our own powers of construction or interference. So little is it at the service of human life, and
so little is this of any consequence to Aristotle, that he can complacently
remark of the knowledge of Anaxagoras and Thales (preeminent *sophoi*)
that its object is "remarkable, admirable, difficult, and divine, but *use-
less.*"[9] Indeed, in this conception, theory was not only nonutilitarian but
nonhumanistic as well.[10] As against the claims of theory, Aristotle considers it "strange to think that [the techne of] politics, or phronesis, is
the best knowledge, since man is not the best thing in the world"—and

does not fail to point out later that there are "other things much more divine in their nature even than man, e.g., most conspicuously, the bodies of which the heavens are framed."[11] Moreover, theory is nonanthropocentric not only because its objects are above man, but also because that within him which enables him to theorize is something more than himself: "it is not in so far as he is man that he will live so [i.e., devoted to theory], but in so far as something divine is present in him."[12]

If theory remains aloof from practical concerns — so that any direct translation from the former to the latter is impossible in principle — there is a sense, nonetheless, in which theory can find utterance in life, and this in a twofold manner. In the first place devotion to theory is a way of life (a *bios*) which, just because it makes demands which are in a sense beyond human nature, requires a lengthy discipline. Aristotle can indeed speak of theorizing as an actualization (*energeia*) which surpasses all others in pleasure, leisureliness, and unweariedness.[13] But such actualization is not for any chance person but only for one who has already been purified through exertion (*meta spoudēs*)[14] — who has undergone something like the *periagōgē*, the turning around of the soul, which Plato speaks of in book 7 of the *Republic*. Since, then, one can equip oneself for a life of theory only through an *askēsis*, we can speak of theory as having a practical, or at any rate educative, import; for it transforms the character of its seeker and possessor and so has ethical substance as its core.[15]

In the second place, this formative aspect of theory is not purely a matter of psychology, altogether independent of the objects of theory. Through an engagement in theoretical pursuits, one opens oneself to the order and harmony of the cosmos, as well as to the transcendent serenity of the divine being. A *mimēsis* is enacted whereby the character of the theorist comes to conform to the qualities of the theoretical objects. To become a theorist is to acquire a disposition which allows the right order of the cosmos and the simplicity of the deity to work their way into one's soul and to become its prototype. In this classic Greek position, human beings are not the measure of all things but find their own true measure through contemplation of an eternal order beyond themselves.

2. The Primacy of Theory and the Questionable Status of Practice

This picture of theory as knowledge that cannot be *applied* in practical life but is nonetheless itself a distinctive life (*bios*) can be reconstructed, in the way in which I have just attempted, from Aristotle's own texts. It has, nonetheless, an undeniably Platonic flavor, and it relies most heavily, in fact, on just two chapters near the end of the *Nicomachean Ethics* (10.7

and 8) which seem to be at odds with nearly all the rest of Aristotle's ethical-political writing, and to contain, in a disconcertingly undiluted form, what one recent commentator has called "ethical Platonism."[16] The trouble with these chapters is not exactly that they sever this highest kind of knowledge from praxis, but rather that they seem to suggest that it is itself the only really worthwhile kind of praxis (or *energeia*), and that there is, therefore, something incorrigibly second-rate about that whole life of praxis through which one engages in the affairs of the *polis* and actualizes the excellences of character, a life which Aristotle analyzed very painstakingly in the rest of the two ethical treatises, as well as in the *Rhetoric* and the *Politics*. If theoretical activity were something which, however elevated its intrinsic satisfactions, was merely a distraction from ethical life, it would not be troublesome in this way. But it seems not so much to distract from, as to compete with, the ethical life. We had been led to believe that the latter deserved all the attention that Aristotle gave it precisely because it was, in his view, the life of full human flourishing (*eudaimonia*); but now we are told bluntly that it realizes *eudaimonia* only in a secondary degree (*deuterōs*),[17] and that perfect (*teleia*)[18] *eudaimonia* resides in theoretical activity. Moreover, we are urged, in the most unequivocal terms, to strive for this perfection: "we must not follow those who advise us, being men, to think of human things, and being mortal, of mortal things, but must, so far as we can, make ourselves immortal, and strain every nerve to live in accordance with the best thing in us [i.e., our theoretical reason]."[19] What confounds us here is that the human things (*ta anthrōpina*) which are now so brusquely discarded are the very things which had been at the center of Aristotle's attention throughout the *Nicomachean Ethics* and been formally allocated to phronesis in book 6.[20] If the ethical life which is taken up with these human affairs now appears, by contrast with the godly life of theory, almost as a cavelike mode of existence, then one begins to ask whether phronesis, for all its suppleness and flair, does not appear, from the vantage point of theory, much as a dog's great sensitivity in smelling and sniffing might appear from the vantage point of phronesis itself.[21]

The difficulty which I have just raised about the relationship between the pursuit of theory, on the one hand, and practical involvement in the *polis*, on the other, is one of the most notorious conundrums facing Aristotelian scholars.[22] Moreover, it is one that might be supposed to require some immediate resolution here. For, as we prepare to follow Aristotle's account of practical knowledge—and especially since our work in Part 1 has heightened our expectations in doing so—how can we be reconciled to the fact that, all his seeming commitment to the integrity of practice notwithstanding, his view of theory still gives him what we might call a reserved position? When we meet this view, rather suddenly, at the end of the *Ethics,* is it not like discovering a trapdoor which had all the time been under us in our reading up to then? Being aware of the threat posed to it by the life of theory, can we have any conviction about Aristotle's conception of the practical life unless we can do something to neutralize this threat at the very outset?

It is not, I believe, open to us to dispute the fact that Aristotle *did* place a higher value on the exercise of the theoretic faculty than on the exercise of phronesis. Nor can we say that although phronesis is inferior to theoretic reason, still it at least has its own sphere of operations in which it is independent of the latter. For Aristotle very clearly subordinates phronesis to, and we might even say instrumentalizes it at the service of, theoretic reason. Moreover, he does this most expressly not in *Nicomachean Ethics* 10 but in the very books on which I shall be relying most heavily in drawing my picture of phronesis: *Nicomachean Ethics* 6 and *Eudemian Ethics* 8.[23] Let us look at the two most explicit statements taken from the closing lines of each of these books. First, from the *E.E.:*

> since man is by nature composed of a ruling and a subject part, each of us should live according to the governing element within himself—but this is ambiguous, for medical science governs in one sense, health in another, the former existing for the latter. And so it is with the theoretic faculty; for god is not an imperative ruler, but is the end with a view to which phronesis issues its commands. . . . What choice, then . . . will most produce the contemplation of god, that choice . . . is best; this is the noblest standard.[24]

And from *E.N.* 6:

> it [phronesis] is not supreme over *sophia* i.e. over the superior part of us, any more than the art of medicine is over health; for it does not use it but provides for its coming into being; it issues orders, then, for its sake, but not to it. Further, to maintain its supremacy would be like saying that the *technē* of politics rules the gods because it issues orders about all the affairs of the state.[25]

These passages leave no doubt as to the superior status of theory. Nonetheless, on analysis, they clear the ground for the approach to phronesis which I shall be taking in the rest of this study. For it is quite clear in both of them that theoretical reason, for all its primacy, does not displace phronesis as the ordering agency in our lives. A life of uninterrupted contemplation that is not inconvenienced even by having to secure the conditions of its own continued existence is a life for a god but not for a human being. For a human being, even if we accept that the highest happiness consists in contemplation and (a different proposition) that all our striving should ultimately be toward this height, still, to order one's life in such a way that the height can be properly enjoyed, or to maintain a *polis* in which it will be reliably provided for and prized, *this* is something that falls not to theoretic reason itself but rather to phronesis. Given that, for Aristotle, the life of contemplation is self-justifying, it is not, however, in the human world in which we live, self-sustaining. And so Aristotle himself (in the second passage above) says that phronesis "provides for its coming into being; it issues orders, then, for its sake."

Aristotle sheds little light on just what kind of considerations might come into play in this exercise of phronesis. Has the life devoted to ethical *aretē* and political engagement some inherent value, or is it to be valued *only* insofar as it contributes to the life of contemplation? Is it conceivable that a character in whom the practice of the virtues had not become a settled habit would still be able to enter into a contemplative life, or must a candidate for such a life already be *spoudaios* (a person of sound character) or, what comes to the same thing, a *phronimos* (one who sees, and is disposed to do, the good in each situation)? If the contemplative life cannot abrogate the life of practice altogether, how are we to understand the relationship between the two? Is there, for instance, an important developmental aspect to be taken into account so that we should envisage *stages* in a person's biography, perhaps seeing a theoretic propensity in a young person's facility in mathematics, which then with greater life-experience yields to a more practical orientation in the stage of adult vigor, which, in its turn, prepares for the fullest flowering of the theoretic faculty as one's advanced years are given over to the contemplation of God? Or is there also an important political dimension to this whole relationship? Should we, in other words, look more to the *polis* than to the individual and see that a life of contemplation will scarcely be possible for anyone unless the life of the citizenry generally is characterized by virtues such as justice and truthfulness (which will ensure a certain tranquillity and absence of discord) and courage (which will ensure a willingness to defend against would-be oppressors)?

It is Aristotle's reticence on questions such as these (which were to find close counterparts in later Christian reflection) which has given such wide scope for the scholarly debate that I mentioned above. The point I have been leading up to here, however, is that for my own purposes in the present study, I do not need to take a position in this debate. For however the primacy of theory is to be interpreted, it does not amount to any kind of imperialism. Rather, the *imperium* remains with phronesis; in both of our passages, it is phronesis which issues commands (*epitattei*).[26] However much, then, the life of theory may relativize praxis (i.e., *ethical* practice—for theory, of course, is itself a praxis in the broad sense of that term) there is nothing in Aristotle which suggests that it can subjugate the latter to itself. It is *this* incommensurability that will be of interest to us: not that a life of practice cannot compare in rewardingness with a life of theory, but rather that practice resists all theoretical pretensions in its direction. Here there can be no question of regarding Aristotle as a Platonist. For if, as is commonly supposed, Plato's basic project was to work out a theoretical knowledge (*epistēmē*) which would be capable of putting the practice of the ethical life and of politics on a radically new footing, Aristotle certainly had no such ambition. To the contrary, he believed that practice required for its guidance its own specific kind of knowledge and, ever mindful of the flat-footedness of theory here, he tried to analyze the peculiar structure of this practical knowledge.

Aristotle's analysis is of course itself a kind of theory. It arises in the context of his *philosophy* of practice which—through clarifying, systematizing, and, to some extent, criticizing the beliefs (*endoxa*) that are implicit in the ethos of his *polis,* attempts to specify the kind of life which brings most well-being and is therefore most worthy of being chosen. But very early in the *Nicomachean Ethics,* in the famous methodological preface, we are disabused of any idea that this philosophy might meet the criteria of theory as *epistēmē* or *sophia.* Its subject matter will not permit the same degree of exactness (*to akribēs*) that we should expect to find elsewhere—in mathematics, for example (and we are aware, of course, that in the *Metaphysics* exactness is highlighted as a property of *sophia* and mathematics is mentioned as an example of it). This subject matter (i.e., human affairs or *ta anthrōpina*) contains so much variety and fluctuation (*diaphoran kai planēn*) that a theoretical account of it can be given only "roughly and in outline" (*pachulōs kai tupōi*) and can do no more than hint at what is true "for the most part" (*epi to polu*).

These early reservations in *E.N.* 1.3 bear on Aristotle's own undertaking of a "theoretical inquiry into practice." Their upshot is to make it all the more important for him, in the course of this inquiry, to clarify the kind of knowledge that comes into play in practice itself. This latter knowledge has to meet the concrete demands of practical situations and thus to make determinate what, on the level of his own general consideration, can be sketched out only "roughly and in outline." It must fit itself to the nature of a domain which lies forever outside the scope of theory as conceived by him: that of contingent or variable being (what he calls *ta endechomena allōs echein,* literally things that can be otherwise) and, more specifically, those things which, subject to certain limitations, are within the rational power of human beings to change. This rational power does not yield the universal and necessary knowledge of theory. But it does yield *knowledge;* it is able to make out truth (*alētheuein*), to distinguish between it and falsity, and to regulate the domain of practice in the light of this distinction.

3. The Place of Techne and Phronesis, and of the Distinction between Them, in Aristotle's Writings

So much by way of a preliminary identification of the area of our concern and of its delimitation from and justification over against 'theory'. The subsequent course of our investigation will revolve around a distinction which we must now introduce within this area itself (what we have so far called the 'practical' in a broad sense of that term) between the 'productive' and the 'practical' (in Aristotle's stricter sense). Production (*poiēsis*) has to do with making or fabrication; it is activity which is designed to bring about, and which terminates in, a product or outcome that is separable from it and provides it with its end or *telos. Praxis,* on the other hand, has to do with the conduct of one's life and affairs primarily as a citizen of the *polis;* it is activity which may leave no separately identifiable outcome behind it and whose end, therefore, is realized in the very doing of the activity itself. (We may therefore say that while "*praxis* and *prakton* are identical, *poiēsis* and *poiēton* are different.")[27]

To these two specifically different modes of activity, *technē* and *phronēsis* correspond, respectively, as two rational powers which give us two quite distinct modes of practical knowledge. The distinction between the two types of *knowledge* derives from what for Aristotle seems to be the prior distinction between the two kinds of *activity:* "making and acting are different . . . so that the reasoned state of capacity to act [i.e., phronesis] is different from the reasoned state of capacity to make [i.e., techne]";[28] and, again: "phronesis cannot be . . . techne . . . because action and making are different kinds of thing."[29] Techne provides the kind of knowledge possessed by an expert in one of the specialized crafts, a person who understands the principles (*logoi, aitiai*) underlying the production of an object or state of affairs, e.g., a house, a table, a safe journey, or a state of being healthy. Phronesis, on the other hand, characterizes a person who knows how to live well (*eu zēn*). It is acquired and deployed not in the making of any product separate from oneself but rather in one's actions with one's fellows. It is personal knowledge in that, in the living of one's life, it characterizes and expresses the kind of person that one is.

The distinction between phronesis and techne which I have just introduced — and which is clearly recognizable as the prototype of the concepts brought to life in different contexts by our different authors in Part 1

—will occupy us in the rest of our study. We ought to begin, however, by asking how significant or well-founded it was for Aristotle himself. What is the profile in his writings of each pole of the distinction? And how much prominence does he give to the distinction itself?

In response to the first of these questions, we must acknowledge a considerable degree of asymmetry: whereas techne, as we shall see, is very deeply embedded in the core of his metaphysics and is therefore almost ubiquitous throughout his work, phronesis, by contrast, is what might almost be regarded as a 'deviant' concept. Apart from scattered and infrequent references to it in other parts of the ethical treatises, it is analyzed only in *E.N.* 6, and even its treatment there, although subtle and fine-textured, is still far from systematic. Both the confinement of phronesis to a single portion of the Aristotelian canon and its treatment there in a fragmentary and unsystematic fashion are, we may judge, symptomatic. For phronesis represents what has come to be justly regarded as a characteristic strain in his philosophical anthropology but one that, nonetheless, hangs loosely in his overall scheme of things. It is the notion through which he allows into knowledge, as well as into the proper ordering of human affairs, the greatest degree of flexibility, openness, and improvisation. As such, it must occupy an ambiguous place in the kind of grand hierarchy of knowledge—rising from the lowest data of the senses right up to the highest and most universal 'first philosophy'—that is outlined in the first two chapters of the *Metaphysics*. In fact, phronesis does not appear at all in this classic schema of the "degrees of knowledge," though techne is accorded an integral place. (And the same is true of the parallel outline in *Posterior Analytics,* 2.19). There is a complexity and multi-layeredness in the concept of phronesis which would make it an extremely uncomfortable fit in any such schematization.

Apart from his treatment of its two terms, what of Aristotle's treatment of the distinction itself? In the earlier books of the *Ethics* we must face the embarrassing fact (embarrassing, that is, for a thesis such as mine, which tries to show that in setting up phronesis as the paradigm of ethical knowledge Aristotle was setting limits to the applicability of techne) that Aristotle turns quite unselfconsciously to techne in order to clarify or illustrate points about the virtues. In *E.N.* 1, for example, after *eudaimonia* has been identified as the final end, the first approach to formulating its nature is prompted by a consideration of the craftsperson:

> just as for a flute-player, a sculptor, or any *technitēs*, and, in general, for all things that have a function or activity, the good and the well is thought to reside in the function, so would it be for man if he has a function. Have the carpenter, then, and the tanner certain functions or activities and has man none? Is he naturally functionless?[30]

Or again, in the middle of a passage about bearing one's misfortunes, Aristotle writes:

> the man who is truly good and wise, we think, bears all the chances of life becomingly and always makes the best of circumstances, as a good general makes the best military use of the army at his command and a shoemaker makes the best shoes out of the hides that are given to him; and so with all the other *technitai*.[31]

Similarly, when he is discussing the way in which we acquire virtues (or 'excellences', as the revised Oxford translation renders *aretai*) his immediate point of comparison is techne: "excellences we get by first exercising them, as also happens in the case of the technai as well. For the things we have to learn before we can do, we learn by doing, e.g. men become builders by building and lyre-players by playing the lyre; so too we become just by doing just acts, temperate by doing temperate acts, brave by doing brave acts."[32] Or again the concept of the mean, which is central to Aristotle's whole theory of the virtues, far from having an exclusively ethical import, is introduced as an idea which is already well established in the technai and for this very reason should command attention in the field of the virtues: "If every knowledge (*epistēmē*) does its work well by looking to the mean (*to meson*) . . . and good *technitai* . . . look to this in their work . . . excellence . . . must have the quality of aiming at the mean."[33] Or as a final example of the pervasiveness of techne even in Aristotle's ethical thought, we may take his partiality—which was hardly less pronounced than Plato's—for the medical analogy.[34] Many times the virtuous person is presented as one who looks to the good of his soul in a way similar to that in which the doctor looks to the health of the body. And even in *E.N.* 6 we find that when Aristotle is analyzing ethical reasoning, the only actual example he gives is medical—and therefore frankly technical.[35]

There is one passage early in the *E.N.* (2.4) where Aristotle explicitly *denies* an analogy between works that proceed from techne and actions that proceed from excellence of character (*aretē ēthikē*). Even here, however, although he wants to emphasize the difference between productive and ethical endeavors, he does not advert to the distinction between techne and phronesis. Indeed not only does he not advert to the latter distinction—in a context which might have seemed especially hospitable to it—but he marks the difference that he is concerned with in a way that might be taken implicitly to undermine it. For the distinction between techne and phronesis is a distinction between two kinds of *knowledge*. But in the passage to which I am referring the difference between productive and ethical activity is outlined in a way which, far from suggesting that

each calls into play a distinctive knowledge of its own (techne and phronesis, respectively) suggests rather that one of them (i.e., production according to techne) involves as a necessary and indeed sufficient condition
a particular kind of knowledge, whereas the other (i.e., virtuous action)
scarcely involves knowledge at all. If a man produces correct sentences,
we are given to understand, then we can attribute the techne of grammar
to him only if he does so according to knowledge that he himself possesses (and not, therefore, simply according to chance [apo tuchēs] or to
someone else's knowledge): "A man will be proficient in grammar, then,
only when he has both done something grammatical and done it grammatically; and this means doing it in accordance with the grammatical
knowledge in himself."[36] Aristotle does not mind conceding that virtuous
action also implies an intimate relationship with the self of the agent (a
more intimate relationship, indeed, than that which exists in the case of
the technai—for, whereas we can consider a work of techne on its own
merits without any reference to its producer, a virtuous action can never
be identified as such without reference to the disposition of the agent who
performs it); but in the spelling out of this relationship the role of knowledge is very conspicuously downplayed:

> if the acts that are in accordance with the excellences have themselves a
> certain character it does not follow that they are done justly or temperately.
> The agent must also be in a certain condition when he does them; in the
> first place he must have knowledge, secondly he must choose the acts, and
> choose them for their own sakes, and thirdly his action must proceed from
> a firm and unchangeable character. These are not reckoned in as conditions
> of the possession of the technai, *except the bare knowledge;* but as a condi-
> tion of the possession of the excellences knowledge has little or no weight,
> while the other conditions count not for a little but for everything.[37]

The fact that Aristotle not only continually and quite casually invokes the model of techne in his discourse about the virtues but also shuns
the opportunity to introduce phronesis on the one occasion in the early
books of the *E.N.* when he is careful to reject techne as an appropriate
model in the ethical sphere raises the question of just how significant or
well-founded the distinction between techne and phronesis was in his
thought. The only explicit statement and analysis of it occurs in *E.N.* 6
(chs. 4 and 5). Apart from this we may take it as being referred to (though
not by name) on those occasions when intellect is classified as theoretical,
productive (i.e., techne) or practical (i.e., phronesis).[38] Moreover, since the
analysis in *E.N.* 6 bases it, as we have seen, on the distinction between
two different kinds of activities—those whose ends lie outside them
(*poiēseis*) and those which are their own ends (*praxeis*)—we may also per-

haps take it as being obliquely referred to on the many occasions (e.g., in the very opening sentences of the *E.N.*) when this latter distinction is made. Furthermore, this latter distinction itself seems to be based on, or at least closely related to, *another* distinction, the celebrated one that is made in the *Metaphysics* between the concepts of process (*kinēsis*) and actuality (*energeia*). (A *kinēsis* is a process within a set limit [*peras*] toward an end [*telos*] and exists only as long as the limit has not been reached and the end does not yet exist; it is *atelēs* or *ou teleia*. An *energeia*, on the other hand, has no as yet unreached limit in that its end, or complete condition, already exists in it at any moment of its duration; it is an *entelecheia*.)[39] Praxis, whether it be virtuous action or the activity of thinking, seems to be coextensive with *energeia;* and while poiesis cannot be said to be coextensive with *kinēsis*—since the latter occurs also in the changing world of nature—it still supplies the paradigm examples of the latter (e.g., building a house), by analogy with which natural processes themselves can be made intelligible. And so we might discern in this metaphysical distinction, at a further remove again, an implicit reference to our cognitive distinction between techne and phronesis.

On the basis of what has just been said, the distinction between techne and phronesis may seem to have been secure enough in Aristotle's thought. It was, moreover, highly characteristic, in that it marked one of the most conspicuous ways in which he departed from Plato: while his concept of techne, as we shall see, remains very close to Plato's,[40] he radically altered the theoretical connotations which 'phronesis' had had in Plato's usage of it.[41] This alteration was part of the revisionist loosening of ethics from metaphysics which was implicit in his critique of Plato's idea of the Good and which required that ethics and the study of human affairs generally should be provided with their own distinctive, nontheoretical mode of rationality.

Despite all this, the fact remains that for any analysis of the distinction between techne and phronesis—and, indeed, as I have said, for the only analysis we shall find of phronesis—we have to look exclusively to *E.N.* 6. Even there, the discussion is brusque, amounting to no more than a few highly compressed and in some cases quite cryptic remarks. The fact is that Aristotle did not take any great pains to clarify or make explicit the ground, import, or ramifications of this distinction which, we may judge, was nevertheless of considerable significance in his thought. It is this unforthcomingness—combined of course with the great fruitfulness which the distinction has shown itself to have in its reincarnations in modern/contemporary philosophy—that motivates the inquiry we now undertake. Aristotle gives us nothing on a plate, and yet it may be worthwhile to develop, as explicitly and systematically as we can, what is for the most part left implicit and fragmentary in his own texts. The picture which will emerge is in some respects, I believe, an ironic one: phronesis, a concept which was not very firmly jointed into his overall scheme, emerges, nonetheless, with a good deal of inner coherence; conversely, techne, one of the most domesticated of all his concepts, reveals different strands which are left curiously intertwined and which, if they are unraveled, betray a deep tension in his thought.

4. Aristotle's 'Official' Concept of Techne: Its Essential Reference to Fabrication and Its Closeness to Theory

Of the two concepts, techne is the one which Aristotle took over more directly from Plato and at the same time embedded more deeply in his own conceptual schema. It also, as we shall see, departs least from the mold of theory and in fact remains so close to the latter that it might be said (notwithstanding the fact that we have already separated off the whole realm of the practical from theory) to introduce within the broad field of practice a dialectic between a theoretical approach and the more practical or experiential approach represented by phronesis. As the more established of the two concepts, then, and the one closest to theoretical knowledge, techne is the concept with which we may best begin.

In *E.N.* 6, techne is defined as a *hexis meta logou poiētikē,* a "reasoned state of capacity to make." It is thus quite straightforwardly linked to making (poiesis), i.e., the generation of "things whose source (*archē*) is in the producer and not in the product." (Such things [*poiēta*], then, are different from natural things [*phusika*], which have the source of their generation in themselves, and from necessary things—the objects of *sophia*—which are ungenerated.) This efficient causality of the maker is an element in a process in which other factors are also causally at play: the material (*hulē*), which gives the maker something to work on and gives the product the solidity and durability to exist as an artefact in the world; the form (*eidos*), which is realized in the material and gives the finished product its specific character; and the end (*telos*) of the making, which may be looked on either as the realized form itself or, beyond that, as the use it serves in people's lives.

When the maker is able to bring these causal factors together under his rational direction he may be said to possess the relevant techne—e.g., of building in relation to the making of houses or of cobbling in relation to the making of shoes. Techne is not itself a useful thing but rather a generative source (*archē*) of useful things, a habitual ability (*dunamis*) of the maker through which he can reliably produce and reproduce them.[42]

He has an understanding of the purpose (*telos*) of the things he makes—dwelling, in relation to houses, or walking comfortably, in relation to shoes. He does not determine this end (hence Aristotle says that he does not deliberate about it)[43] but finds it already established and setting the limit (*peras*) within which his techne operates. The end determines the form, and it is in his knowledge of this form that his techne essentially resides: "from techne proceed the things of which the form is in the soul."[44] From this knowledge he can work out in his mind, through a process of deliberation, the steps which need to be taken in order to induce the form in the matter; and the actual process of making is the execution, usually in reverse order, of the steps outlined in the deliberative process. His techne is, then, the source of the maker's mastery of his trade and of his ability therefore not only to accomplish a successful result (which any handy person might be equally capable of) but in doing so to give a rational account (*logos*) of his procedures—an account which is rational precisely insofar as it can trace the product back to the "causes" (*aitiai*) to which it owes its being.

The concept of techne which I have just outlined was a philosophical construction involving a considerable transformation of the meaning that the word 'techne', with its various derivatives, had had in ordinary parlance since Homeric times. As such it played a crucial role in the attempt by the Socratic philosophers to articulate a notion of rationality that would be more public and reliable than anything previously available. At the same time, however, it did not involve a complete rupture with pre-philosophical experience. To the contrary, it remained rooted in one such experience which had a powerful fascination for the Greeks—i.e., the experience of successful fabrication in various crafts. Jaako Hintikka speculates that the cause of this fascination was quite simply the fact that "of all human activities the activity of the craftsman is likely to have the most concrete and clearly definable product," or, as we might rephrase this, it is the activity where, with least ambiguity, success can be achieved and assessed. This fact was no less compelling for the philosophers than it was for those of sturdy common sense. It presented them with "the temptation to discuss all and sundry phenomena in terms of their outcomes." And when the Socratic philosophers yielded to this temptation—a yielding which involved, perhaps, such a fundamental 'prejudice' that it was hardly as conscious as a 'temptation'—they became unable to "conceptually master a situation without somehow subsuming it under the concept of an end (*telos*)."[45] Thus was established in Greek philosophy—and, we might add, in the whole subsequent tradition of Western rationality—the ascendancy of what Hintikka calls the "paradigm of the craftsman." Techne came to have a huge prestige, not only immediately in the different spheres of making or poiesis (where it was already greatly admired), but mediately through the techne-based explanatory constructs that came to seem appropriate in many different fields.

This tendency to see techne as a source of comprehensive explanatoriness—so that it was virtually coincident with rationality itself—reached its most complete expression in Aristotle's philosophy. For him techne is reason as source of purposive change in the world; but even the other great source of purposive (as distinct from haphazard) change—i.e., nature as an active principle in all living things—could be understood only by analogy with it. Not only is techne in itself the rational source of the order that human agency brings into the world, it is also the primary model in terms of which we can understand the intelligibility that we find already existing in the natural order. In fact the core concepts of Aristotle's metaphysics are shaped by this model; the concepts contained in the doctrines of potency and act and of hylomorphism (which is a partial aspect of the more comprehensive doctrine of the four causes adumbrated above) first reveal themselves in the context of skillful fabrication. And so it is scarcely surprising that when Aristotle puts these concepts to work in analyses of such diverse topics as animal morphology, change (*genesis*), sexual reproduction, and life or soul (*psuchē*), we find techne being constantly invoked as a stock-in-trade exemplar or analogue. *Ex professo* treatments of techne *per se* are in fact rare in Aristotle's writings (one can really only mention *E.N.* 6.4 and *Meta.* 1.1). But the fact that it exhibited more perspicuously than anything else his basic conceptual schema—and that it was indeed the matrix from which this schema was first derived—means that it is frequently turned to for pedagogical purposes when this schema is being deployed throughout the whole range of his writing in physics, biology, psychology, and metaphysics.

The intimate connection between techne and rationality resided not only in the fact that techne was accorded such great significance and scope as a theoretical tool. The way in which its own inner structure as a form of productive knowledge was conceived by the Socratic philosophers—and quite apart, therefore, from the almost limitless extrapolations that it seemed to be capable of—also brought it very close to *epistēmē*. For Plato, far from its being merely practical in any sense which might be taken to imply inferiority, it was a leading paradigm or prefiguration of the kind of true *epistēmē* which the philosopher himself seeks. Over and over again we find Socrates exposing his interlocutors' grasp of basic moral concepts by showing how unfavorably it compares with the reliable and "well-tied down" knowledge of the craftsman. Even Socrates' argument in book 1 of the *Republic* that justice is not a techne (which as we saw in chapter 2 Collingwood has called "one of the cases of brilliant resis-

tance" to the tendency "to look for instances of craft in all kinds of likely
and unlikely places") does not count against this. For here Socrates was
critical of the craftsman not because his techne was not genuine knowledge but rather because it was restricted to one field. If the same kind
of knowledge could be made available in the ethical sphere it would be
so powerful as to be *identical* with virtue. And, for Socrates himself,[46]
this was not the "Socratic paradox" that it has been taken to be by many
of his commentators, but rather (in Hintikka's words) "a mighty challenge
to the theoretical thinker to spell out the definitory what-knowledge"[47]
which, if it were available, would be the equivalent in the moral sphere
of what each techne is in the field of its own specific *poiēsis*.

   What makes Aristotle decisively important from the point of view
of the present work is the fact that even though he found this model of
a theoretically inclined techne a convenient reference point in discussing
ethical matters, still in relation to these matters he ultimately *resisted* it.
In several places in both the *Nicomachean* and the *Eudemian Ethics* he
argues explicitly against Socrates' position, and in *E.N.* 6 he outlines his
notion of phronesis as specifically ethical knowledge in a direct contrast
with techne. What makes this so significant and so worthy of out attention, however, is precisely the fact that it was an *exception:* that, apart
from his analysis of ethical knowledge, Aristotle remained on the high
ground of techne which he had inherited from Plato and that for him
too, as for Plato, techne was strikingly theoretical in its aspiration as knowledge.[48] It does not correspond to our present-day notion of 'craft', and
the usual translation of it as 'art'—a straight transliteration of the Latin
'*ars*'—is misleading to a modern mind, which assumes as commonplace
a strong distinction between 'art' and 'science'; although neither of these
terms is suitable, the latter would in fact be a better rendering of 'techne'.

   The *locus classicus* for this theoretical emphasis in Aristotle's conception of techne is the first chapter of the *Metaphysics.* There the man
of techne is firmly distinguished from the man who works merely by memory or from experience: "we think that *knowledge* and *understanding* (*to
ge eidenai kai to epaiein*) belong to techne . . . and we suppose *technitai*
to be wiser (*sophōterous*) than men of experience . . . because [they] know
the why and the cause (*to dioti kai tēn aitian*)."[49] Since he is concerned
above all with the forms of things in which resides their intelligibility,
the *technitēs* aims not just to deal with particular cases but to reach "one
universal judgement about similar objects. For to have a judgement that
when Callias was ill of this disease this did him good, and similarly in
the case of Socrates and in many individual cases, is a matter of experience; but to judge that it has done good to all persons of a similar constitution, marked off in one class, when they were ill of this disease . . .

this is a matter of techne."[50] Or, as we are also told, "if a man does wish to become master of a techne or *epistēmē* he must go to the universal, and come to know it as well as possible."[51] Furthermore, a master of a techne is in a position to teach: "the man of techne can transmit his knowledge to others," and this, too, suggests a strong resemblance between his knowledge and theory, for, as we are told elsewhere, "every science is thought to be capable of being taught, and its object of being learned."[52]

Since techne was productive knowledge and so (like nature and chance) led to the generation of things that are neither necessary nor eternal, it could not, to be sure, be *epistēmē* in the full sense. Still, if one prescinds from the ontological status of their respective objects and from the cultural valuation of 'leisurely' over productive pursuits—which, as we have already seen, accompanied the birth of philosophy itself—it is hard to see any significant difference between techne and *epistēmē*. Indeed, over and over again Aristotle seems to use them interchangeably. (Medicine, for instance, is one of his most frequently cited examples of a techne; but sometimes it is discussed as an *epistēmē*.[53] Conversely, mathematics and in particular geometry, which are usually regarded as *epistēmai*, are sometimes regarded as *technai*.[54] And, indeed, we can find passages in which medicine and geometry are regarded as both technai and *epistēmai*.)[55] Moreover, Aristotle did not scruple to speak of "productive *epistēmai*"[56] and "theoretical technai." The latter expression, in fact, gestures not to the point which I have just been making—that techne resembles *epistēmē* as a form of knowledge—but rather to the fact that even *within epistēmē itself* there is a techne at work, i.e., logic, which governs reasoning and produces correct arguments. And we may note, finally, that this close relationship between techne and theory remained in the tradition. Aquinas, for instance, saw quite clearly that in contrast to phronesis (*prudentia*), techne (*ars*) is very close to theory (*scientia*): "when the theoretical reason makes something, an argument for instance, then it proceeds according to fixed and classical methods which is the rule of *ars* rather than of *prudentia*. One may envisage a theoretical *ars* but scarcely a theoretical *prudentia*."[57]

5. Technai of the *Kairos,* and Their Affinity with Phronesis

What I have just been outlining is what might be called Aristotle's 'official' concept of techne. This concept provides a foil against which we might immediately begin to set off our other notion, i.e., phronesis. Before going on to the distinction between techne and phronesis, however, we should notice that this 'official' concept, which makes techne coter-

minous with poiesis, involves a selectivity which does not do justice to
the full range of Aristotle's use of the term 'techne'. Two kinds of examples
which he uses quite familiarly seem to raise problems here. First there
are activities such as gymnastics or the playing of a musical instrument,
which we might want to describe as performative rather than productive
since they do not leave behind them as deposits durable, reified products.
At least twice Aristotle refers to musical performance in a way that implies
that while it is a techne, it is *not* concerned with production; and in the
course of doing so he contrasts it with other, straightforwardly productive
technai (such as house-building) in a way that makes the latter out to
be not coterminous with, but rather a subclass of, techne *simpliciter*.[58]
He thus loosens the essential connection between techne and *poiētikē* in
E.N. 6 (where techne is defined as a *hexis meta logou poiētikē*). Indeed,
by speaking of a techne whose exercise is a praxis and not a poiesis, he
seems to buck the careful alignments (between poiesis and techne and
praxis and phronesis) which are laid down in the latter text.

   The second kind of techne which seems problematic in the light
of *E.N.* 6.4's identification of techne with *productive* knowledge, and
which I want to dwell on here, might be illustrated by such examples as
military strategy, navigation, or even the important case of medicine. Unlike the case of musicianship, one may indeed speak here of a definite
result which is achieved by, and endures after, the exercise of the techne —
in successful cases, something like victory, a safe journey, or a person's good
health. This result, however, is more a state-of-affairs than a durable product, and rather than having disposable materials upon which he can impress a preconceived form, the *technitēs* here is more readily thought of
as intervening in a field of forces, or as immersing himself in a medium,
in which he seeks to accomplish a propitious end. If these cases diverge
significantly from the standard paradigm of fabrication, however, this fact
does not seem to have impressed Aristotle. We do not find in his writing
any explicit differentiation of them from the technai such as building that
are exercised in simple reification. Nor do we find any analysis looking
for some commonality in them which would help to identify them as a
class and to furnish us with a *concept* of them. From various passages in
which Aristotle, as it were, betrays his thinking about them, however, we
may say that what characterizes these technai is a close relationship —
which does not obtain in the case of the more straightforwardly productive technai — with the opportune (*ho kairos*) and luck or chance (*tuchē*).

   The relationship with the *kairos* is brought out most clearly in the
critique of Plato's Idea of the Good in *E.N.* 1.6. Here Aristotle points out
that 'good' is an analogical term which is predicated in different senses
in each of the categories, and he goes on to show that there is not — as,

on Plato's position, there should be — just one science dealing with the good "but . . . many sciences even of the things that fall under one category, e.g., of opportunity (for opportunity in war is studied by strategy, and in disease by medicine)."[59] The relationship with luck appears in a discussion of luck in the *Eudemian Ethics* where the point is made that even foolish people are often successful in matters controlled by fortune and that this holds even "in matters involving techne, [but into which] chance largely enters, e.g., strategy and navigation."[60] And indeed we can cite a passage which, significantly, seems not only to relate these technai with luck but, at least by implication, to *deny* any relationship between luck and *productive* technai: "Among the products of thought, some never occur spontaneously — e.g. a house or a statue . . . but with some aim; but others occur by chance too — e.g. health and preservation."[61]

These elements of opportunity and luck are interesting ones that form a kind of penumbra around the clear light of rationality that the Socratic philosophers were trying to reveal. They remain unassimilated by reason and stand, we might even say, in intractable opposition to it. As Aristotle himself puts it: "Where there is most of mind and reason, there is least of chance, and where there is most chance, there is there least mind,"[62] or again "those occupations are most truly technai in which there is the least element of chance."[63] Now it is easy to identify techne with reason here and to see as its defining element precisely the overcoming or transcending of chance; in the words of one of the Hippocratic authors, "they did not want to look into the naked face of chance, so they turned themselves over to techne." These words are quoted by Martha Nussbaum in *The Fragility of Goodness* and they express, in fact, one of the central themes of her book. The essence of techne is revealed in the Promethean myth: all the technai were divine gifts to creatures who, without them, would have remained nakedly exposed to "ungoverned contingency" or *tuchē*. The basic polarity is between "living at the mercy of *tuchē* and living a life made safer or more controlled by (some) techne."[64] And, viewed in the light of this polarity, techne is "a deliberate application of human intelligence to some part of the world, yielding some control over *tuchē*."[65]

Any work on the conceptual geography of techne surely must give considerable prominence to the dialectic with *tuchē*. This dialectic is more complex, however, than what is suggested by a straightforward polarity. There are, it would seem, some technai which gain their ends not so much by overcoming chance as by confining their sphere of operations to domains where chance has little or no foothold. That the technai of fabrication or reification — which are covered unproblematically by the analysis of techne in *E.N.* 6.4 — are of such a kind may be gathered from the

casual remark in the *Analytics* which I have just quoted: "Among the products of thought, some never occur spontaneously — e.g. a house or a statue
. . . but with some aim; but others occur by chance too — e.g. health and
preservation."[66] Here we find grounds for saying that some technai, by
setting for themselves an end which can be attained through a circumscribed process within their direct control, make themselves invulnerable
to chance; others, however, are involved in areas where, since they are circumscribed by no fixed limit (*peras*),[67] the play of chance is simply ineliminable. Being subject to chance, these latter technai cannot aspire to
the same kind of mastery that obtains in the others. Success is to be achieved
in them not so much by keeping one's gaze fixed on the preconceived
form which one will impose on the material, as by a flexible kind of responsiveness to the dynamism of the material itself. It is sensitivity or attunement rather than mastery or domination that one strives for. One's
actions may have to be quick and decisive but they arise within a pattern
of a certain kind of passivity. This is the meaning of grasping the *kairos;*
one's active intervention has skillfully waited until one's polyvalent materials — be they the wind and waves in play upon one's boat or the changing humors in the sick body — are at their most propitious, i.e., are most
able to help, or least able to hinder, the accomplishment of one's end.
If chance is one's enemy in these technai, then one succeeds not by trying
to defeat her but rather by trying to win her over. This is what I take to
be meant by the words of Agathon which Aristotle quotes without gloss
in *E.N.* 6.4: "techne loves *tuchē* and *tuchē* loves techne."[68] *Tuchē* favors
the *technitēs* who has paid court to her.

Love, of course, like war, is not without its stratagems. One of the
meanings which the word 'techne' had for the prephilosophical Greeks
and which it did not lose was 'device', in the sense not simply of something devised but of a 'ploy'.[69] And if the technai which I am focusing
on were involved less in imposing a form on the material than in turning
some of the energy in the material to their own advantage, they did this,
characteristically, through some kind of *outwitting*. Since the materials
of these technai were in more or less capricious motion and did not, therefore, have the stability — and hence relative passivity — of, for example, stone
or wood, adepts here had to compensate for their inability to provide any
accurate specification of the route (the *ta pros to telos*) to their end by
an alert and agile intelligence, capable of improvisation and of a ready
response to opportunity.

That such an intelligence was widely recognized and cultivated among
the Greeks has been forcefully argued in the work of M. Detienne and
J.-P. Vernant. The generic concept under which these two French scholars
have reconstructed a whole semantic field is that of *mētis* or "cunning

intelligence."[70] They show that in a wide range of activities—which seems to include conspicuously just those technai which I am now considering, from hunting and snaring to money-making, navigating, or medicine— the Greeks prized very highly a talent for making out against the odds of greater strength, a talent which combines "flair, wisdom, forethought, subtlety of mind, deception, resourcefulness, vigilance, opportunism, various skills, and experience acquired over the years . . . [and] is applied to situations which are transient, shifting, disconcerting and ambiguous, situations which do not lend themselves to precise measurement, exact calculation or rigorous logic."[71] (The "wily" Odysseus, described by Homer as *polumētis*—i.e., possessed of many stratagems which made him equal to the most unforeseen situations—might be taken as the prototypical figure here.) Part of Vernant's and Detienne's thesis is that this whole field of intelligence was systematically suppressed in the official picture of the Greek mind which was painted by the philosophers, the most influential hand here of course being Plato's. And they claim, further, that this picture was so successful and has been so enduring that only with their own quite heterodox work of "excavation" have the significance and coherence of the whole suppressed range of meanings and images that cluster around the concept of *mētis* been brought to light again.

It is worthwhile, I believe, to relate Detienne's and Vernant's thesis to our own exploration of techne, as well as to Hintikka's thesis about the "preponderance of the paradigm of the craftsman" which we have already met. They emphasize that they are "not writing a history of ideas," quite simply because Greek thought has left no *concept* of *mētis;* the latter "was never explicitly formulated, never the subject of a conceptual analysis or of any coherent theoretical examination"; it does not figure in "what Greek intelligence had to say about itself when it composed theoretical treatises on its own nature."[72] Now this view of things seems to be borne out by what we find in Aristotle's treatment of the technai. A concept of techne does indeed emerge, but it is one which leaves unassimilated just those technai in which the play of chance and the need for cunning are most conspicuous. If the very general paradigm of teleology which Hintikka finds in the Socratic notion of the craftsman was installed in the concept of techne, Detienne's and Vernant's work alerts us to the key features which were *excluded* by this installation—excluded even though they were perfectly well instantiated in familiar activities which Aristotle would never have thought of gainsaying as *examples* of techne.

I shall be going on presently to outline the concept of phronesis by drawing out systematically the contrast between it and the concept of techne. Here, however, we should notice the *affinity* between phronesis and the philosophically orphaned technai which we are now adverting to. In a passage in *E.N.* 2.2, Aristotle writes:

> The accounts we demand must be in accordance with the subject-matter; matters concerned with conduct and questions of what is good for us have no fixity any more than matters of health. The general account being of this nature, the account of particular cases is yet more lacking in exactness; for they do not fall under any techne or set of precepts but the agents themselves must in each case consider what is appropriate to the occasion, as happens also in the techne of medicine or of navigation.[73]

In laying down here as a general principle that the matter (*hulē*) has a determining role with respect to the kind of account (*logos*) that will be available, Aristotle tells us that in the case of ethics the fact that its matter is praxis brings it about that the *logos* here can be given only roughly and in outline (*tupōi kai ouk akribōs*). Indeed so multiform and hetero- geneous are the materials and circumstances of praxis that they cannot be considered to fall under any "techne or set of precepts (*paraggelia*)" at all. There is no systematic body of knowledge that can adequately com- prehend them, and when Aristotle comes, later on, to consider the '*or- thos logos*' that regulates them the best he can do, faced with the im- possibility of giving a determinate content to this *logos*, is to define it obliquely as a *logos* such as the *phronimos* would work out—and then try to specify the kind of resourcefulness of intelligence and character, be- yond the confines of any specific techne, that the *phronimos* must have. In the context of our present discussion, what is most interesting in the above passage is that Aristotle, having declared that the regulation of mat- ters of praxis falls under no techne—and having already compared mat- ters of conduct with matters of health in respect of the lack of fixity which characterizes them both—immediately goes on to point out the affinity between such regulation and what goes on in medicine and navigation. He seems to be saying, or at any rate implying, that medicine and naviga- tion are technai the exercise of which should be deemed to be especially analogous with the living of a virtuous life—so much so, indeed, that *they can scarcely be said to be technai at all.* For, no more than ethics, they cannot enshrine general rules that would offset the requirement that the agents themselves must, in each case, think out what is appropriate to the occasion, or, literally, spy out that which conduces to the *kairos* (*ta pros ton kairon skopein*).

We might pause here to ask whether Aristotle's choice of medicine and navigation as examples at the end of this passage is in fact significant. Could he have made the same point and referred instead to, say, building or cobbling? The decisive thing in the passage, after all, is the shift from

the level of a general account to particular cases, and should our eye, therefore, be caught not by medicine and navigation as special technai, but
rather by *particular* cases in *any* techne? Perhaps Aristotle's point is that
in any area of techne at all (even apparently straightforward areas of reification such as building or cobbling), once we descend to particular cases
of dealing with *this* or *this,* we are no longer securely within the governance of the techne, which always remains limited to *general* rules. This
reading would seem to be supported by the first chapter of the *Metaphysics,* in which, as we have already seen, the man of techne is granted an
expertise with respect to *classes* of persons suffering from different classes
of disease but is still not guaranteed to be able to deal well with Socrates
or Callias suffering from this disease now. And even more striking confirmation is provided in the *Rhetoric:* "None of the technai theorizes about
individual cases [*skopei to kath' hekaston*]. Medicine, for instance, does
not theorize about what will help to cure Socrates or Callias, but only
about what will help to cure any or all of a given class of patients: this
alone is subject to techne [is *entechnon*] — individual cases are so infinitely
various that no knowledge of them is possible [they are *apeiron kai ouk
episteton*]. In the same way the theory of rhetoric is concerned not with
what seems reputable to a given individual like Socrates or Hippias, but
with what seems so to men of a given type."[74]
    The relationship between the general and the particular, which has
just been raised by my question about the possible significance of Aristotle's choice of examples, is one of the most important issues that needs
to be examined in any attempt to clarify his consideration of practical
knowledge. In the next chapter and later on in this one, we shall see that
the subtlety of his treatment of this issue in relation to praxis is one of
the great strengths of his analysis of phronesis; and in chapter 10 I shall
try to show that his lack of explicitness in treating of the same issue in
relation to poiesis — and therefore in relation to the specifically productive activities that are canonized in his official definition of techne — is
a serious weakness in his analysis of techne. Here, however, I want simply
to indicate that there are grounds for ascribing to Aristotle the idea that
in some technai individuals are more exposed to what is *apeiron* in particular cases and less equipped by their stock of formulated knowledge
to deal with it than is the case in other technai. Given his usual disregard
for niceties of distinction with respect to his stock examples of techne it
is helpful to find a passage in the *Eudemian Ethics* where he addresses
a question not unlike the question I have just raised: "One might then
raise the problem — why do doctors deliberate about matters within their
science, but not grammarians? The reason is that error may occur in two
ways (for we may err either in reasoning or in perception when we are

engaged in the very act), and in medicine one may go wrong in both
ways, but in grammar one can do so only in respect of the perception
and action, and if they enquired about this there would be no end to
their inquiries [*eis apeiron hēxousin*]."[75] Here Aristotle seems to distinguish implicitly two types of technai: (i) technai whose exercise always involves deliberative reasoning or *logizein,* because there is always a question of how to get from one's general knowledge of the *eidos* to an ultimate
action (*to eschaton*) that is within one's power to do now, and (ii) technai
where there is no question of things being in our power anyhow (in a way
yet to be determined by the deliberation) since all rules are exhaustively
formulated and universally binding, e.g., the standard spelling or grammar of a language. This interpretation of the passage seems to be borne
out by another remark which Aristotle lightly drops in a parallel passage
in *E.N.* 3.3: "Now every class of men deliberates about the things that
can be done by their own efforts [*peri tōn di' hautōn praktōn*]. And in
the case of exact and self-contained sciences there is no deliberation, e.g.,
about the letters of the alphabet (for we have no doubt how they should
be written); but the things that are brought about by our own efforts,
but not always in the same way, are the things about which we deliberate,
e.g., questions of medical treatment or of money-making. And we do so
more in the case of the techne of navigation than in that of gymnastics,
inasmuch as it has been less exactly worked out [*diēkribōtai*]."[76] It seems
clear from these two extracts that Aristotle did envisage a kind of scale
in respect of the degree to which different technai could encompass the
complexity of individual cases within their general rules and prescriptions;
and even if we are left to guess as to how high on this scale productive
technai (e.g., house-building or saddle-making) might be situated, it is
at least clear that medicine and, more especially, navigation are at the
lower end of it. Moreover, it is just because of their being at this lower
end that, when they are to the fore, it is a comparison and not a contrast
with phronesis that is likely to occur to Aristotle and to us.

In fact, Detienne and Vernant regard Aristotle's analysis of phronesis as the nearest thing to be found in classical Greek philosophy to
a recognition of the kind of intelligence which, in general, was studiously
outlawed by this same philosophy. This Aristotelian analysis, they believe,
"expresses a desire to embrace . . . the types of knowledge that are subject to contingency and directed to beings affected by change," and it "re-
habilitates conjectural knowledge and the type of intelligence that proceeds obliquely."[77] It is easy to regard this type of knowledge either as
morally neutral or as a form of knavery and moral deviousness and to see
Machiavelli as its philosophical spokesman. Part of Aristotle's achievement,
however, was precisely to bed into his conception of ethical knowledge—

i.e., the knowledge of a character which is oriented to the good — much of the suppleness and flexibility which were already well recognized as requirements in areas such as oratory and politics as well as in navigation or hunting.

Aristotle's openness to enlisting *mētis* for the ethical life is eminently comprehensible from the viewpoint of a kind of contemporary philosophy which has assimilated *mētis* into its own strategies of reflection. Detienne and Vernant claim that *mētis* must "be tracked down . . . in areas which the philosopher usually passes over in silence or mentions only with irony or with hostility so that, by contrast, he can display to its fullest advantage the way of reasoning and understanding which is required in his own profession."[78] Moreover they also maintain that such tracking down is something that had not really been attempted until their own pioneering work broke the "prolonged silence on the subject of cunning intelligence" which had been maintained in the whole field of classical scholarship right down to the present. While I am not competent to assess this judgment on their discipline, I do want to point out that what they are attempting to rehabilitate in contemporary scholarship (and what, by their own admission, Aristotle had tried at least partially to rehabilitate in ancient philosophy) is something which Wittgenstein has already made at home in the very working procedures of contemporary philosophy. In the final sentence of their book, they suggest that the "prolonged silence," which they have tried to break, has been due to the fact that "the concept of Platonic Truth . . . has never really ceased to haunt Western metaphysical thought." But if this is so, is it not appropriate that the most intrepid efforts in recent philosophy to exorcise the ghost have (as in Wittgenstein's case) resorted to ploys which would take the reader unawares and, as it were, trick him or her out of ingrained assumptions and habits of thought — or (as in Gadamer's case) have appealed crucially to the precedent of Aristotle's analysis of phronesis?

6. The Distinction between Techne *Poiētikē* and Phronesis

I have just been trying to show that if Aristotle worked out a concept of techne along the lines drawn out in section 4, the denotation of the term 'techne', in his usage, included activities whose characteristic features are scarcely captured by that concept and which bring into play, in fact, a quite different conceptual paradigm — one which bears strong family resemblances with phronesis. All of this was something of an interlude, however, for my primary concern is to mark out what I have been calling the 'official' concept of techne (the one which is defined in *E.N.*

6.4 as *poiētikē*, i.e., oriented to fabrication,[79] and in *Meta.* 1.1 as concerned essentially with universals) and to establish the contrast between it and phronesis. Later on (in another interlude in chapter 9 and throughout chapter 10) I shall try to show that this concept can itself be deconstructed if certain questions are pressed against it. But for now I want simply to spell out Aristotle's understanding of it, and to show the lines along which a *distinction* emerges between it and phronesis.

In *E.N.* 6, as we have already seen, this distinction is derived quite unceremoniously from what seems to be a prior distinction between poiesis and praxis. In chapter 4 (on techne) we are told: "making and acting are different . . . so that the reasoned state of capacity to act [i.e., phronesis] is different from the reasoned state of capacity to make [i.e., techne]"; and again in chapter 5 (on phronesis): "phronesis cannot be . . . techne . . . because action and making are different kinds of things." In the light of these leading statements, we need to consider both how action and making differ, and how this difference determines the difference between phronesis and techne.

Action and making are distinguished by Aristotle thus: "while making has an end other than itself, action cannot, for good action (*eupraxia*) itself is its end."[80] In aiming at an end other than itself, making fits smoothly and comprehensively into a means-end framework: within it, materials and tools can be viewed as means used by the maker to bring about his end product; or it itself as an overall process can be seen as a means to the achievement of the final product (or *ergon*) as end; or, looking beyond the making process to the wider context of use, the end product may itself be seen as means toward the fulfillment of other, higher ends in people's lives (leather and cobbling are means to shoes, but shoes are means to comfortable walking).[81] Now although Aristotle introduces praxis as a kind of activity whose end is *not outside* it, it is noticeable that he does not entirely set aside the telic mold: praxis, we are to understand, is *its own end*. And elsewhere, a little terminological flexibility gives him a word, bearing the impress of this mold, for such an activity, namely *entelecheia* (which is a counterpart to *energeia* in his restricted sense of that term; both terms pick out the same activities: ones whose *telos* or *ergon* is in themselves *qua* activities and not therefore in anything separable that may result from or endure after them). Still, even if Aristotle does not put us especially on our guard here, we shall not grasp what is most distinctive about praxis—and what therefore has a shaping influence on the kind of knowledge that we find in phronesis—unless we see that it involves nothing less than what Gadamer calls a "fundamental modification" of the means-end framework.[82]

The absence of disposable materials and of a substantial end product (which immediately makes praxis more elusive to our conceptual net than poiesis) has as its other side the presence of the agent, who is invested in his action more completely than the producer is in his product. Whereas the latter can stand outside his materials and allow the productive process to be shaped by the impersonal form which he has objectively conceived, the agent on the other hand is constituted through the actions which disclose him both to others and to himself as the person that he is. He can never possess an idea of himself in the way that the craftsman possesses the form of his product; rather than his having any definite 'what' as blueprint for his actions or his life, he becomes and discovers 'who' he is through these actions. And the medium for this becoming through action is not one over which he is ever sovereign master; it is, rather, a network of other people who are also agents and with whom he is bound up in relationships of interdependency.

It may appear that this notion of action which I have just introduced has been distinguished from making only at the cost of cutting it adrift from any governance by knowledge and that it owes far more in fact to Arendt than to Aristotle.[83] I want to try to show, however, that support for it can be found in Aristotle's own texts. Easiest to vindicate is the interpersonal dimension. While it may be true of the philosopher that "even when by himself, [he] can contemplate truth" (though even he "can perhaps do so better if he has fellow-workers") such self-sufficiency is unavailable to the person involved in praxis: "the just man needs people towards whom and with whom he shall act justly, and the temperate man, the brave man, and each of the others is in the same case."[84] Elsewhere in the *Ethics,* Aristotle reflects: "Surely it is strange, too, to make the blessed man a solitary . . . man is a political animal and one whose nature is to live with others."[85] And all of this is of course most famously expressed in the second chapter of the *Politics,* where man's sociability is linked with the fact that he "is the only animal who has the gift of speech" and it is contended that "he who by nature . . . is without a state, is either a bad man or above humanity."[86]

What then of the suspicion that the characterization of praxis given above does little justice to the role of knowledge in praxis? This suspicion is well grounded only if we are already committed to a particular conception of knowledge; but it is this conception, I believe, that we are being asked to relinquish as an appropriate model of the type of *practical* knowledge that is to be found in phronesis. Over against the uncompromising intellectualism of the Socratic equation of virtue with knowledge, phronesis is put forward as a type of knowledge that emerges within a person's striving or desire: "of the part [of the soul] which is practical and intellectual the good state is truth in agreement with right desire" (*orthē orexis*).⁸⁷ This appetitive element is not something separate from knowledge proper, which merely provides the undifferentiated energy, as it were, to translate the terminus of the knowing process into action. Rather, we have here a kind of knowledge whose whole finality is intrinsically toward action ("a man has phronesis not by knowing only but by acting").⁸⁸ This unity of knowledge and striving is expressed when Aristotle tells us that *prohairesis* (purpose or choice), which is the origin of action and cannot exist without both intellect and a moral condition of the mind, "is either desiderative thought or intellectual desire, and such an origin of action is a man."⁸⁹

If we attend now to this fact that phronesis arises within the whole striving that a person *is,* the distinction between it and techne will begin to open up for us. Like techne, phronesis is described as a *hexis meta logou,* a reasoned state, but Aristotle adds: "yet it is not only a reasoned state; this is shown by the fact that a state of that sort may be forgotten but phronesis cannot."⁹⁰ Technai can be forgotten as well as learned, one can distance oneself from them, acquire them or not acquire them, one can (to use Gadamer's terms) "possess" them, and in the security of this possession, "apply" them.⁹¹ They are at one's disposal, moreover, in a way that allows one to determine the direction in which they will be applied. This is brought out by Aristotle's designation of them as "powers of opposites" (*dunameis tōn enantiōn*): a person who possesses the techne of medicine, for instance, is capable of bringing about not just health but also illness; his techne, as such, can be deployed in either direction at his behest.

The way in which phronesis differs from techne here is expressed by Aristotle in a very compressed sentence which needs some unpacking: "while there is such a thing as excellence in techne, there is no such thing as excellence in phronesis; and in techne he who errs willingly is preferable, but in phronesis, as in the [ethical] excellences he is the reverse."⁹² Let us begin with the first part of this sentence. One obvious way of interpreting it would be by taking (any particular) techne as an open field where one may attempt the relevant performance or production and where, when one does so successfully (or meets the relevant standards), one may be said to display "excellence in [the particular] techne." Phronesis, on the other hand, might be taken not to be an open field in this sense—which allows for different degrees of success and even for someone's failing in his techne—because phronesis implies, by definition, excellent performance; and so, rather than there being excellence *in* phronesis, phronesis simply *is* an excellence.⁹³ Now while this interpretation is correct, I believe, in what it attributes to 'phronesis', with respect to techne one thing counts decisively against it: the fact that at the end of *E.N.* 6.4 Aristotle writes 'true' into the definition of 'techne' and introduces the term *'atechnia'* (absence of techne) for false reasoning (or unsuccessful endeavor) in this sphere.

In another attempt to interpret the first part of our sentence, *'aretē'* might be read as ethical excellence and so Aristotle might be taken to mean that while the execution of a work, strictly *qua* actualization of one's techne, is morally neutral, it may *also* be weighted with moral value. One man is making a table (perhaps not very well) for a poor person, while another is playing the flute (perhaps excellently) for the S.S. in Auschwitz; even though the former may be much less 'excellent' in his respective techne than the latter, he may still be said to display, in a sense that the latter does not, excellence *in* techne — and this might be taken to be Aristotle's sense for "*technēs . . . aretē.*" This interpretation seems to be borne out in other places. In *E.N.* 6.2, we are told that *dianoia . . . heneka tou kai praktikē* [i.e., phronesis] "rules [*archei*] the productive intellect [i.e., techne] as well, since every one who makes makes for an end, and that which is made is not an end in an unqualified sense (but only relative to something i.e. of something) — only that which is *done* [*prakton*] is that; for good action [*eupraxia*] is an end and desire aims at this."[94] This sentence very explicitly subordinates one's accomplishments as a *technitēs* to one's wider concerns as a human being; and one might then say that it is only within this subordination, and not within the narrow realm of techne itself, that *aretē* accrues or does not accrue to one's techne. If medicine enables one to produce health *and* disease, then one might say that it ceases to be a mere *dunamis* (*tōn enantiōn*) and becomes an *aretē* only in a doctor who is reliably committed to *health.* The technical competence of such a doctor will be infused with a solicitude for his patients that will incline him to respond to late-night calls; and, as a person, he will differ from, e.g., the kind of doctor mentioned by Aristotle in the *Politics,* whose medical practice has become a vehicle for his acquisitiveness.[95]

The point made in this interpretation can quite congruously be attributed to Aristotle. I believe that the point being made *in the present sentence* (1140b21–22), however, has to do not so much with the way in which phronesis complements or completes techne as with differences between techne and phronesis in respect of the excellence (and, more particularly, the depth of engagement of the person in the display of this excellence) which each of them, as modes of knowledge, properly manifests. Quite apart from the moral value which the exercise of a techne may assume from the context within which it is inserted, techne, in any case, has its own excellence. When Aristotle says that this is an excellence *in* techne (literally, 'of techne'—*aretē technēs*) and that there is no corresponding excellence *in* phronesis, he is perhaps hinting that techne is more self-contained as a form of knowledge than phronesis is and that, because of this self-containment, excellence may be ascribed to it *per se* even if at the same time its application in the production of a concrete outcome may be so interfered with by factors extraneous to itself that this outcome will in fact be lacking in excellence. The external factor might be some ulterior purpose of the *technitēs* himself or it might simply be some resistance in the materials which, while defying the best efforts of his techne, still does not betray a lack of excellence in the latter. (The first case might be illustrated by a master potter who produces a *bad* pot for pedagogic purposes with his apprentices — and therefore, of course, without being implicated in any *ethical* badness — and the second case seems to be envisaged by Aristotle himself when he says in the *Rhetoric:* "its function [i.e., rhetoric's *qua* techne] is not simply to succeed in persuading, but rather to discover the persuasive facts in each case. In this it resembles all other technai. For example, it is not the function of medicine simply to make a man quite healthy, but to put him as far as it may be on the road to health; it is possible to give excellent treatment even to those who can never enjoy sound health."[96] A passage like this appears to support Gadamer's emphasis on a clear distinction in the case of techne between 'possession' and 'application', so that we can ascribe to the techne as possessed, or *aretē,* which is undiminished by any "painful imperfection"[97] that may be involved in its application.) Now in the case of phronesis, which cannot be thus circumscribed as a form of knowledge, things are different; a fault in concrete action indicates an absence of excellence which is really an absence of phronesis itself.

This (third) interpretation will become more plausible if we look now at the *second* part of our sentence: "and in techne he who errs willingly is preferable, but in phronesis, as in the excellences he is the reverse." What is meant here, I think, is this: a voluntary mistake in techne reveals the control that one has over its exercise; one's skill is at one's disposal, is one's own to give or to withhold; and the deliberate withholding of it, masked as a mistake, is no sign of absence of skill; it is a sign, rather, of the extent to which the skill is subject to one's deliberate will. An unintentional mistake, on the other hand, shows that one's techne itself is not secure and that there is nothing that one's will can do to prevent this. The case is otherwise with phronesis, because here the will which might finesse with a mistake is already engaged, and so is not in reserve to do this. In relation to one's phronesis, one has no discretionary powers to be exercised by some superordinate self. Here one is fully engaged and whatever mistakes one makes must be put down to oneself; they cannot be ascribed to one's lack of skill (as in the case of involuntary mistakes in techne) or to some covert intention of one's own which makes one master of the mistake (as in voluntary mistakes in techne).

This reading of a fairly opaque sentence from book 6 of the *Nicomachean Ethics* is confirmed, I think, by the first chapter of book 8 of the *Eudemian Ethics*, in which mistakes are again mentioned, but this time within the context of a very explicit treatment of instrumentality (the core which had been left unstated in the *E.N.* sentence) and a very elaborate argument to show that phronesis does not fit into an instrumentalist mold. The chapter begins by pointing out how things can be used. An eye, for instance, can be used just to see; or, by squinting with it, to see double; or—more bizarrely—to sell it or to eat it (an eye for a tooth!). And it goes on: "knowledge may be used similarly; it is possible to use it truly or to do what is wrong, e.g. when a man voluntarily writes incorrectly, thus using knowledge as ignorance, like a person using his hand as a foot—dancing-girls sometimes use the foot as hand and the hand as a foot."[98] Next, the question is put as to whether justice, as an ethical excellence, might also exemplify the same structure, for if "all the excellences are kinds of knowledge, one might use justice also as injustice, and so one would be unjust and do unjust actions from justice, as ignorant things may be done from knowledge."[99] The answer to this is that justice can*not* be so used,[100] one cannot stand aside from one's virtue and let it be deflected in the manner that one's knowledge can be deflected in one's actual conduct. For, in the case of knowledge, a split is possible between one's real state and the behavior that one shows to the world or between what one *is* and what one *does*. But it is precisely this split that is impossible in the case of virtue: "while one cannot indeed from knowledge *be* ignorant, but only make mistakes and do the same things as one does from ignorance, in the case of justice a man cannot even *act* from it in the way that he will act from injustice."[101]

And now the main question is put, for which the earlier examples were only a preparation: what about phronesis? Where does *it* fit in this scheme? Surely it can be accommodated in the same structure of use (or misuse) as knowledge and techne, for "since phronesis is knowledge and something true, it may behave like knowledge; one might act unphronetically though possessed of phronesis, and commit the errors of the unphronetic."[102] Aristotle's reply to this is that phronesis can*not* be appropriated for unphronetic acts. The key proposition in a complex argument[103] is this: "over other kinds of knowledge, then, there is something superior that diverts them; but how can there be any kind of knowledge that diverts the highest knowledge of all? There is no longer any knowl-

edge or *nous* to do this."[104] And so he concludes the chapter with a characteristically ambivalent allusion to Socrates: "the Socratic saying that
nothing is stronger than phronesis is right. But when Socrates said this
of knowledge he was wrong. For phronesis is an excellence and not a species of knowledge, but another kind of cognition" (*gnōsis*).

We can return now, in the light of the passages which I have just
analyzed, to the contrast between phronesis and techne. What we have
seen is that whereas in the case of techne a split may be envisaged between what we might call its *being* and its *use* (or, in Gadamer's terms,
between its "possession" and its "application") in the case of phronesis
and praxis, on the other hand, there is no such split. The praxis is to be
attributed wholly and without the possibility of extraneous intervention
to phronesis itself. Both are so intimately related that phronesis comes
into its own only in the situations that draw the self into action. And
since before one's involvement in these situations one's knowledge is never
fully possessed, in them it is never merely applied. We may look at this
as an assimilation of action to being—seeing in all genuine praxis a manifestation of the being of the *phronimos*. But equally we may see it the
other way: that all genuine phronesis is absorbed into action—action as
an ineluctable movement that a person can never step out of. The ineluctability resides in the fact that in our lives we can never freeze our assets,
nor is there ever a period of respite in which we might prepare ourselves
for action as if that were something in which we were not already involved.
Or, as Gadamer puts it: "we are always already in the situation of having
to act."[105] All our actions occur within this unavoidable context of movement in our lives and hence are always imbued with a certain dynamism
that transcends any single act. We must not, of course, overemphasize or
misconstrue the nature of this dynamism. For the movement is not only
always edging into the ever new present; it is also deeply layered with its
own past. Each new act arises within the terrestrial magnetism of our past
acts, which lie sedimented in our habits. (This, we may note, is Aristotle's
own imagery in his very stark comment in *E.N.* 3 about the person who
can no longer resist the pull of bad habit: "he has thrown away his chance,"
he tells us, "just as when you have let a stone go it is too late to recover
it.")[106] The point I am making here about phronesis is that it does not
stand outside or above this temporal dispersion of our lives. And this is
an important part of the reason why it cannot be instrumentalized. Whatever issues from it, by way of action, already has the full weight of ourselves behind it and so can be instrumentalized not by ourselves but, if
at all, only by someone else who may try to use what we have done for
his own ends. The point here, however, is that such a person will not be
able to manipulate *himself* in the same way.[107]

7. Meeting Two Difficulties That Stem from Aristotle's Usage

The interpretation of phronesis which I have just been presenting comes up against two particular difficulties in Aristotle's own linguistic usage. In the first place, while I have been arguing for the nondisposability of the agent's self—so that the self appears not within the field that can be surveyed by phronesis but rather in the very activity of phronesis itself—Aristotle himself, however, has no compunction about linking 'phronesis' with some variant of the reflexive pronoun *hautos* and speaking several times in *E.N.* 6, of "phronesis about oneself" (*phronēsis peri hauton*). In the second place, I have been trying to show that the whole conceptual framework of instrumentality, which is so well fitted to the analysis of techne, can provide only negative formulations in relation to phronesis and praxis and that we must continually stretch our thinking beyond it if we are to catch the movement of the self as agent.[108] But how do we square this with the fact that Aristotle himself seems quite comfortably to conduct his analysis of phronesis in instrumentalist terms, using the concepts of end and means (*telos* and *pros to telos*) as his constant stock-in-trade?

Substance is given to the first *aporia* by Aristotle's reporting of ordinary usage: "It is for this reason that we think Pericles and men like him have phronesis, viz., because they can see what is good for themselves," whereas (a little later), "we say Anaxagoras, Thales and men like them have wisdom [*sophia*] but not phronesis when we see them ignorant of what is to their own advantage."[109] Again in another place we are told that "it is to that which observes well the various matters concerning itself that one ascribes phronesis," and two consequences are drawn from this: first, that "we say that some even of the lower animals have phronesis, viz., those which are found to have a power of foresight with respect to their own life," and, second, that phronesis must be different from *sophia* because otherwise "if the state of mind concerned with a man's own interests is to be called wisdom [*sophia*] there will be many wisdoms [a plainly unacceptable conclusion]."[110] And finally we are told that "Phronesis also is identified especially with that form of it which is concerned with a man himself—with the individual."[111]

It is surely significant that in *all* these cases where the reflexive form occurs with phronesis Aristotle qualifies his remarks with some such phrase as *legomen* or *dokei* ("we say that," "we think," "it seems," "is thought to"). What he is doing here is registering carefully according to his customary method the *endoxa* or received opinions of his contemporaries, and although this method betokens the respect which, in general, he has for these opinions, it does not imply his own endorsement of them in the present case.[112] In fact, in the last and longest passage where the connection of phronesis with the reflexive is sustained,[113] it is not at all clear from Aristotle's tone that he sees this use of "phronesis about oneself" as connoting anything more than the shrewdness of the selfish man who knows how to take the main chance and not let civic responsibilities get in the way of private gain. And when at the end of the passage he makes two comments that are clearly in his own name, they are markedly circumspect: "yet perhaps one's own good cannot exist without household management, nor without a form of government. Further, how one should order one's own affairs is not clear and needs inquiry."[114] Aristotle is here opposing any simple identification of phronesis with a facility in finding where one's own benefit lies; the self is revealed only within a network of relationships and communal responsibilities, and the function of phronesis is not to maximize a 'good' that one already knows and can come to *have,* but rather—a much more difficult task—to discover a good that one must *become.*

Our second difficulty concerns Aristotle's own quite unselfconscious use of the terminology of end and means. This use gave rise to a great deal of scholarly dispute in the nineteenth century about the role of phronesis. Julius Walter's view, that phronesis has no part in fixing ends but is limited to deliberating about means, became the dominant one. Clearly this view, which was further entrenched in this century by Werner Jaeger's support,[115] is frankly intrumentalist and cuts against all that I have been saying above. To be sure, the subsequent work of D. J. Allan has been influential in undermining Jaeger's authority and in restoring to phronesis some role in apprehending the end.[116] But what are we to make of the fact that Aristotle's formulations in the *E.N.* have given rise to this whole debate? Rather than coming down on either side, we need only recognize that Aristotle's open prepositional phrase *ta pros to telos* (translated as 'means') as well as the term *telos* itself are insufficiently differentiated for the analytic task which he tries to carry out with them. They embrace *two* meanings which need to be distinguished; and one of these is noninstrumental and therefore badly rendered by our English words 'ends' and 'means'.

We find help here in the commentaries of Greenwood and H. H. Joachim. That there is a noninstrumental sense of 'means' in *E.N.* 6 seems to be implied by Greenwood when he distinguishes between what he calls "external" and "component" means. An external means is always directed to "an end wholly distinct from itself" (as when I take an airplane to get to Paris), whereas a component means actually makes up its end, as in the case where suet, flour, and currants are means to the end pudding or, better, going to a movie is means to the end of having an enjoyable evening. Greenwood points out, "that the two notions of means are really combined in the sixth book's definition of phronesis, or—as it would be truer to say—that they were never properly distinguished from each other, but were both confusedly taken into account, artificially unified by their possession of a common name."[117] A similar point is made by Joachim, who speaks of "ends whose means are at the same time constituents of the ends" as "immanently teleological structures" and goes on: "The means to the end in the sphere of conduct are themselves constituent parts of the end, valuable and desirable in themselves—for they are the ends and it is they. The end and object of the brave man is the realization of bravery . . . and the acting bravely which is the means to his end is itself the end desired."[118]

Returning from his commentators to Aristotle himself, we find confirmation of their views in his statement that "action cannot [have an end other than itself]; for good action is itself its end."[119] And when we find him speaking as if action were merely a means (e.g., at 1145a5–6) we shall avoid being confused if we interpret "means" (*ta pros to telos*) here in a decisively noninstrumental manner. Since the "end" itself remains to be determined even in the process of assembling the "means," and cannot be securely fixed prior to or independently of this process, the consideration of means can never be simply a matter of instrumental efficiency. Aristotle's recognition of this fact seems to be brought out in the distinction he makes between phronesis and "cleverness" (*deinotēs*). Cleverness, he tells us, "is a faculty . . . such as to be able to do the things that tend toward the mark we have set for ourselves, and to hit it. Now if the mark be noble the cleverness is laudable, but if the mark be bad, the cleverness is mere villainy."[120] With this calculative ability, to which virtue or vice would attach only externally and *per accidens,* Aristotle contrasts phronesis as an intellectual virtue whose exercise is internally motivated by a desire for the good, a desire whose fulfillment it itself determines in each instance.[121] That Aristotle wanted to emphasize the point which he makes with this contrast seems evident from the fact that it is essentially the same point which he had already made a little earlier in his analysis of deliberative excellence (*euboulia*), a sub-virtue of phronesis. Deliberative excellence obviously involves a kind of rightness or correctness, but "there being more than one kind of correctness, plainly *euboulia* is not any and every kind: for (1) the incontinent and bad man (if he is clever)[122] will reach as a result of his calculation what he sets before himself, so that he will have deliberated correctly, but he will have got for himself a great evil. Now to have deliberated well is thought to be a good thing; for it is this kind of correctness of deliberation that is *euboulia,* viz. that which tends to attain what is good."[123]

'Deliberative excellence' is perhaps too effete a term to bring out the significance of Aristotle's refusal here to allow merely calculative or technical ability as a candidate for the kind of reasoning which guides practice. In terms which are familiar to us from Part 1, we are entitled, I believe, to see in this refusal a rejection of the methodological distinction between normative or 'value' questions on the one hand, and technical or functional questions on the other: a distinction which can then be used as a basis for claiming that a whole set of technical inquiries is 'value-free' and therefore immune from critical reflection, while critical reflection itself is 'ideological' and therefore devoid of objectivity. What Aristotle is here insisting on — and it is a point which we have already met in the Aristotelianism of Newman — is the fact that one will not be good at finding the 'means' toward certain 'ends' unless one is a person who already appreciates and is striving toward these 'ends'.[124]

It is not just the distinction between end and means, nor the distinction which (following Gadamer) I introduced earlier between possession and application, that must be relativized if we are to come to a proper understanding of phronesis. We must also see that any distinction between the universal and the particular which would simply include the latter under the former is unsustainable. The 'universal' ideas that make up one's habitual practical-moral knowledge — such as justice, bravery, truthfulness — cannot be 'stamped' on each act or situation, nor do they provide the kind of specification for action that a craftsman's working out of the *eidos* of his product provides. In Gadamer's words, Aristotle "does not regard the guiding principles that he describes as knowledge that can be taught. They have only the validity of schemata. They always have to be made concrete in the situation of the person acting."[125] Phronesis itself, then, is not a knowledge of ethical ideas as such, but rather a resourcefulness of mind that is called into play in, and responds uniquely to, the situation in which these ideas are to be realized. The difference here is pointed out when Aristotle tells us that "to know what is just and what is unjust requires, men think, no great wisdom" and goes on: "but how actions must be done . . . in order to be just, to know *this* is a greater achievement than knowing what is good for the health; though even there, while it is easy to know that honey, wine, hellebore, cautery, and the use of the knife are so, to know how, to whom, and when these should be applied with a view to producing health, is no less an achievement than that of being a physician."[126] (It is interesting that at this stage, in *E.N.* 5, when Aristotle has not yet clarified, through the analysis of phronesis, the precise type of knowledge that informs us about "how actions are to be done," the closest analogy for it which he can find — and he acknowledges its limitations — is with a techne of the kind that has to find the *kairos* and reckon with what is *apeiron kai ouk epistēton* in each individual case.)[127]

The point of this analogy with medicine—which is to point up the discrepancy between general, already formulated knowledge and the kind of insight demanded by concrete cases—is further developed by Aristotle in a famous discussion of equity (*epieikeia*). The idea of justice which can be given in a general statement, and incorporated into written law, is defective *precisely because of its universality* and so needs to be corrected by the judgment of equity—which is defined as "a correction of law where it is defective owing to its universality":

> All law is universal [*katholou*], but about some things it is not possible
> to make a universal statement which will be correct . . . the error is not
> in the law nor in the legislator but in the nature of the thing, since the
> matter [*hulē*] of practical affairs is of this kind from the start. When the
> law speaks universally, then, and a case arises on it which is not covered
> by the universal statement, then it is right, when the legislator fails us and
> has erred by over-simplicity, to correct the omission—to say what the legis-
> lator himself would have said had he been present, and would have put
> into his law if he had known.[128]

This discussion of equity at the end of *E.N.* 5 which, in referring so frankly to the "error that arises from the abstractness of the statement," points to the need for experience—for what a person could be aware of only "if he had been present"—prepares the way for the discussion of phronesis which is to follow in *E.N.* 6. Phronesis is committed to a pursuit of the good, a good, moreover, which is rooted in a definite ethos with its own favored dispositions and habits. Still, this good cannot be determined in advance of the actual situations in which it is to be realized. And so phronesis, as the kind of knowledge that makes one sensitive to it, is characterized at least as much by a perceptiveness with regard to concrete particulars as by a knowledge of universal principles.

A few related points have now emerged in our consideration of phronesis: its noninstrumental character, and its mediation of the universal and the particular in a way that puts a premium on experience and perceptiveness rather than on formulated knowledge. These points have emerged in the contrast that we have drawn in the latter part of this chapter between phronesis and techne *poiētikē:* a contrast which made it clear that phronesis is not a cognitive capacity that one has at one's disposal but is, rather, very closely bound up with the kind of person that one is. Our emphasis in drawing this contrast followed in particular from our analysis of the chapter in the *Eudemian Ethics* that marked an important difference between knowledge and virtue and then went on to show that phronesis falls on the side of virtue rather than of knowledge. To bring

these points about phronesis which we have now met into a fuller and
more coherent picture we must try to clarify further the relationship between phronesis and virtue and, in particular, to determine more precisely the status of phronesis as knowledge. I take up this task in the next
chapter.

9. The Circle between Knowledge and Virtuous Character: Phronesis as a Form of Experience

1. Aristotle's Reserve about the Role of Knowledge in Virtue: The Emergence of a Circle between Phronesis and Character

Our central text, book 6 of the *Nicomachean Ethics,* is devoted to an analysis of what Aristotle calls "intellectual virtues" (*aretai dianoētikai*) — i.e., virtues of a type which had already in book 1 been distinguished from "ethical virtues" (*aretai ēthikai*).[1] Phronesis (which occupies the bulk of book 6) is, then, an *intellectual* virtue. What differentiates it from the four other intellectual virtues (*technē, nous, epistēmē* and *sophia*) listed and discussed in book 6, however, is precisely the intimacy of its relationship with *ethical* virtue. Indeed, with phronesis the whole distinction between intellectual and ethical virtues becomes strained. For while phronesis is a virtue of the rational part of the soul (the *logistikon*), which gives direction to the nonrational part (which is *alogon*), still this virtue can exist in the rational part only if the nonrational part is already inclined to the ethical virtues. Moreover, if we suppose that the latter of these two points was at least as important to Aristotle as the former, we get a good sense, I believe, of where the center of gravity is in his analysis of phronesis and of the tensions that are at play in it. He could unhesitatingly rebuke Socrates for regarding knowledge as a sufficient condition of virtue;[2] indeed, from his own stance within an established ethos with its favored dispositions, it had to be shown that knowledge was even a necessary condition. As he puts it in a most characteristic remark: "things just and noble (*kalon*) and good for man . . . these are the things which it is the mark of a good man to do" (*ha tou agathou estin andros prattein*).[3] And so there is actually a case to be made here *against* knowledge: "we are none the more able to act for *knowing* them [the just, noble, and good] if the excellences are states [*hexeis*], just as we are none the better able to act for knowing the things that are healthy and sound, in the sense

275

not of producing but of issuing from the state of health; for we are none the more able to act for having the techne of medicine or of gymnastics."[4]

This objection — introduced in almost the only formal use of the dialectical method that occurs in book 6 — is no mere straw man of an imaginary opponent, but might claim considerable sanction from the way of thinking to which Aristotle himself was committed.[5] And so, since it forced him, as he put it, "to go more deeply into things," there is much to be gained from looking closely at how he deals with it. The kind of knowledge argued against in the objection, clearly, is a detached knowledge *about* something, a knowledge whose significance resides solely in its content and is unaffected by the manner of its possession by the knower. It is third-person knowledge in the sense that, as in the analogy used, the person himself does not need it, since either he *is* already healthy, or, if he is not, the doctor can supply it.

In his answer to the objection, in which he has the task of vindicating the role of phronesis, Aristotle does not defend this kind of knowledge nor deny that possessing it does not make one *praktikos*, "able to do." His argument, rather, seems to be that the health analogy is instructive in showing that the primary sense of health is not what produces health, as medical knowledge does, but rather the *state* of health from which healthy acts spring; the case is similar in the ethical sphere except that here the state of being virtuous (in the full sense of *kuria aretē*, and not merely of an *aretē* that comes by nature or by habituation) itself necessarily includes knowledge of a different kind to what medical knowledge is in the sphere of health, and for which there is, in fact, no counterpart in the health sphere at all.

The rejection here of the medical model (which, as we have already seen, Aristotle was so drawn to in other places) is significant confirmation of the nondisposable nature of phronesis, i.e., of the impossibility of separating out of phronetic action an element of knowledge as possessed and another element of application. For medicine might have seemed a particularly attractive analogue not just because ethical virtue can easily be conceived as a kind of spiritual health, but also because medicine is a techne which, as Aristotle himself says in the *Metaphysics*, "may reside in the patient, but not *qua* patient"[6] — or, as he otherwise makes the same point, which a doctor may possess and then apply to himself *qua* other. But in fact it is just this dealing with oneself *qua* other that is to be excluded from phronesis and praxis. We might almost say that Aristotle shows a preference for situating ethics nearer to a natural than to a technical process and that he is left then with the problem of finding room for knowledge within this 'natural' process. The knowledge that he is trying to conceive is one that arises within a moral state as its natural intuitiveness and not an independently achieved knowledge that can precede the state and be architectonic with respect to it.

To see how this way of saying things is supported in Aristotle, let us now look directly at his argument in response to the objection. It can be reconstructed in a number of steps. First, in accordance with his characteristic placing of acts in the context of their underlying dispositions, there is a refusal to consider an action apart from its relation to the agent: "some people who do just acts are not necessarily just."[7] And so the 'just' actions of these persons are not properly just—even though on the level of what we might call external behavior they conform with those of the just person. For, and this is the second step, the action of the just person, which may seem to be replicated by the 'behavior' of these others, has an inner dimension that the replicas lack. While the latter may be performed "either unwillingly or in ignorance or for some other reasons than for the sake of the action itself," the actions of the just person, on the contrary, are done for *their own sake*. And (the third step) what makes these actions be for their own sake is the fact that they are done through purpose (*dia prohairesin*). One might expect Aristotle to clinch the argument immediately by saying that what constitutes 'purpose' is of course practical knowledge and so—putting the steps together—being virtuous requires practical knowledge. But in fact his unpacking of the notion of *prohairesis,* which now follows, emphasizes not knowledge but virtue or excellence of character (*aretē*).

It is virtue, he states baldly, that causes the purpose to be right; and although he concedes that seeing what has to be done in order to achieve this purpose requires a cognitive power (the 'cleverness' [*deinotēs*] which we have already met),[8] still he is immediately at pains to point out that the cognition required here must itself be infused by moral virtue. He explicitly repudiates any merely calculative efficiency with respect to means, any ability that could serve indifferently all ends whether good or bad and to which goodness, then, would accrue only incidentally. The cleverness required here is, in Aristotle's words, "an eye of the soul" which is fixed on the good; and what makes it so fixed—thereby transforming it into *phronēsis*—is ethical goodness. And so, while we tend to speak of virtue *and* phronesis, strictly speaking, as we see on closer examination, in phronesis virtue is already present. For the good—which it is the function of phronesis to discern—"is not evident except to the good man."[9]

We have in the notion of phronesis, then, ethical knowledge in a very full sense: not just knowledge that directs ethical action, but knowledge that must itself be constantly protected and maintained by good character. Aristotle had in fact made this perfectly clear in a parenthesis in an earlier chapter of *E.N.* 6 when he introduced the virtue of *sōphrosunē* (temperance) and postulated an etymological link between it and phronesis: "We give temperance its name of *sōphrosunē*, that is 'preserver of' (*sōizousa*) phronesis."[10] It was precisely this link with *sōphrosunē* that identified phronesis as moral knowledge and distinguished it from other kinds of knowledge (such as "the belief that the triangle has or has not its angles equal to two right angles")[11] that are not subject to the perversions of pleasure and pain and so do not need the protection of *sōphrosunē*. In the case of "opinions concerning what is to be done," the intemperate man "fails to see any such principle (*archē*) — to see that for the sake of this or because of this he ought to choose and do whatever he chooses and does; for vice is destructive of the principle."[12]

To return now to Aristotle's argument in favor of knowledge as a necessary condition of virtue: we have seen that this argument was interrupted just when it seemed about to be clinched. No sooner has he carved out a place for knowledge than he immediately relativizes it and with an unexpected twist goes on, not to consolidate the place of knowledge, but rather to show that the really important factor is the virtue that must suffuse this knowledge. And so the chapter (chapter 12) which opened, it had seemed, with the primary intention of demonstrating that knowledge, in the form of phronesis, is necessary to virtue concludes its argument by stating just the converse of this: "Plainly therefore, it is impossible that a man who is not good should be phronetic."

But, in fact, this completes only one phase of Aristotle's argument. He goes on immediately to introduce that last chapter of *E.N.* 6 by saying that "we must inquire further concerning excellence." And now he proceeds to carry out an analysis on virtue that is almost identical with the one he has just carried out on knowledge. Parallel to the previous critique of *deinotēs*, of natural, but morally indifferent cleverness, we now have a critique of natural virtue (*phusikē aretē*) which shows that the latter falls short of true virtue (*kuria aretē*) in much the same way that cleverness has already been shown to fall short of phronesis. The two critiques are mirror images of each other: what is lacking in natural cleverness on its own and must be present in order to transform it into phronesis is virtue; what is lacking in natural virtue on its own and must be present in order to transform it into genuine virtue is cleverness. This latter lack in mere natural virtue is pointed out by way of analogy: "as a strong body which moves without sight may stumble badly because of its lack of sight,"[13] so also it happens in this case, i.e., in the case of the man well equipped by nature with virtuous inclinations but "devoid of *nous*."

There is, then, a remarkable circularity in Aristotle's analysis of the relationship between virtue and knowledge. If one starts from the side of knowledge, one analyzes the need for virtue. If one starts from the side of virtue, one analyzes the need for knowledge. Aristotle does both, and the culmination of book 6 is reached with this statement: "It is clear, then, from what has been said, that it is not possible to be good in the strict sense without phronesis nor phronetic without moral excellence."[14]

2. The Key to Understanding the Circle Is 'Experience'

What are we to make of this circle? How does it make intelligible the relationship between virtue and phronesis as knowledge? In our reading of Gadamer we have already seen the 'hermeneutical circle' that persists at the heart of all understanding. It was of this circle—which was not to be reduced "to the level of a vicious circle or even of a circle which is merely tolerated"—that Heidegger said: "in it is hidden a positive possibility of the most primordial kind of knowing." If we explore the circle that we have just met in Aristotle's ethical/political thought, we shall, I believe, find (in phronesis) a kind of knowing that is as primordial as— and in fact is very closely related to—what Heidegger has in mind.[15]

It is clear that what leads Aristotle into this circle is, in one sense, a dissatisfaction with nature: he wants to get beyond merely natural cleverness and merely natural virtuous inclinations. But the circle which he describes precisely in order to do this has, as its inner rationale, nature (*phusis*) in another sense. Both of these different senses of 'nature' are, in fact, to be found in the later chapters of book 6. The first sense, which he wants to get away from, is present in his critique of natural virtue; here he means by *phusei*, natural in the sense of *innate*, as is made clear when he speaks of our possessing these virtues "immediately from birth" (*euthus ek genetēs*).[16] But two chapters previously, although he uses the same word, *phusei*, he has in mind another, more complex meaning of 'natural' when he tells us that *nous*, the faculty of apprehending particulars, is a "natural possession" (*phusei . . . echein*). From what immediately follows in this passage it is clear that what he means here by 'natural' is *not* what is innate, but rather *what is acquired by experience:* he speaks of *nous*, which as we shall see is a very important component of phronesis, and qualities which are closely cognate with it, such as sympathetic judgment (*gnōmē*) and understanding (*sunesis*), as belonging 'naturally' to certain ages or stages of our lives. It may seem strange that Aristotle should use the word 'natural' here to characterize what is learned in the course of maturing into a way of life; for, from one point of view (e.g., that of our contemporary debates about 'nature' and 'nurture'), it seems to be the very *opposite* of his first sense of nature as innate endowment or prowess. He uses it, however, because what he seems to have in mind here is a different opposition, i.e., between what is learned in the ordinary course of affairs and what must be learned through a process of instruction. It is in contrast to the stricter demands of an explicitly pedagogic process, then, that what we might call 'experiential' learning can be regarded as 'natural.' This becomes clear when he goes on to say that no one is naturally in possession of *philosophical* wisdom (*sophia*) — for this *does* require a special training or discipline — whereas in the sphere of *practical* wisdom (phronesis), "we ought to attend to the undemonstrated sayings and opinions of experienced and older people or of *phronimoi* not less than to demonstrations; for because experience has given them an eye they see aright."[17]

Now the notions of *nous* and of experience, associated with the second sense of natural, and brought out in the quintessential sentence that I have just quoted, are, I think, the key to understanding the circle of knowledge and virtue in Aristotle. At the point where the *aporia* is reached in his critique of cleverness, Aristotle says: "the state [*hexis*] [i.e., in this case, phronesis] cannot come to belong to this *eye of the mind* [i.e., cleverness] without excellence." And at the corresponding point in the critique of merely natural (innate) virtue, he locates the weakness of the latter in the fact of its being *"without sight."* Now I am suggesting that what explains the circularity of attributing the correctness of vision or insight in transformed cleverness (i.e., phronesis) to virtue and, contrariwise, of attributing the correctness of insight in virtue to phronesis is that both knowledge and virtue are moments in the more comprehensive process of *experience*, which, as the passage cited above tells us, is what really gives *"an eye."* In other words, if we want to find a synthetic unity beyond the negations of the dialectic of knowledge and virtue, then it is to the notion of experience that we should turn. It would of course be absurd to claim that Aristotle formulates these three ideas (of knowledge, virtue, and experience) in terms of thesis, antithesis, and synthesis. I am suggesting, however, that when he points out the incompleteness of both knowledge and virtue, taken on their own, and fills up what is wanting in each by an appeal to the other — without ever posing the question of which of the two is more ultimate (which if it were answered either way would have precluded the possibility of a *reciprocal* completion) — he is supported in this by an implicit notion of experience which is perhaps the real ultimate. We might then say that knowledge and virtue taken on their own as concepts are abstractions that must be negated or successively 'sublated' in order to express the concrete and unitary experience of the virtuous person in action.

Is this an implausibly Hegelian interpretation of Aristotle? And, in any case, is 'experience' not a notoriously obscure concept, a kind of philosophical abyss in which other concepts are more likely to become lost or blurred rather than clarified? In response to the first question, it has to be admitted that Aristotle himself did not take pains to relate explicitly either phronesis or virtue to experience, but he has, I believe, left us the materials that permit us to do so in his name. To find them we must look beyond *E.N.* 6. His most extensive discussion of 'experience' is in the first chapter of the *Metaphysics*. His approach to experience there is in fact much the same as what has been our own approach to phronesis all along: he works out his concept of it through a carefully drawn distinction and contrast between it and techne. Besides this chapter and the parallel text in *Posterior Analytics* 2.19, the best sources are the last chapter of the *E.N.*, where the transition to the *Politics* is being made and where the need for experience is very much stressed in a discussion of the kind of knowledge that can give insight into character, and *E.N.* 1.3, which contains the famous remarks on method that are really remarks on the kind of person who would be a suitable student to sit in on Aristotle's own lectures — an *experienced* person, as it turns out. If we go on to examine these passages we will, I think, discover — in response to the second question above — that 'experience', in Aristotle's account of it, is far from obscure and provides a way of mediating 'phronesis' and 'virtue' that makes the circle described by Aristotle between these two concepts a good deal more intelligible.

3. Interlude: The Nonassimilation of 'Experience' Raises Questions about Techne in *Metaphysics* 1.1

In the only glimpse of 'experience' that we got in *E.N.* 6 we saw a contrast between it and what needed to be taught. Since a characteristic feature of techne is precisely its teachability, it need come as no surprise to us now in turning to the first chapter of the *Metaphysics* to discover that the notion of experience is developed there in a kind of dialectical interplay with the notion of techne:

> [T]echne arises when, from many notions gained by experience, one universal judgment about similar objects is produced. For to have a judgment that when Callias was ill of this disease this did him good, and similarly in the case of Socrates and in many individual cases, is a matter of experience; but to judge that it has done good to all persons of a certain constitution, marked off in one class . . . this is a matter of techne.[18]

Now there is a real ambivalence in Aristotle's attitude to experience, which focuses on particulars, and techne, which rises to the universal. On the one hand, techne is superior:

We suppose *technitai* to be wiser than men of experience (which implies that wisdom depends in all cases rather on knowledge); and this because the former know the cause, but the latter do not. For men of experience know that the thing is so, but do not know why, while the others know the 'why' and the cause.[19]

This superiority of techne over experience was incontestable for Aristotle; universality and explanatory power were the innermost achievements of knowledge, and insofar as techne possessed them, it was a paradigm of even the highest knowledge, *sophia,* to which the philosopher himself aspired. And yet, on the other hand, this superiority does not tell the whole story. For "*technitai* are wiser not in virtue of being able to act, but of having the theory [*logos*] for themselves and knowing the causes [*aitiai*]."[20] There seems to be a resistant element in practice which relativizes the undoubted superiority of techne. And so Aristotle concedes that:

With a view to action experience seems in no respect inferior to techne, and we even see men of experience succeeding more than those who have theory without experience. (The reason is that experience is knowledge of individuals, techne of universals, and actions and productions are all concerned with the individual; for the physician does not cure a *man,* except in an incidental way, but Callias or Socrates or some other called by some such individual name, who happens to be a man. If, then, a man has theory without experience, and knows the universal but does not know the individual included in this, he will often fail to cure; for it is the individual that is to be cured.)[21]

In this passage Aristotle recognizes that what makes knowledge theoretically powerful does not coincide with what makes it practically effective; and whilst recognizing this, he still very deliberately makes theoretical power the defining characteristic of techne. 'Experience' then remains in the background to account for successful practice. Techne arises from experience through some process of induction and generalizing insight; but it can, it seems, become sealed off from the experiential base and remain concentrated on generalizations. On the other hand, an experienced person may be adept at solving problems that are presented by new experience—even though he has not, as it were, formally passed through any universal propositions or major premises at all.[22]

Such is the picture that emerges from the first chapter of the *Metaphysics.* What seems missing from this picture is some conception of how techne *qua* techne can be complemented by experience in order to give a more masterly and reliable way of handling practical (or, more precisely, productive) problems than would be available to experience alone. In other words, while Aristotle describes the movement from experience to techne, he does not offer any satisfactory account of the movement back from techne to experience. And so techne seems to remain aloof from experience, abstracted from it, rather than a higher ordering that has directive power within it.

My overall purpose here is to elucidate Aristotle's notion of experience as a way into a deeper understanding of phronesis and, more particularly, of the reciprocal relationship between phronesis and virtuous character. I shall digress for a moment, however, to address some remarks specifically to Aristotle's concept of techne (i.e., the 'official' concept which in *E.N.* 6.4 is defined as *poiētikē* and in *Metaphysics* 1.1, as we have just seen, is given a strongly theoretical slant). In the previous chapter,[23] this notion served as a foil against which I developed my account of phronesis. Having first separated out what I called the technai of the *kairos*,[24] I accepted techne *poiētikē* straightforwardly as source of the knowledge which guides making and, without interrogating it as such but simply taking my cue from some terse remarks in *E.N.* 6.4, tried to bring out the different kind of knowing that stems from phronesis as the guide of action. My effort in all this was to show how phronesis, unlike techne, can respond to the subtleties of action. Now, however, in the light of what we have just seen, I want to interject a question concerning techne in its own right. Can 'techne', in Aristotle's conception of it, respond even to the subtleties of *making,* or is it, even as maker's knowledge, a lame concept? I shall only indicate very briefly in this section the grounds that seem to me to give substance to this question. Although I shall then be returning to the main line of inquiry in the present chapter, this digression — prompted by a reading of *Metaphysics* 1.1 — will have served to anticipate some of the issues that will launch us into a very much more extensive examination of techne in the next chapter.

The misgiving which I want to introduce about 'techne' concerns its ability to do justice to, for example, the gifted carpenter who, when confronted with crooked walls and warped timber, contrives, nonetheless, to produce an excellent finished job. Such an exercise of skill would seem to call into play something analogous to what *epieikeia* is in the realm of law, i.e., an ability to bend or stretch or go beyond the rules in order to come up with the best solution in each case. We may indeed recall that in the discussion of equity in *E.N.* 5 Aristotle himself pointedly draws on the builder's trade for an analogue of *epieikeia:* "when the thing is indefinite the rule also is indefinite, like the lead rule used in making the Lesbian moulding; the rule adapts itself to the shape of the stone and is not rigid."[25] But no such element as this seems to be incorporated by Aristotle in the *concept* of techne that we have so far become familiar with. To the contrary, this concept remains unrelentingly formal—in a literal sense that is clear in another passage from the *Metaphysics:*

> from techne proceed the things of which the form is in the soul . . . e.g. . . . health is the formula and the knowledge in the soul. The healthy subject, then, is produced as the result of the following train of thought; since *this* is health, if the subject is to be healthy *this* must first be present, e.g. a uniform state of body, and if this is to be present, there must be heat; and the physician goes on thinking thus until he brings the matter to a final step which he himself can take. Then the process from this point onward, i.e. the process towards health, is called a 'making'. Therefore it follows that in a sense health comes from health and house from house, that with matter from that without matter; for the medical techne and the building techne are the form of health and of the house. . . . Of productions and movements one part is called thinking and the other making,—that which proceeds from the starting-point and the form is thinking, and that which proceeds from the final step of the thinking is making. . . . The active principle then and the starting-point for the process of becoming healthy is, if it happens by techne, the form in the soul.[26]

A passage such as this, I believe, tells us too little about this thinking from the form and how it relates to making. The account of techne that it gives seems too rigid. It gives no consideration to what is perhaps the most interesting aspect of production, namely, the devising of a *new* form[27] (which is thinkable in architecture, if not in medicine; the design for a new type of house, for example). And it throws no light on those cases in which we might want to say that the full-fledged form is simply not available at the outset to guide our thinking (as its 'starting point') but only gradually emerges through a process that involves both thinking *and* making. What is strikingly absent from Aristotle's treatment of techne, in other words, is, in the first place, any account of what we might want to call 'creativity' and in the second place, any scope for what we would call 'experiment'—i.e., a making that is indeed guided by thinking but which, perhaps more importantly, is designed to provide materials for further thinking.[28]

While both of these absences are significant, the second one, the absence of any element of experimentation, is perhaps the more telling; for it shows that although techne is put forward by Aristotle as productive knowledge, it nonetheless remains in a profound sense contemplative. It resides in a knowledge and a thinking which are aloof not only from experience but also, it seems, from the very process of making itself. Having described masters of techne (in *Metaphysics* 1.1) as knowing "the 'why' and the cause," Aristotle then goes on to say that they are "more valuable and discerning and wiser than manual workers," who "like inanimate objects, produce effects, as fire burns, without knowing what they are doing."[29] The separation here between the master craftsman (*architektōn*) and the mere manual worker (*cheirotechnēs*) seems to consolidate in practice the more analytic separation between 'thinking' and 'making' that we saw in the previous passage. We do not get any sense of a making that is itself intelligent, endowed with a know-how which is learned and actualized in the very process of making. The intelligibility of making seems to be fully constituted by a thought process which is independent of the process of making. It does not seem to matter, then, whether the manual worker who implements the design of the 'master craftsman' is the master himself or someone else. If it is someone else, it will suffice that he carry out his instructions precisely, if blindly. And if it is the master himself, his 'thinking' will not be susceptible to 'feedback' received in the actual execution of the plan; for this thinking is strictly architectonic or 'ruling' and so remains invulnerable to any modification suggested in the actual process of material construction.[30]

4. The Appeal to Experience in *Nicomachean Ethics* 10.9 and 1.3

I set out (at the end of §2 above) to examine Aristotle's notion of experience, looking to 'experience' as a synthetic notion which might help us to understand the complementary relationship between phronesis and virtuous character. But, in exploring Aristotle's notion of experience, I have been led into a critique of his notion of techne. 'Experience' has been approached only negatively as that which is not assimilated by the notion of techne — so that its nonassimilation weakens the latter as a conception of productive or, in the broad sense, practical knowledge. I have shown that Aristotle himself was aware that experience gives an immediate familiarity with particulars that is necessary for successful practice; it was not this, however, but rather a mastery of general knowledge and a consequent ability to analyze and explain that he enshrined in the concept of techne.

It is a weakness in Aristotle's position here, I have argued, that he does not show how techne and experience can link up fruitfully in order to provide a masterly practice. He is left with a stark separation between a theoretical techne and a mindless manipulation of actual material. Successful performances of craft, or their products, are not, we may judge, explainable in terms of this separation. 'Experience', on the other hand, could have removed this difficulty by providing a medium in which the separation between a theoretic or contemplative techne and a blind dealing with material could be undercut, and the activity of production rendered more inherently intelligible — and intelligent.

Our first look at 'experience' in Aristotle, then, has focused on it as the shadow side, as it were, of techne. We can approach it more directly now, maintaining continuity with what we have just seen and at the same time coming back closer to a consideration of phronesis, if we turn to an issue, raised in the last chapter of the E.N.,[31] which seemed to confront Aristotle with a problem about techne and which, as a consequence, forced him to invoke in very unambiguous terms the need for experience. The issue in question is the nature of politics or statesmanship, which, as skill in the making of good laws (and hence, indirectly, of good people), might have been expected to conform to the paradigm of techne, so that the same would have been true of the statesman as of other craftsmen: "if a man wishes to become master of a techne or science he must go to the universal, and come to know it as well as possible"[32] — and be able, in consequence, to teach the techne to others. But with respect to statesmanship, Aristotle is forced to ask:

> [I]s a difference apparent between statesmanship and the other sciences and technai? In the others the same people are found offering to teach the technai and practising them, e.g. doctors or painters; but while the sophists profess to teach politics, it is practised not by any of them but by the politicians, who would seem to do so by dint of a certain faculty [*dunamis*] and experience [*empeiria*] rather than of thought [*dianoia*]; for they are not found either writing or speaking about such matters (though it were a nobler occupation perhaps than composing speeches for the lawcourts and the assembly), nor again are they found to have made statesmen of their own sons or of any other of their friends. But it was to be expected that they should if they could; for there is nothing better than such a skill that they could have left to their cities, or could choose to have for themselves, or, therefore, for those dearest to them. Still, experience seems to contribute not a little; else they could not have become politicians by familiarity with politics; and so it seems that those who aim at knowing about politics need experience as well.[33]

Should we conclude from this passage that politics is simply unique and so an exception to the general paradigm of techne? Or might we draw the more radical conclusion that politics is, rather, a revealing counterexample to the paradigm, containing a lesson which, if it were generalized, would lead to a critique of the paradigm itself? In other words, might we take the acknowledged falling apart of theory and practice in the field of politics as a *denouement* of the tenuous connection between theory and practice in Aristotle's general account of techne and poiesis?

An adequate answer to this latter question requires a detailed discussion which must be deferred to the next chapter. We can notice here, however, that the final chapter of the *E.N.* provides a more sensitive and 'empirical' treatment of the relationship between thinking and doing (or, more precisely, making) than we have found in his more general remarks about techne. It makes clear that, in the case of politics, Aristotle never allowed its proper *terminus* in *action* to become obscured — even though, as I have tried to argue, in the general case of techne, its issue in the act of production *was* obscured by an excessively contemplative emphasis. What offered itself as knowledge in the field of politics was required to vindicate itself in the context of action. Not only, indeed, was action the *terminus* of knowledge and the *locus* of its vindication; it was also the *source* of political knowledge. And so not only could political knowledge never lose sight of its directionality *toward* action but also — and for the same reason — it had to arise *from* action. The man who had no experience of the action with which politics was concerned was thereby disqualified from claiming any valuable knowledge with respect to it. In other words, knowledge in this area was involved in precisely that *experimental* or 'feedback' relation to practice that we found missing from Aristotle's account of techne.

In the passage quoted, Aristotle tells us that those who practice politics do so "by dint of a certain faculty and experience rather than of thought"; "they are not found writing and speaking *about* such matters," nor do they manage to teach their skill to others. In sum, they do not possess a techne with respect to politics. On the other hand, as he goes on to show immediately after the above passage, those who do profess to possess such a techne can deliver nothing in practice; and the reason for this is simply that their profession is not based on experience: "they say it is possible to select the best laws — as though even the selection did not call for understanding [*sunesis*], and as if a right judgement [*to krinai orthōs*] were not the crucial factor."[34] And as if judgment itself did not depend on experience, for only "people experienced in any department judge rightly the works produced in it." So that while there may indeed be a theoretical study of politics, nevertheless such a study "seems useful to experienced people, [but] to the ignorant it is valueless"; those who approach it "without a practised faculty will not have right judgement . . . though they may perhaps become more intelligent in such matters."[35]

There is a clear rejection here of the pretensions of any theoretical techne and, as a corollary, an equally clear affirmation of the need for judgment — which, as we have already seen, is classified in *E.N.* 6 as a subvirtue of phronesis — and consequently for that experience which is the necessary seedbed of judgment.[36] We can better understand the significance of judgment (phronesis) and experience if we see that the rebuff to a theoretical politics—which provides the context in which they are invoked—follows and is closely connected to another rebuff that Aristotle had just given to a theoretical ethics. The final chapter of the *E.N.*, from which I have been quoting, had begun with a round denial of the adequacy of a theoretical approach in ethics:

> where there are things to be done the end is not to survey and recognize the various things, but rather to do them. . . . Now if arguments were in themselves enough to make men good, they would justly . . . have won very great rewards . . . but as things are, while they seem to have power to encourage and stimulate the generous-minded among the young, and to make a character which is gently born, and a true lover of what is noble, ready to be possessed by excellence, they are not able to encourage the many to nobility and goodness. For these . . . have not even a conception of what is noble and truly pleasant, since they have never tasted it. What argument would remould such people? It is hard, if not impossible, to remove by argument the traits that have long since been incorporated in the character. . . . argument and teaching, we may suspect, are not powerful with all men, but the soul of the student must first have been cultivated by means of habits for noble joy and noble hatred, like earth which is to nourish the seed. For he who lives as passion directs will not hear argument that dissuades him, nor understand it if he does. . . . The character, then, must somehow be there already with a kinship to excellence, loving what is noble and hating what is base.[37]

Now, the very existence of politics is in one sense a direct consequence of the failure of reason, which Aristotle here describes with an impassioned beauty reminiscent of Plato. Were reason on its own able to carry the day with regard to men's actions, there would be no need for politics—in this sense, that rational discourse and an entirely noncoercive education would do directly what politics can attempt only indirectly. But as things are, we need politics to devise a way of dealing (through law and sanctions) with that element which has the power to unseat reason in the conduct of our lives, i.e., *character*. One might perhaps have hoped that in politics (as a second attempt to install goodness in men's living—a pure rationalism in ethics, let us say, having been tried and found wanting), reason would have been able to cut its losses, as it were, and here at least to reinstate itself as ruler. But even here, as we have already seen, reason had to yield priority to experience and judgment.

I said above that we could "better understand" the significance of experience and judgment if we took these two critiques of theoretical reason together. This is because both critiques reveal a close structural connection between experience and judgment, on the one hand, and character,

on the other. Theoretical reason, as a ruler of action, first founders on
the rock of character; then when politics tries to negotiate this rock, it
in turn must relinquish any hope of relying on reason alone and be guided
rather by experience. These two failures of reason can be related if we say
that it is through experience that character is formed, reveals itself, and
can be learned about. When it *is* learned about—when, in other words,
it is not just an opaque presence in experience but becomes aware of itself—
then experience is not merely experience but contains judgment or phronesis as well. It is such judgment or phronesis—rooted in experience—and
not theoretical reason that the statesman needs in order to formulate and
enact the kind of laws and regulations that have the best chance of fos-
tering virtuous character, and its fruit, i.e., virtuous living. And this is
because it is through them (experience and judgment) and not through
theoretical reason that we gain an apprehension of character in the first
place. "They have not even a conception of what is noble and truly pleasant *because they have never tasted it* [*ageustoi ontes*]" (emphasis mine).
Without the taste, i.e., the experience, of virtue, theoretical discourses about
it are a noisy gong, a clashing cymbal.

The relationship between experience, judgment and character, which
I have just analyzed in the final chapter of the *E.N.* is stated also, in more
compact form, in the remarks on method in *E.N.* 1.3. There, too, having
described politics as the 'master techne', Aristotle nonetheless goes on immediately to warn us that "we must be content . . . to indicate the truth
roughly and in outline . . . speaking about things that are only for the
most part true." And this disavowal of theoretical pretensions is again linked
to judgment and experience: "A man who has been educated in a subject
is a good judge of that subject," but one can be properly educated in politics only if one is experienced: "a young man is not a proper hearer of
lectures on political science; for he is inexperienced in the actions that
occur in life, but its discussions start from these and are about these." And
it is not just that being inexperienced he will not really understand such
discussions (which indeed he will not) but rather that the whole point
of such discussions, anyhow, is not just knowledge but action: "his study
will be vain and unprofitable, because the end aimed at is not knowledge
[*gnōsis*] but action [*praxis*]." And so the lack of experience that is in question here is really a lack of character: "It makes no difference whether he
is young in years or youthful in character [*ēthos*]; the defect does not depend on time, but on his living and pursuing each successive object as
passion directs. For to such persons . . . knowledge brings no profit."[38] The
relationship between experience, judgment, and character that is postulated here, as a necessary replacement for pure theory, is the same as that
which we have already seen in *E.N.* 10.9.

5. Phronesis and Character as Modalities of Experience

We have now come back to the circle between phronesis and character. But given the route through which we have returned to it, we should
be in a position to understand better the sense in which experience may
be said to be its *ratio*. We are accustomed to looking at phronesis as
knowledge that will *guide* action; but the circle resides in the fact that
phronesis also *arises from* good action (as something to which we are already habituated). We cannot have the knowledge to help us to *become*
good unless we already *are* good. All Aristotle's strictures on theoretical
knowledge in ethics and politics really come back to this. To interpret *E.N.*
1.3, therefore, as simply a programmatic confession of 'empiricism' rather
than 'rationalism' in political philosophy misses much of the point. For
Aristotle is not simply making an epistemological point about the standards of rigor to be expected of political knowledge — that they are different, for example, from those governing mathematical knowledge. More
substantially, he is making the point that the standard of knowledge here
is *action,* and that this standard is *internal* to it even *qua* knowledge. The
real defect of 'theory' is that it "brings no profit" with respect to the formation of character. And the reason for this defect is that character has
played no part in the formation of theory. If we want to form our characters, in fact, there is nothing for it but to act: "It is by doing just acts
that the just man is produced, and by doing temperate acts, the temperate
man; without doing these, no one would have even a prospect of becoming good." And Aristotle goes on immediately after this sentence in *E.N.*
2 to deliver perhaps his most stinging rebuke to theory: "But most people
do not do these, but take refuge in theory [*logos*] and think that they
are being philosophers and will become good in this way, behaving somewhat like patients who listen attentively to their doctors, but do none
of the things they are ordered to do. As the latter will not be made well
in body by such a course of treatment, the former will not be made well
in soul by such a course of philosophy."[39]
    But if to have real ethical knowledge (which is not 'theory' but
phronesis) one must already *be* good — and if, moreover, one becomes good
just by doing — does this not mean that such knowledge is redundant, at
best an adornment of a state that is in itself already complete? Has one
not given priority to character (being/action) over knowledge and so abandoned the circle? No, for it is not the case that one is first of good character, and *then* can have phronesis. Rather, being phronetic is itself part
of what it means to be of good character.
    To see how this is so we must first remember that character is not
the natural[40] inclination which to some degree prompts all people to good

acts and which is remarkable in some as an effortless attunement to the good.[41] Such an innate quality (which is really *preter*natural in that it is more a gift of the gods than a property of the persons themselves)[42] may well be the motivating source of good acts, but virtuous character in the full sense (*kuria aretē*) is the disposition that grows out of and naturally[43] results from the repeated performance of good acts—and then becomes itself a motivating source of good acts. Second, we must remember that while we speak of 'good acts' preceding and leading to the formation of character, still, goodness in the strict sense is to be ascribed not to them but rather to acts that are mediated through an already established character. Just because "the acts that are in accordance with the excellences have themselves a certain character it does not follow that they are done justly or temperately"; to be properly good, they must be done "*as* just and temperate men do them,"[44] i.e., as the expression of "a firm and unchangeable character."[45] Now it is precisely at the transition from what we might call 'naive' actions (whether they be prompted simply by a person's innate nature or by a desire to conform with the law, under the 'educative' influence of political institutions) to actions that spring from and are an expression of character, that phronesis arises. If one has reached the stage of a stable virtuous character, then one will be found to already possess phronesis as well.

But we still have to explain how or in what sense this is the case. To do so it will be helpful if we now reintroduce the notion of experience and determine more precisely the relationship which, as we have already seen, obtains between it and 'character'. We might look at things this way: when one performs good acts (whatever be their source) one undergoes these acts or experiences them. Now repeated experiences of them gives *experience* in Aristotle's rather technical sense. In other words, through the repetition of single actions, which can be retained in memory, we gradually acquire that experience which Aristotle describes as "the power of systematizing them" or "the whole universal that has come to rest in the soul (the one beside the many, whatever is one and the same in all those things)."[46]

I am suggesting that the model of induction that Aristotle gives in *Posterior Analytics* 2.19 might be taken as a model of moral development. We need only suppose that the individual impressions that supply the initial data are, in this case, one's perceptions (and indeed actions) in ethically salient situations; then the stabilization within the soul that constitutes 'experience' in the general process of induction, constitutes 'character' in the particular process of moral development. And when Aristotle goes on to give his famous image—"It is like a rout in battle stopped by first one man making a stand and then another, until the original formation has been restored; the soul is so constituted as to be capable of this process"[47] — this seems to be at least as apt a picturing of moral development as it is of the formation of conceptual knowledge.[48]

This move — of interpreting 'character' as 'experience'— is not made by Aristotle himself.[49] But it seems to me that it is simply a formalization of the relationship that we have already seen to exist between experience and character in certain key passages at the beginning and end of the *E.N.* — and of course in book 6. The advantage of making this move is that it immediately solves our problem of how knowledge can be identified as a constitutive element of character. For if we understand character as experience in the way I have suggested then knowledge is already written into it; in its inner structure it is cognitional. It does not develop through a spontaneous process of growth such as occurs in the living things of nature. The dynamism whereby it comes into being is, rather, the dynamism of knowledge itself. And the stability or consistency that it achieves is the same stability or consistency that a higher level of universalization introduces into the flow of our perceptions. This is a natural (in the second sense of "natural") acquirement only in the irreducible sense that "the [human] soul is so constituted as to be capable of this process."

So far we have shown that the dynamics and structure of ethical being replicate those of knowledge and that in this context character (*aretē ēthikē*) may be understood as experience (*empeiria*). But our original problem was to explain the relationship of phronesis to character, and this remains to be done. In the light of what we have just seen, we should be able to do so if we can show the relationship of phronesis to *experience*.

Aristotle himself nowhere attempts a systematic account of the relationship between phronesis and experience. But we shall not be out of step with his scattered remarks about them both if we look at things this way: 'experience' signifies an achieved state that is the fruit of universalizing and consolidating the meaning of many previous discrete impressions; this primary significance is most perspicuously present in our use of the phrase "an experienced person." Now when a person is experienced we might say that the virtue through which he or she exploits that experience or puts what has been learned from it to work — and in the process learns more and so further develops and refines his or her experience — is phronesis. Phronesis is what enables experience to be self-correcting and to avoid settling into mere routine. If experience is an accumulated capital, we might say, then phronesis is this capital wisely invested.

Looked at in this way, phronesis is simply a continuation of the dynamism whereby, as we have already seen, experience arises out of memory and memory out of individual perceptions (or, in the ethical context of experience as character, of individual acts). We have already seen that in

An. Post. 2.19 Aristotle identifies "the techne of the craftsman and the theoretical knowledge of the scientist" as the two modes of knowledge (techne in the sphere of coming to be, and science in the sphere of being) that arise from experience and are the culmination of the whole inductive process. It will be remembered that (although I did not criticize *epistēmē* as theoretical knowledge) I suggested that the place of techne in this scheme undermined its status as *productive knowledge.* The reason I gave for this view was that Aristotle allowed techne to become anchored in universals in such a way that it could apparently become disconnected from the experience from which it had originated. The standpoint of a master of techne was that of a third-person analyst who stood outside the experience from which he was generalizing; indeed it was in no way essential to the integrity of his techne that this experience should be his own rather than someone else's.[50] This rupture between techne and experience had damaging consequences, I suggested, for Aristotle's conception of poiesis, given that techne was the central element in the latter conception. Or perhaps what we might more justifiably say is that Aristotle did not make a sufficiently clear distinction between techne as the systematic analysis of production and techne as the productive knowledge that actually informs the agent in the act of producing.[51]

Now to say that phronesis may be understood as the dynamic element of experience is to assign to it a place in the inductive sequence that corresponds to the place that Aristotle actually assigns to techne (in *An. Post.* 2.19). But in the case of phronesis, we may notice, the difficulties I have alleged in respect of techne do not arise. For phronesis does not ascend to a level of abstraction or generality that leaves experience behind. It arises from experience and *returns into experience.* It is, we might say, the insightfulness—or, using Aristotle's own metaphor, "the eye"—of a particular type of experience, and the insights it achieves are turned back into experience, which is in this way constantly reconstructed or enriched. And the more experience is reconstructed in this way, the more sensitive and insightful phronesis becomes—or, rather, the more the experiencer becomes a *phronimos.*

This close two-way relationship between phronesis and experience, this poise that phronesis is able to maintain within experience, is grounded in a concreteness or concern with particulars that characterizes them both.[52] Experience is concrete in that, while it stabilizes the succession of individual and particular impressions and does this through a process of universalization, still, the universals that it reaches continue to include a *reference to the particulars,* which are thus preserved in experience and remain retrievable in the light of the nonsuppressive universal. This, at any rate, is how I understand Aristotle's words when he describes experience as "the whole universal that has come to rest in the soul (the one beside the many, whatever is one and the same in all those things)." Now phronesis, too, is concrete; it must also take cognizance of particulars, because "it is concerned with action, and action is concerned with particulars."

Immediately after this sentence Aristotle goes on to reveal the very close connection between the concreteness of phronesis and that of experience and, in the same breath, to put his finger on the weakness of theoretical knowledge, and of techne too insofar as it is overcommitted to theory:

> This is why some who do not know, and especially those who have experience, are more practical than others who know; for if a man knew that light meats are digestible and wholesome, but did not know which sorts of meat are light, he would not produce health, but the man who knows that chicken is wholesome is more likely to produce health. Now phronesis is concerned with action; therefore one needs both kinds of knowledge, but particularly the latter.[53]

We might spell out the import of this example as follows: In the first place, the reason for the theoretician's ineffectiveness is that he does not possess the premise ('chicken is a light food') which would connect his generalization ('all light foods are wholesome') with the conclusion ('chicken is wholesome') that is necessary for action. In the second place, the man of ordinary experience, on the other hand, without knowing the premise that all light foods are wholesome nevertheless knows that chicken is wholesome (although he does not, of course, know it *qua* conclusion; in the words of *Meta.* 1.1 he does not know the 'why'—which is stated in the combination of the two premises—but only the 'fact that') and so has knowledge that is "more practical." But there is also a third possibility: the fact that the 'theoretician' does not possess the 'minor' premise tells us something about the way in which he does possess the major premise: he possesses it without reference to more specific descriptions (or, again in the words of *Meta.* 1.1, "he has the theory without the experience and recognizes the universal but does not know the individual included in this").[54] But he might have possessed it *'experientially'*, in which case he would have retained the particular, 'chicken', in his universal, 'light food'—and his universal would then have been "the one beside the many" and not (as it is) the one separated from the many. Now this third possibility might be called 'phronetic experience' and distinguished both from 'theory' and from what I have called 'ordinary experience.' It is to be distinguished from 'ordinary experience' in that, while it retains familiarity with particulars, it still contains a greater pressure toward universalization, toward a kind of knowledge that can handle light foods as well as chicken—and can handle the latter in the light of the former:[55] phronesis "needs *both* kinds of knowledge." But when Aristotle adds "but particularly the latter," we are perhaps justified in thinking that it is even more important to distinguish 'phronetic experience' from 'theory'. It may lag behind theory in the degree of formal universality possessed by its major premises, but it has the advantage over theory that it can redeem *all* the minor premises implicitly contained in each of its major premises and thus maximize its contribution to action.[56]

6. *Nous,* or Perceptiveness with Regard to 'Ultimate Particulars,' as a Crucial Element in Phronesis

What I have been saying confirms the closeness of the relationship between phronesis and experience; I have gone so far as to suggest that phronesis is a particular type of experience — experience that is inwardly impelled toward greater and more 'fruitful' universalization. In thus regarding phronesis as the dynamic element through which experience is deepened, we should not overlook the particular acts through which this deepening is accomplished. These are acts of insight into *particulars,* and we need to focus on them at the point of their emergence, at the moment of their novelty, prior to their assimilation into the habitual pattern of experience.

In doing this, however, we are not helped by the example of Aristotle's that I have just analyzed. For characteristically an act of phronetic insight involves knowledge that is more concrete and more proximately related to action than either of the propositions mentioned in the example. For even the proposition 'chicken is wholesome' — which Aristotle exempts from the charge of arid generality — is itself a universal proposition and so cannot bring us all the way to action, which "has its sphere in particulars." In fact, while I have discussed it as a conclusion in Aristotle's example, in a really practical syllogism it would itself be a major premise, and we would need to supply a new minor, 'this is a chicken'[57] (leading to the conclusion 'this is wholesome'). But even this is not a really practical syllogism. For the property of being 'wholesome' which 'this' possesses still needs to be connected with the property 'to be eaten', and this latter property needs to be further specified as 'to be eaten *by me now*'. And even if we say that there is an analytic connection between 'wholesome' and 'to be eaten' — i.e., that 'wholesome' *means* 'to be eaten' — still we will need some other premises to get in the reference to me now. And apart from other major premises (such as, e.g., 'All humans should eat wholesome food only' or 'All humans should eat when they need food') and unproblematic minors (such as 'I am a human') there will need to be at least one minor (such as 'I need food now') that expresses an insight into my particular situation at the moment.

Now premises that express an insight into particulars ('this is a chicken', 'I need food now') may be called ultimate premises;[58] it is they which make practical reasoning *practical*. This point is made very clear in *E.N.* 7, where it is argued that moral weakness (*akrasia*) can occur only in someone whose grasp of the particular premise (which is described as "the opinion which is active" and as "what determines action") is weakened. It is also very clear in the *De Anima:* "Since the one premiss or judgement is universal and the other deals with the particular (for the first tells us that such and such a kind of man should do such and such a kind of act, and the second that this is an act of the kind meant, and I a person of the type intended), it is the latter opinion that really originates movement, not the universal; or rather it is both, but the one does so while it remains in a state more like rest, while the other partakes in movement."[59] Without these particular premises, we might say, the whole syllogistic apparatus is, in relation to the ethical life, like a mechanical digger that is perched too high to get its teeth into the soil. Nor will any amount of syllogizing produce these premises. They are available — as we saw when I first introduced the notion of experience — only to those of whom it may be said that "because experience has given them an eye they see aright." This eye comes, in fact, through phronesis. A very essential part of the role of phronesis, then, is to supply appropriate and finely discriminated ultimate minor premises. (Its *full* role might be outlined[60] as [a] supplying these premises; [b] mobilizing them within a context whose adequate explication, in the case of our example, would involve, in addition to the major premises I have mentioned, some ultimate major that would link 'wholesome' via 'healthy' to a conception of the good life [*eudaimonia*]; and [c] supplying this major which, when fully elaborated — as perhaps it need never be for single actions, but only for the characteristic orientation revealed in one's life[61] — will be quite a complex proposition, setting out a notion of *eudaimonia* that is "irreducibly plural"[62] in that it embraces several different virtues. This ultimate major is no more derivable from syllogisms than are the ultimate minors. Much of the analysis that has been devoted in the literature to the 'practical syllogism', then — a phrase that occurs in fact only once in Aristotle's works[63] — touches on only one aspect of the work of phronesis, [b] above. It misses much that is essential, for it does not explain how phronesis apprehends nonsyllogistically[64] both the ultimate minor and ultimate major premises which ensure that the knowledge generated by their coming together — which can indeed be presented syllogistically — will be, respectively, both practical and of the good.)

It is the role of phronesis in supplying the ultimate *particular* premise that I especially want to examine. As I have already indicated, the insight into particulars contained in this premise is the *moving* element[65]
of phronesis in that it strikes out beyond the habitual or stabilized knowledge of universals that is formulated in the major premises. (This 'moving' knowledge is of course involved in a close reciprocal relation with the
habitual knowledge; it is an actualization that would be impossible or
at least highly improbable without the latter, and that at the same time
contributes—at least in the case of the person who is still moving toward
moral maturity—to the latter's development and enrichment.) As the source
of insight into particulars—or "eye" that enables one "to see aright"—
phronesis is assimilated by Aristotle to his concept of *nous* (variously
translated as "intuitive reason" [Ross], "intuition" [Thompson], "inductive reason" [Greenwood]). In the first of the two passages in which he
does this, Aristotle *contrasts* phronesis with *nous:*

> It [phronesis] is opposed, then, to *nous;* for *nous* is of the definitions, for
> which no reason can be given, while phronesis is concerned with the ulti-
> mate particular [*eschaton*], which is the object not of knowledge but of
> perception—not the perception of qualities peculiar to one sense but a
> perception akin to that by which we perceive that the *eschaton* is a triangle;
> for in that direction too there will be a limit.[66]

In this passage, Aristotle is pointing out how phronesis might be considered as the opposite of the *nous,* which he had earlier listed with phronesis as one of the five intellectual virtues (the others being *technē, epistēmē*
and *sophia*). The opposition resides in the fact that *nous* is the intuitive,
undemonstrable grasp of first principles which are the source of all scientific knowledge or the limit to which *all* chains of deductive reasoning
must be traced back, whereas phronesis grasps what is entirely particular
or is the limit from which *no* deductions can be made.

But in the second passage Aristotle assumes that the nature of this
very opposition is such as to imply a significant likeness between the two—
for it reveals the *intuitive* character of both of them insofar as they lie
at the limits of argument—and so to warrant the extension of the meaning of '*nous*' to embrace both the apprehension of the primary premises
in the theoretical sphere *and* the apprehension of ultimate particulars in
the sphere of practice. And so:

> *Nous* is concerned with the ultimates in both directions; for both the pri-
> mary definitions and the ultimates are objects of *nous* and not of argu-
> ment, and in demonstrations *nous* grasps the unchangeable and primary
> definitions, while in practical reasonings it grasps the last and contingent

fact, i.e. the second proposition. For these are the starting-points of that for the sake of which, since the universals are reached from the particulars; of these therefore we must have perception and this is *nous*.[67]

Having explained Aristotle's use of *nous* to signify the aspect of phronesis that apprehends ultimate particulars, we must now examine more closely what he says about this apprehension in the above two extracts. We are faced, in fact, with two tantalizingly difficult passages which bristle with awkward problems of interpretation and philosophy.

"[T]he ultimate particular, which is the object not of knowledge but of perception": this is a preliminary, negative way of isolating the ultimate particular — the latter is not to be apprehended within the schemes of necessity and universality that are formulated in scientific knowledge. But what does this tell us? Does it imply that the ultimate particular is the individual substance, the numerically distinct existing thing, the 'this' in the premise 'this is a chicken' that we have already met? An attempt might be made to answer this question in the negative by showing that this premise *can* be scientifically generated. 'Chicken', after all, is a natural species, and are not the properties of species — in a nonevolutionary perspective such as Aristotle's — invariable, and so the object of *epistēmē?* And does this *epistēmē* not provide — through the reading off of carefully prepared checklists of properties — a technique for identifying deductively the species to which individuals belong? And does this not mean that the individual thing, the 'this', *is,* at least in some sense, the object of scientific knowledge — and so, according to our text, *not* the *eschaton* or ultimate particular?

We can begin to answer these questions by looking more closely at what is involved in an act of identification that is performed through reading off a scientifically validated checklist of properties. Such an act of identification, it turns out, is impossible without acts of perception that are not themselves scientific. The general knowledge enshrined in the checklist does indeed provide a technique of identification, but this technique can be *applied* only by those who are capable of *perceiving* in a certain way *what is before them.* And while the availability of a technique seems to exclude haphazardness or the element of hit-or-miss in the making of identifications and to give a kind of infallibility to them, in fact this infallibility is not greater than that of the acts of perception that are inevitably involved. And one of the points that Aristotle seems to be making (by his use of *nous* and *eschaton*) is that there is nothing outside these perceptions themselves from which they can be derived or that can be referred to as a norm of their correctness.

The technique at issue here is essentially a form of deduction, and the above point can be restated as follows: one can indeed contrive to make the judgment 'this is a chicken' the conclusion of a syllogism, or the consequent of an implication. In this case, the checklist will be the composite middle term contained in both premises, or stated in the antecedent and in the implication which links antecedent and consequent, thus:

If this has the properties A, B, C, D, etc., then this is a chicken,
This has the properties A, B, C, D, etc.
Therefore this is a chicken.

But the point I believe Aristotle is making is that the antecedent (or particular premise) here cannot itself be syllogistically derived; or if it can, then at some point along the line a syllogism is reached whose minor premise is *not* syllogistically derived. As Aristotle says: "One must come to a stop somewhere. The stopping-point is an act of perception (*aisthēsis*) performed by *nous*."[68]

We have just seen that the recognition of 'this' as a chicken — even when it is mediated through a framework of scientific knowledge — cannot be made without crucial acts of perception. But is this enough to assure us that this recognition is of the *eschaton?* If the crucial perceptions, being several, are of, for example, two-footedness, featheredness, etc., and if the aggregation of these into 'chicken' is not itself an act of perception, must we not then say that the *eschaton* is not the chicken but, if anything in this example, the individual properties? For a proposition that truly expresses an apprehension of the *eschaton* must we not go to one that cannot be syllogistically derived, where the stopping-point is really reached because there are not other apprehensions that can be set up as sufficient evidence for it?

But perhaps we need to examine more closely the relationship between apprehension and its articulation in propositional or syllogistic form. There is no reason to suppose that the structure of our apprehensions must correspond to the structure of their articulation. It may be that we apprehend something as, for example, a chicken in one unitary act of recognition, which is only subsequently decomposed into the elements that are set out separately in the minor premise. And perhaps it is the case that such immediate recognitions can sometimes be reconstructed analytically so as to yield appropriate syllogisms (as in the chicken example) and that sometimes they *cannot.* In either case it seems clear that the immediacy of an apprehension, whether or not it can be subsequently mediated, is what gives it access to the *eschaton.* The *eschaton,* then, picks out less a sphere of objects than a mode of knowing; it is what corresponds to *nous* and its characteristic *aisthēsis.* Our questions then must be directed to this *aisthēsis,* about which little has become clear so far, apart from its being an immediate recognition.

7. Suggested Examples of 'Ultimate Particulars' Elucidated by Reference to *De Anima* and Wittgenstein

Aristotle tells us—in the first of our two passages on *nous*—that it is "not the perception of qualities peculiar to one sense but a perception akin to that by which we perceive that the *eschaton* is a triangle." What does he mean by the geometrical comparison? On one interpretation, it might be taken to mean not the act of recognizing the particular figure before me for what it is—in this case a triangle, in other cases, a parallelogram, a circle or whatever. Rather, intrinsic significance might be given to the choice of *triangle,* which might be seen to exemplify the *eschaton* or ultimate particular precisely because it is the *simplest* regular figure into which more complicated rectilinear figures can be analyzed or is a limit in the descending series of polylateral figures.

Although this is a received interpretation of this example,[69] it seems to me that its restrictive focus misses Aristotle's point. What he is drawing attention to, I believe, is the *immediacy* with which we apprehend a figure to be a triangle, and the contrast that exists therefore between the latter and a more polylateral figure such as an octagon, in the case of which we might need to go through the operation of counting the sides before being able to recognize it as the specific figure it is. To understand this point, though, in strict terms of the limit of a series seems to me to go too close to the mathematical nature of the example to allow for appropriate generalization to the field of phronesis. (And we should not forget that earlier in this same chapter Aristotle had drawn attention to the dissimilarity between expertise in geometry or mathematics and phronesis.)[70] The significant point that Aristotle is surely making is that the immediate apprehension of a figure as a triangle is of such a status that one must presuppose its occurrence in a person before one can get off the ground, as it were, in teaching him any of the theorems in which the various properties and relations of the triangle are demonstrated. And, furthermore, if he cannot recognize the figure before him as a triangle it is not at all clear how one could ever teach him *this.* Similarly, then, in the field of phronesis one can get nowhere with talk of general moral principles or rules with someone who lacks *nous;* such general moral talk is lost on someone who does not have the 'eye' to perceive certain features of the situation in which action is called for.

But now what can we say more specifically about this immediate perception in the field of phronesis? Anthony Kenny points out that "Aristotle nowhere gives an example . . . of what is perceived by this phronesis-nous." Kenny himself goes on to suggest that: "Presumably instances of the kind of thing he has in mind would be the perception that

A needs cheering up, that B is being offensive, and one is hurting C's feelings; an awareness one might say of the morally relevant features of one's action and the situation in which one is acting."[71] These examples are good ones and can, I think, be supported if we go back to what Aristotle says in the passage which we are analyzing. "Not the perception of qualities peculiar to one sense. . . ." What is being driven at here is made clear in the discussion of perception in the *De Anima*: "I call by the name of special object of this or that sense that which cannot be perceived by any other sense than that one and in respect of which no error is possible." To these 'proper sensibles' he then contrasts "common sensibles [which] are movement, rest, number, figure, magnitude; these are not peculiar to any one sense, but are common to all. There are at any rate certain kinds of movement which are perceptible both by touch and by sight."[72]

The inclusion of "figure" in this list of "common sensibles" throws light on the triangle example which I have just analyzed; Aristotle may mean to suggest that a triangle can be perceived by touch as well as by vision and that the triangularity, therefore, which is immediately apprehended is not what is either seen or touched. But if we can rightly suppose that Aristotle's list in the *De Anima*—confined as it is to physical or mathematical qualities—does not exhaust the potential range of the concept which he has defined, then there is no reason why we should not extend it so as to make it inclusive of Kenny's examples. Such an extension is, in fact, suggested by some remarks of Wittgenstein's:

> Think of this too: I can only see, not hear, red and green,—but sadness I can hear as much as I can see it.
>
> Think of the expression "I hear a plaintive melody." And now the question is: "Does he *hear* the plaint?"
>
> And if I reply: "No, he doesn't hear it, he merely has a sense of it" —where does that get us? One cannot mention a sense-organ for this 'sense'. . . .
>
> One might say of someone that he was blind to the *expression* of a face. Would his eyesight on that account be defective?[73]

Can we not say that predicates such as 'sad' and 'plaintive' (Wittgenstein) or 'offended' and 'hurt' (Kenny), even though they are not explicitly considered by Aristotle as 'common sensibles', nonetheless do fall under this latter concept? This opens up a whole field of what (following Kenny) we might call 'morally relevant' qualities, to be apprehended not by "the perception of qualities peculiar to one sense," but rather by the perception of *phronesis-nous*. 'Perception' is a good word to use here for *aisthēsis* only if we detach it from the narrow epistemological context in which it signifies a lower level of cognitional operation and understand it, rather, in the sense in which we speak of someone as being 'perceptive'.[74] 'Insight', which I used several times earlier, is perhaps a better word.[75] I suggest that the potential richness of Aristotle's highly condensed remarks about *phronesis-nous* can be appreciated if we envisage a range of examples such as the following:

"I am taking out my frustrations with the boss on the children."

"I am making distractions for myself in order to avoid making this decision."

"Mary is embarrassed because alcoholism has been mentioned."

"An inordinate fear of failure is preventing John from revealing his full potential in class."

"James is causing trouble in class because he's bored with work that's too undemanding for him."

What is perceived in these examples or, better, what one has insight into, is something that might not be at all apparent to others who, at least in the case of the last three examples, are also present in the situation but do not, as Aristotle says, have an 'eye' for it (or a 'nose' for it, to use Wittgenstein's phrase in a discussion at the end of the *Investigations* which seems to me to bear a remarkable similarity to Aristotle's passages on *nous*).[76] And, of course, the person who has the insight may himself or herself come to it only by displacing a previously secure and apparently adequate perception of the situation; there may be a quality of revelation or of 'dawning' about his or her recognition of what is really going on.

It will be noticed that there is an explanatory element in most of the examples which I have given; e.g, troublemaking is related to boredom which is related to lack of challenge. Someone might argue that because of this complexity, because there is in fact a knowledge of *causes* involved, these are not examples of the *eschaton* which is apprehended by *nous*. It seems to me, however, that it is a mistake to lay down a kind of atomic simplicity as a uniform criterion of the *eschaton*. The usual interpretation of Aristotle's triangle example, of course—which sees the triangle as the last, unanalyzable rectilinear figure—suggests this mistake; it sets us to look for some kind of primitive facts that would have the same status in the practical-moral field that the triangle has in the geometry of plane figures. But I have already argued against this interpretation in the context of my view that we should be looking to a mode of knowledge which is immediate and 'intuitive' rather than to a range of objects which are analytically simple. As I have already suggested, I see no reason why objects of our intuitions ('perceptions', 'insights') must be simple; even such an apparently uncomplicated perception as 'this is a chicken' can, as I have shown, be resolved into a syllogism whose composite middle term shows that the object in question, a chicken, is by no means simple.

A justification of my list of examples must, however, take the analysis a little further. For the complexity of the chicken involves only the aggregation of properties needed for a *description*. My examples, on the other hand, involve the apprehension of relationships that are, at least in some degree, *explanatory*. To understand why it may be legitimate to take these as examples of the *eschaton*, we must focus on the whole role of phronesis and not just on its specialized function as *nous*. In this wider context, we will see that 'this is a chicken' (apart from its seeming perhaps embarrassingly trite) is in fact a special, unrepresentative example of what may be apprehended by *phronesis-nous*. For once 'this' is established as a chicken, then a chain of universal or 'scientific' knowledge can be mobilized which will supply intermediate premises—(a) and (b) below—that will link 'this' with the ultimate major premise that indicates the constituents of the good life:

(a) All chickens are light food;

(b) All light foods are wholesome or health-producing, and

(c) Health is a component of *eudaimonia* and so is to be cultivated by me as a human being.

Now in the normal case of phronesis premises of the type contained in (a) and (b) are not so easily available to one. There is no scientific knowledge, already mapped-out, to mediate between one's particular apprehensions and the doing of the good in the way that a general knowledge of dietetics mediates between the identification of a particular food and the cultivation of health. In other words, insofar as health is the object of a scientific techne,[77] i.e., medicine and its subsidiary disciplines such as dietetics, it is a special case of *eudaimonia;* in the *general* case, the pursuit of the good cannot be calculated for one by the mediation of any science: and this precisely is the *raison d'être* of phronesis as an irreducible mode of knowledge in its own right.

Because of the absence of systematic knowledge that would supply intermediate *explanatory* premises in the general realm of practice, if one's practical knowledge is to be rich and finely differentiated it must compensate for this absence by getting as thorough a grasp of the concrete particular as it can; and this grasp falls to the intuitive capacity of *phronesis-nous*. If these insights of *phronesis-nous* do not contain an explanatory power in themselves, then there will be no systematically established explanatory knowledge that they can be plugged into, as it were, in order to boost their contribution to practice. To illustrate this point: if I identify James only as a troublemaker, this will not be at all adequate to specify the most helpful response on my part. Even if I understand his troublemaking in terms of boredom, this still does not inform me sufficiently. But if I see both the troublemaking and the boredom in the light of insufficiently demanding work-chores, then I am in a position to consider what I may best do in response. And the essential point is that *not all* troublemaking children are bored, nor is *all* boredom perhaps a response to present work demands. If I am to grasp this constellation of trouble-making/ boredom/ lack of challenge, I must grasp it here and now in the particular case of James. It is for this reason that I consider it a case of the *eschaton*. Explanatory knowledge may be involved in the sense that 'because' is used in its formulation, but it is not *general* explanatory knowledge; the object of the 'because' is inscribed in the particular situation and can be perceived only concretely.[78]

A final point to be noticed about these non-simple particulars which, in my interpretation, embody the *eschaton*, is that they do not necessarily present themselves as particulars prior to the occurrence of insight. Taking Aristotle's example of the triangle again, if we think of this in terms of a figure which stands out unproblematically from its background and which I immediately recognize as a triangle, then again we are not helped to understand the characteristic case of *phronesis-nous*. The latter is better understood if we think rather of a highly complex configuration with lines intersecting in many directions, and perhaps with different colors providing elements of distraction or camouflage, in which—perhaps only after inspecting it for some time—I recognize a triangle that was, we might say, latent in it and that only now stands out to my perception. This is a better analogue of *phronesis-nous* insofar as the latter is usually not about objects, but about actions, motivations, gestures, expressions, events, or situations that are involved in a flux; and it may be that only with the phronetic insight itself is a particular pattern made to stand out in a way that escaped notice before the occurrence of the insight.[79] This may be illustrated by the example in which I came to recognize that what I am doing is making distractions for myself in order to avoid making a decision. Here my behavior is understood in a new way that shows me that particular actions that I may previously have regarded as quite disparate and that I may have had separate descriptions for, in fact have an underlying commonality that constitutes them, from a particular point of view, as the one action of *avoiding a decision*.

8. The Openness of the Phronetic Approach, and How It Differs from Deductivism

I have been focusing on the moments of insight that occur through *nous*. We must now relate this analysis of *nous* more explicitly to our earlier discussion of the circle between knowledge and character and of 'experience' as what helps us to understand this circle. It is a circle which we found running through *E.N.* 6 from the early statement that "part of the intellect that is concerned with action does its work well when it reaches truth in agreement with right desire," to the statement in the last chapter which we regarded as the culmination of the whole book: "It is plain then after what has been said that it is not possible without phronesis to be really virtuous, nor without virtue to be phronetic." The purpose of our discussion was not to try to break this circle by assigning priority to either of the two reciprocal terms but rather to try to understand *its ratio as a circle*. The central unifying concept I looked to in doing this was the notion of *experience*. Our account of Aristotle's notion of experience unfolded in the context of some critical remarks about his notion of techne; the latter appeared as a defective concept of productive knowledge insofar as it does not satisfactorily integrate experience. In the critical cases of statesmanship and ethical inquiry, the incapacity of techne to provide an adequate model appeared simultaneously with the need for experience, judgment and character, three notions which were clustered together in some significant passages from books 1 and 10 of the *E.N.* In analyzing these passages, I showed the close connection which they imply between experience and character, and I went on to suggest how this connection might be more systematically determined by assigning to character the same place that Aristotle assigns to experience in his outline of the inductive process in *An. Post.* 2.19. In order to read this latter text in this way—to see it as containing a model of *ethical* and not simply of cognitional development—we needed only to suppose that the initial impressions which get the whole process under way are not simply sense impressions of the external world but are rather the impressions of one's own *praxeis* or actions.

Having secured the connection between experience and character—having shown that character *is* experience—I then tried to bring out the connection between experience and phronesis. I suggested that phronesis is a perfected form of experience in that it is the virtue which makes the experience of some people (the *phronimoi*) not just the accumulated systematization of their past actions and impressions, but a dynamic orientation to bring this systematization into play and allow it to be tested by present circumstances, to draw from it what is relevant and to see where it does not fit—in the former case consolidating it and in the latter extending or modifying it. I expressed this point through a number of metaphors, looking at phronesis as the growing edge of experience or as experience wisely invested rather than as dead capital. The essential point is that phronesis is a habit of *attentiveness* that makes the resources of one's past experience flexibly available to one and, at the same time, al-

lows the present situation to 'unconceal' its own particular significance—
which it may do comfortably within the terms of one's experience or else
only by evincing as insight which, while it could not occur without one's
past experience, still transcends, and so enriches, it. Now it was in order
to focus on this dynamic aspect of phronesis that I dwelt on the insights
of *nous*. For these are the 'moments' in which experience is quickened,
the moments in which experience becomes more than what it is in Aristotle's schematization of its place in induction and reaches a higher level.
This level is not that of techne or *epistēmē*, however. For these latter include reference to the particular only as abstractly represented in general
rules, formulae, definitions, and demonstrations which can be taught,
whereas the higher level reached when experience becomes phronesis must
be continually renewed in one's insightful dealings with particular situations, and is a *hexis,* a formed disposition, only insofar as one is capable
of such repeated renewals.

If one could have a techne or a science of practice, then, rather than
attentively submitting one's experience to the demands of the situation,
one could consult instead the recipes or rules of the techne; but to think
that one can have such a techne is to succumb to what Gadamer calls the
"illusion of experience perfected and replaced by knowledge."[80] As an internal perfection of experience, phronesis is not a completed state of knowledge that can be made the object of instruction. On the contrary, there
is an openness in the experience of the *phronimos,* and through this openness he or she is continually involved in a learning process. This is a point
which, as we have already seen, is well made by Gadamer:

> experience [*Erfahrung*] itself can never be science [*Wissenschaft*]. It is in
> absolute antithesis to knowledge [*Wissen*] and that kind of instruction that
> follows from general theoretical or technical knowledge. The truth of ex-
> perience always contains an orientation towards new experience. That is why
> a person who is called 'experienced' has not only become such through ex-
> periences but is also open to new experiences. . . . the experienced person
> . . . is particularly well-equipped to have new experiences and to learn from
> them. The dialectic of experience has its own fulfilment not in definitive
> knowledge, but in that openness to experience that is encouraged by expe-
> rience itself.[81]

These words are from Gadamer's section on experience and *not* from
his section on Aristotle. Can we nonetheless find evidence for such an emphasis on openness and learning in the latter's conception of phronesis?
Such an emphasis is, first of all, I believe, implicit in the central role that
he gives to *deliberation* in his account of phronesis and especially in his
description of the excellence that characterizes the deliberations of the

phronimos. Deliberative excellence (*euboulia*) is a "rightness of the *in-quiring* intellect"; it is to be contrasted not only with knowledge (which by definition can never be wrong) but also with opinion: "since, while opinion is not inquiry but already assertion, the man who is deliberating, whether he does so well or ill, is searching for something and calculat-ing."[82] Again, the understanding (*sunesis*) of the *phronimos* is explicitly distinguished from scientific knowledge in general and from "the particu-lar sciences such as medicine . . . or geometry; for understanding . . . is about things which may become subjects of questioning."

Further support for an emphasis on openness and learning in our conception of phronesis comes from the dialectic between experience and insight which is to be found in *E.N.* 6 — even if Aristotle does not make it as obvious as we might have liked. This dialectic consists in the fact that it is the experienced person who has insight, and yet conversely it is only through insights that experience is enriched. The first point here we have already seen in Aristotle's statement that "our powers correspond to our time of life and that a particular age brings with it *nous* and judg-ment"—so that it may be true of experienced and older people that "be-cause *experience has given them an eye they see aright.*"[83] For the con-verse point here we must go back to the second passage on *nous* which I quoted above (at note 67): "in practical reasonings it [i.e., *nous*] grasps the last and contingent fact, i.e. the second proposition. For these are the starting-points of that for the sake of which, since the universals are reached from the particulars; of these therefore we must have perception and this is *nous.*" What we have here is not a logical analysis of the practical syl-logism, but rather a remark about the *development* of practical-moral knowledge cast in syllogistic terms; the 'major' premise (the statement of the 'end') represents the weight of our habitual experience, the 'minor' premise the particular insight of the moment. Logical analysis assumes a major premise, stating the end, as the starting-point of a practical syllo-gism; but what we are shown here is that every major premise that repre-sents one's present habitual outlook must itself have been built up through the accumulation of particular insights. For instance, one is unlikely to have a habitual major premise that puts a value on being sensitive to the feelings of others unless one has had particular 'experiences', over some time, of 'seeing' the effect of one's behavior on others.

It may be well to make more explicit at this point the degree to which we fail to understand phronesis if we confine our attention to the "practical syllogism."[84] I have already noted how partial an aspect of the exercise of phronesis syllogizing is, in that the latter cannot itself generate either the ultimate major or the ultimate minor premises, which must, therefore, be delivered to it from some other source. The further point

I want to make here is that this other source is *not* always *phronesis-nous*.
An example prompted by Elizabeth Anscombe will illustrate the point:[85]
'Adultery is wrong: this is a married woman; therefore it is wrong for me
(not being her husband) to sleep with her'. I do not regard this as involving phronesis because the minor premise, 'this is a married woman' is presumably supplied by an acquisition of uncomplicatedly factual information and not by an act of insight or of *aisthēsis*.[86] (I say "presumably"
because one might, I suppose, conceive of an accomplished Don Juan who
had developed an 'eye' for married women — in situations where the straightforward eliciting of such information could prove damaging to his chances;
but then, even if this were the kind of case envisaged in the example,
such an 'eye' would be the *nous* not of phronesis, but of *deinotēs* "the
quality which defines the man whom the Greeks call a *panourgos*, a sly
one or a rogue, the man who is endowed with a disturbingly oversubtle
intelligence.")[87]

I regard it as important to distinguish practical syllogisms such as
the above from practical syllogisms that are involved in the exercise of
phronesis because there is an approach to ethical practice which tries to
construe *all* practical-moral issues and situations along the lines of the
above example; and it is important to see that this approach, a *deductivist*
one, is *not* the phronetic approach for which I have been arguing; indeed,
if it were adhered to, this approach would make phronesis quite obsolete.
The deductivism of this approach lies in its assuming a definite set of moral
rules which provide major premises ('adultery is wrong') and also descriptions ('married') which make minor premises ('this is a married woman')
unproblematically available. In contrast to this deductivism, the phronetic
approach takes as its point of departure the *problematicity* of minor
premises; the hardest thing about being virtuous, perhaps, is just being
able to *see* what is really significant in different situations. Whereas in
the deductivist approach, the challenge in ethical life is mainly a matter
of the will, for the phronetic approach it is very much a matter of a particular kind of *knowledge*.

Making this point gives me an opportunity to notice the affinity
between Aristotle's view and that of Socrates. I should like to do this, however, not in the negative way that Aristotle himself does it but by reference to one of Plato's most persuasive contemporary apologists, Iris Murdoch. According to Aristotle,[88] Socrates did not think that vice could ever
take the form of moral weakness (*akrasia*), where (overcome by passion)
one acts contrary to what one knows. Such was Socrates' regard for knowledge that he could not countenance the possibility that "when knowledge
was in a man something else could master it and drag it about like a slave."
Accordingly, for him vice must be accounted a form of ignorance. Aris-

totle thinks that this view "plainly contradicts the apparent facts." Nonetheless, when he has worked out his own position some pages later, he finds an ingenious way of both saving the appearance *and* granting validity to Socrates' position. The knowledge that one abandons, or acts against, in the state of *akrasia*, he suggests, is the knowledge of particulars which is formulated in the minor premise. And so "because the last term is not universal nor equally an object of scientific knowledge with the universal term, the position that Socrates sought to establish actually seems to result; for it is not what is thought to be knowledge proper [*kuriōs epistēmēs*] that the passion overcomes (nor is it this that is 'dragged about' as a result of the passion) but perceptual knowledge [*tēs aistētikēs*]."[89]

The negative accord with Socrates that Aristotle contrives to establish here (negative in that it amounts to saying only that neither of them holds that universal premises are dislodged in bad actions) is in danger, it seems to me, of slighting his own position on ethical knowledge as I have been teasing it out. For the kind of knowledge that seems to be relegated here as *mere* perceptual knowledge (and not therefore "knowledge proper") is in fact, especially on the evidence of the two crucial passages on *nous*, the nerve of properly *ethical* knowledge or phronesis. But beyond simply trying to protect Aristotle's position from possible misconstruction arising from his own somewhat rhetorical concession to Socrates, I want to argue for a deeper agreement between it and Socrates' position. I shall do this briefly and obliquely by pointing out the illuminating similarity between the position which I have been attributing to Aristotle and certain aspects of the ethical viewpoint which Iris Murdoch puts forward, "under the banner of Plato," in *The Sovereignty of Good* (London: Routledge and Kegan Paul, 1970).

Murdoch roundly attacks (what was at least in the late 1960s) the prevailing orthodoxy in British moral philosophy. She does so because in her view genuine moral life should stretch one beyond adherence to rules toward the pursuit of some—albeit unattainable—*perfection;* and it is just this latter notion that she finds completely absent in analytic philosophy. What the pursuit of perfection requires above all is the ever renewed habit of *attention*, which is a spiritual energy to rouse oneself from the sluggishness of ordinary experience and to *see*. This attention, Murdoch's version of the Platonic vision of the Good, is a continuous struggle against fantasy and the pull of the lazy, greedy self in order to see the moral reality of each situation in which one is to act. It is, I believe, closely akin to the kind of attentiveness and insightfulness which my interpretation has found in Aristotle's notion of *phronēsis-nous*. Moral vision does not give us the transparent knowledge that is available to the Cartesian ego— which then assigns responsibility for its execution to the will, though it

may be against the grain of passion and inclination. Rather, the very seeing itself is of a kind which "pleasant and painful objects destroy and
pervert,"[90] which therefore requires the safeguard (sōizousa) of a temperate
disposition (sōphrosunē),[91] and which one can hope to become capable
of only as one is deepened and matured by experience.[92] I find the comparison with Murdoch's view helpful here not only because it re-emphasizes
a point which I have been making—namely, that Aristotelian phronesis,
more than simply directing us to good action, is itself already the fruit
of a life devoted to the love of good action—but also because it implies
the need to develop ever greater moral sensitivity rather than a closed deductivist code or—what has often been read into Aristotle and what
Platonists just as often have been anxious to oppose—a connoisseurship
of undemanding moral moderation.[93]

9. The Relationship between Universals and Particulars in the Sphere of Phronesis and *Eupraxia*

The crux of moral awareness that we are attending to here will be
illuminated further if we analyze more closely the relationship between
'universal' and 'particular' which obtains in the sphere of phronesis and
eupraxia. I have just expressed a reservation about the way in which Aristotle's strategy in responding to Socrates in E.N. 7 exploits a distinction
between knowledge of universals and knowledge of particulars. That this
distinction was significant in his whole approach to moral action might
seem to be confirmed in other places in his writings: "It is well to judge
separately [chōris krinein] the statement of the cause and the demonstrated
fact," we are told in the E.E., and again in E.N. 6: "error in deliberation
may be about the universal or about the particular; we may fail to know
either that all water that weighs heavy is bad, or that this particular water
weighs heavy."[94] When Aristotle makes statements like these, his logical
concern for the distinction between the two broadly different kinds of
premises that must operate in a practical syllogism is to the fore. This
concern is in danger of misleading us, however, about the proper nature
of phronesis. Indeed the example of 'heavy water', like the chicken example that I have already analyzed, does not serve Aristotle well. (Cf. Wittgenstein's remark: "a main cause of philosophical disease—a onesided diet:
one nourishes one's thinking on only one kind of example.") It is in fact
an example of what we might call technical as distinct from phronetic
reasoning—though *this*, unfortunately, is a distinction which Aristotle does
not make.

In technical reasoning, universals are already available to us which

may be said to 'contain' or 'include' the particulars. They give us generalized, systematic knowledge which can come into play in the determination of action—once we establish empirically that we have an actual 'instance' before us. Once I establish that, for example, this liquid is heavy
water or this food is chicken, I can call into play the general knowledge
that heavy water is unwholesome or that chicken (being a light food) is
wholesome, in order to ban the former or recommend the latter in an
invalid's diet. In the sphere of phronesis, however, practical-moral universals cannot unproblematically cover or include particular cases, because
they contain in themselves an element of indeterminateness which is removed only through confrontation with the particular case. (There is a
parallel here with the universal enjoinments of a legal code which, because of their very determinateness, must be *corrected*, for the sake of equity,
in their application to particular cases.)

Aristotle's conception of moral universals—i.e., *virtues*—not only
leaves them indeterminate, however; it also includes the mental-moral habit
which, mediating them in the particular case, renders them determinate.
This habit, built into the definition of each virtue (when this virtue is
possessed in its full stature [as *kuria aretē*]) be it courage, justice, magnanimity or whatever, is phronesis. One can be virtuous, can actualize the
virtue in one's life as distinct from merely possessing a theoretical construct of it, only through phronesis and the insights it gives one into how
each situation calls for or allows the exercise of a particular virtue—or a
particular modulation of different and perhaps conflicting virtues, for example, "justice and kindness, loyalty and fairness, honesty and the will
to please."[95]

This point is expressed by Aristotle through his concept of the mean
(*hē mesotēs*), and a discussion such as the present one is, I believe, the
best context in which to understand this concept. It does not, contrary
to what is sometimes supposed, install an ideal of ultrasobriety or moderation (a meaning reinforced by some of the associations of 'prudence', the
word most often used to translate phronesis);[96] rather it indicates that the
accomplishment of virtue calls for a concrete mediation between what one
already knows of the demands of a virtue and the opportunities and limitations of the present situation. To be virtuous *now* calls for a unique
modification, unspecifiable in advance, and by no means easy to determine in the situation itself: "hence . . . it is no easy task to be good. For
in everything it is no easy task to find the middle . . . anyone can get
angry—that is easy—or give or spend money; but to do this to the right
person, to the right extent, at the right time, with the right motive, and
in the right way, that is not for everyone, nor is it easy. . . ."[97]

Being virtuous is difficult because it involves finding one's way through what Aristotle, following the Pythagoreans, calls the *apeiron* — i.e., the un-circumscribable range of potentially noticeable features and the conse-quently unlimited possibilities of action that inhere in each situation — and settling on the one best and most appropriate response.[98] As to how this is to be done, Aristotle can offer no more specific guidance than to say that it is to be "determined by reason [*logos*] and in the way in which the *phronimos* would determine it."[99] That the *phronimos* can, in fact, depend very little on *logos* in the strict sense of principle or reason is made very clear at the end of this discussion; for the matters he has to deal with are concerned with particulars and so, as Aristotle bluntly asserts, "the decision rests with *aisthēsis*."[100]

The above statements are to be found in the general discussion of virtue in *E.N.* 2. Although Aristotle, as he later shows, is well aware that they are annoyingly insufficient, he leaves them hanging until the begin-ning of book 6. He makes it clear there, however, that the whole discus-sion of phronesis on which he is about to embark is intended to deal with the questions which were left begging in book 2. To say that the mean is to be determined by the right principle, he now admits, "though true, is by no means illuminating . . . if a man had only this knowledge he would be none the wiser." And so "it is not enough merely to have estab-lished the truth of the above formula; we also have to define exactly what the right principle [*orthos logos*] is and what is the standard that deter-mines it."[101] And so at this point Aristotle launches into his analysis of the intellectual virtues, especially phronesis.

A reader who found the position of book 2 vague or evasive may be no more satisfied by the analysis of book 6, however; or perhaps we should say that he will be 'wiser' only in seeing why satisfaction of the kind he was seeking is unattainable. For what the analysis of book 6 pro-vides is not a principle or a standard that can be consulted so as to deter-mine for us what to do in given situations. If such a principle were avail-able, there would be no need for phronesis. Aristotle offers, instead, an account of the kind of resourcefulness of mind and character that is needed precisely because of the unavailability of any such principle. And so this account — Aristotle's theory of phronesis — is, in a strong sense, negative; for while bringing out, very subtly, the ramifications of phronesis' adher-ence to particulars, it still remains an account of why an account in the more usual sense — i.e., that which can be set out in a techne — is not pos-sible. This point is well put, in another context, by Stuart Hampshire: "Reflection on moral intuitions may not result in a relatively simple theory which satisfactorily, if roughly, explains these intuitions as derivable from more general principles. Rather it may result in a theory which explains why no such simple theory is to be found, and why no such simple deriva-tions are to be expected."[102]

If Aristotle's ethical 'theory' is one that disabuses us of theory, it does this mainly by showing us that the ethical agent must give up the kind of attachment to generalized knowledge that prevails, legitimately, in theoretical fields. This is the nub of what remains a real disagreement between him and Socrates. The latter's conduct in inquiring what is justice, bravery, etc. "was reasonable, for he thought all the excellences to be kinds of knowledge so that to know justice and to be just came simultaneously; for the moment that we have learned geometry or building we are builders and geometers." Aristotle concedes that this is "correct with regard to theoretical knowledge, for there is no other part of astronomy or physics or geometry except knowing and contemplating the nature of things which are the subjects of those sciences." But with regard to virtue the case is different: "For we do not wish to know what bravery is but to be brave, nor what justice is but to be just. . . ." And here clearly there is a discrepancy between *knowing* and *being* or *doing*. This discrepancy is brought out clearly in a passage a little later: "For there are some who, through thinking it to be the mark of a philosopher to make no arbitrary statement but always to give a reason [*legein meta logou*], often unawares give reasons foreign to the subject and idle . . . by which reasons even men experienced and able to act are trapped by those who neither have nor are capable of having practical and constructive intelligence."[103]

The point of these remarks from the *E.E.*, I should emphasize, is not that knowledge is *not* constitutive of virtuous being and acting. Their point, rather, is to mark a decisive difference between the perspective of theory and the perspective of practice, and to indicate that if we want to get inside the perspective of practice then we must envisage knowledge of a type different from that of the people whose misplaced claims have been criticized. Those who possesses this other type of knowledge, i.e., the *phronimoi,* are different from both types mentioned in the above passage. They neither go in (at least not *qua phronimoi*) for theoretical discussions *nor* are they trapped by them like men of experience (what I have called 'ordinary experience' as opposed to 'phronetic experience')[104] who have no hold on a *logos* at all.[105] When Aristotle says a few lines after the above passage that "one should attend more to perceived facts," he is, one assumes, indicating broadly the *phronimos*' approach: not to disregard reason and principle and yet to attend to them only within the context of an even closer attention to concrete situations. (In fact, we have already met a formulation from *E.N.* 6 which in different words expresses exactly the same weighting: "But phronesis is practical and therefore one needs both kinds of knowledge [i.e., of the universal and of the particular] *but particularly the latter* [i.e., of particulars].")

At this point, having brought out its concern with particulars and the depth of its inextricability from experience, I conclude my analysis of 'phronesis'. With this concept, Aristotle unrelentingly construes moral knowledge from the standpoint of the first person agent and never slides into thinking that the perspective of the third person analyst (or theoretician) can replace this standpoint or obviate the need for insights of the kind which only it can provide. This is the great merit of 'phronesis', and it is this, I have wanted to suggest, which still makes it worthwhile for us to rediscover Aristotle — not only mediately (as in Part 1) through the recent philosophers who have retrieved the phronetic stand in his thought, but also at closer quarters in his own texts.

This point, at which we complete our examination of phronesis, might seem the appropriate point at which to conclude our whole inquiry into Aristotle. For our aim from the beginning has been to bring into relief the nonrationalist (indeed the antirationalist), i.e., the *phronetic*, strand of his thought, and this we have now done. In the first chapter of Part 2, I suggested that despite its having come to be regarded as perhaps the most characteristic concept of Aristotle's ethical/political thought, phronesis might still be regarded, within the terms of his overall philosophy, as a 'deviant' concept.[106] It does not fit comfortably with the classic concepts of 'form', 'matter' and 'end', and in fact we have built up our picture of it largely by developing the contrast between it and the notion which most smoothly and successfully exemplifies and articulates these concepts, i.e., the notion of techne. Having separated out what I call the phronetic strand in his thought, we might regard the *telos* of our inquiry into Aristotle as having been now achieved. However, we are in a position now, I believe, to probe more deeply precisely into the central concept of techne (and through it into the core of Aristotle's philosophy), which up to now has served only as a foil against which to bring out the more 'eccentric' notion of phronesis. We have so far been emphasizing the polarity between a 'theoretical' approach (operative in techne) and an 'experiential' approach (operative in phronesis). We can now go beyond this and ask whether this polarity which, as embodied in techne and phronesis, we have taken to represent a fruitful distinction, cannot also be shown to be *implicit in Aristotle's treatment of techne itself,* where (because it remains implicit) it represents, rather, a failure on his part to make a distinction he ought to have made; a failure, moreover, that has contributed significantly to the very rationalism from which, ironically, we have been looking to him — through the notion of phronesis — for deliverance. We shall take up this question in the next chapter, which will be devoted to a much closer analysis of techne than we have attempted thus far.

10. Beyond the 'Official' Notion of Techne: Recovering the Experiential Background

1. Aristotle's Failure to Distinguish between Techne as an Ability to Analyze and Techne as an Ability to Make

It will be helpful first of all to recapitulate briefly what we have seen of techne so far. In chapter 8, I distinguished technai which contrive, through strategy and a talent for improvisation, to bring about a desired outcome in a shifting field of forces (e.g., navigation, generalship, money-making, rhetoric) from technai which work on stable materials in a straightforward process of fabrication (e.g., house building, sculpture, cobbling, weaving). I saw a resemblance between the former (which I called technai of the *kairos*) and phronesis, whereas the latter (which are the paradigm examples of technai *poiētikai,* and set the pattern for what Aristotle has to say in his *ex professo* discussions of techne) provided us with a foil against which to bring out what is distinctive about phronesis. In a brief interlude in chapter 9, §3 I expressed reservations about 'techne *poiētikē*', seeing it as reposing too much mastery in the mind of the *technitēs* and as not doing justice to feedback that one can receive from the materials in the actual process of making. This conception of techne, I suggested, commits it too much in the direction of theoretical knowledge (*epistēmē*) and does not satisfactorily integrate it with experience (*empeiria*). Without being developed in the previous chapter, these misgivings served a useful pedagogical function in a discussion whose primary aim was to elucidate phronesis. They will now be developed and, in fact, will set the direction of our inquiry in the present chapter as we examine techne in its own right and no longer, therefore, simply with a view to sharpening the profile of phronesis.

This 'official' concept of techne (which was delineated in chapter 8, §4, distinguished from phronesis in chapter 8, §6, and made the target of interjected criticisms in chapter 9, §3) is in conspicuous continuity with Plato and at the same time is deeply implicated in such unmistakeably Aristotelian doctrines as those of act and potency, hylomorphism, and the

315

four causes. It assigns a central place to the *telos* and the *eidos* which the *technitēs* must keep an eye on in order to make the chosen product. It it precisely knowledge of the *eidos* that constitutes one as a *technitēs*, putting one in a position to make the product: "from techne proceed the things of which the form is in the soul."[1] Aristotle's emphasis, however, seems to be less on the making than on the knowledge. What he stresses in the first chapter of the *Metaphysics*, as we have seen, is a "universal judgement about similar objects," an understanding not only of what can be accomplished (the *hoti*) but of its underlying rationale (the *dia tin' aitian*), and a consequent ability to render an account of the productive process and thereby to objectify it for the purposes of instruction. This type of knowledge seems to be more essential to techne than the ability to make: Aristotle can admit without embarrassment, in the same chapter, that the man of techne, despite his knowledge, might not be able—indeed might be less able than the man of mere experience—to respond to the particular condition of Socrates or Callias so as to heal him. (And this position of *Meta.* 1.1, as we saw later, is accurately reflected in the 'light foods' example in *E.N.* 6.7.)

The key source for this notion of techne is *Meta.* 1.1, and we might suppose that its pronouncedly theoretical slant is a reflection of Aristotle's preoccupation there, which is with marking out different levels of knowledge leading up to the summit of *sophia*. Techne arises as a stage or increment in the ascent of knowledge toward the highest universality, difficulty, accuracy, explanatory power (i.e., grasp of 'causes'), autonomy, and authoritativeness—the six properties which he ascribes to *sophia* in the following chapter. His interest in techne then, at this point, is to identify what we might call its degree of participation in *sophia* under the rubric of these six properties. (Thus the man of techne is said to be *sophōteros*, i.e., more endowed with *sophia*, than the man of mere experience.) If we turn now, however, to the chapter at the heart of Aristotle's *practical* philosophy (i.e., *E.N.* 6.4) that is concerned both to distinguish techne from *epistēmē* and *sophia* (as well as from phronesis and *nous*) and to bring out its relation with poiesis, should we not expect to find a rather different emphasis from that which I have just adumbrated from the *Metaphysics*?

The key phrase that is used repeatedly in *E.N.* 6.4 to define techne is *hexis meta logou (alēthous) poiētikē*. This phrase, which brings together two distinct elements—the rational (*logos*) and the productive (*poiētikē*)— is translated by Ross as "a state of capacity to make involving a (true) course of reasoning" and by Rackham as "a rational (and true) quality concerned with making." In Ross's translation, clearly, the predication of *hexis* by *poiētikē* is to be taken in a strong sense: if one possesses a techne then one can make, one's techne issues or can issue in poiesis—and through

it in a *poiēton* (just as phronesis issues in good praxis). If we want to stay
close to *Meta.* 1.1's notion of techne, however, we might hold with Rackham's version and see it as involving a difference of interpretation and
not simply of translation: his "rational quality concerned with making"
makes *hexis* more intimate with *meta logou* than with *poiētikē*, and so
might be taken to suggest that techne gives one (true) knowledge *about*
production — without thereby putting one in a position of *being able to
produce*.[2] This different interpretation of *poiētikē* can be made to resound
throughout the whole of *E.N.* 6.4. The *logos* involved in techne can be
taken as one that is not necessarily directive *in* the process of making but
is rather *about* the latter, i.e., gives one an expertise in analyzing the
process — without thereby enabling one to engage successfully in it. And
when Aristotle introduces a verb for exercising a techne, *technazein*, and
tells us that it means "to contemplate how a thing is to be brought into
being" (*theōrein hopōs an genētei ti*),[3] it seems possible to suppose that
a person might be adept at this *theōrein* and still remain inept in the
act of production itself. Again, when techne is characterized as *poiēseōs*
('to do with production' or, literally, 'of production'), or *peri genesin* ('about
coming into being'), or *peri to endechomenon* ('about the variable') these
phrases seem as open to a 'contemplative' (or 'theoretical') as to a 'productive' interpretation. Finally, we may note that while the designation of
techne as a *hexis* does indeed mean that it is "well entrenched . . . relatively
stable and hard to change,"[4] this still does not imply that its activity or
energeia is poiesis and not simply *theōrein an hopōs genētei ti;* that there
need not be anything odd about its being the latter is borne out indeed
by the fact that Aristotle does not hesitate to call *epistēmē* a *hexis*.[5]

I ought to acknowledge immediately that the interpretation of techne
in *E.N.* 6.4 which I have just given is perverse. No one, so far as I know,
has ever supposed that when Aristotle introduces *oikidomikē* in E.N. 6.4
as the example from which, with a minimum of fuss,[6] he generalizes to
his notion of techne, he has in mind anything other than the rational
capability that is manifested in actually building real houses: the very notion of a *technitēs* who never makes anything — a cobbler who never makes
a pair of shoes or a weaver who never makes a piece of cloth as much as
a builder who never makes a house — seems a self-evident nonsense. What
is the point, then, of trying to show that this is a *possible* interpretation
of *E.N.* 6.4?

The point is to demonstrate that in such an important text as *E.N.*
6.4 (which is, after all, the only chapter in the whole *corpus* which is devoted exclusively to techne) Aristotle's usage does not clearly discriminate
between two meanings which we might have in mind when reading him,
namely: (i) techne as an excellence of knowledge that possesses explana-

tory power (i.e., that grasps the *aitiai*—the 'causes' or explanatory principles[7] of an artefact's coming into being), and (ii) techne as an excellence in bringing about an actual concrete effect. We can go further, I believe, and say that throughout Aristotle's whole treatment of techne no explicit or systematic distinction is made between (i) and (ii)—i.e., between techne as an excellence of a *knower* whose *intentional* object is poiesis (the sphere of artificial generation [*genesis*] of works [*erga, poiēta*] whose forms [*eidē*] are ends [*telē*] to which determinate means are correlated) and techne as an excellence of a *maker* whose *real* object is a *poiēton* (an actual product). And since Aristotle did not distinguish clearly between these two different notions, he does not seem to have raised, with any degree of explicitness, questions about the relationship between them. When he wrote the *Rhetoric* (whose title is '*Technē Rhētorikē*') did he thereby show himself to be a *technitēs* in this area? Or is the *technitēs* here the accomplished speaker who has a high rate of success in persuading audiences? And might someone like Aristotle who excels in writing a treatise in this area still prove to be an incompetent speaker himself?[8] Or, conversely, might one be a reliably successful practitioner and still be unable to formulate an explanatory account of one's practice?[9] Or, if one can furnish such an account, is this a different kind of account from the one that Aristotle provides in his treatise? And if it is, what is the relationship between the two kinds of account?

We may try to answer these questions on Aristotle's behalf, but they are questions which he himself does not seem to have regarded as profitable—or, perhaps more accurately, which his conceptual scheme did not encourage him—to raise. Whatever the value of pursuing all of these questions, there is one consequence of the conceptual scheme which is, I believe, worth attending to. I do not in fact want to claim that according to, e.g., *E.N.* 6.4, possessing a techne implies no ability to be successful in achieving appropriate outcomes (*erga*). What I do want to claim, however, is that such an ability involves to a significant degree what I have been calling an experiential element and that this element, although not absent from Aristotle's thought, all too easily slips through the mesh of his conceptual net when he is formally discussing techne. I shall try to show, then, in the rest of this chapter, that Aristotle did appreciate the indispensability of experience in the exercise of a techne but nonetheless allowed this appreciation to be overshadowed by his greater concern for the explanatory knowledge possessed by the *technitēs;* that his overall framework, or characteristic approach to the analysis of problems, was in certain respects inimical to the elucidation of the experiential background at play in the activity of the *technitēs;* and that there are nonetheless important elements in his thought (particularly the concepts of matter [*hulē*], nature [*phusis*], and soul [*psuchē*]) which provide grounds for an emphasis on experience.

2. Evidence of Two Different Tendencies in Aristotle's Treatment of Techne

If my reservations about Aristotle's conception of techne so far have hinged on its unsatisfactory assimilation of 'experience', what evidence is there, nonetheless, of his recognition of the role played by experience in the performance of the *technitēs?* Let us look first at the opening chapter of *E.N.* 2 where technai are regarded as comparable to moral virtues in a context where both of these (technai and virtues) are contrasted with natural faculties of sense:

> It was not by often seeing or often hearing that we got these senses, but on the contrary we had them before we used them, and did not come to have them by using them;[10] but excellences we get by first exercising them, as also happens in the case of the technai as well. For the things we have to learn before we can do, we learn by doing, e.g. men become builders by building and lyre-players by playing the lyre.[11]

and some lines later:

> Again, it is from the same causes and by the same means that every excellence is both produced and destroyed, and similarly every techne; for it is from playing the lyre that both good and bad lyre-players are produced. And the corresponding statement is true of builders and of all the rest; men will be good or bad builders as a result of building well or badly. For if this were not so, there would have been no need of a teacher, but all men would have been born good or bad [at their techne].[12]

The context here is that of learning or acquiring technai and, in this context, clearly, Aristotle was not in the least inclined to construe techne as a form of contemplation; that it might reside in some expertise in analysis, or in apprehending causes, that could be acquired apart from repeated efforts to achieve mastery in production, through continual engagement with one's materials, is a possibility that he does not even discuss. The notion of techne he is entertaining here is indeed not just nontheoretical but even in a sense antitheoretical: a little later in *E.N.* 2, after he has once again repeated his doctrine of the primacy of *energeia* or practice for the formation of virtue ("it is correct, therefore, to say that a man becomes just by doing just actions and temperate by doing temperate actions; and no one can have the remotest chance of becoming good without doing them"), he goes on to scorn the theoretical approach of those who try to avoid the commitment of practice by *epi de ton logon katapheugontes*—a phrase which is translated by both Rackham and Thompson as "having recourse to theory" but which might be taken to imply a discreditable flight or retreat into the *logos*, better expressed by Ross's "taking refuge in theory."

In the two passages which I have quoted above we find a solid basis for Aristotle's later characterizations, in *E.N.* 6, of techne as a *hexis* and as an *aretē*, characterizations which, despite what I have said about *epistēmē* as a *hexis*, do not sit easily with a theoretical conception but suggest, rather, a fixed orientation to *act* (or *make*) in a determinate manner. When he says, just before the passages quoted, that in virtues we "are made perfect by habit"[13] and, a little after them, that "our states [*hexeis*] are formed out of the corresponding activities"[14] it is, in fact, through an appeal to cases of acquiring specific technai, just as much as to specifically ethical cases of becoming courageous or temperate, that he demonstrates the force of these statements. Moreover, the reference to teaching at the end of the second passage shows us that teachability as a property of techne need not suggest, as I have hitherto assumed, a *corpus* of knowledge that has been disengaged from particular contexts and circumstances and so made available for transmission. For teaching of the kind intended here, quite clearly, must involve the apprentice *technitai* in a process where they work with their materials and have the teacher at hand to point out mistakes and to suggest ways forward toward mastery. And indeed we might already have picked up just such a notion of instruction in the very first sentence of *E.N.* 2 where it is stated that intellectual virtue (which is how techne is later categorized in book 6) "is for the most part both produced and increased by instruction, and therefore requires *experience* and time."

Here, then, in the first chapter of *E.N.* 2 is an unequivocally experiential techne which neither resides in, nor is to be transmitted by, theoretical formulae and which, accordingly, must be learned the hard way by dint of repeated practice—practice in the very act of building or lyre-playing, etc. And yet, if we go on just a few chapters, we will find that a more theoretical notion of techne is reinstated and that all that had been gained in the way of an experiential emphasis in the passages which I have just quoted is briskly and, it would seem, inconsistently set at nought. In *E.N.* 2.4 Aristotle states:

> the products of the technai have their goodness in themselves, so that it is enough that they should have a certain character, but if the acts that are in accordance with the excellences have themselves a certain character it

does not follow that they are done justly or temperately. The agent also must be in a certain condition when he does them; in the first place he must have knowledge, secondly he must choose the acts, and choose them for their own sakes, and thirdly his action must proceed from a firm and unchangeable character. These are not reckoned in as conditions of the possession of the technai, *except the bare knowledge;* but as a condition of the possession of the excellences, knowledge has little or no weight, while the other conditions count not for a little but for everything.[15]

There is a disavowal here, without any explanation, of the analogy which had been posited only a few chapters previously between virtues and technai insofar as both of them can be acquired only experientially or through repeated practice. The two conditions over and above knowledge (i.e., purposiveness and fixity of disposition) which are here ascribed to virtue, *but denied to techne,* are precisely those which are based on repeated practice (*pollakis prattein*). And with their exclusion from techne, we seem to be left again with a 'theoretical' techne, i.e., one constituted by nothing else "except the bare knowledge" (*plēn auto to eidenai*).

In his commentary on this passage, Aquinas cannot be accused of going beyond what is at least implicit in it when he says: "A man can be a good artist [*artifex; technitēs*] even if he never chooses to work according to art [*ars; techne*] and does not persevere in his work."[16] For the essential perfection of *ars* resides in the knowledge of the *artifex,* and nothing is added to this perfection, it would seem, if it goes on to manifest itself in the act of completing a work. (This point of Aquinas is, in fact, echoed by Gadamer, whose analysis of techne, we may recall,[17] is based on a distinction between 'possession' and 'application': "With the design of the object and the rules of its execution, the craftsman proceeds to carry it out. He may be forced to adapt himself to particular circumstances; i.e., not be able to carry out his design as originally intended. But this does not mean that his knowledge of what he wants is made more perfect. Rather he simply omits certain things in the execution. What we have here is the application of his knowledge and the painful imperfection that is associated with it.")[18]

Aquinas officially adopts this position, basing it on Aristotle but developing and systematizing, as he often does, what remains inchoate and implicit in Aristotle's own formulation. In the first article of the tract on *prudentia* in the *Summa* he says that "the achievement of *prudentia* consists not solely in thinking about a matter [*in consideratione*] but also in applying oneself to do something [*in applicatione*]," and in this he sees a contrast between *prudentia* and *ars* — a contrast, moreover, for which he claims Aristotle's authority: "hence the Philosopher says that *pruden-*

tia is not solely a rational quality like *ars*."[19] I take this to be a gloss on
Aristotle's words at 1140b28 that "phronesis is not a *hexis meta logou* simply [*monon*]." I call it a gloss rather than a straight quotation because
Aristotle himself does not actually say — as Aquinas does — that *ars* (techne)
is a *hexis meta logou* simply. But from the context in which this line occurs in the *E.N.* (at the end of 6.5) Aquinas's construction seems to me
both shrewd and justifiable. And of course the point here is that it lends
further support to the 'theoretical' notion of techne which, as I have already tried to show, might be read even into *E.N.* 6.4.

This point about *ars* as *sola consideratio* or *solum cum ratione* is
developed more systematically by Aquinas in a later article. There are,
he says, three acts of the practical reason:

> The first is taking counsel [*consiliari*] which is inquiry in order to
> discover. The second is forming a judgement (*judicare*) on what has been
> discovered. *So far we have not left theory* [*speculativa ratio*]. But practical
> reason which is meant for the doing of something pushes on further: it
> has a third act which is to command [*praecipere*]; this consists in bringing
> into execution [*applicatio*] what has been thought out and judged. And
> because this approaches more closely to what the practical reason is for,
> it is the principal act of the practical reason and so of *prudentia* as well.
> This is indicated by a comparison of *prudentia* with *ars, the perfection of
> which lies in judging and not in commanding.* For the *artifex* who deliber-
> ately breaks the rules of his *ars* is reckoned a better *artifex* as keeping a
> sound judgement of what they are, than one who involuntarily breaks them,
> from a fault it would seem of judgement. With prudence, however, it is
> the reverse, as noted in the *Ethics*. . . .[20]

I quote this text from Aquinas because I take it to be — albeit in
different language, and without advertence on Aquinas's part — an explication of Aristotle's point in the passage from *E.N.* 2.4 where techne, unlike
virtue, is contracted to merely knowing (*auto to eidenai*) and also because
it gives us an occasion to link this latter passage with the sentence from
E.N. 6.4 on involuntary mistakes which Aquinas does advert to. This
sentence is at 1140b22–24: "in techne he who errs willingly is preferable,
but in phronesis, as in the excellences he is the reverse."[21] On Aquinas's
interpretation of this gnomic statement, the only failure that really counts
against a person's techne, i.e., an involuntary failure, must be a failure
of judgment. (And this accords with the point of the passage from Gadamer quoted three paragraphs above). But why, I want to ask, should we
not conceive an involuntary failure of a *technitēs* as one where he may
indeed have an adequate judgment of the work but is unable — despite
all his best efforts — precisely to *realize this in his materials*? If the point

of Aristotle's remark *is* to place such failures outside the essential sphere of techne, then this is further confirmation of a 'theoretical' notion of techne (and therefore of a 'weak' sense of *poiētikē* in *E.N.* 6.4.).[22]

This emphasis on knowledge as the defining property of techne — even if it is withdrawn from productive activity so that it never issues forth in a product — which I have brought out (and, with Aquinas's help, made quite explicit) in the passage from *E.N.* 2.4 can seem puzzling if it is set beside the opening words of the same passage: "the products of the technai have their goodness in themselves, so that it is enough that they should have a certain character." One might have expected that this emphasis on the *object* in the case of techne — this understanding (which is after all quite central to the whole distinction between praxis and poiesis and the corresponding distinction between phronesis and techne) that whereas the *telos* of ethical virtue may be within the agent as a personal perfection, the *telos* of a techne is in a real object made — would have suggested a conception of techne that could not be defined so exclusively in terms of a knowledge-excellence in the *technitēs* himself. One might have expected, rather, a notion of techne that would establish an effective relationship between the *technitēs*, his materials, and the finished product. It is just such a relationship, however, that is missing, I believe, from what we have so far seen of Aristotle's account of techne. To be sure, when the finished product is there before us its perfection resides in itself and it no longer matters what state the *technitēs* is in — or whether indeed he is even still alive. We can still ask, however, how this perfection *came to be* there through the agency of the *technitēs*; and to this question, I believe, we have not yet got a satisfactory answer from Aristotle. For all that techne is said to be *peri genesin*,[23] just how it actually accounts for *genesis* has still not become clear.

If we turn now to *Metaphysics* 9.8, however, we find remarks which *do* seem to be in harmony with an artefact's perfection being in the artefact itself, which reiterate an *experiential* dimension to techne, and which *do* ensure an effective relationship between the *technitēs* and his product. First, the emphasis on experience which we met in *E.N.* 2.1 but which then seemed to be negated by *E.N.* 2.4 is reaffirmed: "it is thought impossible to be a builder if one has built nothing or a harper if one has never played the harp; for he who learns to play the harp learns to play it by playing it, and all other learners do similarly."[24] Then, in contrast to *E.N.* 6.4, which (at least on my stubborn reading of it) remained inconclusive on this point, the *energeia* of techne as a potency (*dunamis*) is clearly specified as the act of *producing* (and not merely, therefore, of *theōrein about* producing): "the actuality [*energeia*] is the end [*telos*], and it is for the sake of this that the potentiality is acquired. For animals

do not see in order that they may have sight, but they have sight that
they may see. And similarly men have the techne of building *that they
may build.*"[25] And then, further on, an effective relationship between the
technitēs and his product is written into the notion of techne. In fact Aristotle finds a remarkable way of expressing this transitivity of the *energeia*
of building, an *energeia* which in one sense is obviously a perfection of
the *technitēs* himself but which, as he now goes on to affirm, more properly resides in the object made. He begins by repeating our familiar distinction between praxis and poiesis, taking as his examples seeing and
building; whereas the *energeia* of seeing is complete in itself (in his own
coinage it is an *entelecheia*), the act of building, by contrast, cannot be
complete *without a house:* "while in some cases the exercise [*chrēsis*] is
the ultimate thing (e.g. in sight the ultimate thing is seeing, and no other
product besides this results from sight), but from some things a product
follows (e.g. from the techne of building there results a house as well as
[*para*] the act of building)."[26] But even the "as well as" is hardly appropriate here if we are to express the internality of the relationship between
the act and the product:

> For the act of building is the thing that is being built, and comes to be—
> and is—at the same time as the house. Where, then, the result is something
> apart from the exercise, the actuality is in the thing that is being made
> [*hē energeia en tōi poioumenōi estin*], e.g. the act of building is in the
> thing that is being built and that of weaving in the thing that is being
> woven, and similarly in all other cases, and in general the movement is in
> the thing that is being moved.[27]

In these passages from the *Metaphysics,* Aristotle goes as far as anyone could go to conceive of a techne that is essentially productive (i.e.,
that comes into being only with and in the product). From this standpoint we can make sense of the opening remark in the passage from *E.N.*
2.4 that "the products of the technai have their goodness in themselves,
so that it is enough if they should have a certain character." What we cannot so easily understand, however, is the remainder of this passage in which,
as I have shown, Aristotle suggests that because the *poiēton* is separate
from the *technitēs* the perfection of the latter is a more truncated perfection than that of the moral agent (whose *ergon* may be within himself),
consisting of mere knowledge and not depending on the purposiveness
and fixity of disposition that come from repeated practice. What seems
to get lost from view here is the point that we have just seen clearly in
Meta. 9.8, i.e., that the goodness (*eu*) which is ascribed to the *poiēton*
can exist in it only because the very act of building of the *technitēs* himself has come to exist in it.

Once made, the *poiēton* has indeed been released into the world complete unto itself (at least so long as the disposition of its materials is preserved from external interference or from inner decay.)[28] It is true that a virtuous person is never in this way frozen (he is not, we might say, "like a physician in a painting, or like a flute in a sculpture which, despite its name, will be unable to do the office which the name implies");[29] he is rather constantly being called upon to prove his virtue in new deeds.[30] And it is also true that techne exists for the sake of the product rather than for the sake of the *technitēs* himself, a point (much stressed by Plato) which Aristotle makes in the *Politics* when he points out that whereas the master-slave relationship is based on the master's self-interest, the relationship of husband to wife and children is "essentially for the good of the governed, as we see to be the case [he immediately goes on] in medicine, gymnastic, and the technai in general, which are only accidentally [as when a doctor treats himself] concerned with the good of the *technitai* themselves."[31] Granted all this, however, it is hard to see why, in the *ordo fieri* or from the point of view of *genesis,* the act of producing a *poiēton* should not require something analogous to the hinterland to knowledge, by way of experience, practice, and secure accomplishment, which is recognized by Aristotle as necessary for the practice of a virtue. For, albeit that we can form a contrast between the unrelentingness of moral existence and the fixed composure of an achieved work of techne, still this work required, in its *genesis,* an investment of the maker, and, in fact, we can say that so long as it exists it never ceases to bear upon itself its maker's stamp. This latter point, indeed, is one which Aristotle himself makes — in a wry aside in a discussion not of techne but of friendship. He is wondering (at the beginning of *E.N.* 9.7) why it is that benefactors love those whom they have benefitted more than the latter love them. He first considers that perhaps this is just a special case of the creditor, really out of self-interest, having an unreciprocated solicitude for his debtor. But he quickly rejects this; "the cause," he thinks, "would seem to be more deeply rooted in the nature of things; the case of those who have lent money is not even analogous." The true analogy, he then goes on to suggest, is with the case of the *technitēs:*

> This is what happens with *technitai* too; every man loves his own handiwork better than he would be loved by it if it came alive; and this happens perhaps most of all with poets. For they have an excessive love of their own poems doting on them as if they were their children. This is what the position of benefactors is like; for that which they have treated well is their handiwork, and therefore they love this more than the handiwork does its maker. The cause of this is that existence [*to einai*] is to all men a thing to be

chosen and loved and that we exist by virtue of activity [*energeia*] (i.e. by living and acting), and that the handiwork *is*, in a sense, the producer in activity; he loves his handiwork, therefore, because he loves existence. And this is rooted in the nature of things; for what he is in potentiality, his handiwork manifests in activity.[32]

Although the above passage might in some respects be considered vintage Aristotle, it is not in character with his more *ex professo* remarks about techne.[33] We still have the problem, I believe, of explaining why it is that experience, repetition, and self-investment are so explicitly recognized as the necessary complements of knowledge for the practice of a virtue, while in his account of techne, on the other hand, they so often seem to disappear behind the facade of an apparently self-sufficient knowledge.

3. Aristotle's Neglect of the Role of Experience in Techne Related to His Characteristic Approach to *Genesis*

Perhaps the first thing to appreciate about this problem is that it arises within the order of becoming (*ordo fieri*) and that Aristotle had his own particular way of handling the latter. His preferred procedure was to analyze already-constituted beings and only through retrospective inferences from within this discourse of *being* to shed light on the process of *becoming*. A classic statement of this preference is in the opening chapter of his biological treatise, *De Partibus Animalium:*

> Another matter which must not be passed over without consideration is whether the proper subject of our exposition is that with which the earlier writers concerned themselves, namely, the way each thing is naturally generated, or rather the way it *is* [*pōs esti*]. For there is no small difference between these two views. The best course appears to be that we should follow the method already mentioned — begin with the phenomena presented by each group of animals, and when this is done, proceed afterwards to state the causes of those phenomena — in the case of generation too. For in house building too, these things come about because the form of the house is such and such, rather than its being the case that the house is such and such because it comes about thus. For the generation is for the sake of the substance and not this for the sake of the generation.[34]

Aristotle is discussing here the procedure to be adopted by himself in the conduct of a scientific inquiry. But it is interesting — and highly characteristic — that he can assimilate this issue so easily to the issue of procedure in the exercise of a techne, and can even justify his own viewpoint on scientific inquiry by claiming a convergence between it and the view-point of the *technitēs*. There is no significant difference with regard to methodology, it would seem, between issues of explanation and issues of production. For Aristotle, methodological issues are brought back to on-tological ones; the procedures of the investigator and of the *technitēs* are comparable because so are their respective objects—namely, natural be-ings and artefacts—a point made here in the context of biology but which also runs right through book 2 of the *Physics* as well as through much of the *Metaphysics*.[35] The fundamental similarity between them in Aris-totle's viewpoint, it would seem, is that from both of them novelty is sys-tematically excluded. In the passage just quoted, he is not just making the unexceptionable point that we must first establish empirically the *ex-plicanda* or the phenomena to be explained. More fundamentally, he is saying that the explanation can only be in terms of a *prior reality* that formally contains all that exists in the phenomena to be explained. These phenomena, therefore, can never be explained as the outcome of a pro-cess of emergence, where this process itself—and not some pre-existent, already-informed reality—supplies the explanation. In the order of ex-planation one's viewpoint on *genesis* is of course inevitably retrospective; but Aristotle is not only always looking backward but backward and straight through *genesis*, we might say, to a complete reality that precedes it. *Genesis* is itself completely transparent and reveals to us when we inspect it, from the vantage point of its outcome, only a being that was already constituted as the *archē* of the outcome, prior to the occurrence of *genesis* at all. This point is made by Aristotle, clearly and vividly, when he goes on, imme-diately after the passage quoted, to attack Empedocles for holding the contrary view:

> Empedocles, then, was in error when he said that many of the characters presented by animals were merely the results of incidental occurrences dur-ing their development; for instance, that the backbone is as it is because it happened to be broken owing to the turning of the foetus in the womb. In so saying he overlooked the fact that propagation implies a creative seed endowed with certain powers [*dunamis*]. Secondly, he neglected another fact, namely, that the parent animal pre-exists, not only in account [*logos*] but actually in time. For man is generated from man. . . . The same state-ment holds good also . . . for the products of techne [*epi tōn technastōn*] . . . [where] the agent [*to poiētikon*] is pre-existent, such as the statuary's techne.[36]

What concerns me here is not just the fact that Aristotle, in his *ex post factum* explanation of animal morphology, excludes, as a principle of intelligibility, all that belongs essentially to the process of becoming,

all, in other words, that was not written into the essence of a pre-existing
reality which is formally identical with the *explicandum* and which alone
supplies its explanation. My primary concern, rather, is his assumption,
expressed very clearly in the last line of the above passage, that the position occupied by the biological scientist—which allows him to possess the
explanatory form (on the other side as it were of all that transpires in the
process of development)—is *equally* available to the *technitēs*. What, for
the scientist, is an explanatory form is, for the *technitēs*, a productive form.
And the fact that the *technitēs* stands not at the *terminus* of a development but at its originative source seems to make no significant difference:
genesis is not one whit more inscrutable from the vantage point of its
beginning than it is when surveyed retrospectively after its completion.
Aristotle is saying that in the case of explanation not only can the formula
(or *logos*) be discovered by the scientist *post factum* (a quite unproblematic claim) but that it actually existed before the fact began to come into
being. In which case, we must note, the whole history which left deposits
for the scientist to explain is strictly inessential.[37] Aristotle should have
no objection in principle, we may suppose, if his scientist were transported
in some fantastic time machine back to the source—if there is a source—
of this history: for back at the source all that enters into his explanations
ought in principle to be available to him. And if this position, which I
have attributed to an Aristotelian scientist, seems a bizarre development
of what Aristotle actually says, it is in fact no different from the position
which he himself explicitly attributes to the *technitēs;* for, in his conception, the latter *is* there before the fact (which in this case is the *poiēton*)
with a contemplative grasp of its formula and hence with the power to
set it on its way to realization.

   Aristotle's systematic occlusion of the process of *genesis*, the implications of which for his notion of techne I have been exposing through
an analysis of an especially perspicuous passage in *De Partibus Animalium*,
in fact runs through the *Metaphysics* and the *Physics*. Its conceptual expression is in terms of his distinction between actuality (*energeia*) and
potency (*dunamis*), and his affirmation of the priority of actuality; his
distinction between form and matter, his affirmation of the ungeneratedness of form,[38] and his reduction of matter to a remainder concept, in
itself devoid of intelligibility; and his overarching teleology which reaches
its culmination in his assimilation to one another of efficient, formal and
final causality[39] (so that only matter remains outside this unified and comprehensive explanatoriness). This suggestion, that *genesis* is squeezed out
of his conceptual scheme, is clearly at odds with Aristotle's own view that
one of the main strengths of this scheme was precisely its ability to explain change or becoming;[40] I have been suggesting that, at least in the

case of some kinds of *genesis,* he does not so much explain it as explain it away.[41]

In the foregoing, I have been attempting to answer the question: Why does an experiential dimension to techne remain so relatively un-expressed by Aristotle? I have suggested that his inattention to 'experience' in the context of techne is all of a piece with his inattention to 'history' or 'process' in the wider context of becoming. His aversion to granting any significant status, in the case of animal evolution, to "incidental oc-currences during their development (*genesis*)"[42] is continuous with his reluctance to acknowledge that there might be a genuinely experimental element in the process of poiesis. In wanting to bring more into focus an ineluctably experiential component of techne, I am wanting, Aristotle might say, to introduce just that kind of haphazardness which he criti-cized in Empedocles[43] — where the disposition of a thing (in Empedocles' case, a backbone; in my case of a techne, let us say a watercolor picture) is "indebted to" events that occur unpredictably in its gestation (in the one case in the womb, in the other in the meetings of canvas, paints, brush and a hand charged[44] with perceptiveness and imagination). I want to go on to ask now, however, whether within the terms of Aristotle's own discussion — albeit that (if there is truth in what I have said in this section) its overall structure is inhospitable to this purpose — there are any chinks, as it were, through which an experiential emphasis might appear.

4. The Role of Matter in Aristotle's Thought Supports an Emphasis on Experience

To this end, perhaps the most profitable place to look is to his treat-ment of the concept of matter (*hulē*). The hylomorphic theory is indeed, as I have already intimated, quite basic to the conceptual context of Aris-totle's notion of techne: to the extent that the distinction between form and matter is emphasized, to just that extent is there a basis for a formal-istic or theoretical conception of techne. A clear expression of this connec-tion occurs, for instance, in *Meta.* 7.7 in a passage which I have already quoted: "Therefore it follows that in a sense health comes from health and house from house, that with matter from that *without matter;* for the medical techne and the building techne *are* the form of health and of the house (and I call the essence substance without matter)."[45] At the same time, we have to be equally clear that Aristotle's hylomorphism as-serts a distinction between form and matter, but not a separation: so that what are analytically distinct are, in fact, concretely united. And only some lines after the above passage in which he speaks of the form without mat-

ter as identical with the techne, he speaks, with different emphasis, of
the *logos* of the concrete unity which is the *poiēton:* "But is the matter
an element *even in the logos?* Well, we describe in both ways what bronze
circles are; we describe both the matter by saying it is bronze, and the
form by saying that it is such and such a figure. . . . The bronze circle,
then, *has its matter in its logos.* "⁴⁶ But if the matter is present in the *logos*
of the *poiēton,* must it not also be present in the *logos* of techne (which
is the *archē* of the *poiēton*), i.e., the *logos* which appears in Aristotle's
definition of techne as a *hexis meta logou poiētikē* in *E.N.* 6.4?

There is a significant passage in the *Eudemian Ethics* which seems
to support and even strengthen this thought. Aristotle is discussing Socrates' identification of virtue with knowledge:

> Socrates, then, the elder, thought the knowledge of excellence to be the
> end, and used to inquire what is justice, what bravery and each of the parts
> of virtue; and his conduct was reasonable, for he thought all the excellences
> to be *kinds of knowledge,* so that to *know* justice and to *be* just came
> simultaneously; for the moment that we have learned geometry or building
> we are builders and geometers. Therefore he inquired what excellence is,
> *not how or from what it arises.* This is correct with regard to theoretical
> knowledge, for there is no other part of astronomy or physics or geometry
> except knowing and contemplating the nature of the things which are the
> subjects of those sciences. . . . But the end of the productive sciences is
> different from science and knowledge, e.g. health from medical science,
> law and order (or something of the sort) from political science. Now to know
> anything that is noble is itself noble; but, regarding excellence, at least,
> not to know what it is but *to know out of what it arises is most precious.*
> For we do not wish to know what bravery is but to be brave, nor what justice
> is but to be just, just as we wish to be in health rather than to know what
> being in health is.⁴⁷

It is interesting that in this passage ethical and productive knowledge (i.e.,
phronesis and techne) are regarded as being on all fours with each other—
so that the distinction between them which is so important in *E.N.* 6.4
is not made at all. This latter distinction, however, is unimportant when
the whole point of the passage—and this is what makes it so instructive
in the context of my present discussion—is to mark a decisive difference
between productive (or ethical) knowledge and theoretical knowledge.
"Knowing and contemplating the nature" are not enough in the case of
productive knowledge; the latter must know not only the what but also
"how and from what it arises" (*pōs ginetai kai ek tinōn*). And so even
though it is the apparently theoretical formulation, *poiētikai epistēmai,*
that is used here for technai, quite clearly what is being picked out by

it is an explicitly nontheoretical conception of techne, significantly different in emphasis from the conception with which we have become familiar from our previous analysis.

When Aristotle says "not to know what it is but to know out of what it arises is most precious," one may take it that he means by "out of what it arises" the material, and that he is positing knowledge of this as most precious specifically for the *technitēs* (and the ethical agent).[48] This point is made more sharply in *Physics* 2.2:

> The technai, therefore, which govern the matter and have knowledge are two, namely the techne which uses the product and the techne which directs the production of it. That is why the using techne also is in a sense directive; but it differs in that it knows the form, whereas the techne which is directive as being concerned with production knows the *matter.* For the helmsman knows and prescribes what sort of form a helm should have, the other from what wood it should be made and by means of what operation.[49]

In this passage, we can discern a different emphasis from that of the more exclusively 'formal' accounts of techne that I have already quoted from the *Metaphysics.* Aristotle is much nearer here to making explicit a point which — even though it is central to his disagreement with Plato — can often recede in his writings: form *is* a disposition of matter. And this is especially consequential for anyone who must make things; it is more permissible, it seems, to speak of the commissioning patron of a work as being concerned with the form than to speak thus of the maker, who is all the time immersed in the materials from which he must try to induce the form.[50] Some lines after the above passage, in fact, Aristotle explicitly states the point I have made earlier about the distinctness but inseparability of the two elements in hylomorphism:

> How far then must the student of nature know the form or essence? Up to a point, perhaps, as the doctor must know sinew or the smith bronze (i.e. until he understands the purpose of each); and the student of nature is concerned only with things whose forms are separable indeed, but do not exist apart from matter.[51]

In the context of the present discussion, what is especially interesting in this difficult[52] passage is the way it unobtrusively inverts the emphases proper to the physicist or natural philosopher (theoretician) on the one hand and to the physician (practitioner) on the other; the former is interested in the form to the same extent that the latter is interested in the *matter.* The question which now arises is whether this difference can be taken to be more than merely notional; whether it implies, for instance, that the knowing (*eidenai*) of the bronze which is attributed to the smith can never be expressed (as the physicist's knowledge presumably can be expressed) in formal statements apart from his actual poiesis itself.

"Apart from" is a vague phrase to use here and I shall try to make its meaning more precise; in doing so I shall examine more carefully the status of the *logos* that is possessed by a *technitēs*. Since we first met this *logos* in *Meta.* 1.1 I have tended to assume that it is of such a nature as to transcend particular facts (the *hoti* of *Meta.* 1.1) and productive situations, and that its expression is in an abstract formula which, because of its abstractness, is in principle (and given the fulfillment of certain specifiable conditions in terms of previous learning) communicable to anyone. But I want to quote now a passage which has the unusual advantage of setting the *logos* in an interlocutory context; and if we attend to this *context* (if, in contemporary jargon, we attend to the 'pragmatics of communication')—something which Aristotle himself does not do—we may gain an understanding of the *logos* which remains hidden so long as we focus only on the explicit *content* of what Aristotle says about it. To say (as Democritus does) that configuration and color disclose the essences of the various animals

> is too simple—it is much the same as if a woodcarver were to insist that the hand he had cut out was really a hand. Yet the physiologists, when they give an account of the development and causes of the animal form, speak very much like such a *technitēs*. What are the forces by which the hand or the body was fashioned into its shape? The woodcarver will perhaps say, by the axe or the auger; the physiologist, by air and by earth. Of these two answers the woodcarver's is the better. For it is not enough for him to say that by the stroke of his tool this part was formed into a concavity, that into a flat surface; but he must state the reasons why he struck his blow in such a way as to effect this, and for the sake of what he did so; namely, that the piece of wood should develop eventually into this or that shape.[53]

This passage not only brings Aristotle's account of techne unusually close to the nitty-gritty of the actual making process but in it we find the *logos* being enunciated by the *technitēs* himself in response to questions which are put to him. And clearly such questions[54] as why "he struck his blow in such a way" can be put only by someone who is *present with him* as he goes about his task. What this brings home to us, then, is that the *logos,* which is articulated primarily by the *technitēs* himself, is intelligible only to someone who is closely observing the process of poiesis, following each step in the actual transaction between the *technitēs* and his materials. Moreover, it is altogether possible that this 'someone' may not only be the auditor of the articulated *logos,* but may, by pointed questioning, already have played an important role in helping the *technitēs* himself to perform his articulation, to bring into discourse, or to make into a true *logos* what might otherwise have remained immersed in his movements with his materials. And the *logos,* even when it has been fully articulated, continues to be marked by this fact about its genesis. Consequently, it can never become an abstract, context-free formula for the replication, by an indefinite series of other craftsmen, of what *this* craftsman has done.

This way of understanding the *logos* seems to me to be the most insightful way of understanding these words of Aristotle's which we have already met: *"matter is in the logos."* It also, I may say, recalls to our minds the point that has already emerged about the kind of teaching that is appropriate to technai;[55] perhaps teaching is but a specialization of the interlocution that we have just seen in which an experienced and attentive person gets the *technitēs* to reflect in new ways, with a view to refining the skills, on the *why* of what he is doing. And, finally, I should say that our present way of looking at the *logos* of techne recalls, in a manner which I have already said would be desirable, Aristotle's account of equity (*epieikeia*) in *E.N.* 5.[56] According to that account the moral *aretē* of justice has a *logos* that cannot be expressed in the written law, which is always universal and for this reason in need of a kind of correction which can be made only by a person "who is present there" in the very situation of action; and this person can formulate the equitable (i.e., the "correction of law where law is defective on account of its generality") only in a special ordinance, a *logos* which is able to take account of the indefiniteness (*to aoriston*)[57] which belongs to the situation itself.[58] Similarly, I am suggesting, the *logos* of techne as an intellectual virtue lies not so much in general formulae as in specific accounts that are always measured to particular acts of production; and it is the ability, reliably, to produce such accounts that is the *hexis meta logou* of techne. Moreover, we cannot fail to find it significant, in the light of my present discussion, that the factor which Aristotle singles out in *E.N.* 5.10 as the cause of the defect in universalized law—and hence of the need for equity as its correction—resides in "neither the law itself, nor in the lawmaker" but rather in the *material of action*" (*tōn praktōn hulē*).[59]

Here we have returned to the theme of the comparison/contrast between techne and ethical *aretē* which we have already examined in *E.N.* 2. The analogy that I have just argued for between techne and the ethical *aretē* of justice confirms a previous comparison which we have seen Aristotle himself make between technai and ethical *aretai* generally in *E.N.* 2.1.[60] But this comparison, we may recall, was interrupted soon afterwards in *E.N.* 2 when technai were said to require nothing "except the bare knowledge," whereas ethical *aretai* were acknowledged to require, in addition to knowledge, an expansive experiential background. But it is worth pointing out that the negations contained in this latter contrast seem themselves in turn to be negated—so that the positive comparison or analogy is reinstated—in a passage in *E.N.* 5.9 just prior to the analysis of equity that I have been discussing. Aristotle is arguing against the view that acting justly or unjustly "lies easily within people's power"—in the sense that a just man could effortlessly "lie with his neighbor's wife or strike a person or slip someone a bribe," or that the unjust person could perform deeds of shining virtue. What this view ignores, Aristotle thinks, is precisely the stable disposition which lies behind our actions, gives them their moral stamp (in the words of book 6, makes them *kuria aretē*) and is *not* so easily within our power. And to show this Aristotle reaches quite unproblematically for a medical, i.e., technical, analogy: one might as well say that "to know [*eidenai*] what honey, wine and hellebore, cautery and surgery are" is easy. Indeed, such knowing is easy, but for the "task of being a doctor" (*ergon . . . iatron einai*) it is not sufficient; one is not a doctor unless one knows "how, to whom, and when to administer [these things —honey, etc.] with a view to producing health." Aristotle uses an interesting phrase to characterize this factor which is over and above straightforward knowledge *of* medicine: *to hōdi echonta*, which is translated by Rackham as "a certain disposition of mind," by Ross as "a certain state of character," and which literally means something like "having in such a way as to . . .". What is involved here, quite clearly, is a kind of discriminating resourcefulness that will be available only to one who has been informed by a wealth of experience, and the point I am making is that Aristotle in this passage attributes this both to the virtuous person *and* to the *technitēs*.[61]

5. Implications of the Analogy between Techne and Nature

In the previous section, I have been suggesting that it is by reference to Aristotle's notion of matter that we can best find a space within his conceptual schema for a less theoretical or less formal notion of techne. In leaning in this direction, I have been following out what is, in a sense, most characteristic in Aristotle's thought. For while 'form' (*eidos*) is an inextinguishably Platonic concept, Aristotle was the first Greek thinker to remove '*hulē*' from the ordinary currency in which it meant simply 'wood' and to make it a technical term, designating his new concept of matter.[62] I want now, in the present section, to expand the foregoing discussion by turning to a major strand in Aristotle's analysis of techne which is closely related to his position on matter but which we have not yet examined, namely, the parallel which he draws between techne and nature (*phusis*). We very frequently come across the two terms 'techne' and '*phusis*' used together disjunctively (sometimes with *tuchē* [chance] making up a tripartite division)[63] to indicate quite different ways in which change may come about: in the one case—*apo technēs*—when the *archē* is separate from the thing in which the change happens and in the other (*phusei*) when the *archē* is immanent in the thing itself; in the latter case the *telos* unfolds from within, while in the former it is introduced through the external agency of a maker who is *entechnos*, i.e., who possesses the appropriate techne.[64] Given this commonplace disjunction in Aristotle's listing of the modes of change, however, what is significant is not the obvious *difference* between nature and craft, but rather the fact that he sees such striking similarities or analogies between them and indeed analyzes both of them so unproblematically in terms of the same conceptual structure.

"Art imitates Nature" (*hē technē mimeitai tēn phusin*) is the most celebrated expression of the analogical relationship between the two,[65] and before analyzing the meaning of this phrase, we can immediately notice that here again Aristotle is moving beyond Plato. For while Nature and Art are indeed closely related by Plato, still for him nature receives *ab extra* from Art (i.e., the craft of the Demiurge in the *Timaeus*) the order (*taxis*) and organization (*kosmos*) which it manifests; in itself nature is without any power to produce order, form, or beauty. For Aristotle, however, the function fulfilled by Plato's god or cosmic demiurge is *immanent* in nature. In itself *phusis* is a principle of ordered change and thus, far from needing the ministrations of an external demiurge, it is intrinsically demiurgic. This transposition of Plato's cosmic craftsman in fact lies behind Aristotle's formula, 'techne imitates nature': it is easy to see that techne imitates nature if nature itself has already been understood in terms of techne. As Solmsen points out, since "Aristotle's entirely new concept of nature . . . has been fathered (or godfathered) by craft it is not astonishing that Aristotle, looking from the vantage-point of this concept of the crafts, persuades himself that craft follows the pattern of nature."[66]

What motivates my interest in the techne-*phusis* relationship is an anticipation that Aristotle's discussion of this theme might lead to a change of emphasis in his conception of techne. In being drawn into a relationship with 'nature'—so that it can even be said to imitate 'nature'—is 'techne' not likely to undergo subtle modification so that what will come into relief will be not so much the element of premeditation and planning as a certain 'natural' fluency in accomplishing results? After all, when we came across 'nature' in our discussion of phronesis in the previous chapter we saw a link between *phusei* and *experience*, and if Aristotle's concept of techne is now to be related to *phusis,* might we not expect it thereby to become more experiential in emphasis?

If this is our anticipation, however, we ought to notice immediately that there is much in Aristotle's discussion which works against it. For, as I have just pointed out, when he sees techne as imitating nature, his concept of nature is one that has already been conceived in the light of his concept of 'techne'. And despite the halo that the phrase 'techne imitates nature' came to have in the subsequent tradition,[67] its place in Aristotle's own discussion is in fact quite precarious. In *Physics* 2 (which is the classic text) we find that the analogy between techne and nature is invariably deployed from the other side: techne is the primary analogate which is used to elucidate nature and not the reverse. Moreover, this is true even in the two passages where techne is said explicitly to imitate nature.[68] Given then that insofar as this analogy goes Aristotle's overwhelming tendency is to set techne up as the paradigm which he uses to illustrate various points about nature, it is not at all clear what there is in nature which could, so to speak, react back on this paradigm in order to modify it. If nature has itself already been cast in the mold of techne, how can it provide any basis for loosening this mold?

To answer this question we need to take account of a fact which is not at all highlighted in Aristotle's own text, viz., that two fundamentally different orders of analysis are in play here depending on which way he turns the analogy. When he says that techne imitates nature, he seems to be making an *ontological* point: nature is ontologically prior,[69] its order and purposiveness primordially established; techne then is the artifice of nature's highest but most helpless creature who is born "unshod, unclad, unarmed"[70] but who, precisely through his techne, can make good his weakness, put himself on the right side of nature, and even carry to completion what nature, left to her own devices, would leave fallow or even diseased.[71] On the other hand, when he — much more frequently — shows how nature imitates techne he is making a *pedagogical* point,[72] i.e., not denying the ontological priority of nature, but rather assuming it, and then proceeding to explain what is ontologically prior, i.e., nature, by what *quoad nos* is more *perspicuous,* i.e., techne.[73] And the greater perspicuity of techne he might have taken as simply a reflection of the fact that we ourselves deliberately take up craft activities and, having them reliably at our disposal, are in a strong position to make their constitutive structure stand out.[74]

If the ontological point still stands, however — that techne only carries forward what nature has already disposed and is bound to follow her paths — are there then grounds for attributing to nature something primordial or something that remains opaque insofar as it can*not* be gleaned

from what we take to be our homely familiarity with our own craft activities? Is there, in other words, something in nature that has still not
been grasped even when the pedagogical efficacy of 'techne' has been fully
exploited? And is this something that is not only to be grasped in nature
but that also has implications for techne insofar as it supplies an independent basis for saying 'techne imitates nature' and thereby saves the meaning of this statement from circularity (where the 'nature' that 'techne' is
said to imitate has already been defined in terms of this 'techne' itself)?

In arguing for an affirmative answer to these questions, I shall look
to passages where Aristotle, rather than simply extrapolating from 'techne'
in order to develop a concept of nature, seems, on the contrary, to get
a different kind of purchase on techne by considering it in close juxtaposi-
tion with nature. "If a house, e.g. had been a thing made by nature, it
would have been made in the same way as it is now by techne; and if
things made by nature were made not only by nature but also by techne,
they would come to be in the same way as by nature."[75] Here, clearly, the
assimilation of techne and nature to each other is very close, and there
seems to be as much encouragement to think of techne as naturelike as
to think of nature as technical. Later in the same chapter, Aristotle goes on:

> when an event takes place always or for the most part, it is not accidental
> or by chance. In natural products the sequence is invariable, if there is no
> impediment. It is absurd to suppose that purpose is not present because
> we do not observe the agent deliberating. Techne does not deliberate. If
> the ship-building techne were in the wood, it would produce the same re-
> sults by nature. If, therefore, purpose is present in techne, it is present also
> in nature. The best illustration is a doctor doctoring himself: nature is like
> this.[76]

The implication of these two passages seems to be something like
this: both techne and nature are generative and work toward an end; nature already shows its resourcefulness by bringing to completion, in an
orderly process, its own natural products. It therefore requires no impossible stretch of the imagination to suppose that in the case of *artificial*
products, the techne might be in the material, i.e., the material might
somehow be able to assemble itself into the finished *ergon*. If this were
the case the process would be just as orderly and sequenced as it is now
when it is indebted to the techne of the craftsman, but, in fact, with the
removal of the craftsman, techne as an immanent potentiality of the material
would now *be phusis*. We will immediately want to interject, of course,
that this cannot be the case, since techne and *phusis* are different and
the difference resides precisely in the fact that things of nature have their
archē in themselves (*en hautois*), while things of techne have their *archē*

in another (*en allōi*), viz., the *technitēs*.[77] And yet a force still remains
in the two passages: they encourage us not to be so impressed by the intervention of the *technitēs* as to suppose that it inaugurates a new realm
that is entirely different from *phusis*.[78] For we would not be too far from
the truth if we were to imagine the craftsman's activity itself as but a strategic
detour through which nature goes (and in which it surrenders its own name)
in order to bring about a new class of beings (artefacts) which it can neither
produce nor reproduce through its normal channels.[79] And Aristotle goes
a surprising distance to assure us that the terrain (of techne) through which
this detour passes is not a very alien one, when he remarks: "[even] techne
does not deliberate" (*kaitoi kai hē technē ou bouleuetai*).

This latter remark is surprising because, as we have seen earlier, the
analysis of *genesis apo technēs*, in the important seventh chapter of *Meta*.
7 places deliberation at the very heart of the exercise of a techne.[80] Artificial generation is there divided into *noēsis* and *poiēsis* — poiesis being
the execution, in reverse order, of the steps which have already been worked
out (intentionally) in the process of *noēsis*. And this process of *noēsis* is
precisely the process of deliberation, which is briefly illustrated (in the
case of medicine) in this same chapter,[81] and is given its classic exposition
in *E.N.* 3.3. It is when Aristotle comes closest to taking seriously his dictum 'techne imitates nature' that he has to play down the role of deliberation; for deliberation, as a consciously intelligent process, is obviously not
to be attributed to nature. And so the whole contemplative or theoretical
side of techne — the working out of a form *in the mind of the technitēs*,
prior to any engagement with the material ("techne indeed consists in
the account of the product without its matter")[82] — recedes from view. But
what kind of concept of techne are we now left with? Perhaps one in which
noēsis and poiesis are not separable, linear sequences, such that one re-
traces in reverse order the steps marked out by the other, but are, rather,
interwoven in one process which is at the same time intelligent *and* productive, and must be said to go on in the materials as much as in the
mind of the *technitēs*.

6. Implications for 'Techne' of Aristotle's Account of Change

Do Aristotle's own words entitle us to speak of *technazein* as going
on in the materials? "If the shipbuilding techne were in the wood, it
would produce the same results by nature. . . ." This remark is suggestive, but it remains *hypothetical*; clearly Aristotle can entertain the idea
in it, but can he actually embrace it? He can hardly do so if it is taken
to mean that techne is in the material as a *dunamis* which is fully in the

material's possession, for to do so would be to abolish the distinction between techne and *phusis* altogether. However, we have already met a remark which suggests that techne is in the material in the sense that it is in the latter— and not therefore just in the mind of the *technitēs*—that techne is actualized: "The act of building is in the thing that is being built . . . the actuality is in the thing that is being made . . . in general the movement is in the thing that is being moved".[83] Moreover, the import of this remark from the *Metaphysics* is reinforced in the work with which we are at present most occupied, i.e., the *Physics:* "When what is buildable, in so far as we call it such, is in fulfilment [*entelecheia*], it is being built, and that is the [the act of] building. And similarly with learning, healing . . .";[84] or again "the actuality [*energeia*] of the buildable as buildable is the process of building."[85]

These statements contain two closely related theses that are quite fundamental to Aristotle's analysis of causation and change: when A brings about a change in B (1) the agency of A and the patiency of B are *one act,* and (2) this act resides in the patient, B. The classic exposition of these theses is in *Physics* 3.3. It is there explained that the distinction between A's agency and B's patiency is only a notional one; the two phrases are simply different *descriptions* of what is a single *reality:* "there is a single actuality of both alike, just as one to two and two to one are the same interval, and the steep ascent and the steep descent are one—for these are one and the same, although their definitions are not one. So it is with the mover and the moved."[86] Aristotle wants to avoid postulating any *tertium quid* between A and B, any mysterious influx into B that emanates from A and is, while the process is still going on, traversing some metaphysical space or 'in-between' that somehow provides a medium between them. It might seem that his only way of avoiding the insoluble problems attendant on such a postulation would be by adopting the even more absurd position that "to teach will be the same as to learn, and to act the same as to be acted on—the teacher will necessarily be learning everything that he teaches, and the agent will be acted on."[87] But in fact Aristotle is not driving himself into this absurdity; he does not want to hold that teaching and learning *mean* the same, but that a teacher's teaching and a pupil's learning *are* the same event.

> Nor is it necessary that the teacher should learn, even if to act and to be acted on are one and the same, provided they are not the same in respect of the account [*logos*] which states their essence . . . but are the same in the sense in which the road from Thebes to Athens and the road from Athens to Thebes are the same. . . . [I]t by no means follows from the fact that teaching is the same as learning, that to learn is the same as to teach, any

more than it follows from the fact that there is one distance between two things which are at a distance from each other, that being here at a distance from there and being there at a distance from here are one and the same. To generalize, teaching is not the same as learning, or agency as patiency, in the full sense, though they belong to the same subject, the motion [*kinēsis*].[88]

For the purpose of my own discussion, I want to accept without quarrel the first of Aristotle's two theses—the one so adroitly explained and defended in the above passage. But what about the second thesis which asserts that the actual event of change (which may be described—tracing from Thebes to Athens, as it were—as the agency of A, or—tracing in the opposite direction—as the patiency of B) occurs in the patient B? There is, I believe, an awkward fact that counts against this thesis and, drawing on a recent book on the *Physics*, I want to suggest a revision of it, that would both take account of this fact and at the same time remain compatible with the first thesis. The awkward fact is that even if a hot body can cause another body adjacent to it to be heated, without itself apparently having to do anything, the case is otherwise with, say, building—which is Aristotle's staple example of *genesis apo technēs*. For granted that (in terms of the distinction between poiesis and praxis, or between *energeia* and *kinēsis*) change in the builder cannot be what building *means,* nonetheless without some obvious change in the builder, no building will take place. The inescapable fact is that if the builder himself does nothing—if he never raises a hand, exerts pressure, consults drawings—then there will be no process of building; and it is hard to see how these necessary movements can be said to exist in the building materials and not in the builder himself.

In her book *Nature, Change and Agency in Aristotle's Physics,* Sarah Waterlow draws attention to this fact and, in response to it, proposes an ingenious recasting of the second thesis above, a recasting which certainly goes well beyond anything Aristotle himself says but which, nevertheless, can claim to derive a certain impetus from a tendency that is clearly present in his thought. Waterlow's proposal is that what we call agent and patient should be regarded, *while the process of change is actually going on,* not as two separate entities, but rather as forming one reality, an organic unity, as it were, which is the real subject of change. The factor in Aristotle's thought which might lend support to this proposal is the centripetal tendency, particularly evident in his approach to 'substance', which led him to look for some unifying principle that would bring together under one superordinate *telos* what might otherwise be regarded as a multiplicity of discrete objects and changes. The paradigm instance of this, of course, is his approach to the complex living organism which is always the subject of the functions of its different parts, no matter how autonomous or separate these latter functions might—from a point of view other than that of the complete organism—appear to be. It is as an extension of this way of thinking that Waterlow proposes to view neither agent nor patient, but a unity which is indeed materially constituted by both of them, as the real subject of change: "What happens in the one [the agent] and what happens in the other [the patient] have the same end and are from the same principle. Such a consideration justifies thinking of one body (in the ordinary sense of 'one body') as an organic unit; so let it justify a similar view in this case."[89] Our language and our conceptual habits leave us ill-equipped to deal with this unified subject of poiesis; hence Waterlow's recourse to the paradigm of a living organism in order to express her meaning:

> Of course the two distinct beings are materially continuous, both before and after, with the one subject of the concrete change as it actually occurs. But is this a reason for supposing that during the change there were two actually distinct beings involved? Surely not, any more than the fact that different simple bodies are yielded up when an organism decomposes would be, for Aristotle, a ground for saying that they were actually present as their distinct selves during the life of the creature.[90]

The reason, it would seem, why we are driven to analogy here in order to avoid being misled by the language which is 'native' to the topic of change is that this language is already a language of analysis, projecting onto the reality of change, in the guise of an apparently unavoidable description, a particular conceptual schematization. On Waterlow's supposition, however, "we would not be able to distinguish one being as that in which the new state happens, and the other as that which contributes to this without itself suffering the new state. For this distinction presupposes that the concrete event has already been conceptually split into the active and passive aspects. It seems then that considered prior to analysis, this event occurs in a single subject, which only *upon* analysis reveals different factors, an agent and a patient."[91]

Waterlow's purpose is to express the reality of change, and her way of doing this is a *via negativa:* a quite radical stripping away of the conceptual baggage which obscures the nature of this reality:

> In the change as a concrete unitary event there are not different entities to *be* agent and patient. The active and passive of the verb, from this point of view, are used of the change itself only derivatively, on the basis of an actual distinction, existing only *ante* and *post eventum.* We cannot even

call the two beings the 'potential agent and patient', since this implies that they could be actually so. But they could be actually so only in the actual change and *in* the actual change they are not distinct and therefore not agent and patient.[92]

But perhaps we will ask why this particular conceptual baggage has accumulated around our thinking about change, or why our language has been analytically biased in the way that it has. Why is it so difficult in our understanding the reality of change to let go of solid, spatially and perceptibly discrete entities? Perhaps one answer to this question is simply in terms of a lapsarian tendency to naive realism that is endemic in all our thinking, as creatures extroverted to an "already out there now real."[93] But Waterlow suggests a more particular answer when she writes: "If we and Aristotle find this account [i.e., her own account, which undercuts all the customary distinctions] incredible, the reason, I suggest, does not lie with the concept of change as such, but with the structure of the concepts we use to describe our own practical activities."[94] When we get involved in an activity of poiesis, we usually have the opportunity of thinking about it in advance and of framing an intention. Then when we enter into the making we suppose ourselves to be enacting what has already been mapped out in our intention. But in our intention we could not help thinking of ourselves as distinct from that with which we were going to interact and so we suppose that in the making too—which we take to be simply a real production of the content which has already existed intentionally in our mind—the object-to-be-changed is distinct from ourselves. As Waterlow puts it: "The point of view of the voluntary agent is one for which the 'halves' already present themselves as distinct."[95]

We must now return to our own discussion of techne and see what has been gained for it from this excursus on Aristotle's analysis of *kinēsis* and Waterlow's adventurous reconstruction of it. We went to this analysis seeking support for our view (developed above in §5) that Aristotle's assimilation of techne to *phusis* argues against a conception of techne as a deliberative process, enacted solely in the mind of the *technitēs*. This support seems to have been amply forthcoming. For Aristotle has gone so far as to deny any real distinction between the actualization of the *technitēs qua* agent and the actualization of the material *qua* patient in the process of its becoming the finished product; and this seems to enforce the view of *technazein* that we have been trying to establish, namely, that it transpires not only in the mind of the *technitēs* but also *in his engagement with his materials*. Moreover, this view is even more explicitly implied by Waterlow's reconstruction of Aristotle. For this reconstruction does not just establish a close bond between the *technitēs* and his material by seeing the actualization of the former as occurring in the latter (which is Aristotle's own position); it goes further and asserts that while the poiesis is going on the *technitēs* and the material are actually a concrete unit. And furthermore, it is worth noting that, in working out this position, Waterlow's analysis, like my own, pushes techne very firmly in the direction of nature. By way of making sense of her idea of one unitary being which somehow embraces both *technitēs* and materials, she appeals (as we have seen) to the analogy of a natural substance. And in doing so she also quite deliberately alters the direction in which Aristotle himself invariably works this analogy: "Now although Aristotle's analogies . . . between natural and artificial change are intended to illustrate the former by the latter, why should we not reverse the analogy and regard the artifex and his material as forming, in the change, a concrete organic unity, as if the material were an extension of his own body?"[96] The degree of involvement, or rather identification, that we find here between the *technitēs* and his material seems to argue decisively against any conception of techne which sees it as being consummated in mere knowledge or as residing solely in the mind of the *technitēs*.

7. Aristotle's Account of 'Soul' Supports a Conception of Techne as Embodied

There is one factor which I have not taken into account at all in the previous section and which may go a fair distance to explain the contrasting emphases that have appeared throughout this chapter in Aristotle's conception of techne. I have just been attending to his analysis of the *technitēs in actu* and to Waterlow's very sharp focus on the *event* of poiesis itself rather than on what is the case *ante* or *post eventum*. Formally considered, however, is techne not something that exists *ante* the event? In other words, is it not properly speaking a *dunamis* and an *archē*, i.e., a power or capacity possessed by the craftsman which can be appealed to as the explanatory source of the event of poiesis? And, as such, must it not exist in the craftsman, before any poiesis is enacted, as a habitual possession (*hexis*) which makes him really different from a person without techne (*atechnos*) and which, *post eventum*, can be appealed to as the explanation (*aitia*) for his productive successes as against the latter's failures? And if it thus resides in the craftsman even when he is not exercising it, must we not say that techne is essentially immaterial and that, as such, Aristotle could hardly avoid thinking of it as a knowledge-excellence? Here is a passage which will sharpen the point of these questions:

[T]hings are called movers in two ways. Both that which contains the origin of the motion is thought to impart motion (for the origin is first among the causes), and also that which is last in relation to the moved thing and the coming-to-be . . . [thus] we speak of the doctor and of the wine as healing. Now . . . in action, there is nothing to prevent the *first agent* being unaffected, while the *last agent* only acts by suffering action itself. For if things have not the same matter, the agent acts without being affected; thus the techne of healing produces health without itself being acted upon in any way by that which is being healed. But the food, in acting, is itself in some way acted upon; for, in acting, it is simultaneously heated or cooled or otherwise affected. Now the techne of healing corresponds to an origin [*arché*], while the food corresponds to the last [*eschaton*] (i.e. contiguous) mover. Those active powers, then, whose forms are not embodied in matter are unaffected; but those whose forms are in matter are such as to be affected in acting.[97]

In this passage — which strongly recalls the *Meta.* 7.7 passages which gave us our first intimation of a contemplative bias in techne[98] — Aristotle is making a distinction whose effect seems to be to insulate techne from the actual interaction in which the material is changed. As originative source, techne seems to coincide with the process of *noēsis* which terminates (or reaches its *eschaton*) in the *thought* that wine is desirable; but when the wine is *actually* being administered, Aristotle does not seem to think of it (let alone the patient to whom it is being administered) as embodying the techne. It looks as if techne has already been actualized in the *noēsis* (i.e., the deliberation of the *technitēs*) before poiesis begins between the 'last agent' and the material. Aristotle's anxiety to keep techne thus removed from the material interaction seems to derive from his unwillingness to allow that techne might be susceptible to modification or change;[99] and he preserves it from this possibility through asserting that it "does not have its form in matter" (*mē en hulēi echei tēn morphēn*). The question we are now left with is: how exactly does the immaterial techne of medicine relate to the wine which, being material, is licenced to engage in the actual process of poiesis? Or, more acutely (and taking Aristotle's own example in *Meta.* 7.7), how does the doctor's immaterial techne relate to his own material activity of rubbing — when the *eschaton* reached in deliberation about a particular patient is not 'give him wine' but 'rub him'?

There is another passage (tucked away, characteristically, in a discussion of animal reproduction where we find another easy deployment of the techne-*phusis* analogy) which will, I believe, bring us closer to Aristotle's answer to this question than any of the more central texts that we have so far examined. In trying to explain the cooperation of male and female to produce the new offspring, he reaches for a striking analogy with craft, viewing the male as craftsman and the female as material (it is not his biology, be it noted, but what he uses as *explicans,* namely, his conception of techne, that interests us here): "the male contributes the principle of movement (*archēn kinēseōs*) and the female the material (*hulēn*). This is why the female does not produce offspring by herself, for she needs a principle, i.e something to begin the movement in the embryo and to define the form it is to assume."[100] Granted this, however, "the birth must take place in the female," just as, in the case of the crafts, "all workmanship and the ultimate [*eschatē*] movement imparted to matter must be connected with the material concerned, as, for instance, architecture is *in* the buildings it makes."[101] (This is a straight application of our familiar thesis 1 on change.)[102] Now Aristotle believes that the male seed does not contribute materially to the reproductive process. What then is its role, or what kind of contribution does it make to the material, all of which is supplied by the female? The same role, the same contribution, that the techne of the craftsman makes in the *genesis* of the artefact. But what is *this* role and *this* contribution? "No material part comes from the carpenter to the material, i.e. the wood in which he works, nor does any part of the carpenter's techne exist within what he makes."[103] This seems simply to reinforce the distinction which we have seen in the previous passage between the techne as *archē* and the wine (or the rubbing) as *eschaton;* techne is immaterial and so is in some sense aloof from the *genesis* which transpires in the material — and in which therefore the wine (or the rubbing) can be involved. But, of course, techne cannot be *completely* aloof, and now Aristotle goes on to specify how, even though it contributes nothing material, it is still effective in the process:

> the shape and the form [*hē morphē kai to eidos*] are imparted from him to the material by means of the motion he sets up. It is his hands that move his tools, his tools that move the material; it is his knowledge of his techne, and his soul, in which is the form, that move his hands or any other part of him with a motion of some definite kind. . . . In like manner, in the male of those animals which emit semen, nature uses the semen as a tool and as possessing motion in actuality, just as tools are used in the products of any techne for in them lies in a certain sense the motion of the techne.[104]

When Aristotle says here: "it is . . . his soul [*psuchē*], in which is the form, that move[s] his hands" he might seem to be committing himself to a picture of the soul as a kind of chief executive who issues orders (*archei*) which are carried along down a chain of command into the process and — eventually — the product of manufacture. This 'order' consists in a conception of the *eidos* which is to be induced in (if not imposed on) the materials and also in a specification of the series of steps, beginning with the *eschaton* (which is 'last' only in the chief's — i.e., the soul's — thinking), through which his operatives (hands, tools, etc.) will implement it (i.e., the order and, through it, the *eidos*). It is essential in this picture that the chief himself never visits the shop floor and has only a one-way communication with his operatives; they cannot report back to him or seek any modification of his order; their function is simply to execute, as his is simply to order. Finally, it is to be noted that techne fits into this picture altogether as the possession of the chief; it is source or *archē* and things come about from (*apo*) it, but it itself is not affected by anything coming back from the material which receives form from it.

The picture of the soul which I have just sketched might be called a 'mentalist' one, and clearly it fits with the 'mentalist' conception of techne with which I have all the time been taking issue. Not only is this picture easily read into the passage cited above, but it can also be claimed to be fairly extensively in evidence throughout Aristotle's writings;[105] moreover, as eminent a commentator as Ross does nothing to discredit it when he uses 'mind' as a synonym for 'soul': "The form is present in the builder as being known by him and as filling his *mind*."[106] It is not, however, Aristotle's maturest view of the soul and, for the light which it may throw on 'techne', let us now consider briefly what this latter view in fact is.

In *De Anima* 1.3 Aristotle argues against a conception of the soul held by some of his predecessors:

> The view we have just been examining, in company with most theories about the soul, involves the following absurdity: they all join the soul to a body, or place it in a body, without adding any specification of the reason [*dia tin' aitian*] of their union, or of the bodily conditions required for it. Yet such explanation can scarcely be omitted; for some community of nature is presupposed by the fact that the one acts and the other is acted upon, the one moves and the other is moved; but it is not the case that *any* two things are related to one another in these ways. All, however, that these thinkers do is to describe the specific characteristics of the soul; they do not try to determine anything about the body which is to contain it, as if it were possible, as in the Pythagorean myths, that any soul could be clothed in any body — an absurd view, for each body seems to have a form and shape of its own. It is as absurd as to say that the techne of carpentry could embody itself in flutes; each techne must use its tools, each soul its body.[107]

When he says here, in relation to soul and body respectively, that "one acts and the other is acted upon," Aristotle is using the language of dualism. Everything else in the passage, however, conspires to subvert the dualistic picture by showing that the relationship between soul and body, so far from being purely extrinsic, is possible at all only because of a 'community of nature' (*koinōnia*) between them: the soul is inconceivable without the 'containing body' (*tou dexomenou sōmatos*), which must be of a special character. Indeed, as Aristotle later goes on to point out, the soul *is* the special character of this body. Both are given to us only as already composing a unity: "we can dismiss as unnecessary the question whether the soul and the body are one: it is as though we were to ask whether the wax and its shape are one, or generally the matter of a thing and that of which it is the matter."[108] Given this unity, i.e., the fact that soul is the way of being and acting of a body which has the capacity to receive it (and which is not a human body at all until it has received it), it is, in fact, better to speak not of the soul as acting but rather of the person who is the souled body (or the embodied soul): "It is surely better not to say that the *soul* pities or learns or thinks but rather that the man does this with his soul."[109]

In setting out this conception of the soul, Aristotle finds it convenient to illustrate important points through reference to techne. Thus, immediately before the sentence I have just quoted about the preferability of speaking of the person and not the soul as agent, he writes: "to say that it is the soul which is angry is as if we were to say that it is the soul that weaves or builds"—something which is manifest nonsense (he implies by the absence of further comment, let alone argument). In the preceding passage, he illuminates the intimacy between soul and body by suggesting that the relationship between them is like that between a techne and its own proper tools; just as carpentry cannot conceivably be realized without tools fitted to carry out the functions of cutting, hammering, planing, etc., so too the soul depends intrinsically for its actualization on a body of a special character. Or, again, when he illustrates the soul-body relationship by a physiological one, he immediately goes on to illustrate the latter in turn by a techne-based one. The soul is to the body, he suggests, as its proper functioning is to a sense organ: "Suppose that the eye were an animal—sight would have been its soul, for sight is the substance [*ousia*] of the eye which corresponds to the account [*logos*], the eye being merely the matter of seeing; when seeing is removed the eye is no longer an eye, except in name—no more than the eye of a statue or of a painted figure."[110] And this point, he now shows, can be made just as easily in relation to a craftsman's tool (an axe). Although, as he concedes,[111] we cannot *properly* speak of the axe having a soul, still its soul, *if* it had one would be its power or function (of cutting). And so we have a double analogy: "as sight and the power of tool are, so is the soul" (*hōs d' hē opsis kai hē dunamis tou organou, hē psuchē*).[112]

At this point we ought to notice a curious circularity. We have turned to an elucidation of soul in order to deepen our understanding of techne. (The immediate motive for this was our need to interpret Aristotle's remark that it is his soul which moves the *technitēs'* hands—which move his tools, which in turn move the material. But in fact the importance of 'soul' for an understanding of 'techne' was already apparent at the beginning of this section when we acknowledged that as an active power (*dunamis*)—and not therefore as something that exists only in the moment of actual poiesis—techne must reside immaterially in the soul of the *technitēs*. And indeed from the time we first met techne, soul has played an important part in its conceptualization: "from techne," we discovered very early on, "proceed the things of which the form is in the soul.")[113]

If it is critical for us to understand 'soul' in order to understand techne, what we have just found, however, is that in his most developed treatment of the soul, Aristotle appeals by way of illustration—and as if its exemplary value for this purpose is already securely established—to techne. Now I believe that when Aristotle is treating techne here only obliquely (i.e., when his focus is on *psuchē*) he nonetheless gives us more light— or at any rate a different light, and one more favorable to the nonmentalist interpretation that I have been trying to develop—on it (techne) than he does in his more *ex professo* remarks about it (e.g., in *E.N.* 6.4 and *Meta.* 1.1).[114] I propose, therefore, to spell out more explicitly than he does himself what the fact of its being able to function so smoothly as an exemplar of the soul tells us about techne.

First let us take up the point that Aristotle does not mean by 'soul' what modern philosophers have often meant by 'mind': a disembodied instrument of thinking and reasoning.[115] Soul is essentially embodied; it is that through which the 'body' is endowed with all its modulated capacities for movement and action. It is present in the whole body and in all its parts; it makes each integral part capable of its specific functioning and thus is to the unified human body what sight is to the eye. When Aristotle says that techne is in the soul, therefore, we can certainly interpret this to mean that it is in, e.g., the hand. Without the presence of soul we might have an inert lump of flesh but not a human hand. The very potentiality for dexterity and coordinated action which makes it a human hand is already due to this presence of soul. And when this raw potentiality is gradually disciplined into actual capacities for specific types of skilled activity, techne is present, we may say, as much in the hand as in the soul; it is what makes the hand of a *technitēs* different from the hand of an unskilled person.

When Aristotle says, then,[116] that "it is his knowledge . . . and his soul, in which is the form, that move his hands," we need not think of the soul as an extrinsic agent directing, through its knowledge (contained in the 'mind'), soulless, knowledgeless hands. Or, again, when he counts techne as one of those "active powers whose forms are not embodied in matter"[117] we can deem him to be speaking only half the truth. For while techne is not indeed embodied in the matter of a particular artefact – so that with the disintegration of the latter it too would cease to exist – nonetheless it is embodied in the souled matter of the human body in such a way that it can, through repeated actualizations, lead to the generation of an indefinite number of particular, specifically characterized, artefacts. To say that techne is immaterial is not to remove it to some transcendently 'mental' or 'spiritual' dimension, but rather to attribute it to that particular kind of matter (i.e., the human body) which is not self-enclosed as other material things are but is, rather, capable of influencing certain other kinds of things (or, in the case of medicine, things of the same kind as itself) in determinate ways.

The notion of an embodied techne which we have just found to be implicated in Aristotle's discussion of soul will be consolidated if we look more closely at what is said in this discussion about tools. First, tools have been likened to the body: as the body is to the soul so its proper tools are to a techne. And since the soul (as we have just seen) cannot exist at all except through the body, is it not likewise the case, therefore, that a techne cannot exist except through its tools? We would not be able to even conceive, we might say, of technai such as surgery, sailing, or snaring if we did not know what scalpels, sails, and nets are; these technai have no other way of being exercised except through these tools, and so what constitutes a person as a *technitēs* in these areas is precisely a proficiency with these tools. And this is reinforced by the second point which we have seen Aristotle make about tools: the soul of a tool – if we could speak properly of its having a soul – would be its functioning (in Aristotle's example the soul of an axe would be cutting, just as the soul of an eye would be seeing). But since the first point has already likened techne itself in relation to its tools as soul to body, is it not therefore the case that the techne *is* the functioning of the tools ("in them lies, in a certain sense, the motion of the techne")[118] – or, treating it more strictly as a *dunamis*, the ability on the part of the *technitēs* to bring the tools into the state of actualization which is their proper functioning?

While arguing thus against what I have been calling a 'mentalist' concept of techne and stressing its embodiedness, I do not want to deny any part to knowledge ("it is his soul wherein is the form and his *knowledge* [*epistēmē*] which moves his hands"): it is a question only of clarifying the *kind* of knowledge that is involved here and the conditions to which it is subject. In the previous chapter we saw that phronesis transcends the sort of propositional knowledge that can be acquired by someone who simply has a good 'mind'. As conceived by Aristotle, it is available only to a person whose character has already been formed in a particular direction — though it in turn comes to inform this character. Now although in the case of techne we have a great deal less explicitness on Aristotle's part — and indeed, as we have seen, no lack of obstacles in our way — the upshot of the whole analysis in the present chapter is to suggest that techne can and ought to be conceived in a similar way. Just as Aristotle very clearly recognized the role of the passions in the acquisition and exercise of phronesis, so in (at least some cases of) techne a similar role ought to be recognized for what we might call the sensori-motor system. If the *phronimos* possesses knowledge that is inseparable from a certain ordering of his passional life, similarly the knowledge of the *technitēs* is inseparable from a certain development and attunement of his sensory and motoric capacities — and indeed of his passional life, too, insofar as the latter must be able to submit to the discipline of the task. Techne is a *hexis poiētikē,* and the *technitēs'* possession of the form is *poiētikē* only if it extends into his hands' capacity for movement. Indeed not only his mode of possession of the form, but the form itself (insofar as it too is *poiētikē*) carries an intrinsic reference to excellences that are rooted in the body. The forms which are the specific objects of different technai cannot be comprehended adequately in the mind, either through a generalized, treatiselike knowledge or through a process of 'deliberation'.

8. 'Deliberation' Reconsidered, and Conclusion

We are now in a better position to look more closely at Aristotle's account of deliberation, which, as we have been aware all along, is crucial to the conception of techne both as an *archē* and as essentially 'mental'. In a significant passage from the *Metaphysics* (which we met in our interlude on techne in the last chapter and which is echoed in some of the passages we have just been considering) we find this:

> From techne proceed the things of which the form is in the soul . . . e.g.
> . . . health is the formula and the knowledge in the soul. The healthy subject, then, is produced as the result of the following train of thought; since *this* is health, if the subject is to be healthy *this* must first be present, e.g. a uniform state of body, and if this is to be present, there must be heat; and the physician goes on thinking thus until he brings the matter to a final step which he himself can take. Then the process from this point onward, i.e. the process toward health, is called a 'making'. Therefore it fol-

> lows that in a sense health comes from health . . . that with matter from
> that without matter; for the medical techne . . . [is] the form of health.
> . . . Of productions and movements one part is called thinking and the
> other making,— that which proceeds from the starting-point and the form
> is thinking, and that which proceeds from the final step of the thinking
> is making.[119]

What disconcerts in this passage is the unidirectionality of the thinking
(*noēsis*), which proceeds from the form to a specification of a treatment
for the sick person—apparently without need for close attention to his
actual condition. He is 'patient' to the very full extent of being on the
receiving end of a poiesis, while the *noēsis* which informs this poiesis does
not, apparently, need to be 'patient' to him in the sense of carefully observing or diagnosing his condition. This *noēsis* consists rather in what,
in the chapter on deliberation in *E.N.*, is called 'analysis' (*analusis*),[120] literally a freeing-forth or releasing of what is already contained in the form.
And that it is 'analytic' in a strong sense is brought out by the fact that
Aristotle does not scruple to compare it with a geometrical inquiry: "the
person who deliberates seems to inquire and analyse in the way described
as though he were analysing a geometrical construction."

This geometrical comparison is surprising in the light of Aristotle's
acknowledgement, in introducing deliberation as a topic for discussion
earlier in this chapter (*E.N.* 3.3), that he would be dealing here with a
kind of thinking where certainty or clear definition are not available:

> about eternal things no one deliberates . . . nor about the things that . . .
> always happen in the same way. . . . And in the case of exact and self-
> contained sciences there is no deliberation. . . . And we do so [i.e., deliber-
> ate] more in the case of the techne of navigation than in that of gymnastics,
> inasmuch as it has been less exactly worked out [*diēkribōtai*], and again
> about other things in the same ratio, and more also in the case of the tech-
> nai than in that of the *epistēmai;* for we have more doubt about the former.
> Deliberation is concerned with things that happen in a certain way for the
> most part, but in which the event is obscure [*adēlois*], and with things in
> which it is indeterminate [*adioriston*].[121]

From the tone of these remarks which lead into the discussion of deliberation, one might have expected that what would be emphasized in this
discussion would be the unreliability of one's purchase on the relevant
realities, the elusiveness of sure judgment, the need for subtle strategies,
and indeed the often ambiguous nature of what can be counted as success. But what we get instead is not only schematic but quite cut-and-
dried:

> We deliberate not about ends but about what contributes to ends. . . . Having set the end they [viz., *technitai*—doctor, orator, and statesman are the examples which have just been mentioned] consider how and by what means it is to be attained; and if it seems to be produced by several means they consider by which it is most easily and best produced, while if it is achieved by one only they consider how it will be achieved by this and by what means *this* will be achieved, till they come to the first cause, which in the order of discovery is last . . . [but] first in the order of becoming [*genesis*].[122]

The very distinction between end and means which underpins this whole analysis and is posited at the beginning without argument is, to say the least, highly problematical. For it is certainly not always the case that we know the end in advance, in such a way as to obviate the need for deliberation about it. Often we are not just trying to calculate the means to our end but are, rather, trying to work out what a worthwhile and feasible end in our situation is. To say that the general's end is victory and that his deliberation therefore is only about the means to achieve it is to gloss over the fact that much of his most difficult pondering may be about just what would count as victory here or—where 'victory' may be impossible—what would be an acceptable compromise, or—failing even that—a not dishonorable defeat. And the same is true if we take the example Aristotle himself uses of the doctor, or our own example of the teacher (which, despite our silence about it, was the catalyst for this whole study). Every good doctor or teacher will certainly have a rich conception (however inadequately, if put to it, he or she might articulate it) of what 'health' or 'education' is. But to think that the problems can now be reduced to simply calculating 'means' to 'produce' this 'health' or 'education' is greatly to underestimate the complexity of the task. Rather than having the end unproblematically available from the beginning—in such a way that it apparently provides a clear-cut criterion against which the candidacy of different possible means can then be evaluated—in one's deliberation one may in fact be defining or redefining the very end. What is an acceptable level of health for this person, given the damage already done by illness, his constitutional make-up and the tolerances it lays down, the undesirable side-effects of powerful drugs, his environment and life-circumstances? Or what is a worthy educational goal for this pupil, given the depth of difficulty she experiences in certain areas, the effects on other pupils of a disproportionate amount of one's time given to helping her, the level of parental support that is available to her, or the probabilities in relation to the kind of job (if any) she is likely to have later on?

Even granted a situation where one already knows one's end, Aristotle's treatment of deliberation as a form of means calculation is oversimplified. He assumes that when the *technitēs* has several options and wants to determine which of them is easiest and best (and quite apart from the unmentioned possibilities of *conflict* between the easy and the good, and the vexing problems of how to resolve such conflict) he can do so apparently without any recourse to action and entirely, therefore, through thinking. In other words, this thinking does not seem at any point to need to provide itself with fresh information available only by trying something out and *then* considering what results. There is no element in it of the tentative or the provisional which would lead one to make active interventions precisely in order to learn from them. The consideration of *possibility* here is extraordinarily terse. "And if we come on an impossibility we give up the search . . . but if a thing appears possible (*dunaton*) we try to do it."[123] But why, we want to ask, does this doing seem to be the *terminus?* What if the doing should turn out (despite its appearance in thought) to be actually impossible, or if, though possible, it should *fail*, or in some way fall short of the 'easiest and best', or produce consequences other than those one had anticipated? Why is Aristotle so disappointingly silent on all these possible eventualities? And why, in particular, does he not recognize that *noēsis* might *feed* itself on them?

These doubts which I have just raised about Aristotle's conception of deliberation may now be related to our discussion of techne. Aristotle seems to suggest that techne lies either in a body of knowledge that has been fully systematized so as to provide strict and ready-made guidance to the *technitēs* or—in the much more frequent cases where such an "exact and self-contained" science is not available—in a process of deliberation, along the lines we have just seen, where the *technitēs* has to inquire (or engage in a process of *zētēsis*) about what is to be done—but where such inquiry can nonetheless be described as 'analytic' in that it runs along tracks that are very clearly laid down by the (prior) possession of the form or end. Now if our criticisms of this account of 'deliberation' (that it is blind to the frequent need to bring the end itself—and not just the means—into focus in one's deliberation, and that it ignores the advantages of a hypothetical or experimental approach in trying to achieve one's end) have brought us beyond Aristotle, I believe nonetheless that they harmonize, in a way that the criticized account of deliberation itself does not, with the conception of the *technitēs'* mode of possession of the form or end which I have shown to be implicit in Aristotle's own remarks about soul. For what these remarks about the soul taught us was that without a sensitivity and responsiveness of the body (through hands, eyes, etc.) the 'mind' of the *technitēs* cannot comprehend the form. And such sensitivity and responsiveness, we may judge, play a large part in supplying the data that help one to redefine, as needs be, one's end, or to determine, as one goes along, and with a discrimination and judiciousness that would be impossible through a mere mental analysis, the "easiest and best."

I indicated earlier that it may come as a surprise to find deliberation cast in such formalized terms, given that in introducing it Aristotle had very clearly recognized the ill-defined nature of its terrain. There is something else in this introduction, however, which — outweighing his concessions to 'doubt', 'obscurity' and 'indeterminateness'—'rationalized' his conception of deliberation and made it suitable as the core of his 'official' notion of techne. Deliberation is what makes choice (*prohairesis*) rational (*meta logou kai dianoias*),[124] and moreover it is concerned with "things [that] can be brought about by our own efforts (*di' hēmōn*] . . . [and] that are in our power (*eph' hēmin*],"[125] since "the moving principle [*archē*] is in ourselves."[126] Now this idea of a rational *archē* (and of man as architectonic in the world) is one of Aristotle's deepest commitments; it is, I believe, what accounts for the unsatisfactory nature of his analysis of deliberation and of techne; and ultimately it is what I have been chipping away at most throughout this chapter. Responding perhaps to the low esteem in which 'banausic' activities were held by aristocratic Greeks (if not also reflecting Socratic contempt for the body), Aristotle (like Plato) dignified the crafts by investing them with a knowledge that would be a sovereign source of the forms that characterize their respective products. Dispensing with the Platonic 'other world' and with an epistemology of *anamnēsis*, he committed himself to a much more 'inductive' conception of knowledge.

The question I have been raising (in different guises), however, is whether, for all its undoubted power, this conception can really account for the degree of sovereignty which Aristotle seems to repose in techne as *archē*. What he underestimates, I have tried to argue, is not so much the need for a great deal of first-hand experience in the *acquisition* of a techne (he acknowledges this frequently enough) as the continuing need for such experience in the *exercise* of it. In this exercise it is not just that (as he stresses) the material is passive, but that the *technitēs* should know how to be passive also and that this passivity should be conceived as an element in his very techne. Speaking of change in *De Anima*, Aristotle says: "sometimes it terminates in the soul and sometimes it starts from it, perception e.g. coming from without."[127] Now when he is speaking formally of techne, Aristotle gives the impression that everything comes *from* it, and in doing so he neglects the role, *in technē itself*, precisely of perception or, better (and echoing our discussion of *aisthēsis* in the previous chapter), of *perceptiveness*.

If I have been making a case against Aristotle, I have been doing so, of course, with help from himself: what is neglected in the *ex professo* treatment of techne that I have tried to 'deconstruct' can be reconstructed (I have argued) from the more oblique remarks that occur in various contexts in which 'techne' is not so much analyzed *per se* as deployed pedagogically in the analysis of other concepts. The *ex professo* concept of techne served earlier (ch. 8, §6) as a foil against which to bring out the distinctive features of phronesis; what has emerged in the alternative concept, however, is what might be called a 'phronetic' techne, i.e., one whose responsiveness to the situation is not fully specifiable in advance and which is experiential, charged with perceptiveness, and rooted in the sensory and emotional life. Moreover, this alternative concept might be said to make paradigmatic those technai which I earlier called technai of the *kairos* and compared with phronesis.[128] Whereas the 'official' concept tends to assimilate these technai to a paradigm of fabrication (e.g., in Aristotle's habitual way of handling medicine), in the alternative concept fabrication itself is seen to be a process where involvement and fluidity—which are only more *obvious* in technai of the *kairos*—are ineliminable.

It may be noted that the tension that I have been finding in Aristotle, as the first great systematic thinker of the Western tradition of reason, is one that has a strong resonance in contemporary criticism of the 'logocentrism' of this tradition. Recent 'deconstructionist' and 'postmodernist' thought has taken issue strongly with a monopolistic reason defined as masterful, autonomous, technocratic and logocentric; and it has done so in the name of what has been suppressed by this monopoly: materiality, contingency, vulnerability, nature, and embodiment. That the kind of detailed exegesis of ancient canonical texts undertaken here in the second part of our study is not at all extraneous to this contemporary criticism should be evident from the fact that in quarreling with (what I have taken to be) Aristotle's rationalist account of techne I have found support for an alternative conception of it precisely by giving full weight to what he has to say about matter, nature, and embodiment. I need to point out, however, that if both phronesis and (the alternative notion of) techne have been elaborated over against a rationalist conception, they are not on that account irrational. The analysis here has not been inspired by, nor does it support, any desire to abandon the *logos* altogether. To the contrary, it has been for the sake of continuity with a tradition that, far from outlining kinds of knowledge that are *aneu logou*, I have been trying simply to understand the *kind* of *logos* that may be involved when Aristotle describes both phronesis and techne as *meta logou*.

With these broad remarks, I conclude my analysis of techne and indeed of the whole conceptual field of techne/poiesis and phronesis/praxis in Aristotle. In the Epilogue I shall try to make more explicit both the relationship of this analysis to our discussion of modern thinkers in Part 1 and the implications of our whole study for those contemporary problems of knowledge and action that have been our concern from the beginning.

Epilogue

As Aristotle's voice—with those of our other interlocutors—fades away, what are we left with? A conversation does not lend itself to summary, and if there were conclusions that could be easily detached from the foregoing chapters, this would imply—contrary to expectations I tried to establish in the Introduction—that although this book is about praxis it may be approached in the mode of poiesis. Still, a reader who has persevered thus far may expect some appropriate stocktaking, and I shall attempt to show here where I believe our inquiry has brought us, what upshot it has for practical affairs, and how it relates to other work that is going on in philosophy.

1. The Main Themes

All the partners in the conversation have been speaking to what may be called the 'human condition'. A 'condition' is something that the person who is 'in' it may find excessively difficult to be aware of, let alone to define. And since the human condition is one that *everyone* is in, it presents difficulties which allow no one a privileged standpoint on them from outside. These difficulties are the ones that have kept the Western tradition of philosophy going at least since the time of Socrates. A philosopher, of course, may not recognize them as stemming from a condition, and his or her philosophy may be an attempt (perhaps a magnificent attempt) to construct just such a standpoint. This has certainly not been the way with any of the philosophers who have been met in this book, and the first thing I shall do here is to reaffirm not so much the kind of condition it is, as the major implications we have seen of its being a *condition* at all.

We have seen that the knowing person can never quite catch up with how he or she knows; in achieving knowledge he or she is always already beholden to assumptions, antecedent interests and tacit procedures which are not themselves known—if to be known means to be fully available for inspection and certification by consciousness. This is so even for those knowers (namely, scientists) who work in carefully circumscribed areas, on well-defined problems, and with a high degree of control over their operations; or at least it is the case when they are doing research of a kind which, when it is successful, makes a genuine advance in the science in which they are engaged. It is much more clearly the case, however, for persons whose knowledge is acquired and deployed in areas that are informal, or unsystematic, or have not, for whatever reason, become the object of scientific study. These are settings in which people invariably not only know but act; where their knowledge is intimately connected with ways of conducting themselves, relating with others, getting things done. Now it is possible not to see these areas as inherently contingent, due to the very nature of the matters with which they deal (as Aristotle supposed), but rather to see their lying outside the scope of scientific management up to the present time as a matter of contingency, as a state of affairs that can and ought to be altered. It can seem an attractive project to establish in each of these areas a systematic body of generalized knowledge, or a method laying down explicit rules and procedures, that will supplant the understanding and judgment of practitioners and ensure success in the relevant performance or production. In the present study this project has been identified as that of converting the rationality implicit in these areas (if before such conversion they are conceded to be rational at all) into *technical* rationality; it has been recognized as a powerful project, both in the modern world and, in a more limited way, in the ancient world; and, as a project which seeks to overcome the conditionality of human life, its possibility of fulfillment has been strongly contested.

In questioning the attainability of technical mastery over these areas an alternative to the technicist picture has been developed. In this alternative picture, practical knowledge has been shown as a fruit which can grow only in the soil of a person's experience and character; apart from the cultivation of this soil, there is no artifice for making it available in a way that would count. In exposing oneself to the kind of experience and acquiring the kind of character that will yield the requisite knowledge, one is not the kind of epistemic subject that has been canonized by the modern tradition of philosophy. One is at the same time a feeling, expressing, and acting person, and one's knowledge is inseparable from one as such.

One's perception of and response to situations is 'aesthetic' in that it is mediated through feelings. These feelings become clear only as they are expressed and this expression is not something that can be managed technically. There are perceptions, interpretations, and judgments all the time at play in expressive activity, but these are available to one only as a person already committed to this activity—and never, therefore, as a detached ego. Moreover their adequacy to the situation and the truth of what they say about one's own involvement in it are a function of emotional dispositions that have already become established; they depend on nothing less than one's integrity as a person—where this integrity cannot be ensured just by the deliberate activity of the will.

To speak of 'action' as well as (though not as separate from) knowledge and expression is to advert to the network of relationships within which one finds oneself, and to the hazardousness of one's undertakings within this network—the unpredictability, open-endedness, and frequent irreversibility of what these undertakings set in train. No one is exempt from action in this sense (a sense which allows that speech often *is* action); it is through it that one discloses and achieves the unique identity that distinguishes one as a person; and at the same time it reveals the depth of one's interdependence with others. When a craftsperson 'acts' on suitable materials in order to produce an artefact which is comfortably within his or her proficiency, there is a predictability about success which is commensurate with this proficiency itself. However, when one's actions are not imposed on materials but are directed toward other persons, such mastery is not attainable. One cannot determine in advance the efficacy of one's words and deeds. Efficacy turns out to be a form of influence; it lies not so much in one's own operation as in the cooperation of others. The nature and extent of this cooperation cannot be counted on beforehand, and even afterwards one cannot be sure just what it has been.

What has just been about the way in which the outcomes of action elude the agent's grasp—so that they are indeed, in a literal sense, 'outcomes' (Anglo-Saxon for 'events') and not products—has followed from the *plurality* of distinct agents with whom one is thrown together. However, the depth of one's nonsovereignty does not derive only from this fact that there are many different centers of initiative within the network of human relationships. It is also related to two basic and closely interconnected factors that are common to all agents, being constitutive of the web within which they all find themselves. The first of these is *historicity*. As a knowing, feeling, and acting person in the present, one always carries the weight of the past—one's own and one's community's: a weight which leans heavily on one's projecting into the future. This is the past as tradition, which means the past as present—all the more present because of its being for the most part implicit and prereflective, active from behind one, as it were, rather than something one can place before one as object. Or, to change the plane of the image, tradition may be thought of as what is *underneath* us, continually exercising a kind of gravitational pull. Not that it necessarily makes for a deadweight; for the ground to which it connects us by a thousand invisible filaments, in our thought and in our being, can be a sustaining one, making possibilities substantial and actual.

The compromised state that one finds oneself in, as a historical being, can make the uncompromised position of the technician appear in an attractive light; and the history of technique, and in particular the history of its modern expansion, has been an attempt to overcome history—to create "the peculiar semblance of post-histoire."[1] This is only a semblance, because, for example, those who promote the behavioral objectives model of teaching are themselves involved in a deeply historical project, whose roots, as this study has tried to show, lie deep in Greek philosophy. Such a project involves a loss of significant substance as the price to be paid for its gains in rigor and apparent control. But fascination with the gains serves to distract attention from the losses which they entail.

The second factor which limits an individual's sovereignty and binds one to the web of human relationships is *language* and, more particularly, language as speech. This factor, of course, is not separable from that which we have just been considering, since language is itself deeply historical: it has become what it is through a wayward development over time, a process of gathering, combining, profiling, recessing, discarding, and layering meanings, interests, perceptions, and values—and all of this directed by no higher logic or plan than what can be reconstructed as the life of the particular language itself. What is important here is not just the way in which language is bound to the past—so that it is the dominant mode of being of tradition—but more especially the way in which it binds those who use it—i.e., everyone—to the past. In a sense, of course, no one really *uses* language; no one, that is, constructs thoughts within his or her subjectivity and *then* employs words which can best convey these thoughts to a public. Rather thinking itself is already within language; even when, as a creative or radical thinking, it does not fall into the obvious pathways of the language (i.e., its clichés) but strains to cut fresh paths, it still remains within it—just as (to change images from land to sea) a daring sailor is in the wind and on the waves with which he contends.

This fact—that as a thinker one always finds oneself within the encompassing element of language—can also be seen as compromising the sovereignty of thought; for words already have all kinds of tugging effects, and if one's thought must be freighted in them, how can it be straight and true? One response to this question has been the technicist one: to escape from the eddies of ordinary language and either to freeze existing words (now become technical terms) into one precise, fixed and unambiguous meaning, or to invent new words which from the start will have just such a meaning. The other response, which is a defense of the practical or 'phronetic', does not accept the question as given, for it does not see 'sovereignty' as either possible or desirable, nor does it assume that thought must be straight in order to be true. This second response appreciates the kind of *buoyancy* that language gives to thought. And, without hoping for escape to another element altogether, it accepts that thinking is a tension-filled activity which, already unmoored on language, still tries to find poise and direction in it. And this is true for *all* thinking. Everyone who nego-tiates his or her way through a practice — and not just the poet or paradigm-breaking philosopher — may be thought of as a sailor (navigation caught our attention in ch. 8, §5 as one of the nontechnical technai which open toward phronesis).

The last parenthesis, with its advertence to the work on Aristotle in Part 2, will have come as something of a jolt. For almost everything in this Epilogue so far has seemed to refer back to Part 1. The points made about knowledge, the expression of feeling, and the open-endedness of action were very truncated versions of what had been met, respectively, in the chapters on Newman, Collingwood, and Arendt. And in pointing to historicity and language we were touching on the central issues of the chapters on Gadamer and Habermas. What exactly, then, is Aristotle's relationship to all this? Or, what comes to the same thing, how has Part 2 complemented Part 1?

Historicity and language are certainly not made thematic in Aris-totle's writings. However, the dialectic that we saw in Part 1 between over-coming (or escaping from) *history* and *language,* and, on the other hand, surrendering to them and still finding a way forward within them, is the same dialectic that, on my account of Aristotle in Part 2, obtains in rela-tion to *experience:* the dialectic between a mode of knowledge (techne) which can legislate securely for experience — on the basis of having done a clean job of abstracting universal features from it and thereby having transcended it — and, on the other hand, a mode of knowledge (phrone-sis) which itself remains experiential, since the universals within its grasp are always modifiable in the light of its continuing exposure to particu-lar cases.

What kind of relationship am I positing here between historicity and language as the characteristic themes of our modern philosophers (which, when unpacked, contain the other themes of nondetached knowl-edge, the nondisposability of the self in emotional expression, and the vulnerability of action within the communal matrix) and Aristotle's con-ception of experience (which clearly has been the pivotal notion in Part 2)? One might read the two themes explicitly back into Aristotle. It could be claimed, for instance, that his account of the development of experi-ence is — if only by being a developmental account — historical; it shows him to be well aware, for instance, that different intellectual excellences, precisely insofar as they depend in different degrees on experience, correspond to different stages of life: gifted mathematicians may be found among the young, but not *phronimoi*. And it might be added that he was not in danger of construing experience in individualistic terms; the well-established Greek sense of the importance of the polis, with its formative ethos, made him aware that experience in Sparta will be significantly different from experience in Athens. This claim might then be extended to language; Gadamer, we may recall, has been able to find in Aristotle's account of the development of experience an excellent depiction of how we learn to speak—albeit that Aristotle himself did not fasten on the linguistic element, as such, in this development.[2]

While there is merit in these claims, we must allow, nonetheless, that the preoccupation with historicity and language that we met in Part 1 is distinctively post-Cartesian and is not, as such, to be found in Aristotle. Still this preoccupation disposes us favorably to what *is* to be found in Aristotle and specifically to the point and value of the distinctions and relations which he worked out with the concepts of phronesis, praxis, techne, poiesis, and *empeiria* (experience). There is, I believe, a very illuminating parallel between language as the field of interpretation and speech, and the practical field in which one acts. By speaking of a 'parallel' here, I intend to imply that all practice is not *just* linguistic (I say this because it has been urged against Gadamer by some critics that his 'linguistification' of experience or his assimilation of praxis to the activity of interpretation—which, for him, is a form of speech—involves an idealist foreshortening of experience and praxis;[3] but Gadamer's claim is only that interpretation is a form of praxis, and not, conversely, that all praxis is just interpretation). At the same time, while not wanting to collapse one into the other, I want to suggest that the fields of language and of action are importantly similar, and thus can throw light on each other.

In both fields, there is a tension between closure and openness, and an ever renewed—never antecedently guaranteed—mediation between universal and particular. The closure lies, in the one case, in one's command of the language and, in the other, in one's already acquired experience and formed *ēthos*, both of which bias one in a definite direction. The openness lies, in the one case, in the infinity of the language itself, its inexhaustible capacity for new utterance and, in the other, in the uncircumscribable range of differently nuanced situations in which, as an agent, one may find oneself. In both cases, as *em-peiros* (experienced) one has brought things within a *peras* (fixed limit); but this achievement is always precarious insofar as in both cases one remains cast out on the *a-peiron* (the limitless — of which, for the Greeks, the sea was a favorite example). The *empeiros* meets the challenge of the *apeiron* with the benefit of universals, in the one case with an established linguistic competence and, in the other, with major premises for practical syllogisms; and yet, on the actual occasion of utterance or action, this universal element proves itself flexible enough to unite with a fine pereception of what the particular occasion calls for: so that the achieved unity *is* the utterance, *is* the action.

What happens here in the actualization (*energeia*), in the moment, of a whole background of habit is extremely difficult to articulate. As a phenomenon, it is more apparent, I believe, in language — in the everyday miracle of speech — than it is in the web of our practical affairs, where we are doing more than speaking. But, when one tries to get a purchase on the dynamics that are involved in both cases, it is Aristotle's concepts — worked out with respect to practice in the wide sense — that still, I believe, offer most help. With the concepts that we have explored in Part 2 — not just the central ones already mentioned here, but the whole cluster of ancillary ones such as the *kairos* (the opportune), the *mesotēs* (the mean) in which the *kalon* (the fitting) is realized, *euboulia* (deliberative excellence) and the *aisthēsis* (insight) of *nous* — Aristotle gave us resources for thinking about the rationality of practice which, far from being exhausted, we can now, aided by preoccupations of our own, come to appreciate better.

The philosophy presented here as Aristotle's gives much scope to improvisation and indeterminateness, to what I have called the 'experiential' — where *empeiria* always has to reckon with the *apeiron,* and where it reckons with it justly when it becomes phronesis. It may be asked, however, how *this* Aristotle sits with the perhaps more familiar Aristotle, the philosopher of stability — of predetermined forms, immutable species, and rigorously demonstrative knowledge. I have not tried to answer this question. To the contrary, my analysis in the final chapter has opened it up as a question. In that chapter I have tried to show how far the 'experiential' or 'phronetic' element in Aristotle's thought might not just be seen as a concession to the contingency of interhuman *praxis* but might also act as a wedge to open up our understanding of human dealings with the material world (in *poiēsis*) — leading to a reevaluation of the role of 'matter' (*hulē*) and of nature (*phusis*), and to a greater emphasis on personal embodiment. I should confess, however, to a certain violence in my treatment of Aristotle in that chapter; and I see the analysis there as more tentative than that in other chapters, as broaching a line of questioning (that may be wrong-headed) rather than as presenting a conclusive judgment.

2. Import for Practices

After this resume of the main themes of the book, the question
arises: What is the upshot of all this for specific practices? The point of
departure for the whole study was a dissatisfaction with a prestigious contemporary model of teaching, and the cause of dissatisfaction was identified early on as the assimilation of *practical* problems to a technical mode
of rationality—something which, it was claimed, is also to be discerned
in other practices, e.g., in psychotherapy, in management approaches, and
in modes of political organization. Perhaps it will be felt, however, that
the exposure of the limits of technical rationality and the exploration of
the contours of practice that we have since undertaken, however illuminating as an essay in philosophical anthropology, have no clear import for
particular practices. It may be contended that every significant practice
or profession circumscribes a specific theater of operations within which
it defines its own goals, procedures, and criteria of success; that in doing
so it legitimately brackets out such *generic* features of experience as historicity and finitude; and that the whole point of particular professions,
indeed, is precisely to limit the sway of these features of experience-as-
such and, by establishing well-defined competencies, to ensure reliable
control of *specific* types or aspects of experience. Moreover, a contemporary
attempt to retrieve Aristotle's 'praxis' may be deemed implausible when
this notion, as concerned with the simply human (*ta anthrōpina*), referred
to the public interaction of citizens who, as a minority served by the
many, were unencumbered by specific tasks, while citizens of a modern
society, by contrast, spend most of their time earning a livelihood in a
specific occupation and, outside this, are increasingly *privatized*. And it
may further be pointed out that Aristotle himself quite happily consigned
specific areas of skill to techne, so that outside the luxury of full-time
devotion to *eudaimonia* (which included contemplative activity, of course,
as an even more valued component than involvement in public affairs)
he had no reservations about technical rationality.

The first of these difficulties is raised on the basis of simply asserting
what is now the status quo in industrialized societies where the attempt
has been made to construe specific tasks as value-neutral and to immunize
them, so to speak, against the human condition. It is just this attempt,
however, that has been in question throughout this book: not the *fact*
of the attempt—for that has always been granted—but whether what it
actually achieves is what it professes to achieve, and whether it doesn't
have a shadow side which it is unable to account for within its own terms.
True, this question has, at various stages, been pitched at a general level,
as in the account of Habermas's critique of technicism in chapter 6, §5.

But it is not that the critique cannot touch specific areas of endeavor, but rather that it is not *confined* to any one area. Moreover, in other places our questioning has in fact focused on a specific area—particularly in the opening three chapters. With respect to the difficulties raised about Aristotle, it may simply be noted that he did *not* sanction any deployment of a techne cut loose from phronesis. We saw his explicit statement that practical intellect (phronesis) governs (*archei*) productive intellect (techne).[4] And phronesis not only supervened on techne *ab extra* (which was more the case when the techne constituted mastery over something exclusively material—as in the example of the carpenter putting his skill at the disposal of either the S.S. or of a needy person)[5] but could also be an intrinsic element in the exercise of the techne itself (in cases where the techne was ineluctably interpersonal as, e.g., in a military commander's display of courage or magnanimity in the conduct of a campaign or, more significantly, in the orator's employment of a rhetoric which—despite its being called a techne—was oriented to successful persuasion only within the context of a concern for the true and the good).[6]

Having made these defensive points, I want to clarify more positively the kind of implications our philosophical reflection has for the conduct of specific practices. I shall rely heavily on Gadamer's clarification of the role of hermeneutics vis-à-vis the practice of interpretation—which, as we have seen,[7] itself draws heavily on Aristotle's understanding of the import of his lectures in practical philosophy for the actual conduct of his hearers. Although the reflection we pursued here is, of course, theoretical, it is nonetheless paradoxical in its effect. For it is a form of theory whose whole import is to vindicate practical knowledge—and thereby to severely curtail the claims of theoretical knowledge on practice. It not only exposes the limitations of the kind of theory that informs the technical approach but it also recognizes the modesty of its own contribution to practice. Its role is not to instruct or dictate to practitioners. It does not offer any countermodel to the technical model. Nor is its argument merely moralistic—preaching how things *ought* to be to a world that is no better disposed to philosophical than it is to religious homiletics. It draws attention not to what ought to be, so much as to what *is* the case anyhow—even though the technicist project does not recognize it and even tries to suppress it. "It is not my intention," Gadamer writes in the Introduction to *Truth and Method*, "to make prescriptions for the sciences or the conduct of life, but to try to correct false thinking about what they *are*." And so he offers his work not as "a methodology of the human sciences, but an attempt to understand what the human sciences truly *are*, beyond their methodological self-consciousness, and what *connects them with the totality of our experience of world*."[8] "My real concern," he says elsewhere, "is philosophic: not what we do or what we ought to do, but what *happens* to us over and above our wanting and doing."[9] And so he presents his hermeneutics as a type of reflection which "enlightens the modern attitude of making, producing and constructing about the *necessary conditions to which it is subject.*"[10] To explain the type of relationship that I envisage between the present work and the conduct of particular practices, I shall offer a brief commentary on these statements of Gadamer's.

As human being we give ourselves to — or find ourselves in — projects through which we shape our environments and our relationships with each other. In the history of this projecting, particularly since the rise of modern science in the seventeenth century, we have moved more and more into a position where, as 'subjects', we confront a world which is ours to objectify and control. And, increasingly, the substance of our human lives has become part of this objectified world over which we exercise mastery. Our lives are resolved into a series of projects, and all of these projects — all "our wanting and doing," our "making, producing and constructing" — occur within this overall project or 'frame' of mastery itself. It is this frame which defines the scope of our ambitions and the meaning of success; our attitudes, our modes of thought, the very questions which are our problems arise already within this framework or else are smoothly, and inexorably, assimilated into it.

The task of philosophy — or, at any rate, of the type of philosophy explored here — has been to avoid being absorbed into this frame and, by maintaining a space for reflection outside it, to articulate its limits and to draw attention to aspects and dimensions of existence which do not appear within the frame but which, nonetheless, continue to give human life its density and even make the frame itself possible. These things, whose presence philosophy must make noticeable (and which were summarized in the previous section), are not noumenal truths whose recognition would suspend or annul our ordinary involvements; they are, rather, "what happens to us" in these involvements, or what is already given in "the totality of our experience of world," prior to our objectifications and prior to any understanding of ourselves as being capable, through our will, of shaping our affairs. They are the "necessary conditions" of human experience, which all our projects at mastery actually build on but which, despite our ambitions, we cannot supplant or co-opt: there will be no project to make them cease to operate or operate only on its terms.

I have been claiming that the features of human experience that the philosophers in this book have brought to our attention cannot be expunged from specific practices. I have not focused on what is specific about any one practice, however, and if these features are a common factor in *all* practices, then how much light do they throw on any of them? In the case of teaching, for instance, which first motivated this study, nothing has been said that a teacher could recognize as properly characteristic of her task—even if the task is conceived only in the broadest terms (as involving an interaction between A and B where A intends to promote the learning or human development of B)—and without reference, then, to particular issues about the teaching of different things to people of different ages and backgrounds, in groups of different sizes, with different degrees of institutional formality, etc. This book enables us to come to grips with the behavioral objectives model of teaching only at the level of general assumptions: not in fact as a model of teaching *as such,* but rather as a model of human interaction. And so, from the point of view of a teacher—as from that of a practitioner in any other single field—can it not still be said that there is a flight from concreteness here, a flight into what might be called 'bad universals'?

Two points can be made in answer to this question. First, the most crucial clarification about teaching occurs at the level at which we decide what kind of interaction it is. A decision at this level has the heaviest consequences not only for how we understand but also how we go about doing it. The concepts of 'technique' and 'practice' may seem like high-level abstractions, but the different orientations that each of them establishes ramify into the most minute details of how a teacher will set about the task. If it is true that teaching is not a process of making which can be judged exclusively on its end-results, and that teaching methods are never merely means but are intrinsically related to some ends—perhaps unintended ones; that the open-endedness and hazard of action haunt what a teacher does; that, no matter how much she strives to remain 'in role,' she unavoidably expresses 'who' she is; that her character, with its fusion of emotion and reason, is always 'on the line'; that she acts within the field of an individual and communal 'effective history'—which is the more effective for operating pre-judgmentally; and that her own greatest effectiveness or 'power' is realized in moments not of manipulation but of inter-*play*—if all this is true then it is true *willy-nilly*. It is not something that happens by default in the case of the careless teacher, which another teacher, however, can obviate by taking the necessary technical steps. And, ironically, a highly technical mode of teaching is not only inescapably exposed to the factors I have mentioned, but is *more* exposed to them than a practical or 'phronetic' mode. For the technicist mode gives the *illusion* of bringing everything under control: it confines the teacher's attention within the technical frame—without informing her that these factors are not now nonexistent but simply unattended to. In the other approach, however, a teacher habitually understands her task as involving these factors, and the reason to which she is committed — i.e., phronesis — is fitted to them.

This brings us to the second point to be made in response to the charge of a flight from concreteness. Phronesis is precisely the kind of reason which, as including practical *nous,* has developed an 'eye' (Aristotle) or a 'nose' (Wittgenstein) for what is salient in concrete situations. The *phronimos* does not, indeed, lack knowledge of universals; a mathematics teacher, for instance, (alongside his thorough understanding of the concepts and relations involved in, e.g., quadratic equations) will have a whole stock of largely unformulated knowledge about the kind of pedagogical aids (with respect to these equations) that, in general, tend to work well, the typical difficulties to be anticipated or pitfalls to be avoided, the sorts of questions and promptings that in the past have tended to work well, etc. As part of this general knowledge, he can even be said to possess 'techniques'— i.e., strategies which, given that at a particular juncture phronesis has isolated a specific problem as needing solution or a particular goal as worthy of pursuit, can be relied on, when certain conditions are fulfilled, to solve the problem or to achieve the goal. The crucial thing about phronesis, however, is its attunement of the universal knowledge and the techniques to the particular occasion, so that they are deployed in relation to "the right person, to the right extent, at the right time, with the right aim, and in the right way . . . [which] is not for every one, nor is it easy."[11] (Here I am implicitly distinguishing techniques, as just defined, from Technique, as a general form of rationality, and allowing that techniques are not excluded *a priori* from a 'practical' style of teaching; the point about them, however, is that they are far from being used all the time in teaching, and when, how, and in what circumstances they are to be used — or, having been tried, are to be amended or abandoned — can be decided not by Technique but only, on the spot, by phronesis.)

Even if the argument here has been conducted on what might be considered difficult philosophical terrain, it is still, then, an argument precisely in defense of the concreteness of a practice such as teaching. A good teacher might find that a work such as this did little, directly, to improve her practice — other than to help her to articulate it better. The value of such articulation, however, is not to be underestimated. For even good teachers can easily be intimidated by the sophistication, apparent power, and high prestige of technicist approaches. Insofar as they do not have the conceptual resources to articulate the nature of their enterprise, they are vulnerable; hardly able to avoid frustration and resentment at what they intuitively recognize as Procrustean advances from technocratic 'educationalists', they may still lack confidence in the integrity or respectability of what they already do well.

What these teachers lack is not phronesis but rather 'practical philosophy'. It is not important that every teacher should be a philosopher. What is important, however, is that in the educational community—which rightly is the *whole* community—a discourse should be available in which the nature of teaching as a practice can be articulated and thereby *defended*. With the help of such a discourse and the arguments which it will nourish, real debate about educative teaching becomes possible. In such a debate, approaches to research in education, for example, or to whatever teacher-training that at present holds the high ground can be strongly challenged. Teachers will be encouraged to see *themselves* much more as researchers—and thus to become members of a profession that reflects on itself with a higher degree of universality and explicitness—rather than being simply *consumers,* and often indeed simply *objects,* of research carried out by experts (the word 'expert' would thus recover something of its original meaning of 'experienced'). And student-teachers will devote more time to practice teaching, and perhaps less to lecture courses in 'educational theory'—adapting Aristotle's view that "it is by doing just acts that the just man is produced, and by doing temperate acts the temperate man; without doing these, no one would have even a prospect of becoming good [although] most people do not do these, but take refuge in theory [*logos*]."

Questioning the role of theory here does not commit me to a narrowly pragmatic conception of teaching (or of any other practice); my deep misgivings about the ascendancy of *technicist* theories of teaching should not be understood to imply that all teaching is good simply if it is non-technical. To the contrary, one thing I can concede to technicism is that it is an understandable response to the morass—the stale routine or sheer chaos—to which teaching can deteriorate when it is not practiced intelligently. The kind of intelligence needed here is not easily acquired; the trouble with technicism, however (as we have seen from our very first chapter on Newman), is that it is an attempt to supplant rather than to develop it. In being initiated into the practice of teaching, student-teachers need not only experience in the classroom but also the right conditions for reflecting on this experience—so that reflectiveness (which we have all the time been clarifying under the name of 'phronesis') can become more and more an abiding attitude or disposition.

The main aim of 'educational studies' should be to contribute to the development of this disposition. I see no reason to be narrow in our conception of what may constitute these studies. Certainly the study of literature or history, physics or mathematics, art or drama, psychology or sociology (without technicist blinkers) could—even for those who will not teach them as school subjects—contribute to this development, and so I lament the growing tendency to regard such a 'liberal' element as dispensable from what are called (with increasing accuracy, I fear) teacher-training programs. What follows much more directly from the whole line of argument of the present work, however, is that an important role should be given in such programs to practicing teachers who are not only *phronimoi* but are also well-equipped to teach apprentice-teachers to become *phronimoi*. For (as no one saw more clearly than Dewey) not all 'experience' is educative; or, in Aristotle's words, "it is from playing the lyre that both good *and bad* lyre-players are produced. And the corresponding statement is true of builders and of all the rest; men will be good or bad builders as a result of building well or badly. For if this were not so there would have been no need of a teacher."[12] A student-teacher will not become proficient *just* by trying his hand in the classroom; left to himself, he may be only reinforcing bad habits. He needs a teacher who will help him to reflect on what he is doing. Such a teacher, though not a theoretician in our modern sense—or in the sense which, as we just saw, Aristotle scorns—will nonetheless be able to evince the *logos* of good practice (i.e., the kind of *context-bound logos* which we met, in relation to the sculptor, when interpreting the phrase "matter is in the logos").[13] And she will have developed those specialized subvirtues of phronesis that Aristotle calls 'understanding' (*sunesis*) and 'sympathetic judgment' (*gnōmē*):[14] her own experience and reflection will have ripened into a special gift for understanding the difficulties that another (in this case the aspirant teacher) may experience in the same field and for offering him counsel that will help him to find his feet. (A large element in counseling, as we now know—and, given the kind of forbearance and friendship that are implicit in *gnōmē*, have no reason to suppose that Aristotle did not know—consists in listening and in helping the other to identify and articulate the problem.) Not all teachers, of course, will have these qualities, and it is important to recognize that when one who does have them engages with an 'apprentice', what goes on between them will be very different from the drilling and slavish imitation that obtained in the old (pre-technicist) 'monitorial' system.

In touching on educational matters here I have not endeavored to do justice to them or to spell out the full implications of this study for them. (I have said nothing, for instance, about curriculum development, or assessment and evaluation, both of which tend at present to be strait-jacketed by technicist assumptions. And, a more serious omission, in focusing on the teacher, I have said nothing about how education might be conducted if we took seriously the unity of experience—in knowledge, expression, and action—of the *pupil* and saw the educative task as one of helping him not only to acquire skills but, more importantly, to become a *phronimos*.) I have intended only to show that there are such implica-

tions and to do so as an *illustration* of what is also the case, and could
be demonstrated, with respect to other practices. There is work to be done
in mediating between the kind of philosophy that is espoused here and
what goes on in these different practices, and in the case of education,
certainly, this work has been under way, and even gathering momentum,
over the past decade.[15] My own priority here, however, has been with practical philosophy—i.e., with the articulation of modes of knowledge, action, and experience that are central to every important practice. In the
present section I have concentrated on this philosophy *as practical*, suggesting that such articulation is essential to the defense of these practices,
that without it they are in great danger not only of losing their integrity
but even of not recognizing that they have lost it. I shall conclude, however, by considering some problems that it must face *as philosophy*.

3. Bearings in Philosophy

In *Two Theories of Morality*, at the point in his discussion where
he makes the transition from Aristotle's theory to Spinoza's, Stuart Hampshire identifies what he sees as the crucial stumbling block to any contemporary espousal of Aristotelian ethics. Having acknowledged with respect
to Aristotle's ethical theory that "there is no comparably clear and comprehensive theory superior to his in the power to explain the range of our
moral intuitions," he nonetheless concludes that because of what he calls
"the barrier of modernity," it must be considered "incorrigibly incomplete."
At this barrier, we cannot help noticing a "missing element" in Aristotle's
moral universe, namely, the specifically modern notion of *freedom*. Because this notion is missing, for Aristotle, "nature and freedom are not
in opposition. In a reasonably ordered social environment a character and
moral temperament will develop naturally by habituation." In contrast
to this harmonious dispensation, which is characterized by Hampshire as
"pre-lapsarian"—in that it does not involve "some imagined redemption
or salvation following upon a fallen state, a state of bondage"—the modern position, with respect both to "ethics as a philosophical inquiry" and
to "first-order moral anxieties," is altogether more vexed. For, to the modern consciousness, nature "is entirely uniform in the regular correlations
of causes and effects"; and if this is so, if natural phenomena, "including
changes within the souls of men," make up a field of determinism, then
"there is a philosophical problem surrounding the idea of a morally responsible agent who has his own character to make and who is free to
choose between good and evil; for it seems that his character directly and
his choices indirectly must be the effects of innate and environmental con-

ditions combined and that he cannot ultimately be responsible for them even though he ought to be responsible for them."[16]

Hampshire is pointing out here, although he does not put it in these terms, that modern ethics has to face a challenge which Aristotle's ethics never had to face: that of modern science. For Aristotle, science was limited to the necessary and immutable, so that the changeable world of human affairs lay outside its ken. Phronesis, unchallenged by science, was then left to bring order and coherence into this world of affairs. Modern science, on the other hand, with the resourcefulness of its methods for isolating and correlating variables in the phenomenal field, has shown itself ever more capable of explaining human behavior and social organization — and thereby taking the ground from under the older tradition of reflection about human affairs. This is precisely the technicist project that we have become familiar with throughout this work. The threat that it poses to ethics is, at the limit, the suppression of the ethical sphere altogether.

In terms of Hampshire's characterization of a distinctively modern opposition between nature and freedom, technicism may be viewed as the project of resolving this opposition by absolutizing nature and thereby abolishing freedom. And it is unsurprising, then, if modern ethical thought, with the need to vindicate freedom, has turned to a critique of nature, at least insofar as this concept is understood as having any reference to human life and thought. This critique has taken various forms. In analytic philosophy it has appeared — in a characteristically 'logical' form — in a sustained attack on the 'naturalistic fallacy'. On the Continent, it has had a more 'metaphysical' turn, in the idea, for example, that 'man is a weakness at the heart of nature' (Sartre), and the ethics of pathos or of defiance that have followed from this idea. Perhaps more significant than either of these forms has been that philosophy of history which, through a self-conscious anticipation of human evolution, has put modern thought in a far more distanced relation with nature than Aristotle could have envisaged. For the latter, nature set limits within which human striving took place; the elements in relation to which the cultivation of a good life (*eu zēn*) and of ethical excellence (*kuria aretē*) took place were stable and not ultimately within the power of human beings to change. Modern philosophy of history, on the other hand, sets itself in opposition precisely to 'nature', and exposes the latter — or at any rate *human* nature — as itself a historical determination. It is interested in limits not because they provide a stable framework, but, on the contrary, because they indicate what is to be overcome or 'sublated' if humankind is to progress to the next stage of its historical development. Historical consciousness, then, is informed by the spirit of criticism in relation to limits; it tries to discern in them the relations of power or constraint that hold back further stages of human emancipation.

Against the background of this philosophy of history—and given the technicist prohibition on ethical questions—*criticism* became the characteristic style of moral/political reflection. And historical materialism and psychoanalysis—or more potently, a combination of the two—might be said to have become the home to which the most serious ethical/political concern migrated. Both Marx and Freud went to some lengths, in their own writings, to understand human beings as part of nature; in doing so they saw themselves as scientists and (motivated, respectively, by a disdain for 'bourgeois ideology' and a concern for 'analytic neutrality') strongly disclaimed any substantive moral commitments. But despite their compromises with a scientistic *Weltanschauung*, both of them projected in their writings (albeit, in Freud's case, with great sobriety) "some imagined redemption or salvation following upon a fallen state, a state of bondage." Both of them provided theoretical bases for practices that would enable human beings to claim for themselves the lost humanity which no merely empirical science could have told them they had lost; and in both cases these practices can be shown—on careful reconstruction and, it may be, against the *verba ipsa* of their founders—to be at variance with the techniques of modern science. In this sense both of them were moralists—indeed, I am suggesting, the most advanced moralists of modernity: they held up a picture of how society and the individual ought to be and act. But their pictures were like photographic negatives, in that they highlighted what remains dark in the conventional pictures, namely, the significance and value of exploited labor and repressed desire. Both images emerge only through criticism of the conventionally accepted pictures. They do not represent *humanity* as a state, as the actualization of certain preferred dispositions. Instead, they propose a process of *humanization* which is in both cases a struggle against various forms of dehumanization which must be understood and surpassed. Marx did indeed envisage a real ending to 'prehistory', and therefore a *terminus* to revolutionary struggle; but he was deliberately slow to anticipate what the new person of truly human history would be like. And even if Freud had a surer picture of the mature person, he did not underestimate the element of struggle; analysis remains, in principle and preferably in practice too, interminable.

From the viewpoint of any thinking that has come through this mill of modern philosophy, the complicity of phronesis with an established way of life must rob it of the detachment with which to criticize this—or any other—way of life. On this side of modern critique the defining characteristic of reason is its very agility in folding itself back from all substantive commitments, its ability to maintain a posture of unrelenting suspicion. The rootedness, then, of phronesis, i.e., the fact that it is an intellectual virtue only because it is the intelligence of a favored set of moral virtues within an established political system, must appear as simply the token of its incorrigible complacency. "To an Oxford man . . . the Nicomachean Ethics has become, mentally speaking, bone of his bone and flesh of his flesh";[17] but is that not so only because Aristotle's ethics of the mean serves as a convenient rationalization of upper-middle-class life? The *phronimos,* who has no sense of a broken world, looks suspiciously like the English gentleman. And, transferred to a different cultural milieu, this same charge has been renewed recently in Germany, where neo-Aristotelianism has been linked with neo-conservatism and what has been called 'the ideology of phronesis' has been seen as a front for elitism and antidemocratic nostalgia.[18]

What I have just sketched, taking off from Hampshire's conception of the antinomy between nature and freedom, has been one 'narrative' of modern philosophy; and we have seen the problem it creates for Aristotle: his conception of the *voluntary agent*[19] falls too far short of the modern conception of the *free subject.* There is another narrative, however, more particularly of twentieth-century philosophy, which may be sketched. This second narrative also involves a contesting of the imperialist claims of technical reason.[20] The movement that is to be discerned in it, however, not only takes on technicism, but also rejects the idea of the modern subject and the whole Cartesian framework which supports it—Cartesianism being understood not just as an epistemology but as an anthropology, a whole vision of the nature of the human person.

Now the retrieval of phronesis which has been undertaken in the present work might be seen as part of this second broad movement in philosophy. What this movement represents is philosophy's *kenosis*—its divesting itself of godlike notions and coming to accept that it cannot have and therefore must no longer aspire to a god's-eye view of the human condition. And this movement away from detachment, sovereignty, and imperturbability has at the same time been a movement into and a taking upon itself the burdens of finitude, contingency, situatedness. In subverting the Cartesian subject, it has been reincarnating the real person in the world of history and language, action and involvement with other people —and, of course, in his/her own affective and bodily being.

Given that Cartesianism was *par excellence* an epistemology, i.e, a defense of knowledge, the crisis that must be faced by its deconstructors manifests itself as a problem about knowledge. Now that the self-enclosed certainty of the *res cogitans*—and all its modern successors—has been discarded, the specter that haunts the new philosophical landscape is that of skepticism or relativism. In the particular strand of philosophy that the present work has tried to appropriate this problem must be met by phronesis. The question is: can phronesis lay this specter or, in folding itself so closely into the texture of the *lebenswelt,* has it forfeited any basis on which it could make claims to objectivity and truth?

These questions — the one about freedom or the possibility of critical distance as the basis of an emancipatory project and the one about knowledge or normative foundations — are closely related. Both of them are posed from the perspective of modernity and come together, in fact, in the work of the philosopher whom I have cast as the most tenacious defender of modernity, Jürgen Habermas. In Habermas's view, it is because phronesis lacks the normative basis that would support the universalism of his own cognitivist or 'discourse ethics' that it so easily falls in as an apologist for the status quo; having no rational basis of its own, it is available as an ideological cloak for positions whose real basis is *power.* Now it is a feature of Habermas's philosophy that he has wanted both to defend the project of freedom and emancipation set out in my first narrative *and* at the same time (more pronouncedly in his later work) to appropriate critically much of the movement that has been depicted in the second narrative (especially the shift from a subjectivist to an intersubjectivist frame). This latter appropriation has been critical in that its purpose has been precisely to help to 'reconstruct' the Enlightenment project — all the better to defend it — and that it has also involved a very trenchant rejection of the two movements within the second narrative which have prospered most conspicuously in recent years (and to an extent that could scarcely have been predicted only a little over a decade ago when Hampshire was conceding the undisputed high ground to modernity), namely, 'neo-Aristotelianism' and 'post-modernism'.

The broad context I have just sketched, within which the plausibility of a retrieval of phronesis may be most critically evaluated, is the scene of lively debate in contemporary moral and political philosophy.[21] In this book I have been exploring the tradition of phronesis from the inside, attempting to *understand* it sympathetically, and to *disclose* it in a way that might make it convincing; but I have not formally been concerned with *justifying* it. The current debate is about whether phronesis deserves to be retrieved, whether the type of rationality that it embodies is viable in today's world; my own task, however, has been the more modest one of clarifying what phronesis is. This task, of course, is not irrelevant to the debate and might indeed be considered a prerequisite to it: If phronesis is to be dismissed, then one ought to be very sure that the conception of it that has been found wanting is a fair and adequate one. My effort here has been to furnish such a conception. One would scarcely commit oneself to this labor, of course, unless one felt that phronesis had much to offer; and certainly this feeling has given a strongly persuasive tone to what I have written. It is already a sign of the vigor of phronesis that it is so much at the center of current debate, and the fact that its opponents impute an incurable dogmatism to it makes it all the more incumbent on its defenders to participate in this debate with genuine openness. The Epilogue to the present study is not the place for full-scale participation in it. But having already adopted the offensive strategy of exposing the difficulties inherent in Habermas's position (see the final section of chapter 7), I want to conclude by acknowledging that his questions do indeed raise difficulties about phronesis which my presentation of it has not, as such, addressed. And I want to point out summarily the lines along which these difficulties might be met.

If phronesis has been appropriated as a slogan of 'neo-conservative' ideology, I take this to be an abuse from which it needs to be rescued rather than evidence of anything intrinsic to it. To be sure, 'phronesis' can be mystified so that it comes to connote a higher faculty of judgment which cannot and need not account for itself, a 'flair' which can be possessed only by the cultivated few, a 'good taste' that goes with 'good breeding'. But such an esoteric phronesis, with its aristocratic and authoritarian implications, is not the one that has been expounded in these pages. To the contrary, what we have seen supports an argument for participative democracy. All along we have seen that with respect to human affairs there are no experts: no one has a privileged standpoint from which he or she can hand down judgments to which others can only defer. This does not mean, of course, that everyone's judgment on a particular issue at a particular time is equally true—for this would only mean that none of them was true and that truth itself, indeed, was a nonsense. Aristotle did not think that everyone was a *phronimos,* nor had he any hesitation in regarding certain outstanding individuals as exemplary embodiments of it—for example, Pericles in the sphere of politics.[22] The important point, however, was that praxis, as concerned with *ta anthrōpina,* was for every citizen; one could realize one's humanity only through *eupraxia,* and since for this one required phronesis every citizen, without exemption, had the task of becoming a *phronimos* with respect both to personal and to political matters (the two, of course, being interdependent). So far from its being the case, then, that phronesis has antidemocratic leanings, a healthy democracy depends on its wide cultivation as a vernacular virtue among the citizenry. As a mode of political organization democracy has, deeper than its formal procedures, certain ethical requirements. It is when these are not met that there is no defense against tyranny. And this (as Part 1 made quite clear) is all the more acutely the case today when, in addition to the despotisms that were common in Aristotle's time, we have to cope with the anonymous and deceptively benign tyranny that subjects what properly are domains of praxis to technical imperatives.

This defense of its democratic credentials, I need hardly say, rests on a belief that 'phronesis' neither depends on nor contributes to Aristotle's reasons for legitimating slavery and thus severely restricting the extension of citizenship. And while separating phronesis from this tenet of Aristotle's political philosophy, I want also to distance it from the 'neo-Aristotelianism' which combines a strong animus against modernity with an attempted restoration of Aristotle's doctrine almost as a *depositum fidei.* This kind of canonical Aristotelianism easily succumbs to pessimistic 'culture criticism' and reactionary and elitist politics. And it may indeed be read into the work of even so deeply historical and fallibilist a thinker as Alasdair MacIntyre (who is prepared to jettison what he calls Aristotle's "metaphysical biology" and who, having been through the mill of modern philosophy, is more than able, rather than simply inveighing against the latter from the vantage point of a *philosophia perennis,* to enter into the most vigorous dialectics with it). From the somber suggestion at the close of *After Virtue* that, the barbarians now being inside the gates and in power, a good life may be possible only in small semimonastic communities, as from the "disquieting suggestion" in the opening chapter that there is "grave disorder" in the moral usage of "the actual world which we inhabit," it is hard to see how the book's Aristotelianism can be a reconstruction of anything in this world — and not an external, extremely unsympathetic judgment on it.

While I resist MacIntyre's "drastic conclusion", there are two features of his argument in *After Virtue* which I do not disavow. The first is his identification of Nietzsche as crucial adversary of Aristotle.[23] Nietzsche has not figured in the present work, but I believe what is presented here is an alternative to, and in competition with, the various brands of postmodernism which, under Nietzsche's inspiration, flourish in contemporary philosophy, for example, in the works of Foucault, Derrida, Rorty, and Lyotard. Two metaphors for the life of practice have recurred throughout my argument, one that of the *sea* through which, like a sailor, the speaker and agent must navigate his or her passage, and the other (which comes from Wittgenstein, and gives this work its title) that of the *rough ground* to which we must always return. The two metaphors are different, but each of them hits at something essential in the practical life: one, a need for flexibility and improvisation, the other a need for rootedness and (in Clifford Geertz's term) "thickness." The contrast that is implicit in both metaphors is with *ice,* and it is by reference to this image that I can characterize the two things I have sought to avoid. Looked at from the sea, the ice is that of technicism, which fixes everything into crystalline purity and thereby freezes all movement. But, looked at from the land, the ice is that of post-modernism, which allows one not indeed to walk but to skate and to perform the most dazzling pirouettes. Post-modernist thinkers are glad to have unburdened reason of the heavy responsibility that had been assumed by the classical tradition of modern thought, with its universalist and emancipatory aspirations. And they embrace 'dispossession' as the post-modern mode of existence. They do so not only by way of deconstructing the Cartesian subject but, more radically, as a protest against 'logocentrism' (Derrida) or against "the massive and repressive order of Aristotle."[24] As dispossessed, one must have "the strength to forget the past" (Nietzsche), seek nothing more stable than the "temporary contract," and find meaning only in "the quest for paralogy" (Lyotard).[25]

At the end of the previous chapter I *linked* my reconstruction of the "order of Aristotle" to post-modernism and I have since located within the same narrative of contemporary philosophy both this post-modernist discourse and the whole line of reflection traced in this book around the concept of phronesis. There are, I believe, points of affinity between the two of them (e.g., language is a major preoccupation in both, and Gadamer's emphasis on the playfulness, 'eventuality', and inexhaustibility of language finds strong echoes in Lyotard).[26] The dedication of post-modernist thought to *novatio,* however, creates a kind of vertigo. And its shortcomings can be well illustrated, I believe, by reference to the *second* feature in MacIntyre's argument which I want to preserve, namely, his emphasis on *practices.* In the previous section I have stressed the way in which, with the help of a range of Aristotelian concepts, one can formulate the capacity for appropriate responses to particular situations which is essential to good performance in any practice. However, the Aristotelian perspective also alerts us to the fact that the good practitioner has been formed by a history of participation in the practice itself. His or her experience of serving the end or *telos* of the practice — and recurrently trying to discover what this concretely requires — has laid down certain dispositions (*hexeis*) of character which, through discipline and direction, enable and energize. A practice is not just a surface on which one can display instant virtuosity. It grounds one in a tradition that has been formed through an elaborate development and that exists at any juncture only in the dispositions (slowly and perhaps painfully acquired) of its recognized practitioners. The question may of course be asked whether there *are* any such practices in the contemporary world, whether the wholesale encroachments of Technique have not obliterated them — and whether this is not the whole point of MacIntyre's recipe of withdrawal, as well as of the post-modern story of dispossession.

I have argued in the previous section that technicism cannot finally obliterate the practical texture of our engagements: that even a putatively self-enclosed and agent-proof mode of interaction will be infiltrated by the kind of factors mentioned in the previous section, (p. 367). Such a quasi-transcendental argument, however, can hardly disguise the fact that if the practical can now survive only as a kind of guerrilla presence on the margins of an entrenched Technique, then this is a type of practice which neither fits Aristotle's account nor can be looked to as a reliable matrix for ethical formation. Still, despite all the huge pressures toward functionalism and fragmentation, I want to affirm what we have already seen affirmed by both Gadamer and Habermas (against the apocalyptic diagnoses of Heidegger and Adorno), i.e., the stubborn resistance of practical forms of life.[27] In the end this is a matter less of philosophical argument than of one's basic sense of the world. Education, the area of my own special concern, has been as exposed as any other social activity to functionalist imperatives. The school system has become the major mechanism for carrying out social selection and accreditation, and at the same time, as sociological evidence shows, it tends overwhelmingly to confirm — being itself powerless to offset — deep inequalities that already exist. It is thus tightly enmeshed in the 'steering media' of money and power. And yet, in my experience very many teachers (not to speak of parents), albeit that their engagement with young people is stretched out on a linear timetable and subjected to standardized examinations, still manage to create a humane space for their pupils' learning. They do so because they have not lost the sense that practice has the sort of open texture that I have described and because they bring to it (in addition to competence in their subject matter) the variations it calls for of good temper, friendliness, love of truth, and ready-wittedness,[28] as well as of the larger virtues of courage and justice.[29] Teachers can continue to bring these qualities to their teaching only if there is a shared ethos among their colleagues which prizes and sustains them. Such an ethos is at the heart of what I have been calling a practice, and I am claiming that, against all the odds, there are schools and staffrooms in which it is still recognizable (and again I am only taking teaching as my most familiar example).

If individual teachers depend on the ethos of a school, it is no less true that the latter is itself highly vulnerable to the overall ethos of a society, expressed in and conditioned by the ways it organizes institutions, allocates resources, disposes of power and wealth. Although practices are devoted (as MacIntyre stresses) to goods "internal" to themselves, it is not sensible — or Aristotelian — to see them as closed spheres, the integrity of which can be ensured by a naive moralism. To the contrary, as I have stressed in Part 1 (and here no one was more helpful than Habermas), the difficulties encountered by different practices are quite generalized: they have assumed "the proportions of a life form, of the 'historical totality' of a life-world." An adequate response to them calls for a phronesis which not only is attuned to the ends of particular practices but also has a wider sense of the interdependency of these ends with other ends and policies within the overall society. At this level, phronesis must be capable (beyond anything Aristotle could have envisaged when he said that practical reason must rule productive reason) not only of setting limits to techne but also of appropriating and directing the potential of techne itself. It has the task (in Gadamer's words) "of integrating the monologic of the sciences into the communicative consciousness [which] includes the task of exercising practical, social and political reasonableness." Here, given the complexity of modern conditions of life, phronesis reaches its extreme outer limits—a point which Habermas, who perhaps more than any other philosopher does not evade the complexity, is in a position to make.

While acknowledging the need for and the difficulty of this superordinate, political phronesis, I am led by the prejudice of my own point of departure in this book to a different though complementary emphasis. Concern for the wider issues and the larger political good does not cancel out more specific practices nor in the dialectic of our actual lives can engagement in the latter be deferred until more comprehensive solutions are available. To concentrate on this point (without denying the truth of its converse) does not entail a conservative acquiescence in the perpetuation of current injustices or the smooth running of existing institutions. It does entail, however, finding *some* good in current practices—however fragile and in need of transformation. In an important essay to which I have already referred, Herbert Schnädelbach holds it against contemporary Aristotelians that their "basic premise is that *the Good is already in the world*" (so that "there is no need to introduce it from some abstract and ideal sphere").[30] I have indeed been affirming this—even though the enormous and systematic evil in the world would be denied only by a fool or a knave. The good exists (as several traditions tell us) in hidden places, in lives of unrecorded heroism. Insofar as it gains a reliably public space, however, it does so through specific practices in which people cooperate toward shared ends, the achievement of which helps to form their characters but which they themselves must continue to redefine. That these practices are hugely threatened is not in doubt. Where are the resources to defend them?

The endless capacity to 'deconstruct' or to invent new moves that is envisaged by post-modernism demands of the individual an extraordinary masterfulness and, while this may make sense in the aesthetic field, I do not see how it could be incorporated into practices generally—if indeed its whole point is not to subvert all such practices as I have been speaking of. This is one kind of decenteredness which contemporary philosophy seems to offer: resignation to the corruption of established solidarities, and reliance on self-generating and self-justifying inventiveness to produce for each moment something better — or, nihilistically, just to *produce.*

The other kind of decenteredness invites one away from this vortex into an ideal consensus-seeking community. If one forfeits identity here it is in order to regain it at a higher level of universalization, in a commitment to maxims that will have demonstrated their worthiness to be accepted by anyone who could be involved in the situation. I have already made clear my difficulty with this. One's ability to discern the good (or the 'right', if we must accept the restrictiveness of 'deontological' ethics) at the level of the ideal community will be severely conditioned by the ability that one has acquired in an actual community. "Each state of character has its own ideas of the noble and pleasant," Aristotle says, so that "argument and teaching, we may suspect, are not powerful with all men." The point here, once again, is not to reject reason but to recognize a *specific type* of reason. Much in the conduct of practical affairs depends on singular judgments which cannot be derived from, and answer to epistemic conditions different from those of, idealized discourse. A person's capacity for judgments that inform practice is deeply embedded in the history of his or her engagement in that specific domain of practice — even when these judgments are creative ones that disclose the ends of the practice in a new light. From the viewpoint of the second kind of decenteredness, it follows from this unavoidable contextuality that 'phronesis', not being "a concept of practical reason that meets the criteria of procedural rationality," must "dissolve into flat common sense."[31] Phronesis does indeed depend on a common sense that has built up around particular practices. And this common sense can indeed go flat. What I have been trying to show throughout this study, however, is that phronesis is precisely the leaven that keeps this from happening.

No philosophy can ensure that this leaven will continue to act in the substance of shared ways of life. By the same token, however, the resilience of phronesis can be missed by a philosophy whose reserve about the *lebenswelt* is the obverse of its inflated claims for reason — just as it can also be missed by a philosophy which is anxious to overthrow the tradition of reason altogether. The finitude, i.e., the limitedness, of human existence — and therefore of human reason — has been a main theme of all the philosophers who have been met in this book. An acknowledgment of finitude, however, is not at all a commitment to pessimism. As developed here, it is rather an espousal of phronesis as the kind of reasonableness that is fitted to our finite mode of being; and it puts no *a priori* restrictions on just how resourceful this finite human reason may,

in different situations and on different occasions, show itself to be. To be
sure, 'practical philosophy' is no more capable than any other kind of philosophy of determining how events will fall out or how successful our historical undertakings will be. It does us no small service, however, when
it exposes the one-sided and indeed illusory nature of what a technicist
culture counts as 'success', and when it brings to our attention certain conditions which do not cease to be constitutive of our human mode of being
even when much energy is expended in denying them. If we are persuaded
by the philosophers who have developed the central argument of this book,
we are directed to a particular mode of engagement in our actual communities; we are made clear-eyed about what threatens the integrity of
the practices that are at the heart of these communities; and at the same
time we are given reason to hope that these practical ways of life have
the resources continually to reassert themselves.

Notes

Introduction

1. W. J. Popham, "Objectives and Instruction," in *Instructional Objectives*, American Educational Research Association Monograph Series on Curriculum Evaluation (Chicago: Rand McNally, 1969), pp. 32–33.

2. For fuller development of these points, and documentation of them in the relevant literature, see J. Dunne, "Teaching and the Limits of Technique: An Analysis of the Behavioural Objectives Model," in *Irish Journal of Education* 22 (1988): 69–91.

3. B. S. Bloom, T. Hastings, G. Medaus et al., *Handbook of Summative and Formative Evaluation* (New York: McGraw Hill, 1971), p. 33.

4. R. E. Mager, *Preparing Instructional Objectives*, rev. 2nd ed. (Belmont, Calif.: David S. Lake, 1975), p. 68.

5. Popham, p. 38, and B. S. Bloom, ed., *Taxonomy of Educational Objectives*, Handbook 1: *Cognitive Domain* (London: Longmans, 1979), pp. 6–7.

6. Rüdiger Bubner, *Modern German Philosophy* (Cambridge: Cambridge University Press, 1981), p. 204.

7. Given that in philosophical parlance the word *'modern'* is often taken to refer to a seventeenth- and eighteenth-century affair — viz., the working out of the classic epistemological discussion from Descartes to Kant — and that it has also become a highly charged term in the polemics of 'post-modernist' writers, its use here is less than happy. However, I have found no better term to designate a group of thinkers which includes one from the nineteenth alongside four from the present century.

8. Bernard Williams, *Ethics and the Limits of Philosophy* (London: Collins, Fontana Press, 1985), p. vi. In fact the theme of this book is quite close to that of the present study, and Williams's attitude to the characteristic preoccupations of German philosophy is more eirenic than that of most 'analytic' philosophers.

9. See, e.g., the excellent essays in *On Metaphor*, ed. Sheldon Sacks (Chicago: University of Chicago Press, 1978).

10. *Republic* 435a.

11. Rorty, *Philosophy and the Mirror of Nature*, (Oxford: Blackwell, 1980), p. 318.

12. Ibid., p. 372.

13. *Nicomachean Ethics* (hereafter *E.N.*) 1.6.

14. *Seventh Letter* 344.b.

15. See *Republic* 1; *Gorgias* 481ff.

16. See J. Taminiaux, "Merleau-Ponty: From Dialectic to Hyperdialectic," p. 172

383

in *Dialectic and Difference: Finitude in Modern Thought*, ed. and trans. R. Crease
and J. T. Decker (Atlantic Highlands, N.J.: Humanities Press, 1985).

17. I shall mention two conspicuous examples. The first—since I was no more inclined to exclude than to include 'neo-Aristotelians'—is Adasdair MacIntyre. One of
the "characters so essential to the dramatic scripts of modernity," whom he trenchantly
exposes, is "the expert who matches means to ends in an evaluatively neutral way."
Such an expert (who has "no genuine counterpart in Aristotle's scheme or indeed in
the classical tradition at all"—which always insisted on the inseparability of excellences
of intelligence from those of character) acts out "the peculiar managerial fiction embodied in the claim to possess systematic effectiveness in controlling certain aspects
of social reality." This is a *fiction* quite simply because—given "the particular and peculiar ways in which [in human life] predictability and unpredictability interlock"—"the
kind of knowledge which would be required to sustain it [i.e., the claim] does not
exist." And, this being the case, what we have in our business organizations (and,
I should add, to the degree that the kind of thinking manifested in the behavioral
objectives model comes to prevail, in our schools) is "not scientifically managed social
control, but a skilful dramatic imitation of such control. It is histrionic success which
gives power and authority to our culture. The most effective bureaucrat is the best
actor" (MacIntyre's writing this coincided with Reagan's becoming President) (*After
Virtue* [London: Duckworth; Notre Dame, Ind.: University of Notre Dame Press,
1982]), pp. 71, 98, 72, 102).

The second, less combative, philosopher whom I have in mind as a potential partner in the conversation (and whom my friend John Doyle has well described, I believe,
as "the English Gadamer") is Michael Oakeshott. Oakeshott has written the classic
essay on conversation as the true home of the human mind and has also very explicitly
attacked rationalism (which he traces back to the *Discourse on Method* and the *Regulae* of Descartes as well as to the *Novum Organon* of Bacon and shows to have been
very effectively criticized, early in its career, by Pascal) by insisting on a distinction
(whose Aristotelian provenance, however, he does not advert to) between technical
and practical types of knowledge. "The Rationalist," he writes, "holds that the only
element of *knowledge* involved in any human activity is technical knowledge, and
that . . . practical knowledge is really only a sort of nescience which would be negli-
gible if it were not positively mischievous. The sovereignty of 'reason', for the Rationalist, means the sovereignty of technique." (See "The Voice of Poetry in the Conversation of Mankind," esp. pp. 197–204, and the title essay, esp. pp. 7–20, in *Rationalism
in Politics and Other Essays* [London: Methuen, 1962].)

1. J. H. Newman's Appeal to Phronesis in *A Grammar of Assent*

1. See his seven letters to the *Times* (republished as "The Tamworth Reading Room"
in *Discussions and Arguments on Various Subjects* [London: Longman and Green,
1907]) in response to a speech on education by Sir Robert Peel, and *A Letter Addressed to His Grace the Duke of Norfolk on the Occasion of Mr. Gladstone's Recent
Expostulation* (London: Pickering, 1875) in response to some remarks of Gladstone's
on the baleful political influence of current Roman Catholic teaching in Gladstone's

pamphlet, *The Vatican Decrees in their Bearing on Civil Allegiance: A Political Expostulation* (London: John Murray, 1874–75).

2. J. H. Walgrave, O.P., *Newman the Theologian* (London, 1960; English translation of *Newman, Le Developpement du Dogme,* Paris, 1957), p. 19. See also Edward J. Sillem, *John H. Newman, the Philosophical Notebooks,* Vol. 1: *General Introduction to the Study of Newman's Philosophy* (Louvain: Nauwelaerts, 1969), ch. 3, §1, on "His Intellectual Isolation." Newman's thought, of course, was not without its sources, and for a thorough account of them see ibid., ch. 4 (and also John Coulson, *Newman and the Common Tradition* [Oxford: Clarendon Press, 1970], ch. 5 of which is especially interesting on the shared ground between Newman and Coleridge). It is significant, however, that in his account Sillem is more often drawing attention to Newman's reactions against, or reservations about, his important forebears rather than to what he takes positively from them (see, e.g., his remarks on Whately, Newman's teacher at Oxford, and on Bacon, Locke, and Mill). Apart from Aristotle (the Aristotle of the *Ethics* rather than of the *Organon*) the authors to whom Newman was most indebted in a positive sense were the early Church Fathers, especially Clement and Origen, and Bishop Joseph Butler, whose classic work *The Analogy of Religion* (1736) profoundly influenced him. Interestingly, he gave a wide berth to German philosophy. He read carefully H. M. Chalybaus's *Historical Development of Speculative Philosophy from Kant to Hegel* (translated by A. Edersheim, with an Introduction by Sir William Hamilton, Edinburgh, 1853) but never read any of the original works. His sense of German philosophy—and the basis of his indifference to it—seems to be well summed up in the characteristic comment which he wrote in his copy of Chalybaus, apropos the attempt to build a system founded ultimately on one principle: "is not that an assumption that it must be *one?* Aristotle speaks of *archai*" (quoted in Sillem, p. 228).

3. 'Temporal distance' is an important concept in the hermeneutics of Gadamer; see below, ch. 4, §4. In saying that Newman was isolated in his own time, I do not mean that he was aloof from its preoccupations and problems, or that he saw himself writing *sub specie aeternitatis*. To the contrary, few thinkers in nineteenth-century England had as keen a sense of the historicity of thought—his own included—as Newman (his *Essay on the Development of Christian Doctrine* [1845; edited with Introduction by J. M. Cameron, Harmondsworth: Penguin, 1974] was quite seminal in introducing historical consciousness to the study of Christian theology, and R. G. Collingwood had a point when, apropos the great ripening of this consciousness in the nineteenth century, he put Newman's contribution in theology on all fours with Darwin's contribution in biology, Hegel's in philosophy, and Marx's in economics [*Speculum Mentis,* p. 53]). "We are ourselves necessary parts of the existing system, out of which we have individually grown into being, into our actual position in society. Depending therefore on the times as a condition of existence, in wishing for other times we are, in fact, wishing we had never been born. Moreover it is ungrateful to a state of society, from which we daily enjoy so many benefits, to rail against it." Thus Newman expresses his belongingness to his own time. But he immediately goes on: "Yet there is nothing unbecoming, unmeaning, or ungrateful in pointing out its faults and wishing them away." It was his role as critic of contemporary orthodoxy that set

Newman apart in his own time, and what I shall be trying to show is that there is
not a little truth, as applied to himself, in his remark: "if there is anything at once
new and good, years must elapse, the writer must be long dead, before it is acknowledged and received."

4. See especially ch. 3, §1 and §3, and ch. 6, §5.

5. Our main text, *An Essay in Aid of A Grammar of Assent* (London 1870; new
Oxford edition, edited by I. T. Ker, Oxford: Clarendon Press, 1985; all page references
will be this edition, hereafter *G.A.*) is divided into two parts, each of five chapters;
and only one chapter in each part (chs. 5 and 10) is devoted—by way of applying
the general argument of the other chapters—to specifically religious matters.

6. Part of what Newman hoped to show was that the faith of a simple, unlettered
person has just as good grounds to be considered reasonable as that of a learned theologian. In another context Alasdair MacIntyre has recently written: "In place of the
hierarchical relationship of intellectuals to plain persons we might entertain the hope
of developing a form of social conversation in which professors are as likely to learn
from farmers or coalminers as *vice versa*" ("Moral Arguments and Social Contexts:
A Response to Rorty," in *Hermeneutics and Praxis,* ed. Robert Hollinger [Notre Dame,
Ind.: University of Notre Dame Press, 1985]). This hope had been expressed by Richard Rorty, but in fact MacIntyre believes that it can be realized only given "the existence of a certain type of tradition-bearing community" (a type which is certainly not
coincident with civil society in the age of bourgeois liberalism, and which, MacIntyre
seems to suggest, can exist in such a society, if at all, only in small, semimonastic enclaves). Now for Newman the church was, or ought to be, just such a community, and
that its teachers and theologians could have something to learn from the ordinary
faithful was something which he argued in *On Consulting the Faithful in Matters of
Doctrine* (1859; republished, edited and with an Introduction by John Coulson, London: Collins, 1961) a work which greatly raised the hackles of the then ecclesiastical
authorities but which can be seen in retrospect to have prepared the way for the Second Vatican Council's Constitution on the Church, *Lumen Gentium.* It is interesting,
in the light of what we shall be seeing of Newman's appropriation of the notion of
phronesis, that one of the five ways in which, on his account, the *sensus fidelium* can
be seen as "tradition-bearing" is through "a sort of instinct or *phronema*" (see ibid.,
pp. 73–74).

7. "Nothing, then . . . about Faith . . . is inconsistent with the state in which
we find ourselves by nature with reference to the acquisition of knowledge generally,
a state in which we must assume something to prove anything, and can gain nothing
without a venture" ("The Nature of Faith in Relation to Reason," in *Fifteen Sermons
Preached before the University of Oxford,* first published 1843, republished by Christian Classics, Westminster, Md., 1966; hereafter *U.S.*).

8. "Religious Faith Rational," p. 191, in *Parochial and Plain Sermons* (London:
Rivingtons, 1868); quoted by Nicholas Lash in his Introduction to an edition of *G.A.*
(Notre Dame, Ind.: University of Notre Dame Press, 1979), p. 6.

9. *G.A.,* p. 185.

10. *G.A.,* p. 205.

11. *G.A.,* p. 214.

12. In passing over the first part of the book, on "Assent and Apprehension," I

am omitting any consideration of its most celebrated topic, i.e., the distinction between 'real' and 'notional' assent (and the related issue of the role of the imagination), though we shall find strong echoes of this in our discussion of Aristotle in Part 2. I am also passing over some important issues which would be material to any adequate account of how Newman avoids the charge to which—as he himself was aware—his position is most vulnerable, namely, that of relativism.

13. *G.A.*, p. 173 and p. 171.

14. *G.A.*, p. 219.

15. *G.A.*, pp. 228–229.

16. *G.A.*, p. 195.

17. *G.A.*, p. 218.

18. *G.A.*, p. 229.

19. *E.N.* 6.8; 1142a14–15.

20. *G.A.*, p. 221.

21. *G.A.*, pp. 220–221; *E.N.* 6.4; 1143b11–13.

22. *G.A.*, p. 226.

23. *G.A.*, p. 231.

24. *E.N.* 2.6; 1107a1–2. Here and in the citation at n. 27 below I depart from the Revised Oxford translation.

25. *G.A.*, p. 185.

26. *E.N.* 6.11; 1143a35–1143b11.

27. *E.N.* 6.1; 1138b21–23.

28. *G.A.*, p. 202.

29. *E.N.* 6.11; 1144a29–37.

30. *E.N.* 6.5; 1140b13–14.

31. *G.A.*, p. 277.

32. *G.A.*, p. 205.

33. *G.A.*, p. 231.

34. *G.A.*, p. 230. In opposing Aristotle's thesis on the unity of the virtues, Newman anticipates perhaps the most robustly Aristotelian book of recent times, namely, *After Virtue*, in which Alasdair MacIntyre does the same.

35. The phenomenological character of Newman's method has been noted by several commentators. See Edward J. Sillem, *John H. Newman, the Philosophical Notebooks*, 1:127–130; A. J. Boekraad, *The Personal Conquest of Truth According to J. H. Newman* (Louvain, 1955), pp. 138–140; and J. M. Cameron, "Newman and Locke: A Note on Some Themes in An Essay in Aid of a Grammar of Assent," in *Cardinal Newman Studien*, number 9 (Nuremberg: Glock, 1974), p. 197.

36. *G.A.*, p. 222.

37. Gadamer, *Truth and Method* (London: Sheed & Ward, 1975), pp. 239–240; see below ch. 4, end of §1.

38. *G.A.*, p. 242–243.

39. "Faith and Reason Contrasted as Habits of Mind," *U.S.*, p. 187. Newman uses these phrases in relation to faith, as distinguished from reason; but here he is referring to 'reason' in the narrow rationalist sense and not in the more expansive sense which he himself ultimately wants to defend—and which allows that faith itself is reasonable.

40. One of Newman's great strengths as a writer is the way he illustrates his points

with apposite examples, and especially characteristic of the *Grammar* are fine analyses
of the factors coming into play, and dividing the protagonists, in a number of controversies well-known at the time—e.g., one involving the relative merits of various emen-
dations of Shakespearean texts (pp. 177–180), or another about the provenance of
some of the writings traditionally attributed to Virgil, Horace, Livy, and Tacitus (pp.
192–193), or another, in historiography, about the stringency of evidence required in
studies of the early Greek and Roman periods (pp. 234–239). More significant than
the illustrative materials worked over by Newman in the *Grammar,* however, is the
fact that the context which motivated him to write the book—and sustained him through
the frustrations of twenty years of attempting to do so—was a discussion, conducted
in private correspondence over many years, between himself and William Froude, a
scientifically enlightened, agnostic friend of his. This exchange, candid, mutually respectful, deeply probing, and still without issue (in the sense that both parties retained their basic positions) when it ended with Froude's death, gave Newman ample
opportunity to reflect on the degree to which what really moved and directed particular minds was implicit, circuitous, and ramified—and therefore gave little scope
to formal argumentation conducted on neutral ground.

41. *G.A.,* p. 176.
42. *G.A.,* p. 180.
43. See especially Kuhn's *The Structure of Scientific Revolutions* (Chicago: University of Chicago Press, 1962) and Feyerabend's *Against Method* (London: New Left Books,
1975).
44. Hilary Putnam, *Meaning and the Moral Sciences* (London: Routledge and Kegan
Paul, 1978), p. 72.
45. Ibid., p. 73.
46. Ibid., p. 70.
47. Ibid., p. 72.
48. *G.A.,* p. 210.
49. *G.A.,* p. 196.
50. *G.A.,* p. 223.
51. *G.A.,* p. 205.
52. *G.A.,* pp. 181–182.
53. *Meaning and the Moral Sciences,* p. 75.
54. *L.D.,* xv, p. 381; quoted by Ker in his Editor's Notes to *G.A.,* p. 388.
55. *U.S.,* p. 224.
56. *U.S.,* p. 204.
57. *U.S.,* p. 231.
58. *U.S.,* p. 230.
59. *U.S.,* p. 227.
60. *G.A.,* p. 246.
61. See below, ch. 4, end of §1.
62. *The Structure of Scientific Revolutions,* p. 200.
63. "Objectivity, Value Judgement and Theory Choice," p. 331 in T. S. Kuhn, *The
Essential Tension: Selected Studies in Scientific Tradition and Change* (Chicago: University of Chicago Press, 1977).

64. Bernstein, *Beyond Objectivism and Relativism* (London: Basil Blackwell, 1983), p. 55.

65. Ibid., p. 69.

66. *G.A.*, p. 171.

67. *G.A.*, p. 196.

68. *G.A.*, p. 212.

69. *G.A.*, p. 208.

70. *L.D.*, xxi, p. 146.

71. Martha Nussbaum, *The Fragility of Goodness* (Cambridge: Cambridge University Press, 1986), p. 294.

72. Myles Burnyeat, "Aristotle on Learning to be Good," in A. O. Rorty, ed., *Essays on Aristotle's Ethics* (Berkeley: University of California Press, 1980), p. 87.

73. David Wiggins, "Weakness of Will, Commensurability, and the Objects of Deliberation and Desire," in ibid., p. 256.

74. See *Politics* 3.12; 1283a3–13.

75. On this view, which has been most fully developed by Nussbaum in *The Fragility of Goodness*, Aristotle's philosophy of action is compatible with a view of tragedy in which culpability cannot be attributed to the tragic figure. But for an argument which contests Nussbaum's interpretation of Aristotle and her view of tragedy, see Alasdair MacIntyre, *Whose Justice, Which Rationality?* (Notre Dame, Ind.: University of Notre Dame Press; London: Duckworth, 1988), p. 187.

76. As early as 1829 Newman was writing of the "incommensurability . . . of the human mind"—"since each mind pursues its own course and is actuated in that course by ten thousand indescribable incommunicable feelings and imaginings" (*L.D.*, ii, p. 60; quoted by Ker, *G.A.*, p. xxiii).

77. *G.A.*, p. 170.

78. *G.A.*, p. 233.

79. *The Structure of Scientific Revolutions*, p. 4.

80. Ibid., p. 152.

81. Ibid., p. 150.

82. Ibid., p. 151.

83. Ibid., p. 158.

84. Ibid.

85. Ibid., p. 148.

86. Ibid., p. 109.

87. Ibid., p. 110.

88. Ibid., p. 148.

89. Ibid., p. 152.

90. Ibid., p. 94 (emphasis added).

91. Ibid., p. 204. The idea of understanding as having an unavoidably circular structure and as being an unforced 'happening'—rather than a project of the ego or the will—will reemerge with central significance later on in our discussion of Gadamer (see below, ch. 4, §3 and §8).

92. A striking characteristic of both books is the way in which they make their respective cases through appeal to, and analysis of, particular *examples* of knowledge.

Kuhn's book is replete with cases from the history of science, and Newman's (as we saw in note 41 above) abounds in examples from many different fields, including science. Going beyond the *Grammar*, however, perhaps one may say that the example which is most brilliantly analyzed by Newman is that of his own 'step into' Roman Catholicism: his *Apologia Pro Vita Sua* (1865; edited and with an Introduction by M. J. Svaglic [Oxford: Clarendon Press, 1967]) is one of the great classics in the literature of conversion.

93. *G.A.*, p. 175.

94. *G.A.*, p. 239.

95. *G.A.*, pp. 236–237.

96. Kuhn twice invokes the notion of 'tacit knowledge' developed by Michael Polanyi (p. 44 and p. 191). He does so in the context of making the point that a paradigm is something operative in the practice of scientists and not a set of explicit theorems to which they are reflectively committed; it is "knowledge embedded in shared exemplars . . . which is misconstrued if reconstructed in terms of rules that are first abstracted from exemplars and thereafter function in their stead" (p. 192).

97. *G.A.*, p. 202.

98. *G.A.*, p. 266.

99. The relevance to their theme of this Aristotelian analysis is not developed by either Kuhn or Putnam (though the latter does refer briefly to Aristotle's being "profoundly right" on practical knowledge [see *Meaning and the Moral Sciences*, p. 5], and Bernstein is able to link persuasively Kuhn's viewpoint with Gadamer's [see *Beyond Objectivism and Relativism*, esp. part 1]). Our authors can be said to follow Aristotle, however, insofar as, recognizing the pursuit of science (or, more generally, of knowledge) as a practice, they are keen to acknowledge and respect the facts—what Aristotle calls the *hoti*—of this practice (or set of practices), rather than to subject it to some theoretical preconception. And this is the basis of their opposition to rationalists. Thus Wiggins sees himself as arguing against the kind of philosopher who "values his pet theory above the phenomena" (p. 214), Putnam argues that Mill and Nagle are "misrepresenting what actually goes on," and so "promulgate an ideology in the pejorative sense of 'ideology'" (p. 75), while Newman himself, in a characteristic passage, writes of Locke that "instead of . . . being content with the mind as God has made it, he would form men as he thinks they ought to be formed, into something better and higher, and calls them irrational and indefensible, if (so to speak) they take to the water instead of remaining under the narrow wings of his arbitrary theory" (p. 109). It is ironic, perhaps, that while the 'incommensurability thesis' commits our authors to the view that 'facts' are available only as already within the embrace of some theoretical construction of them, they still affirm this thesis itself on the basis that it does justice to the *phainomena*, i.e., the *facts of knowledge* in different fields—more justice, indeed, than rationalism, which satisfies the theoretical proclivities of its adherents only by flying in the face of these facts.

100. *G.A.*, p. 232.

101. *G.A.*, p. 231.

102. *G.A.*, p. 179.

103. *G.A.*, pp. 171–172.

104. *G.A.*, pp. 173–174.

105. See below, ch. 5, §3.

106. *The Idea of a University* (London: Longmans, Green, 1925), p. 426.

2. R. G. Collingwood's Critique of Techne in *The Principles of Art*

1. Collingwood, *The Principles of Art,* first published, Oxford: Clarendon Press, 1938 (hereafter *P.A.*).

2. *P.A.*, p. 9.

3. *P.A.*, p. 17.

4. For Collingwood's elaboration of these six points, see *P.A.*, ch. 2, §1.

5. *P.A.*, p. 17.

6. Ibid.

7. *P.A.*, p. 18.

8. Ibid. It is a characteristic consequence of the idealist tendency in Collingwood's thought that poetry does not, in this respect, differ from more 'material' technai; for the ultimate aim of the cobbler or carpenter or weaver, in his view, is the production not of material things, a pair of shoes, a cart, or a piece of cloth, but rather of "a state of mind in his customers, the state of having these demands [i.e., for the shoes, etc.] satisfied" (*P.A.*, p. 18).

9. *P.A.*, pp. 15–16.

10. *P.A.*, p. 6.

11. *P.A.*, p. 5.

12. *P.A.*, p. 31.

13. *P.A.*, p. 34.

14. *P.A.*, p. 19.

15. *P.A.*, p. 18.

16. The two examples adduced by Collingwood are Plato's argument that justice is not a techne (*Republic* 330d–336a) and "Aristotle's rejection (*Metaphysics* Λ) of the view stated in Plato's *Timaeus,* that the relation between God and the world is a case of the relation between craftsman and artifact" (*P.A.*, p. 18). (For a discussion by Collingwood of Aristotle's analysis in *Meta.* Λ, see *The Idea of Nature* (posthumously prepared for publication by T. M. Knox; [Oxford: Clarendon Press, 1945]) pp. 82ff.).

17. Both magic and amusement involve *representation,* which, since it is a matter of craft-skill, Collingwood also disqualifies as a genuinely artistic activity. Ch. 3 of *P.A.* is an attack on representational theories of art *per se* – i.e, leaving aside the fact that, as specific cases of the more generic 'technical theory', they are in fact, logically, already undermined by the critique of the latter.

18. For a fuller elaboration of Collingwood's unusual notion of 'magic', see *P.A.*, ch. 4.

19. A particular work of art may of course have the characteristics of both amusement and magic; Shaw's plays are paradigm examples of amusement for the educated classes but, as Collingwood points out, Shaw can *also,* e.g., send a theater audience home indignant about how men treat their wives.

20. So, he believes, was Plato: the banishment of the artists in the *Republic* he interprets as a prophetic denunciation of the shallow amusement-art which in Plato's

own time was replacing the magico-religious art of, e.g., the Olympian sculptures and the Aeschylean drama (see *P.A.*, pp. 46–52 and pp. 97–99).

21. See *P.A.*, p. 95.

22. "... of the two warring creeds which are dividing the inheritance of nineteenth-century liberalism, communism appears to have tongue, eyes and fingers, and fascism only teeth and claws" (*P.A.*, p. 71). That, as between these two creeds, Collingwood came to sympathize more with communism is very clear from the sombre final chapter of his *Autobiography* (Oxford: Clarendon Press, 1939; with Introduction by Stephen Toulmin, Oxford University Press paperback, 1978), written the year after the completion of *P.A.* and within a year of the outbreak of the Second World War.

23. *P.A.*, p. 77. It should be clear that I am not saying here that connectedness with "a robust way of life" is a necessary condition for art. It is a condition which, in fact, can hardly be said to be fulfilled for artists in contemporary industrialized societies; but this means not that the latter cannot on that account produce great art but only that such art as they do produce will be highly unlikely to serve a magical function.

24. *P.A.*, p. 29.
25. *P.A.*, p. 22.
26. *P.A.*, p. 26.
27. *P.A.*, p. 20.
28. *P.A.*, p. 29.
29. *P.A.*, p. 28.
30. *P.A.*, p. 125.
31. *P.A.*, p. 26.
32. *P.A.*, pp. 26–27.

33. As I mentioned in the Introduction, what originally motivated this book was my strong antipathy to the assumption made by proponents of the behavioral objectives model that to resist their program of extending a technical logic into teaching was *ipso facto* to renounce any prospect of seeing teaching as a rational practice.

34. *P.A.*, p. 125.
35. *P.A.*, p. 129.
36. *P.A.*, p. 235.

37. *P.A.*, p. 215. In reserving the term 'consciousness' for one distinct level of mental functioning, in *P.A.*, Collingwood is giving it a strict sense which does not obtain in normal usage—where, e.g., we would certainly speak of higher intellectual operations as 'conscious'—and which indeed is not retained in his own later and in some ways more systematic work, *The New Leviathan* (Oxford: Clarendon Press, 1942), where it is used to refer to *all* levels.

38. *P.A.*, p. 207.
39. *P.A.*, p. 224.
40. *P.A.*, p. 215.
41. *P.A.*, p. 216.
42. *P.A.*, p. 224.
43. *P.A.*, p. 218.
44. *P.A.*, p. 219.

45. Collingwood, who was a contemporary of Freud, was able to see that the latter's undertaking "has already won a great place in the history of man's warfare with the powers of darkness" (*P.A.*, p. 221); he interpreted psychoanalysis, in fact, as "bearing the same relation to the general principles of mental hygiene laid down by Spinoza that the detailed inquiries of relativistic physics bear to the project for a 'universal science' of mathematical physics as laid down by Descartes." (*P.A.*, p. 220). He was not, however, an uncritical admirer of psychoanalysis; quite apart from his circumspection about whether it has really succeeded in providing the means to "rescue" people from corruptions of consciousness, he was vehemently critical of Freud's attempts to extrapolate from studies in mental pathology to generic issues in anthroplogy (see his note on *Totem and Taboo*, *P.A.*, p. 77).

46. This ambiguity is very revealingly brought out by Philip Rieff in *Freud: The Mind of the Moralist* and in his later book *The Triumph of the Therapeutic*. It has also been analyzed in philosophical interpretations of Freud which have shown how the scientistic bias of his conceptual system ill-fitted it for articulating the inherently hermeneutical character of the psychoanalytic interaction (see, e.g., Paul Ricoeur, *Freud and Philosophy: An Essay on Interpretation*, and Jürgen Habermas's essays on Freud discussed below, ch. 6, §3).

47. *P.A.*, p. 111 (emphases added). In holding that expression is constitutive of becoming conscious, Collingwood was following a line of thinkers who took the same view, e.g., in England, Coleridge in poetics and Nettleship in (idealist) philosophy. (For helpful background to the sources of Collingwood's aesthetics, see Peter Jones, "A Critical Outline of Collingwood's Philosophy of Art," in Michael Krausz, ed., *Critical Essays on the Philosophy of R. G. Collingwood* [Oxford: Clarendon Press, 1972] pp. 42–44). This view may be contrasted with the view held by the psychologist Carl Rogers, who, like Collingwood, distinguishes between an organismic level of experience and a conscious level of awareness and sees that, as in Collingwood's "corrupt consciousness," there can be a lack of congruence between the two levels (he defines "congruence," a central concept in his theory of psychotherapy, as an "accurate matching of experience with awareness"). Rogers differs from Collingwood, however, in regarding 'expression' as a further level where, on a *discretionary* basis, one communicates what is going on in one's awareness—so that a person can be congruent on *three* levels, "in what he is experiencing at an organismic level, in his awareness at the conscious level, and in his words and communications." For Collingwood "expression" arises not at the third level (whose existence, of course, he would not deny) but rather at the second level—which is why he speaks of it as making "a clean breast of things" and sees "perfect sincerity" as a hallmark of good art. (See Carl Rogers, *On Becoming a Person* [London: Constable, 1961], pp. 283–284, and *P.A.*, p. 115).

48. *P.A.*, p. 244.

49. *P.A.*, p. 238.

50. At the level of consciousness two kinds of emotion are distinguished by Collingwood: (a) psychic emotions which have been converted by the activity of attention into conscious emotions, and (b) what he calls "emotions of consciousness," i.e., emotions such as love, envy, or shame that have an intrinsic reference to some sense of *self* and so are never merely psychical (though just as psychical emotions, once con-

verted, can be expressed at the conscious level, so, conversely, emotions of consciousness can also find expression at a psycho-physical level, e.g., the quickened pulse of
love, the blush of shame etc.) (see *P.A.*, pp. 232–234).

51. *P.A.*, p. 239.

52. *P.A.*, p. 226 and pp. 226–227.

53. See *P.A.*, p. 226. (In *The New Leviathan*, 6.45–6.57, Collingwood grants to
Hobbes a deeper understanding of language as intrinsic rather than extrinsic to consciousness.)

54. For Collingwood's relation to T. H. Green and F. H. Bradley (who, if they
were not Hegelians, were the English philosophers most conversant and least out of
sympathy with Hegel) see *Autobiography*, chs. 3 and 4. The systematic intention and
scope of his own philosophical project are most perspicuous in his early work, *Speculum Mentis, or The Map of Knowledge* (Oxford: Clarendon Press, 1924), which contains a chapter on art. For the most ambitious attempt to find in all Collingwood's
later writings a coherent development of the inchoate program of *Speculum Mentis*
see Louis O. Mink, *Mind, History and Dialectic* (Bloomington: Indiana University
Press, 1969).

55. Collingwood had his own way of stating these limitations. As "the lexicographer can never be victorious in his running fight with the vagaries of context" (*P.A.*,
p. 258), so the grammarian "is not a kind of scientist studying the actual structure
of language; he is a kind of butcher, converting it from organic tissue into marketable
and edible joints. Language as it lives and grows no more consists of verbs, nouns,
and so forth than animals as they live and grow consist of forehands, gammons, rump-
steaks and other joints" (*P.A.*, p. 257). And the logician formulates proposals (about
the isolability of 'propositions' or 'statements', about their substitutability for each
other, and about rules governing their manipulation) which, even when taken in conjunction with what the lexicographer and the grammarian have to offer, so far from
specifying a language, aim at "the conversion of language into something which, if
it could be realized, would not be language at all" (*P.A.*, p. 262).

56. *Philosophical Investigations*, §108 (emphasis Wittgenstein's), 2nd ed., trans.
G. E. M. Anscombe and R. Rhees (Oxford: Basil Blackwell, 1976). Wittgenstein speaks
of this "crystalline purity" as a "preconceived idea" and as a "requirement" rather than
"a result of investigation." (Ibid., §107.) Similarly, Collingwood emphasizes that logic
consists of "assumptions" which are in fact "proposals" (*P.A.*, p. 262)—just as grammatical units are "devised" and not "discovered" (*P.A.*, p. 256).

57. *P.A.*, p. 238.

58. *P.A.*, p. 244.

59. See *P.A.*, p. 227.

60. *P.A.*, p. 263.

61. Ibid.

62. *P.A.*, p. 262.

63. This is a point which we shall meet later in Gadamer; see especially ch. 5,
§3, text between nn. 39 and 43.

64. *P.A.*, p. 266 (see also p. 243). Collingwood here goes on to hold not just that
when language (as intellectualized) communicates thought it always *also* expresses emotion but, more, that it is precisely *through* the expression of emotion that it commu-

nicates thought at all. (For his development of this provocatively strong claim, see
P.A., pp. 266ff.) This assumes, of course, that emotions arise not just on the psychic
level in their crude state, nor at the conscious level as a charge on the activity of expressing what had been merely psychic, but also at the third level as a charge on the
activity of intellectual thinking. If the expression of emotion at this third level is, *qua*
the expression of *intellectual* emotion, our way of communicating the thought whose
charge it is, it is also of course, *qua* expression of emotion *simpliciter,* an artistic activity. And an implication of this is that a work of art can (and most great works of art
in fact do) carry a high intellectual content. A work's having a 'universal' theme, then,
does not at all disqualify it as a work of art—provided that it is a genuine emotional
response to the contemplation or working out of this theme and not a hackneyed
generalization that is expressed in it. This is a point which the whole thrust of Collingwood's argument tends to neglect, but see *P.A.*, pp. 45–46.

    65. *P.A.*, p. 263.

    66. *P.A.*, p. 298. We will be reminded later of this point (which is also made in
An Essay on Philosophical Method [Oxford: Clarendon Press, 1933], ch. 10, §4) when
we see how Gadamer presents his hermeneutics as a style of thinking in which the
ancient enmity between dialectic and rhetoric is overcome (see below, ch. 5, §5). I
may say that it is a point which is more easily made in the present philosophical climate (characterized by a revival of interest in rhetoric and by a growing convergence,
in style as well as in preoccupations, of philosophy and literary theory—e.g., in writers
as different from each other as Jacques Derrida and Stanley Cavell) than in the climate
in which Collingwood had to make it.

    67. *P.A.*, p. 298.

    68. See *P.A.*, p. 56 and p. 323, and below, text at n. 121.

    69. *P.A.*, p. 285.

    70. *P.A.*, p. 112.

    71. *P.A.*, p. 113.

    72. *Metaphysics* 1.1; 981a10–11. See below, ch. 8, §4 and ch. 9, §3.

    73. Ibid. (emphasis added).

    74. What we meet here is close to the "natality" which, as we shall see in the next
chapter, Hannah Arendt relates not just to the fact of biological birth but to the new-
ness which characterizes every genuine 'action'. For a comparison of her concept of
action with Collingwood's concept of expression, see next chapter, §3, text between
nn. 36 and 37.

    75. See n. 64 above.

    76. See Collingwood's demonstration of the variety of emotions that may on dif-
ferent occasions be expressed when someone says: "The chemical formula of water is
H_2O" (*P.A.*, p. 265).

    77. See below, ch. 3, §5 at n. 66 and ch. 8, §3 at n. 39.

    78. Collingwood is not embracing here a notion of originality which would imply
a denial of the importance of artistic tradition or an assertion of the need for radical
novelty in a work of art. This notion of originality he regards as a prejudice of "aesthetic individualism," a doctrine which, as we shall see, he roundly dismisses (pointing out, as he does so, what promiscuous borrowers and copiers Shakespeare, Handel,
Beethoven, and Turner, for example, were). See *P.A.*, pp. 318–320.

79. *P.A.*, p. 282.

80. *P.A.*, p. 285.

81. *P.A.*, p. 284.

82. *P.A.*, p. 278 (emphasis added).

83. *P.A.*, pp. 279–280. A work *might* simultaneously serve art and politics; but if it does, the politics in question will be characterized by openness—i.e., be able to tolerate the *exploration* of political emotions. Conversely, if there is "any kind of political order whose realization involves the use of the muzzle, no one can serve that kind and at the same time serve art" (*P.A.*, p. 280). In fact with the final words of his book Collingwood implies that if an artist really serves his art he cannot help but serve the polity too—precisely by not trying to do so, and whether or not this service is recognized. For "no community altogether knows its own heart; and by failing in this knowledge a community deceives itself on the one subject concerning which ignorance means death. For the evils which come from that ignorance the poet . . . suggests no remedy, because he has already given one. The remedy is the poem itself. Art is the community's medicine for the worst disease of mind, the corruption of consciousness."

84. *P.A.*, p. 291.

85. Ethics was the area which received most of Collingwood's attention as a university teacher, and his writing of *An Essay on Philosophical Method* was closely connected with lectures on ethics which he had been giving over the previous decade. The most mature expression of his moral philosophy, however, is to be found in *The New Leviathan*, Pt. 1.

86. See end of n. 47 above, and the last sentence in the passage quoted at n. 99 below; see also Alasdair MacIntyre, "Moral Philosophy: What Next?" p. 15, and Quentin Bell, "Bad Art," p. 163, in Stanley Hauerwas and Alasdair MacIntyre, eds., *Revisions* (Notre Dame, Ind.: University of Notre Dame Press, 1983).

87. *Autobiography*, pp. 101, 102, 104.

88. Ibid., p. 106.

89. Ibid., p. 105.

90. *P.A.*, pp. 303–304.

91. *P.A.*, p. 304. The emphasis on seeing here does not prevent Collingwood from holding at another place in the book that "painting is not a visual art," that Cézanne, for instance, paints not so much what he sees as what a blind man might feel in groping through a space, and that a spectator's response to his work is not so much visual as a total imaginative experience in which what Bernard Berenson called "tactile values" and motor sensations come into play. (See *P.A.*, pp. 144–151.) *Mutatis mutandis*, the same can be said of other art media—e.g., music gives an imaginative experience in which visual and kinesthetic as well as auditory elements are involved.

92. See especially ch. 9, §1 and §2.

93. *P.A.*, p. 290. Collingwood attributes a role here to art which is very close to the role which he attributes to *history* in the *Autobiography:* "What history can bring to moral and political life is a trained eye for the situation in which one is to act" (p. 100). In arguing that *both* art and history have the particular as their object, he may seem to be directly at odds with Aristotle, who argues, notoriously (at *Poetics*

9.1451b6–11), that whereas history deals with particulars, poetry deals with a higher universal; but see n. 64 above.

94. See David Wiggins, "Deliberation and Practical Reason," in A. O. Rorty, ed., *Essays on Aristotle's Ethics* (Berkeley and Los Angeles: University of California Press, 1980), p. 237.

95. *P.A.*, pp. 112–113.

96. *E.N.* 2.9; 1109a26–28.

97. 'Betraying' emotion is "exhibiting the symptoms" of it (e.g., "turning pale and stammering" when feeling fear) and seems to be — though Collingwood does not say so — the same thing as *psychical* expression of it (see *P.A.*, pp. 121–122). 'Catharsis' is the somewhat more active process whereby emotion is 'discharged', so that "we have worked it off and are rid of it" (*P.A.*, p. 110).

98. *P.A.*, p. 281.

99. *P.A.*, p. 283.

100. *P.A.*, pp. 283–284.

101. See below, ch. 9, §1–§5.

102. See, e.g., Richard Wollheim, "On an Alleged Inconsistency in Collingwood's Aesthetics," in Michael Krausz, ed., *Critical Essays on the Philosophy of R. G. Collingwood*, pp. 68–78.

103. *P.A.*, p. 130.

104. *P.A.*, p. 139.

105. *P.A.*, p. 134.

106. *P.A.*, p. 305.

107. *P.A.*, p. 107.

108. Ibid.

109. *P.A.*, pp. 110–111.

110. This concept is essentially the same as what he develops more fully, with specific reference to historical understanding, under the rubric of *'re-enactment'*, in *The Idea of History*, ed. T. M. Knox (Oxford: Clarendon Press, 1946), pt. 5, §4, and in the *Autobiography*, ch. 10.

111. *P.A.*, p. 141.

112. *P.A.*, p. 140.

113. *P.A.*, p. 311.

114. *P.A.*, p. 118.

115. *P.A.*, p. 316.

116. Publication may mean no more than showing one's work to one or two friends. Thus, to take an extreme case, although Hopkins's poems were published only posthumously — and although the circumstances that caused this were undoubtedly a severe affliction to him as an artist — still they were already published, in a real, if only minimal, sense, when they were shown to his poet-friend, Bridges.

117. *P.A.*, p. 314.

118. *P.A.*, p. 315.

119. *P.A.*, p. 314.

120. *P.A.*, p. 315.

121. *P.A.*, p. 323 and p. 322.

122. *P.A.*, p. 326.

123. *P.A.*, p. 320.

124. *P.A.*, pp. 315–316.

125. *P.A.*, p. 316 (emphasis added).

126. *P.A.*, p. 317.

127. Ibid.

128. Ibid.

129. The phrase 'linguistic turn' (which gained currency as the title of a collection of essays edited by Richard Rorty in 1967) has become a tag for marking the shift toward language as the privileged locus of philosophical reflection, in which the traditional problems of epistemology, philosophy of mind, ethics, etc., are to be resolved or re-focused—or dissolved altogether. The seminal text here of course is Wittgenstein's *Philosophical Investigations*, first published in 1953 (though completed some years earlier), a decade and a half later than *P.A.*

130. As we shall see, both Arendt and Gadamer are hostile to the notion of 'expression' because of what they see as its subjectivist implications (see below, ch. 3, n. 38 and ch. 4, n. 40). I should like to advert here, however, to Maurice Merleau-Ponty, who embraces the idea of 'expression', and seems to me both (a) to be close to Collingwood in what he says about it *and* (b) to have a nonsubjectivistic, indeed, precisely an anti-subjectivistic, concept of it.

(a) Merleau-Ponty is like Collingwood: in his aliveness to what is missed in any attempt to study language purely as a datum for science ("Taking language as a *fait accompli*—as the residue of past acts of signification and the record of already acquired meanings—the scientist inevitably misses the peculiar clarity of speech, the fecundity of expression"); in not being lured by the project of an *ideal* language, a perfect system of signification ("It [language] is never composed of absolutely univocal meanings which can be made completely explicit beneath the gaze of a transparent constituting consciousness. It will be a question not of a system of forms of signification clearly articulated in terms of one another . . . but of a cohesive whole of convergent linguistic gestures which will be defined less by a signification than by a use-value"); in rejecting the view of language as an *instrumentality* for conveying a pre-existing meaning ("Expressive speech does not simply choose a sign for an already defined signification, as one goes to look for a hammer in order to drive a nail or for a claw to pull it out. It gropes around a significative intention which is not guided by any text, and which is precisely in the process of writing the text"); in showing that expression arises not at the level at which I communicate with others but at that at which I become *aware* myself ("this act of expression . . . is not . . . a second-order operation we supposedly have recourse to only in order to communicate our thoughts to others, but our own taking possession or acquisition of significations which otherwise are present to us only in a muffled way. . . . For the speaking subject . . . to express is to become aware; he does not express just for others, but also to know himself what he intends"); in stressing the *originary* quality of expression ("The words, lines and colours which express me come out of me as gestures. They are torn from me by what I want to say as my gestures are by what I want to do. In this sense there is in all expression a spontaneity which will not tolerate any commands, not even those which I would like to give to myself"); in seeing speech, verbal language, and indeed all art as being rooted in and continuous with a language of total *bodily gesture* ("If we want to understand language as an originating operation, we must . . . compare . . . [it] to other arts of expression, and try to see it as one of these mute arts"; and "it is the expressive operation of the body, begun by the smallest perception, which is amplified into painting and art"); and in seeing that despite, or rather because of, being rooted in the body, expressiveness is *ineliminable* from all language and, far from being a superfluity of some kinds of thinking activities, is at the heart of *all* thought— including philosophy ("no language ever wholly frees itself from the precariousness of mute forms of expression . . . in this sense the privilege language enjoys over painting or the practices of life remains relative; and . . . expression is not one of the curiosities that the mind may propose to examine but is its existence in act"— so that the "meaning of philosophy is the meaning of a genesis . . . and it is still expression").

(b) Merleau-Ponty goes to great pains to show (in an argument directed at Andre Malraux) that one would be wrong, just because the expressivity of modern painting and literature so manifestly involves a rejection of representation (which Collingwood, too, of course, excludes from his notion of art; see n. 17 above) to construe modern(ist) art as "a return to subjectivity . . . [and] to bury it in a secret life outside the world." As against this, what he tries to show is that the artist cannot express himself without expressing the world, and that when he expresses the world the full significance of what he does can become clear to him only through others. The painter "finds in the shape of things the same questioning and the same call he never stops responding to . . . without . . . ever being able to say (since the distinction has no meaning) what comes from him and what comes from things." The work of art is not so much "absolute creation in an aggressive solitude . . . [as] a response to what the world, the past, and the completed works demanded." And the painter "is no more capable of seeing his paintings than the writer is capable of reading his work. It is in others that expression takes on its relief and really becomes signification." The problem presented by modern painting (and, analogously, by all modern art-forms) is "completely different from that of the return to the individual"; it is "the problem of knowing how one can communicate without the help of a pre-established Nature which all man's senses open upon, the problem of knowing how we are grafted to the universal by that which is most our own." This way of seeing the problem, as we shall see, is very close to Gadamer's way of seeing the great problem of the 'one and the many' in language. Gadamer responds to this problem with a reflection on dialectic, which he understands as a movement which is unaccountable for in terms of individual subjectivity—and which, therefore, he supposes, undercuts the notion of "expression." The curious point I want to draw attention to, however, is that Merleau-Ponty develops a response which, closely resembling (I believe) Gadamer's, appeals to the notion of dialectic—but understands *dialectic precisely as expression:* "dialectic is what we call by another name the phenomenon of expression, which gathers itself up and launches itself again through the mystery of rationality." (All quotations above are from Maurice Merleau-Ponty, "Indirect Language and the Voices of Silence" and "On the Phenomenology of Language" ("le langage indirect et les voix de silence" and "sur la phénoménologie du langage" in *Signes* [Paris: Gallimard, 1960], pp. 49–122) in *Signs,* trans. Richard C. McCleary (Evanston: Northwestern University Press, 1964), pp. 39–97.

131. *P.A.*, p. 249.
132. *P.A.*, p. 250.
133. See above, §4, text at n. 90.
134. *P.A.*, p. 248.
135. *P.A.*, pp. 248–249.
136. *P.A.*, pp. 249–250.
137. *P.A.*, p. 250.
138. *P.A.*, p. 251.
139. See esp. ch. 4, §4, and the latter half of §8; and ch. 5, §3, esp. text at n. 42.
140. We also find, I may point out, the same emphasis on language as universal and constitutive that we shall find in Gadamer; with the latter's well-known dictum, "Being that can be understood is language," compare equally compact remarks of Collingwood's: "His world is his language," or "The world he has come to know is a world consisting of language" (*P.A.*, p. 291 and p. 292).
141. We have already met this Aristotelian image in Newman (above ch. 1, §2, text at n. 18) and for Aristotle's own use of it see below, ch. 9, §3, text at n. 25.
142. *P.A.*, p. 251.
143. *P.A.*, p. 309.
144. *P.A.*, p. 311.

3. Hannah Arendt's Distinction between Action and Making in *The Human Condition*

1. See below, ch. 10, §1 and §2.
2. See below, §5.
3. Arendt's analysis seeks to clarify the distinctions and relationships between *three* primordial categories: action, making, and labor. Since it is only the first two of these that fall within my overall theme, I confine attention to Arendt's treatment of them. I may briefly note, however, that labor is a process through which we are immersed in nature, repetitiously and endlessly reproducing the needs of life. Making — or work (*ergazōai*) in the sense of an activity that produces a work (*ergon*) — rises above the imperatives of nature by creating a *world* (rather than a habitat) of durable objects; on each occasion, its linear sequence — from planning through execution to final attainment of the particular object which is its *telos* — gives an experience of mastery and release. The cyclical process of labor, by contrast, having no transcendent *telos*, is condemned to an unremitting struggle with nature's implacable demands on the species. (By way of illustration here, one might say that one of the things that is at issue between feminist critics and defenders of the woman's traditional role in the home is whether 'housework', which is undeniably laborious, can become work or action.) Marx's thought is gravely flawed, for Arendt, because of what she sees as his uncritical attitude to labor and in particular his failure to distinguish it properly from work and action.
4. For Arendt, the 'social' is not the same as the 'public' world and so, in repudiating a mere social type, she is not recommending any withdrawal into the privacy of specifically modern forms of subjectivity. To the contrary, the actions that reveal one as distinct require a public space where one undergoes their consequences in the

full light of 'appearance'. In modern 'society' such a public space where people really speak and act together has become more and more attenuated as politics has been reduced to a form of national housekeeping or bureaucratic administration of economic affairs. Whereas for the Greeks the *polis* was the space where citizens escaped from the largely economic life of the domestic sphere (i.e., the *oikia*), the modern state has itself become economized, and it is in the domestic or private sphere that people now seek escape in 'authentic' personal fulfillment. Although privacy has much greater prestige in modernity than it had among the ancient Greeks, Arendt sees it — no less than the shared public world — as radically threatened by the rise of 'society'. As a sphere of intimacy and intensified feeling, it (modern privacy) may indeed be seen as a protest (whose great prophet was Rousseau) against the ever greater encroachments of society; but for Arendt the weakness caused by its separation from the reality of 'appearance' makes it incapable of offering any real resistance to the tendency whereby even its own forms of subjective experience become fabricated commodities. (For the Greeks, by contrast, privacy, even if it was not at all the arena for the pursuit of excellence, was still secure. It formed the complement or backdrop to the public domain; as the place where the necessities of life were mastered, it gave one a stable base from which to venture into the *polis* as well as a place where one could find the temporary respite which one needed from the relentless exposure of public life.)

5. *The Human Condition*, (Chicago: University of Chicago Press, 1958) (hereafter *H.C.*), p. 43.
   6. *H.C.*, p. 322.
   7. *H.C.*, p. 181.
   8. *H.C.*, p. 179.
   9. *H.C.*, p. 26 (emphasis added).
   10. *H.C.*, p. 179.
   11. Ibid.
   12. *H.C.*, p. 180.
   13. *H.C.*, pp. 182–183.
   14. *H.C.*, p. 183.
   15. *H.C.*, pp. 183–184.
   16. *H.C.*, p. 183.
   17. *H.C.*, p. 186.
   18. *H.C.*, p. 190.
   19. *H.C.*, p. 233.
   20. *H.C.*, p. 190.
   21. *H.C.*, p. 192.
   22. *H.C.*, p. 184.
   23. *H.C.*, p. 201.
   24. *H.C.*, p. 200.
   25. *H.C.*, p. 234.
   26. *H.C.*, p. 203.
   27. *H.C.*, p. 230.
   28. *H.C.*, p. 220.
   29. This view has been perhaps most influentially propounded by Leo Strauss;

see especially *Natural Right and History* (Chicago: University of Chicago Press, 1953), ch. 5.

30. *H.C.*, p. 230.
31. *H.C.*, p. 223.
32. *H.C.*, p. 225.
33. *H.C.*, p. 222.
34. *H.C.*, p. 225.
35. *H.C.*, p. 220.
36. *H.C.*, p. 229.

37. This statement seems true of Arendt's presentation in *The Human Condition*. It should be said, however, that in some other works—most notably *On Revolution* (London: Faber, 1963) and *Men in Dark Times* (London: H.B.J. Books, 1968)—she does find some flickering examples of action in modernity, not just among the founding fathers of the American republic or those involved in the Paris commune, but more recently in the Hungarian Revolution of 1956 and in some of the civil disobedience campaigns against the Vietnam War. Had she lived to see them, one feels sure that she would have regarded recent events in Eastern Europe (perhaps especially in Czechoslovakia) as providing spectacular examples of 'action'.

38. The structural similarity in the respective arguments of Collingwood and Arendt which I advert to here does not imply substantive agreement between them. The fact that "expression" plays the same kind of role in Collingwood's argument that "action" plays in Arendt's implies neither that Arendt would see the need, in the *aesthetic* field, for an argument similar to what she has developed in the field of politics, nor—even if she did—that she would look to 'expression' as its central concept. In fact, from passing remarks which she makes about art in *The Human Condition*, it seems clear that Arendt is not only happy to regard artistic activity as essentially fabrication but that she is particularly scornful of the idea of it as 'expression': "The artist, whether painter or sculptor or poet or musician, produces worldly objects, and his reification has nothing in common with the highly questionable and, at any rate, wholly unartistic practice of expression" (*H.C.*, p. 323, n. 87). Arendt's hostility to 'expression' here stems from her insistence on the "inherent worldliness of the artist" (ibid.) and her opposition to the growth of 'private' subjectivity, which she sees as a protest against the increasing determinism of modern *society*—but as no substitute for the *public*, i.e., genuinely political, space which has been usurped by the 'social' (see note 4 above). Later on we shall see that very similar reservations are entertained by Gadamer about the notion of 'expression' (see ch. 4, n. 40). The question raised by these reservations (which may be taken to reflect Heidegger's influence on Gadamer and perhaps on Arendt too) is whether Collingwood, for all his opposition to conscious contrivance as the source of art objects, is not still captive to the whole philosophy of consciousness which was inaugurated by Descartes and whose radical deconstruction might almost be taken to be definitive of all the best contemporary endeavors in philosophy—however disparate or divergent from each other, in other respects, these endeavors may be. I have tried to deal with this question in sections 5 and 6 of the previous chapter; for the view that 'expression'—even Collingwood's version of it—need not carry subjectivistic implications, see especially the extended reference to Merleau-Ponty in ch. 2, n. 130.

39. *H.C.*, p. 229.

40. The point that Arendt is making here is close to the point that Max Weber made with his famous distinction between substantive and formal rationality, or which Max Horkheimer and Theodor Adorno made with their "critique of instrumental reason" (the title of a book by Horkheimer). Later on we shall see Jürgen Habermas — influenced by these three thinkers, but also by Arendt — making much the same point (see below, ch. 6, §5, and n. 12).

41. *H.C.*, p. 157.

42. *H.C.*, p. 154.

43. Ibid.

44. *H.C.*, p. 220.

45. *H.C.*, p. 222.

46. *H.C.*, p. 238.

47. *H.C.*, p. 234.

48. *H.C.*, p. 236.

49. *H.C.*, p. 244.

50. Ibid.

51. *H.C.*, pp. 240–241.

52. *H.C.*, p. 241.

53. Ibid.

54. *H.C.*, p. 243.

55. Ibid.

56. *H.C.*, pp. 237–238.

57. *H.C.*, p. 238.

58. Ibid.

59. *H.C.*, p. 230.

60. If Arendt's book has a hero, perhaps it might be said to be Jesus. Despite the fact that Christianity has given "unquestioned priority . . . to the *vita contemplativa* over all kinds of human activities," Arendt attributes this to the influence on the Christian tradition of Greek philosophy and not of its founder; for in her view the "only activity Jesus of Nazareth recommends in his preachings is action" (*H.C.*, p. 318). Elsewhere she maintains that his "insights into this faculty [i.e., action] can be compared in their originality and unprecedentedness with Socrates' insights into the possibilities of thought" (ibid., p. 247). Jesus' particular genius lay in his insight into *forgiveness*: "The discoverer of the role of forgiveness in the realm of human affairs was Jesus of Nazareth" (ibid., p. 238). Moreover his enjoinment to forgive did not stem from the fact that God forgives and that we should therefore do likewise; on the contrary, forgiveness is primarily a *human* response which corresponds to the condition of beings who truly "know not what they are doing," and it is only if a person forgives others that he may then hope that God will forgive him.

61. *H.C.*, p. 207.

62. The distinction I advert to here between 'conceptual' and 'real' is one that is not made by Arendt, though the import of her analysis would, I think, be clarified and strengthened by making it. One might take Arendt to be saying that 'action' and 'making' *denote* two quite different kinds of reality, i.e., that the activities which they respectively pick out belong in two mutually exclusive classes. On this position, if a

particular activity is judged to be a case of 'making', then it cannot also be a case of 'action'; and the converse is also true. If this is Arendt's position, she is hardly correct. For there are surely some cases where a person is involved in an activity of making which may *also*, though from a different *perspective*, be regarded as an instance of acting. Consider the case of a doctor* (let us say in an underground movement) or of a writer—who, for Arendt, if not for Collingwood, is a maker. When Yeats asked— in respect of his own play *Cathleen nī Houlihan*—"Did that play of mine send out/ Certain men the English shot?" was he not acknowledging that his work, even in spite of him, had become an 'action'? Or, to take a contemporary and more striking example, has not the dramatic work of Václav Havel—with the 'disclosure', uncertainty, and irreversibility to which it has exposed him— all the hallmarks of action? But if this is so, then the distinction between making and acting is a *conceptual* or *analytic* one, providing two sets of criteria for identifying activities, so that some activities might in fact satisfy both sets. Nor would the distinction, looked at in this way, lose its force. For it may well be that the historical development which Arendt analyzes has brought about conditions in which the criteria for action are becoming more and more difficult, if not impossible, to fulfill; and if this is the case then our understanding of this development is greatly enhanced by the distinction which she has spelled out in her book. I may point out that if Arendt does not clarify the logical status of her distinction between making and acting she does not differ much in this from Aristotle. For, as we shall see later, he did not go to any great pains to clarify the status of his corresponding distinction between poiesis/techne and praxis/phronesis (see below, ch. 8, §3).

*Medicine belongs—with, e.g., navigation, military strategy, and rhetoric—in a group of activities which are in an ambiguous positon *vis à vis* Arendt's *and* Aristotle's distinctions, in that they are specific *technai* and so do not, as such, seem to involve action or praxis, while they are, at the same time, not concerned with fabrication in any straightforward sense, either. Arendt does advert to the distinctiveness of these technai (*H.C.*, p. 207) and seems to acknowledge a close affinity between them and action—insofar as they might be considered performative as much as productive. They will be of some significance in my own analysis in Part 2, where I shall try to show that although Aristotle 'officially' (in *E.N.* 6.4) defines techne as *poiētikē*—i.e., as having to do with making or fabrication in Arendt's sense—he still works, less formally, with these other technai which this definition does not fit (see below, ch. 8, §5).

63. *P.A.*, p. 17.

64. *H.C.*, p. 230.

65. *H.C.*, p. 196.

66. Ibid., pp. 206–207. Although Arendt's glossing in this passage of key terms of Aristotle (terms in ordinary usage to which he was quite self-consciously assigning a new technical meaning, beyond even that of Plato) is generally sound, there is an inaccuracy. Aristotle does not use '*ateleis*' as a predicate of activities that have no end external to themselves (i.e., of *energeiai*); to the contrary, he uses it of activities whose ends *are* external to them in the sense that it is only with the completion of the activities that the ends are achieved; the activities in themselves are essentially *processes* whose ends are *not yet* achieved—and it is in this sense that they are *ateleis*. *Poiēsis* is the paradigm example of such a process, having its end fully external to it (e.g.,

in the finished house or pair of shoes); but Aristotle also considers, e.g., slimming as an example of an activity that is *atelēs*. The generic term which he uses to cover *all* "atelic" processes is *kinēsis* — which includes, but is not coterminous with, poiēsis. (See *Metaphysics* 9.6 and 9.7, esp. 1048b18–25; and below, ch. 8, §3, text immediately after n. 38.)

I may mention here one other — and, in the light of our own theme, more significant — occasion where Arendt's reading of Aristotle seems unreliable. To support her claim that like Plato, Aristotle, too, "tends to invert the relationship between work and action in favor of work" she points to two passages in the *Metaphysics* where the threefold distinction is made between practical, productive, and theoretical intellect, and where, as she supposes, the order in which these occur is *hierarchical,* implying a superiority of the productive intellect over the practical (*H.C.,* p. 301). But this reading (despite the fact that techne is indeed much closer in spirit to *epistēmē* than phronesis is [see below, ch. 8, the latter part of §4]) hardly seems warranted by the two passages and is, in fact, explicitly contradicted in a passage in the *Ethics* (to which Arendt makes no reference), which, having affirmed practical intellect as the only kind of intellect that can move something, goes on to tell us that it "rules the productive intellect as well, since everyone who makes makes for an end, and that which is made is not an end in the unqualified sense (but only an end in a particular relation, and the end of a particular operation) — only what is *done* is that; for good action *is* an end . . ." (*E.N.* 6.2, 1139b1–3).

67. *The Fragility of Goodness* (Cambridge: Cambridge University Press, 1986 [hereafter *F.G.*]), p. 3.

68. *H.C.,* p. 234.

69. *H.C.,* pp. 195–196.

70. *F.G.,* p. 21. In picking out action as "the exclusive prerogative of man," Arendt notes that "neither a beast nor a god is capable of it" (*H.C.,* pp. 22–23). Both she and Nussbaum of course are echoing Aristotle's famous assertion (in the context of making the point that man "alone of all the animals is furnished with the faculty of language") that "the man who is isolated . . . must be either a beast or a god" (*Politics* 1.2).

71. *F.G.,* p. 8.

72. *F.G.,* p. 318.

73. From Nussbaum's viewpoint (despite her concern to extricate *aretē* from any narrowly moral context — she speaks, characteristically, of "the quick tense splendor of human excellence" [*F.G.,* p. 342]), there would seem to be too much of Nietzsche in Arendt's emphasis on "glory" (see *H.C.,* p. 180) or "greatness" (*H.C.,* pp. 205–206) as the seal of action; and it must also seem regrettable that, having rescued action from the type of rationality that prevails in fabrication, Arendt fails to provide any adequate account of an *alternative* type of knowledge or rationality that can inform it. And here Aristotle must seem superior to Arendt in that his reaction to Plato, far from prompting any kind of 'romantic' picture of action, led to a very refined analysis of the kind of action-guiding knowledge that is phronesis. (see *F.G.,* ch. 10 on "nonscientific deliberation"). While both Nussbaum and Arendt always remain aware of the deep attractiveness of the Platonic drive for rational control, which they nevertheless want to resist, the form of Nussbaum's resistance is more *sober:* when, early

on, she gives us two lists, A and B, of qualities which fall on either side of the polarity which she is exploring throughout the book (very summarily, between "control" and "fragility"), she is careful to alert us to the fact that the one which she wants to defend is not exclusive or extreme: "It is important to notice that B is not the polar opposite of A: it is the balanced combination of the elements stressed and cultivated in A with the elements that A avoids and shuns" (ibid., p. 20).

74. *F.G.*, p. 393.

4. The Play of Phronesis and Techne in Hans-Georg Gadamer's *Truth and Method*

1. See below, ch. 6, §3.

2. Originally published as *Wahrheit und Methode: Grundzüge einer philosophischen Hermeneutik* (Tübingen: Mohr, 1960), now vol. 1 of Gadamer's *Gesammelte Werke* (Tübingen: Mohr, 1986); English version trans. and ed. Garret Barden and John Cumming (London: Sheed & Ward, 1975). In citing all references I shall follow the established practice of giving page numbers in both the English (hereafter, *T.M.*) and the German (2nd ed., 1965, hereafter, *W.M.*) texts.

3. See, for example, the easy use of phronesis, untranslated, in Richard Rorty's *Philosophy and the Mirror of Nature* (Oxford: Basil Blackwell, 1980) esp. p. 319 and ch. 8, in Richard J. Bernstein's *Beyond Objectivism and Relativism* (Oxford: Basil Blackwell, 1983), esp. pt. 3, and in Alessandro Ferrara's "On Phronesis," in *Praxis International*, vol. 7, no. 3/4 (autumn 1987/spring 1988).

4. Gadamer acknowledges Heidegger's influence in opening up not only hermeneutics but also — through his seminar on the *Ethics* in 1923 — the potential richness and serviceability of Aristotle's treatment of practical knowledge in *E.N.* 6. See, e.g., "Martin Heidegger and Marburg Theology," in *Philosophical Hermeneutics*, a selection of essays (with one exception) published in *Kleine Schriften* (Tübingen), ed. and trans. David E. Linge (Berkeley and Los Angeles: University of California Press, 1977), pp. 200–202; "Hermeneutics and Historicism," Supplement 1 in *T.M.*, pp. 489–490; *W.M.*, p. 511; and "Martin Heidegger" in *Philosophical Apprenticeships* (*Philosophische Lehrjahre* [Frankfurt am Main, 1977] with one additional essay), trans. Robert R. Sullivan (Cambridge, Mass.: M.I.T. Press, 1985), pp. 47–49.

5. *T.M.*, p. 278; *W.M.*, p. 295.

6. The first part of *Truth and Method* is devoted to a reflection on art. This reflection, in fact, "points in the same direction" as the reflection on the human studies (and especially on their central activity of interpretation) that is undertaken in the second part of the book. Gadamer's target in the latter is "historical consciousness," just as in the former it is "aesthetic consciousness"; but both of these are only different versions of modern subjectivism, which is the underlying target of the whole book and the ontological alternative to which is developed through the reflection on language in the third part. I shall not focus on Gadamer's treatment of art but shall outline his main hermeneutical themes as they emerge out of his discussion of textual interpretation in the second part. I should point out, however, that these themes can also embrace the appreciation of works of art. For Gadamer's overall strategy is such that "[A]esthetics has to be absorbed into hermeneutics" and, conversely, "hermeneutics has to be so determined as a whole that it does justice to the experience of art"

(*T.M.*, p. 146; *W.M.*, p. 157). The fact that I shall not be drawing attention to aesthetic considerations as such will not therefore prevent the latter from being implicitly present in our discussion. In particular, the themes of play and of language as the self-presentation of being that we shall meet later have a very intimate role in Gadamer's hermeneutically aware aesthetics. On the relationship between Gadamer's aesthetics and Collingwood's, see n. 40 below.

7. These essays are now brought together in vol. 2 of Gadamer's *Gesammelte Werke* (Tübingen: Mohr, 1986). Two important collections in English translation are *Philosophical Hermeneutics* (hereafter *P.H.*) and *Reason in the Age of Science* (*Vernunft im Zeitalter der Wissenschaft* [Frankfurt: 1976]) with two additional essays, trans. Frederick G. Lawrence (Cambridge, Mass.: M.I.T. Press, 1981).

8. "Practical philosophy" is the usual translation of the German expression *Praktische Philosophie*, which is itself a translation of the Latin *philosophia practica*. In view of the ambiguity of this phrase in English ("philosophy of practice" would, I think, be a better translation), it should be pointed out that it connotes not an attempt to make philosophy "practical" or "applied"—so that it will earn its keep—but rather a discipline which takes the practical realm as the object of its inquiry and at the same time recognizes that the peculiar nature of this object inevitably affects its own status as theory. Practical philosophy in this sense is Aristotle's discovery; it was based on his rejection of Plato's attempt to construct a theory of ethics and politics which would be continuous with, and meet the strict criteria of, theory as *epistēmē* or *sophia* (see below ch. 8, §2).

9. There was, of course, a pre-history of hermeneutics which stretched back very far indeed. Plato, for instance, was involved in hermeneutical issues when he was arguing about how Homer was to be read, as, more particularly, were the early Church Fathers or, much later, the Reformers in their approaches to Scripture. In all cases where texts were both familiar, in that they were still actively pondered and deferred to, and alien, in that they came from a different and perhaps quite distant world, hermeneutical issues arose. In pre-modern hermeneutics, however, these issues were considered relatively unproblematical, and in the case of theology, for instance, hermeneutics remained a minor subdiscipline very firmly under the control of dogmatics. It was only with the radical break with the past brought about by historical consciousness in the eighteenth and nineteenth centuries that these issues were transformed into ones of major methodological significance, so that in the religious sphere, for instance, they were to prove capable of shaking dogmatic theology to its very foundations. Although with Gadamer the significance of these issues becomes even more radical—so that they become virtually coextensive with the subject matter of philosophy itself—his analysis, as we shall see later (especially in his appeal to the precedents of religious and legal hermeneutics), serves to confirm a truth in the old approaches which had been forfeited by the new hermeneutics.

10. We have already met and criticized this notion in Collingwood. See above, ch. 2, §5, text at n. 110.

11. *T.M.*, p. 166; *W.M.*, p. 177.

12. *T.M.*, p. 164; *W.M.*, p. 175.

13. *T.M.*, p. 175; *W.M.*, p. 187.

14. *T.M.*, p. 258; *W.M.*, p. 274.

15. *T.M.*, p. 210; *W.M.*, p. 224.

16. *T.M.*, p. 212; *W.M.*, p. 226.

17. *T.M.*, pp. 239–240; *W.M.*, pp. 254–255.

18. With the work of Kuhn, Feyerabend, and others, it is, of course (as we saw in ch. 1, §3), no longer as predominant as it was a few decades ago. For a discussion which very adroitly links Gadamer's work with this "post-empiricist philosophy of science," see Bernstein, *Beyond Objectivism and Relativism*, esp. pt. 1.

19. *T.M.*, p. 229; *W.M.*, p. 244.

20. *Being and Time*, trans. by John Macquarrie and Edward Robinson (Oxford: Basil Blackwell, 1962; hereafter *B.T.*), p. 182; *Sein und Zeit* (Tübingen: 1926; hereafter *S.Z.*), p. 143 (emphasis added).

21. *B.T.*, p. 185; *S.Z.*, p. 145.

22. *B.T.*, pp. 191–192, *S.Z.*, p. 150.

23. *B.T.*, p. 194; *S.Z.*, p. 153.

24. *B.T.*, p. 195; *S.Z.*, p. 153.

25. *B.T.*, p. 428; *S.Z.*, p. 376.

26. *T.M.*, p. 232; *W.M.*, pp. 247–8.

27. *T.M.*, p. 244; *W.M.*, p. 260 (emphasis added).

28. What Gadamer is partly getting at here — that traditionalism is no substitute for tradition — is well expressed by Merleau-Ponty when (paraphrasing Husserl) he speaks of tradition as "the power . . . to give to the past not a survival, which is the hypocritical form of forgetfulness, but a new life, which is the noble form of memory" ("Indirect Language and Voices of Silence," *Signs* [Evanston, Ill.: Northwestern University Press, 1964], p. 59).

29. *T.M.*, p. 244; *W.M.*, p. 260.

30. *T.M.*, p. 245; *W.M.*, p. 261. The way in which Gadamer puts pressure on himself here is very comparable, I think, to an occasion which I shall advert to later (see below, ch. 9, §1) where Aristotle, in trying to secure the place of phronesis as a form of practical-moral knowledge, makes things provocatively difficult for himself by introducing, as a dialectical position, the view that virtuous practice is already well established without any need of the reasonableness of phronesis. We see in both cases the "art of strengthening", which Gadamer elsewhere suggests is at the heart of dialectic: "A person who possesses this art will himself seek for everything in favour of an opinion. Dialectic consists not in trying to discover the weakness of what is said, but in bringing out its real strength." (*T.M.*, pp. 330–331; *W.M.*, p. 349) It is only when we concede the full weight of what conspires, in each case, against the transcendence that is normally taken to be a criterion of knowledge that we can adequately understand the kinds of knowledge that both Gadamer and Aristotle are trying to elucidate.

31. *T.M.*, pp. 246 and 247; *W.M.*, pp. 261 and 263 (emphasis added).

32. *T.M.*, p. 249; *W.M.*, pp. 264–265.

33. *T.M.*, p. 250; *W.M.*, pp. 265–266.

34. *T.M.*, p. 250; *W.M.*, p. 265.

35. *T.M.*, p. 251; *W.M.*, p. 267.

36. *T.M.*, p. 261; *W.M.*, p. 277.

37. Ibid. Here, as in many other places, the German word Gadamer uses is not

tradition but *Überlieferung*, which, more strongly than the English word 'tradition,' conveys a sense of the enduringly active character of what is handed down.

38. Gadamer's word for 'thing', *die Sache*, is one of the most crucial and constantly recurring terms in *Wahrheit und Methode*. Its frequent rendering in the English translation as 'object' is unfortunate, since Gadamer's express purpose in appealing to it is precisely to undercut the notion of 'objectivity' as a correlative of methodically disciplined 'subjectivity'. Clearly, *die Sache* has to do with what is the case and asserts itself, irrespective of our desires, projections, or plans. We have to be careful, however, about how we understand "irrespective" here. Although, in speaking frequently of *die Sache selbst*, Gadamer is strongly echoing Husserl's famous formulation of the task of phenomenology as "back to the things themselves," he does not believe that Husserl's own transcendental method allowed a satisfactory performance of this task. At the same time, however, when thinkers (such as his teachers and colleagues Hartmann, Löwith, and Kruger) reacted against neo-Kantian idealism and transcendental constitution-analysis by affirming some variant of a metaphysics of being-in-itself, Gadamer believes that their notion of 'being' remains tied to the notion of subjectivity (and 'will') simply by being conceived in such explicit opposition to it. (See "The Nature of Things and the Language of Things," *P.H.*, pp. 69–81.) What Gadamer himself means by *die Sache* cannot be briefly formulated; the whole of *Wahrheit und Methode* might indeed be seen as an attempt to do so. But there is certainly an echo of Aristotle's fundamental postulate in bk. 1 of the *Ethics* that inquiry into practical affairs has to fit its mode of procedure and the scale of its ambition to its subject matter (*hulē*). And there is also a strong echo of Hegel's notion of dialectic as a process through which the thing is revealed (in one place, dialectic is described as "an activity of the thing itself, an activity that unlike the methodology of modern science, is a passivity, an understanding, an event" (*T.M.*, p. 422; *W.M.*, pp. 440–441). We shall see, however, that there is a great deal more humility in Gadamer's dialectic than there is in Hegel's: a humility that is brought about by his deeper reflection on the linguistic character (*Sprachlichkeit*) of our experience of the world. Ultimately, for Gadamer, the meaning of *die Sache* is held in the meaning of *die Sprache* (language); although words can easily be made mere instruments of our will, language is still the place where — paradigmatically in the tentative unfolding of a conversation or in the miraculous appropriateness of a poem — beyond our intending or willing, the thing appears.

39. See *T.M.*, p. 212; *W.M.*, p. 227.

40. I do not want to overstate the affinities here. Although Collingwood's aesthetics, like Gadamer's hermeneutics, is an attack on technicist assumptions, from Gadamer's perspective the question must arise as to whether it is at all radical enough in dismantling the subjectivist framework which holds these assumptions in place. Collingwood's theory of consciousness is a finely differentiated one which allows for "passivity"—and therefore limits the controlling agency of the ego—in the expression of emotion; but does it not still remain a version of that "philosophy of consciousness" whose entire spell Gadamer is trying to break? This question is given a particularly sharp focus by the fact that Collingwood accords such centrality to the concept of 'expression'. For this is a concept about which Gadamer is especially circumspect: in an appendix to *Truth and Method* he tells us that the "whole of our investigation shows why the concept of 'expression' [*Ausdruck*] must be purified of its modern subjectivist

flavour," and again that "the critique of the psychologisation of the concept of expression runs through the whole of our present investigation." Moreover in "Hermeneutics and Historicism," a Supplement to *Truth and Method*, he argues that Collingwood's central concept of 're-enactment' in *The Idea of History* is flawed by psychologistic assumptions (see *T.M.*, pp. 467–469; *W.M.*, pp. 485–487, and n. 90 below). In my own response to Collingwood, in ch. 2, §6 above, I anticipated Gadamer's perspective and tried to 'purify' Collingwood's position in *The Principles of Art* (a work, incidentally, which Gadamer does not consider) of its 'subjectivist flavor'; I also pointed out by reference to Merleau-Ponty (n. 130), that the concept of 'expression' *per se* need not carry subjectivistic implications.

41. See above ch. 1, §2, text at n. 39.

42. *G.A.*, p. 353.

43. *T.M.*, p. 329; *W.M.*, p. 348. "Dialectic" has, of course, come to be associated more with Hegel than with Plato. For Gadamer's appreciation of the superiority of Platonic dialectic, however, see below, ch. 5, n. 41.

44. *T.M.*, p. 331; *W.M.*, p. 349.

45. Gadamer's own explication of Aristotle's concept of phronesis, in the context of a concern with hermeneutical problems which were certainly outside Aristotle's horizon, may itself be taken as a paradigm example here. My own reading of Newman, as I mentioned at the time, attempted to do something similarly constructive with the 'temporal distance' that separates Newman's era from our own.

46. That the conversational nature of interpretation precludes appeal to any more ultimate yardstick outside the conversation is a point which we met earlier in Collingwood. Rejecting the possibility of the conversational parties' having "any absolute assurance" of understanding each other correctly, Collingwood maintains that the only available assurance is one that grows "progressively stronger as conversation proceeds. . . . The question whether they understand each other *solvitur interloquendo*. If they understand each other well enough to go on talking, they understand each other as well as they need; and there is no better kind of understanding which they can regret not having attained" (*P.A.*, p. 251).

47. *Philosophy and the Mirror of Nature*, p. 321.

48. *T.M.*, p. 268; *W.M.*, p. 285.

49. Although the English expression here is an unhappy one, it is not easy to find any compact equivalent for the German phrase which means something like "a consciousness that is aware of its own exposure to the continuing efficacy of the past"; the hyphen in the English term is important because it is not consciousness but rather history which is 'effective'.

50. See *T.M.*, p. 524, n. 200 and pp. 216ff; *W.M.*, p. 285, n. 1 and pp. 231ff.

51. *T.M.*, p. 269; *W.M.*, p. 285.

52. It seems to me that what we meet here in Gadamer has a very close parallel in a bold analysis of Aristotle's conception of change (*kinēsis*) by Sarah Waterlow which we will meet in part 2 (ch. 10, §6). As Gadamer is trying to show that the duality of reader and text is annulled in the actual process of reading, so Waterlow tries to undercut a like duality between agent and patient in the process of change: "In the change as a concrete unitary event there are not different entities to be agent and patient. The active and passive of the verb, from this point of view, are used of the

change itself only derivatively, on the basis of an actual distinction, existing only *ante* and *post eventum*. We cannot even call the two beings the 'potential agent and patient' since this implies that they could be actually so. But they could be actually so only in the actual change and *in* the actual change they are not distinct and therefore not agent and patient." Just as Gadamer, at this point, may create unease in a reader by dissolving what seem like basic categories, so Waterlow acknowledges, at this point in her analysis, that we may "find this account which undercuts all the customary distinctions incredible." Waterlow's position here might indeed be regarded as more radically deconstructive than Gadamer's; for it grates more on our intuitions to admit the case here in relation to the interaction of material substances than to grant it in the case of a cognitive — and therefore already less 'solid' — process such as reading or understanding. In fact, what Waterlow points out as the cause of our incredulity here is, I believe, just what Gadamer is trying to subvert throughout the course of *Truth and Method*. For Waterlow the difficulty resides in "the structure of the concepts we use to describe our own practical activities" — or, in other words, "the point of view of the voluntary agent," which we adopt when "we intend to produce some change in an object other than ourselves." This structure or point of view trips us into misconstruing the reality both of our own practical achievements and of the interaction of material substances to which we inadvertently extrapolate it. Waterlow does not see it as part of her purpose to provide "further discussion of the issues that open up here"; but what she is getting at is, I suggest, very close to what Gadamer is getting at when he tells us that his main concern is "not what we do or what we ought to do, but what happens to us over and above our wanting and doing" — or when he highlights the role of hermeneutics as a "corrective" that "enlightens the modern attitude of making, producing and constructing about the necessary conditions to which it is subject." (Quotations from Gadamer and Waterlow here are from the foreword to the 2nd edition of *Truth and Method*, and *Nature, Change and Agency in Aristotle's Physics* [Oxford: Clarendon Press, 1982], pp. 202–203.)

53. *T.M.*, p. 273; *W.M.*, p. 289.
54. *T.M.*, p. 263; *W.M.*, p. 279.
55. *T.M.*, p. 273; *W.M.*, p. 290.
56. Ibid.
57. The German word that Gadamer mainly uses is *Anwendung*, though he does also use *Applikation*, a derivative from the Latin *applicatio* (which he mentions [*T.M.*, p. 274; *W.M.*, p. 291] as a Pietistic contribution to hermeneutical theory but which was also in fact used by Aquinas in his analysis of *prudentia* [see below, ch. 10, §2, text between n. 18 and n. 19]).
58. This is a phrase Gadamer himself used to characterize the development of ideas in *Truth and Method* at a colloquium in Belfast in March 1985.
59. See the section headed "The Hermeneutical Significance of Aristotle", *T.M.*, pp. 278–289; *W.M.*, pp. 295–307.
60. *T.M.*, p. 289; *W.M.*, p. 307.
61. *T.M.*, p. 472; *W.M.*, p. 491.
62. *T.M.*, p. 491; *W.M.*, p. 512.
63. See n. 7 above.
64. "Hermeneutics as Practical Philosophy" in *Reason in the Age of Science*, p. 109.

65. *T.M.*, p. 280; *W.M.*, p. 296.
66. Ibid.
67. *T.M.*, p. 288; *W.M.*, p. 305.
68. "Hermeneutics as Practical Philosophy," pp. 106–107.
69. Ibid., p. 107.
70. Ibid., pp. 107–108.
71. While his hermeneutical philosophy is the main source of Gadamer's renown, he has also, of course, had a parallel (and indeed profoundly complementary) career as a philologist and exegete. In his *laudatio*, Habermas speaks of him as "this philosopher who has been accustomed to characterize himself with the remark that he is a student of Heidegger and has learned the craft of classical philology" ("Urbanizing the Heideggerian Province," in J. Habermas, *Philosophical-Political Profiles*, trans. Frederick G. Lawrence [London: Heinemann, 1983]). He has in fact published a study of Plato's and Aristotle's ethical theory (*Die Idee des Guten zwischen Plato und Aristoteles* [Heidelberg, 1978]), translated with Introduction and Annotation by P. Christopher Smith as *The Idea of the Good in Plato and Aristotle* (New Haven: Yale Univ. Press, 1986). I do not refer to this book in the text because it does not, I believe, alter the picture of phronesis that is presented in *Truth and Method*. It does, however, attempt to bring out what Gadamer sees as the profound unity of Plato's and Aristotle's thought—and to show that even the latter's famous critique of the Idea of the Good reveals a methodological difference rather than substantive disagreement. (For other references to the Platonism of Aristotle, see below, ch. 5, §5).
72. *T.M.*, pp. 287–288; *W.M.*, p. 305.
73. *T.M.*, p. 310; *W.M.*, p. 329.
74. *T.M.*, p. 311; *W.M.*, p. 330.
75. *T.M.*, p. 316; *W.M.*, p. 335.
76. Ibid.
77. Ibid.
78. All the quotations in this and the next paragraph are from *T.M.*, pp. 317–321; *W.M.*, pp. 336–340.
79. *The Human Condition*, p. 207.
80. *T.M.*, p. 324; *W.M.*, p. 343.
81. *Sunesis* and *gnōmē* are described by Aristotle as having the same objects as phronesis—i.e., particular actions (*eschata*)—and the same reference, so that the people who are credited with them are identical with the *phronimoi*. Cf. *E.N.* 6.11; 1143a.25–33.
82. *T.M.*, p. 288; *W.M.*, p. 306.
83. *T.M.*, p. 322; *W.M.*, p. 341.
84. *T.M.*, p. 324; *W.M.*, p. 343.
85. Here we may note the close affinity between Gadamer's basic hermeneutical attitude and that of Paul Ricoeur. Ricoeur has argued for what he calls an "affirmative hermeneutics" to counter the "hermeneutics of suspicion" which was deployed so devastatingly by the great "masters of suspicion," Marx, Nietzsche, and Freud. (See *Freud and Philosophy: An Essay on Interpretation*, trans. Denis Savage [New Haven: Yale University Press, 1970].) Gadamer's position here will come into clearer relief when I discuss his disagreements with Habermas, whose "critical theory," like that of his

forebears in the first generation of the Frankfurt School, has, of course, quite crucially built on the insights of both Marx and Freud. It is interesting that despite what Ricoeur himself has called his "great proximity" to Gadamer ("A Response by Paul Ricoeur," p. 36 in *Hermeneutics and the Human Sciences: Essays on Language, Action, and Interpretation*, ed., trans., and introduction by John B. Thompson [Cambridge: Cambridge University Press, 1981]) he very pointedly does not take Gadamer's side in his very even-handed discussion of the Gadamer-Habermas debate. (See "Hermeneutics and the Critique of Ideology" in ibid. and below, ch. 6, §4.)

86. *T.M.*, p. 325; *W.M.*, p. 344.

87. *T.M.*, p. xxvi; *W.M.*, p. xxiv.

88. The difficulties here, as we shall see presently, are formidable: "the nature of language is one of the most mysterious questions that exist for man to ponder on" (*T.M.*, p. 340; *W.M.*, p. 359). What makes it so mysterious for Gadamer, as for anyone else, is well expressed by Seamus Heaney: "A human being pondering the nature of language is not unlike a snowman attempting to comprehend the nature of snow, for the snowman's instruments of cognition are no less snowy than the human being's are wordy" ("Words Alone?" p. 12, in Vincent Greaney and Brendan Molloy, eds., *Dimensions of Reading*, [Dublin: The Educational Company of Ireland, 1986]). Or as the same point is made less vividly by Gadamer himself: "all thinking about language is already once again drawn back into language. We can only think in a language and just this residing of our thinking in a language is the profound enigma that language presents to thought" ("Man and Language," p. 62 in *P.H.*).

89. Aristotle is aware that 'play' (*paidia*) is a form of non-instrumental activity and (as Collingwood points out in a section of play in his chapter on art in *Speculum Mentis*) even considers whether it might not be a good definition of God's activity. So far from seeing it as a concept with rich potential for ontological illumination, however, Aristotle adopts a moralistic and dismissive attitude to it; its most noteworthy features for him are frivolousness and childishness (*paidia* was derived from *pais*, a child), and so he sees it as unworthy of being chosen for its own sake. Indeed, in his own hierarchy of values, he recommends a frankly instrumentalist attitude to it; rather than working in order to play, we ought to play in order to work; play in other words, is justifiable only because it refreshes and relaxes and so makes one better able for the exertions of work (*ascholia*). Work itself, of course, was not self-justifying either, but was to be subordinated to leisure (*scholē*), the only sphere in which well-being (*eudaimonia*) was to be achieved — through the practice either of the ethical virtues or, better, of contemplation — and which alone, therefore, was self-justifying ("everything we choose we choose for the sake of something else — except *eudaimonia* which is an end"). Play, then, had a very low status indeed, being subordinate to work and, in particular, being quite distinct from leisure (see *E.N.* 10.6 and Friedrich Solmsen, "Leisure and Play in Aristotle's Ideal State," in *Kleine Schriften*, vol. 2 [Hildesheim, 1968]).

The importance of language for Aristotle is perhaps most evident in his famous differentiation of man, in the second chapter of the *Politics*, on the basis that he "alone of the animals is furnished with the faculty of language" (*logon echōn*). It will be clear from the discussion in the next chapter, however, that *logos* here is quite different from the concept of language entertained by Gadamer (and indeed many other twentieth-century philosophers).

90. Gadamer pays generous tribute to Collingwood as the source of the "logic of question and answer" which he develops at this point in his discussion, while trying to extricate it from some of the idealist implications of Collingwood's own rather sketchy formulation of it (in chapter 5 of his brief *Autobiography*, which, incidentally, was translated into German, with an introduction by Gadamer [Stuttgart, 1955]). There is also a critical discussion of Collingwood's *The Idea of History* in "Hermeneutics and Historicism" (supplement to *T.M.*) in which Gadamer tries to show that if Collingwood had remained faithful to his insight into the logic of question and answer he would have avoided the error of asserting that "thought can be placed in different contexts without losing its identity." In fact, Gadamer believes that Collingwood, his best intentions notwithstanding, does not succeed in extricating "thought" from the "psychological particularity" of the thinker, so that "the dimension of hermeneutical communication which is passed through in every act of understanding still escapes him" (*T.M.*, pp. 467–469; *W.M.*, pp. 485–487). On this last point, see my discussion of Collingwood in ch. 2, §6 and n. 40 above.

91. *T.M.*, p. 325; *W.M.*, p. 344.

92. *T.M.*, p. 337; *W.M.*, p. 356.

93. *T.M.*, p. 338; *W.M.*, p. 357. Gadamer acknowledges that there are, of course, questions that we cannot now ask, even though they are meaningful in the sense that we can understand how they were once asked, e.g., questions about perpetual motion or questions that were asked before the sphericity of the earth was discovered. In these cases there has been a radical rupture; the presuppositions of the questions have entirely collapsed. The horizon of present questioning cannot really 'fuse' with the horizons of these 'obsolete' questions, although the drastic discontinuities which make this the case can, perhaps, be intelligibly reconstructed as crucial moments within the development of an ongoing tradition of inquiry. Gadamer's point is that such reconstruction—which is undertaken on the basis of the established superiority of the vantage point of the present—is in no way normative for our general relationship to the past; much of what comes down to us in the form of 'tradition' simply does not allow us such a superior vantage point in its regard; and in fact we only encounter it in the 'fusion' of its questions and our own.

94. *T.M.*, p. 326; *W.M.*, p. 345.

95. Ibid.

96. *T.M.*, p. 330; *W.M.*, p. 349.

97. *T.M.*, p. 330; *W.M.*, p. 348.

98. *T.M.*, p. 329; *W.M.*, p. 348.

99. *T.M.*, p. 330; *W.M.*, p. 349.

100. See esp. pp. 91–99; *W.M.*, pp. 97–105.

101. *T.M.*, p. 94; *W.M.*, p. 100.

102. *T.M.*, p. 93; *W.M.*, p. 99.

103. *T.M.*, pp. 95–96; *W.M.*, pp. 101–102.

104. *T.M.*, p. 98; *W.M.*, p. 104. In one of the rare references to empirical work in his writings, Gadamer points to the research of von Weizsäcker on the "tension-filled" interaction between the mongoose and the snake as an apposite illustration of the dynamics of the game. A less esoteric illustration is to be found in the work of the American psychologist W. Timothy Gallwey, elaborated in such books as *The*

Inner Game of Tennis, The Inner Game of Golf, and *The Inner Game of Skiing.* Gallwey has his own jargon in these books, but his basic thesis could, I think, be accurately formulated in terms that are now familiar to us from Gadamer: to cultivate the "inner game" is simply to find ways of stopping the interference that comes from one's projecting subjectivity and to surrender to the bouyancy of the game itself. In the context of my overall study I may say that Gallwey's books provide an interesting example of work whose basic premise is precisely a keen recognition of the limits of technique. And although he himself does not at all advert to the philosophical tradition, his conceptual stock-in-trade bears eloquent tribute to the enduringness of Aristotle's basic categories. Later on, I shall have occasion to examine the way in which Aristotle works out the relationship between techne and the unconscious teleology of nature (*phusis*), as I analyze such remarks as "techne imitates nature" or "techne exists to aid nature and to make up its deficiencies." But here is a typical piece from Gallwey which might have come straight out of Aristotle: "The word 'technology' may sound antithetical to your concept of . . . what is natural. But nature *is* technical. What is *un*natural is the use of technique to replace what is natural . . . my objection has been to the use of technical information about the golf swing replacing and interfering with the body's natural ability to learn. Technique is most useful when it *supports* natural ability" (*The Inner Game of Golf* [London: Jonathan Cape, 1981], p. 103; and see also below, ch. 10, §5).

105. In the *Logic,* as Gadamer points out, Hegel quotes Plato and makes an "explicit appeal to the Greek concept of methodology", which for him was much superior to the "external reflection" of modern method. (See *T.M.,* p. 421; *W.M.,* p. 439, and "Hegel and the Dialectic of the Ancient Philosophers," in *Hegel's Dialectic: Five Hermeneutical Studies* [*Hegels Dialektik: fünf hermeneutische Studien,* Tübingen, 1971], trans. P. Christopher Smith [New Haven: Yale University Press, 1976], pp. 5–34.)

106. "On the Problem of Self-Understanding," p. 54 in *P.H.*

107. Ibid., p. 55.

108. Ibid., p. 57.

5. Language, Hermeneutics, and Practical Philosophy

1. *T.M.,* p. 411; *W.M.,* p. 429.

2. "On the Origins of Philosophical Hermeneutics," p. 179, in *Philosophical Apprenticeships.*

3. *T.M.,* p. 401; *W.M.,* p. 419.

4. *T.M.,* p. 375; *W.M.,* p. 392. Cf. Newman's strictures on the scientific-technical assault on words, the attempt to "circumscribe and stint their impact as much as possible . . . to make them as much as possible the calculi of notions which are in our absolute power, as meaning just what we choose them to mean" (*Grammar of Assent,* p. 214); and for Collingwood's concurrence, also, with Gadamer here, cf. above, ch. 2, §3.

5. *T.M.,* p. 368; *W.M.,* p. 384.

6. *T.M.,* p. 377; *W.M.,* p. 394.

7. *T.M.,* p. 406; *W.M.,* p. 424.

8. *T.M.,* p. 363; *W.M.,* p. 379.

9. Gadamer tells us that: "Insofar as they are my constant companions, I have

416   Notes to pages 140–147

been more formed by the Platonic dialogues than by the great thinkers of German Idealism" ("On the Origins of Philosophical Hermeneutics," p. 184). But he also concludes an essay on "The Heritage of Hegel" by affirming Hegel as one "whose challenge I try to pose to myself, in positive as well as in negative aspects, whenever I can" (*Reason in the Age of Science*, p. 63). See below, n. 41.

10. "Man and Language," p. 67 in *P.H.*

11. *T.M.*, p. 406; *W.M.*, p. 424.

12. *T.M.*, p. 411; *W.M.*, p. 429.

13. *T.M.*, p. 346; *W.M.*, p. 362.

14. *T.M.*, p. 349; *W.M.*, p. 365.

15. It is briefly adverted to on p. 274 and p. 341 (*W.M.*, p. 291 and p. 360).

16. *T.M.*, p. 359; *W.M.*, pp. 375–376.

17. *T.M.*, p. 365; *W.M.*, p. 381.

18. *T.M.*, p. 364; *W.M.*, p. 380.

19. *T.M.*, p. 411; *W.M.*, pp. 429–430.

20. *T.M.*, p. 377; *W.M.*, p. 394.

21. *T.M.*, p. 390; *W.M.*, p. 407.

22. *T.M.*, p. 388; *W.M.*, p. 405.

23. *T.M.*, p. 392; *W.M.*, p. 409.

24. Given this extreme brevity, a remark of Gadamer's in one of his later essays, where he is referring to this passage in *Posterior Analytics* 2.19, seems exaggerated: "It is Aristotle once again who gives us the most extensive description of the process in which one learns to speak." Gadamer acknowledges, incidentally, that his move of taking this passage as an accurate depiction of how one learns to speak a language was first made in the commentary of Themistius. Later on (ch. 9, §5) I shall take it to be an equally good account of the dynamics of ethical development.

25. *T.M.*, p. 391; *W.M.*, p. 409.

26. This is a phrase which, as we shall see later, Habermas uses, in the spirit of Vico, in his own critical recapitulation of the tradition.

27. *T.M.*, p. 418; *W.M.*, p. 437.

28. "The Nature of Things and the Language of Things," p. 75, in *P.H.*

29. Wittgenstein is not mentioned in *Truth and Method*, but in two of his later essays Gadamer adverts to the "noteworthy convergence" between "Wittgenstein's critique of Anglo-Saxon semantics" (including his own *Tractatus*), which led to the pragmatics of language-games in the *Philosophical Investigations*, and Heidegger's critique of "the ahistorical art of phenomenological description," which led to the hermeneutics that Gadamer himself has so conspicuously developed. See "Philosophical Foundations," pp. 126–127, and "The Phenomenological Movement," pp. 173–177, in *P.H.*

30. Cf. St. Paul, 1 Corinthians 1:23.

31. *T.M.*, p. 341; *W.M.*, p. 360.

32. "The Nature of Things and the Language of Things," p. 77, in *P.H.*

33. See *T.M.*, p. 415; *W.M.*, p. 433.

34. "Man and Language," p. 67, in *P.H.* For a consummate discussion of this aspect of language, see Merleau-Ponty's essay "Indirect Language and the Voices of Silence," in which he shows "that the idea of complete expression is nonsensical, and that all language is indirect or allusive — that it is, if you wish, silence" (in *Signs*, translated

and introduced by Richard C. McCleary ([Evanston, Ill.: Northwestern University Press, 1964], p. 43; "Le Langage indirect et les voix du silence," in *Signes* ([Paris: Gallimard, 1960], p. 54).

35. *T.M.*, p. 425; *W.M.*, p. 444.

36. *T.M.*, pp. 415-416; *W.M.*, p. 434.

37. Gadamer uses the English word 'statement' (*W.M.*, p. 352) when he refers admiringly to the way in which Collingwood's 'logic of question and answer' undermined the fixity of 'statements'. 'Aussage' is the word he uses later on, when he deepens this critique through his own reflection on language.

38. *T.M.*, p. 355; *W.M.*, p. 371. The point that Gadamer is making here is the same point that he makes in a later essay where he maintains that *genuine* rhetoric is actually coincident with dialectic, and—with a more eirenic attitude to Plato than he shows in *Truth and Method*—that this was Plato's point in the *Phaedrus*, as well as being an assumption of Aristotle's in the *Rhetoric*. See below, latter part of §5.

39. *T.M.*, p. 426; *W.M.*, p. 444.

40. *T.M.*, p. 353; *W.M.*, pp. 369-370.

41. Here Gadamer is only echoing Plato's lament about the way in which a written text "drifts all over the place, getting into the hands not only of those who understand it, but equally of those who have no business with it; it doesn't know how to address the right people and not to address the wrong. And when it is ill-treated and unfairly abused it always needs its parent to come to its help, being unable to defend or help itself" (*Phaedrus* 275e). (Gadamer of course would not agree with Plato here that the rescuer must always be the parent, i.e., the author; the whole point of his subversion of the *mens auctoris* as the norm of interpretation is that others can prove themselves to be "the right people," precisely by their ability to "awaken" the meaning of the text in contexts and idioms that could never have been envisaged by its author.) Such was Plato's keen sense of this vulnerability of the written word that there was a core of his own teaching, as he tells us in the *Seventh Letter* (341c), that he was unwilling ever to commit to writing. But even his writings themselves, we must notice, attempt to overcome the fixity of their written state by incorporating into themselves something of the life and movement of conversation.

For all the dexterous moves whereby Gadamer distances himself from Plato and Hegel, it is still clear that they remain for him the great masters of philosophical writing. Of Plato he remarks: "The literary form of the dialogue places language and concept back within the original movement of the conversation. This protects words from all dogmatic abuse." Plato has the advantage over Hegel, one might infer, that his Dialogues retain the openness (and invariably, indeed, the inconclusiveness) of actual conversation. Despite Gadamer's great admiration for Hegel, despite, indeed, his regarding Hegel as the peerless interpreter of Greek thought ("whoever wants to learn from the Greeks has always first to learn from Hegel"), he is still, very characteristically, more in sympathy with the modesty of the Greeks than with the ambition of Hegel. Although Hegel gives us "a magnificent reminder of what dialectic was and is" (by his attempt to make "fluid and subtle the abstract determinations of thought," which means "dissolving and remoulding logic into the procedures of language, and the concept into the meaningful power of words, which ask questions and give answers") he is still "unsuccessful" insofar as in the end his dialectic disappears into absolute knowledge. Hegel provides a masterly formulation of the nature of dialectic; but he over-reached himself in supposing that with this formulation the issue of the dialectic could be determined. Gadamer remarks of the great enterprise which he both admires and at the same time constantly fights against: "Hegel's dialectic is a mono- logue of thinking that seeks to carry out in advance what matures little by little in every genuine conversation." (See *T.M.*, pp. 332–333; *W.M.*, p. 351) The impossibility of ever getting beyond this "little by little" approach may be linked to one of Hegel's own concepts, 'substance' (*Substanz*), i.e., the historically pre-given conditions that limit every use of reason. And in one place Gadamer provocatively characterizes his whole inquiry in a way that brings it very close to Hegel's but actually *reverses* the direction of the latter: "This almost defines the aim of philosophical hermeneutics: its task is to move back along the path of Hegel's phenomenology of mind until we discover in all that is subjective the substantiality that determines it" (*T.M.*, p. 269; *W.M.*, p. 286). (Gadamer has published a volume of essays on Plato and another on Hegel: see *Dialogue and Dialectic: Eight Hermeneutical Studies on Plato*, trans. P. Christopher Smith [New Haven: Yale University Press, 1980] and *Hegel's Dialectic: Five Hermeneutical Studies*, trans. P. Christopher Smith [New Haven: Yale Univer- sity Press, 1976].)

42. *T.M.*, p. 331; *W.M.*, p. 350.

43. Ibid. This "memory of what originally was the case" was very strikingly brought home to me in a lesson recently with a class of six-year-old children on the topic of 'living things'. We were making a preliminary survey of things that could be said to be alive when Katie suggested: 'books'. Asked why she thought they are alive, she instantly replied: "books talk when they are read"; and Jason immediately added: "yeah, they have lots of tongues." When I said I did not quite see this, he explained: "their pages are their tongues"!

44. *T.M.*, p. 340; *W.M.*, p. 359.

45. See "Man and Language" p. 65, in *P.H.*, where Gadamer writes that an "es- sential feature of the being of language seems to me to be its I-lessness."

46. *T.M.*, p. 420; *W.M.*, p. 439.

47. *T.M.*, p. 414; *W.M.*, p. 432.

48. *T.M.*, p. 404; *W.M.*, p. 422.

49. *T.M.*, p. 428; *W.M.*, p. 447.

50. *T.M.*, p. 432; *W.M.*, p. 450.

51. *T.M.*, p. 446; *W.M.*, p. 464.

52. Op. cit., p. 35.

53. "On the Problem of Self-Understanding," p. 56 in *P.H.* This gamelike qual- ity of language—or, in other words, the fact that, in its historical development, lan- guage has a life of its own which eludes any technocratic ambitions which might be entertained in its regard—was beautifully expressed by Dr. Johnson in the Preface to his *Dictionary of the English Language:* "The tropes of poetry will make hourly en- croachments, and the metaphorical will become the current sense . . . and the pen must at length comply with the tongue . . . to enchain syllables, and to lash the wind, are equally the undertaking of pride, unwilling to measure its desires by its strength."

54. *T.M.*, p. 439; *W.M.*, p. 457.

55. This phrase is from the lines of Rilke which Gadamer takes as epigraph for

Truth and Method and which, like every happy epigraph, contains, in compact form, the whole meaning of the book.

56. See above, end of §1.

57. *T.M.*, p. 391; *W.M.*, p. 409.

58. "Letter on Humanism," p. 197 in Martin Heidegger, *Basic Writings*, ed. with introduction by David Farrel Krell (London: Routledge and Kegan Paul, 1978).

59. Cf. Habermas's *laudatio*, "Urbanizing the Heideggerian Province," which sees Gadamer's work as "urbanizing" "the thick-skinned uniqueness and originality" of Heidegger's thought (in Jürgen Habermas, *Philosophical-Political Profiles*, trans. Frederick G. Lawrence [London: Heinemann, 1983], pp. 189–197).

60. *T.M.*, p. 441; *W.M.*, p. 459.

61. Ibid.

62. I am paraphrasing here Nussbaum's formulation of the three issues that she regards as "central" to her inquiry in *The Fragility of Goodness* (see pp. 6–7).

63. The *linguistic* constitution of what Aristotle refers to as "the appearances" (*ta phainomena*) was most persuasively demonstrated by G. E. L. Owen in his groundbreaking article "Tithenai ta phainomena" (published originally in S. Mansion, ed., *Aristote et les problèmes de méthode* (Louvain, 1961), pp. 83–103; also reprinted in anthologies on Aristotle edited by Barnes, Sorabji, and Schofield, and by Moravcsik, as well as in Owen's collected writings, *Logic, Science, and Dialectic*, ed. M. C. Nussbaum (London: Duckworth, 1986). For an excellent discussion (inspired by but going beyond Owen) of the significance of "saving the appearances" in Aristotle's whole methodology of ethical-political inquiry, see Nussbaum, *The Fragility of Goodness*, ch. 8.

64. In fact, the *Rhetoric* mentions (at 1362b19) the power of speaking (*dunamis tou legein*) in a comprehensive list of goods that is later put under the jurisdiction of phronesis (at 1366b20).

65. "The Heritage of Hegel," p. 56, in *Reason in the Age of Science*.

66. "Letter on Humanism," p. 199.

67. "Letter on Humanism," p. 197.

68. "The Heritage of Hegel," p. 57.

69. Ibid., p. 58.

70. It is perhaps not out of place to mention here that a review in an English church journal was able to support its view of *Truth and Method* as a "typical German" work by pointing out that on one page (p. 455) "we find Gadamer commenting on Löwith commenting on Heidegger commenting on Nietzsche!" (*Heythrop Journal*, vol. 18, no. 2, 1977, p. 200). The sparseness of Newman's references to other thinkers in the *Grammar* was quite deliberate; it followed from his belief that, in treating of matters of knowledge and conviction, "egotism is true modesty."

71. "The Heritage of Hegel", p. 58.

72. Ibid.

73. Ibid.

74. "Hermeneutics as a Theoretical and Practical Task," p. 126 in *Reason in the Age of Science*.

75. See n. 64 above.

76. I say "insofar as" here because of course modern technique has supplanted

the old *technai* precisely by its incorporation of a modern science which was quite outside the horizon of Greek thought. For fuller discussion of the discontinuity as well as the continuity between Greek techne and modern technique, see the next chapter on Habermas, §2 and esp. n. 24.

77. "Hermeneutics as Practical Philosophy," p. 111 in *Reason in the Age of Science.*

78. Ibid., p. 117.

79. Ibid., p. 116.

80. Ibid., p. 117.

81. Ibid.

82. See below, ch. 8, §3, esp. text at n. 30 to n. 37.

83. For the kind of "free play within set limits" which characterizes the relationship between *ēthos* and *phusis,* and which enables Gadamer to see Aristotle's use of *phusis* in an ethical-political context as having a critical rather than dogmatic function, see *T.M.,* pp. 284–286; *W.M.,* pp. 302–304.

84. "Hermeneutics as a Theoretical and Practical Task," p. 117.

85. See below ch. 9, n. 61.

86. Cf., in the same essay p. 118 where Gadamer more or less suggests that Aristotle set himself the question which Kant felt he had been set by Rousseau, about the place and purpose of moral theory. I shall take this a step further and show how Aristotle by no means took it as self-evident that even the "first-order" rationality of phronesis was necessary to the man favorably endowed with good natural instincts (see below ch. 9, §1).

87. "Hermeneutics as a Theoretical and Practical Task," p. 117.

88. Ibid., p. 131.

89. Ibid., p. 118.

90. Ibid., p. 133.

91. Ibid., p. 118.

92. Ibid., p. 134.

93. Ibid., p. 135.

94. Ibid.

95. "Hermeneutics as Practical Philosophy," p. 112.

96. *T.M.,* Introduction, p. xiii; *W.M.,* p. xxvii.

97. Cf. Richard Rorty's notion of "edifying philosophy" and especially his discussion of Gadamer as an exemplary exponent of it in *Philosophy and the Mirror of Nature,* ch. 8, §1; pp. 357–365.

98. "Hermeneutics as a Theoretical and Practical Task," p. 114.

99. Ibid.

100. Ibid., p. 119.

101. Ibid.

102. *T.M.,* p. 278; *W.M.,* p. 295. C1.4f. also *E.N.* 1.6 and "Hermeneutics as a Theoretical and Practical Task," p. 120.

103. This dictum occurs in his chapter on Marburg in *Philosophical Apprenticeships.* I have used the more felicitous translation of it as quoted by Habermas in "Urbanizing the Heideggerian Province," p. 190.

104. Gadamer makes this comment that "Plato was no Platonist" in the context of some remarks on the close relationship between philosophy and poetry; but it is

characteristic of him that elsewhere in the same essay he is able to suggest a perspective on Platonism according to which "the first Platonist would be none other than Aristotle himself"! (See "On the Origins of Philosophical Hermeneutics," p. 193 and p. 186.)

105. "Hermeneutics as a Theoretical and Practical Task", p. 122.

106. This viewpoint—i.e., a defense of Phaedrus against Socrates or, in other words, of rhetoric against the imperialist claims of dialectic—was trenchantly argued by Robert Pirsig in his best-selling philosophical novel *Zen and the Art of Motorcycle Maintenance* (New York: William Morrow, 1974; Bantam Books, 1975).

107. "Hermeneutics as a Theoretical and Practical Task," p. 120.

108. Ibid., p. 121.

109. Ibid., p. 122.

110. Ibid., p. 123. In relation to my own point of departure for the present study (see above, Introduction, §1) I may point out that Gadamer immediately goes on to remark here that "even though it is supposed to make good citizens, Aristotelian politics does not actually treat education as productive philosophy [i.e., as a formulable techne]. Instead, Aristotle deals with it . . . as practical philosophy."

111. "On the Origins of Philosophical Hermeneutics," p. 183.

112. *E.N.* 1141a20–22. (I depart from the Revised Oxford translation.)

113. On the "overshadowing" mentioned here, see below, ch. 8, §2.

114. For Gadamer's gloss on this phrase of the later Heidegger, see "The Heritage of Hegel," p. 68, n. 34; and also "Hegel and Heidegger," in *Hegel's Dialectic: Five Hermeneutical Studies.*

115. "On the Origins of Philosophical Hermeneutics," p. 183.

116. "Hermeneutics as Practical Philosophy," pp. 109–110.

117. "On the Scope and Function of Hermeneutical Reflection," p. 28 in *P.H.*

118. "On the Origins of Philosophical Hermeneutics," p. 178. A very similar point comes up nicely when Gadamer is responding to what he sees as a failure on Richard Bernstein's part to appreciate the *continuity* here: "In your expression 'critique of tradition or of contemporary society', 'or' is then used in a way that I cannot understand" (in a letter by Gadamer, published as an appendix in *Beyond Objectivism and Relativism*).

119. "The Universality of the Hermeneutical Problem," p. 10 in *P.H.*

120. Ibid.

121. "On the Origins of Hermeneutics," p. 182. When Gadamer speaks here of the "monologic" of the sciences as something that in itself is still outside—and needs to be mediated into—the "communicative consciousness" of ordinary speech he is making a point which Arendt makes very trenchantly in the prologue to *The Human Condition:* "The reason why it may be wise to distrust the political judgment of scientists *qua* scientists is not primarily their lack of 'character'—that they did not refuse to develop atomic weapons—or their naïveté—that they did not understand that once these weapons were developed they would be the last to be consulted about their use—but precisely the fact that they move in a world in which *speech* has lost its power. And whatever men do or know or experience can make sense only to the extent that it can be spoken about" (p. 4, emphasis added).

122. "Hermeneutics as a Theoretical and Practical Task," p. 137.

123. *T.M.*, p. 417; *W.M.*, p. 436.
124. "The Universality of the Hermeneutical Problem," pp. 10–11 in *P.H.*
125. Letter by Gadamer, appendix in Bernstein, *Beyond Objectivism and Relativism*, p. 264.
126. Ibid.
127. Ibid., p. 262.

6. The Distinction between Praxis and Technique in the Early Philosophy of Jürgen Habermas

1. On the close connection between Habermas's driving philosophical intentions and his perception of the Germany of his youth, see the first few pages of the Introduction in R. J. Bernstein, ed., *Habermas and Modernity* (Cambridge: Polity Press, 1985).

2. I have in mind here the Popper of *The Open Society and Its Enemies*, vol. 2: *The High Tide of Prophesy: Hegel and Marx* (London: Routledge and Kegan Paul, 1948). Popper's philosophy of science has also been a favorite target in Habermas's polemics against 'positivism' in his earlier writings. See Habermas, "The Analytical Theory of Science and Dialectics," in Theodor W. Adorno et al., *The Positivist Dispute in German Sociology*, trans. Glyns Adey and David Frisby (London: Heinemann, 1976) and *Theory and Practice* (abridged version of *Theorie und Praxis*, 4th ed. [Frankfurt am Main: Suhrkamp Verlag, 1971]) trans. John Viertel (London: Heinemann, 1974; hereafter *T.P.*), pp. 276ff. The emphasis on "fallibilism" in Habermas's later work, however, shows signs—as he himself has acknowledged—of Popper's influence. See Peter Dews, ed., *Habermas, Autonomy and Solidarity*, Interviews with Jürgen Habermas (London: Verso, 1986; hereafter, *A.S.*), p. 50.

3. For a classic attack on Heidegger, see Theodor W. Adorno, *The Jargon of Authenticity*, trans. Knut Tarnowski and Frederick Will (London: Routledge and Kegan Paul, 1973). Habermas himself has confessed to an early infatuation with Heidegger—who, in fact, "strongly influenced" his doctoral dissertation—but this did not survive his period as an assistant to Adorno in the mid-1950s (see *A.S.*, p. 150). Heidegger's "Dionysian messianism" has come to represent for him the "radical gesture of a break with modernity" which, "under Nietzsche's banner," may be seen either as an attempt to "step over the threshold to post-modern thought" or as a "revolutionary renewal of pre-modern energies, most often reaching back to archaic times." Habermas's own philosophy, as we shall see, is very definitely an attempt, a heroic attempt one might say, to defend modernity (which is essentially the legacy of the Enlightenment) not only against recrudescences of a pre-modern spirit but also against the many beguiling versions of post-modernist relativism that one finds in writers such as Derrida, Rorty, and Lyotard. See "Questions and Counterquestions," in Bernstein, ed., *Habermas and Modernity*, p. 229, n. 6 and, for Habermas's most developed critique of Heidegger, *The Philosophical Discourse of Modernity* trans. by F. Lawrence (Cambridge: Polity Press, 1987), pp. 131–160.

4. Most of this group of thinkers fled Germany to the United States where they came together in the Institute for Social Research in New York. For a thorough account of the vicissitudes of the school, see Martin Jay, *The Dialectical Imagination:*

A History of the Frankfurt School and the Institute for Social Research 1923–1950 (London: Heinemann, Educational, 1973). For a more extended treatment that embraces Habermas's contribution to the development of the key ideas of the school, see David Held, *Introduction to Critical Theory* (London: Hutchinson, 1980).

5. "Questions and Counterquestions," p. 216 in Bernstein, ed., *Habermas and Modernity*. The invocation of Freud did not imply any concession to irrationality. For in giving new recognition to dreams, neurotic symptoms, and parapraxes, as well as to the basic instinctual urges which find roundabout expression in them, Freud's object was precisely to bring this whole sphere of the irrational within the scope of *rational* investigation. And in addition to the rationality which prevailed in Freud's own theoretical inquiries, insofar as these inquiries could be said to have been *interested* (in a sense which Habermas himself develops; see n. 24 below), their interest was in extending the "primacy of intellect" in people's lives—so that "where id was there shall ego be."

6. See especially M. Horkheimer, *The Eclipse of Reason* (New York: Seabury Press, 1947) and T. Adorno and M. Horkheimer, *Dialectic of Enlightenment* (English translation of *Dialektik der Aufklärung* [Amsterdam: 1947]) (London: Verso, 1979).

7. For a very sympathetic discussion by Habermas of Marcuse's unquenchable optimism see "Psychic Thermidor and the Rebirth of Rebellious Subjectivity," in Richard J. Bernstein, ed., *Habermas and Modernity*. For Habermas's more formal strictures on Marcuse's epistemology, however, see n. 25 below.

8. Habermas's relation to Kant would be a study in itself. Several perceptive commentators on his earlier work (up to *Erkenntnis und Interesse* [Suhrkamp Verlag, 1968], trans. Jeremy J. Shapiro as *Knowledge and Human Interests* [London: Heinemann, 1972], hereafter *K.H.I.*) noted how insistently Kant peers out from behind the more immediately visible shapes of Marx and Hegel. (See Richard J. Bernstein, *The Restructuring of Social and Political Theory;* Thomas McCarthy, *The Critical Theory of Jürgen Habermas* [London: Hutchinson, 1978]; and Rüdiger Bubner, *Modern German Philosophy* [Cambridge: Cambridge University Press, 1981].) These Kantian proclivities have become more explicit in his later work where the analysis of three provinces of reason bears a marked resemblance to the threefold differentiation of Kant's three critiques. If the Kantianism of his early work could be interpreted as a kind of regression which betrayed his intentions, he is now "relieved" to acknowledge his "stubbornly Kantian way of putting things" (*A.S.*, p. 127), though he is still very anxious to qualify the sense in which the formal analysis of his own "universal pragmatics" makes *transcendental* claims (see below, ch. 7, §1).

9. See, e.g., Jürgen Habermas, "Legitimation Problems in the Modern State," pp. 201–204, in *Communication and the Evolution of Society* (London: Heinemann Educational, 1979); the book is comprised of essays, mainly from *Zur Rekonstruktion des historischen Materialismus* (Frankfurt am Main: Suhrkamp Verlag, 1976), translated by Thomas McCarthy (hereafter *C.E.S.*). For recent debate on neo-Aristotelianism and its implications for modernity, see H. Schnädelbach, "What is Neo-Aristotelianism?" and M. P. d'Entrèves, "Aristotle or Burke? Some comments on H. Schnädelbach's 'What is Neo-Aristotelianism?'" *Praxis International*, vol. 7, no. 3/4 (Oct. 1987, Jan. 1988), pp. 225–237 and pp. 238–245 respectively.

10. Terminologically, a distinction between 'technique' and 'praxis' straddles two

distinctions of Aristotle's. What he distinguished from *techne* was *phronēsis* (and not *praxis*); and conversely what he distinguished from *praxis* was *poiēsis* (*and not techne*). The first pair of terms connoted kinds of *knowledge* and the second pair kinds of activity with which the former were respectively correlated. (See below, ch. 8, beginning of §3 and §6.)

11. *Theorie des kommunikativen Handelns* (Frankfurt am Main: Suhrkamp Verlag, 1981) or *The Theory of Communicative Action*, trans. Thomas McCarthy, vol. 1: *Reason and the Rationalization of Society*, and vol. 2: *The Critique of Functionalist Reason* (Boston: Beacon Press, 1984 and 1987); hereafter *T.C.A.*

12. "Introduction: Some Difficulties in the Attempt to Link Theory and Praxis," in *T.P.*, p. 2. In a footnote to "The Classical Doctrine of Politics and Its Relation to Social Philosophy," Habermas writes: "The study of Hannah Arendt's important investigation [i.e., *The Human Condition*, or *Vita Activa* as it was called in its German edition] and of H. G. Gadamer's *Wahrheit und Methode* (Tübingen: 1961) have called my attention to the fundamental significance of the Aristotelian distinction between *techne* and *praxis*" (*T.P.*, p. 286, n. 4). He has also written sympathetically of Arendt's work (see "Hannah Arendt's Communications Concept of Power," in *Social Research* 44 (1977), pp. 3–24; and "Hannah Arendt on the Concept of Power" in Habermas, *Philosophical-Political Profiles*, pp. 171–187), while a protracted debate with Gadamer, in which he has appropriated as well as rejected ideas of his elder partner, has been of considerable significance in the working out of his philosophy (see §4 below).

13. The interpretative method that Habermas practices under the rubric of 're-construction' is, I believe, well formulated by Collingwood, who, like Habermas, is a 'dialectical' philosopher (see Louis O. Mink, *Mind, History and Dialectic: The Philosophy of R. G. Collingwood*, esp. pp. 16–23): "An erroneous philosophical theory is based in the first instance not on ignorance but on knowledge. The person who constructs it begins by partially understanding the subject and goes on to distort what he knows by twisting it into conformity with some preconceived idea . . . [therefore] a special method of analysis must be used. This consists in isolating the preconceived idea which has acted as the distorting agent, reconstructing the formula of the distortion, and re-applying it so as to correct the distortion and thus find out what it was that the people who invented or constructed the theory were trying to say" (*P.A.*, p. 107). (It should be noted that what Collingwood means here by 'reconstructing', as a particular type of critical interpretation, is not the same as the more generic concept of 'reconstruction' that he uses to characterize *all* interpretation. In fact what I have done (ch. 2, §5) with his concept of 'reconstruction' in the latter sense was precisely to 'reconstruct' it in the former sense.

14. "The Classical Doctrine of Politics," p. 45, in *T.P.*

15. Ibid.

16. *T.P.*, Introduction, p. 3.

17. *T.P.*, p. 44.

18. *T.P.*, p. 3.

19. *T.P.*, p. 61.

20. Aristotle had written: "the minute accuracy of mathematics is not to be demanded in all cases, but only in the case of things which have no matter. Therefore

its method is not that of natural science, for presumably all nature has matter." (*Metaphysics* 2.3.995a15–17).

21. "The Classical Doctrine of Politics," *T.P.*, p. 61.

22. Ibid.

23. "Interest" in this sense is a basic framework within which knowledge is assembled and action pursued. Habermas claimed that there are three such interests which are grounded in the very structure of human existence itself. Their scope is universal in that all knowledge is constituted by one or other of them. "Interest," therefore, does not have the same meaning that it has in the more familiar contexts of psychoanalytic or Marxist critiques of "rationalization" or "ideology" which try to show—on the individual and social levels, respectively—that "the manifest content of statements is falsified by consciousness's unreflected ties to interests, despite its illusions of autonomy" (*K.H.I.*, p. 311). In both of these cases, knowledge is called into question once its relation to interest is made transparent; the interest for which the knowledge is a vehicle and a disguise corrupts it as knowledge. In Habermas's sense, however, knowledge is possible at all only as already constituted by an interest. This means that the interests which he explicates are not particular ones, the spuriousness of whose claims could be exposed by critique; they are, rather, "interests of the human race as a whole and not of an individual epoch, a specific class or a surpassable situation." In this different sense of interest, indeed, psychoanalytic and Marxist critiques are themselves "interested"; they are directed to the unmasking of particular interests in the psychic and socioeconomic domains—and thereby to undeceived understanding of the mechanisms through which these interests find devious satisfaction—only because *they are themselves already committed to the interest of mature autonomy* (*Mündigkeit*) whose implications, with respect to personality development and sociopolitical arrangements, respectively, they try to spell out. This latter interest in what Habermas calls the *emancipatory* one, and psychoanalysis and Marxism are, in fact, the paradigm examples of knowledge that is constituted by it. Apart from it and the *technical* interest which I am dealing with here in the text, the other defining interest is the *practical* one, which is related to praxis and which, in Habermas's view, is constitutive of what he calls the "hermeneutical sciences." While the distinction between the practical and the technical seems clear enough (it is after all only another formulation of the distinction which concerns us throughout the present work), the distinction between the practical and the emancipatory seems more problematic. Presumably they are not exclusive of each other in that emancipatory knowledge is also practical. But is the converse necessarily true? An answer to this question might be thought to be crucial not simply to our understanding of Habermas but also to our judgment of how well both Aristotle and our other interlocutors—for whom critique has not been conspicuously important—can withstand the challenge of his work. As thus formulated, however, the question itself has been undercut by the fact that in his later work Habermas has abandoned (though not repudiated) the whole category of "interest" and replaced it with a different conceptual framework. (See *A.S.*, p. 198, and below, ch. 7, §1.) Still what lies behind the question will not go away, and later on we shall find it reemerging, albeit in a different guise, with respect to the later work also.

24. In emphasizing here the discontinuity between Greek theory and modern science, Habermas underestimates, I believe, both the extent to which the Greek con-

ception of theory—even if it eschewed any utilitarian function—was inspired by the
techne paradigm and, conversely, the extent to which a theoretical bias characterized
their notion of techne itself. The first of these points is strongly made by Hintikka
who insists that Plato saw genuine knowledge as *maker's* knowledge; not only in the
case of moral knowledge (and the famous "Socratic paradox") but in all other cases,
too, real knowledge is power. The second (and in the present context more important)
point is easily established, I believe, in relation to both Plato and Aristotle and will
emerge clearly in my own analysis of techne later on (see below, ch. 8, §4). Both of
these points together seem to show that the uniqueness of modern science and technology does not lie, as Habermas suggests, in their having brought about for the first
time an intimate connection between theory and production; for this connection was
already present in the way in which 'techne' functioned as a paradigm of genuine
theory (*epistēmē*) for the Greeks as well as in the strongly theoretical bias of techne's
own internal structure. (Hintikka, in fact, goes so far as to argue for a clear anticipation of modern science in Aristotle's analysis of technical deliberation in *E.N.* 3.3;
the comparison there of deliberation with geometrical analysis (1112b21–22) prompts
him to suggest that "precisely the same conceptual model" lies at the root both of
Aristotle's notion of productive reasoning and of "one of the first and foremost methodological ideas of modern natural science" ("Practical vs. Theoretical Reason—An
Ambiguous Legacy" pp. 90–91 in Jaako Hintikka, *Knowledge and the Known: Historical Perspectives in Epistemology* [Dordrecht: Kluwer, 1974]). I do not find this
suggestion very plausible; it is insensitive to the context of the passage, which in fact
immediately goes on to repudiate the mathematical analogy and which also explicitly
contrasts deliberation with science. The point remains, however, that Aristotle's notion of techne was very closely connected with *his* notion of theory.)

25. Habermas's acceptance of modern natural science as genuine historical progress is brought out most clearly in his polemical (albeit friendly) response to Marcuse
in the important essay, "Science and Technology as Ideology" (in *Toward a Rational
Society* [London: Heinemann, 1971; hereafter, *T.R.S.*], pp. 81–122). In the radical critique of such books as *One-Dimensional Man: Studies in the Ideology of Advanced
Industrial Society* (London: Routledge and Kegan Paul, 1964) and *Eros and Civilization: A Philosophical Inquiry into Freud* (London: Allen Lane, 1969), Marcuse had
convicted modern science of harboring at its core a project of domination: the oppres-
sion of man by man in modern society is but a necessary consequence of the domination of nature by man in modern science. And he seemed to envisage the possible
replacement of this science of domination by a new science that would, as it were,
allow Nature to speak for itself as a respected partner, rather than put it on the rack
of complete objectification. (It is worth pointing out that Marcuse's views here have
a long tradition in German philosophy, which [in Gadamer's words, *T.M.*, p. 417; *W.M.*,
p. 436] "has constantly tried to supplement the new science of physics by a philosophical and speculative science. . . . We need only recall Goethe's objection to Newton,
which was shared by Schelling, Hegel and Schopenhauer.") Habermas gives short shrift
to any such romantic conception of an alternative natural science; he is quite content
to leave natural science to the technical interest (which is one of quite unabashed mastery and control) and to reserve an interactive framework (i.e., that of the *practical
interest*) for the hermeneutical sciences whose irreducibility to the natural sciences

he does want to insist on — precisely through his distinction between these two "knowledge-constitutive interests."

26. *T.P.*, p. 255.

27. See n. 23 above.

28. *T.P.*, p. 9.

29. *T.R.S.*, p. 113.

30. T. McCarthy, *The Critical Theory of Jürgen Habermas*, p. 35.

31. *T.R.S.*, p. 98.

32. McCarthy, *Critical Theory of Jürgen Habermas*, p. 36.

33. *T.P.*, pp. 168–169.

34. *K.H.I.*, p. 55.

35. *T.P.*, p. 169.

36. Gadamer, in particular, has contested this point; see especially "On the Scope and Function of Hermeneutical Reflection," *P.H.*, pp. 18–43.

37. *K.H.I.*, pp. 281–282.

38. *K.H.I.*, pp. 261–262.

39. *K.H.I.*, p. 283.

40. *K.H.I.*, p. 284.

41. *K.H.I.*, chs. 7 and 8.

42. *K.H.I.*, p. 179.

43. For Gadamer, critique has its home in "sociology," (when the latter remains faithful to the "authentic epistemological interest which distinguishes true sociologists from technicians of social structure" [*P.H.*, p. 40]) and he makes no attempt to mitigate the differences between this discipline and hermeneutics: "the purpose of sociological method as emancipating one from tradition places it at the outset very far from the traditional purpose and starting point of the hermeneutical problematic with all its bridge-building and recovery of the best of the past" (ibid., p. 26). Or, again, "The history-embracing and history-preserving element runs deep in hermeneutics, in sharp contrast to sociological interest in reflection as basically a means of emancipation from authority and tradition." Gadamer throws out not just a wry remark, one feels, but a cry from the heart, in the concluding words of his letter to Richard Bernstein: "to make me into a sociologist is something no one will succeed in doing, not even myself" (Bernstein, *Beyond Objectivism and Relativism*, p. 265).

44. Habermas himself seems to acknowledge this when he distinguishes the practical and the emancipatory interests and sees the *former* as the defining interest of the hermeneutical sciences.

45. Habermas, *On the Logic of the Social Sciences*, translated by Shierry Weber Nicholsen and Jerry A. Stark (Cambridge, Mass.: M.I.T. Press, 1988), p. 16. It should be noted that the German original of this work (*Zur Logik der Sozialwissenschaften*) was first published (as a special issue of the journal *Philosophische Rundschau*) in 1967 and that what Habermas then called the "dominant conception" of social science is now — not least because of his own influence — much more vigorously contested.

46. *T.M.*, p. 340; *W.M.*, p. 360 (emphasis added).

47. I quote here from the extract from *Zur Logik der Sozialwissenschaften* translated as "A Review of Gadamer's Truth and Method" in *Understanding and Social*

Inquiry, edited by Fred R. Dallmayr and Thomas A. McCarthy (Notre Dame: University of Notre Dame Press, 1977), p. 357.

48. *Understanding and Social Inquiry,* p. 360.

49. See especially "The Scope and Function of Hermeneutical Reflection" in *P.H.* and the twofold *replik* to Habermas in *Hermeneutik und Ideologiekritik* (Frankfurt, 1971), parts of which are translated into English in *Continuum* 8 (1970).

50. *T.P.,* p. 264.

51. *T.P.,* pp. 254–255.

52. *T.P.,* p. 258.

53. *T.P.,* pp. 262–263.

54. *T.P.,* p. 255.

55. *T.P.,* p. 270.

56. *T.P.,* p. 275.

57. *T.R.S.,* p. 103.

58. *T.R.S.,* p. 104.

59. *T.R.S.,* p. 105.

60. *T.R.S.,* p. 110.

61. *T.R.S.,* p. 112.

62. Ibid.

63. *T.R.S.,* p. 113.

64. Ibid. (emphases Habermas's).

65. *T.P.,* p. 256.

7. Habermas's Later Philosophy: Ambiguities of Rationalization

1. See especially the postscript to the second German edition of *Erkenntnis und Interesse* (*K.H.I.,* pp. 351–380) and the introduction to the fourth German edition of *Theorie und Praxis* (*T.P.,* pp. 1–40).

2. In an interview in November 1984, Habermas affirmed that he still considered "the outlines of the argument" developed in *Knowledge and Human Interests* to be correct and that "I do not believe that I have changed any more in my fundamental orientations than was necessary to hold true to them in altered historical circumstances" ("A Philosophico-Political Profile," *A.S.,* p. 152 and p. 188).

3. See *T.C.A.,* vol. 1, ch. 1, §3, especially pp. 88–90.

4. "Over these gods and their struggles it is *fate*—and certainly not any 'science' —that holds sway" (quoted by Habermas, *T.C.A.,* vol. 1, pp. 246–247, emphasis added). Thus Weber remarked of the "new polytheism," which was his ironic way of characterizing the fragmented state of modern culture in the wake of secularization.

5. It may be recalled that I began my account of Habermas's "modernization" of the concept of praxis, by adverting to his response to Weber (see ch. 6, beginning of §3. above). This response was in the important essay "Science and Technology as Ideology." *The Theory of Communicative Action* might be seen as in large part a development of the central ideas of that essay, and if it can be said to have, among its huge cast, a leading protagonist, it is Weber (see *T.C.A.,* vol. 1, pp. 143–271 and pp. 345–365, and vol. 2, p. 264).

6. See especially *The Philosophical Discourse of Modernity.*

7. That Habermas's later philosophy is so avowedly a *defense* of "the modern project" *and* that it identifies precisely Nietzsche and (to a lesser degree, it must be acknowledged) Aristotle as the crucial adversarial reference points makes it especially pertinent to the argument of Alasdair MacIntyre's *After Virtue*. For the "drastic conclusion" which MacIntyre argues in this book is that "nothing less than the *rejection* of a large part" of "the ethos of the distinctively modern and modernising world . . . will provide us with a rationally and morally defensible standpoint from which to judge and to act" (p. viii, emphasis added). Moreover, in developing this argument, MacIntyre too makes Nietzsche the key protagonist; for him, however, Nietzsche is not, as he is for Habermas, the philosopher who radically rejects the Enlightenment but rather the one who most ruthlessly draws out the *implications of its failure;* Nietzsche's nihilism is not so much a scandal to the Enlightenment as its ultimate *denouement.* His "negative proposal to raze to the ground the structures of inherited moral belief and argument" (p. 238) has, therefore, a "terrible plausibility"—unless it should turn out to be the case that we have more to look to in our *whole* tradition than the Enlightenment inheritance itself. MacIntyre in fact argues that the modern project had to be undertaken in the first place only because "a moral tradition of which Aristotle's thought was the intellectual core was repudiated in the transitions of the fifteenth to the seventeenth centuries" (p. 110). He can then interpret the failure of this project as "nothing other than a historical sequel to the rejection of the Aristotelian tradition," and go on to formulate (in the cardinal chapter, "Nietzsche or Aristotle") what for him is the "key question": "can Aristotelian ethics or something very like it after all be vindicated?" (p. 111). The rest of the book is an attempt to answer this question with a resounding yes.

In their respective readings of the tradition (and diagnoses of our present condition), the directions traveled by MacIntyre and Habermas are provocatively and intriguingly different. Although the memory of Nazism makes it impossible for Habermas to be complacent about Nietzsche, he can still be relatively benign to a playful thinker like Richard Rorty, on the basis that (as Peter Dews puts it in his Introduction to *A.S.*) "a liberal-universalist safety-net was always tacitly spread beneath the high-wire of the new Nietzscheanism." MacIntyre's argument, however, is precisely that this is no saftey-net: the best minds of the Enlightenment (Kant, Diderot, Hume, Smith et al.) failed to provide an autonomous basis for morality—not because they "were not adroit enough in constructing arguments," but rather because they "were inheritors of a very specific and particular scheme of moral beliefs, a scheme whose internal incoherence ensured the failure of the common philosophical project from the outset" (p. 49). Moreover, the most ingenious contemporary apologists for this project of liberal Enlightenment (such as Rawls, Nozick, Dworkin, and Gewirth), *as inheritors of the same legacy,* can no more avert its failure than could their intellectual forebears of the two previous centuries. It is because Habermas is so acutely aware of the weaknesses and distortions of this very legacy and yet *still* tries to show that it can be reconstructed from within ("there is no cure for the wounds of Enlightenment other than the radicalized Enlightenment itself")—without surrendering to the unpalatable dogmatism of a hoary Aristotelianism—that one laments his absence from MacIntyre's argumentative narrative. Not just the fact that he is undoubtedly "adroit enough in constructing arguments" but also the fact that his command of the whole tradition is as impressively sweeping as MacIntyre's own (as well, incidentally, as the fact that the kind of "reconstructed" Marxism which he espouses would allow him both to concede what is damaging in MacIntyre's interpretation of Marxism as in the end parasitic on liberalism, and at the same time—as his friendliness to North American pragmatism shows—not to disown the liberalism implicit in a *communicative* version of Marxism) make him the most formidable opponent of MacIntyre's polemical thesis. (Interestingly, in a book which contains a kind of sociological equivalent of MacIntyre's philosophical argument, i.e., in Geoffrey Hawthorn's *Enlightenment and Despair* [Cambridge: Cambridge University Press, 1976] Habermas's work is assimilated—and, indeed, in a new Conclusion to the second edition [1987] is given special treatment with Rawls's work—as part of the "grand project of social theory" which was "misconceived" and is, indeed, "finished"!)

8. "What is Universal Pragmatics?" in *C.E.S.*, p. 23.

9. See the Excursus immediately after the chapter on Derrida in *The Philosophical Discourse of Modernity* (hereafter *P.D.M.*) pp. 185–210.

10. See *P.D.M.*, lecture 3 (on Marx) and lecture 6 (on Heidegger).

11. Although Habermas identifies four validity claims, the claim to comprehensibility has nothing like the status of the other three claims in the overall development of ideas in *T.C.A.* A threefold structure continually recurs in the book which is always traceable back to the differentiation between the first three claims (see n. 13 below). These claims might then be said to have the same kind of overall significance that the three knowledge-constitutive interests had in his earlier work, and it is noteworthy that they correspond closely to Kant's three Critiques.

12. Habermas's formulation here is very close to that of Bernard Lonergan, who also sees assent to an unconditionality which is reached through the actual fulfilment of conditions as the crucial moment in being reasonable (see *Insight: A Study of Human Understanding* [London: Longmans, 1958], pp. 279–281). Both Lonergan and Habermas construct very comprehensive philosophies through the systematic development of what are essentially epistemological distinctions (Lonergan's three levels of "cognitional process" in *Insight* do the same kind of work that the three cognitive interests do in Habermas's early writings). From their cognitivist bases, both can develop critical and utopian perspectives (compare "bias" in Lonergan with "systematically distorted communication" in Habermas, or "cosmopolis" with the "ideal speech situation"). Each of them is a "transcendental" thinker (a kind of Kant of Thomism and of Marxism, respectively) who can defend his theory retorsively—i.e., by showing that it must be performatively presupposed even by those who would explicitly reject it—while at the same time insisting that it is fallibilist or, in a broad sense, empirical. Both have tried to mend fences between their respective, often dogma-prone, traditions and the sciences (an appropriation of the genetic structuralism of Piaget is a conspicuous feature of the work of both). What is problematic about both of them in the end, perhaps, is just what kind of light can be thrown on issues of empirical/historical density by theories of such a quasi-transcendental cast.

13. Typical of Habermas's penchant for systematization is the way in which he correlates the three main types of validity claim (to truth, rightness, and truthfulness or authenticity) with three different types of discourse (the scientific, the practical, and the aesthetic) as well as with three different functions of speech acts (the proposi-

tional, the illocutionary, and the expressive), three different "worlds" (the objective world, the common social world, and the subjective world to which a person himself has privileged access), and three different aspects of the "reproduction of the life-world" (cultural reproduction, social integration, and personality formation or individuation).

14. "A Philosophico-Political Profile," *A.S.*, p. 169.

15. See n. 19 below.

16. See *A.S.*, p. 184.

17. "The Dialectics of Rationalization," *A.S.*, p. 107.

18. "The Normative Content of Modernity," *P.D.M.*, p. 338.

19. The concept of a "steering medium" is one that Habermas appropriates in a selective and characteristically "reconstructive" manner from Talcott Parsons (see especially *T.C.A.*, vol. 2, pp. 180–185 and 256–282). The essence of such a medium is that it regulates interactions in a "deworlded" zone where communication in ordinary language, with all its proneness to misinterpretation and disagreement, is replaced or bypassed. As "relief mechanisms that reduce the expenditure of communication and the risk of disagreement" (p. 181) steering media set up predictable schedules which autonomize interactions and thereby unburden agents of responsibility for them. To Habermas it is only sensible that a modern age which has opened up such space for, and exposed itself so much to the hazards of, discursive consensus-seeking in the symbolic reproduction of the lifeworld (i.e., in the spheres of culture, social relationships, and child-rearing/socialization practices) should try to spare itself these hazards in the sphere of material reproduction.

20. The above quotations are from *T.C.A.*, vol. 2, pp. 339 and 340; the emphases are Habermas's own.

21. Anthony Giddens gives this line to the "critical" (as opposed to "sympathetic") voice in his fork-tongued essay on *T.C.A.*, "Reason without Revolution" in *Habermas and Modernity*, p. 120.

22. *T.C.A.*, vol. 2, p. 334. In ch. 6, §3 above, we saw Habermas's earlier reconstruction of Marx; for his later, more developed, version of this, see *T.C.A.*, vol. 1, pp. 334–356.

23. *P.D.M.*, p. 363. The compensatory mechanisms mentioned here are those of the welfare state. It is interesting that Habermas, who sees the welfare state as the fourth stage in a historical progression from the bourgeois, through the constitutional and the democratic states, and who is certainly not blind to the achievements of this whole Enlightenment line of development, offers a pungent critique of welfare policy in *T.C.A.* Interventions by the state apparatus, he tries to show, can ameliorate the distorting effects of a capitalist economy only by causing further distortions in the life-worlds of the beneficiaries: "The net of welfare-state guarantees is meant to cushion the external effects of a production process based on wage labor. Yet the more closely the net is woven, the more clearly ambivalences of *another sort* appear. . . . The situation to be regulated [that of, e.g., sickness, disability, unemployment, old age] is embedded in the context of a life-history and of a concrete form of life; it has to be subjected to violent abstraction, not merely because it has to be subsumed under the law, but so that it can be dealt with administratively. . . . The more the welfare-state . . . spreads a net of client relationships over private spheres of life, the stronger are the anticipated pathological side-effects of a juridification that entails both a bu-

reaucratization and a monetarization of core areas of the lifeworld" (*T.C.A.*, vol. 1, pp. 362–364). Moreover, these antinomies are not resolved but only reinforced by recourse to what Habermas (improbably echoing Philip Rieff; see *The Triumph of the Therapeutic*, London: Penguin University Books, 1966) calls "the therapeutocracy"; of attempts to dejuridify ways of dealing with family conflicts, he remarks: "Replacing the judge with the therapist is no panacea; the social worker is only another expert, and does not free the client of the welfare-state bureaucracy from his or her position as an object" (p. 370).

24. *T.C.A.*, vol. 2, pp. 395 and 392. The contemporary protests which Habermas sees as objectively the most significant, as well as the ones which his own theory is best equipped to explain, are those of the "new politics," concerned with "defending and restoring endangered ways of life" rather than (as the "old politics") with problems that arise in the "domains of material reproduction." It is interesting to see Habermas's obvious attraction to this new politics and at the same time his circumspection about it. He recognizes that it is discontinuous with both bourgeois and trade-union emancipation struggles, that in some cases it can serve as a cloak for privilege (e.g., in some single-issue campaigns such as against comprehensive schooling or for 'old world' environments that have become enclaves for the rich) and that its "revaluation of the particular, the natural, the provincial," etc., can betoken a sentimental refusal to take up the challenges of a differentiated modern culture. At the same time his sympathies clearly lie with, e.g., feminism, with "youth and alternative movements for which a critique of growth sparked by themes of ecology and peace is the common focus," and, in general, with "an alternative practice" that "tries out new ways of cooperating and living together" and is "directed against the profit-dependent instrumentalization of work in one's vocation, the market-dependent mobilization of labor power, against the extension of pressures of competition and performance all the way down into elementary school" (see ibid., pp. 391–396).

25. See, e.g., ibid., pp. 183, 263, 302, 366.

26. Ibid., pp. 355–356.

27. *A.S.*, p. 174. Habermas's being "skeptical of the thesis that the essence of the public sphere has been liquidated in postliberal societies" (*T.C.A.*, vol. 2, p. 389) is part of his attempt to free himself from the "totality thinking" which he sees as an excessively burdensome legacy taken over by Adorno and Horkheimer from the "philosophy of history." A move toward what might be considered a more moderate position *politically* was linked, then, to an *epistemological* move which (importantly motivated, on Habermas's own admission, by his reading of analytic philosophy and by his skirmishes with Popper) reflected growing "doubts about whether concepts of totality, of truth, and of theory derived from Hegel did not represent too heavy a mortgage for a theory of society which should also satisfy empirical claims" (*A.S.*, p. 152). Habermas's friendliness to North American Pragmatism (e.g., in Dewey) contrasts strongly with the contemptuous attitude to it of the earlier generation of the Frankfurt School.

28. *A.S.*, p. 109.

29. *T.C.A.*, p. 328.

30. Ibid.

31. One might say that the aesthetic has come to play a role very similar to that of the emancipatory in Habermas's earlier work. While the distinctions between

knowledge-constitutive interests have given way in the later work to distinctions between domains of discourse, two elements of the earlier schema seem to survive intact
in the later one (the technical and practical interests, seem to carry over, in other words,
into cognitive/instrumental and practical/moral discourses respectively). The object
of the third interest, then, i.e., emancipation, seems now to be assigned diffusely to
all three discourses — but *in a special way*, it would seem, to the third area of discourse
(which, strictly should be called "criticism" rather than "discourse"; see *T.C.A.*, vol. 1,
p. 20 and p. 42) i.e., the aesthetic.

32. *T.C.A.*, vol. 2, p. 397.
33. *A.S.*, p. 172. Examples which Habermas gives here are the projections by Bau-
delaire of "those experiences of a mobilized, concentrated, metropolitan life-world
which surfaced like a new continent in nineteenth century Paris," those by Kafka and
Musil of "the experiential space of the collapsing Austrian Imperial and Royal Mon-
archy," and those by Celan and Beckett of "a world transformed by Auschwitz."
34. *P.D.M.*, p. 340.
35. *T.C.A.*, vol. 2, p. 329.
36. Ibid., p. 398.
37. See nn. 23 and 24 above.
38. *T.C.A.*, vol. 2., p. 329.
39. Ibid., p. 400.
40. *T.C.A.*, vol. 1, p. 65.
41. *T.C.A.*, vol. 2, p. 342.
42. "Questions and Counterquestions," in Bernstein, ed., *Habermas and Modernity*, p. 211.
43. *T.C.A.*, vol. 2, p. 397.
44. Ibid., p. 326.
45. See "Questions and Counterquestions," p. 207.
46. Ibid., pp. 207–208.
47. See the references to *T.C.A.* in n. 31 above.
48. In one place where Habermas excludes from his theoretical purview intuitions
of wholeness which we may have from our actual culture or tradition, he does so because they "cannot be *generalized* in the same way as the standards which we use in
judging processes that involve learning" (*A.S.*, p. 170, emphasis added).
49. *T.C.A.*, vol. 2, p. 327.
50. *A.S.*, p. 109.
51. *A.S.*, pp. 109–110.
52. *T.C.A.*, vol. 2, p. 400.
53. *H.C.*, pp. 179–180.
54. *T.C.A.*, vol. 1, p. 335.
55. *T.C.A.*, vol. 1, pp. 100–101.
56. *A.S.*, p. 162.
57. *A.S.*, p. 126.
58. Ibid.
59. *A.S.*, p. 127.
60. "A Reply to My Critics," in J. B. Thompson and D. D. Held, eds., Habermas
Critical Debates (London: Macmillan, 1982), p. 235. Cf. *A.S.*, p. 174. Habermas's reti-

cence here about the positive elements of utopia is one which he claims, with some justification, to be canonical in the Marxist tradition.

61. *A.S.*, pp. 160-161. Although Habermas's conception of philosophy is in one respect "weak" or "restrictive"—in that it abstains from offering or defending any particular worldview—in another respect, as he himself is well aware, "he is defending an outrageously strong claim in the present context of philosophical discussion." For whereas most twentieth-century moral philosophy has been committed to some version of relativism, emotivism, or non-cognitivism, he is quite insistent that ethics is a field for *rational* argument, where we can properly speak of *knowledge*. If he is (deliberately) "weak" on ethical substance, then, he is "strong" on epistemological grounding; his whole later philosophy, whose purpose was to "reconstruct the normative foundations of critical theory," aims precisely to make explicit the kind of rationality or knowledge that is involved here.

62. Habermas would see, e.g., Rawls's "veil of ignorance" as a "pure" philosophical construct, but the rest of *A Theory of Justice*, including the famous two "principles," as "engaged" political argument on the part of "a committed liberal," or "a citizen of the United States with a certain background." He applauds Rawls for this commitment to substantive argument in the public realm—as he himself indeed has been applauded by Richard Rorty for his interventions in public debates in Germany. (Rorty mentions his "yeoman work" in confuting contemporary apologists for Nazism, and adds: "Habermas, almost alone among eminent philosophers of the present day, manages to work as Dewey did, on two tracks. He produces both a stream of philosophical treatises and a stream of comment on current events. I doubt that any philosophy professor since Dewey has done more concrete day-to-day work in the political arena, or done more for the goals of us social-democrats" ["Thugs and Theorists, A Reply to Bernstein," *Political Theory*, Nov. 1987, pp. 574 and 580, n. 31].) Habermas is still keen to insist, however, that the two roles of the philosopher can be distinguished and that an awareness of the difference in status between the arguments advanced in each context remains important: in one case these arguments "move within the horizon of a shared tradition from the start," whereas in the other they are ones which "are *binding*, not just for us here and now, being members of a particular community, but which claim to be true, simply true" (*A.S.*, p. 205).

63. *A.S.*, p. 171.

64. *A.S.*, pp. 207-208. The "Aristotelian argument" mentioned here resonates throughout the *Ethics*, but its most explicit statement is in the famous methodological preface (1.3) and in the final chapter (10.9) which marks the transition to the *Politics*. I shall be attending closely to both of these texts in ch. 9, §4.

65. "What is Universal Pragmatics?" p. 15 in *C.E.S.*

66. "The Heritage of Hegel," p. 58.

67. "Hermeneutics as a Practical and Theoretical Task," p. 131.

68. *A.S.*, p. 102.

69. Ibid.

70. *A.S.*, p. 155. Needless to say, Habermas finds much more in common with Adorno than with Heidegger. Even if he regards it as misconceived, he still sympathizes with the former's attempt to "salvage the particular as the intangible, the injured, the victimized—that necessarily falls through the grasp of all discursive or iden-

tifying thought" and only "finds an echo in the powers of a wordless mimesis" (*A.S.*, p. 102 and p. 155). Despite this sympathy, however, he sees Adorno's philosophical project leading into a cul-de-sac; and ironically (in the light of the profound differences between them) this cul-de-sac allows an unfortunate comparison with Heidegger: "When one is oriented to questions of truth and does not misunderstand oneself in the process then one should not try, as Heidegger and Adorno both did, to . . . wager on a higher level of insight, on the thinking of Being or on a mindfulness of tormented nature" (ibid., p. 127). For critical discussion of Adorno, see "Theodor Adorno: The Primal History of Subjectivity—Self-Affirmation Gone Wild," pp. 99–109 in *Philosophical-Political Profiles*, *T.C.A.*, vol. 1, pp. 366ff., and *P.D.M.*, ch. 5, pp. 106–130.

71. *A.S.*, p. 139.

72. See above, ch. 4, §7, penultimate paragraph.

73. *A.S.*, pp. 139–140. The voice of "Critical Theory" which echoes most strongly in this passage is that of Walter Benjamin; see especially his "Theses on the Philosophy of History" in *Illuminations*, ed. with an Introduction by Hannah Arendt, trans. H. Zohn (London: Cape, 1970); also *P.D.M.* pp. 11–14, and Habermas's essay, "Walter Benjamin: Consciousness-Raising or Rescuing Critique?" in *Philosophical-Political Profiles*, pp. 129–163.

74. *A.S.*, p. 106 (emphasis added).

75. Cf. MacIntyre's chapter, "Liberalism Transformed into a Tradition," in *Whose Justice? Which Rationality?* (Notre Dame, Ind.: University of Notre Dame Press; London: Duckworth, 1988), pp. 326–348.

76. This is the theme of *P.D.M.*, which is Habermas's most intensely argued book.

77. *T.C.A.*, vol. 2, p. 108.

78. Ibid., p. 110.

79. See *Phenomenology of Spirit*, trans. A. V. Millar (Oxford: Oxford University Press, 1977) pp. 252ff.

80. *Critique of Practical Reason*, trans. L. W. Beck (Indianapolis: Bobbs-Merrill, 1956), p. 30.

81. Ibid., p. 429 (emphasis added).

82. "A Reply to My Critics," p. 262.

83. *A.S.*, p. 169.

84. "Questions and Counterquestions," p. 215.

85. Ibid.

86. "Reply to My Critics," p. 262.

87. Ibid. "Happiness" of course carries echoes of the Greek *eudaimonia*, and while Habermas, unlike Aristotle, is clearly squeamish about unpacking it in terms of the "good," his preferred notion of "health" is one which also came very naturally to both Aristotle and Plato, and is in fact pervasively present in their ethical-political writings. (See below, ch. 8, n. 34.)

88. *A.S.*, p. 170.

89. See *T.C.A.*, vol. 2, pp. 400–403.

90. *A.S.*, p. 171.

91. "Questions and Counterquestions," p. 214.

92. See "Moral Development and Ego Identity," pp. 69–94 in *C.E.S.*

93. Ibid., p. 90 and p. 93.

94. The "reconciliation" is, one might say, an attempt to wed Kohlberg with Freud, a wedding which can seem at all plausible, however, only because the Freud we meet here has been sanitized in his passage through "ego psychology" (a revisionist movement within psychoanalysis which has tended to emphasize the *rational* side of Freud's picture of human personality, thereby making him more congenial to Habermas's overall designs; for Habermas's references to particular ego psychologists, see *C.E.S.*, p. 220, n. 7). For a penetrating critique of Habermas on Freud by a practicing psychoanalyst, see Joel Whitebrook's "Reason and Happiness," pp. 140–160 in Bernstein, ed., *Habermas and Modernity*, and "The Problem of Nature in Habermas," in *Telos* 40 (1979), pp. 41–69. Whitebrook tries to show that it is only by glossing over the stubborn intractability of the id that Habermas can so unproblematically turn Freud to account; his approach "fails to capture the sense of 'an inner foreign territory' which is a hallmark of Freudian thought," and it is this failure that allows him to suppose, in "an almost glib manner," that "everything is potentially transparent" (*Habermas and Modernity*, p. 157).

95. *T.P.*, p. 44.

96. *Whose Justice? Which Rationality?* p. 143. MacIntyre can point to Aristotle's very explicit use of this method of inquiry in the first book of the *Metaphysics*, but he also urges that the latter's ethical-political thought is a similar, only more implicit, attempt to take over the achievements and resolve the *aporiai* of Pericles, Sophocles, Thucydides, and Plato.

97. Quoted by Joel Whitebrook in "Reason and Happiness," p. 223, n. 24.

98. Rüdiger Bubner, *Modern German Philosophy*, p. 204.

Interlude

1. See above, ch. 4, §6, after n. 67.

2. Engberg-Pedersen, *Aristotle's Theory of Moral Insight* (Oxford and New York: Clarendon Press, 1983), pp. vii–viii.

3. Ibid., p. viii.

4. It is noteworthy that the most sustained forum for serious scholarship on Newman has been the *Cardinal Newman Studien* published at Nuremberg. And Collingwood, who during his lifetime was an outsider in English philosophy and indeed at Oxford (the contemporary philosopher that he was closest to was the Italian, Croce) has received hardly less attention in Germany (helped by Gadamer's influence) than in England or America.

5. There has been some movement in recent years to break down the sectarian divisions between these two different traditions in philosophy; a philosopher whose work has done much to highlight convergences between them is Richard J. Bernstein. See his *Praxis and Action* (London: Duckworth, 1972); *The Restructuring of Social and Political Theory* (London: Methuen, 1976); and *Beyond Objectivism and Relativism* (London: Basil Blackwell, 1983). (All three works published in the U.S. at Philadelphia: University of Pennsylvania Press.)

6. Wilfrid Sellars, "The Soul as Craftsman" in *Philosophical Perspectives* (Springfield, Ill.: C. Thomas, 1967), p. 5.

8. Theory, Techne, and Phronesis: Distinctions and Relations

1. For occurrences of this threefold distinction, see, e.g., *E.N.* 1139a27–28; *E.N.* 1178b20–21; *Meta.* 1025b25; and *Top.* 145a15–16.
2. See especially *An. Prior.* 1.
3. This combination is made most explicit at *E.N.* 6.7.1141a17–20, where it is said that the *sophos* "must not only know what follows from the first principles, but must also possess truth about the first principles. Therefore *sophia* must be *nous* combined with *epistēmē* — *epistēmē* of the highest objects which has received as it were its proper completion."
4. Cf. *Meta.* 1.2.
5. Cf. *E.N.* 6.3.1139b20–24.
6. *E.N.* 10.7.1177b4–5.
7. *Meta.* 982b12; 20–21.
8. *E.N.* 1177b1–4.
9. *E.N.* 1141b6–7 (emphasis added).
10. This sense is retained in Heidegger's "Letter on Humanism" (*"Brief über den Humanismus,"* trans. F. A. Capuzzi and J. G. Gray, in D. F. Krell, ed., Martin Heidegger *Basic Writings* [London: Routledge and Kegan Paul, 1987], pp. 193–242), which strongly echoes Aristotle's point here.
11. *E.N.* 6.7.1141a20–22; 1141a34–1141b2.
12. *E.N.* 10.7. 1177b26–28.
13. See *E.N.* 1777a23 and 1177b22.
14. See *E.N.* 1177a1–8, where this is said of *eudaimonia* as a life of excellence; it is not negated when the next chapter goes on to claim that the highest, if not indeed the only, *eudaimonia* resides in *theōrein.*
15. This aspect of edification seems very foreign to the sense of 'theory' which is enshrined in modern science. It is not entirely without resonance, however, in twentieth-century thought. Perhaps its most exalted expression is to be found in Husserl, who saw phenomenological reflection as a mode of liberation from the 'natural' attitude, and described it (in *The Crisis of the European Sciences* [Evanston, Ill.: Northwestern University Press, 1979]) as "a novel practice . . . whose aim is to elevate mankind to all forms of veridical norms through universal scientific reason, to transform it into a fundamentally new humanity, capable of absolute self-responsibility on the basis of absolute theoretical insight" (quoted by J. Habermas in *K.H.I.,* p. 305). A more sober conception of the moral rewards of theoretical engagement is to be found in Simone Weil: "If we concentrate our attention on trying to solve a problem of geometry, and if at the end of an hour we are no nearer to doing so than at the beginning, we have nonetheless been making progress each minute of that hour in another more mysterious dimension. Without our knowing or feeling it, this apparently barren effort has brought more light into the soul. The result . . . may very likely be felt . . . in some department of the intelligence in no way connected with mathematics. . . . So it comes about that a geometry problem . . . may be of great service one day, provided we devote the right kind of effort. . . . Should the occasion arise [it] can one day make us better able to give someone in affliction exactly the help

required to save him, at the supreme moment of his need" ("Reflections on the Right
Use of School Studies with a View to the Love of God", pp. 67–76 in *Waiting on God*
[Glasgow: Collins, 1978]; "Réflexions sur le bon usage de études scolaires en vue de
l'amour de dieu," pp. 72–80 in *Attente de dieu* [Paris: La Colombe, 1950]). And even
Freud (who is so much more 'modern' than either Husserl or Weil and more anxious,
in particular, to embrace the modern notion of 'science') saw a moral import as intrinsic to theoretical pursuits. In *The Future of an Illusion,* he asserts that while the
eclipse of religion may be dangerous in its impact on ordinary folk—whose morals
have always needed the supercharge of religion—it will have no detrimental effects
on theorists who, precisely by becoming theorists (i.e., by submitting to what Freud
calls the "primacy of intellect"), will apparently have inoculated themselves against
the possibility of moral disease. (See the standard edition of the *Complete Psychological Works of Sigmund Freud,* trans. and ed. J. Strachey [London: Hogarth, 1961],
21:39.)

16. See Martha C. Nussbaum, *The Fragility of Goodness* (Cambridge: Cambridge
University Press, 1986) pp. 373–377.

17. *E.N.* 1178a9.

18. *E.N.* 1178b7.

19. *E.N.* 1177b31–34.

20. At 1140b20–21 we are told that phronesis is a "rational disposition towards
action" (*hexin einai meta logou . . . praktikēn*) which is "concerned with human things"
(*peri ta anthrōpina*).

21. In fact in *E.N.* 6.7 Aristotle acknowledges, without embarrassment, that "we
say that some even of the lower animals have phronesis," whereas in *E.N.* 10.8 he finds
an opportunity to point out that "none of the other animals is happy, since they in
no way share in contemplation."

22. Treating an extensive literature very schematically and selectively, one might
identify three positions that have been taken on this issue: (i) Aristotle accords a strict
priority to the life of theory: it is the sole constituent of *eudaimonia,* and practical
life—being entirely instrumental to it—should decrease that it may increase; (ii) Aristotle regards theoretical activity as the highest but not the sole constituent of *eudaimonia;* it is most worthy of pursuit, but only within bounds that are set by phronesis,
and never in such a way that the demands of ethical virtue are relativized by it; and
(iii) Aristotle's position remains stubbornly inconsistent; there is no satisfactory way
of reconciling the two conflicting sets of demands. (i) might be called the *strong* position; it was supported, among the older commentators by Grant, and more recently
by Cooper. (ii) might be called the *moderate* position and was held by Stewart, and
more recently by Gauthier and Jolif, and Keyt. (iii) might be called the *skeptical* position and attributed to Ackrill (who maintains that Aristotle's view of the nature of
man, postulating, as it does, an impossible "coalition" of the divine and the human,
is "unintelligible"—so that his position on *eudaimonia* cannot avoid being "broken-
backed") and to Nussbaum (who suggests that *E.N.* 10, chapters 6 through 8, in their
present setting, are quite likely to have been inserted by someone other than Aristotle—
though they may well be of his authorship, and do in any case express a kind of intellectualism [a residual Platonism] to which he remained "in some ways deeply attracted"—even though it was "out of step" with all that is most characteristic in his

mature ethical-/political writings). See John M. Cooper, *Reason and Human Good in Aristotle* (Cambridge, Mass.: 1975), esp. pp. 155–180; J. L. Ackrill, "Aristotle on Eudaimonia" in A. O. Rorty, ed., *Essays on Aristotle's Ethics* (Berkeley and Los Angeles: University of California Press, 1980), pp. 15–33; Martha Nussbaum, *The Fragility of Goodness*, pp. 373–377; and David Keyt, "Intellectualism in Aristotle," in *Paideia*, Special Aristotle Issue, 1978, pp. 138–154. For the references in Grant, Stewart, and Gauthier and Jolif, see Keyt, p. 155, nn. 21 and 28; and for a more complex division of positions than I have suggested here on this much-disputed issue, see ibid., p. 143ff.

23. *E.N.* 6 — together with *E.N.* 5 and 7 — is one of the 'common' books which, in the manuscript tradition, occur both in the *Nicomachean* and the *Eudemian Ethics*. The question as to which of the two treatises they properly belong to has long been an issue for Aristotelian commentators and has generally been settled in conjunction with the problem of deciding the chronological order of the two treatises. The orthodox position (associated in this century especially with Jaeger, but supported also by the classic commentary of Gauthier and Jolif, and by Rowe in a monograph in 1971) has been that the *Nicomachean Ethics* is the later and more mature work and that the three disputed books therefore belong to it. This position has, however, been the object of a powerful and many-pronged attack by Anthony Kenny in *The Aristotelian Ethics* (Oxford: Oxford University Press, 1978). Kenny is frank about his purpose, which is "to attack, and I hope demolish this dogma" (what I have called the orthodox position) and "to settle in a definitive manner the original context of the disputed books" (pp. 2 and 4). He refrains from committing himself to a comparative dating of the two treatises and maintains, in any case, that previous scholars have been guilty of a "serious methodological error" in deciding the provenance of the three books on the basis of such a dating. Instead, he is satisfied that he has shown that the chief arguments which have been used to demonstrate that "the *Eudemian Ethics* is early and immature are built on sand" and that he has "presented a succession of arguments, historical, philological, and philosophical, to prove that [the common books] fit within the Eudemian framework very much better than they fit within the Nicomachean framework in which they have been so long read" (p. 238). Although lacking the competence to judge on this issue, I find the philosophical component of Kenny's argument, which includes acute observations about phronesis and *eudaimonia*, persuasive. For critical reviews of Kenny's book, see T. H. Irwin in *Journal of Philosophy*, 77, no. 6 (1980): 338–353, and J. M. Cooper in *Nous* 15 (1981): 381–392. In any case, one thing now seems clear and will, I hope, be reflected in what follows: The *Eudemian Ethics* is not to be neglected, as for a long time it was, as a source of some of Aristotle's finest analyses.

24. *E.E.* 1249b9–19.

25. *E.N.* 1145a6–11.

26. At *E.N.* 1145a9 and *E.E.* 1249b15.

27. This is a typically succinct formulation of L. G. H. Greenwood in his classic *Aristotle, Nicomachean Ethics Book Six, With Essays, Notes and Translation* (Cambridge, 1909; reprint New York: Arno Press, 1973).

28. *E.N.* 1140a2–5.

29. *E.N.* 1140b1–4.

30. *E.N.* 1.7.1097b25–30.
31. *E.N.* 1.10.1100b35–1101a6.
32. *E.N.* 2.1.1103a31–1103b2.
33. *E.N.* 2.6.1106b8–16.
34. Aristotle's use of medical analogies in working out his ethics is a study in itself. For interesting articles on it see Werner Jaeger, "Aristotle's Use of Medicine as Model of Method in His Ethics," *Journal of Hellenic Studies* 77 (1957): 54–61; G. E. R. Lloyd, "The Role of Medical and Biological Analogies in Aristotle's Ethics," *Phronēsis* 13 (1968): 68–83; Michael J. Seidler, "The Medical Paradigm in Aristotle's Ethics," *The Thomist* 42 (1978): 400–433; and Martha Nussbaum, "Therapeutic Arguments: Epicurus and Aristotle," in M. Schofield and G. Striker, eds., *The Norms of Nature* (Cambridge: Cambridge University Press, 1985), pp. 31–74. For illuminating discussion of the whole medical background to Aristotle's conception of virtue as a mean, see Theodore Tracy, *Physiological Theory and the Doctrine of the Mean in Plato and Aristotle* (The Hague: Mouton, 1969), esp. §4, pp. 157ff.
35. I am alluding here to the example of "light foods" at *E.N.* 6.7.1141b18–21, which I analyze in some detail later (see ch. 9, §5, text at n. 53).
36. *E.N.* 1105a23–26.
37. *E.N.* 1105a28–1105b3 (emphasis added).
38. See n. 1 above.
39. See *Meta.* 9.6.1048b18–34.
40. See n. 48 below.
41. We need to be careful in speaking of "Plato", for in Plato's later work—especially in the *Laws*—phronesis is used in a sense which is in fact very close to Aristotle's. (See also n. 46 below.)
42. This is a point nicely made by Aristotle at the very end of *De Sophisticis Elenchis* when he criticizes earlier sophists who "used to hand out rhetorical speeches to be learned by heart. . . . For they used to suppose that they trained people by imparting to them not the techne but its products, as though any one professing that he would impart a form of knowledge to obviate any pain in the feet, were then not to teach a man the techne of shoe-making or the sources whence he can acquire anything of the kind, but were to present him with several kinds of shoes of all sorts—for he has helped him to meet his need, but has not imparted a techne to him." To impart a techne to someone is to enable him to produce things *by his own initiative*, and to do so *methodically*—a point brought out in the *Rhetoric* when Aristotle says that those things are *entechna* which are *dia tēs methodou kai dia hēmon* (*Rhet.* 1355b38).
43. See *E.N.* 3.3.1112b11–16.
44. *Meta.* 7.7.1032a32–1032b1. At 1032b13 and 1034a23 Aristotle even says that techne *is* the form.
45. These quotations from Hintikka are from "Plato on Knowing How, That and What," in *Knowledge and the Known, Historical Perspectives on Epistemology* (Dordrecht: Kluwer, 1974), pp. 41–42.
46. One will implicitly distinguish "Socrates himself" from Plato if one follows Terence Irwin in *Plato's Moral Theory: The Early and Middle Dialogues* (Oxford: Clarendon Press, 1977). Irwin there maintains that while the "craft analogy" (CA in his

abbreviation), which "argues from the character of specialized crafts to conclusions about the character of virtues" (p. 71), is one of Socrates' two main methodological resources — the other being the 'cross-examination' (*elenchos*) — it is rejected by Plato in the middle dialogues (*Meno, Symposium, Phaedrus,* and *Republic* from the beginning of book 2 onwards). According to Irwin, "Plato criticizes the CA . . . insists that the CA misrepresents the proper status of virtue by making it worthwhile only for its consequences . . . rejects those parts of Socrates' theory which depend on craft-principles [e.g., the denial of incontinence] and retains the parts which depend on elenchos-principles. Moral knowledge will emerge from, and will be justified by, the elenchos, but it will not meet the conditions of a craft" (p. 174). On the degree of explicitness which Irwin attributes to this Platonic criticism of Socrates within the dialogue-form, which after all still retains Socrates as chief protagonist, see p. 323, n. 63. But for an approach to the Dialogues which is more sensitive to the philosophical import of their literary and dramatic form and which consequently is more circumspect about identifying a distinctly Socratic or Platonic voice, see, e.g., Rosemary Desjardins, "Why Dialogues?" pp. 110–125, or Charles Griswold, Jr., "Plato's Metaphilosophy: Why Plato Wrote Dialogues," pp. 143–167, in Griswold, ed., *Platonic Writings and Platonic Readings* (New York and London: Routledge, 1988).

47. Hintikka, p. 41.

48. The following quotation from the *Gorgias* shows both the theoretical inclination in Plato's conception of techne and its remarkable resemblance to Aristotle's account of techne in *Meta.* 1.1 that I am about to discuss in the text: "I said that in my opinion cookery differed from medicine in being, not a techne, but a routine, pointing out that the other, that is, medicine, has investigated the *nature* of the subject it treats and the *cause* of its actions and can give a *rational account* of each of them, whereas its counterpart, which is exclusively devoted to cultivating pleasure, approaches it in a thoroughly unscientific way, without once having investigated the nature of pleasure or its cause; and without any pretense whatever to *reason* and practically no effort to *classify*, it preserves by *mere experience* and routine a *memory* of what usually happens, thereby securing its pleasures" (*Gorgias,* 500e–501a, emphases added). On the other hand, it should be noted that a less theoretically inclined, more experiential techne is not absent from Plato's writings; for an exemplary formulation of it from the *Statesman,* see n. 128 below.

49. *Meta.* 1.1.981a24–30.

50. *Meta.* 1.1.981a6–12.

51. *E.N.* 10.9.1180b20–22.

52. *E.N.* 6.3.1139b25–26.

53. E.g., *E.N.* 1143a3–4, where it is considered as the science of health, on all fours with geometry as the science of magnitudes.

54. E.g., *Meta.* 981b23–24 speaks of *hai mathēmatikai technai,* and at *Topics* 170a31 geometry is called a techne.

55. E.g., *Rhet.* 1355b28–31, where medicine and geometry are treated as *epistēmai* and technai without distinction.

56. E.g., at *Meta.* 1046b3.

57. *Summa Theologiae,* 2a–2ae, q.47, a.2, ad 3. It is interesting to find an echo of this remark of Aquinas's in Gadamer, who insists that "I cannot really make sense

442 Notes to pages 254–260

of a phronesis that is supposed to be scientifically disciplined," although he is happy
to add: "I can imagine a scientific approach that is disciplined by phronesis" (a letter
by Hans-Georg Gadamer, in Bernstein, *Beyond Objectivism and Relativism* [Oxford:
Blackwell, 1983], p. 263).

58. Both of these passages are in the *Magna Moralia*. The first speaks of "the
technai of making" as those which "have some other end beyond the making; for instance, beyond house-building, since that is the techne of making a house, there is
a house as its end beyond the making, and similarly in the case of carpentry and the
other technai of making." And it then goes on to speak of playing the harp as a techne
which is *not* a techne of making, since "beyond playing the harp there is no other
end, but just this is the end, the activity and the doing." In a similar vein, the second
passage speaks of a class of technai where "the end and the activity are the same, and
there is not any other end beyond the activity," and immediately adds that this class
is illustrated by the case of the flute-player—to whom "the activity and the end are
the same (for to play the flute is both his end and his activity)"—but not by that of
the builder, for "the techne of house-building . . . has a different end beyond the
activity" (see *M.M.* 1.34.1197a4–11 and 2.12.1211b26–31).

59. *E.N.* 1096a31–33.

60. *E.E.* 1247a5–7.

61. *An. Post.* 2.11.95a3–6.

62. *M.M.* 2.8.1207a4–6.

63. *Pol.* 1.11.1258b35.

64. *The Fragility of Goodness*, pp. 94–95.

65. Ibid., p. 95.

66. *An. Post.* 2.11.95a3–6.

67. One might say that these areas tend toward the *apeiron*, i.e., that which is
without limit and therefore uncontrollable. The sea, which is so obviously the site
of the navigator's techne, is often described by Greek writers as *apeiron*.

68. *E.N.* 1140a19–20.

69. Aristotle himself uses '*technikos*' in this sense at *Rhet.* 3.15.1416b7. It is a sense
which is also retained in the English words 'crafty' and 'artful', which are adjectival
forms of the words most often used to translate techne.

70. See M. Detienne and J.-P. Vernant, *Cunning Intelligence in Greek Culture
and Society*, trans. J. Lloyd (Sussex: Harvester Press, 1978), originally published as *Les
Ruses d'intelligence: la Metis des grecs* (Paris, 1974).

71. *Cunning Intelligence in Greek Culture and Society*, pp. 3–4.

72. Ibid., p. 3 and p. 4.

73. *E.N.* 2.1.1104a2–10.

74. *Rhet.* 1.2.1356b30–34.

75. *E.E.* 1226a34–1226b2.

76. *E.N.* 1112a33–1112b6.

77. *Cunning Intelligence in Greek Society and Culture*, p. 316 and p. 317. Detienne and Vernant do not provide any textual support for this thesis, but the following might be adduced. *Eustochia* (translated by Ross as "skill in conjecture" but
literally "a good aim") and *anchinoia* (readiness of mind or quick-wittedness), which
are terms identified by them as belonging within the field of *mētis*, occur in the dis-

cussion of *euboulia* (excellence in deliberation) in *E.N.* 6.9; and although Aristotle in fact distinguishes them from *euboulia* (which is a very important ingredient of phronesis) his taking the trouble to do this—i.e., his recognizing them as *plausible candidates* in unpacking the latter notion—shows his awareness of the similarities between the field of *mētis* and what he was trying to bring out with his notion of phronesis. Moreover in *De Virtutibus et Vitiis* (the Aristotelian provenance of which is admittedly uncertain) "*to anchinōs chrēsasthai . . . tōi logōi* (translated by Solomon as "the sagacious use of word") together incidentally with grasping the *kairos*, is put within the province of phronesis (see 1250a34). Again, the end of praxis (in relation to which phronesis is our guide) is said to be "attuned to the *kairos*" at *E.N.* 1110a13–14. And in *E.E.* 2.3, when the notion of virtue as a mean is illustrated by a list in which each virtue is matched with its corresponding excess and defect, in the case of phronesis the defect is simplicity or naiveté (*euētheia*), while the excess is *panourgia* (sly roguery), a term mentioned by Vernant and Detienne as associated with *mētis*.

78. Ibid., p. 4.

79. House-building (*oikodomikē*) is the sole example mentioned by Aristotle in *E.N.* 6.4 at 1140a7.

80. *E.N.* 6.1140b6–7.

81. Cf. *E.N.* 1139b1–3: "every one who makes makes for an end, and that which is made is not an end in the unqualified sense (but only relative to something, i.e. of something)."

82. *Truth and Method,* p. 286; *Wahrheit und Methode,* p. 304. Cf. D. Monan's remark to the same effect: "The very retention of the ends/means scheme to express an action as being its own goal demands a transformation in the meaning given to the schema itself" (*Moral Knowledge and Its Methodology in Aristotle* [Oxford: Oxford University Press, 1968], pp. 68–69).

83. See above, ch. 3.

84. *E.N.* 10.7.1177a30–34.

85. *E.N.* 9.9.1169b16–19.

86. *Pol.* 1.2.1253a2–10. The inherently interpersonal nature of the practice of the virtues is also stressed at, e.g., *E.N.* 1130a7–8; 1178a10–13 and 1178b5–6; but perhaps more eloquent than any individual passage is the fact that two whole books of the *E.N.* (8 and 9) are devoted to *friendship,* which is said to be "most necessary with a view to living. For without friends no one would choose to live." Although odd passages might be cited which emphasize self-sufficiency rather than interdependence, they occur only in contexts where the sense of praxis is restricted to contemplative activity (see, e.g., *Pol.* 7.3.1325b16–21).

87. *E.N.* 6.3.1139a29–31.

88. *E.N.* 7.10.1152a8–9.

89. *E.N.* 6.2.1139b4–5.

90. *E.N.* 6.5.1140b28–30.

91. See *Truth and Method,* p. 283; *Wahrheit und Methode,* p. 300.

92. *E.N.* 1140b21–24.

93. Cf. Gilbert Ryle's distinction between 'task verbs' and 'achievement verbs', *The Concept of Mind* (London: Penguin, 1986), pp. 143ff.

94. *E.N.* 1139a36–1139b4.

95. At *Pol.* 1.9.1258a10–14, Aristotle writes: "The quality of courage, for example, is not intended to make wealth, but to inspire confidence; neither is this the aim . . . of the physician's techne; but . . . health. Nevertheless, some men turn every quality or techne into a means of getting wealth; this they conceive to be the end, and to the promotion of the end they think all things must contribute."

96. *Rhet.* 1.1.1355b10–14.

97. *Truth and Method*, p. 284; *Wahrheit und Methode*, p. 301.

98. *E.E.* 8.1246a33–36.

99. *E.E.* 1246a36–1246b1.

100. This theme of the possible misuse of cognitive power is of course thoroughly Platonic. Another interesting Aristotelian instance of it occurs in the *Rhetoric* where rhetorical skill is defended even though it can be misused: "if it is objected that one who uses such power of speech unjustly might do great harm, *that* is a charge which may be made in common against all good things except excellence" (1355b2–5).

101. *E.E.* 1246b2–4 (the translation here is my own).

102. *E.E.* 1246b4–6.

103. The argument, as elaborate, I believe, as any which is to be found in Aristotle, is in fact a series of *reductio ad absurdum* arguments against each of the guises which the position being argued against can take on if one supposes, as Aristotle does, that the rational and nonrational parts of the soul are distinct and that different combinations of perfection or its lack may be found in each.

104. *E.E.* 1246b8–11. The final sentence here confirms the point which I argued in §2 above, namely that the primacy of theoretical reason does not imply any overlordship in the realm of practical affairs; in this realm phronesis provides the highest form of knowledge there is.

105. *Truth and Method*, p. 283; *Wahrheit und Methode*, p. 300.

106. *E.N.* 3.1114a17–18.

107. Alasdair MacIntyre argues cogently that a person's inability to predict and hence manipulate his own future actions is in fact a limit on his ability, as a third person observer and operator, to predict or manipulate *another person's* future actions (see *After Virtue*, p. 91).

108. *The Self as Agent* (Atlantic Highlands, N.J.: Humanities, 1978) is in fact the title of an unjustly neglected book by the Scottish philosopher John MacMurray which, with its companion volume of Gifford Lectures, *Persons in Relation* (Humanities, 1979) carried through—quite independently of the major moves in continental philosophy which were reviewed in Part 1 of this study—its own reversal of the Cartesian (and indeed, in MacMurray's view, Greek) hegemony of the thinking ego over the acting person-in-relation.

109. *E.N.* 1140b7–10 and 1141b4–6.

110. *E.N.* 1141a25–26; 26–28; 29–31.

111. *E.N.* 1141b29–31; see also 1142a1–2.

112. See the remark at *E.N.* 7.1: "We must . . . set the phenomena before us and, after first discussing the difficulties, go on to prove, *if possible*, the truth of all the reputable opinions . . . or, *failing this*, of the greater number and the most authori-

tative" (1145b1–5, emphases added) and, for an excellent account of this method, Nussbaum, *The Fragility of Goodness*, ch. 8.

113. *E.N.* 1141b30–1142a11.

114. *E.N.* 1142a9–11. It is not entirely clear from the context whether *skepteon* is pointing up the need for a general inquiry by Aristotle himself or some other philosopher about how a person may best manage his affairs, or a concrete growing-wiser-in-the-course-of-experience on the part of the *phronimos* about his own affairs specifically. The former position is taken by Stewart, Ross, and Thompson; the latter by Grant and Greenwood. For Greenwood's unusually long and, I believe, persuasive argument defending his interpretation, see *Nicomachean Ethics, Book Six, with Essays, Notes and Translation*, pp. 193–194.

115. See W. Jaeger, *Aristotle, Fundamentals of His Development*, trans. R. Robinson, (Oxford: Clarendon Press, 1934) e.g., at p. 242: "Its [i.e., phronesis's] function is . . . to discover the right means of attaining the end determined by the moral will."

116. See D. J. Allan, *The Philosophy of Aristotle* (London, 1952), pp. 180–182, and "Aristotle's Account of the Origins of Moral Principles," ch. 5 in J. Barnes, M. Schofield and R. Sorabji, eds., *Articles on Aristotle*, vol. 2, *Ethics and Politics* (London, 1977).

117. Greenwood, p. 48.

118. H. H. Joachim, *The Nicomachean Ethics* (posthumously published lectures of 1902–1917, ed. by D. A. Rees, Oxford, 1951), p. 188. More recently this point has been made by W. F. R. Hardie in *Aristotle's Ethical Theory*, (2nd ed., Oxford: Clarendon Press, 1980), pp. 13–14 and by Alasdair MacIntyre, who distinguishes between "internal and external means to an end" and claims that although this distinction "is not drawn by Aristotle himself . . . it is an essential distinction to be drawn if we are to intend what Aristotle intended" (*After Virtue*, p. 172).

119. *E.N.* 1140b6–7.

120. *E.N.* 1144a24–27.

121. Cf. *M.M.* 1197b22–26: "it is the part of the *phronimos* and of phronesis to aim at the best things, and always to choose and do these, but it is the part of cleverness and the clever man to consider by what means each object of action may be effected, and to provide these."

122. I depart here from the Revised Oxford Translation, staying with Ross, who inserts *ei deinos* ("if he is clever"), for *idein* at line 19. Kenny calls this a "brilliant emendation" (*Aristotle's Theory of the Will*, p. 105); in any case it chimes with my purpose, which is to link this passage on *euboulia* with the later passage on *deinotēs*.

123. *E.N.* 1142b17–22.

124. The conception of *euboulia* in *E.N.* 6.9 involves, I believe, a synthesis of the concepts of *boulē* (or *to bouleuesthai*, i.e., 'deliberation') and *boulēsis* (i.e., 'wish') in *E.N.* 3.3 and 3.4. For the concept of deliberation in 3.3 was a purely technical one, concerned solely with means; the apprehension of ends was then assigned to the separate faculty of 'wish' in the following chapter. *Boulēsis* does not occur in *E.N.* 6, and it may be taken to be assumed into *euboulia* or the more embrasive phronesis, neither of which had occurred in *E.N.* 3.

125. *Truth and Method*, p. 286; *Wahrheit und Methode*, p. 303.

126. *E.N.* 9.1137a9–17.

127. See above, §5, text before n. 74.

128. *E.N.* 5.10.1137b13–24. This extract may recall a passage from the *Phaedrus* about this unhappy lot of the written word when its author cannot continually accompany it on its travels in order to guard it against misinterpretation (we met this passage in the context of Gadamer's insistence on the need to rescue the 'statement' from the 'alienation' of the written state and to restore it to the matrix of living speech; see above, ch. 5, n. 41). An even closer parallel to it, however, is to be found in the *Statesman:* "Law can never issue an injunction binding on all which really embodies what is best for each. . . . The differences of human personality, the variety of men's activities, and the inevitable unsettlement attending all human experience make it impossible for any techne whatsoever to issue unqualified rules holding good on all questions at all times. . . . It is impossible then for something invariable and unqualified to deal satisfactorily with what is never uniform and constant. . . . How could any lawgiver be capable of prescribing every act of a particular individual and sit at his side, so to speak, all through his life and tell him just what to do?" (*Statesman,* 294b–295b.) The tone here is as quintessentially 'experiential' as anything that we shall find in Aristotle, and shows how oversimplified is any straightforward contrast between him and Plato.

9. The Circle between Knowledge and Virtuous Character

1. See *E.N.* 1.13.1103a3–10.

2. *E.N.* 1144b18–21 and 28–30.

3. *E.N.* 1143b22–23.

4. *E.N.* 1143b24–28.

5. Perhaps the strongest statement of this way of thinking occurs in the *Magna Moralia:* "Speaking generally, it is not the case, as the rest of the world think, that reason is the principle and guide to virtue, but rather the feelings. . . . Wherefore a right disposition of the feelings seems to be the principle that leads to virtue rather than the reason" (1206b,17–29). St. George Stock refers to this passage as "the crowning word of Peripatetic Ethics, for which we wait in vain in *E.N.* or even in *E.E.*" (Introduction to *Magna Moralia, Eudemian Ethics,* and *De Virtutibus et Vitiis,* in the Oxford edition of the works of Aristotle, edited by W. D. Ross, vol. 9, p. xxi).

6. *Meta.* 5.12.1019a18–19.

7. *E.N.* 6.1144a13–14. By contrast, works of techne *can* be considered apart from their relationship to their maker; for (as we are told in *E.N.* 2.4) they "have their goodness [*eu*] in themselves."

8. See above, ch. 8, §7, text at n. 122.

9. *E.N.* 1144a34.

10. *E.N.* 1140b11–12.

11. *E.N.* 1140b14–15.

12. *E.N.* 1140b18–20.

13. *E.N.* 1144b10–12.

14. *E.N.* 1144b30–32. This circle is restated in the discussion of *theoria* in *E.N.* 10.8: "Phronesis, too, is linked to excellence of character, and this to phronesis, since

the principles of phronesis are in accordance with the moral excellences and rightness in the moral excellences is in accordance with phronesis" (1178a16–19).

15. This is of course why at the heart of Gadamer's exploration of the hermeneutical circle we find his analysis of phronesis. See above, ch. 4, §3.

16. *E.N.* 1144b6.

17. *E.N.* 6.11.1143b11–14. My interpretation of *phusei* here tallies with that of Engberg-Pedersen; see *Aristotle's Theory of Moral Insight* (Oxford: Clarendon Press, 1983), pp. 216–217.

18. *Meta.* 1.1.981a5–12.

19. *Meta.* 1.1.981a25–30.

20. *Meta.* 1.1.981b5–6.

21. *Meta.* 1.1.981a12–24.

22. The point at issue here will be illustrated and further clarified later (see below, end of §5 and §6) when I advert to this passage from *Meta.* 1.1 in the context of an analysis of Aristotle's "light foods" example at *E.N.* 6.7.1141b18–21. Just before introducing this example, Aristotle in fact repeats essentially the same point as *Meta.* 1.1: "some who do not know, and especially those who have experience, are more practical than others who know."

23. See above, ch. 8, §6.

24. See above, ch. 8, §5.

25. *E.N.* 5.10.1137b29–32.

26. *Meta.* 7.7.1032a32–1032b23.

27. This point is adverted to by J. Hintikka: "The most striking feature of Aristotle's theory [of *kinēsis* (change)—one of the principal spheres of which is techne (*phusis* or nature being the other)] is that the change always has as its beginning an actual instantiation of the same 'form' as the outcome, existing potentially during the change. This actual individual may be a member of the same species as the outcome ('man begets man') but it may also be the form realized in the mind of a conscious producer of the outcome according to a plan. In all cases, however, there will have to be such an antecedently existing form which initiates the *kinēsis:* the mover or agent will always be the vehicle of a form . . . which, when it acts, will be the source and the cause of the change. . . . From this it follows that whenever it is true to say that a certain universal ('form') exists potentially, there must have been an earlier exemplification of the same universal actually existing" (*Time and Necessity: Studies in Aristotle's Theory of Modality* [Oxford: Clarendon Press, 1973], p. 106). As Hintikka points out elsewhere (*Knowledge and the Known* [Dordrecht: Kluwer, 1974], p. 44), the conception of the fine arts and of technology implied by this doctrine of *kinēsis* was inevitably based on and limited by the notion of *imitation (mimēsis).*

28. The absence of experimentation from Greek science has often been remarked. Sambursky, for instance, in *The Physical World of the Greeks* (trans. from the Hebrew by M. Dagut [London: Routledge and Kegan Paul, 1987]) writes: "with very few exceptions the ancient Greeks throughout a period of eight hundred years made no attempt at systematic experimentation." Sarah Waterlow (who quotes this remark) gives a very succinct explanation of why experimentation was ruled out in principle by Aristotle's metaphysics of a natural substance (*Nature, Change and Agency in Aristotle's Physics* [Oxford: Clarendon Press, 1982], pp. 33–34). The absence of experimentation

from Aristotle's notion of *techne* remains puzzling when we consider that techne is precisely what he distinguished from nature (both being sources of change in the world). But this distinction was never allowed to open up a real chasm between techne and nature; in the end it is always the analogy between them that Aristotle insists on. See below, ch. 10 §5.

29. The starkness of this contrast is slightly modified when Aristotle goes on to say that "inanimate objects produce each of their effects somehow by nature [*phusei*]; and manual workers by habit" (*ethos*) (981b4–5).

30. It is noteworthy that the sharpness with which *Meta.* 1.1 states the distinction between the architect and the manual worker—evacuating all thinking from manual work and reposing it solely in the superior function of the architect—does not occur in *E.N.* 6.8, where, in the context of his discussion of phronesis, Aristotle applies the same distinction to politics. There he treats legislation (*nomothetikē*) as architectonic, but when he compares those who apply and develop the law through particular enactments with manual workers (*cheirotechnai*) there is no pejorative intent. He does not question the propriety of attributing *politeuesthai* to these workers, for not alone are they the only ones who act (*monoi gar prattousi*) but the object of their action is *bouleutikē*, namely, that which requires deliberation, i.e., real thinking out and not merely mindless activity (see 1141b25–30). All of this seems to confirm that the theoretical bias which vitiates his account of techne-poiesis is not evident in his account of phronesis-praxis, and to suggest, moreover, that politics is not readily assimilable to Aristotle's official concept of techne (a point which will now emerge in §4).

31. *E.N.* 10.9.

32. *E.N.* 1180b20–22.

33. *E.N.* 10.9.1180b31–1181a12.

34. *E.N.* 1181a17–18.

35. Quotations here are from the last chapter of *E.N.* 1181a18–1181b12.

36. Two different words, *gnōmē* and *krinein*, are used for judgment in *E.N.* 6 and 10 respectively, but it seems clear that the two words are very close in meaning and are intimately related to phronesis; the *phronimos* is one who has good judgment about his own actions and the affairs of others.

37. *E.N.* 1179a35–1179b31.

38. All quotations in this paragraph are from *E.N.* 1.3.

39. *E.N.* 2.4.1105b12–18.

40. This is in the first sense of 'natural' that we met above in §2 at n. 16.

41. In his commentary on the *Ethics*, Aquinas adverts to three aspects of this natural inclination, two of which are common to *all* and the third of which is variable as between individuals. This natural inclination "can be considered first on the part of the reason, since the first principles of human conduct are implanted by nature, for instance, that no one should be injured, and the like; next, on the part of the will, which of itself is naturally moved by the good apprehended as its proper object; last on the part of the sensitive appetite according as, by natural temperament, some men are inclined to anger, others to concupiscence or passions of a different kind either too much or too little, or with moderation in which moral virtue consists. The first two are common to all men" (St. Thomas Aquinas, *Commentary on the Nicomachean*

Ethics, bk. 6, lect. 11, par. 1277, trans. C. I. Litzinger, O.P. [Chicago: Regnery, 1964]).

42. Cf. *E.N.* 10.9.1179b20–23: "some men think that we are made good by nature, others by habituation, others by teaching. Nature's part evidently does not depend on us, but as a result of some divine causes is present in those who are truly fortunate."

43. Cf. the second sense of 'natural' in §2 above, second paragraph.

44. *E.N.* 2.4.1105b8–9.

45. *E.N.* 2.4.1105a33.

46. *An. Post.* 2.19.100a2 and 6–8.

47. *An. Post.* 2.19.100a12–14 (I depart here from the Revised Oxford translation which reads *alkēn* for *archēn* at line 13).

48. Gadamer, as we have already seen (ch. 5, §1, after n. 19), takes this image in *An. Post.* 2.19 as a powerful picture not just of concept-formation but of how a person learns to speak a language. When I take it to depict the process of moral development, I do not mean to deny the uniqueness of the latter or the sense in which character is different from experience *simpliciter;* the two developments, in other words, need not be collapsed into each other nor need we exclude the possibility of a person's being cognitively or linguistically sophisticated and yet a moral laggard (or, conversely, of being backward in many areas of knowledge and yet morally mature). For a reordering of one's emotions is involved when recurrent perceptions and actions consolidate into dispositions of character. It is true that the specifically ethical knowledge acquired through this development (i.e., phronesis) can be brought into play not only in situations in which one has to act oneself but also in situations in which *others* have to act. In the latter case it is the knowledge conferred by 'understanding' (*sunesis*) and 'sympathetic judgment' (*gnōmē*), two subvirtues of phronesis that Aristotle introduces in *E.N.* 6.12 and 11. (Understanding deals with "matters that cause perplexity and call for deliberation" and its sphere, therefore, is the same as that of phronesis; but it differs from the latter in that "phronesis issues commands since its end is what ought to be done or not to be done; but understanding only judges" (1143a8–10). Such judgments may be about "what someone else *says* about matters with which phronesis is concerned" (1143a14–15) but ultimately they are "about things to be *done*" (1143a34–35). Understanding as the capacity for judgment seems to be complete for Aristotle only when it includes *gnōmē,* which is the capacity for sympathy or considerateness in one's concrete judgments of what is right or equitable). Both *sunesis* and *gnōmē* are linked very intimately with phronesis and the point to be made here (cf. 1143a25ff.) is that, although they focus on the actions of others, we cannot possess either of them unless we have had our *own* considerable moral experience.

49. The nearest Aristotle comes to making this point explicit is, I think, in two highly condensed lines (at 1143b4–5) in the middle of a passage on *nous* which we shall meet presently (see below, text at n. 67 and after n. 83). Greenwood makes a comment on these lines which seems very close to my present point: "the phenomena of *ēthismos* or habituation are well-known, and habituation is not only a kind of moral induction itself but is accompanied by an intellectual process that is inductive in the strict sense" (Greenwood, *Nicomachean Ethics Book Six,* p. 70).

50. This is clear, e.g., in the first paragraph of the *Rhetoric:* "the subject can plainly

be handled systematically, for it is possible to inquire the reason why some speakers succeed through practice and others spontaneously, and everyone will at once agree that such an inquiry is the function of a techne" (1354a8–11).

51. The *analytic* sense of techne is revealed in the sentence from the *Rhetoric,* quoted in the previous note, or in the passage we have already seen from *Meta.* 1.1 about techne as the ability to "analyze and explain" or to know "the reason why" rather than "the fact that." On the other hand it is an *active* sense of techne that is suggested at *E.N.* 6.4 where it is described as a "reasoned state . . . which is capable of production" or a "productive state which is truly reasoned." Aristotle's failure to distinguish these two senses of techne, which I advert to here, will be a major theme of the next chapter.

52. Cf. *E.N.* 6.8: "while young men become geometricians and mathematicians and wise in matters like these, it is thought that a young man of phronesis cannot be found. The cause is that the latter is concerned not only with universals but with particulars, which become familiar from experience, but a young man has no experience, for it is length of time that gives experience."

53. *E.N.* 1141b16–22 (I depart here slightly from the Revised Oxford translation).

54. *Meta.* 981a21–22.

55. The distinction I make here tallies with a point Aristotle makes a couple of chapters later in his analysis of *euboulia:* "But it is possible to attain even good by a false deduction and to attain what one ought to do but not by the right means, the middle term being false; so that this too is not yet *euboulia*—this state in virtue of which one attains what one ought but not by the right means" (*E.N.* 6.9.1142b22–27). Here Aristotle says that the *falsity* of middle terms abrogates *euboulia;* in the earlier passage I am interpreting him as saying that the *absence* of middle terms abrogates phronesis (which includes *euboulia* as a subvirtue).

56. At the level of the present example, it is doubtful if phronetic experience syllogizes at all; the syllogism is only a formal reconstruction of what is already accomplished by that cumulative systematization which *is* experience.

57. There is an example of such a premise elsewhere in *E.N.* 6: "we may fail to know either that all water that weighs heavy is bad, or that this particular water weighs heavy." This example occurs at the end of a passage that is parallel to the one I have been analyzing and where it is again affirmed that "phronesis . . . is concerned with particulars, which become familiar from experience" (*E.N.* 6.8). In the discussion of moral weakness in *E.N.* 7 Aristotle gives another example of such a premise and clearly contrasts it with a universal one: the incontinent person knows that "'such and such food is dry': but whether 'this food is such and such', of this the incontinent man either has not or is not exercising the knowledge."

58. 'Ultimate premise' is not a phrase that Aristotle uses. But when he uses '*eschaton*' he often clearly means 'ultimate particular', and by an ultimate premise I mean one whose subject is an ultimate particular.

59. *De. An.* 3.11.434a16–22.

60. What I describe here as the 'full role' of phronesis accords with Anthony Kenny's schematic presentation of phroneis as comprising three elements: (1) an apprehension of the ultimate ends of action, (2) *euboulia,* and (3) an apprehension of particulars. In my account, the added major premise(s) would be (1), the minor prem-

ise(s) would be (3), and mobilizing (3) within the context of (1) would be (2). (See *The Aristotelian Ethics*, pp. 171–172).

61. See Kenny's remark: "We are not in the *Ethics* given an instance of a virtuous initial premise: unless we say that the whole *Ethics* is meant to provide one" (*Aristotle's Theory of the Will* [London: Duckworth, 1979], p. 150). Compare this with Anscombe's remark: "Aristotle's grand universal premise is that blessedness is activity in accordance with virtue, especially intellectual virtue. The argument for this as the true premise is the *Nicomachean Ethics* itself" ("Thought and Action in Aristotle," in *New Essays in Plato and Aristotle*, ed. R. Bambrough [London: Routledge and Kegan Paul, 1965], p. 155). When taken in the context of the point I am now making (i.e., that supplying the ultimate universal premise is part of the role of phronesis), these remarks of Anscombe and Kenny suggest one way of answering a question that is sometimes raised about phronesis and the *Ethics*. Was Aristotle's own activity in writing the *Ethics* an exercise of phronesis or of a different type of (theoretical) thinking? Due regard for the involvement of phronesis with the concrete situation and the particular action might suggest the latter. On the other hand, insofar as one sees the *Ethics* as itself the formulation of the ultimate universal premise (à la Kenny and Anscombe) one can say that it not only analyzes phronesis (in bk. 6) but *exercises* it (throughout the work). If the question then arises as to how this thinking—which proceeds by argument and is manifestly discursive—can be considered as an act of *nous*—which, according to Kenny, is the faculty of *intuiting* the ultimate major premises—perhaps an answer is given by Monan when he suggests that "the key word to describe Aristotle's method in determining what actions are good . . . as well as in identifying the supreme good for man . . . is *reflection*, which unfolds, and renders explicit, the truth-value and the guarantees already contained in the prephilosophical experience itself." This is a method which "reveals the identity of the supreme good by *reflecting* on the prephilosophical affective experience of value grasped in the practice of the moral as well as the intellectual virtues" (*Moral Knowledge and Its Methodology in Aristotle*, p. 153). *Nous*, we might say, is the intuitive element in the "prephilosophical experience" of the *phronimos*, and Aristotle's *Ethics* is a reflective articulation of what is implicit in this. Aristotle himself must be a *phronimos* in order to be the kind of ethician he is. Otherwise, he would fall foul of his own words (in the last chapter of *E.N.*) against those who "have not even a conception of what is noble and truly pleasant, since they have never tasted it."

62. This is Stuart Hampshire's phrase in discussing Aristotle (*Two Theories of Morality* [Oxford: Oxford University Press, 1977], p. 17).

63. At 1144a31. T. Ando (*Aristotle's Theory of Practical Cognition* [The Hague: Martinus Nijhoff, 1971], p. 222) gives some significance to this fact that the term occurs only once. On the other hand it must be remembered that the concept is discussed at length in the context of the analysis of moral weakness in *E.N.* 7 (1146b35–1147b19) as well as in *De Anima* 3.11 and *De Motu Animalium*.

64. Aristotle makes it very plain of course that even the scientific or demonstrative syllogism presupposes an extra-syllogistic source of knowledge, e.g.: "Now induction is of first principles and of the universal and deduction proceeds from universals. There are therefore principles from which deduction proceeds, which are not reached by deduction" (1139b28–31).

65. This premise is 'moving' not only in the sense that it strikes out beyond our habitual knowledge to give us a more particular knowledge of the 'here and now', but also in the sense that through this particularization, it moves us to *action*. For a statement of this latter sense, see the passage from *De Anima* quoted in the text at n. 59.

66. *E.N.* 6.8.1142a25–29.

67. *E.N.* 6.11.1143a35–1143b5.

68. In fact Aristotle is here only reiterating a point he had already made in *E.N.* 3.3: "nor indeed can the particular facts be a subject of it [deliberation], as whether this is bread or has been baked as it should; for these are matters of perception. If we are to be always deliberating, we shall have to go on to infinity" (1112b33–1113a2). His point here is close to Wittgenstein's point near the beginning of *Philosophical Investigations:* "Explanations must come to an end somewhere." There the shopkeeper is supposed to be using 'five red apples' as the formula of a technique for providing what the customer wants. But, as Wittgenstein shows, in order to *use* the words in this way the shopkeeper must be in possession of some intuitive ways of acting which are not specified by the formula itself. While agreeing with Aristotle in postulating the need for an end to explanations, Wittgenstein differs from him in seeing this end not as a perception but as an irrefragable way of *acting*. See *On Certainty*, p. 110: "As if giving grounds did not come to an end sometime. But the end is not an ungrounded proposition: it is an ungrounded way of *acting*"; or again, for a passage where the difference with Aristotle is more explicit, ibid., p. 204: "giving grounds, however, justifying the end comes to an end; — but the end is not certain propositions striking us immediately as true, i.e. it is not a kind of *seeing* on our part; it is our acting which lies at the bottom of the language-game." Aristotle is more Wittgensteinian than he might seem here, however; for, as I am trying to make clear in the text, only persons who have become habituated to *act* in certain ways will be capable of the kind of *perception* which he is drawing attention to.

69. It is implicitly held by, e.g., Rackham, Thompson, and Kenny in their translations (see, respectively, Loeb edition of the *Ethics*, p. 350, note g; Penguin edition p. 216, with Tredennick's note; and *The Aristotelian Ethics*, p. 172). It is also, incidentally, Gadamer's interpretation in *Truth and Method* (p. 287). It is implicitly rejected, however, by Ross, Hardie (who adopts Ross's translation), and Greenwood (see his translation on p. 109 and his long note, pp. 197–199). For an incidental analysis of the triangle, and of its relation to other polylateral figures (e.g., the quadrilateral) which *supports* this interpretation, see *E.E.*, 2.6.1222b32–38.

70. At 1142a11–20.

71. *The Aristotelian Ethics*, p. 172.

72. *De An.* 2.5.418a11–20.

73. *Philosophical Investigations*, Pt. 2, pp. 209–210.

74. The basis for a distinction of the kind I am making here between perception in a narrow sense and moral perceptiveness is certainly to be found in Aristotle. In discussing involuntariety in *E.N.* 3.1, he mentions cases where "a person might mistake his son for an enemy . . . or mistake a sharp spear for one with a button on it or a heavy stone for a pumice stone." All these are mistakes in what I am calling the narrow sense of perception, and what is significant is that Aristotle (by regarding them

as involuntary) explicitly places them outside the sphere of moral evaluation: a person who made such a mistake could not, on that account, be morally reproved. But clearly, on Aristotle's analysis, a person who makes mistakes, or does not see, in the sphere of *phronēsis-nous is* blameworthy: to lack *nous* is also to lack the good character which facilitates and is reinforced by it.

75. Wiggins and Nussbaum helpfully use the terms "situational appreciation" and "discernment" respectively. (See Wiggins, "Deliberation and Practical Reason," p. 233 in A. O. Rorty, ed., *Essays on Aristotle's Ethics* (Berkeley: University of California Press, 1980) and Nussbaum, "The Discernment of Perception: An Aristotelian Conception of Private and Public Rationality," in J. Cleary, ed., *Proceedings of the Boston Area Colloquium in Ancient Philosophy,* vol. 1 (1985): 151–201.

76. When Wittgenstein speaks here of "knowledge of mankind," and asks: "Can one learn this knowledge?" his answer is quintessentially Aristotelian and might indeed have come straight from *E.N.* 6: "Yes, some can. Not, however, by taking a course in it, but through '*experience*'" and ". . . what one acquires here is not a technique; one learns correct judgments. There are also rules, but they do not form a system, and only experienced people can apply them right" (*Philosophical Investigations,* Pt. 2, p. 227).

77. In fact we have already seen that there are good grounds for *not* regarding medicine as scientific in this way: it was a conspicuous example of those technai of the *kairos* which, I suggested, are similar rather than dissimilar to phronesis (see above, ch. 8, §5).

78. Aristotle himself, in *De Anima,* gives an example of an act of perception which incorporates a 'because': "perceiving by sense that the beacon is fire, it recognizes in virtue of the general faculty of sense that it signifies an enemy, because it sees it moving." 'Common sense' here not only apprehends something but, as in my examples, also puts an interpretation or explanation on it.

79. Heidegger has made much of interpreting *alētheia* (truth) as *a-lētheia* (i.e., the negative prefix *a* with a derivative of *lanthanein,* 'to escape the notice of') so that truth — in what Heidegger regards as its primordial sense — means unconcealment. (See *Being and Time,* pp. 262ff.) Cf. also Wittgenstein's concepts of "noticing an aspect," "seeing as," and "dawning" in the discussion of the "duck-rabbit" in *Philosophical Investigations* (Pt. 2, §xi).

80. *Truth and Method,* p. 324 (*Wahrheit und Methode,* p. 343).

81. *Truth and Method,* p. 319 (translation slightly amended; *Wahrheit und Methode,* p. 338).

82. *E.N.* 1143a6. I am appealing here, in support of my argument, to the notion of deliberation in this passage of *E.N.* 6.9 and not to the one in *E.N.* 3.3 (and *Meta.* 7.7); for criticism of the latter, see above, §3, and below, ch. 10, §8.

83. *E.N.* 1143b9–15.

84. The significance of the "practical syllogism" can be contested on the grounds (a) of its inherent shortcomings, and (b) that Aristotle's account of practical knowledge is not in any case as heavily dependent on it as has sometimes been supposed. Critics who tend to argue (a) are, e.g., Mure (*Aristotle* [London: Benn, 1932], p. 148, n. 1 and p. 211, n. 3) and Hintikka (who calls the practical syllogism "one of Aristotle's less happy inventions" [*Knowledge and the Known,* p. 89]); among those who argue

(b) are Hardie (*Aristotle's Ethical Theory* [Oxford: Clarendon Press, 1980], p. 213) and Kenny (who largely follows Hardie; see *Aristotle's Theory of the Will*, pp. 111ff.).

85. See Anscombe, "Thought and Action in Aristotle," in R. Bambrough, ed., *New Essays on Plato and Aristotle*, p. 151.

86. My point here is, I believe, related to a point which Aristotle himself makes about the case of adultery in *E.N.* 2.6: "not every action . . . admits of a mean; for some have names that already imply badness, e.g, . . . adultery, theft, murder; for all of these and suchlike things imply by their names that they are themselves bad, and not the excesses or deficiencies of them. . . . Nor does goodness or badness with regard to such things depend on committing adultery with the right woman, at the right time and in the right way." Since, for Aristotle, adultery is wrong *per se,* cases of it fit unproblematically into a deductivist mold; and phronesis is reserved, then, as is made clear at the beginning of *E.N.* 6, for types of action for which a good can be found in a mean between two extremes (see below, §9, after n. 95). This point of Aristotle's is related to the point I am making in that minor premises are less likely to prove problematical in cases where absolute prohibitions are in force. Even in the latter cases, of course, problems can arise, e.g., a question posed by Geach, namely, "is this a case of killing someone or just a case of not taking special care to keep someone alive?" (*The Virtues* [Cambridge: Cambridge University Press, 1977], p. 89).

87. Detienne and Vernant, *Cunning Intelligence in Greek Society and Culture,* pp. 316–317.

88. I shall be referring here to the discussion of moral weakness (*akrasia*) in the first three chapters of *E.N.* 7.

89. *E.N.* 1147b13–17.

90. *E.N.* 1140b13–14.

91. Cf. *E.N.* 1140b11–12.

92. Cf. *E.N.* 1143b11–14.

93. One such Platonist—to whom, in fact, Murdoch is indebted for her notion of 'attention'—is Simone Weil (see especially "l'Attention et la volonté," pp. 134–142, in *La Pesanteur et la grâce* [Paris: 1948]). In one essay, Weil speaks of the unavailingness of "the vocabulary of middle values," the main begetter of which she clearly regards as Aristotle: "A village idiot in the literal sense of the word, if he really loves truth, is infinitely superior to Aristotle in his thought, even though he never utters anything but inarticulate murmurs. He is infinitely closer to Plato than Aristotle ever was. He has genius, while only the word talent applies to Aristotle. If a fairy offered to change his destiny for one resembling Aristotle's he would be wise to refuse unhesitatingly" ("Human Personality", in *Simone Weil, An Anthology,* edited with an introduction by Sian Miles [London: Virago, 1986], p. 87). Despite the immoderateness of this extract, I confess to finding Weil's vision compelling, and what I have been doing in the text is not so much rejecting her Platonism as trying to show one way in which it may be said—with Gadamer, and *pace* Weil herself—that "Aristotle was the first Platonist."

94. *E.N.* 1142a20–23.

95. The examples are Stuart Hampshire's in *Two Theories of Morality* (p. 20). Hampshire sees it as a merit of Aristotle's theory of the virtues that it allows for conflict between virtues—which is a palpable feature of ordinary experience—whereas theo-

ries (e.g., utilitarianism) which try to establish a "single criterion of moral judgments" tend to stifle or ignore such conflict. It is not clear how this view squares with Aristotle's own affirmation of the unity of the virtues at the end of *E.N.* 6. It is interesting that in *After Virtue* Alasdair MacIntyre quarrels with Aristotle on the question of the unity of the virtues, but in a later book, *Whose Justice, Which Rationality?* (Notre Dame, Ind.: University of Notre Dame Press; London: Duckworth, 1988), has changed his viewpoint and (gesturing to Aquinas) defends the unity thesis.

96. For a forceful disavowal of these associations, with respect to the classical tradition of phronesis and *prudentia*, see Josef Pieper, *Prudence*, trans. from German by R. and C. Winston (London: Faber and Faber, 1954). Cf. also Maritain's comment that "old *prudentia* in its genuine sense" is "not our bourgeois and timorous prudence" (*Creative Intuition in Art and Poetry* [London: Harvill Press, 1954], p. 48).

97. *E.N.* 2.9.1109a24–29.

98. Cf. *E.N.* 2.6.1106b28–33.

99. *E.N.* 2.6.1107a1–2.

100. *E.N.* 2.9.1109b23.

101. *E.N.* 6.1138b25–34.

102. Hampshire, *Two Theories of Morality*, p. 4.

103. Quotations in this paragraph are from *E.E.* 1.5.1216b5–1217a7.

104. See above, last paragraph of §5.

105. That is, those who know conclusions but do not know them *qua* conclusions of a practical syllogism.

106. See above, ch. 8, §3, text between n. 29 and n. 30.

10. Beyond the Official Notion of Techne

1. *Meta.* 7.7.1032a34–1032b1.

2. I have brought out this possibility of different interpretations as between Ross and Rackham, but it also exists *within* Ross's translation. For while he renders four consecutive occurrences of "*hexis . . . poiētikē*" as "capacity to make," the fifth (and last) occurrence (at 1140a21) he gives as "a state concerned with making."

3. There is a variant reading of 1140a11–12 which inserts *kai* after *technazein* so that *theōrein* is used conjunctively with *technazein* and not as explanatory of it. Ross adopts this reading (as does Greenwood) and translates: "contriving *and* considering how something may be brought into being." This does not lessen my difficulty, however, for the question then becomes: if *technazein* is not identical with *theōrein*, how then is it related to it?

4. D. S. Hutchinson, *The Virtues of Aristotle* (New York and London: Routledge and Kegan Paul, 1986), p. 32.

5. E.g., at 1139b31. One might, of course, think that this designation of *epistēmē* as a *hexis* is itself odd. For *hexis* is often regarded as proper to the sphere of the *affections*, and thus as limited to dispositions of character, i.e., moral virtues. A text to support this view is, e.g., *E.N.* 2.5.1105b25–26: "The *hexeis* are the things in virtue of which we stand well or badly with reference to the passions." But although excellence of character is indeed the paradigm case of *hexis*, it is nonetheless only a *case;* the concept itself has to do with fixity of orientation and as such has more gen-

eral applicability. Moreover, when Aristotle is discussing the general concept (in his discussion of 'quality' [*poiotēs*] — of which *hexis* is a species — in the *Categories*) he explicitly includes *epistēmē* as an example of *hexis:* "A *hexis* differs from a condition [*diathesis*] in being more stable and lasting longer. Such are the branches of knowledge and the virtues. For knowledge seems to be something permanent and hard to change if one has even a moderate grasp of a branch of knowledge, unless a great change is brought about by illness or some other such thing" (*Categories* 8.8b26–34). And again some lines later: "It is obvious that by a *hexis* people do mean what is more lasting and harder to change. For those who lack full mastery of a branch of knowledge and are easily changed are not said to be in a state (*hexis*) of knowledge." See also *Physics* 7.3, where Aristotle distinguishes among *hexeis* (a) those of the body (*tou sōmatos*), such as health and fitness; (b) those of the emotions (*tēs psuchēs*); and (c) those of the *intellectual* part (*tou noētikou merous*).

6. As Greenwood remarks of 1140a6–10: "the argument of this sentence is hardly more than a categorical statement." See the rest of Greenwood's characteristically acute comment on this sentence (p. 182).

7. "The Greek *aitia* and the corresponding adjective *aitios* can be applied to anything that is 'guilty of' or 'responsible for' a thing, or to the account of which, for praise or blame, the thing may in any sense be put down" (Wicksteed, in a note to the Loeb edition of the *Physics,* p. 127).

8. The verb which Aristotle uses in the *Rhetoric* for the kind of systematization of a field that he undertakes in this work is *technologein* (e.g., at 1354b17 and 26–27; 1355a19; and 1356a11 and 17). Our question here might therefore be reformulated thus: Can one be skilled in *technologein* and still be incompetent at *technazein?*

9. One thinks here of Newman's "distinction between ratiocination as the exercise of a living faculty in the individual intellect and mere skill in argumentative science" — where the former as "a process of reasoning is more or less implicit and without the direct and full advertence of the mind exercising it" — a distinction which he illustrates with several examples, among which is that of "the judge who, when asked for his advice by a friend on his being called to important duties which were new to him, bade him to always lay down the law boldly — but never give his reasons — for his decision is likely to be right, but his reasons are sure to be unsatisfactory" (*Grammar of Assent,* p. 196, p. 190, and pp. 196–197).

10. The contrast Aristotle draws here between sense-faculties, on the one hand, and excellences of character or productive skills, on the other, does not seem tenable if we bear in mind that there are *excellences of sense* and that in some cases these can be acquired only by the most diligent practice. See, e.g., F. Franck, *The Zen of Seeing* (London: Wildwood House, 1973); Aldous Huxley, *The Art of Seeing* (London: Chatto and Windus, 1943); and, for an interesting discussion of the need to develop, through practice, a particular kind of ocular vision as an intrinsic element of Vision in the philosophico-religious sense, David Michael Levin, *The Opening of Vision, Nihilism and the Postmodern Situation* (New York: Routledge, Chapman and Hall, 1988).

11. *E.N.* 2.1.1103a28–34.

12. *E.N.* 2.1.1103b6–13.

13. *E.N.* 2.1.1103a25–26.

14. *E.N.* 2.1.1103b21–22.

15. *E.N.* 2.4.1105a27–1105b5 (emphasis added).

16. St. Thomas Aquinas, *Commentary on the Nichomachean Ethics,* book 2, Lecture 4, paragraph 284 (trans. C. I. Litzinger, O.P.).

17. See above, ch. 4, §6, text before n. 67.

18. *Truth and Method,* p. 284.

19. St. Thomas Aquinas, *Summa Theologiae,* 2a.,2ae., q.47, a.1,ad3 (trans. T. Gilbey, O.P.).

20. Ibid., q.47, a.8 (emphasis added).

21. I have analyzed this sentence in ch. 8, text after n. 97.

22. By 'weak' here I mean one that imputes to techne an analytic concern with poiesis but not (this would be the 'strong' sense) an ability to carry out poiesis.

23. *E.N.* 6.4.1140a11.

24. *Meta.* 9.8.1049b29–32.

25. *Meta.* 9.8.1050a9–12 (emphasis added). This point had been made earlier in *Meta.* 9.2 when it was explained that, as potentialities, technai are "principles of change in another thing" (1046b3–4), and also in the 'philosophical lexicon' of *Meta.* 5 where, among other definitions of *archē,* we find this one: "that by whose choice that which is moved is moved and that which changes changes," so that among examples of things called *archai* are "the technai . . . and of these especially the architectonic technai" (1013a10–14).

26. *Meta.* 9.8.1050a23–26.

27. *Meta.* 9.8.1050a28–34 (emphasis added); cf. also *Physics* 3.1 and 3.2.

28. Cf. *Phys.* 2.1, where Aristotle states precisely this point: that, as objects of techne, they are frozen while, as composed of particular materials, they are of course destructible.

29. *De Part. Anim.* 641a1–3. There is in fact a most remarkable (*thaumasiotaton*) example in Aristotle's writings of a statue which was *not* frozen: "the statue of Mitys at Argos [which] killed the author of Mitys' death by falling down on him when he was looking at it" (*Poetics* 9. 1452a7–9)!

30. See above, ch. 8, §6, last paragraph.

31. *Politics* 3.6.1279a1–2.

32. *E.N.* 9.7.1167b32–1168a9. Benefaction of this kind has of course come in for severe and justifiable criticism in the context of recent approaches to community development, education, and aid-programs of various kinds. But it should be noted that Aristotle himself would not have regarded it as an element in properly human relationship, i.e., friendship, and that in fact he provides a basis for its radical critique, from the point of view of the recipient, when he goes on: "to the benefactor that is noble which depends on his action, so that he delights in the object of his action, whereas to the patient there is nothing noble in the agent, but at most something advantageous, and this is less pleasant and lovable. What *is* pleasant is the activity of the present, the hope of the future, the memory of the past; but most pleasant is that which depends on activity, and similarly this is most lovable. Now for a man who has made something his work remains (for the noble is lasting), but for the person acted on the utility passes away." Intellectualist and aristocratic assumptions are sometimes regarded as putting Aristotle beyond the pale for modern radical thought, but (quite apart from Marx's own great admiration for him) what he is saying here

is very close to the essential point of, e.g., Paulo Freire's *Pedagogy of the Oppressed* (London: Penguin, 1970).

33. I say it is vintage Aristotle in that the notion of *energeia* as an actualization or flourishing of a reality's innermost powers is indeed quite basic to his thinking (and as such it formed the medieval, or more specifically, the Thomist, conception whose commonplace expression was in such dicta as *"agere sequitur esse"* and *"bonum est diffusivum sui"*). But this is clearest in his consideration of the living things of nature and of man as a moral-political being, where the flourishing is in each case a fulfillment of an *inner* principle. In the case of techne, however, the externality of its *telos* seemed to place it, the passage I have quoted notwithstanding, rather outside this perspective. And it is significant that even in the passage quoted the example of techne chosen by Aristotle is poetry, i.e., the most immaterial of technai; in general, the relationship between the *technités* and his materials was always in danger of being seen by him as one of unfreedom rather than of unfolding. Cf. his remarks on *banausia* in the *Politics,* and also the thrust of his argument for the primacy of contemplation in *E.N.* 10. Or consider the following: "where there are two things of which one exists for the sake of the other, they have nothing in common except that the one receives what the other produces. Such, for example, is the relation in which workmen and tools stand to their work; the *house and the builder have nothing in common, but the techne of building is for the sake of the house*" (*Pol.* 1328a28–33). The words I have emphasized here seem very much at odds with the whole point of the passage from the *E.N.*'s discussion of friendship.

34. *De Part. Anim.* 640a10–19. The final lines of this passage re-echo a point which Plato had already made — e.g, in the *Philebus,* where he speaks of "becoming for the sake of being" and gives as an illustration the fact "that shipbuilding goes on for the sake of ships rather than that ships are for the sake of shipbuilding" (see 54a,b,c.).

35. See below, §5.

36. *De Part. Anim.* 1.1.640a20–31.

37. Cf. above, ch. 4, §7 for Gadamer's remarks about the absence of "an inner dimension of historicality" from Aristotle's notion of experience and for his own attempt to correct the one-sidedness of this notion by appeal to Hegel and Aeschylus.

38. See *Meta.* 7.8.1033b1–18.

39. See *Phys.* 2.7.198a25–27, where the coincidence of efficient, formal, and final causation is stated but hardly explained. The pivotal role seems to be played by the formal cause. This is the final cause too insofar as it is the *tou heneka,* or the "for-the-sake-of-which," toward which the whole process is directed. (In the case of poiesis, we might of course say that there is a *more* final cause than the formed thing itself, i.e., the use it serves in people's lives; the final cause of the builder's activity then would be the formed house, certainly, but beyond this the purpose of shelter and dwelling.) The perhaps less obvious equation between the formal cause and the efficient cause may be construed thus: the man is efficient cause of the house only because he is a builder, and he is a builder only because he possesses the techne of building (cf. *Phys.* 195b23–24), which is then the ultimate (*akrotaton*) source of his "efficiency"; but it (the techne) *is* the form. (See W. D. Ross, *Aristotle's Physics: A Revised Text with Introduction and Commentary* (Oxford: Clarendon Press, 1979), pp. 36–37 and pp. 41–42.)

40. In *Phys.* 1.8 Aristotle presents hylomorphism (which includes privation [*sterē-sis*] as an aspect of matter) precisely as an answer to the ancients' perplexity about becoming: "It was through failure to make this distinction that those thinkers gave the matter up, and through this error that they went so far astray as to suppose that nothing else comes to be or exists apart from what is itself, thus doing away with all becoming. . . . If they had come in sight of this nature, all their ignorance would have been dispelled" (191b12–34). In this chapter, too, Aristotle points out that, as well as his form/matter-privation schema, his potency/act distinction also offers a solution to the problem of becoming; but he refers us to other places (presumably *Meta.* 9 and 7.7–9) for a more developed account of this.

41. If Aristotle did fail to offer an adequate account of *genesis,* this failure would hardly have surprised his former teacher at the Academy. For Plato, according to Friedrich Solmsen, "considers the realm of genesis as opaque to human reason" and as accessible only through symbol and myth (see Solmsen, "Nature as Craftsman," *Journal of the History of Ideas,* 24:484–485). That Aristotle's reason accounted for change only in a very limited respect—and in fact ruled out the possibility of any radical change—is most evident in *Meta.* 7.8 where he argues for the ungeneratedness of form. His theory of change, i.e., his answer to the problem of Parmenides about the possibility of any change, *presupposes* the reality of forms and so is unable to account for the generation of these forms themselves (without getting involved in an infinite regress), which he therefore regards as *ungenerated.* Having gone through these moves in the first part of *Meta.* 7.8, he immediately goes on to differentiate his position from that of Plato by arguing that there is no need to attribute a separate existence to these forms. But for all that Aristotle's forms are immanent in concrete substances, *genesis* remains just as 'opaque' in his theory as it did in Plato's.

42. *De Part. Anim.* 640a21.

43. From the role played by Empedocles in the present discussion, it is no surprise to find Ross (*Aristotle* [London: Methuen, 1923]) regarding him as an early anticipator of Darwin's theory of evolution. But for a contrary view which sees more of Darwin in Aristotle than in Empedocles, see W. Charlton, *Physics Books 1 and 2* (Oxford: Oxford University Press, 1970) pp. 121–122.

44. The notion of 'charging' that I use here is one that is familiar to Aquinas and it is interesting to note that he uses the same term, *applicatio,* for it which, as we have already seen, he uses for the proper act of *prudentia.* For instance, in *S.T.* 2a2ae, q.47, a.3 ad3, in an obvious reference to the passage on *nous* which I analyzed earlier (see above, ch. 9, §6), we find this: "Aristotle says that *prudentia* . . . lies in an internal sense seasoned by memory and experience and so ready to meet the particular facts encountered. Not that an internal sense is the main seat of prudence, for prudence is mainly in the reason, but that prudence by a certain application (*per quemdam autem applicationem*) reaches to internal sensation." In a note on this use of *'applicatio',* Gilbey, in the English Blackfriars edition of the *Summa,* writes of a "charging or loading of one ability or active disposition by a higher within the unity of a single psychological and moral being" (vol. 36, p. 13, note h).

45. *Meta.* 7.7.1032b11–14 (emphasis added).

46. *Meta.* 7.7.1033a1–5 (emphasis added). An exact parallel to the point I have been making here occurs in *Physics* 2.9. Aristotle is making a distinction there be-

tween necessity and teleology, stressing the latter as an explanatory factor that is superordinate to the former. Bricks and stones and wood are necessary for a house but there is in this necessity no power to make a house. It is nonsense to say that "a wall of a house necessarily comes to be because what is heavy is naturally carried downwards and what is light to the top, so that the stones and foundations take the lowest place, with earth above because it is lighter, and wood at the top of all as being the lightest. Whereas, though the wall does not come to be *without* these, it is not *due* to these, except as its material cause: it comes to be for the sake of sheltering and guarding certain things." And while "[n]ecessity is in the matter . . . that for the sake of which is in the *logos.*" Having said all this, however, Aristotle concludes this final chapter of *Physics* 2 with these words, which tally with the point I have been making in the text: "Perhaps the necessary is present also in the *logos.* For if one defines the operation of sawing as being a certain kind of dividing, then this cannot come about unless the saw has teeth of a certain kind; and these cannot be unless it is of iron. For in the *logos* too there are some parts that stand as matter. Necessity is *also* in the *logos* of the thing; if we define the function of sawing as a certain way of dividing, the dividing cannot take place unless the saw has teeth of such and such a kind, and these cannot be unless they are made of iron. There are also in the *logos* certain parts which function, so to speak, as the (necessary) material for the *logos.*"

47. *E.E.* 1.5.1216b2–25 (emphasis added).

48. In the *general* case, Aristotle gives clear priority to knowledge of the form as, e.g., at *De Part. Anim.* 640b22ff.: "For it is not enough to say what are the stuffs out of which an animal is formed . . . if we were discussing a couch or the like [i.e., an object *apo technēs*], we should try to determine its form rather than its matter (e.g., bronze or wood). . . . For the formal nature is of greater importance than the material nature."

49. *Phys.* 2.2.194a36–194b7. Cf. two remarks in the *Politics:* "there are some technai whose products are not judged solely or best by the *technitai* themselves . . . the user or in other words the master of the house will be an even better judge than the builder, just as the helmsman will judge better of a rudder . . ."; and again: the ruled "may be compared to the maker of the flute, while his master is like the flute-player or user of the flute" (1277b28–29).

50. I am emphasizing here the distinction between the "higher order" commissioning techne concerned with form and the making techne, in order to highlight the maker's involvement with the material. But I should say that for Aristotle (as for Greek thought generally) the organic place that a techne had within a living hierarchy of technai was very significant; and this is in extreme contrast to the contemporary state of affairs in which innovations in production set the agenda to which use (now reduced simply to consumption) must accommodate. For a contemporary re-affirmation of the Greek position, see Heidegger: "Only if we are capable of dwelling, only then can we build." Heidegger attempts "to bring out somewhat more clearly that building belongs to dwelling and how it receives its essence from dwelling" ("Building Dwelling Thinking," in Martin Heidegger, *Basic Writings,* ed. with introduction by David Farrell Krell [London: Routledge and Kegan Paul, 1978]).

51. *Phys.* 2.2.194b10–14. For a passage parallel, see *De Anima* 1.1.403b2ff.

52. The Greek lines here are condensed and difficult to translate. As Cornford

remarks in a footnote in the Loeb edition, their "reading and punctuation were debated by the ancient commentators and remain doubtful" (p. 125, note d).

53. *De Part. Anim.* 1.1.641a5–14.

54. Such questions would seem to be apposite examples of what Kenny means by "wherefore questions" in an interesting discussion of *logos heneka tinos* as the obverse of deliberation and practical (or more particularly, of technical) syllogizing. See *Aristotle's Theory of the Will,* pp. 114–117.

55. See above, this chapter, §2, second paragraph.

56. See above, ch. 9, §3 at n. 25. Earlier, when I first dealt with this account (ch. 8, §7, penultimate paragraph), I assumed that it was intended by Aristotle as a preface to his discussion in *E.N.* 6 of phronesis and *not* of techne.

57. Aristotle, in fact, identifies *matter* with the indefinite (*to aoriston*) at *Phys.* 4.2.209b10: *esti de toiouton hē hulē kai to aoriston.*

58. See *E.N.* 5.10, esp. 1137b11–30.

59. *E.N.* 5.10.1137b19.

60. See above, this chapter, beginning of §2.

61. See *E.N.* 5.9.1137a5–25.

62. Cf. Solmsen's remark: "That no Greek thinker before him [Aristotle]—with the possible exception of Plato in one or two passages . . . ever employs the word in the sense of 'matter' is entirely natural; for none had arrived at a concept of matter" ("Nature as Craftsman in Greek Thought," p. 492). On the other hand, when Ross points out that "the material cause . . . is writ large in the whole history of Greek thought" (*Aristotle's Physics,* p. 37), he can claim Aristotle's own authority for this view: "If we look at the ancients, natural science would seem to be concerned with the matter. It was only very slightly that Empedocles and Democritus touched on form and essence" (*Phys.* 2.2.194a20–22; cf. *Meta.* 1.3).

63. This triple division of principles of coming-to-be has a Platonic background. For this as well as its occurrence in Aristotle, see A. Mansion, *Introduction à la physique aristotélicienne* (Paris: 1945), pp. 94–97.

64. There is a strong affinity between this distinction between techne and *phusis,* and our central distinction between techne and phronesis. The *telos* of phronesis, too, i.e., virtuous action, is an immanent one, and it was this fact which led me to speak (ch. 9, §1, after n. 6) of phronesis as the "natural intuitiveness" of a virtuous person.

65. The meaning of this phrase cannot be reduced to a simple endorsement of 'representational' art, i.e., to a thesis about the content of art. Cf. James Joyce's remark: "'*Hē technē mimeitai tēn phusin*'—this phrase is falsely rendered as: 'Art is an imitation of Nature.' Aristotle does not here define art; he says only Art imitates Nature and means that the artistic *process* is like a natural process" (quoted in Sheldon Brivic, "Joyce and the Metaphysics of Creation," *The Crane Bag* [Dublin], vol. 6, no. 1 [1982]: 13 [italics mine]). Joyce wrote this (in March 1903) in notes he made on the *Poetics.* Perhaps he had at hand Butcher's *Aristotle's Theory of Poetry and Fine Art* (with a critical text and translation, first published in Edinburgh, 1894) which makes substantially the same point (on p. 116).

66. Solmsen, "Nature as Craftsman in Greek Thought," p. 488.

67. See Anthony J. Close, "Commonplace Theories of Art and Nature in Classical Antiquity and in the Renaissance," *Journal of the History of Ideas,* 30 (1969): 467–

486, and "Philosophical Theories of Art and Nature," ibid., 32, especially pp. 170–176 on Aristotle.

68. At *Phys.* 2.2.194a22ff. the sentence begins: "If . . . techne imitates nature" but goes on not, as we should expect, to draw a conclusion about techne based on the example of nature but, on the contrary, to infer from the conduct of technai certain guidelines for the study of nature. And at *Phys.* 2.8.199a15ff., where Aristotle uses a somewhat different formulation ("generally techne in some cases completes what nature cannot bring to a finish, and in others imitates nature"), he immediately follows it with a sentence which is supposed to be its consequent but in which techne is the model and nature the imitator ("If, therefore, artificial products are for the sake of an end so clearly also are natural products").

69. If nature is to be accorded 'ontological priority' in the present context, then its teleological character must be supported by argument that is *independent* of the analogy with techne. That such support is available may be gathered from John Cooper's contention that the arguments for teleology in nature which "press the analogy between artistic activity . . . are not very good arguments and there are reasons for thinking that Aristotle did not think his view rested primarily on them." Cooper points out that Aristotle's first and most elaborate argument for natural teleology in *Physics* 2.8 does not appeal to the analogy with techne and concludes from this that "we must reject the suggestion that is sometimes made that this analogy is central and fundamental to Aristotelian natural teleology" (J. Cooper, "Aristotle on Natural Teleology," in *Language and Logos: Studies in Ancient Greek Philosophy*, ed. M. Schofield and M. C. Nussbaum [Cambridge: Cambridge University Press], 1982), pp. 197–198).

70. *De Part. Anim.* 4.10.687a24.

71. This idea of techne as completing or filling up the deficiencies of nature occurs in the sentence in *Physics* 2.8 quoted in note 68 above, and also in the well-known remark in the *Politics* (1337a,1–2) that "the deficiencies of nature are what techne and education seek to fill up." As the latter remark—from the discussion of education at the end of the *Politics*—makes clear, human nature quite as much as external nature is completed by techne, and so not just, e.g., medicine and gymnastics but intellectual and moral formation (*paideia*) as well as politics itself (cf. *Pol.* 1.2.1253a2: "man is *by nature* a political animal"—*anthrōpos phusei politikon zōion*) are rooted in, and are a completion of, nature.

Attention should be drawn here to the *Protrepticus*—an early work of Aristotle's Academic period, only fragments of which have come down to us—which contains what is probably his clearest and most explicit statements of the priority of nature and of techne's role in bringing about its completion:

> [t]hat which comes into being according to nature does so for an end, and is always constituted to better purpose than the product of techne: for *nature does not imitate techne, but vice versa;* techne exists to aid nature and to fill up its deficiencies. For some things nature seems able to complete by itself without assistance, but others it does with difficulty or cannot do at all—in the matter of birth, to take an obvious example; some seeds generate without protection, whatever ground they fall into, others need the techne of farming as well; and similarly some animals attain their full nature by themselves, but man needs many technai for his preservation. . . . If then techne imi-

tates nature, it is from nature that the technai have derived the characteristic that all their products come into being for an end" (*The Works of Aristotle*, vol. 12: *Select Fragments*, ed. David Ross, p. 44, emphasis added).

It is very noticeable in this passage how firmly Aristotle keeps to nature as model and techne as imitator; this is in striking contrast to *Physics* 2 where the analogy is constantly being worked from the other direction. I may say, incidentally, that this passage also provides a basis for a distinction which entered the tradition between (i) technai which cooperate with nature, using it as an active principle, e.g., farming, medicine, education, and (ii) technai which produce artefacts quite discontinuous with nature, even though they depend on her for their materials, e.g., carpentry and shipbuilding. A claim for the Aristotelian provenance of this distinction is usually supported (e.g., by Aquinas in *Summa contra Gentes* 2:75) by reference to *Meta.* 1034a8–30; but the above passage seems to provide a much fuller warrant for it.

Another passage from the *Protrepticus* which, far more explicitly than any passage in the *Physics*, sees techne as the imitator and servant of nature is the following:

> For as all skilful physicians and most gymnasts agree that those who are to be good physicians or gymnasts must have experience of nature, so it is agreed that good legislators must have experience of nature, and indeed much more than the former. For the former are producers only of bodily excellence, while those who are concerned with the excellences of the soul and undertake to give instruction about the well-being and the ill-being of the state need philosophy far more. As in the mechanical technai, the best instruments have been borrowed from nature (e.g. in carpentry the ruddled line, the rule, and the lathe were suggested by the surface of water and by the rays of light, and it is by reference to these that we test what is to our senses sufficiently straight or smooth), similarly the statesman must borrow from nature and reality certain limits by reference to which he will judge what is just, noble, or advantageous; for as those tools excel all others, so the law that conforms best with nature is the best. (*The Works of Aristotle*, vol. 12, p. 48)

72. Analogy is a pedagogical and not a probative device. In other words, *given* that A is like B in certain respects, then we can exploit our (or our listeners' or pupils') greater familiarity with B in order to elucidate certain aspects of A. In order, then, for analogy to get off the ground, as it were, a prior assumption or argument must have established that the necessary relationship between A and B actually exists. But analogy can be a dangerous device in cases where the very richness of the explanation which it seems to yield can obscure the fact that its *validity* has not in the first instance been established, i.e., that the analogy with B provides us with no more than an interesting way of looking at A—which *may*, in fact, be *false*. I take it that Aristotle avoided this mistake by his affirmation independently of the analogy (see n. 69 above) of the ontological priority of nature. (A good example of the mistake is Freud's critique of religion in *The Future of an Illusion* which is the teasing out of an analogy [between the structure and stages of phylogenesis and those of ontogenesis], the basis of which is never demonstrated. Freud exploits for a polemical purpose the properly pedagogical efficacy of analogy.)

73. In doing this, he is only following his own advice, given at the beginning of

Phys. 1: "the natural way . . . is to start from the things that are more knowable and clear to us and proceed towards those which are clearer and more knowable by nature; for the same things are not knowable relatively to us and knowable without qualification. So we must follow this method and advance from what is more obscure by nature, but clearer to us, towards what is more clear and more knowable by nature" (184a16–21).

74. If this was Aristotle's working assumption, then he may be compared with Vico, who thought that we are more at home with our own products than with the things of nature and so contrasted the clarity of our knowledge of "*il munde della nazione*" (the world of history and politics—he was more impressed by technai such as rhetoric and politics than by material crafts) with the relative muddiness of our knowledge of "*il munde della natura.*" This idea of Vico's might seem eminently post-Cartesian and unAristotelian. But in fact Vico was a critic of Descartes and tried to rehabilitate the humanistic tradition, including Aristotelian phronesis, against the rise of objectivistic science and its extension into the regulation of life. In the context of Part 1 of the present study, it is worth noting that both Gadamer and Habermas canvas Vico's significance in a tradition of thought that goes back to Aristotle; see *Truth and Method*, pp. 19–24 and *Theory and Practice*, pp. 43–46.

75. *Phys.* 2.8.199a12–15.

76. *Phys.* 2.8.199b24–32.

77. Another way of expressing this difference is to say that an artefact has a substantial form but not a *soul:* "it is not the kind of body whose whatness and formula [*to ti ēn einai kai ho logos*] is a soul"—where 'soul' is "a power [of a living thing] of setting itself in movement and arresting itself." (This is from *De Anima* 2.1.412b13ff.—a passage which begins, interestingly, with the words: "Suppose that . . . an axe were a *natural* body. . . .")

78. Cf. Heidegger: "Not only handcraft manufacture, not only artistic and poetical bringing-into-appearance and concrete imagery, is a bringing-forth, *poiēsis. Physis,* also, the arising of something from out of itself, is a bringing-forth, *poiēsis. Physis is indeed poiēsis in the highest sense*" ("The Question Concerning Technology," *Basic Writings*, p. 293, emphasis mine).

79. Aristotle does not disagree with Antiphon's remark which he cites in *Phys.* 2.1: "[I]f you planted a bed and the rotting wood acquired the power of sending up a shoot, it would not be a bed that would come up, but wood . . ."! (193a12–14).

80. See above, ch. 9, §3 at n. 26. According to Ross (*Aristotle's Physics*, pp. 530–531), Cornford (Loeb edition of *Physics*, 1–4, p. 178, note a), and Charlton (*Physics, Books 1 and 2*, p. 125), Aristotle is referring here only to the "exact and self-contained sciences" in which, as he tells us in *E.N.* 3.3, there is no possibility (or need) of deliberation (see above, ch. 8, §5, at n. 76). A different and, I believe, better interpretation comes into view if we consider that it was a cardinal point in Aristotle's theory of deliberation that no one deliberates about ends ("a doctor does not deliberate whether he shall heal, nor an orator whether he shall convince, nor a statesman whether he shall produce law and order, nor does anyone else deliberate about his end. Having set the end, they consider how and by what means it is to be attained" [1112b12–16]). It can therefore be maintained that when Aristotle says so perfunctorily—and without qualification—that "techne does not deliberate," he means "about ends." Although

this might seem unlikely, given that by 'deliberate' he virtually *means* 'deliberate about means', still it becomes more plausible if we go on to ask: where does the end come from if not from deliberation? For the answer to this, according to a significant line in *E.E.* 2.10 is: *from nature:* "the end is always something good by nature." And so if we are to have an explanation of the remark in *Phys.* 2.8 the best explanation, I suggest, is this: Aristotle is trying to argue for a strong analogy between techne and nature. He has to acknowledge that nature quite obviously does not deliberate. This seems immediately to jeopardize the analogy, since techne so conspicuously *does* deliberate. His way of protecting the analogy, then, is by urging us to see the limit of, and to look beyond, the deliberative function of techne; for all technical deliberation, no matter how sophisticated, occurs only within the already established context of a *telos*. And, as we have just seen, he is in a position to add, by way of reinforcing the analogy, that what *does* work out this *telos* is precisely *nature*. This is the explanation which is, in fact, implicit in the analysis in my text.

81. See the passage at the beginning of §8 below.

82. *De Part. Anim.* 1.1.640a31–32.

83. See text above, §2 at n. 27.

84. *Phys.* 3.1.201a16–18.

85. *Phys.* 3.1.201b8–10.

86. *Phys.* 3.3.202a18–21.

87. *Phys.* 3.3.202b2–5.

88. *Phys.* 3.3.202b11–21.

89. Waterlow, *Nature, Change, and Agency in Aristotle's Physics* (Oxford: Clarendon Press, 1982), p. 201.

90. Ibid., p. 202.

91. Ibid., p. 201.

92. Ibid., p. 202.

93. This is a celebrated phrase among those familiar with the 'critical realist' philosophy of Bernard Lonergan. See *Insight: A Study of Human Understanding* (London: Longmans, 1957), esp. ch. 8, §§1 and 2, pp. 245–254.

94. Waterlow, *Nature, Change and Agency in Aristotle's Physics*, p. 202.

95. Ibid., p. 203.

96. Ibid., p. 201. This passage might indeed be taken to imply not just a very close assimilation of techne to nature but an actual identity between them if we take this point of Ross: "In fact the *only* difference between art and nature is that in artistic activity, agent and patient are *disjoined*, while in natural activity they are conjoined in one individual" (*Aristotle's Physics*, p. 43). Waterlow avoids this implication, however, by pointing out the "important disanalogy" that the "organic unit" of artifex-material exists as a unit only during the change, to be replaced after it by two separate substances—whereas "it would be a strange natural substance indeed whose natural change necessarily resulted in its own dissolution" (p. 201).

97. *De Gen. et Cor.* 1.7.324a27–324b7.

98. See above, ch. 9, §3.

99. Aristotle's anxiety to keep techne immune from any change, and the close connection that this implies between techne and merely contemplative thought—i.e., thought that has no finality toward an external *ergon*—are brought out in a casual

remark in *De Anima* 2.5: "what possesses knowledge becomes an actual knower by a transition which is either not an alteration of it at all (being in reality a development into its true self or actuality) or at least an alteration in a quite different sense. Hence it is wrong to speak of a wise man as being 'altered' when he uses his wisdom, just as it would be absurd to speak of a builder as being altered when he is using his skill in building a house" (417b5–9). This remark occurs in the context of an important discussion which I shall have occasion to come back to later in the text.

100. *De Gen. Anim.* 1.21.730a27–30.

101. *De Gen. Anim.* 1.22.730b4–8.

102. See above, this chapter, §6, second paragraph.

103. *De Gen. Anim.* 1.22.730b12–14.

104. *De Gen. Anim.* 1.22.730b14–23.

105. This evidence has been assembled most systematically by F. Nuyens (*L'évolution de la psychologie d'Aristote* [Louvain:1948]) who argues that Aristotle's account of the soul-body relationship is not unreconstructedly hylomorphic. There are, Nuyens argues, two other views of this relationship that obtrude in his writings: (a) a dualistic view which occurs especially in his earlier academic works and (b) an instrumental view which is suggested by certain formulations that he is not averse to using even in *De Anima*. The picture I have sketched is something of a hybrid of these two views.

106. W. D. Ross, *Aristotle's Physics*, p. 37 (emphasis added).

107. *De An.* 1.3.407b13–26.

108. *De An.* 2.1.412b6–8.

109. *De An.* 1.4.408b13–15.

110. *De An.* 2.1.412b18–22.

111. At 412b15–17.

112. *De An.* 2.1.413a1.

113. See above, ch. 8, §4, at n. 44.

114. In terms of the strategy of our inquiry, the relationship here between techne and *psuchē* parallels closely the relationship we have already explored between techne and phusis. In each case Aristotle is using techne pedagogically, i.e., in order to explicate what he takes to be the more obscure concepts of nature and soul. But my argument is that both of these pedagogical uses of techne turn out in fact to be pedagogical *about techne itself*: although this can hardly be said to be Aristotle's intention, something new is learned about 'techne', since in neither case does our understanding of it remain unchanged when 'techne' is pressed into service in the way in which it is.

115. Gilbert Ryle, however, should be mentioned as the philosopher who most conspicuously does *not* mean this. *The Concept of Mind* (London: Penguin, 1986) is interesting in the present context because it reflects both sides of Aristotle that I have been trying to bring out. On the one hand, its debunking of the "Ghost in the Machine" is really a restatement, stylish and unencumbered by exegesis, of Aristotle's position in *De Anima*. On the other hand, its attack on the "intellectualist legend" (which involves the "absurd assumption . . . that a performance of any sort inherits its title to intelligence from some anterior internal operation of planning what to do") is actually, though not avowedly, an attack on Aristotle's accounts (so central to his official concept of techne) of *noēsis* and *boulē* in *Meta.* 7.7 and *E.N.* 3.3 respectively. In fact Ryle's criticisms of this 'legend' harmonize with my own criticisms of Aristotle's

notion of techne (esp. in ch. 9, §3 above, and ch. 10, §8 below). For Ryle, there is no "shadow action [*noēsis*] covertly prefacing the overt action [poiesis]" (p. 26); "when we describe a performance as intelligent, this does not entail the double-operation of considering and executing" (p. 30); "'thinking what I am doing' does not connote 'both thinking what to do and doing it'. When I do something intelligently, i.e. thinking what I am doing, I am doing one thing and not two. My performance has a special procedure or manner, not special antecedents" (p. 32); "the exercise of intelligence in practice cannot be analyzed into a tandem operation of first considering prescriptions and then executing them" (p. 40).

116. In the passage cited in the text at n. 104 above.
117. See the passage in the text at n. 97 above.
118. We have met this phrase in the passage cited in the text at n. 104 above.
119. *Meta.* 7.7.1032a32–1032b17.
120. See *E.N.* 3.3.1112b20–24.
121. *E.N.* 3.3.1112a21–1112b9.
122. *E.N.* 3.3.1112b11–24.
123. *E.N.* 3.3.1112b24–27.
124. *E.N.* 3.3.1112a16.
125. *E.N.* 3.3.1112a30–31.
126. *E.N.* 3.3.1112b28.
127. *De An.* 1.4.408b16–17.
128. See above, ch. 8, §5.

Epilogue

1. This is a phrase of Habermas's which we met in ch. 4, §5.
2. See above, ch. 5, §1.
3. See, e.g., the strictures of R. J. Bernstein, a sensitive and sympathetic commentator on Gadamer, in *Beyond Objectivism and Relativism*, pp. 150ff.
4. At *E.N.* 1139a36–1139b4 and above, ch. 8, §6, text at n. 94.
5. See above, ch. 8, §6.
6. See above, ch. 5, §5.
7. See ch. 5, §5.
8. *Truth and Method*, p. xiii; *Wahrheit und Methode*, p. xxvi (emphases added).
9. *Truth and Method*, p. xvi; *Wahrheit und Methode*, p. xiv (emphasis added).
10. *Truth and Method*, p. xxv; *Wahrheit und Methode*, p. xxiii (emphasis added).
11. *E.N.* 2.9.1109a28–29.
12. *E.N.* 2.1.1103b8–12 (emphasis added). It may seem incongruous that I invoke Aristotle's analysis of techne here; but the point he is making about technai in this passage is one that he also makes in the same place about virtues (*aretai*): both of them "we acquire by first having practised them [*energēsantes proteron*]". What I am appealing to in techne here, and in my recall, presently, of the example of the sculptor, is something that we met precisely in the context of reconstructing a strongly *experiential* dimension to techne and arguing that this dimension serves to bring techne close to, rather than to distinguish it from, phronesis.
13. See above, ch. 10, §4 at n. 53.
14. See above, ch. 9, n. 48.

15. See the writings of a number of educationalists deeply influenced by the work of the late Laurence Stenhouse, e.g., Shirley Grundy, *Curriculum: Product or Praxis* (London: Falmer Press, 1987); Wilfred Carr and Stephen Kemmis, *Becoming Critical: Education, Knowledge and Action Research* (London: Falmer Press, 1987); and various writings of John Elliot, especially "Educational Theory, Practical Philosophy and Action Research," *British Journal of Educational Studies* 35 (1987). Or, again, coming from two quite different backgrounds are the writings of Joseph Schwab on 'the practical' (see especially I. Westbury and N. I. Wilkof, eds., *Science, Curriculum and Liberal Education: Selected Essays of Joseph J. Schwab* [Chicago: University of Chicago Press, 1978]) and Donald Schön on the "reflective practitioner" (see *The Reflective Practitioner: How Professionals Think in Action* [London: Temple Smith, 1983]).

16. See Hampshire, *Two Theories of Morality* (Oxford: Oxford University Press, 1977), pp. 54–58.

17. St. George Stock, Introduction to *Magna Moralia, Eudemian Ethics*, and *De Virtutibus et Vitiis*, in vol. 9 of *The Works of Aristotle*, edited by W. D. Ross (Oxford: Oxford University Press, 1975), p. v.

18. See Herbert Schnädelbach, "What is Neo-Aristotelianism," *Praxis International* 7, no. 3/4 (Oct. 1987/Jan. 1988), pp. 225–237.

19. See *E.N.* 3.1–5.

20. Technicism is the military wing, so to speak, of positivism—both of them being the endorsement of the claims of a specific mode of knowledge: the latter, its claim to exclusive legitimacy *qua* knowledge and the former its claim to overwhelming effectiveness *qua* basis for action. And nearly *all* philosophy now, whatever other fronts it may fight on, involves a rear-guard action against positivism—one in which its own very existence is at stake—for, in Habermas's words, "that we disavow reflection *is* positivism."

21. See, e.g., D. Rasmussen, ed., *Universalism vs. Communitarianism*, and S. Benhabib, and F. Dallmayr, eds., *The Communicative Ethics Controversy* (both Cambridge, Mass.: M.I.T. Press, 1990).

22. See *E.N.* 6.5.1140b8–10.

23. See *After Virtue*, ch. 9.

24. This phrase is Frederic Jameson's, paraphrasing Lyotard, in his Foreword to the latter's *The Post-Modern Condition: A Report on Knowledge*, trans. G. Bennington and B. Massumi (Manchester: Manchester University Press, 1986).

25. Ibid., p. 66.

26. See ibid., p. 81, and "Presentations," p. 125 in A. Montefiore, ed., *Philosophy in France Today* (Cambridge: Cambridge University Press, 1983).

27. See above ch. 5, §4, text after n. 65 and ch. 7, §4, text after n. 66.

28. See respectively chs. 5, 6, 7, and 8 of *E.N.* 4.

29. See respectively *E.N.* 3.3–9 and *E.N.* 5.

30. Schnädelbach, "What Is Neo-Aristotelianism?" p. 233.

31. This is Jürgen Habermas's charge in his essay "Lawrence Kohlberg und der Neoaristotelismus," in Habermas, ed., *Erläuterungen zur Diskursethik* (Frankfurt: Suhrkamp, 1991), p. 90. The translation I use is from an English version of this essay which Professor Habermas sent me after conversing very generously about his work at the World Philosophy Conference at Brighton in October 1988.

Bibliography to Introduction
and Part 1

Adorno, T. *The Jargon of Authenticity.* (Jargon der Eigentlichkeit: zur deutschen Ideologie, 1970.) Translated by K. Tarnowski and F. Will. London: Routledge and Kegan Paul, 1973.

————, ed. *The Positivist Dispute in German Sociology.* (Der Positivismus in der deutschen Soziologie, 1970.) Translated by G. Adey and D. Frisby. London: Heinemann, 1976.

———— and M. Horkheimer. *Dialectic of Enlightenment.* (Dialektik der Aufklärung, 1947.) Translated by John Cumming. London: Verso, 1979.

Arendt, H. *The Human Condition.* Chicago: University of Chicago Press, 1958.

————. *Men in Dark Times.* San Diego: Harvest, 1968.

————. *On Revolution.* London: Faber, 1973.

Aristotle. *Metaphysics, Nicomachean Ethics, Politics, Rhetoric* and *Posterior Analytics,* in The Complete Works of Aristotle. Revised Oxford translation, in Two Volumes, edited by J. Barnes. Princeton: Princeton University Press (Bollingen Series), 1984.

Bacon, F. *Novum Organon.* 1620. Edited by T. Fowler. Oxford: Oxford University Press, 1889.

Barnes, J., R. Sorabji, and M. Schofield, eds. *Articles on Aristotle.* Vol. 2, *Ethics and Politics.* London: Duckworth, 1977.

Benjamin, W. *Illuminations* (Illuminationen: Ausgewälte Schriften, 1969.) Edited, with an Introduction by H. Arendt. Translated by H. Zohn. London: Cape, 1970.

Bernstein, R. J. *Beyond Objectivism and Relativism.* Philadelphia: University of Pennsylvania Press; Oxford: Blackwell, 1983.

————. *Praxis and Action.* Philadelphia: University of Pennsylvania Press; London: Duckworth, 1972.

————. *The Restructuring of Social and Political Theory.* Philadelphia: University of Pennsylvania Press; Oxford: Blackwell, 1976.

————, ed. *Habermas and Modernity.* Cambridge, Mass.: M.I.T. Press; Cambridge: Polity Press, 1985.

Boekraad, A. J. *The Personal Conquest of Truth According to J. H. Newman.* Louvain, 1955.

Bubner, R. *Modern German Philosophy.* Cambridge: Cambridge University Press, 1981.

Burnyeat, M. "Aristotle on Learning to be Good." In A. O. Rorty, ed., *Essays on Aristotle's Ethics,* pp. 69–92. Berkeley: University of California Press, 1980.

Butler, Joseph. *The Analogy of Religion.* Glasgow: Robert Urie, 1764.

Cameron, J. M. "Newman and Locke: An Essay on Some Themes in *An Essay in Aid of A Grammar of Assent.*" In *Cardinal Newman Studien,* vol. 9. Nuremberg: Glock, 1974.

Chalybaus, H. M. *Historical Development of Speculative Philosophy from Kant to Hegel.* Translated from German by A. Edersheim. Edinburgh: 1853.

Collingwood, R. G. *An Autobiography.* Oxford: Oxford University Press, 1939; paper, 1970.

———. *An Essay on Philosophical Method.* Oxford: Clarendon Press, 1933.

———. *The Idea of History.* Oxford: Clarendon Press, 1946; paper, 1961.

———. *The Idea of Nature.* Edited by T. M. Knox. Oxford: Clarendon Press, 1945.

———. *The New Leviathan.* Oxford: Clarendon Press, 1942.

———. *The Principles of Art.* Oxford: Clarendon Press, 1938.

———. *Speculum Mentis or The Map of Knowledge.* Oxford: Clarendon Press, 1924.

Coulson, J. *Newman and the Common Tradition.* Oxford: Oxford University Press, 1970.

Dallmayr, F. R., and T. McCarthy. *Understanding and Social Inquiry.* Notre Dame, Ind.: University of Notre Dame Press, 1977.

Descartes, R. *Philosophical Essays of Descartes.* (Including *Discourse on Method* [*Discours de la méthode,* 1637] and *Rules for the Direction of the Mind* [*Regulae ad directionem Ingenii,* written in 1620s, pub. 1701].) Translated by L. J. Lafleur. New York: Bobbs-Merrill, 1964.

Dewey, J. "Context and Thought." In *On Experience, Nature, and Freedom: Selected Writings of John Dewey,* edited by R. J. Bernstein, pp. 88–110. New York: Bobbs-Merrill, 1960.

Eliot, T. S. "The Waste Land." In *Collected Poems.* London: Faber and Faber, 1974.

d'Entrèves, M. P. "Aristotle or Burke? Some Comments on H. Schnädelbach's 'What Is Neo-Aristotelianism?'" *Praxis International* 7, no. 3/4 (Oct. 1987/Jan. 1988): 238–245.

Ferrara, A. "On Phronesis." *Praxis International* 7, no. 3/4 (Oct. 1987/Jan. 1988): 246–267.

Feyerabend, P. *Against Method*. London: New Left Books, 1975.

Freud, S. *Totem and Taboo*. In the standard edition of the *Complete Psychological Works*, translated under the general editorship of J. Strachey, vol. 13. London: Hogarth Press, 1958.

Gadamer, H-G. *Dialogue and Dialectic: Eight Hermeneutical Studies on Plato*. Translated by P. C. Smith. New Haven, Conn.: Yale University Press, 1980.

―――. *Hegel's Dialectic: Five Hermeneutical Studies*. Translated by P. C. Smith. New Haven, Conn.: Yale University Press, 1976.

―――. *The Idea of the Good in Plato and Aristotle*. (*Die Idee des Guten zwischen Plato und Aristotles*, 1978.) Translated by P. C. Smith. New Haven, Conn.: Yale University Press, 1981.

―――. *Philosophical Apprenticeships* (*Philosophische Lehrjahre*, 1977, with one additional essay.) Translated by R. R. Sullivan. Cambridge, Mass.: M.I.T. Press, 1985.

―――. *Philosophical Hermeneutics*. (Essays selected from *Kleine Schriften*.) Edited and translated by David E. Linge. Berkeley and Los Angeles: University of California Press, 1977.

―――. *Reason in the Age of Science*. (From *Vernunft im Zeitalter der Wissenschaft*, 1976, with two additional essays.) Translated by F. G. Lawrence. Cambridge, Mass.: M.I.T. Press, 1981.

―――. *Truth and Method*. (*Wahrheit und Methode*, 2nd ed., Tübingen: Mohr, 1965.) Edited by G. Barden and J. Cumming. London: Sheed and Ward, 1975.

Gallwey, T. *The Inner Game of Golf*. London: Jonathan Cape, 1981.

Giddens, A. "Reason without Revolution." In R. J. Bernstein, ed., *Habermas and Modernity*, pp. 95–124.

Gladstone, W. E. *The Vatican Decrees in Their Bearing on Civil Allegiance: A Political Expostulation*. London: John Murray, 1874–75.

Habermas, J. *Autonomy and Solidarity*. Interviews edited and introduced by P. Dews. London: Verso, 1986.

―――. *Communication and the Evolution of Society*. (Essays mainly from *Zur Rekonstruktion des historischen Materialismus*, 1976.) Translated by Thomas McCarthy. London: Heinemann, 1979.

―――. "Hannah Arendt's Communications Concept of Power." In *Social Research* 44 (1977): 3–24.

―――. *Knowledge and Human Interests*. (*Erkenntnis und Interesse*, 1968.) Translated by J. J. Shapiro. London: Heinemann, 1972.

―――. *The Philosophical Discourse of Modernity*. (*Der philosophische Diskurs der Modern: Zwölf Vorlesungen* 1985). Translated by F. Lawrence. Cambridge: Polity Press, 1987.

————. *Philosophical-Political Profiles.* (Revised edition of *Philosophisch-politische Profile,* 1981.) Translated by F. G. Lawrence. Cambridge, Mass.: M.I.T. Press, 1983.

————. "Psychic Thermidor and the Rebirth of Rebellious Subjectivity." In R. J. Bernstein, ed., *Habermas and Modernity,* pp. 67–77.

————. "Questions and Counterquestions." In R. J. Bernstein, ed., *Habermas and Modernity,* pp. 192–216.

————. "A Reply to My Critics." In J. B. Thompson and D. Held, eds., *Critical Debates,* pp. 219–283. London: Macmillan, 1982.

————. "A Review of Gadamer's Truth and Method." (From *Zur Logik der Sozialwissenschaften,* 1970.) In F. R. Dallmayr and T. McCarthy, eds., *Understanding and Social Inquiry,* pp. 335–363. Notre Dame: University of Notre Dame Press, 1970.

————. *Theory and Practice.* (*Theorie und Praxis,* 4th, ed., 1971.) Translated by J. Viertel. London: Heinemann, 1974.

————. *The Theory of Communicative Action.* (*Theorie des kommunikativen Handelns* 1981.) Translated by T. McCarthy. Vol. 1, *Reason and the Rationalization of Society* and vol. 2, *The Critique of Functionalist Reason.* Boston: Beacon Press, 1984 and 1987.

————. *Toward a Rational Society.* (Essays from *Protestbewegung und Hochschulreform,* 1969, and *Technik und Wissenschaft als 'Idiologie,'* 1968). Translated by J. J. Shapiro. London: Heinemann, 1971.

Hawthorn, G. *Enlightenment and Despair.* Second edition. Cambridge: Cambridge University Press, 1987.

Heaney, S. "Words Alone?" In V. Greaney and B. Molloy, eds., *Dimensions of Reading.* Dublin: The Educational Company of Ireland, 1986.

Hegel, G. W. F. *Hegel's Logic: Being Part One of the Encyclopedia of Philosophical Sciences* (1830, 3rd edition) Translated by William Wallace. Oxford: Oxford University Press, 1975.

————. *The Phenomenology of Spirit.* Translated by A. V. Miller. Oxford: Oxford University Press, 1977.

Held, D. *Introduction to Critical Theory.* London: Hutchinson, 1980.

Heidegger, M. *Basic Writings.* Edited by D. F. Krell. London: Routledge and Kegan Paul, 1978.

————. *Being and Time.* (*Sein und Zeit,* 1927.) Translated by J. Macquarrie and E. Robinson. Oxford: Basil Blackwell, 1962.

Hintikka, J. *Knowledge and the Known: Historical Perspectives in Epistemology.* Dordrecht: Kluwer, 1974.

Horkheimer, M. *Critique of Instrumental Reason.* Translated by Matthew J. O'Connell et al. New York: Seabury Press, 1974.

————. *The Eclipse of Reason*. New York: Seabury Press, 1974.

Jay, M. *The Dialectical Imagination: A History of the Frankfurt School and the Institute for Social Research, 1923–1950*. London: Heinemann, 1973.

Johnson, S. *Dictionary of the English Language*. London: Macmillan, 1982.

Kant, I. *Critique of Judgement*. (*Kritik der Urteilskraft*, 1790.) Translated by J. C. Meredith. Oxford: Oxford University Press, 1952.

————. *Critique of Practical Reason*. (*Kritik der praktischen Vernunft*, 1788.) Translated by L. W. Beck. Indianapolis: Bobbs-Merrill, 1956.

Kuhn, T. "Objectivity, Value Judgment and Theory Choice." In *The Essential Tension: Selected Studies in Scientific Tradition and Change*. Chicago: University of Chicago Press, 1977.

————. *The Structure of Scientific Revolutions*. Chicago: University of Chicago Press, 1962.

McCarthy, T. *The Critical Theory of Jürgen Habermas*. Boston: M.I.T. Press; London: Hutchinson, 1978.

MacIntyre, A. *After Virtue*. Notre Dame, Ind.: University of Notre Dame Press; London: Duckworth, 1981.

————. "Moral Arguments and Social Contexts: A Response to Rorty." In R. Hollinger, ed., *Hermeneutics and Praxis*, pp. 222–223. Notre Dame, Ind.: University of Notre Dame Press, 1985.

————. "Moral Philosophy: What Next?" In S. Hauerwas and A. MacIntyre, eds., *Revisions*, pp. 1–15. Notre Dame, Ind.: University of Notre Dame Press, 1983.

————. *Whose Justice? Which Rationality?* Notre Dame, Ind.: University of Notre Dame Press; London: Duckworth, 1988.

Mansion, A. *Aristote et les problèmes de méthode*. Louvain, 1961.

Marcuse, H. *Eros and Civilization: A Philosophical Inquiry into Freud*. London: Allen Lane, 1969.

————. *One-Dimensional Man: Studies in the Ideology of Advanced Industrial Society*. London: Routledge and Kegan Paul, 1964.

Merleau-Ponty, M. "Indirect Language and the Voices of Silence." In *Signs*, translated by Richard C. McCleary, pp. 39–83. Evanston, Ill.: Northwestern University Press, 1964.

————. "On the Phenomenology of Language." In *Signs*, translated by Richard C. McCleary, pp. 84–97.

Mink, L. O. *Mind, History and Dialectic: The Philosophy of R. G. Collingwood*. Bloomington: Indiana University Press, 1969.

Newman, J. H. *Apologia Pro Vita Sua* (1865). Edited and with an Introduction by M. J. Svaglic. Oxford: Clarendon Press, 1967.

————. *Discussions and Arguments on Various Subjects.* London: Longmans and Green, 1907.

————. *An Essay in Aid of A Grammar of Assent* (1870). Edited and with an Introduction by I. T. Ker. Oxford: Oxford University Press, 1985.

————. *Essay on the Development of Christian Doctrine* (1845). Edited and with an introduction by J. M. Cameron. Harmondsworth: Penguin, 1974.

————. *Fifteen Sermons Preached before the University of Oxford* (1843). Westminster, Md.: Christian Classics, 1966.

————. *The Idea of a University.* London: Longmans and Green, 1925.

————. *A Letter Addressed to His Grace the Duke of Norfolk on the Occasion of Mr. Gladstone's Recent Expostulation.* London: Pickering, 1875.

————. *Letters and Diaries of John Henry Newman.* Edited by C. S. Dessain, T. Gornall, S.J., and I. T. Ker. Oxford: Clarendon Press, 1961–.

————. *On Consulting the Faithful in Matters of Doctrine* (1859). Edited and with an Introduction by J. Coulson. London: Collins, 1961.

————. *Parochial and Plain Sermons.* London: Rivingtons, 1868.

Nussbaum, M. *The Fragility of Goodness.* New York and Cambridge: Cambridge University Press, 1986.

Oakeshott, M. *Rationalism in Politics and Other Essays.* London: Methuen, 1962.

Owen, G. E. L. *Logic, Science and Dialectic.* Edited by M. Nussbaum. London: Duckworth, 1986.

Pirsig, R. *Zen and the Art of Motorcycle Maintenance.* New York: William Morrow, 1974.

Plato. *Sophist, Republic, Gorgias, Phaedrus, Protagoras, Theaetetus* and *Seventh Letter.* In E. Hamilton and H. Cairns, eds., *The Collected Dialogues of Plato.* Princeton: Princeton University Press, 1961.

Popper, K. *The Open Society and Its Enemies.* Vol. 2, *The High Tide of Prophesy: Hegel and Marx.* London: Routledge and Kegan Paul, 1945.

Putnam, H. *Meaning and the Moral Sciences.* London: Routledge and Kegan Paul, 1978.

Rawls, J. *A Theory of Justice.* Cambridge, Mass.: Harvard University Press, 1971.

Ricoeur, P. *Freud and Philosophy: An Essay on Interpretation.* Translated by D. Savage. New Haven, Conn.: Yale University Press, 1970.

————. "A Response by Paul Ricoeur" and "Hermeneutics and the Critique of Ideology." In J. B. Thompson, ed. and trans. *Hermeneutics and the Human Sciences: Essays on Language, Action and Interpretation.* Cambridge: Cambridge University Press, 1981.

Rieff, P. *Freud: The Mind of the Moralist.* London: Victor Gollancz, 1959; Chicago: University of Chicago Press, 1979.

———. *The Triumph of the Therapeutic.* London: Penguin University Books, 1964; Chicago: University of Chicago Press, 1987.

Rogers, C. *On Becoming a Person.* London: Constable, 1961.

Rorty, A. O., ed. *Essays on Aristotle's Ethics.* Berkeley: University of California Press, 1980.

Rorty, R. *The Linguistic Turn.* Chicago: The University of Chicago Press, 1967.

———. *Philosophy and the Mirror of Nature.* Princeton, N.J.: Princeton University Press, 1979; Oxford: Basil Blackwell, 1980.

Sacks, S. O., ed. *On Metaphor.* Chicago: University of Chicago Press, 1978.

Schnädelbach, H. "What Is Neo-Aristotelianism?" In *Praxis International* 7, no. 3/4 (Oct. 1987/Jan. 1988): 225–237.

Sillem, Edward J. *John Henry Newman, The Philosophical Notebooks.* Vol. 1: *General Introduction to the Study of Newman's Philosophy.* Louvain: Nauwelaerts, 1969.

Solmsen, F. "Leisure and Play in Aristotle's Ideal State." In *Kleine Schriften,* vol. 2. Hildesheim, 1968.

Strauss, L. *Natural Right and History.* Chicago: University of Chicago Press, 1953.

Taminiaux, J. *Dialectic and Difference: Finitude in Modern Thought.* Edited and translated by R. Crease and J. T. Decker. New Jersey: Humanities Press, 1985.

Walgrave, J. H. *Newman the Theologian: The Nature of Belief and Doctrine as Exemplified in His Life and Work.* Translated by A. V. Littledale. London: Chapman, 1960.

Waterlow, S. *Nature, Change and Agency in Aristotle's Physics.* Oxford: Clarendon Press, 1982.

Whitebrook, J. "The Problem of Nature in Habermas." *Telos* 40 (1979): 44–69.

———. "Reason and Happiness: Some Psychoanalytic Themes in Critical Theory." In R. J. Bernstein, ed., *Habermas and Modernity,* pp. 125–139.

Wiggins, D. "Deliberation and Practical Reason." In A. O. Rorty, ed., *Essays on Aristotle's Ethics,* pp. 221–240.

———. "Weakness of Will, Commensurability, and the Objects of Deliberation and Desire." in A. O. Rorty, ed., *Essays on Aristotle's Ethics,* pp. 241–265.

Williams, B. *Ethics and the Limits of Philosophy,* London: Fontana Press, 1985.

Winch, P. *The Idea of a Social Science and Its Relation to Philosophy.* London: Routledge and Kegan Paul, 1958.

Wittgenstein, L. *Philosophical Investigations.* 3rd ed. Edited by G. E. M. Anscombe and R. Rhees and translated by G. E. M. Anscombe. Oxford: Basil Blackwell, 1976.

Wollheim, R. "On an Alleged Inconsistency in Collingwood's Aesthetics." In M. Krausz, ed., *Critical Essays on the Philosophy of R. G. Collingwood.* Oxford: Oxford University Press, 1972.

Yeats, W. B. *Cathleen ní Houlihan.* In *The Collected Plays.* London: Macmillan, 1956.

Bibliography to Part 2
and Epilogue

Aristotle. *Categories.*

———. *De Anima.*

———. *De Generatione Animalium.*

———. *De Generatione et Corruptione.*

———. *De Partibus Animalium.*

———. *De Sophisticis Elenchis.*

———(?). *De Virtutibus et Vitiis.*

———. *Eudemian Ethics.*

——— (?). *Magna Moralia.*

———. *Metaphysics.*

———. *Nicomachean Ethics.*

———. *Physics.*

———. *Poetics.*

———. *Politics.*

———. *Posterior Analytics.*

——— (?). *Protrepticus.*

———. *Rhetoric.*

———. *Topics.*

In *The Complete Works of Aristotle.* Revised Oxford translation, in 2 vols., edited by J. Barnes. Princeton, N.J.: Princeton University Press (Bollingen Series), 1984.

Protrepticus, in David Ross, ed., *The Works of Aristotle,* vol. 12: *Select Fragments.* Oxford: Oxford University Press, 1952.

Ackrill, J. L. "Aristotle on Eudaimonia." In A. O. Rorty, ed., *Essays on Aristotle's Ethics.* Berkeley and Los Angeles, Ca.: University of California Press, 1980.

477

Allan, D. J. "Aristotle's Account of the Origins of Moral Principles." Chapter 5 in
J. Barnes, M. Schofield, and R. Sorabji, eds., *Articles on Aristotle*, vol. 2, *Ethics
and Politics*.

———. *The Philosophy of Aristotle*. 2nd ed. Oxford: Oxford University Press, 1970.

Ando, T. *Aristotle's Theory of Practical Cognition*. 3rd rev. ed. The Hague: Martinus
Nijhoff, 1971.

Anscombe, G. E. M. "Thought and Action in Aristotle." In R. Bambrough, ed., *New
Essays in Plato and Aristotle*, pp. 143–158.

Aquinas, St. Thomas. *Commentary on the Nichomachean Ethics*. Translated by C. I.
Litzinger, O.P. Chicago: Regnery, 1964.

———. *Summa contra Gentiles*. Leonine edition. Rome: Desclée & C.–Herder,
1934.

———. *Summa Theologiae*, cura et studio, P. Caramello. Rome: Marietti, 1950.

Bambrough, R. *New Essays in Plato and Aristotle*. London: Routledge and Kegan Paul,
1965.

Barnes, J., M. Schofield, and R. Sorabji, eds. *Articles on Aristotle*. Vol. 2, *Ethics and
Politics*. London: Duckworth, 1977.

Bernstein, R. J. *Beyond Objectivism and Relativism*. Philadelphia: University of Pennsylvania Press; Oxford: Blackwell, 1983.

———. *Praxis and Action*. Philadelphia: University of Pennsylvania Press; London:
Duckworth, 1972.

———. *The Restructuring of Social and Political Theory*. Philadelphia: University of
Pennsylvania Press; London: Methuen, 1976.

Brivic, S. "Joyce and the Metaphysics of Creation." *The Crane Bag* 6, no. 1 (1982):
13–19.

Butcher, S. H. *Aristotle's Theory of Poetry and Fine Art, With a Critical Text and
Translation of the Poetics*. 4th ed. New York: Dover Publications, 1951.

Charlton, W. *Aristotle's Physics I and II*. Oxford: Oxford University Press, 1970.

Carr, W., and S. Kemmis. *Becoming Critical: Education, Knowledge and Action Research*. London: Falmer Press, 1987.

Close, A. J. "Commonplace Theories of Art and Nature in Classical Antiquity and
in the Renaissance." *Journal of the History of Ideas* 30 (1909): 467–486.

———. (1971) "Philosophical Theories of Art and Nature." *Journal of the History
of Ideas* 32:163–184.

Cooper, J. M. "Aristotle on Natural Teleology." In *Language and Logos, Studies in
Ancient Greek Philosophy presented to G. E. L. Owen*, edited by M. Schofield
and M. C. Nussbaum. Cambridge: Cambridge University Press, 1982.

————. *Reason and Human Good in Aristotle* (Cambridge Mass.: Harvard University Press, 1975).

————. Review of Anthony Kenny's *The Aristotelian Ethics.* In *Nous* 15, (1981): 381–392.

Cornford, F. M. and P. H. Wicksteed. *Aristotle, The Physics.* Loeb edition. London, 1929.

Desjardins, R. "Why Dialogues? Plato's Serious Play." In C. L. Griswold, Jr., *Platonic Writings, Platonic Readings,* New York and London: Routledge, 1988.

Detienne, M. and J. P. Vernant. *Cunning Intelligence in Greek Culture and Society.* Translated by J. Lloyd. Sussex: Harvester Press, 1978.

Elliot, J. "Educational Theory, Practical Philosophy and Action Research." *British Journal of Educational Studies* 25, no. 2 (1987): 149–169.

T. Engberg-Pedersen. *Aristotle's Theory of Moral Insight.* Oxford: Clarendon Press, 1983.

Frank, F. *The Zen of Seeing.* London: Wildwood House, 1973.

Freire, P. *Pedagogy of the Oppressed.* London: Penguin, 1972.

Freud, S. *The Future of an Illusion.* Vol. 21 of *Complete Psychological Works of Sigmund Freud.* Translated and edited by J. Strachey. London: The Hogarth Press 1961.

Gadamer, H.-G. "A Letter by Professor Hans-Georg Gadamer." Appendix in R. J. Bernstein, *Beyond Objectivism and Relativism.*

————. *Truth and Method. (Wahrheit und Methode,* 2nd ed., 1965.) Translation edited by G. Barden and J. Cumming. London: Sheed and Ward, 1975.

Gauthier, R. A. and J. Y. Jolif. *L'Éthique à Nicomaque.* Louvain, 1970.

Gilbey, T., ed. St. Thomas Aquinas, *Summa Theologiae,* vol. 36: *Prudence* (2a2ae., 47– 56). London: Blackfriars and Eyre and Spottiswoode, 1974.

Grant, A. *The Ethics of Aristotle.* London, 1857.

Greenwood, L. G. H. *Nicomachean Ethics Book Six: With Essays, Notes and Translation.* Cambridge: Cambridge University Press, 1909: reprint, New York: Arno Press, 1973.

Griswold, Charles, Jr. "Plato's Metaphilosophy: Why Plato Wrote Dialogues," In Griswold, ed., *Platonic Writings, Platonic Readings,* pp. 143–167. New York and London: Routledge, 1988.

Grundy S. *Curriculum: Product or Praxis.* London: Falmer Press 1987.

Habermas, J. "Laurence Kohlberg und der Neoaristotelismus." In Habermas, ed., *Erläuterungen zur Diskursethik,* pp. 79–99. Frankfurt: Suhrkamp, 1991.

————. *Theory and Practice (Theorie und Praxis,* 1971.) Translated by J. Viertel. London: Heinemann, 1974.

Hampshire, S. *Two Theories of Morality*. Oxford: Oxford University Press, 1977.

Hardie, W. F. R. *Aristotle's Ethical Theory*. 2nd ed. Oxford: Clarendon Press, 1980.

Heidegger, M. *Being and Time*. Translated by J. Macquarrie and E. Robinson. Oxford: Basil Blackwell, 1978.

———. "Building Dwelling Thinking." In Martin Heidegger, *Basic Writings*, edited by D. F. Krell. London: Routledge and Kegan Paul, 1978.

———. "Letter on Humanism." Translated by F. A. Capuzzi and J. G. Gray. In Martin Heidegger, *Basic Writings*, pp. 193–242.

Hintikka, J. "Plato on Knowing How, That and What." In *Knowledge and the Known, Historical Perspectives on Epistemology*. Dordrecht: Kluwer, 1974.

———. *Time and Necessity: Studies in Aristotle's Theory of Modality*. Oxford: Clarendon Press, 1973.

Husserl, E. *The Crisis of the European Sciences and Transcendental Phenomenology: An Introduction to Phenomenological Philosophy*. Translated by D. Carr. Evanston, Ill.: Northwestern University Press, 1970.

Hutchinson, D. S. *The Virtues of Aristotle*. London and New York: Routledge and Kegan Paul, 1986.

Huxley, A. *The Art of Seeing*. London: Chatto and Windus, 1957.

Irwin, T. H. *Plato's Moral Theory: The Early and Middle Dialogues*. Oxford: Clarendon Press, 1977.

———. Review of Anthony Kenny's *The Aristotelian Ethics*. In *The Journal of Philosophy* 77 (1980): 338–354.

Jaeger, W. *Aristotle, Fundamentals of the History of His Development*. Translated by R. Robinson. Oxford: Clarendon Press, 1934.

Jaeger, W. "Aristotle's Use of Medicine as Model of Method in his Ethics." *Journal of Hellenic Studies* 77 (1957): 54–61.

Joachim, H. H. *The Nicomachean Ethics* (Posthumously published lectures of 1902–1917). Edited by D. A. Rees. Oxford: Clarendon Press, 1952.

Kenny, A. *The Aristotelian Ethics*. Oxford: Oxford University Press, 1978.

———. *Aristotle's Theory of the Will*. London: Duckworth, 1979.

Keyt, D. "Intellectualism in Aristotle." In *Paideia*, Special Aristotle Issue, 1978, pp. 138–155.

Levin, D. M. *The Opening of Vision, Nihilism, and the Postmodern Situation*. New York: Routledge, Chapman and Hall, 1988.

Lloyd, G. E. R. "The Role of Medical and Biological Analogies in Aristotle's Ethics." *Phronesis* 13 (1968): 68–83.

Lonergan, B. *Insight: A Study of Human Understanding*. London: Longmans, 1957.

Lyotard, J. F. "Presentations." In A. Montefiore, ed., *Philosophy in France Today.* Cambridge: Cambridge University Press, 1983.

———. *The Post-Modern Condition: A Report on Knowledge.* Translated by G. Bennington and B. Massumi. Manchester: Manchester University Press, 1986.

MacIntyre, A. *After Virtue.* London: Duckworth; Notre Dame, Ind.: University of Notre Dame Press, 1981.

———. *Whose Justice? Which Rationality?* Notre Dame, Ind.: University of Notre Dame Press; London: Duckworth, 1988.

MacMurray, J. *The Self as Agent.* Atlantic Highlands, N.J.: Humanities, 1978.

———. *Persons in Relation.* Atlantic Highlands, N.J.: Humanities, 1979.

Mansion, A. *Introduction à la Physique Aristotélicienne.* Paris, 1945.

Maritain, J. *Creative Intuition in Art and Poetry.* London: Harvill Press, 1954.

Monan, D. J. *Moral Knowledge and Its Methodology in Aristotle.* Oxford: Oxford University Press, 1968.

Murdoch, I. *The Sovereignty of Good.* London: Routledge and Kegan Paul, 1970.

Mure, G. R. G. *Aristotle.* London: Benn, 1932; reprinted New York: Greenwood Press, 1975.

Newman, J. H. *An Essay in Aid of a Grammar of Assent.* Edited by I. T. Ker. Oxford: Clarendon Press, 1985.

Nussbaum, M. C. *Aristotle's "De Motu Animalium."* Princeton: Princeton University Press, 1978.

———. "The Discernment of Perception: An Aristotelian Conception of Private and Public Rationality." In J. Cleary, ed., *Proceedings of the Boston Area Colloquium in Ancient Philosophy,* vol. 1 (1985), pp. 151–201.

———. *The Fragility of Goodness.* Cambridge: Cambridge University Press, 1986.

———. "Therapeutic Arguments: Epicurus and Aristotle." In M. Schofield and G. Striker, eds., *The Norms of Nature,* pp. 310–374. Cambridge: Cambridge University Press, 1985.

Nuyens, F. *L'évolution de la psychologie d'Aristote.* Louvain: 1948; 1973.

Pieper, J. *Prudence.* Translated by R. and C. Winston. London: Faber and Faber, 1957.

Plato. *Meno, The Laws, Symposium, Phaedrus, Philebus, Republic, Gorgias and Statesman.* In E. Hamilton and H. Cairns, eds., *The Collected Dialogues of Plato.* Princeton: Princeton University Press, 1961.

Rackham, H., ed. and trans. *The Nicomachean Ethics.* Vol. 19 of Loeb edition of Aristotle. Cambridge, Mass.: Harvard University Press, 1908; London: Heinemann, 1975.

Rorty, A. O., ed. *Essays on Aristotle's Ethics.* Berkeley and Los Angeles: University of California Press, 1980.

Rorty, R. *Philosophy and the Mirror of Nature.* Princeton: Princeton University Press, 1979; Oxford: Blackwell, 1980.

Ross, W. D. *Aristotle.* London: Methuen University Paperbacks, 1966.

———. *Aristotle's Physics: A Revised Text with Introduction and Commentary.* Oxford: Clarendon Press, 1936; 1979.

Rowe, C. J. *The Eudemian and Nicomachean Ethics: A Study in the Development of Aristotle's Thought.* Cambridge, 1971.

Ryle, G. *The Concept of Mind.* London: Penguin, 1986.

Sambursky, S. *The Physical World of the Greeks.* Translated by M. Dagut. London: Routledge and Kegan Paul, 1987.

Schnädelbach, H. "What is Neo-Aristotelianism?" *Praxis International* 7, no. 3/4 (Oct. 1987/Jan. 1988): 225–237.

Seidler, M. "The Medical Paradigm in Aristotle's Ethics." *The Thomist* 42 (1978): 400–433.

Sellars, W. *Philosophical Perspectives.* Springfield, Ill.: C. C. Thomas, 1967.

Sherman, N. *The Fabric of Character: Aristotle's Theory of Virtue.* Oxford: Clarendon Press, 1989.

Smith, I. A., and W. D. Ross, eds. *The Works of Aristotle.* English translation in 12 vols. Oxford, 1910–1952.

Solmsen, F., "Nature as Craftsman in Greek Thought," *Journal of the History of Ideas,* 24:473–496.

St. George Stock. Introduction to *Magna Moralia, Eudemian Ethics* and *De Virtutibus et Vitiis* In *The Works of Aristotle,* Vol. 9. Oxford: Oxford University Press, 1975.

Stewart, J. A. *Notes on the Nicomachean Ethics.* Oxford: Clarendon Press, 1892.

Taylor, A. E. *Aristotle.* 1919. Reprint. New York: Dover, 1955.

Thompson, J. A. K., trans. *The Ethics of Aristotle.* Revised with notes by H. Tredennick. Harmondsworth: Penguin, 1980.

Tracey, T. *Physiological Theory and the Doctrine of the Mean in Plato and Aristotle.* The Hague: Mouton, 1969.

Waterlow, S. *Nature, Change and Agency in Aristotle's Physics: A Philosophical Study.* Oxford: Clarendon Press, 1982.

Weil, S. *La Pesanteur et La Grâce.* Paris: 1948.

———. "Reflections on the Right Use of School Studies with a View to the Love of God." In *Waiting on God.* Glasgow: Collins, 1978.

Westbury, I., and H. I. Wilkof, eds. *Science, Curriculum and Liberal Education: Selected Essays of Joseph J. Schwab*. Chicago: University of Chicago Press, 1978.

Wiggins, D. "Deliberation and Practical Reason." In A. O. Rorty, ed., *Essays on Aristotle's Ethics* (see above).

Wittgenstein, L. *On Certainty*. Edited by G. E. M. Anscombe and G. H. von Wright, translated by D. Paul and G. E. M. Anscombe. Oxford: Blackwell, 1969.

———. *Philosophical Investigations*. Edited by G. E. M. Anscombe and R. Rhees and translated by G. E. M. Anscombe. 3rd ed. Oxford: Basil Blackwell, 1968.

Index

Ackrill, J. L., 438n.22
Action, Arendt's concept of: and behavior, 89–90; and labor, 400n.3; limits of fore-knowledge in, 92, 102; and making, 12, 95, 97–98, 101, 400n.3; self-disclosure in, 90–91, 116, 359; uncertainty of, 91–94, 98, 102. *See also* Speech
Adorno, T. W., 168–69, 403n.40, 422n.3; Habermas's criticism of, 200–201, 214–215, 432n.27, 434n.70
Aeschylus, 131, 215
Aesthetics: Collingwood on, 55–87; and emancipation, 432n.31; and ethics, 57, 69–75; Habermas on, 203–204; and her-meneutics, 406n.6, 409n.40; and politics, 95–96. *See also* Art
Agent-patient relation, 77, 191, 339–341, 410–411n.52
Aletheia, 151, 453n.79
Allan, D. J., 270
Ambrose, St., 54
Ando, T., 451n.63
Anscombe, G. E. M., 308, 451n.61
Arendt, H., 12, 88–103, 400–405; and Aris-totle, 100–103; on behaviorism, 89; and Collingwood, 94–96; on forgiving and promising, 98–100; and Gadamer, 131–132; and Habermas, 210, 424n.12; on limits of will, 210; on Plato, 96–97; on public and private, 400n.4. *See also* Ac-tion, Arendt's concept of
Art: corrupt consciousness as bad, 62; Gada-mer on, 406n.6; originality in, 395n.78; and politics, 70, 396n.83; technical the-ory of, 55–60; work of, and audience, 75–87. *See also* Aesthetics
Attention, 305, 309
Augustine, St., 65, 145
Austin, J. L., 145, 196

Bacon, F., 384n.17, 385n.2
Behavioral objectives model, 1–8, 117, 130, 191, 360, 367, 392n.33
Bell, Q., 70
Benjamin, W., 435n.73
Bentham, J., 11
Berenson, B., 396n.91
Bernstein, R. J., 44–45, 390n.99, 406n.3, 408n.18, 421n.118, 436n.5, 467n.3
Bloom, B., 2
Bubner, R., 423n.8, 436n.98
Burnyeat, M. F., 46

Callicles, 24
Capitalism: Habermas on, 188–192, 199–203
Cartesianism, 76, 104, 374
Cavel, S., 395n.66
Character: and action, 290; and experience, 289–292, 305, 358; and phronesis, 290–291, 305, 381; and politics, 288–289
Charlton, W., 459n.43, 464n.80
Cleverness (*deinotēs*), 37, 277–278, 280, 308
Coleridge, S. T., 78, 385n.2, 393n.47
Collingwood, R. G., 11–12, 55–87, 391–400; on aesthetic individualism, 79–80; on amusement and magic, 58; and Arendt, 94–96; and Aristotle's ethics, 71–74; on consciousness, 60–63; on expression, 63–69, 75, 77–85; Gadamer and, 116, 409n.40, 414n.90; influences on, 393n.47, 394n.54; on language, 63–68, 81–87; on reconstruction, 78–86; on 'technical the-ory of art', 55–60. *See also* Question and answer, logic of
Communication: systematically distorted, 17, 178; undistorted, 218
Consciousness: Collingwood on, 60–63; cor-rupt, 62–63; 'effective-historical', 119–122, 149–150; freedom of, 61; and lan-

Consciousness (*cont.*)
guage, 81–82; and morality, 72, 74–75;
philosophy of, 81, 196, 402n.38. *See also*
Historical consciousness
Contemplative life, the, 88, 174, 238–242
Conversation: human significance of, 185,
384n.17; as mode of philosophical inquiry, 20–27; as model of interpretation,
84–86, 115, 117–121, 410n.46; as play, 23,
135–137, 148–150
Cooper, J. M., 462n.69, 439n.23
Cornford, F. M., 460–461n.52, 464n.80
Critique, 16–17, 171, 179, 183, 185, 192–194,
201, 373, 427n.43

Darwin, C., 385n.3
Decentering, 204, 208, 215, 219, 222, 380–
381
Deliberation, 250, 306, 344, 350–354; end
and means in, 352–353; excellence in
(*euboulia*), 271–272, 307, 443n.77,
445n.124, 450n.55. *See also under*
Techne
Democritus, 332
Derrida, J., 17, 216, 378, 395n.66, 422n.3
Descartes, R., 14, 81, 402n.38, 384n.17
Detienne, M., 256–257, 260–261
Dewey, J., 29, 370, 432n.27, 434n.48
Dialectic, 24, 136, 139, 147, 399n.130,
408n.30, 409n.38, 417n.41. *See also*
Rhetoric
Dialogues (Plato), 441n.46; Gadamer on,
415n.9, 417n.41
Dilthey, W., 42–43; Gadamer on, 108–109,
111, 115; Habermas on, 182–183

Emancipation, 17, 182, 189, 194–203, 216,
373, 375, 425n.23
Empedocles, 327, 329, 459n.43
End and means. *See* Instrumentality
Energeia, 90, 101, 363, 404n.66, 458n.33;
and *dunamis*, 323–324, 328–329; and
kinēsis, 248; and virtues, 319
Engberg-Pedersen, T., 230–231, 447n.17
Enlightenment, the, 109, 111; Frankfurt
school and, 169; Habermas as defender
of, 17, 168–170, 216, 375, 429n.7; romantic protest against, 108, 111–112
Equity (*epieikeia*), 283, 311, 333–334

Ethics: and aesthetics, 69–75; Aristotelian
and modern, 371–372; Aristotle's method
in, 153–154, 269–270, 419n.63; deductivism in, 308; discourse, 375; medical analogy in, 219, 246, 275–276, 334, 440n.34;
suppression of, 190, 372. *See also* Practical philosophy
Eudaimonia (human flourishing), 238–242,
245, 296, 303, 364, 413n.89, 435n.87,
437n.14, 438n.22
Evans-Pritchard, E. E., 206
Experience: Aeschylus on, 131–132; Aristotle
on, 279–295, 305–306, 313, 318–325,
329; and character, 289–292, 367; and
circle of knowledge and virtue, 280, 305;
and empiricism, 129; Gadamer on, 127–
133; and *genesis*, 326–327; in Habermas,
223; Hegel on, 130–131; historicality of,
129, 328–329; and judgment, 287–288,
453n.76; and language, 143; and moral
development, 289–290; as natural, 279,
335–336; and openness, 306; 'ordinary'
and 'phronetic' distinguished, 294–295,
313; and particulars, 293–294, 361; and
phronesis, 292–295, 361; in Plato,
446n.128; and techne, 281–285, 293,
305; of the 'thou,' 132–133
Experienced person, 130, 133–134, 287, 290,
362–363
Expression: and action, 358–359; Arendt's
critique of, 402n.38; Collingwood on,
63–69, 75, 77–85; and description, 67–
68; as dialectic, 399n.130; of emotion,
63, 77; Gadamer's critique of, 409n.40;
imaginative, 60–63; and language, 64–
69, 82

Feyerabend, P., 40
Finitude, 81, 103, 112, 125, 131, 146–150,
364, 381
Form: ungeneratedness of, 328, 459n.41. *See
also* Hylomorphism; Techne
Foucault, M., 216, 378
Foundationalism: and Newman, 38–39; and
Habermas, 219
Four causes, Aristotle's account of, 249, 316,
458n.39
Frankfurt School, 168–169, 180, 188, 195,
422n.4
Freud, S., 412n.85, 463n.72; Collingwood

Freud, S. (*cont.*)
on, 393n.452; Habermas on, 17, 169,
180–182, 193, 436n.94; as moralist, 373.
See also Psychoanalysis
Friendship, 23, 99, 443n.86

Gadamer, H.-G., 13–15, 104–167, 406–422:
and Aristotle, 105–106, 122–130, 143–
144, 153–163, 306, 321; on the beautiful,
151; and Collingwood, 85, 87, 116; on
conversation, 115, 117–121, 134–137, 148–
150; on 'effective-history', 119, 149, 367;
on experience, 127–133; on finitude, 112,
125, 146–150; on fusion of horizons,
122–124, 149, 184; and Heidegger, 109–
111, 154–155, 166, 379, 406n.4; on hermeneutical circle, 114–115; and Newman,
39–40, 52, 116, 154–155; and nineteenth-
century hermeneutics, 106–109; on play,
135–137; on practical philosophy, 157–
161, 164, 365–366; on prejudices, 109–
118; on questioning, 134–136, 414n.93;
on the 'statement', 54, 116, 147, 417n.37;
on temporal distance, 31, 108, 115, 118–
119; on tradition, 109–115, 120. *See also*
Habermas, J.; Hegel, G. W. F.; Hermeneutics; Interpretation; Plato
Gallwey, W. T., 414n.104
Geach, P., 454n.86
Geertz, C., 377
Genesis, Aristotle on, 326–329
Giddens, A., 431n.21
Gnōmē (judgment), 132, 279, 287–288, 370,
412n.81, 449n.48. *See also* Judgment
Good: idea of (Plato), 23, 46, 162, 412n.71;
and Habermas's proceduralism, 217–218;
and phronesis, 37, 269–270, 275–279. *See
also* Virtue
Greenwood, L. G. H., 270–271, 439n.27,
445n.114, 449n.49, 452n.69, 456n.6

Habermas, J., 16–18, 167–226, 422–436; on
autonomy, 217–218, 425n.23; and Arendt,
210, 424n.12; and Aristotle, 173–177,
223–226, 229–230; on capitalism, 188–
192, 199–203; on communicative action,
17, 194–197, 199, 203, 210; core intuitions
of, 211–212; criticism of Adorno by, 200–
201, 214–215; critique of technicism,
364–365; as defender of Enlightenment,

Habermas, J. (*cont.*)
17, 168–170, 216, 375, 429n.7; on dis-
course(s), 198–203, 207; distinction between morality and ethical life, 217; on
four validity claims, 196–197, 430n.11;
on Freud, 17, 169, 180–182, 193, 436n.94;
on Gadamer, 183–186, 412n.71, 419n.59,
424n.12; Gadamer compared with, 214–
215; on ideal speech situation, 178; justification in, 219–222; on knowledge-
constitutive interests, 175–176, 194,
425n.23; on Kohlberg, 220–222; and liberalism, 200; on G. H. Mead, 216–217;
on modernity, 199–205; and Newman,
211; proceduralism in later philosophy of,
212, 217–222; restricted conception of
philosophy in, 212–213, 218, 434n.61; on
'steering medium', 431n.19; on universal
pragmatics, 196; on welfare state, 189–
190, 431n.23. *See also* Communication;
Critique; Decentering; Emancipation; Heidegger, M.; Marx, K.; Marxism; Rationalization of life-world; Theory and practice
Hampshire, S., 312, 371–372, 375
Hardie, W. F. R., 445n.118, 452n.69, 454n.84
Hawthorn, G., 430n.7
Heaney, S., 413n.88
Hegel, G. W. F., 166, 217; Collingwood on,
385n.3; Gadamer on, 130–131, 136,
409n.38, 415n.105, 416n.9, 417n.41;
Habermas on, 177–178
Heidegger, M., 114, 145–146, 152, 402n.38,
453n.79, 460n.50, 464n.78; on circular
character of understanding, 109–111, 279;
and Gadamer, 109–111, 154–155, 166,
379, 406n.4; and Habermas, 422n.3,
434n.70
Herder, J. G., 139
Hermeneutics: and critique, 183; and epistemology, 22–23; legal and religious, 122–
123; ninteenth-century, 106–109; as philosophy, 106, 164–167; premodern,
407n.9; practical philosophy as model of,
15, 124–125, 157–164; and science, 165–
166; and sociology, 427n.43. *See also* Interpretation; Praxis
Hermeneutical circle, 105, 114, 231
Hexis (state), 249, 316–317, 455n.5
Hintikka, J., 250, 252, 257, 426n.24, 447n.27,
453n.84

Historical consciousness, 106, 112, 372–373, 385n.3
Historicity, 14, 110, 359–362, 364, 385n.3
Hobbes, T., 64, 65, 94, 173
Hölderlin, F., 154
Hopkins, G. M., 397n.116
Horizon(s), 119–121, 210–211; fusion of, 121–124, 149, 184
Horkheimer, M., 68–69, 379, 403n.40, 432n.27
Humboldt, W. von, 139, 195
Husserl, E., 109, 119, 409n.38, 437–438n.15
Hutchinson, D. S., 455n.4
Hylomorphism, 251, 315, 329, 331, 459n.40

Ideology, 176; critique of, 189–192
Incommensurability, 45–50
Instrumentality, 95, 127, 134, 352–353; in teaching, 5–7. See also Phronesis; Techne
Interpretation: 'application' in, 122, 124; practical dimension of, 122, 156, 184, 362; in psychoanalysis, 181; and understanding, 85, 141–143. See also Conversation; Hermeneutics; Reconstruction
Intersubjectivity, 76, 79–83, 92, 100, 132, 194, 217, 359–360, 375
Irwin, T., 439n.23, 440–441n.46

Jaeger, W., 270
Jaspers, K., 119
Jesus, 403n.60
Joachim, H. H., 270–271
John, St., 145
Johnson, S., 418n.53
Joyce, J., 461n.63
Judgment, 4, 35, 73–74, 220–222, 381. See also Gnōmē

Kant, I., 135, 196, 217–218, 423n.8, 430n.11
Kenny, A., 300–301, 439n.23, 445n.122, 450n.60, 451n.61, 461n.54
Keyt, D., 439n.22
Knowledge: epistēmē as, 144, 157, 174, 237–238, 253, 316–317; experiential, 280, 363; general vs. particular, 67–68, 73, 252–253, 259, 310–311, 368; implicit, 41, 210, 390n.96. See also Phronesis; Practical philosophy; Techne; Theory, Aristotle's conception of; Theory and practice

Knowledge-constitutive interest(s), 175–176, 194, 425n.23
Kohlberg, L., 196, 215, 217, 220–222, 436n.94
Krathwohl, D., 2
Kuhn, T., 44–49

Language: Aristotle on, 143–144, 154, 413n.89; and the body, 64–65; Collingwood on, 63–68, 81–87; communicative role of, distinguished, 196; and concept-formation, 144; context-free, 3, 177; expressiveness of, 65–66; field of, parallel with field of action, 362; Gadamer on, 52, 137–154; infinity of, 146–149, 362; learning a, 143, 150; as medium of agreement, 166, 196; Merleau-Ponty on, 398–399n.130; and metaphor, 144; natural, 64, 139–141; Newman on, 51–54; and phronesis, 52, 156, 419n.64; and power, 186, 196; and techne, 152; technical theory of, 66, 143; technical vocabulary in, 139, 415n.4; and thought, 51–53, 138–144; and translation, 141; universality of, 140; and world, 138, 140–141, 150. See also Consciousness; Experience; Expression
Leibniz, F., 139
Life-world (Lebenswelt), 109, 171, 174, 199–200, 381. See also Rationalization of life-world
Locke, J., 15, 64, 65, 390n.99
Logos, 106, 143–145, 312–313, 316–317, 320, 355; as context bound, 332, 370. See also Matter
Lonergan, B., 430n.12, 465n.93
Lyotard, J.-F., 216, 377–378, 422n.3

MacCarthy, T., 206, 423n.8
Machiavelli, N., 94, 173, 260
MacIntyre, A., 70, 224, 377, 378, 384n.17, 386n.6, 387n.34, 429n.7, 444n.107, 445n.118
MacMurray, J., 444n.108
Making (fabrication): Arendt on, 12, 95, 97–98, 101, 400n.3; Collingwood on technicist concept of, 55–60. See also Poiesis
Marcuse, H., 168–169, 423n.7, 426n.25
Maritain, J., 455n.96
Marx, K., 17, 88, 373, 385n.3, 400n.3, 412–413n.85; Habermas's reconstruction of, 178–180, 199–200

Marxism: Habermas on, 188–190, 193–194,
    201–202, 210, 425n.23
Matter, 328–329; and *logos,* 258, 330–331,
    333, 460n.46; subject of a text, 150,
    409n.38. *See also* Hylomorphism
Mead, G. H., 196, 216–217
Mean, Aristotle's concept of the, 246, 311–
    312, 363
Merleau-Ponty, M., 150, 398–399n.130,
    408n.28, 416n.34
Metaphysics, 145, 152–153
Method: Gadamer on, 108, 125–126, 129,
    133, 161; Aristotle's, in ethics, 153–154,
    269–270, 289, 419n.63
Methodology, in Aristotle, 158, 327, 463–
    464n.73
Mill, J. S., 11, 390n.99
Mink, L. O., 394n.54, 424n.13
Modernity, Habermas on, 199–205
Monan, D., 443n.82, 451n.61
Moral: development, 220–221, 289–290, 305,
    307, 449n.48; weakness (*akrasia*), 296,
    308–309
Murdoch, I., 309–310

Natural, two senses of, in *E.N.,* 6, 279, 290–
    291, 448n.40, 449n.43
Nature, Aristotle on techne and, 334–338
Neo-Aristotelianism, 26, 170, 195, 374, 375,
    377, 423n.9
Newman, J. H., 11, 31–54, 369, 384–391; on
    antecedent probability, 43; and Aristotle,
    33–38; and Gadamer, 39–40, 52, 116,
    154–156, 161; and Habermas, 211; on
    Illative Sense, 34–38, 46; influences on,
    385n.2; and Kuhn, 44–49; on language,
    51–54; on persuasion and proof, 44–45,
    49; and Putnam, 40–43
Nicholas of Cusa, 146
Nietzsche, F. W., 88, 155, 377–378, 405n.73,
    412n.85, 429n.7
Nous, 36, 278–280, 295–304, 306–307, 363,
    368
Nussbaum, M. C., 46, 102–103, 255,
    419nn.62,63, 438n.22, 453n.75
Nuyens, F., 466n.105

Oakeshott, M., 384n.17
Objectivism, 104, 126, 183, 185
Owen, G. E. L., 419n.63

Particular, and universal, 123, 127, 252, 272–
    273, 293–304, 310–313, 362–363,
    396n.93, 450n.52
Pascal, B., 384n.17
Peirce, C. S., 44–45
Perception (*aisthēsis*), 73, 273, 298–304, 308,
    363
Pericles, 94, 376
Philosophy: analytical, 13, 372; applied, 22;
    contemporary, 261; of consciousness, 81,
    196, 402n.38; of craft, 55–56; of educa-
    tion, 22; German, 13; Habermas's re-
    stricted conception of, 212–213, 218,
    434n.61; of history, 372; of language, 81;
    limits of, 25; modern, 374; and poetry, 67;
    as a practice, 22; and pre-philosophical
    experience, 212; and scholarship, 19–20,
    229–233. *See also* Practical philosophy
Phronesis: and character, 290–291, 305, 446–
    447n.14; as condition of goodness, 279;
    distinguished from cleverness, 271; and
    equity, 273; and *euboulia,* 271–272; and
    experience, 126–127, 228, 292–295;
    Gadamer on, 124–127, 156, 159, 163; as
    governing techne, 365, 405n.66; Haber-
    mas on, 173, 375; as not only a *hexis
    meta logou,* 264; and Illative Sense, 34–
    38; and instrumentality, 268, 270–272;
    intimacy of knowledge and action in,
    264, 266, 268; and language, 52, 156,
    419n.64; and *logos,* 312; and *mētis* (cun-
    ning), 260–261; as model of understand-
    ing, 124–126, 163; and neo-conservatism,
    374, 376; no excellence in, 264; non-
    disposability in, 126, 267–268, 276; and
    nous, 295–304, 306–307; about oneself,
    269–270; and particular virtues, 311; and
    perceptiveness, 273, 301–302; place of,
    in Aristotle's writings, 245, 314; and poli-
    tics, 286–289, 376; and practical syllo-
    gism, 296–297, 307–308; relation of
    universal and particular in, 272–273,
    293–304, 310–313; scope of, generalized
    by Newman, 37–38; and *sophia,* 269;
    and technai of *kairos,* 272–273; and tech-
    niques, 368; and unavailability of moral
    science, 303, 306, 311–312; virtue as
    condition of, 277–278. *See also* Phrone-
    sis and techne, Aristotle's distinction
    between

Phronesis and techne, Aristotle's distinction between, 9–10, 153, 244, 262–268, 310–311; as based on distinction between praxis and poiesis, 247–248, 262; as departure from Plato, 248; profile of, in Aristotle's writings, 245–249. *See also* Phronesis; Techne

Piaget, J., 196, 217

Pieper, J., 455n.96

Plato, 9, 23–24, 56, 124; Arendt on, 94–96, 405n.73; and Aristotle, 237, 239, 243, 246, 248–249, 251, 288, 308–309, 315, 325, 334–335, 446n.128; Gadamer on, 134–135, 136, 139, 140, 147, 151, 153, 162–163, 407nn.8,9, 412n.17, 417n.41, 420n.104, 426n.24. *See also* Good; Dialogues

Platonism of Aristotle, 162, 240, 309–310, 412n.71, 420n.104, 454n.93

Play, 135–137, 150, 367, 413n.89

Poiesis: act of, in product, 324, 339–342; embodiment in, 343–350; instrumentality in, 262; product of, as producer *in actu,* 325–326, 339–342; 'strong' and 'weak' senses of *poiētikē,* 316–318; unsatisfactoriness of techne as knowledge in, 282–285, 321–323. *See also* Agent-patient relation; Making (fabrication); Praxis and poiesis, Aristotle's distinction between; Techne

Polanyi, M., 42, 390n.96

Politics: Arendt on, 93–97; and art, 70, 396n.83; Habermas on new, 189–190, 432n.24; Aristotle on theory and practice in, 286–289. *See also* Marxism; Phronesis

Popham, W. J., 2

Popper, K., 168, 422n.2, 432n.27

Positivism, 16, 109, 145; in Dilthey, 109, 183; and Habermas, 188, 207, 468n.20; in Marx, 179

Post-modernism, 17, 196, 355, 375, 377–378, 380, 422n.3

Power: Arendt on, 93; Habermas on, 185–186, 375

Practical: dimension of interpretation, 122, 156, 184, 362; distinguished from technical, 175–176, 367–368; knowledge and human sciences, 40–42; loss of distinction between technical and, 186–192. *See also* Practical philosophy; Practice; Technique

Practical philosophy, 157–161, 407n.8; as lacking exactness, 223, 243; rehabilitated by Gadamer, 39, 105; Habermas on, 173–174; as model of hermeneutics, 15, 124–125, 157–164; and specific practices, 365–371. *See also* Practical; Practice; Theory and practice

Practical syllogism, 294–297, 307–308, 453n.84

Practice: circle of knowledge and, 17–18, 72; philosophy as a, 22; rationality of, 3, 7–8, 358; as resistant to theory, 9, 223, 243; specific domains of, 364–371, 378–382; teaching as a, 367, 379; theory as a, 51. *See also* Practical; Practical philosophy; Praxis; Theory and practice

Praxis: critique and, 183, 192–194; difficulty of contemporary retrieval of, 364; Habermas on, 176–186; Habermas's distinction between technique and, 186–192, 423n.10; hermeneutical element in, 183; interpersonal setting of, 263; knowledge in, 263–264; as noninstrumental, 262. *See also* Practical; Practice; Praxis and poiesis, Aristotle's distinction between; Technique

Praxis and poiesis, Aristotle's distinction between, 9–10, 126, 244, 324; as basis of distinction between phronesis and techne, 247–248, 262; and distinction between *energeia* and *kinēsis,* 248

Prejudice(s): Gadamer on, 14, 16, 107, 109–118, 184; unavoidability of, 25–26, 39

Prohairesis (choice), 157, 159, 264, 277

Psychoanalysis, 63, 169, 425n.23; and later Habermas, 193–194, 201; as paradigm of critical theory, 182. *See also* Freud

Putnam, H., 40–43

Question and answer, logic of, 116, 124, 414n.90

Questioning, 134–136, 414n.93

Rackham, H., 316–317, 320, 334

Ranke, F., 108

Rationalism, 8–9, 140; Habermas and, 202; Newman and, 31–33

Rationality: communicative, 171, 200; formal, 177, 188, 195; substantive, 177, 188; technical, 187–190, 358

Rationalization of life-world, 171; through capitalist modernization, 199–200; through communicative rationality, 198, 201–202; Habermas's reservations about, 202–209; limits of, 209–212, 218

Rawls, J., 429–430n.7, 434n.62

Reconstruction: interpretation as, 78, 84–86; as critical interpretative method, 172, 424n.13

Relativism, 45, 140, 374–375, 387n.12

Rhetoric, 148, 161–162, 365, 419n.64, 449–450n.50; and dialectic, 54, 139, 163, 395n.66, 417n.38, 421n.106, 444n.100

Richards, I. A., 65

Ricoeur, P., 393n.46, 412n.85

Rieff, P., 393n.46, 432n.23

Rilke, R. M., 418–419n.55

Rogers, C., 393n.47

Romanticism, 108, 111–112, 140, 166

Rorty, R., 22–24, 119, 378, 386n.6, 398n.129, 406n.3, 420n.97, 429n.7, 434n.62

Ross, W. D., 37, 316–317, 320, 334, 445n.122, 461n.62, 464n.80, 465n.96

Rousseau, J.-J., 159, 420n.86

Ryle, G., 466n.115

Sambursky, S., 447n.28

Sartre, J.-P., 372

Schleiermacher, F., 107

Schnädelbach, H., 380, 423n.9

Schön, D., xi, 468n.15

Science(s), modern: and ethics, 372; and Frankfurt School, 169; and Greek theory, 425–426n.24; Habermas on, 173–174, 426n.25; and hermeneutics, 165–166; as informing practice, 203; social, 184–185; technical interest of, 174–175

Sellars, W., 233

Socrates, 157, 251–252; and Plato, 440–441n.46

Socratic Intellectualism, Aristotle on, 124, 162, 263, 268, 275, 308–309, 313, 330

Solmsen, F., 335, 459n.41, 461n.62

Sophia (wisdom), 238, 253, 316

Sōphrosunē (temperance), 37, 277–278, 310

Soul, Aristotle on, 345–349

Sovereignty, lack of: in action, 93, 99, 100, 117, 359; in play, 137

Speech, 360–361; and action, 90, 359; Arendt on, 421n.121; everyday, 154; uni-

Speech (cont.)
versal and particular in, 362–363; and writing, 66, 148, 162

Stock, St. George, 446n.5

Subjectivism, 75, 81, 83, 87, 135, 184, 406n.6, 409n.40

Subjectivity, 109–110, 114–115, 135–136, 144–145, 152, 155, 366, 374

Sunesis (understanding), 132, 279, 287, 307, 370, 412n.81, 449n.48

Teaching, 1–8, 333, 367–371, 379; and learning, 339. See also Behavioral objectives model; Techne, teachability as mark of

Technai of kairos: 254–261, 315, 355

Techne: as analytic or productive, 158, 317–318, 450n.51; as archē, 249, 335, 337–338, 343, 345, 350, 354, 457n.25; Aristotle's 'official' concept of, 249–253; as contemplative, 284; and creativity, 284; as deliberative, 250, 260, 338, 344, 350–354; different kinds of, on scale of exactness, 260; does not deliberate, 337–338, 464n.80; as dunamis, 249, 343; as embodied, 348–350, 353–354; and epieikeia, 283, 333–334; and epistēmē, 251–253, 405n.66, 426n.24; and ethics, 158, 245–247, 319, 333–334; 'excellence in', 264–266; and experience, 281–285, 293, 305, 318–323, 338; absence of experimentation in, 284, 353, 447–448n.28; foreknowledge in, 56, 59, 328, 447n.27; and form, 250, 284, 316, 329, 345, 348–349; and four causes, 249, 316; Gadamer on, 229; general and particular in, 259; and Habermas's later philosophy, 208; as hexis meta logou poiētikē, 249, 316–317; instrumentality and, 250, 267; knowledge as sufficient condition of, 247, 321–323; learning a, 246, 319, 323, 354; logos in, 250, 330, 332, 333, 355; and matter, 331–334, 338–339, 342–343, 349; mistakes in, 266–267, 322; and nature, 334–338, 343–344; and 'paradigm of craftsman', 250; perception in, 354; performative, distinguished from productive, 254, 404n.62, 442n.58; as pervasive in Aristotle's writings, 245; and politics, 286–287; 'possession' and 'application' distinct in, 266, 321; as 'power of opposites', 264–

Techne (*cont.*)
265; and *sophia*, 316; and soul, 345–349;
teachability as mark of, 253, 281, 286,
320, 333; theoretical emphasis in, 251–
253, 282, 285, 315–316, 321–323, 426n.24,
441n.48; and tools, 347; and luck (*tuchē*),
255–256; user and producer in, 331,
460n.49; wide explanatory use of, by
Aristotle, 251; and knowledge of universals, 281–286. *See also* Phronesis and
techne, Aristotle's distinction between;
Technai of *kairos;* Technique
Technique, 360, 378–379; Collingwood on,
55–60; hegemony of, 187–192, 358, 372;
as ideology, 190–191; need for perceptiveness in applying, 298. *See also* Practical;
Practical philosophy; Practice; Praxis;
Techne
Temporal distance, 31, 108, 115, 118–119,
385n.3
Theory, Aristotle's conception of: 237–243;
ethical import of, 239–242, 437n.15; as a
praxis, 240; limits of, in ethics and poli-
tics, 287–290, 294–295, 312–314, 320.
See also Practical philosophy; Practice;
Theory and practice
Theory and practice, 9, 156–165, 223, 243,
365; Aristotle on, 237–243; Gadamer on,
156–163; Habermas on, 173–175, 194,
213–214, 224–225; in teaching, 367–371.
See also Practical philosophy; Practice;
Theory, Aristotle's conception of
Thomas Aquinas, St., 86, 146, 321–322,
448n.41, 459n.44
Thompson, J. A. K., 320, 445n.114, 452n.69
Thrasymachus, 24
Tradition, 109, 111, 114, 359; authority of,
113, 120; and language, 149, 184, 360;
and reason, 108
Trinitarian theology, 145–146

Tuchē (luck), 27, 153, 155–156, 254–257,
335. *See also* Technai of *kairos*
Tyler, R., 2

Understanding, 151; circle in, 110; and interpretation, 85, 141–143; phronesis as
model of, 124–126, 163; self-understanding, 123, 183–185, 187. *See also* Sunesis;
Verstehen
Utilitarianism, 11, 97

Value-neutrality: in teaching, 6–7; and technical reason, 187–188, 364
Vernant, J.-P., 256–257, 260–261
Verstehen, 42–43, 108
Vico, G., 173, 199, 464n.74
Virtue (*aretē*): conditions for possession of,
247; ethical and intellectual distinguished, 275; knowledge in, 275–276,
278–280; and learning, 246, 320; and the
mean, 246, 311–312; natural and proper
distinguished, 278, 290–291, 448n.41;
and *prohairesis,* 277; and techne, 245–
247, 333–334; unity of, 37, 454n.95

Walter, J., 270
Waterlow, S., 340–343, 410–411n.52, 447n.28
Weber, M., 169, 177, 195, 199–201, 403n.40,
428nn.4,5
Weil, S., 437n.15, 454n.93
Whitebrook, J., 436n.94
Wicksteed, P., 456n.7
Wiggins, D., 50, 390n.99, 397n.94, 453n.75
Williams, B. A. O., 383n.8
Winch, P., 40, 206
Wittgenstein, L., 64–65, 145, 232–233, 261,
301, 310, 368, 377, 394n.56, 416n.29,
453n.79

Yeats, W. B., 138, 404n.62